Seventh Edition

COMPARATIVE CRIMINAL JUSTICE SYSTEMS

A TOPICAL APPROACH

Philip L. Reichel

University of Northern Colorado

330 Hudson Street, NY, NY 10013

Vice President, Portfolio Management:
Andrew Gilfillan
Portfolio Manager: Gary Bauer
Editorial Assistant: Lynda Cramer
Senior Vice President, Marketing: David Gesell
Field Marketing Manager: Thomas Hayward
Product Marketing Manager: Kaylee Carlson
Senior Marketing Coordinator: Les Roberts
Director, Digital Studio and Content Production: Brian Hyland
Managing Producer: Cynthia Zonneveld
Managing Producer: Jennifer Sargunar
Content Producer: Purnima Narayanan
Manager, Rights Management: Johanna Burke

Operations Specialist: Deidra Smith
Creative Digital Lead: Mary Siener
Managing Producer, Digital Studio:
Autumn Benson
Content Producer, Digital Studio:
Maura Barclay
Full-Service Management and Composition:
iEnergizer Aptara®, Ltd.
Full-Service Project Manager: Sadika Rehman
Cover Design: StudioMontage
Cover Art: ecco/Shutterstock
Printer/Binder: LSC Communications
Cover Printer: LSC Communications
Text Font: Times LT Pro

Acknowledgments of third-party content appear on the appropriate page within the text.

Library of Congress Cataloging-in-Publication Data available upon request

2 17

ISBN 10:   0-13-455898-7
ISBN 13: 978-0-13-455898-1

To Eva, Scott, Matt, Tammy, Ella Jo, and A.J.

CONTENTS

Learning Objectives **144**

Countries in Focus **144**

Classification of Police Structures **145**

   Centralized Single Systems: Ghana 147

   Decentralized Single Systems: Japan 149

   Centralized Multiple Coordinated Systems: France 153

   Decentralized Multiple Coordinated Systems: Germany 157

   Centralized Multiple Uncoordinated Systems: Spain 160

   Decentralized Multiple Uncoordinated Systems: Mexico 163

Policing Issues: Police Misconduct **167**

Policing Issues: Global Cooperation **169**

   International Criminal Police Organization (ICPO)—INTERPOL 169

   European Police Office—Europol 171

   South Asian Association for Regional Cooperation—SAARC 172

      Summary 172 • Discussion Questions 173 •
      References 173

Chapter 7 **AN INTERNATIONAL PERSPECTIVE ON COURTS** 176

Learning Objectives **176**

Countries in Focus **176**

Professional Actors in the Judiciary **178**

   Variation in Legal Training 178

   Variation in Prosecution 180

   Variation in Defense 184

The Adjudicators **186**

   Presumption of Innocence 188

   Professional Judges 189

   Jurors and Lay Judges 190

   Examples along the Adjudication Continuum 193

Variation in Court Organization **199**

   France 199

   England and Wales 203

   Nigeria 206

   China 208

   Saudi Arabia 211

      Summary 212 • Discussion Questions 213 •
      References 213

PREFACE

Much has changed in the area of comparative criminal justice since this book's first edition. Those 25 years have seen increased attention to such transnational crimes as terrorism, human trafficking, and maritime piracy, and to the important international crime of genocide. Law enforcement agencies cooperate cross-nationally to prevent, investigate, and combat those crimes, and supranational organizations such as the United Nations, INTERPOL, and Europol serve as conduits allowing global sharing of information.

Concurrent with the increased interest of practitioners has been the attention paid to comparative criminal justice by scholars and researchers. The increasing number of professional journals, books, articles, and conference themes with a comparative justice focus is an obvious indicator; but so too are comments suggesting that developments in the justice system of any single country cannot be fully explored without acknowledging the impact of international and global forces.

Possibly the clearest acknowledgment that comparative justice is an accepted subdiscipline arrives when policy makers, politicians, and practitioners recognize and announce that one's own country can learn from the experiences of other countries. We may be on our way to reaching that point as indicated by the Justice Policy Institute's publication titled *Finding Direction: Expanding Criminal Justice Options by Considering Policies of Other Nations*. There is much to be gleaned, the Institute declared, from the criminal justice policies and practices in other democratic nations. Believing that similarities among nations—democratic principles, for example—make policy opportunities possible, the publication compares the criminal justice policies of Australia, Canada, England and Wales, Finland, and Germany to those of the United States.[1] Several of the criminal justice practices reviewed in this textbook are among those highlighted in the Justice Policy Institute's publication.

These changes are, of course, to everyone's benefit. Current students of criminology and criminal justice have a much better understanding of comparative and international issues than have students of earlier generations. That knowledge is useful when those students become practitioners and increasingly must interact with justice system agents in other countries. In addition, the increased knowledge of different ways that justice is conceived and achieved gives practitioners and policy makers ideas for improving their own system.

It is hoped that the interest in and perceived importance of an international perspective are irreversible. This book is designed to encourage continuation of that interest and to provide a knowledge base about justice in countries around the world.

ORGANIZATION OF THE BOOK

The text is organized in 10 chapters that reflect the material and order of presentation typically found in introductory books on the American system of criminal justice. That is, arrangement proceeds from concern with criminal law through examination of police, courts, and corrections. This organization distinguishes the text from other comparative criminal justice books that present detailed information on only a few specific countries. The result means that this text contains less detail on the criminal justice system of particular countries, but it provides greater appreciation and understanding of the diversity in legal systems around the world.

---

[1] Amanda Petteruti and Jason Fenster, *Finding Direction: Expanding Criminal Justice Options by Considering Policies of Other Nations* (Washington, DC: Justice Policy Institute, 2011), http://www.justicepolicy.org/research/2322.

A benefit of using the same countries for each chapter would be a sense of consistency and depth in the text. However, not every country offers the same level of contrast in all aspects of its criminal justice system. For example, describing German and French policing results in interesting and specific contrasts. If the same countries are used to contrast the trial procedure, their similarity makes us less aware of the variation occurring in that process when other countries are considered.

Fortunately, there is an alternate means for presenting information on law, police, courts, corrections, and juvenile justice. The organization used in this text follows the belief that comparison relies on categorization. That is, to best understand and explain similarities and differences among things, one must start by categorizing them. Chapter 1 provides the rationale for studying other systems of justice and sets down the specific approach used in this text. Chapter 2 explains and distinguishes comparative criminology and comparative criminal justice and then shows crime as a world problem by reviewing types of transnational crime. In doing so, it sets the stage for consideration of the different ways justice systems are organized in attempts to respond to the crime problem. Chapter 3 presents traditional material on American criminal law so that the reader has a familiar and common base to use in the following chapters and concludes with a review of how the war on terrorism affects both substantive and procedural law. Chapter 4 presents four contemporary legal traditions and outlines the basic features of each. Chapter 5 continues material in Chapters 3 and 4 by looking at substantive and procedural criminal law in each of the four legal traditions.

The next four chapters cover the topics of policing (Chapter 6), the judiciary (Chapter 7), corrections (Chapter 8), and juvenile justice (Chapter 9). Countries representing Africa, Asia, Europe, Middle East, North America, Latin America, and Oceania are included in the coverage. Some make frequent appearances (e.g., Australia, China, France, Mexico, Saudi Arabia); others are less recurrent (e.g., Canada, Finland, New Zealand). The text concludes with a concentrated look at the criminal justice system of Japan. This country was chosen for special consideration because it has a history of borrowing from other countries (a point encouraged by comparative studies) and has what many consider to be a very effective criminal justice system. Also, ending the text with an in-depth look at a particular country provides an opportunity to tie together some of the topics and items presented in earlier chapters.

PEDAGOGICAL FEATURES

This edition includes coverage of several new topics and enhanced coverage of others. Popular pedagogical features from earlier editions are continued and, at reviewer request, the number of Web Projects has been increased. Among the new features are an increased use of photographs and graphics to add a visual learning experience and to provide greater readability. Identification of "Countries in Focus" at each chapter's start provides the reader with a global orientation to the chapter's coverage. The goal is to orient students about the regions and nations they will encounter during their reading while making it clear that these countries receive particular attention in the chapter. Earlier editions included "In the News" boxes that highlighted current events, but an increased length of time between editions makes that feature less helpful. However, some of those boxes have been repurposed as "You Should Know!" boxes. Other pedagogical features deserve more specific description.

> *Learning Objectives:* Each chapter begins with specific learning objectives that identify the knowledge and skills students should have after reading the chapter. These objectives are presented in the phrasing of Bloom's taxonomy, which is increasingly used to assist in the assessment of student achievement.

Impact Sections: This feature, which has proven very popular with students and professors, continues in this edition. Each chapter of the text includes an "Impact" section in which topics mentioned in that chapter receive greater attention and questions raised by chapter material are addressed. These sections should encourage mental gymnastics, suggesting things such as links between countries, ideas for improving systems, and ways to encourage more global understanding. Examples include how security measures may explain the global crime drop (Chapter 2) and how soccer and American football can explain differences between common law and civil law (Chapter 5).

You Should Know!: Another popular feature from previous editions is the "You Should Know" boxes. At least one such box appears in every chapter. Each item provides students with helpful background information relevant to chapter topics. Examples include explanations of the role of oaths and evidence in Islamic law (Chapter 5) and the idea of jurors asking questions during a trial (Chapter 7).

Web Projects: The "Web Project" feature has become one of the most popular items in the book. Feedback on these features from students and professors has been extremely positive and this edition honors requests for an increased number of these projects. These projects can be used as assignments by instructors or simply as interesting sites for students to visit. For example, students are encouraged to learn about the United Nations' Global Counter-Terrorism Strategy (Chapter 3), the roles and responsibilities of lay judges in Finland (Chapter 7), and how to use Cornell Law School's death penalty database to answer questions about capital punishment around the world (Chapter 8).

Discussion Questions: One of the most frequently requested additions to the book was a call for discussion questions at each chapter's end. Instructors, especially ones teaching the course online, noted how discussion questions encourage class participation and provide a way to gauge student understanding of chapter material. They also make good assignments for the online students. I have tried to develop them as true items for discussion rather than as essay questions that may be more appropriate for an exam. Suggested essay questions are provided in the Instructor's Manual and Test Bank.

World Maps: Continued in this edition are regional maps that combine to show the world. To help orient students, the first time a country in focus is mentioned in a chapter, reference is made to the specific map containing that country.

General Websites: Also continued is Appendix B with an annotated list of websites that can be helpful to students seeking information for group projects, classroom presentations, and research papers.

NEW TO THIS EDITION

Subsequent editions of criminal justice textbooks are often necessary to update statistics, changes in law, modifications in procedures, and to include, increase, or decrease information about particular topics. All those reasons are relevant to the seventh edition of this book. Actually, a revision to a book that covers justice systems around the world is especially necessary because of the changes constantly occurring on one continent or another. There have been quite significant changes on the world scene since the sixth edition. Important new laws and legislation are having significant impact on the administration of justice in several countries and appropriate sections of the chapters have been modified in this edition to account for those changes.

Pedagogical improvements to the text, as already outlined, are among the more important changes in this edition. In addition to those specifically noted earlier, this edition continues to provide complete case citation for all U.S. federal cases and to rely on primary sources for information. That latter point is worth highlighting since it increases the accuracy of information provided for a country. The Internet makes easily available the laws of many countries, and the countries themselves are increasingly accommodating to English speakers by providing an English-language translation of those laws. In addition, criminal justice agencies in many countries are providing (again, in English) information about their structure and operation. These changes have made it possible to use primary sources to a greater extent than has been possible in the past.

Each chapter of this edition has been modified by additions and deletions. The most notable changes are summarized here to assist instructors as they struggle to keep course material current, accurate, and interesting.

- In Chapter 1, the section on *local* (previously called provincial) benefits of an international perspective has been revised to include intercultural competence as one of the benefits, and to identify both "intercultural competence" and "establishing points of comparison" as specific benefits. Information on the Mérida Initiative (Bilateral Cooperation Efforts) has been updated and the section describing a political approach to an international perspective has been completely revised and now uses United Nations' efforts in Liberia as a specific example of police reform. Two new Web Projects ("Assessing cultural competence" and "Arrested in . . .?") have been added—making a total of four web projects in the chapter.
- Dr. Rosemary Barberet has been added as a co-author for Chapter 2 to improve coverage of theories and to add material on international crime. The chapter title has been modified to reflect the addition of international crime as a key topic and a new chapter introduction provides specific examples of domestic, transnational, and international crime. The new section on international crime reviews its primary forms (genocide, crimes against humanity, and war crimes) and provides information about the role of the International Criminal Court in prosecuting violations of international criminal law.
- Chapter 3's Impact section now uses Canada rather than the United States as a contrast to Mexico when discussing due process, crime control, and corruption. A new Web Project ("A Global Counter-Terrorism Strategy") has been added— making a total of two web projects in the chapter. The section "Liberty, Safety, and Fighting Terrorism" has been revised to have less emphasis on the USA PATRIOT Act and more on legislation generally and now includes the USA Freedom Act of 2015. A new section "Tilting toward Safety and Security" highlights counterterrorism measures taken in the United States and other countries. As a contrast, another new section "Tilting toward Liberty" describes some tempering measures as the United States and other countries seek to balance security and liberty.
- Chapter 4 was the most drastically changed chapter in the last edition as the socialist legal tradition was replaced with the Eastern Asia legal tradition. That change, of course, had ripple effects throughout the rest of the book. Feedback was positive regarding that modification, so the changes for this edition are more modest and occur mostly during coverage of the Islamic legal tradition. For example, discussion of flexibility in Islamic law has dropped mazalim courts and now highlights—and distinguished between—fatwa and ijtihad as key concepts.
- Under Chapter 5's discussion of substantive law in the Islamic legal tradition, coverage of hudud and tazir crimes has been expanded and clarified. And, in a continuing effort to explain and distinguish inquisitorial and adversarial

procedures, additional explanation and examples have been added. Primary among those is a new section "Merging Adversarial and Inquisitorial Processes" that describes how each procedure influences the other. In 2013, an amended version of China's Criminal Procedure Law came into effect, and some of its key features are not included in discussion of procedural law in the Eastern Asia tradition. Finally, a new Web Project allows students to consider the conditions and obstacles of criminal responsibility in Iran.

- New information about the demilitarizing of the French Gendarmerie has been added and recent reform attempts of policing in Mexico receive significant coverage in Chapter 6. There is a new Web Project that provides students with opportunities to compare police agencies in such areas as structure, organization, mission, and training. Still other new Web Projects direct students to the topics of Spain's Civil Guard, to articles comparing police shooting in countries around the world, and to INTERPOL's work. Because the Schengen Convention and European arrest warrants are less newsworthy today than when those topics were first included, they have been replaced with additional information on regional police cooperation.

- Chapter 7's introduction still uses the Amanda Knox case (with all necessary updates) to set the stage for differences in the judicial process and court organization. Specific differences between Italian and American trials are highlighted in a new Web Project. Another new Web Project allows students to consider the implications of Scotland juries being able to return a "not proven" verdict rather than only "guilty" or "not guilty." The section "Lay Judges" has been considerably expanded and now provides more examples of contemporary lay participation. Because of changes to the French penal code in 2014, France has been removed from the Impact box as an example of countries that have concurrent consideration of guilt and sentencing. Court organization was modified in both China and Saudi Arabia since the previous edition of this book, so those sections have been updated.

- Changes in Chapter 8 are primarily updates to statistics, inclusion of the Nelson Mandela Rules on Treatment of Prisoners, and the addition of new information on recent changes in China regarding the use of capital punishment—especially the increased use of suspended death sentences. Also, to still have discussion of incarceration rates across the extremes, Australia replaces South Africa (which current data places among the low-level countries) as an example of the mid-level use of incarceration. Finally, the section on women in prison has been updated.

- One new Web Project in Chapter 9 asks students to consider at what age criminal responsibility begins and another one allows them to compare aspects of juvenile justice proceedings in different countries. Changes in juvenile justice proceeding have occurred in each of the four focus countries since the last edition of this book, and those changes have been incorporated into the narrative.

- Japan introduced a major reform to its justice system in 2009 and that lay judge process is now entrenched as a key feature. As a result, Chapter 10 now includes a new section describing the citizen role in adjudication. Other changes are updates to statistics and additional information about prison sentences.

Although comparative criminal justice enjoys increased attention, it is still in its infancy as a subject matter. As more and more textbooks begin to appear, more scholars attempt cross-cultural research, and more practitioners share ideas, comparative criminal justice will grow to levels we cannot yet appreciate. I hope you will find this book to be a positive contribution toward the advancement of this important field of study.

INSTRUCTOR SUPPLEMENTS

Instructor's Manual with Test Bank. Includes content outlines for classroom discussion, teaching suggestions, and answers to selected end-of-chapter questions from the text. This also contains a Word document version of the test bank.

TestGen. This computerized test generation system gives you maximum flexibility in creating and administering tests on paper, electronically, or online. It provides state-of-the-art features for viewing and editing test bank questions, dragging a selected question into a test you are creating, and printing sleek, formatted tests in a variety of layouts. Select test items from test banks included with TestGen for quick test creation, or write your own questions from scratch. TestGen's random generator provides the option to display different text or calculated number values each time questions are used.

PowerPoint Presentations. Our presentations are clear and straightforward. Photos, illustrations, charts, and tables from the book are included in the presentations when applicable.

To access supplementary materials online, instructors need to request an instructor access code. Go to **www.pearsonhighered.com/irc,** where you can register for an instructor access code. Within 48 hours after registering, you will receive a confirming email, including an instructor access code. Once you have received your code, go to the site and log on for full instructions on downloading the materials you wish to use.

ALTERNATE VERSIONS

eBooks. This text is also available in multiple eBook formats. These are an exciting new choice for students looking to save money. As an alternative to purchasing the printed textbook, students can purchase an electronic version of the same content. With an eTextbook, students can search the text, make notes online, print out reading assignments that incorporate lecture notes, and bookmark important passages for later review. For more information, visit your favorite online eBook reseller or visit www.mypearsonstore.com.

ACKNOWLEDGMENTS

This edition, as with the previous ones, has been possible only because of the support and assistance provided by many colleagues around the world—some of whom I have the great pleasure of knowing rather well and others who have been helpful to a stranger seeking information about their country. Among the former are colleagues Jay Albanese, Rosemary Barberet, Pete Benekos, Karin Bruckmüller, Harry Dammer, Bitna Kim, Alida Merlo, Stefan Schumann, and John Winterdyk. Each of them has provided me with opportunities to expand my knowledge and experiences in comparative and international criminal justice. I thank them all and can only hope that upon reflection they believe their trust was well placed.

I would also like to thank my students at the University of Northern Colorado who, for more than 30 years, provided me with wonderful opportunities to teach and to learn. Their interest in comparative criminal justice encourages a positive view for the future.

Gary Bauer, Portfolio Manager and my editor at Pearson, provided important support, encouragement, and advice as this edition came to fruition. As Managing Producer, Jennifer Sargunar played an essential role in keeping me on task and responding to any concerns or questions. Project Manager Sadika Rehman provided an excellent team for copy editing, typesetting, and other work that is so essential for a book's professional appearance. Special thanks go to Lynda Cramer, Editorial Assistant, who has proven to be invaluable over the years as a person to be relied upon for prompt and helpful assistance with questions of almost any kind. And, of course, the marketing efforts of Thomas Hayward and Derrica Moser are always greatly appreciated.

Finally, acknowledgment also goes to the reviewers who have kindly provided suggestions for the improvement of this book. The following people gave their valuable time and assistance in helping this book come to publication in a better form than was first planned. Thank you to Allan Barnes, University of Alaska—Anchorage; Diana Bruns, Southeast Missouri State University; Sophie Clavier, San Francisco State University; Francis Danso Boateng, Washington State University; James Jengeleski, Shippensburg University; Pamella Seay, Florida Gulf Coast University; and Pietro Toggia, Kutztown University of Pennsylvania.

An International Perspective

LEARNING OBJECTIVES

After studying this chapter, you will be able to:

1. Summarize the local and universal benefits of an international perspective.

2. Distinguish between, and give examples of, bilateral and multinational cooperation.

3. Describe and compare the historical, political, and descriptive approaches to an international perspective.

4. Distinguish, with examples, the functions/procedures and the institutions/actors strategies.

5. Summarize and distinguish the synthetic and authentic classification strategies.

COUNTRIES IN FOCUS

Canada	Liberia
China	Mexico
France	United States

Do you have confidence in the criminal justice system? Over the last several decades, the American public has been disgusted and befuddled at the actions of some justice employees and the workings of parts of the system. On occasion, some police officers have behaved with bias and brutality toward suspects. Some prosecutors seem to have filed criminal charges in a selective manner. Defense attorneys have fallen asleep while their clients have been on trial for their lives. Juries in civil trials have held people responsible for actions that those same people were deemed not guilty of by juries in criminal trials. Correctional officers in prisons have abused inmates, and prison programs have been denounced as having failed to rehabilitate criminals. Is it possible to have confidence in such a system? Well, that depends!

Of 14 national institutions, Americans express the most confidence in the military and the least in Congress. Falling in the low-middle, along with organized labor and television news, is the criminal justice system with 23 percent of Americans expressing either "quite a lot" or a "great deal" of confidence. Admittedly, a less than one-fourth of the population having high confidence in the criminal justice system is not an outstanding statistic. Interestingly, the police as a specific institution was in second place with 56 percent expressing "quite a lot" or a "great deal" of confidence (Norman, 2016). Specific concerns include issues of fairness and the involvement of politics in judicial decisions (Krogstad, 2014; Rasmussen Reports, 2014, 2016):

- Whereas more than half of white voters think the justice system is fair to black and Hispanic Americans, just 9 percent of black voters agree.

- Seventy-five percent of whites have either a great deal or a fair amount of confidence that their local police will not use excessive force on suspects, but only 45 percent of Latinos and 36 percent of blacks had a similar opinion.
- Eighty-two percent of black voters say black Americans receive unfair treatment from the police, but only one-third of whites agree.
- Twenty-two percent of black Americans think most cops are racist. Just 9 percent of white adults agree.
- Only 37 percent of likely U.S. voters believe most judges are impartial and guided by the law, whereas 54 percent think instead that most judges let politics influence their decisions.

Despite concerns about some of our institutions, most Americans think that the United States stands above all other countries in the world (28 percent), and 58 percent say it is one of the greatest countries in the world, along with some others (Tyson, 2014). In another national poll, Americans agreed that in spite of its problems, the American justice system is still the best in the world (American Bar Association, 1999; Rasmussen Reports, 2011a, 2011b, 2011c).

An important question is how so many people can find fault with key parts of the justice system yet still believe the United States is one of the greatest countries in the world and that the American justice system is the best in the world. Do Americans have too idealistic a notion of their own system, or are they simply skeptical about any other country's ability to do better? Such a perspective is reflected in the term *ethnocentrism*, or the belief that one's own way of doing something is the best.

Ethnocentrism has some positive aspects. It encourages pride, confidence, and group identification. When ethnocentrism is attached to one's country, it is a key ingredient in what we call patriotism. Because feelings of patriotism and cultural identity are generally positive attributes that help make a nation strong, it is desirable for citizens to be somewhat ethnocentric about their own social institutions. Indeed, public opinion polls in various countries show that most citizens have confidence in their own country's public institutions—even while recognizing problems with some aspects of those institutions. For example, the Gallup Law and Order Index (comprised of responses to three questions—including "do you have confidence in your local police") found the highest index scores (i.e., feeling most secure) in countries of Southeast Asia, the United States, and Canada (Gallup, 2015). In Australia, Japan, Kenya, Senegal, and the Philippines, at least 60 percent have confidence in their judicial system and courts (Loschky, 2014; Rochelle & Loschky, 2014; Tortora, 2007; Van de Walle, 2009).

As with many other cultural traits, ethnocentrism has negative aspects that oppose its positive ones. When ethnocentrism makes people in one group unwilling to understand and appreciate differences with people from other groups, prejudice and discrimination can result. When ethnocentrism makes it difficult, or even impossible, to be critical about the status quo, society may not experience positive change. If people believe that no other way of doing something can be useful, desirable, or even better than the current way, opportunities for improvement are missed. Preferably, citizens should balance their cultural pride and confidence with a willingness to appreciate and learn from others—even when the "others" are culturally different and geographically separate.

One goal of comparative studies is to extend a person's knowledge of people and cultures beyond his or her own group. After seeing the similarities and differences among countries and their citizens, comparative scholars have a better understanding of their own society and of ways that society might be improved. Importantly, that can be accomplished without loss of pride in one's own country or social institutions. Or, to paraphrase George Santayana, our feet should be planted in our country, but our eyes should survey the world (Santayana, 1905).

WHY STUDY THE LEGAL SYSTEM OF OTHER COUNTRIES?

Taking an international perspective is still a new endeavor in American criminal justice curricula, so it is important to highlight its value. We begin with the premise that contemporary technology has provided a global communications network serving to shrink the world in the perspective of its people. It is a "small world" in terms of common problems! There is every reason to believe that citizens of the world, through their respective governments and businesses, will become increasingly interdependent. As a result, an international perspective has both local and universal benefits. We discuss these as they relate to criminal justice and from the viewpoint of Americans.

Before continuing, a few words regarding the use of the terms *America* and *American* are in order. Some authors are troubled by the use of those terms in sole reference to the United States and its citizens. Such concerns are well founded, because the North American continent is composed of Canada, Mexico, Central America, and the islands of the Caribbean, as well as the United States. Furthermore, because the term *America* does not distinguish either the northern or the southern continent, the citizens of South American countries could also be the subjects of conversation. However, despite the insensitivity its usage may encourage, this text uses *America* as specifically referring to the United States, simply because it is so commonly used that way and because citizens of other North and South American countries are more correctly identified with reference to their specific country. Moreover, although the names Canadians, Peruvians, Mexicans, and Guatemalans allow us to place a citizen with a particular country, a term like *United Statesian* does not roll off the tongue as easily. With apologies to our North and South American neighbors, this book uses *America* and *Americans* to refer to the United States of America and its citizens.

Local Benefits of an International Perspective

Benefits of an international perspective that are best described as local in nature include the development of intercultural competence and establishing points of contrast.

INTERCULTURAL COMPETENCE Intercultural competence is recognized as an important skill for citizens of the twenty-first century. Similar terms such as intercultural awareness and cultural intelligence all refer to the knowledge, skills, and attitudes needed to interact successfully with people from different backgrounds (Deardorff, 2014). Economic and social factors have encouraged (if not required) college and university curricula to be more internationalized and businesses to understand better the variation in global cultures.

In the absence of intercultural awareness, there is an increased possibility of misinterpreting the verbal and nonverbal behavior of persons with whom we are interacting. People in different countries react to inputs differently, communicate differently, and make decisions differently. Ignoring those points leads to miscommunication at best and to distrust at worse. There are a variety of examples of such problems when conducting business across cultures. Meyer (2015) relates the experience of a New York–based financial institution that interpreted the silence of their colleagues in Thailand as indicating the Thais had nothing to contribute during conference calls. Instead, the Thais—for whom jumping into conversations uninvited is deemed inappropriate—were simply waiting for an invitation to comment. In other examples, companies that rely on confrontation and open disagreement as essential for generating creativity and reducing risk find that approach to be essentially unworkable at their offices in many Southeast Asian and Latin American countries where there is a preference for group harmony.

Just as businesses improve their chances for successful interaction through intercultural competence, so too can criminal justice agencies. The most obvious examples are when police in any country are interacting with victims, witnesses, suspects, and members of the public who are from other cultural backgrounds (whether domestic or foreign). An understanding of, and appreciation for, the cultural background of the people involved increases the likelihood of productive interaction. Less obvious examples are when police in one country are interacting with police in another country. With little understanding by police in Country A of how policing is organized in Country B—or how investigations are carried out, evidence gathered, and interrogations conducted—there can be as much confusion, misunderstanding, and distrust as is found in examples of blunders by businesses trying to operate in another country. When describing impediments to cross-national collaboration in combating human trafficking, Reichel (2008) gives examples of differences in what constitutes legal investigation techniques regarding surveillance procedures. One country may require permission from a judge—even if the person is in a public place, whereas public surveillance in another country requires no judicial permission. Requests from one country that police in another country conduct mobile phone interceptions may turn out to be a request for action that is not allowed (or even technologically possible) in the second country. Even knowing what agency or which person in what position to contact when making a request may be hindered by not knowing whether there is a national police force and whether policing is organized at state, province, or local level.

Although intercultural competence is an essential skill for persons and organizations in today's world, that is not the only benefit in learning about other countries. An international perspective also provides us with opportunities to understand, appreciate, and even improve our approach to criminal justice. The following section makes this point by highlighting examples of specific areas where legal systems may differ from one another.

ESTABLISHING POINTS OF CONTRAST Upon realizing that one's own legal system is not the only one possible, it becomes more interesting and more important to scrutinize that system. For example, the rather passive role of a judge in the American trial process takes on new meaning when contrasted with the very active judge under other legal systems. When we read of some European legal systems making use of private citizens as lay judges, it puts the use of citizens on American juries in a new perspective. In this manner, knowledge of alternative systems of justice provides a point of contrast. That contrast, in turn, allows the student a means and reason to gain new insight into a procedure or structure previously viewed as uninteresting and ordinary. A comparative view of legal systems allows us to understand better the dimensions of our own system (Terrill, 1982).

Besides providing new insight and understanding of our system of justice, having a point of contrast can furnish ideas to improve that system. A technique used in one country to combat crime might be successfully adapted for use in another country. For example, do high levels of gun ownership in the United States make high levels of gun violence inevitable? Are there other countries with high rates of gun ownership but low rates of gun crime? Can techniques used by the indigenous Maori people of New Zealand influence the development of restorative justice practices in Toronto, Denver, or Atlanta? Organizations such as the United Nations Office on Drugs and Crime, the International Center for the Prevention of Crime, and the International Corrections

WEB PROJECT
Assessing Cultural Competence

With paper and pencil handy, visit https://www.youtube.com/watch?v=Y6d3e-gcOzo and take the Cultural Competence Self-Test. Without providing specifics regarding your responses, write a paragraph or two that describe your general reaction to the questions asked and the ability of those questions to assess a person's cultural competence. Can assessments such as this one be useful in educational or occupational settings? Why or why not?

and Prisons Association are only a few examples of groups committed to the idea of gathering information on justice-related projects from a wide variety of countries and sharing that information with the world community.

No society can incorporate another culture's legal system in its entirety and expect it to work. Yet certain aspects of another system—modified to account for cultural differences—may operate successfully in a new setting. It is important to note that potentially transferable ideas come not only from countries at similar levels of development but also from less developed countries. For example, Americans are becoming increasingly interested in mediation to settle a variety of legal disputes. As anthropologists remind us, mediation and dispute resolution have a long and distinguished tradition at the tribal and village levels in African and other countries. To ignore the experiences of those systems is imprudent and elitist.

Universal Benefits of an International Perspective

A benefit of comparative studies is to help replace one's traditionally parochial view of the world with a global perspective. Doing so has always been important, but today it is essential. That is because, as *New York Times* columnist Thomas Friedman's book title declares, "the world is flat." By that, Friedman means the people of the world today are able to do business, communicate, entertain, or engage in almost any other activity, instantaneously with billions of others around the globe. Several technological (digital, especially) and political forces have converged, and that has produced a global playing field that allows for multiple forms of collaboration without regard to geography or distance, or soon, even language (Friedman, 2005).

Importantly, just as the world is flat for legitimate enterprises and lawful people, it is flat also for illegal endeavors and criminals. It appears that garden-variety thefts, robberies, and assaults may become less troublesome to society than offenses like the internationalization of organized crime, cybercrime, terrorism, money laundering, and the trafficking of humans. Criminality in this new century seems to have expanded its target beyond private citizens to include communities, governments, and even nations.

Efforts to contain illegal behavior in a flat world require that criminal justice practitioners move about on the playing field as easily as do the criminals. That skill is acquired, in part, by ensuring that those practitioners have an international perspective that helps them understand such things as the similarities and differences in social control mechanisms at domestic and transnational levels and how countries can work together effectively to combat "flat world crime."

Multinational collaboration is occurring, but the needed action requires a level of teamwork that countries of the world are only beginning to consider. Understandably, cooperation often starts with neighboring countries. Their common border not only presents the problem of intercountry crime but also provides both reason and opportunity to do something about it. In addition to such neighbor cooperation, multinational cooperation is occurring as well, as groupings of countries realize the need to develop formal agreements in their quest to control and combat crime. We consider a few examples of both neighbor and multinational cooperation.

NEIGHBOR COOPERATION The shared borders between the United States and Canada and between the United States and Mexico have encouraged bilateral agreements

Bilateral agreements among the North American countries of Canada, Mexico, and the United States are examples of neighbor cooperation.

Ronniechua/123RF

WEB PROJECT
Bilateral Cooperation Efforts

Find the most recent International Narcotics Control Strategy Report (INCSR) at http://www.state.gov/j/inl/rls/nrcrpt/ and open Volume 1: Drug and Chemical Control. Scroll down to the "Country Reports" section and select three countries that interest you. Find the section that describes each country's bilateral cooperation efforts. Write a paragraph or two on how the countries are similar or different in their cooperation with the United States.

among the neighboring countries as each responds to internal and cross-border crime. Oftentimes, the political "spin doctors" present the resulting cooperation between national law enforcement agencies as being more cooperative than is actually true, but each country recognizes the need for collective efforts.

The United States and Canada (see Map A.3) have long-standing agreements on law enforcement cooperation, including treaties on extradition and mutual legal assistance as well as an asset-sharing agreement. The two countries participate in the annual U.S.–Canada Cross-Border Crime Forum to coordinate policy matters and operation procedures so that problems can be more easily resolved. In addition, the two countries have several Memoranda of Understanding (MOU) such as the one designating the U.S. Drug Enforcement Administration and the Royal Canadian Mounted Police as the points of contact for drug-related matters relevant to both countries. Especially important are the Border Enforcement Security Taskforces (BEST) and the Integrated Cross-Border Maritime Law Enforcement Operations (known as "Shiprider"), which conduct regular patrol and boarding operations in locations along the shared maritime border (Bureau for International Narcotics and Law Enforcement Affairs, 2016).

Canada and the United States seem to have found a comfortable version of bilateral cooperation that U.S. officials describe as extensive and highly productive. The collegiality reflected in the U.S.–Canada arrangements has not been so easily duplicated in U.S.–Mexico (see Map A.3) arrangements.

Official policy statements given by the Mexican and U.S. governments proclaim the need for collaborative efforts at stemming cross-border crime—with particular attention to drug trafficking. Specific arrangements include bilateral cooperation between law enforcement agencies, between members of the judiciary, and even between each country's military. The problem is not so much in getting each country to agree on what should be accomplished but rather in how the agreements are actually implemented. Specific concerns are expressed about the way U.S. agencies and personnel seem to take a rather cavalier attitude toward their Mexican counterparts. The result, critics argue, is a situation wherein the United States has the upper hand in a bilateral arrangement between presumably equal parties (for a counterargument, see Aspinwall & Reich, 2016).

When one country takes a dominant position in its dealings with another country, the subordinate country has understandable concerns about protecting its sovereignty. Maria Celia Toro (1999) claims that the United States has used transnational crime concerns (especially drug crimes) as a way to extend its own jurisdiction beyond U.S. borders. She cites as examples the laws providing for grand jury indictments of foreign nationals, the U.S. Supreme Court decisions that refuse to apply the Fourth Amendment to searches by U.S. law enforcement agents in foreign countries (see *United States* v. *Verdugo-Urquidez*, 494 U.S. 259, 1990), and the judicial processing in U.S. courts of defendants who were kidnapped from other countries by U.S. federal agents operating in that country (see *United States* v. *Alvarez-Machain*, 504 U.S. 655, 1992). These acts of extraterritorial enforcement of U.S. antidrug laws pose a threat to Mexican sovereignty, according to many observers.

Deflem counters that the dominant position taken by the United States in its "cooperative" law enforcement arrangements with Mexico simply reflects the nature of international police work wherein national interests are always at stake (Deflem, 2002). He notes that the agreements between Mexico and the United States state that the programs are meant to uphold principles of sovereignty and mutual respect. Nevertheless, it seems to many observers that U.S. law enforcement agencies are the dominant players in every bilateral initiative with Mexico.

United States government responses to claims that its actions do not reflect the principles of equality described in the bilateral agreements tend to be explanations rather than denials. The relative strength of U.S. personnel, equipment, technology, and technical know-how are presented as features that require the U.S. agencies to take the lead in law enforcement efforts. Added to those reasons is the recognition in both Mexico and the United States that corruption is pervasive in Mexican law enforcement.

Current attempts at a more equitable and effective collaborative response are based on the Mérida Initiative, which is a bilateral partnership that includes counterdrug and anticrime assistance for Mexico. Initially, U.S. assistance through the initiative was focused on training and equipping Mexican counterdrug forces, but now it places more emphasis on addressing the weak institutions and underlying social problems that have allowed the drug trade to flourish in Mexico. Specifically, the Mérida strategy focuses on such things as disrupting organized criminal groups, institutionalizing the rule of law, and building strong and resilient communities. The initiative includes a pledge by the Mexican government to intensify its anticrime efforts and a pledge by the U.S. government to address drug demand in the United States and the illicit trafficking of firearms and bulk currency to Mexico (Seelke & Finklea, 2014, 2016).

Mutual cooperation between neighboring nations in fighting cross-border crime seems to be of obvious benefit to both countries, but cooperative efforts are not easily achieved—especially if one country has recognized advantages over the other. A risk associated with transnational policing is the compromising of national sovereignty as countries that are more dominant extend their jurisdiction into subordinate countries. A risk of not engaging in transnational policing is, however, to give a distinct advantage to criminals who might avoid apprehension and prosecution by changing their national identification or location. Can such difficulties be overcome by arrangements between two countries? Is it, in fact, conceivable that many nations could join in an effective cooperative effort against transnational crime and criminals?

MULTINATIONAL COOPERATION   The European Union (EU) is a treaty-based framework that defines and manages economic and political cooperation among its 28 member states: Austria, Belgium, Bulgaria, Croatia, Cyprus, Czech Republic, Denmark, Estonia, Finland, France, Germany, Greece, Hungary, Ireland, Italy, Latvia, Lithuania, Luxembourg, Malta, Poland, Portugal, Romania, Slovakia, Slovenia, Spain, Sweden, The Netherlands, and, until its withdrawal is officially complete, the United Kingdom.

The countries making up the EU remain independent sovereign nations, but they delegate some of their decision-making powers to shared institutions they have created. In this manner, decisions on specific matters of joint interest are made democratically at a supranational level. The three key institutions are the European Parliament, the Council of the European Union, and the European Commission. These institutions produce the policies and laws that apply throughout the EU (Europa, 2016). The European Commission is of particular interest to us, because it provides the institutional structure for cooperative efforts among criminal justice agencies.

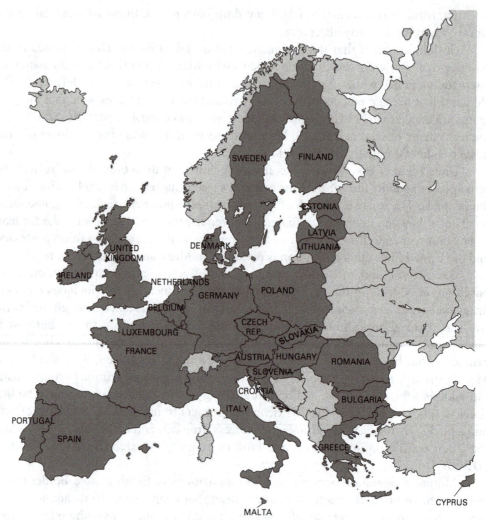

The 28 countries of the European Union (including the United Kingdom until its exit is officially completed) remain independent sovereign nations, but they delegate some of their decision-making powers to shared institutions they have created.

Courtesy of Central Intelligence Agency.

The areas of police and judicial cooperation provide especially good examples of multinational cooperation for justice purposes. Unlike the neighbor cooperation exemplified by the United States and Mexico, the EU tries to achieve cooperation among the institutions and agencies of 28 nations. A realistic goal, from the EU's perspective, is to create a European judicial space that allows Europeans to combat crime and seek justice across borders and throughout the continent.

Just as movement toward a common currency, the Euro, took a rocky but steady course, some believe the EU will follow a similar path as the nations seek agreement on common judicial procedures for investigating, prosecuting, and punishing some criminal acts. After all, the reasoning goes, Europeans increasingly cross their national borders to marry, work, study, buy and sell goods and services, and invest or borrow money. Shouldn't they also be able to seek and receive justice as simply and efficiently from any other EU country?

The tricky part, as you can well imagine, is to provide a specialized supranational judicial structure that combats transnational crime but does not violate the spirit of each country's criminal code or criminal procedure. There are precedents for such a structure. The United States has a federal judicial system that works in harmony with 50 separate state systems. Countries such as Canada and Australia have found suitable ways to have federal laws and enforcement in conjunction with separate provincial and state laws. Of course, it is probably easier to get states and provinces that are part of a single nation to agree to a national judicial space than it is to get separate nations to agree to a supranational judicial space. The EU countries are working hard to achieve such cooperation. For example:

IMPACT

USING MEXICAN JUSTICE

How does one country bring to justice a person who has fled to another country after committing a crime in the first country? The typical technique is through an extradition process wherein the two countries have agreed to surrender the accused individual to the requesting country for trial and punishment. The specifics of such an accommodation are typically laid out in a treaty or other agreement between the countries.

Problems may arise when the countries disagree on key issues regarding the event. For example, the act alleged to have been committed may be a crime in the first country but not in the country where the accused is currently located. For example, parental child abduction offenses are penalized throughout the United States but not generally in Mexico (Duran, 2002). Or, the punishment to which the accused would be subject in the first country may be considered an unacceptable sanction in the other country. Actually, this second point has been a problem for the United States in a number of extradition attempts in which the accused may be subject to the death penalty if found guilty. Because many countries have abolished capital punishment, they are unwilling to release a person under their jurisdiction to a country where the death penalty could be imposed. However, there are alternatives to extradition that show how cooperative efforts between two countries can be rather easily achieved. Consider, for example, the effort of a homicide investigator in a Colorado county.

In 1992, seasonal field supervisors Juan and Aurelia Lara were robbed and killed in a rural area of Colorado's Weld County by a gang of six men—all Mexican citizens. One of the men was arrested and prosecuted in Weld County, but the other five escaped to Mexico. Sheriff's Department Investigator Al Price learned that Article IV of Mexico's penal code provides for other nations to punish criminals using Mexico's judicial system. Using evidence provided by Investigator Price, four of the killers were apprehended in Mexico, convicted by a Mexican court, and sentenced to 35 years of hard labor at a prison near Mexico City.

The process required some techniques not used in traditional U.S. police work. For example, Mexican authorities prefer face-to-face workings with the U.S. police officers rather than relying on phone or fax communication. Written (translated to Spanish) and photographic evidence is required in the Mexican courts; and, as in the United States, particular rules must be followed in a particular order. But, as Investigator Price explained, when you abide by their rules, you get positive results (Mitchell, 1999).

Mexico and the United States do have an extradition treaty, and it has been used increasingly over the last several years. And, in 2005 the Mexican Supreme Court ruled that persons accused of crimes for which the sentence could be life in prison without the possibility of parole could also be extradited (Enriquez & Blankstein, 2005). That ruling is considered a major breakthrough in the U.S.–Mexico extradition relationship because it will facilitate extradition of fugitives facing life imprisonment in the United States (extradition of persons facing execution, however, is still prohibited).

Police departments in some California, New Mexico, and Texas cities have also made use of Article IV, but many police departments remain unaware of the article's potential for accomplishing justice. Even when police are familiar with Article IV, preconceived notions about corruption in Mexico or presumptions about minimal cooperation by Mexican officials have kept attempts at teamwork from even beginning. Maybe an increased interest in comparative criminal justice will result in more individual police departments working together in different countries, regardless of the reluctance of politicians at the national level in each country regarding cooperation.

- Europol (see Chapter 6) has been in full operation since 1999 and, much like Interpol does on a larger scale, it serves to facilitate the sharing of information among EU countries about crimes and criminals. Europol also provides expertise and technical support for operations and investigations engaged in by the member nations.
- Complementing Europol is Eurojust, which enhances cooperation and coordination of the prosecuting authorities in EU countries. Similarly, the European Judicial Network facilitates judicial cooperation.
- European Union countries already rely on each other for protection and security under the Schengen Convention, which has the goal of passport-free travel among the member nations. That means each country must provide strict identity controls at airports, seaports, and land borders for travelers arriving from countries outside the EU. Border checks of travelers moving from one EU country to another are no longer conducted, so the initial identity check becomes crucial for the governments and citizens of other EU countries to which the traveler may go.
- The police of one EU country, under tight constraints, are allowed to pursue criminals across borders into another EU country.
- European arrest warrants replace lengthy extradition procedures with an efficient way of returning suspected criminals to the country where they are accused of committing a serious crime. The warrants can also be used to return fleeing offenders to the country where they were sentenced.

Both bilateral and multinational cooperation in law enforcement present many problems for the countries involved. However, increasing transnational crime suggests that the potential benefits of cooperative efforts might outweigh the problems. A necessary step in achieving that cooperation is an increased understanding of criminal justice systems in the various nations. Thus, more people taking an international perspective toward criminal justice will have definite universal benefits.

APPROACHES TO AN INTERNATIONAL PERSPECTIVE

An author's goal typically instructs the approach used to convey information. A police officer writing her report of a recent arrest tells the story by referring to what she heard, saw, smelled, and touched. That approach is more likely to achieve a prosecution goal than would a report providing biographical information about the suspect without reference to the suspect's behavior at the time of the incident. On the other hand, after a conviction, a presentence investigation written by a probation officer would be of little use if it fully described the event resulting in conviction but provided no biographical information about the offender.

The police officer's descriptive style and the probation officer's historical one are both necessary. The two approaches differ in their appropriateness rather than in their importance. Similarly, the approach used to present information about criminal justice systems throughout the world will depend on the goal sought. There are at least three ways to study different criminal justice systems (Table 1.1). The historical, political, and descriptive approaches afford a structure that we can use to narrow and specify the goal of this text.

Historical Approach

The authors of a report on the state of their country's prison system complain about the heavy cost to the treasury of maintaining prisons. Adding to the problem, prison discipline is minimal and the convicts leave prison more hardened than they entered. The high recidivism rate may be explained by the prison's failure to instill in its inmates any

TABLE 1.1	Approaches to an International Perspective	
Historical Approach	**Political Approach**	**Descriptive Approach**
What mistakes and successes have already occurred?	How does politics affect a nation's justice system?	How is a country's justice system supposed to operate?
What do earlier experiences tell us about the present?	How does politics affect interaction among nations?	What are the main components of a justice system?
How can knowledge of the past prepare us for the future?	How is a country's legal tradition affected by politics?	Who are the main actors in a justice system?

principles of morality or sense of responsibility. The authors go on to tell of another country's prison system that not only shows a financial profit but does so under more humane conditions. Prisoners in the second country are placed under severe but uniform discipline, requiring rigorous work during the day and complete isolation at night. The benefits of this inflexibly uniform system include few recommittals to the prison.

We could argue that the authors' first country is the United States and the second either has a good public relations official or is a place we should send observers in order to get ideas on how to improve the American prison system. Actually, the authors were Gustave de Beaumont and Alexis de Tocqueville. The country criticized was their own nineteenth-century France, and the envied system was the American penitentiary structure in 1831 and 1832 (Beaumont & Tocqueville, 1964). An early nineteenth-century American prison system being coveted as superior to others seems ironic in light of twenty-first-century problems. Yet it is just that type of helpful comparison that the historical approach presents.

Beaumont and Tocqueville toured America when the Pennsylvania and Auburn systems were being touted as solutions to the new idea of imprisonment as punishment. The Frenchmen seemed to initially favor the Auburn system (quite likely for its economic benefits), but by the mid-1840s Tocqueville spoke before the Chamber of Deputies of France in favor of the Pennsylvania system (see Sellin's introduction in Beaumont & Tocqueville, 1964). Despite such wavering, there is no doubt that the two travelers to the United States considered either American penitentiary system as superior to others known at the time. Their report to French citizen provides a classic example of the historical comparative approach. After describing its evolution and objectives, they compare the American system with that of Switzerland and France, explaining why they consider the American system superior and suggesting ways to implement it.

Beaumont and Tocqueville used an international approach for what we earlier called "local benefits." They wanted to improve their system and looked to other countries for suggestions. Their appreciation of the American penitentiary system's historical evolution made it easier for them to see how that system might apply to the French situation. Today their report provides a sense of history for American and French prison systems. Researchers wishing to learn from earlier mistakes and successes in each country will benefit from an international perspective incorporating a historical approach.

An understanding and appreciation of history provide the criminal justice student with information about the present and the future. Like all other social institutions, criminal justice changes over time. Ignoring the past will make it impossible to prepare for inevitable changes of the future in procedures and institutions. As Terrill (1982) explains, the historical approach helps students to understand and be a part of a changing world. Despite the changes always taking place in any society, the problems faced remain remarkably stable. The need for security, justice, and freedom is neither the only nor the least of those problems.

Political Approach

An international perspective that takes a political approach appreciates the importance of understanding how a country's legal system is affected by that country's politics. That point is emphasized by Downie (2013) who—in giving advice on what the United States can do to reform police in three African nations—suggests that political will is the minimum condition for police reform. If the political will is not evident, the United States (or, presumably, any other entity) should probably not get involved. Similarly, when analyzing United Nations and European Union efforts at police reform in Bosnia and Herzegovina, Padurariu (2014) warns that most of the stumbling blocks for implementing police reform lie at the political level.

The point is that understanding a country's criminal justice system requires an understanding of its political system. This principle is most clearly apparent in efforts to build police capacity in post-conflict societies. When defining their protocols for police capacity building, the United Nations noted that the guidelines are based on the assumption that the host government is committed to the establishment of a responsive, representative, and accountable police service (United Nations, 2015). In fact, the first fundamental principle of the UN guidelines notes that police reform is as much a political as a technical matter. To that end, successful police reform requires the involvement of various political or factional divisions and the overcoming of rivalries. Without political will, it is not possible to build an effective police institution.

Individual nations and nations working in collaboration have been involved in building police capacity in post-conflict societies (e.g., in Iraq and Afghanistan), but the United Nations has been the most active of supranational organizations. During the last three decades, the UN Department of Peacekeeping Operations and the UN Development Programme have helped to reform or create new police forces in, to name just a few, Namibia, El Salvador, Bosnia and Herzegovina, Kosovo, Rwanda, Croatia, Sierra Leone, Guatemala, and Liberia. Based on the UN experience, O'Neill (2005) identified several things that are apparent when police reform is attempted. Those include:

- The realization that police reform takes a long time and involves transforming power relations in a society.
- Respect for human rights and effective crime fighting go together.
- It is not sufficient to work only on reforming the police. Effective reform requires paying attention to the broader criminal justice institutions as well.
- Local history, traditions, and culture must be acknowledged in all police reforms. Failing to anchor programs in local realities means failure for those programs.

WEB PROJECT
Politics Around the World

Visit http://www.world-newspapers.com/ or http://www.onlinenewspapers.com/, and from the lists of newspapers around the world choose one paper to read for a full week. With selections such as the *Beirut Daily Star*, the *Canberra Times*, the *China Daily*, the *Guadalajara Reporter*, *The Guardian* (Nigeria), the *Jerusalem Post*, the *Times of London*, the *Toronto Star*, and many others, you should easily find one that attracts your attention. News items related to politics will be found most easily, but during the week you may also come across stories about police, courts, or prisons. At the end of the week, write a few paragraphs that describe your experience of reading a daily newspaper from another country and include specific examples of interesting things you learned.

There have been, in fact, some examples of successful police reform efforts when political factors have been taken into consideration. For example, after the end of Liberia's (see Map A.1) civil war in 2003, the United Nations Mission in Liberia (UNMIL) began working to train and equip new police recruits, advise and mentor senior police officers, and build links between police and prosecutors in Liberia. The Liberia National Police (LNP) had been feared and distrusted by the public, so reform efforts had to immediately address those well-founded citizen concerns. There were some missteps (e.g., all former police were required to reapply for their jobs and that angered experienced officers), but there have been clear signs of progress. The LNP's prewar reputation for abuses and corruption is being cast off, honest police officers who started their career in 2003 have reached senior officer levels where they can positively influence junior officers, ethnicity is no longer a divisive force within the police, and women now comprise 17 percent of the workforce (Downie, 2013).

Serious problems remain for Liberia, however. The LNP's budget is inadequate, a shortage of basic resources makes it difficult for officers to perform their duties, low salaries and the absence of robust professional standards lead to corruption, and public trust of the police remains low. Taking a political approach, we see that many of the problems facing reform efforts are tied to political factors. Downie (2013) explains that the government seems to value loyalty toward the state over service to the people. Against the recommendation of civil society groups, the president continues to have the authority to appoint several of the most senior police officials, including the inspector general of the LNP. As a result, the most senior police executive and some of the other senior police officers have no policing experience or background. Mid-ranked police officers express frustration with their superiors who occasionally give directives based more on political considerations than on proper police procedures.

A country's political system will influence, if not determine, its policing, court, and corrections system. The political approach recognizes the importance of politics in understanding criminal justice at a national and international level. Like the historical approach, the political approach is not the primary one we follow in this text, but it is important nonetheless.

Descriptive Approach

A description of how something should operate provides the necessary basis for analysis and repair. Just as it would be difficult to repair a motor without knowing how that motor is supposed to function, we must understand a justice system's stated organization and structure before we can determine how closely its operation conforms to the model. Description is the essential first step in comparing criminal justice systems. The historical and political approaches are also necessary and will receive occasional attention in this book, but the descriptive approach allows us to gain an overview of a country's justice system so that we can begin to identify similarities and differences among the nations. To that end, this book emphasizes a descriptive approach when presenting information about criminal justice in other countries. Two tactics are possible when a descriptive approach is selected for a cross-cultural textbook. One technique focuses on specific countries and describes the legal system's operation in each country. The result is a text in which the same topics (e.g., law, police, courts, and corrections) are described in a separate chapter for each country (e.g., England, Germany, Australia, and Japan). This strategy provides depth of coverage and gives the reader a strong background in the systems of several countries. An alternative technique focuses on specific components of the criminal justice system and describes how different countries implement those segments. The result is a text wherein a wide variety of countries (again, England, Germany, Australia, and Japan, plus others) are referred to in separate chapters on such topics as law, police, courts, and corrections. This tactic does not provide the reader with detailed information about any two or three specific countries. Instead, the detail centers on the primary components of all systems of justice and uses various countries to highlight the variations. Because the goals of this text include developing a better understanding of the American system of justice and gaining ideas for improving that system, the second technique seems more appropriate. In that manner, we can concentrate on already familiar concepts (i.e., law, police, courts, and corrections) but do so by looking at the diversity that exists in executing those concepts. As noted, the trade-off for showing variance is a less comprehensive review of each country. However, several countries make appearances in at least two chapters, so readers will have a nearly complete portrait of the justice system in some places, such as Germany and France.

STRATEGIES UNDER THE DESCRIPTIVE APPROACH

When differences among standard components of criminal justice systems are explored, the descriptive approach can follow two paths. One emphasizes the institutions and actors, whereas the other highlights specific functions and procedures. This text follows the institutions/actors strategy but occasionally makes use of the functions/procedures strategy as well.

The Functions/Procedures Strategy

Lynch believes cross-national research benefits from a functional rather than organizational or positional description of national criminal justice systems (Lynch, 1988). He argues that there is more similarity of jobs across systems than there is among persons performing those duties. This point becomes apparent in other chapters as we look at examples such as private citizens serving as prosecutors or lay judges, judges actively involved in police investigations, and probation officers who are volunteers rather than paid employees.

The argument Lynch makes is that all countries require that similar jobs be done—they just assign the duties differently. Ingraham provides an excellent example of this approach in his descriptive account of the underlying structure common to the procedural systems of several countries. As he puts it, "Nations may differ from one another in the manner of collecting evidence, the way they sift it, refine it, and evaluate it prior to trial, and the way they present it at trial, but they all have procedures to do these things" (Ingraham, 1987). The comparison model he develops describes procedures under the headings of intake, screening, charging and protecting, adjudication, sanctioning, and appeal. The result is a concise account comparing countries in each of the six categories.

As an example, we consider the way the United States, France (see Map A.10), and China (see Map A.7) respond to the task of charging a defendant and protecting that defendant against abuse by the accusers. The first concern in this process is the need to protect the defendant against prolonged and unnecessary pretrial detention. We are interested not in the particular office or type of agent responsible for ensuring this protection but, rather, in the procedures each country uses.

Police in the United States may detain a suspect for a limited time as part of an investigative stop or investigative detention (*Terry* v. *Ohio*, 392 U.S. 1, 1968), but any prolonged detention requires formal arrest. Rather than setting time limits after which an investigative detention becomes a de facto arrest, the U.S. Supreme Court has simply said that the detention should last no longer than is necessary to accomplish the purpose of the stop (*Florida* v. *Royer*, 460 U.S. 491 at 500, 1983). After a formal arrest, the suspect must be taken to a magistrate who advises the defendant of the charges against him or her and of his or her rights regarding bail and legal counsel. This initial appearance (which is not required in all jurisdictions) typically occurs within 48 hours of arrest—although there has been no U.S. Supreme Court case setting time limits for the initial appearance.

Some jurisdictions require a probable cause hearing in order to provide a judicial (rather than only a police) determination of probable cause to keep a person detained. Where those hearings are required, they must take place "promptly after arrest" (*Gerstein* v. *Pugh*, 420 U.S. 103, 1975), which should not take longer than 48 hours (*County of Riverside* v. *McLaughlin*, 500 U.S. 44, 1991). Based on these restrictions, we would not expect the police to be able to independently detain a suspect for more than 48 hours before a judicial officer reviews the legality of the detention.

The powers of the French police to detain accused persons before trial differ somewhat from those in the United States. In cases of recently committed offenses (in practice, offenses occurring within the preceding 8 days), the police may detain a suspect without a warrant for 24 hours so that an investigation can be conducted (Frase, 2007; Hodgson, 2005; Pakes, 2004). The prosecutor can extend the detention period for another 24 hours upon being shown additional and weighty evidence supporting guilt. The defendant cannot be detained beyond the 24 (or the total of 48) hours unless the prosecutor turns the investigation over to an investigation judge, who can then authorize temporary detention. In order to use temporary detention, the authorized punishment for the alleged offense must exceed 2 years, there must be reason to believe that the accused would respond negatively in the community (e.g., flee, exert pressure on witnesses, or commit new offenses), or judicial supervision must be determined inadequate. Rather than relying on the bail system, France allows the defendant to obtain liberty before trial either with or without "judicial supervision." That procedure is a pretrial release with conditions (e.g., do not leave the area, or report at specific times to particular officials) imposed by the magistrate.

China's Criminal Procedure Law allows the police to detain a suspect for up to 3 days when certain conditions are present (e.g., the suspect is preparing to, is in the process of, or has just committed a crime; criminal evidence is discovered on or near the suspect or in the suspect's home; or there is a chance the suspect may destroy evidence). Under "special circumstances" (undefined in the Criminal Procedure Law), the initial period may be extended up to a total of 7 days. However, in "major cases" (identified in Article 89 of the Criminal Procedure Law as crimes committed across regions, repeatedly, or as part of a gang), the suspect may be detained for up to 30 days (People's Republic of China, 2012).

After the maximum period of 7 days, or, for the major cases, 30 days, the police must obtain permission to formally arrest the suspect. The procurator (see Chapter 7 for an explanation of this "prosecutor-like" position) has up to 7 days to render a decision. The result of all this is that police, on their own authority, can easily subject anyone (given the general definition of "major cases") to incarceration for up to 37 days (Belkin, 2007; People's Republic of China, 2012).

That brief review of how three countries protect citizens against prolonged and unnecessary pretrial detention provides a quick look at the functions/procedures perspective. This approach allows easy viewing of similarities among countries while drawing attention to

WEB PROJECT

Arrested in . . .?

Visit https://www.fairtrials.org/arrested-abroad/arrested-in/, where you will find more than 30 countries listed in the "Arrested in . . ." dropdown box (left margin). Select at least two countries and find the question: "What are my rights upon being detained in . . .?" Write a few paragraphs that describe similarities and differences in the detention rules of your chosen countries.

the basic functions and procedures found in a variety of criminal justice systems. When differences become apparent, they suggest topics of conversation and debate.

For example, Ingraham suggests that by failing to allow limited periods for investigative detention prior to arrest, we in the United States may not be providing suspects the level of protection we think we are (Ingraham, 1987). His position is that the absence of investigative detention provisions forces American police to initiate the arrest process very early. Once the suspect is arrested and confined, pretrial release procedures come into play. American pretrial release relies heavily on bail, and arrested persons are frequently too poor to raise the necessary security. As a result, in providing safeguards against arbitrary and prolonged pretrial detention, the U.S. system actually deprives poor defendants of a measure of protection against being unfairly arrested (Ingraham, 1987). On the other hand, China's ability to hold a person for more than 30 days before formal arrest is required could lessen the likelihood of an unfair arrest but means that an unfair detention can be quite lengthy.

The Institutions/Actors Strategy

A functions/procedures strategy clarifies duties and highlights the similarities among countries but may mask important differences. Also, although that approach makes it easy to organize information for comparing a few countries, it becomes cumbersome when working with a large number of countries.

The other approach is to compare countries on the basis of specific institutions and positions charged with accomplishing particular duties. For example, Ingraham (1987) examines protection against prolonged and unnecessary pretrial detention by describing the functions and procedures used in four countries to accomplish that task. He is not concerned with the specific agency or type of officer responsible for those efforts. The alternative way to approach the topic is to emphasize such institutions as police, courts, and corrections while discussing the assigned duties of people such as police officers, attorneys, judges, and wardens.

Each approach is reasonable and useful. However, for our purposes, the institutions/actors technique is featured because it better enables the viewing of differences and can handle a larger number of countries. The chapters of this book rely on descriptions of institutions and actors, so it is an approach that will soon become very familiar to you.

COMPARISON THROUGH CLASSIFICATION

In a popular parlor game, one person thinks of a person, place, or thing while others try to guess the object using no more than 20 yes-or-no questions. When you consider the infinite number of possibilities, it seems quite presumptuous to believe that we could guess, with no more than 20 questions, what someone else is thinking of. The fact that questioners are successful enough to perpetuate the game is a sobering thought.

A standard approach for players is to ask questions by setting up categories. For example, after determining that the object is a person, questioners may ask if it is male or female. Additional questioning may identify living or dead, famous or infamous, and eventually narrow down the person's occupation, basis for fame, and so forth. This process used to identify the object is dependent upon the player's knowledge and use of classification.

The Need for Classification

Classification refers to the grouping of individual objects into categories based on the object's relationships. Through this process of naming and then grouping items into recognizable categories, we order and summarize the diversity that exists in the world. Its importance for operating in society (rather than simply winning a parlor game) becomes apparent upon realizing that survival of early humans must have been aided by an ability to recognize that individual objects shared certain properties. For example, some items were edible whereas others made people sick. Some animals were helpful; others were lethal. The ability to distinguish the category into which a particular item fell certainly made life more pleasant.

The process of classification and the resulting classification systems have been studied most completely by scientists interested in living organisms (Dunn & Everitt, 1982; Mayr, 1982; Stace, 1989). Terms such as *taxonomy* and *systematics* are familiar from biology classes. The concept of classification, however, is helpful and applicable whenever one has to deal with diversity. From the rather frivolous example of playing "20 Questions," we can move to the more practical one of finding a book in the library. Simply mentioning the prospect of searching for a particular book from a grouping of thousands, in no order whatsoever, is enough to remind us to be grateful for the Library of Congress classification system.

So, there is no argument on the need for classification. Instead, disagreement rests on how to classify, what criteria should be used in the process, and what the ultimate purpose of classification is. We spend some time responding to these questions, because classification plays an important role in the structure of this text. Our guiding principle follows Ehrmann's (1976) argument that categorization is the base for all comparison. The diversity of the world's criminal justice systems requires an understanding of and appreciation for the classification process and the resulting schemes.

Classification Strategies

Rather than tackle the difficult issue of how the classification process should take place (interested readers are referred to texts on macrotaxonomy, mathematical taxonomy, plant taxonomy, and biosystematics), let us consider the idea that each classification strategy has good and bad points. What is "best" in a particular instance depends on the goal sought. It seems more important for our purposes to be aware of what schemes are possible than to try to determine which one is superior.

Two ways of classifying are possible (see Table 1.2). The first is a synthetic strategy resulting in categorization of artificial groups. Classification of this type typically has a special purpose and attempts to bring order to a confusing array of objects. The terms *synthetic* and *artificial* are used with this approach because the ensuing classification is the result of scientists manufacturing a group that categorizes objects based on some criteria of interest to the scientist.

Usually, artificial groups are built around only one or two aspects of the object being classified. For example, a telephone book groups people alphabetically within the 26 groups of letters. A book for hikers may group flowers by color, thereby making identification easier and quicker. The classification of library books uses more criteria (e.g., subject matter and author's last name) but still is essentially a "pigeonholing" exercise for the purpose of bringing order to diversity.

Although synthetic classification strategies have practical applications, such as making it easy to find a phone number, identify a flower, or track down a book, their artificial nature does not allow us to imply or deduce other information about the object. For example, we would not assume that all people listed under S in the phone book are females of German heritage just because our friend Helene Schneider is an Austrian woman. Because nothing else about an object is suggested, beyond the one or two characteristics used in the classification process, synthetic strategies have low predictivity.

The process of classification allows us to summarize diversity and is used in this book to highlight similarities and differences in the criminal justice systems of countries around the world.

limbi007/123RF

TABLE 1.2	Classification Strategies
Synthetic Strategies	**Authentic Strategies**
Results in artificial groups	Results in natural groups
Is based on only one or two aspects of the object	Is based on extensive study of the object
Resulting classification has a practical or special purpose that brings order to diversity	Resulting classification allows some predictivity regarding the group's members

Authentic strategies for classification provide categorization of natural groups. Because this scheme uses a great number of characteristics to categorize objects into groups, it is much more predictive than are synthetic systems. The terms *authentic* and *natural* are appropriate here, because scientists group objects based on factual characteristics shared by members of a group. Unlike synthetic strategies, this approach relies on verified inherent attributes rather than traits assigned or manufactured to meet some purpose that a scientist has. Humans categorized according to last names in a phone book constitute artificial groups. In contrast, humans classified according to some measure of human biology constitute natural groups. Because this classification is based on inherent rather than assigned characteristics, it possesses the quality of predictivity. To illustrate, when scientists determine that everyone in a group of 100 humans drives erratically after imbibing a certain amount of alcohol, it seems safe to hypothesize that all (or most) other humans (i.e., all other members of the same category of living organisms) would be similarly affected. Additional study may require us to revise that initial assumption to allow for variation in size, weight, and so on. Even so, a predictivity exists that is impossible with an artificial grouping. We cannot assume that a poison oak leaf is edible just because, like a lettuce leaf, it is green.

It may seem that its predictivity makes an authentic classification strategy superior to a synthetic one, but both schemes have their good and bad points. Predictivity is desirable, but it is not the sole criterion for judging classification schemes. It may be just as important and interesting to know the evolutionary history and relationships among items as it is to make predictions about the attributes of a particular object in a group. Similarly, the currently observable structure of objects in a specific category requires description and understanding regardless of any need to make predictions. These concerns with historical relationships and contemporary relationships are examples of special-purpose classifications easily handled by synthetic strategies. In these cases, predictivity is not a goal of the categorization, so natural groups are not necessary. Therefore, the classification may be adequately conducted with knowledge of only one or two characteristics of the objects involved.

The Role of Classification in This Book

The classification of living organisms traces its origin at least as far back as Aristotle (384–322 BCE). It is not surprising, therefore, that some authentic systems of classification resulting in natural groups and having significant predictivity are found in biology and botany. The cross-cultural study of criminal justice systems does not share such a distinguished history. As a relatively new area of study, comparative criminal justice has not investigated its various "objects" to the extent necessary to provide authentic systems and natural groups. Today, classification in comparative criminal justice is essentially of the synthetic scheme. Synthetic strategies are important, however, because they successfully serve purposes other than predictivity.

Chapters 2 through 9 of this text are organized around particular classification schemes. Some of those approximate authentic systems with a general purpose, but most are the synthetic type having a special purpose (either historical or contemporary). In both cases, the reader should remember that classification (of either type) is being used to summarize and make sense of diversity. In addition, any classification system should serve as an aid to memory. Presenting information about a topic via a classification scheme should enable you to visualize and conceptualize the material more easily.

A final note of caution is necessary. Some people tend to view a particular classification as equivalent to a scientific theory. As such, the classification could be proved wrong. Viewing a classification in that manner is inappropriate and incorrect (Dunn & Everitt, 1982). Because it is a creation of reason based on accumulation of experienced data, a classification can be neither right nor wrong. It is merely an intelligible summary of information. Its value is determined by its usefulness to others. Importantly, saying that a classification is neither right nor wrong is not the same as saying that it cannot or should not be changed. If it ceases to be useful, it should be modified or discarded.

THE STRUCTURE OF THIS BOOK

This book uses a descriptive rather than a historical or political approach to studying comparative criminal justice. The focus is on the primary components of a large number of nations rather than on providing an in-depth examination of the components in just a few countries. This topical rather than country-by-country approach loses detail of specific countries but compensates by allowing coverage of a larger number of countries and by more clearly identifying system differences. The particular path followed with this descriptive approach emphasizes institutions and actors rather than functions and procedures. Historical and political approaches are not ignored; neither are descriptive accounts of functions and procedures. Yet those devices provide only secondary themes here.

To aid in presenting the descriptive information, classification schemes are built around both synthetic and authentic strategies. The infancy of comparative criminal justice as a field of study requires greater use of synthetic strategies, because these can be built on only one or two criteria. The resulting artificial groups provide a sense of order to the diversity of institutions and procedures in the criminal justice systems we will encounter. The reader should remember to approach the classification in each chapter as a summary of information rather than a scientific theory. Continuing political and cultural changes occurring throughout the world present opportunities to modify the classification scheme as our knowledge of different systems expands.

With the descriptive approach used here, there is a distinct danger of providing incomplete information about some countries. Sociologists are well aware that social groups and organizations have an informal structure as well as the formal one presented to the public. A police department's organizational chart may clearly show a chain of command flowing from the police chief through bureau chiefs to division chiefs and down to section and unit commanders. What may not be shown is the department's informal policy that allows administrators to bypass a level or two when working on certain tasks or with "old friends." For example, earlier this chapter described the procedures used to ensure a suspect's right against prolonged and unreasonable detention for three countries. It would be naive of us to believe that those procedures, in any of the countries, are followed to the letter by each actor every day.

The best way to identify and eventually describe the informal structure and relations of a group or organization is through participant observation over a prolonged period. Unfortunately, comparative criminal justice is a foundling among scientific fields of study. As a result, it has few participant-observation-type research efforts.

Yet the absence of knowledge about informal workings should not preclude the use of a descriptive approach. It should only serve to remind us that there is much to learn about criminal justice organizations in our own country as well as those in other parts of the world. Although the descriptive approach provides information about only the stated workings of criminal justice institutions and actors, when you think about it, we would not want to start anywhere else. After all, it is necessary to understand how something is supposed to work before we can even begin to discern how it varies from the model.

There is a final point to make concerning the structure of this book—and the structure of the world. The last decade of the twentieth century started with dramatic and traumatic world events beginning in the late 1980s. The social, political, and economic changes brought down the Berlin Wall, saw the rise of democracy in former Communist countries, encouraged the reunification of Germany and the breakup of the Soviet Union, and essentially ensured that the world would end the century in a very different place than either experts or laypeople had imagined.

The changes brought opportunities to many people in a variety of occupations, but mapmakers composed one occupational group for whom the events were as frustrating as they were exciting. Throughout the late 1900s, media reported the futility felt by artists responsible for portraying geographic boundaries, encyclopedists attempting to prepare factual entries by publication deadlines, and college professors trying to give accurate lectures on the politics of Eastern European countries. Persons interested in comparative criminal justice were placed in a similar predicament. What if a country's justice system is faithfully and accurately described in February only to find that country operating under a different political system in March? If we wait until April to describe the system, who can say that other changes will not occur in May? During times of rapid geographic change, cartographers continue to make and distribute maps. During times of rapid economic change, economists continue to debate and predict financial issues. Similarly, despite changes affecting government structures and organization, criminal justice scholars continue to describe and analyze justice systems.

Actually, the field of comparative criminal justice has an advantage over some other fields, because even rapid political and economic change cannot easily force similarly paced structural and bureaucratic change. Change does not necessarily occur at the same pace in all parts of a country. After all, tradition is hard to overcome, and change is scary.

The comfort of tradition and the threat of change do not mean that a nation's social institutions can avoid change. The point is not that criminal justice agencies escape modification but rather that what appears to be rapid social change affecting all aspects of a country and its people may be the start of a marathon race rather than a sprint. As you read this book's description of criminal justice in various countries, you will undoubtedly find information that is no longer accurate for that country; you may even read about a country that no longer exists in the form described. Such problems are inevitable in today's dynamic world. However, because people and their social institutions tend to find comfort in tradition and anxiety in change, the discrepancies are likely to be ones of detail rather than of the whole.

Summary

This chapter introduces a book describing the different ways criminal justice can operate. That variability is shown by reference to justice systems operating in countries around the world. The study of criminal justice systems in other countries has specific benefits for our own justice system as well as for international relations. The local benefits include the development of intercultural competence and establishing points of contrast, which can suggest ideas to improve our system. On a broader scale, knowledge of how other countries conceive and implement the idea of "justice" is increasingly necessary. The presence and persistence of cross-national crimes, including terrorism, hijacking, drug smuggling, and organized crime, demand a cooperative international effort. Such an effort is aided when citizens of different countries are familiar with and try to understand and respect the institutions and procedures of other countries. Specific examples include cooperation by neighboring countries and multinational cooperation.

The process of studying assorted criminal justice systems can take at least three approaches: historical, political, and descriptive. This book uses the descriptive approach primarily, with attention focused on the formal workings of organizations and people driving a country's criminal justice system.

The descriptive approach allows for comparison of a number of countries. A problem with such comparison is the overwhelming diversity confronting us as we attempt to find similarities and identify differences among various systems. To aid in the process, each chapter uses a classification scheme that provides order and aids the memory process. The process of classification is achieved through two strategies: synthetic and authentic. Each strategy results in a grouping of objects (artificial or natural groups of objects) having special (the artificial groups) or predictive (the natural groups) purposes.

Discussion Questions

• Although you likely have only limited knowledge of how the justice system operates in other countries (after all, that is one of the reasons you're taking this course), identify a foreign country where you would prefer to be visiting should you be unfortunate enough to be arrested for a crime. What features of that country that you know or believe to be true have influenced your selection? For example, would it be important that you not need to rely on an interpreter when speaking with the police or appearing in court? Was your selection based on visits you have made to the country? On what you have seen in movies or read in books? What features of the American system of justice (e.g., search warrants, jury trials, burden of proof) do you hope the selected country has?

• This chapter's Impact box describes how one local jurisdiction was able to have a person who committed a crime in Colorado successfully prosecuted for that crime in Mexico. In what ways do you think the role of local law enforcement officers will change during the next decade as foreign nationals increasingly commit crimes in a host country and then return to their native country?

References

American Bar Association. (1999, September 25). Perceptions of the U.S. justice system, 1999. Retrieved from http://www.abanow.org/wordpress/wp-content/files_flutter/1269460858_20_1_1_7_Upload_File.pdf

Aspinwall, M., & Reich, S. (2016). Who is Wile E. Coyote? Power, influence and the war on drugs. *International Politics, 53*(2), 155–175. doi:10.1057/ip.2015.43

Beaumont, G., & Tocqueville, A. (1964). *On the penitentiary system in the United States and its application in France*. Carbondale, IL: Southern Illinois University Press.

Belkin, I. (2007). China. In C. M. Bradley (Ed.), *Criminal procedure: A worldwide study* (2nd ed., pp. 91–106). Durham, NC: Carolina Academic Press.

Bureau for International Narcotics and Law Enforcement Affairs. (2016, March). Volume 1: Drug and Chemical Control. *International Narcotics Control Strategy Report*. Retrieved from http://www.state.gov/j/inl/rls/nrcrpt/index.htm

Cole, G. F., Frankowski, S. J., & Gertz, M. G. (Eds.). (1987). *Major criminal justice systems: A comparative study* (2nd ed.). Newbury Park, CA: Sage.

Deardorff, D. K. (2014, May 15). Some thoughts on assessing intercultural competence. National Institute for Learning Outcomes Assessment. Retrieved from https://illinois.edu/blog/view/915/113048

Deflem, M. (2002). *Policing world society: Historical foundations of international police cooperation*. New York, NY: Oxford University Press.

Downie, R. (2013). Building police institutions in fragile states: Case studies from Africa. Retrieved from https://www.ciaonet.org/attachments/26086/uploads

Dunn, G., & Everitt, B. S. (1982). *An introduction to mathematical taxonomy*. Cambridge, UK: Cambridge University Press.

Duran, E. J. (2002). Article IV prosecutions. *FBI Law Enforcement Bulletin, 71*(6), 20–24.

Ehrmann, H. W. (1976). *Comparative legal cultures*. Englewood Cliffs, NJ: Prentice Hall.

Enriquez, S., & Blankstein, A. (2005, November 30). Mexico to extradite more suspects to U.S. *Los Angeles Times*. Retrieved from http://articles.latimes.com/2005/nov/30/world/fg-mexico30

Europa. (2016, June 1). EU institutions and other bodies. Retrieved from http://europa.eu/about-eu/institutions-bodies/index_en.htm

Frase, R. S. (2007). France. In C. M. Bradley (Ed.), *Criminal procedure: A worldwide study* (2nd ed., pp. 201–242). Durham, NC: Carolina Academic Press.

Friedman, T. L. (2005). *The world is flat: A brief history of the twenty-first century*. New York, NY: Farrar, Straus & Giroux.

Gallup. (2015). Global law and order 2015. Retrieved from http://www.gallup.com/services/185798/gallup-global-law-order-2015-report.aspx

Hodgson, J. (2005). *French criminal justice: A comparative account of the investigation and prosecution of crime in France*. Portland, OR: Hart.

Ingraham, B. L. (1987). *The structure of criminal procedure: Laws and practice of France, the Soviet Union, China, and the United States*. New York, NY: Greenwood Press.

Krogstad, J. M. (2014, August 28). Latino confidence in local police lower than among whites. Pew Research Center. Retrieved from http://www.pewresearch.org

Loschky, J. (2014, August 4). Less than half in Africa confident in their judicial systems. Retrieved from http://www.gallup.com

Lynch, J. P. (1988). A comparison of prison use in England, Canada, West Germany, and the United States. *Journal of Criminal Law and Criminology, 79*, 180–217.

Mayr, E. (1982). *The growth of biological thought*. Cambridge, UK: Cambridge University Press.

Meyer, E. (2015). When culture doesn't translate. *Harvard Business Review, 93*(10), 66–72.

Mitchell, K. (1999, April 11). Mexico offers an avenue, but fugitives still on street. *The Denver Post,* pp. 1A, 25A, 27A.

Norman, J. (2016, June 13). Americans' confidence in institutions stays low. Gallup. Retrieved from http://www.gallup.com

O'Neill, W. G. (2005). Police reform in post-conflict societies: What we know and what we still need to know. Retrieved from https://www.ipinst.org/wp-content/uploads/publications/polreferpt.pdf

Padurariu, A. (2014). The implementation of police reform in Bosnia and Herzegovina: Analysing UN and EU efforts. *Stability: International Journal of Security and Development, 3*(1), 1–18. Retrieved from http://dx.doi.org/10.5334/sta.db

Pakes, F. J. (2004). *Comparative criminal justice*. Portland, OR: Willan.

People's Republic of China. (2012). Criminal Procedure Law of the People's Republic of China (amended: March 14, 2012). China Law Translate. Retrieved from http://chinalawtranslate.com/criminal-procedure-law/?lang=en

Rasmussen Reports. (2011a, July 3). 54% say U.S. is nation of liberty and justice for all. Retrieved from http://www.rasmussenreports.com/

Rasmussen Reports. (2011b, July 14). 58% trust jury more to determine guilt or innocence, 27% trust judge. Retrieved from http://www.rasmussenreports.com/

Rasmussen Reports. (2011c, June 11). 61% believe Casey Anthony is guilty of murder. Retrieved from http://www.rasmussenreports.com/

Rasmussen Reports. (2014, December 9). What American thinks: Is the justice system fair for everyone? Retrieved from http://www.rasmussenreports.com/

Rasmussen Reports. (2016, June 8). Voters don't trust judges but think politicians should leave them alone. Retrieved from http://www.rasmussenreports.com/

Reichel, P. L. (2008). Cross-national collaboration to combat human trafficking: Learning from the experience of others. Retrieved from https://www.ncjrs.gov/App/Publications/abstract.aspx?ID=245202

Rochelle, S., & Loschky, J. (2014, October 22). Confidence in judicial systems varies worldwide. Gallup. Retrieved from http://www.gallup.com

Santayana, G. (1905). Patriotism. *Reason in society* (Vol. II). New York, NY: Charles Scribner's Sons.

Seelke, C. R., & Finklea, K. (2014, April 8). U.S.–Mexican security cooperation: The Mérida Initiative and beyond. Congressional Research Service. Retrieved from http://digital.library.unt.edu/ark:/67531/metadc332947/m1/1/high_res_d/R41349_2014Apr08.pdf

Seelke, C. R., & Finklea, K. (2016, February 22). U.S.–Mexican security cooperation: The Mérida initiative and beyond. Congressional Research Service. Retrieved from https://www.fas.org/sgp/crs/row/R41349.pdf

Stace, C. A. (1989). *Plant taxonomy and biosystematics* (2nd ed.). London, UK: Edward Arnold.

Terrill, R. J. (1982). Approaches for teaching comparative criminal justice to undergraduates. *Criminal Justice Review, 7*(1), 23–27.

Toro, M. C. (1999). The internationalization of police: The DEA in Mexico. *Journal of American History, 86*(2), 623–640.

Tortora, B. (2007, January 18). Africans' confidence in institutions—Which country stands out? Gallup. Retrieved from http://www.gallup.com/poll/26176/africans-confidence-institutions-which-country-stands-out.aspx

Tyson, A. (2014, July 2). Most Americans think the U.S. is great, but fewer say it's the greatest. Pew Research Center. Retrieved from http://www.pewresearch.org/fact-tank/2014/07/02/most-americans-think-the-u-s-is-great-but-fewer-say-its-the-greatest/

United Nations. (2015). Guidelines on police capacity-building and development. Retrieved from http://www.un.org/en/peacekeeping/sites/police/documents/Guidelines.pdf

Van de Walle, S. (2009). Trust in the justice system: A comparative view across Europe. *Prison Service Journal, 183*, 22–26.

2

Domestic, Transnational, and International Crime and Justice
With Rosemary Barberet[1]

LEARNING OBJECTIVES

After studying this chapter, you will be able to:

1. Distinguish between comparative criminology and comparative criminal justice.
2. List and provide examples of the two primary problems criminologists face when comparing crime in two or more countries.
3. Name and summarize five grand theory explanations that have been used in cross-national crime research.
4. Distinguish between international crime and transnational crime.
5. Identify and explain at least five types of transnational crime.
6. Summarize international efforts responding to domestic, transnational, and international crime.

COUNTRIES IN FOCUS

Somalia	Switzerland
Sweden	United States

Two high school football players were found guilty on March 17, 2013, of raping a 16-year-old girl the previous summer in Steubenville, Ohio. The case attracted national attention because social media prompted the initial prosecution and later generated publicity about the case. The two young men penetrated the victim with their fingers (considered rape in Ohio), who was drunk and had passed out and thus could not consent to sex. She did not remember what had happened but text messages and cell phone pictures were evidence (Oppel, 2013).

On March 21, 2016, the International Criminal Court (ICC) found Jean-Pierre Bemba Gombo guilty, as military commander, of crimes against humanity (murder and rape) and war crimes (murder, rape, and pillaging). The crimes were committed in the Central African Republic between 2002 and 2003. His trial, which began in 2010, was the ICC's first to focus on the recognition of rape as a war crime. A rebel leader and former vice president of the Democratic Republic of the Congo, he commanded a militia that raped, murdered, and pillaged in the civil war in neighboring Central African Republic. One victim was raped by 12 soldiers. Also, a 10-year-old girl also was raped and, the court was told, her father heard her cries. Additional testimony told of a man being held at gunpoint while at least four soldiers raped his wife. When the man protested, he was then raped himself (Vinograd, 2016).

---

[1]Dr. Rosemary Barberet is Professor of Sociology at John Jay College of Criminal Justice in New York City. Her research and teaching are centered on international criminal justice.

On February 24, 2015, a federal jury in the United States issued guilty verdicts against two Ukrainian brothers living in Canada, on the charge of conspiracy to participate in a racketeering enterprise in connection with a human trafficking scheme. From 2000 to 2007, they operated a human trafficking organization that smuggled young Ukrainian immigrants into the United States via Mexico and then forced them to work for little or no pay. The defendants promised the victims they would earn $500 per month with free room and board by working for their organization. They smuggled the workers into the United States and then put them to work as cleaning crews in retail stores, private homes, and office buildings without paying them. They used physical force, threats of force, sexual assault, and debt bondage to keep the victims in involuntary servitude. One female worker was brutally raped by one of the co-conspirators (U.S. Department of Justice, 2015).

These three incidents are illustrative of domestic, transnational, and international crime—in this case, all involving sexual violence. The Steubenville case is considered domestic crime because it occurred within the borders of the United States. The Ukrainian brothers' human trafficking scheme is categorized as transnational crime—crime that occurs in two or more countries (in this case, Ukraine, Mexico, Canada, and the United States). The third incident, which also involves sexual violence, is international crime, crimes that are part of mass atrocities and shock the conscience of the world.

Domestic crime, transnational crime, and international crime provide the subject matter for the field of study known as comparative or international criminology. From these brief scenarios, you may already be thinking how challenging it is to engage in comparative criminological research. Legal definitions of crime, the reporting and recording of crimes, and the motivations and circumstances surrounding crimes vary so much around the world. Those fascinating topics compose much of the material for this chapter. Also interesting is how countries respond to domestic, transnational, and international crime. That topic, which is the concern for comparative justice scholars, is addressed briefly in this chapter but is the theme for much of the rest of the book.

COMPARATIVE CRIMINOLOGY AND CRIMINAL JUSTICE

Comparative studies in crime and justice cover two independent but overlapping areas. First is the area of comparative criminology for which interest is in the study of crime as a social phenomenon (the focus is more on the crime) and as social behavior (the focus is more on the offender). Second is comparative criminal justice with its interest in determining how various countries attempt to maintain social order and accomplish justice.

This book is about comparative criminal justice and has as its theme the procedures and processes established to identify, adjudicate, and punish law violators in countries around the world. This chapter, however, focuses on comparative criminology because a complete understanding of a country's criminal justice system must include an appreciation of that country's domestic crime and criminals. Similarly, because the phenomenon of transnational and international crime propels much of today's multinational cooperation, it behooves comparative criminal justice scholars to understand transnational crime and criminals.

Comparative Criminology Looks at Crime as a Social Phenomenon

When comparative criminologists study crime as a social phenomenon, they try to identify commonalities and differences in crime patterns among divergent cultures (Smith, Zhang, & Barberet, 2011). There is obvious overlap with the next section because variation in crime rates (crime as a social phenomenon) must first be established before behavioral explanations (crime as social behavior) are offered.

Criminologists seeking to compare crime in two or more countries encounter two primary problems. The first is to ensure that crime data from different countries have been defined, reported, and recorded in a similar manner. The second is compiling crime data in a manner that allows researchers to conveniently compare many different countries. Both problems are addressed here.

COMPARING SIMILAR DATA There is an understandable tendency to compare, contrast, and even rank countries in terms of general and specific crime rates, yet this is too often done without understanding the limits of such a portrayal. Countries increasingly appreciate the importance of comparative work but are concerned that statistics will be used for developing more "best places to live" types of rankings rather than for increasing the understanding of domestic crime issues.

Numerical rankings based on crime data should be undertaken only with caution for very good reasons. Consider, for example, differences in the legal definitions of crime. In the absence of a universally agreed-upon definition of what constitutes a particular crime, there is always the chance that data on a specific crime in two countries do not actually compare similar acts (European Institute for Crime Prevention and Control, 2014).

YOU SHOULD KNOW!
Comparing with Caution

The temptation to compare countries on the basis of reported crime requires significant restraint. Reasons for caution can be grouped under four broad categories (Lewis, 1999; Newman & Howard, 1999):

Statistics Are Political Statements

- The open announcement of a country's official crime statistics is often made only after the information has been rigorously checked for both its "validity" and the impression it creates.
- At times, countries have made crime data available to the United Nations survey but have not provided that information to their own citizens.

Problems in Defining, Reporting, and Recording

- Types of crime that seem comparable are often not (e.g., comparisons of homicide are confounded by how deaths from drunken driving are recorded).
- Many crimes are not reported to the police.
- Some events reported and recorded as crimes may not actually be crimes, and some crimes reported are never officially recorded.
- Decisions to record crimes may be affected by concerns about job evaluation measures or agency performance indicators. That is, there may be political pressures on criminal justice actors to demonstrate more or less crime.

Comparison Problems

- The structure and number of police personnel vary among the countries.

- Whereas some countries count crimes when the police become aware of them, others count crimes only when police forward them for prosecution.

Varying Social Features Affect Crime Rates

- Countries where telecommunications are more common tend to report a higher proportion of crime.
- Countries where household insurance is more developed report a higher proportion of crime, particularly burglary.
- Countries where police forces use more advanced technology tend to find a higher proportion of actual crime.
- Countries with more available medical facilities may have lower homicide rates than countries with less accessible medical facilities.

Similarly, Aebi (2008) has clarified the importance of counting rules that the police follow in each country to record crimes. It makes a difference whether the offense is recorded following the initial report ("input" statistic) or the initial investigation ("output" statistic). As for the counting of multiple offenses (such as a robbery, followed by a rape, then a homicide), some countries count the offenses separately, and others use a principal offense rule (they only count the most serious offense). Notably, regarding continuous offending, countries differ in their counting of incidents of domestic violence when it is experienced by the same person over time.

When providing their crime data for the Sourcebook, countries were asked to indicate when they deviated from the provided definition of a crime. According to the Sourcebook's standard definition, rape means sexual intercourse with a person against her/his will (per vaginam or other). Where possible, the figures include penetration other than vaginal (e.g., buggery), violent intramarital sexual intercourse, sexual intercourse without force with a helpless person, sexual intercourse with force with a child, and attempts. They exclude sexual intercourse with a child without force and other forms of sexual assault (these are counted elsewhere in the Sourcebook). Fifty percent of the countries providing police crime data to the Sourcebook did not follow the standard definition (European Institute for Crime Prevention and Control, 2014, p. 370). If a person simply compared Sweden's (see Map A.10) 2011 rape rate (69.4 per 100,000 population) with that of other countries (11.6 is the mean rate, and 5.5 the median rate) without attention to definitional differences, one would be quite taken aback by Sweden's high rate of rape compared to other European countries. However, Sweden includes in its statistics statutory rape and other forms of nonviolent rape of minors. As von Hofer (2000) explains, Sweden has an expansive definition of rape, counts rapes separately in the case of continuous or multiple offense scenarios, and also defines and counts an offense as rape at the input stage, when the victim reports the crime. And, as we will examine shortly, crime reporting also plays a role: women in Sweden are encouraged to report rape, and public services have been developed to increase trust between women, the police, and other public services in Sweden.

In addition to the problems presented by differences in legal definitions of crime, cross-national comparison of crime rates is hindered by the way crime is reported in countries. For example, the International Crime Victims Survey (ICVS) shows considerable range in how often crimes are reported in different countries (van Dijk, van Kesteren, & Smit, 2007). According to global ICVS results for the years 1996–2015 (van Dijk, 2016), the percentage of victims in capital cities in different regions who reported burglary, robbery, and assault/threats to the police varied from a minority of victims in Bishkek (21 percent), Latin America (29 percent), Eastern Europe (30 percent), and Africa (31 percent), to the majority of victims in the United States (54 percent), the Caribbean (56 percent), and Western Europe (63 percent).

The willingness of victims to report crime is not the only factor affecting reporting rates. Also important are factors such as accessibility to police so that a report can be made (e.g., the number of police stations and telecommunication), the level of insurance coverage available (certainly one reason that automobile theft reporting is high in industrialized countries), and the level of trust that the public has for its police (a population under corrupt or authoritarian rule is less likely to report crime). Finally, the greater the difference in social, economic, and political context between countries, the more unwise it is to make any comparison of their crime rates.

In addition to considering how accurately a crime is reported in countries being compared, it is also necessary to determine how recording practices may vary. Van Dijk and Kangaspunta (2000) highlight differing recording practices by noting that police in some countries are very careful about recording every theft of a bicycle while in other countries the tracking of bicycle thefts may have low—or even no—priority. Rubin, Culp, Mameli, and Walker (2008) systematically discovered anomalies and inconsistencies in crime data series of both INTERPOL and UN data. Also, the efficiency of criminal justice agencies is likely to make a difference. Higher rates of recorded crime in some countries may simply reflect more efficient and thorough systems for reporting and recording crime in those countries. Similarly, low rates of recorded crime rates may simply reflect system inefficiency. The result of all of this is that official crime statistics probably tell us as much about a country's justice organization as about its crime rate.

The danger in emphasizing the problems involved in comparing crime data is that one could infer that nothing can be gained from gathering and analyzing such information. Such a conclusion would be wrong! Part of the job of the comparative criminologist is to ascertain whether crime data can indeed be compared and to invent new ways of measuring crime cross-nationally so that the figures are valid and reliable. Attempts to provide annual rankings of countries according to their crime rates are typically faulty because of different defining, reporting, and recording practices. But that does not mean comparison cannot or should not occur.

COMPARING OVER TIME   One appropriate use of comparative crime data is to identify any changes in crime over time and across nations. Bennett and Lynch (1990) explain that although crime survey results cannot reliably be used to rank countries, they are appropriate for assessing the direction of change in crime. Consider, for example, the interesting observations and intriguing questions that arise upon seeing the global trends for selected crimes from 2003 to 2013 (see Figure 2.1). Violent crimes (measured by police-recorded data for intentional homicide, robbery, and rape) have slightly decreased over the past decade. The decrease is clearer for property crimes: motor vehicle theft almost halved, and burglary has been reduced by more than a quarter. Criminal offenses related to drug trafficking remained relatively stable over time, while drug possession offenses showed an increase since 2003. Of course, these rates are affected by detection and reporting rates. An increase in reported cases might be linked to greater awareness of the crime and a higher reporting rate. The trends in drug possession offenses can reflect changes in the drug market and/or changes in law enforcement.

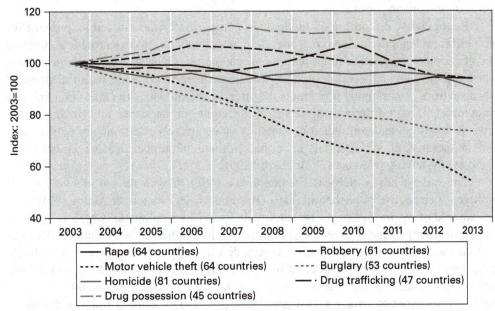

Notes: Trends are calculated as weighted crime rates per 100,000 population relative to the base year 2003. To produce global estimates, the estimated crime rates for each region were weighted according to the share of the region's population in the global population.

Data on drug trafficking and possession refer mostly to persons arrested or prosecuted for those types of crime.

FIGURE 2.1   Global Trends of Selected Crimes, 2003–2013

Source: United Nations. (2015). *State of crime and criminal justice worldwide* (Figure 1, p. 5). Paper presented at the Thirteenth United Nations Congress on Crime Prevention and Criminal Justice, Doha, Qatar. Paper retrieved from https://www.unodc.org/documents/data-and-analysis/statistics/crime/ACONF222_4_e_V1500369.pdf.

WEB PROJECT

Overcoming Comparison Problems

Download UNODC's International Classification of Crime for Statistical Purposes, Version 1.0 at http://www.unodc.org/documents/data-and-analysis/statistics/crime/ICCS/ICCS_English_2016_web.pdf and read pages 11–21. Write a few paragraphs that explain how this initiative tries to overcome some of the methodological problems associated with cross-national comparison of crime data. Do you think they were reasonably successful in identifying the key problems and in the manner in which they propose to overcome them?

As we will see later in this chapter, these are the types of questions that comparative criminology tries to answer when it views crime as social behavior. The point here is that these interesting and important questions are unlikely to be considered unless crime data are compared across countries. As long as it is done with caution, crime data can and should be compared cross-nationally.

USING UNITED NATIONS CRIME DATA   Several organizations are making available some key statistics on crime and justice in countries around the world. Especially important data sets today are those provided by the United Nations Office on Drugs and Crime (UNODC).

Beginning in the 1970s and continuing today, the periodic *United Nations Survey on Crime Trends and the Operations of Criminal Justice Systems* has become increasingly sophisticated, but also more general in terms of questions asked. In addition to providing data on reported crimes, responding countries are also asked to provide information about the operation of their criminal justice system through data on arrests, convictions, and prison population.

Recognizing the problems inherent in comparing crime rates among countries with different legal definitions of crime, the United Nations surveys provide a standard classification of crime definitions and justice categories. Over the years, countries have adapted their own statistical definitions and procedures to coincide with the standard UN categories. A remaining problem is the often fragmented way the questionnaire may be completed, with different officials from different bureaucracies introducing sometimes inconsistent and contradictory statistics as a country's questionnaire is filled out, and the fact that, on average, only about half of the total number of UN member states complete the survey (Newman & Howard, 1999).

The surveys are available to the public at a UNODC website and in a very useful multiyear perspective published in 2010 (Harrendorf, Heiskanen, & Malby, 2010). As an example of the usefulness of the survey data, consider homicide, which is an especially interesting crime for comparison purposes. In addition to being universally considered the most serious of offenses, homicide rates appear to be especially reliable indicators of the actual occurrence of that crime and many comparative criminologists rely on homicide data for theory testing (see Koeppel, Rhineberger-Dunn, & Mack, 2015, for a review; Newman & Howard, 1999, pp. 12–13). Table 2.1 shows the homicide rates for selected countries in Africa, the Americas, Asia, Europe, and Oceania.

Comparing countries within a geographic region as done in Table 2.1 (using UN geographic regions) can be useful for comparisons, but one cannot be sure what is represented by those groups. Regional groupings are often made without a clear idea of what ties the countries in a region together—other than geographical proximity. For example, comparing countries in Africa with ones in Asia may not be as helpful as a comparison of countries based on their official language—which would help draw attention to the importance of cultural factors rather than simply geographic ones. The point is, there should be some reason for how countries are grouped—and oftentimes that

TABLE 2.1	Homicide Rates for Selected Countries by Region (Latest Year, 2010–2013)		
	Rate per 100,000 Population		**Rate per 100,000 Population**
AFRICA		**ASIA**	
Egypt	3.4	Japan	0.3
Uganda	10.7	Israel	1.48
Namibia	17.2	Turkey	2.6
South Africa	31.0	Philippines	8.8
AMERICAS		**EUROPE**	
Canada	6	Norway	2.2
United States	4.7	England & Wales	1.0
Chile	3.1	France	1.04
Jamaica	39.3	Ukraine	4.3
Honduras	90.4	Russian Federation	9.2
OCEANIA			
Australia	1.1		
New Zealand	0.9		

Source: Table developed from data in United Nations Office on Drugs and Crime. (2014). *Global study on homicide 2013* (Table 8.1, pp. 122–133). Retrieved from https://www.unodc.org/gsh/.

reason is based on a theory that is being tested. For example, as we will see subsequently, some crime theories find it helpful and relevant to group countries on the basis of modernization or civilization indicators.

Building on the achievements of the United Nations Survey on Crime Trends and the Operations of Criminal Justice Systems, UNODC has proposed a new mechanism for gathering official crime data: the International Classification of Crime for Statistical Purposes (ICCS) (United Nations Office on Drugs and Crime, 2015). This classification system for crime mirrors the one developed by the World Health Organization for the international classification of diseases (and links to it) and proposes standard definitions for crime data to be used worldwide. The ICCS is in its development and implementation phase.

USING INTERNATIONAL CRIME VICTIM DATA Because official crime statistics from police sources require victims to report an offense, there is concern that cross-national comparison of crime statistics may compare reporting habits as much as crime incidents. In an attempt to reduce the data loss that occurs when relying on police reports of crime, individual countries make greater use of victimization surveys, which have been found to provide a more complete picture of crime's occurrence.

At the international level, this move toward victim surveys as a means to compare crime cross-nationally has relied on the International Crime Victims Survey. Since the first survey sweep in 1989, the ICVS has conducted five sweeps with the most recent being the 2004/2005 International Crime Victim Survey—although surveys for the 2010/2015 sweep have been distributed and are currently being returned. All survey data are available electronically for researchers (http://wp.unil.ch/icvs/codebooks/), but many will find the reports summarizing the survey findings to be sufficient for most purposes (e.g., see van Dijk et al., 2007).

Overall victimization rates in industrialized countries show relatively high counts (above 20 percent of the respondents in each country) in England and Wales, Iceland, Ireland, and New Zealand. Countries with relatively low counts (10 percent and less) included Hungary, Japan, and Spain. Australia, Canada, Sweden, and the United States show rates near the average of 16 percent (van Dijk et al., 2007). As with police crime rate data, the real value of cross-national crime victim statistics is in identifying trends over time rather than showing one-time rankings of countries. When analyzing trends from the ICVS sweeps, there is a general consistency in country positions over the years. England and Wales, Estonia, the Netherlands, and New Zealand have consistently ranked high relative to others, while Austria, Japan, and Portugal consistently show low overall victimization.

The crime and victimization data available to comparative criminologists today provide a wealth of information. As long as the necessary methodological cautions are understood and accounted for, scholars and practitioners will be able to compare crime occurrence, crime trends, victimization, and other topics of importance for a more complete understanding of domestic crime. As noted earlier, however, comparative criminology is also interested in advancing theoretical explanations of criminal behavior. Crime and victimization data are also necessary for that goal, as we see in the next section.

Comparative Criminology Looks at Crime as Social Behavior

When looking at crime as social behavior, criminologists develop and test theories about crime's etiology—that is, its causes, origins, and distribution. Traditionally, those theories have been used to understand domestic crime in a particular country. When theories about crime are developed and tested in or across two or more countries, criminology is more accurately called comparative criminology (Beirne & Nelken, 1997; Newman & Howard, 2001).

Howard, Newman, and Pridemore (2000) identify three general frameworks that are commonly employed as comparative criminologists attempt to explain the variation of crime rates among nations: grand theories, structural theories, and theories relying on demographic characteristics. A thorough examination of how criminological theory is applied to cross-cultural and international crime statistics is not possible in this book. However, that subject is important enough to warrant at least a brief description of

---

YOU SHOULD KNOW!

Victimization Rates

Information from victimization studies can be quite useful for increasing our understanding of crime within countries. The following are examples of information learned from the *International Crime Victims Survey* of 30 participating countries (van Dijk et al., 2007).

- Because the 10 countries with the highest victimization rates comprise both very affluent and less affluent countries, one might question the conventional wisdom about poverty as a dominant root cause of common crime.
- Countries with low victimization rates are fairly heterogeneous, both geographically and in terms of affluence.
- Whether crimes are reported to the police depends mostly on the seriousness of the crime and whether such a report is needed for claiming insurance. For example, nearly all car and motorcycle thefts are reported but few sexual behavior offenses were reported.
- Victims in Australia, Denmark, and Switzerland are among those expressing satisfaction with the way the police treated their case, whereas victims in Estonia, Greece, and Mexico express little satisfaction with the police.
- Fear of crime (measured by belief that a burglary will take place in one's home in the coming year) is most widespread in Bulgaria, Greece, and Poland. Such feelings are least common among the public in Canada, the Netherlands, and the Nordic countries.

theories from one of these general frameworks. Because they have played a greater role in cross-national research to date, we look at examples of grand theory explanations.

- **Modernization Theories**—Grand theories typically assume that a single theoretical construct has significant impact on a nation's crime level. Shelley's *Crime and Modernization* (1981) is an early example of this methodology. As the title indicates, Shelley uses empirical evidence to show that modernization provides the best theoretical explanation for crime's evolution in recent history. Specifically, she suggests that social processes accompanying industrial development have resulted in conditions conducive to increased criminality, such as loosened family ties, instability of family, and lack of supervision of youthful members of a family.

- **Civilization Theory**—Another type of grand theory uses a comparative historical approach to show a link between crime and civility. For example, these civilization theorists note that murder was more common in the Middle Ages than it is now and that it dropped dramatically in the seventeenth, eighteenth, and nineteenth centuries. This seems to directly contradict modernization theory because it suggests that violent crime, at least, decreased rather than increased as modernization dismantled traditional family and community bonds. Elias attributes the decline to the gradual introduction of courtly manners (e.g., eating with a knife and fork, refraining from urinating in public) that transformed a violent medieval society into a more peaceful modern one (Elias, 1982; Stille, 2003). Modernization and civilization theories are not necessarily contradictory, however. Shelley, for example, modified her initial reliance on modernization as the key explanatory variable in favor of a synthesized modernization–civilization perspective, which suggests that a more civilized society has lower volumes of violent crimes because people exercise more internal control over their behavior as others increasingly depend on them (Heiland & Shelley, 1992). However, the modernization–civilization proponents argue that violence directed against the self (e.g., suicide, drug abuse) will occur more often as civility increases.

- **World System Theory**—Other grand theories take politics as the key construct. World system theory, for example, draws from the Marxist perspective to explain that as capitalism expands, it disrupts indigenous cultures and traditional means of subsistence. The resulting exploitation from the outside and new inequalities within disrupt political and legal formations and create class conflict (Howard et al., 2000). This perspective treats industrialization and urbanization as the outcomes of capitalist expansion. Unlike the modernization perspective, which sets modernization as a key predictor of crime rates, the world system perspective uses modernization only as an intervening variable. In this way, it argues that the effect of industrialization and modernization depends on how modes of production interact with one another.

- **Opportunity Theories**—Opportunity theories suggest that the occurrence of crime is best understood as the result of modern economies and social organization that provide increased opportunities to engage in criminal behavior. More goods are purchased as expanding economies create more expendable income, and those goods become available for theft. Technological gains produce smaller and more portable electronic devices that are easily stolen. Changes in social organization (e.g., both spouses working and increased leisure time mean more hours of the day when the home is unoccupied) result in less guardianship over household items and more opportunities for theft.

- **Feminist Theory**—Feminist theories examine how indicators of gender inequality influence crime rates, particularly gender differences in crime rates (perpetration of crimes by men or women, and victimization of women or men) and differences in rates of gendered crimes (domestic violence, for example). This is a large body of research that has generally been undertheorized (Hunnicutt, 2009) and new indicators of gender equality are now emerging that can be used in cross-national research (Barberet, 2014).

Howard et al. (2000) note that tests of grand theories have produced conflicting results. For example, Bouley and Vaughn (1995) studied violent crime in Colombia and found support for grand theories with respect to the crimes of theft and robbery but not for the more violent crimes of assault and homicide. Similarly, Schichor's (1990) study of homicide and larceny rates indicated that development is likely to be accompanied by increased property and decreased violent crime. Gillis (1994) claims that civilization theory is supported in his study of violent crime and suicide in France from 1852 to 1914. Gillis found that the climbing literacy rate during that period was associated with a decrease in the rate of crimes of passion and an increase in the suicide rate. Opportunity theory seems supported in studies such as that by LaFree and Birkbeck (1991), which uses victimization data in Venezuela and the United States to show that robbery typically involves public domains, lone victims, strangers, and incidents taking place outside buildings. Should comparative criminologists continue to find that crimes occur in similar situations, regardless of country, we will have valuable information about criminal acts—although our knowledge about motivation to commit those acts will not necessarily be advanced.

The hypotheses that emerge from feminist criminological theory are varied and results are conflicting. For example, Yodanis (2004) used data from the International Crime Victims Survey with United Nations statistics and found that the educational and occupational status of women in a country is related to the prevalence of sexual violence against women: where status is high, prevalence is low. Chon (2016) used homicide data from the World Health Organization to examine the relationship between gender inequality and female homicide victimization. He found that the relationship disappeared when controlling for income inequality and ethnic heterogeneity.

Regarding this point, our review has emphasized how comparative criminology seeks to measure and explain domestic crime cross-nationally. The crime and victim data sets are designed to measure the occurrence and reporting of criminal acts within a particular country. Comparative criminologists then use that information to identify similarities and differences in crime types and occurrence (i.e., crime as a social phenomenon) or to extend our understanding of criminal behavior (i.e., crime as social behavior). The twenty-first century brought a new, nondomestic type of crime to intrigue and challenge comparative criminologists. These transnational crimes are not confined to national borders but have an impact across many nations.

TRANSNATIONAL CRIME

Criminologist Jay Albanese (2011) explains that transnational crime today is similar to what city gangs and Al Capone were to the last century. The analogy is especially appropriate given the link to organized crime in both time periods and the difficulty law enforcement had and has in combating the resulting criminal acts. Few comparative criminologists would disagree with his assessment of transnational crime's importance in contemporary society. As a simple indication of the increasing globalization of crime, consider just the following (Di Nicola, 2005; McLaughlin, 2005; U.S. Drug Enforcement Administration, 2005):

- Europol dismantled one of the most efficient cybercrime organizations, led by Russians who had managed to extort millions of euros from online users across more than 30 countries by persuading them to pay spurious police fines for improper use of the Internet. The criminal threat was essentially a form of online extortion called ransomware and relied on malware that locked a user's computer and sent a message in the form of a fake police warning, demanding 100 euros to unlock. The Russian head of the crime network was arrested in Dubai and 10 other people were arrested by the Spanish police (Minder, 2013).

- INTERPOL's Operation Pangea targeted the illegal online sale of medicines and medical devices, involving some 193 police, customs, and health regulatory authorities from 103 countries, and resulting in 393 arrests worldwide and the seizure of more than $53 million worth of potentially dangerous medicines, including fake cancer medication, substandard HIV and diabetes testing kits, counterfeit dental equipment, and illicit surgical equipment. Nearly 5,000 websites selling illicit pharmaceuticals were suspended (INTERPOL, 2016a).

IMPACT

THE GLOBAL CRIME DROP AND THE SECURITY HYPOTHESIS

Comparative criminologists seek to explain differences and similarities in crime across countries and over time. This means trying to figure out why crime goes up as well as why crime goes down. The latter has evolved as a relatively new area of research in light of recent evidence that for certain crimes around the globe (see Figure 2.1) and particularly in the industrialized world, it appears that we face a "global crime drop."

One of the more promising explanations for this global crime drop is the security hypothesis, developed by Jan van Dijk and inspired by Ronald Clarke and Graeme Newman, among others, and tested by a range of researchers in Europe, Canada, and the United States using official crime data as well as data from victimization surveys. This hypothesis, in sync with opportunities theory, argues that improvements in the quality and quantity of security measures have meant lower crime rates for a variety of crimes. In short, the researchers argue that popular items for theft have simply become harder to steal because of security devices, and that this has a domino effect on other crimes (Farrell, Tilley, Tseloni, & Mailley, 2008; van Dijk, Tseloni, & Farrell, 2012).

This would seem a rather simple explanation for a crime drop, but it is more complex than it looks. In order to argue that security measures are the key driver to a crime drop, researchers must look at specific crimes, the availability and uptake of security measures that are commonly used to counter them, and whether the types of crime attempts or modus operandi that reflect that use have failed or declined. Competing explanations must be falsified. In this case, because the claim is global, this must be done cross-nationally in order to argue that the security hypothesis is globally viable. Finally, the relationships between crimes must be clarified. Researchers have coined two additional hypotheses for this purpose: the debut hypothesis and the keystone hypothesis. The debut hypothesis argues that if the numbers of some crimes committed by novices fall, others that those offenders would have progressed to, had their initial crimes been successful, will also fall. The keystone hypothesis argues that when some crimes are instrumental for other crimes (motor vehicle theft, for example, is a common precursor to other crimes such as burglary), if the first crime falls, the other crimes will as well.

What has the research shown? Tseloni, Mailley, Farrell, and Tilley (2010) document the global crime drop and the relationship between crimes. All crime types they examined (theft from cars, theft from person, burglary, assault, and car theft) declined, especially after 1995. The results suggest that the set of factors that set off the crime drop first impacted burglary and car theft, then theft from a car and personal theft, and only belatedly assaults. Farrell, Tseloni, Mailley, and Tilley (2011), examining vehicle theft in England and Wales and Australia, show that electronic immobilizers and central locking were particularly effective in decreased car theft. They suggest that decreased car theft may have caused drops in other crimes including violence. Killias and Lanfranconi (2012), in contrast, argue that global crime trends can mask individual countries' differences that must be considered in context. Switzerland (see Map A.10) has seen a recent 15-year increase in violent crime, which Killias attributes to the deregulation of bars, pubs, and restaurants, and the increase in nighttime public transportation. This chapter in comparative criminology shows us that given good data, comparative criminologists can work to explain not only increases in crime, but also decreases. Even so, finding universal laws applicable around the globe is a challenging task.

Transnational Crime Types

Transnational crimes encompass a variety of distinct activities. Nine types are discussed here with a brief note explaining each. Notable by its absence in this grouping of transnational crimes is transnational organized crime. A common feature of any transnational crime is the organized effort involved in the inception and perpetration of the crime. A single person might be able to conceive and begin a crime in one country, move through several other countries in the process of accomplishing the crime, and then complete it in yet another country, but the likelihood seems very remote. Much more likely, and certainly more efficient, is the reliance on several individuals and groups in many countries working together to complete the crime. Rather than having a separate category called transnational organized crime, this list assumes that each of the specific crime types has an organized crime component.

CYBERCRIME   Cybercrime is one of the fastest growing crime areas as criminals increasingly rely on the speed, convenience, and anonymity offered by modern technologies. The cost of cybercrime worldwide is estimated at some $400 billion (CSIS, 2014; INTERPOL, 2016c).

Computers are linked to criminal activity in three general ways (Rantala, 2005):

- **Cyber attacks**, wherein the computer system itself is a target of the criminal act. These acts against computers or their services include obtaining illegal access to a system, preventing legitimate access by others, theft of services provided by the computer, or causing damage to a computer or its data—increasingly, to large data systems and infrastructure.
- **Cyber theft** occurs when the computer is used as a tool in committing a crime. Typically, this involves the theft of money and other things of value, including intellectual property.
- **Other computer security incidents** include spyware, adware, hacking, phishing, and theft of other information regardless of whether the breach was successful or any damage or losses were actually sustained.

CORRUPTION   Corruption is recognized as a domestic issue since it undermines a country's political, social, and economic stability. But it also contributes to global crime since transnational criminals are aided in their illegal activities by the complicity of corrupt public officials. In 2000, the UN General Assembly realized that a treaty against corruption, independent of the United Nations Convention against Transnational Organized Crime, was needed and established a committee for its negotiation. The United Nations Convention against Corruption (UNCAC) entered into force on December 14, 2005.

At the most basic level, corruption is the abuse of entrusted power for private gain. Often the power abused is that attached to a public office that one holds as a result of

Cybercrime, one of the fastest growing crime areas, has estimated costs to the global economy running to billions of dollars.

Borislav Marinic/123RF

YOU SHOULD KNOW!
Cybersecurity, Human Error, and Social Science Research

Many experts in cybersecurity are turning their attention to human error, as well as to important findings in behavioral science and economics that explain both how cybercriminals perpetrate their crimes as well as how victims fall prey to their schemes. In doing so, they are acknowledging that it is not enough to build bigger and better cybersecurity in the more traditional sense, and importantly that cybercriminals are way ahead of the game compared to those who work to deter them.

Many cyber attacks occur because of user choice of poor passwords and users clicking on links in emails. The 10 most common passwords in 2015 were 123456, password, 12345678, qwerty (the string of top letters used by the left hand on a keyboard), and 12345. Requirements to change passwords frequently, it seems, are counterproductive with busy employees. Most of us choose new passwords that are very related to our previous ones (and thus are less secure) so that we can remember them. Researchers looking at the human compatibility of password policies have discovered, for example, that encouraging employees to use complex combinations of letters, numbers, and symbols does not work. Rather, long strings of real words are easier to remember, and still deter hackers.

If user behavior has its vulnerabilities, perhaps social science can also find similar vulnerabilities among cyber attackers. Economists and computer scientists have followed digital trails to expose and analyze how illegal cyber businesses operate. This knowledge of business structure then helps them discover sectors that are more vulnerable to detection than others. They can see how criminal systems form and dissolve, grow and are taken down, and they can track the flow of money. Looking at motivations and incentives, instead of building cyber walls, may be the next generation of cybersecurity studies, and go a long way toward uniting social science research in the service of criminal justice practice (Waldrop, 2016).

election or assignment. UNCAC calls on countries to criminalize not only basic forms of corruption such as bribery and the embezzlement of public funds, but also trading in influence and the concealment and laundering of the proceeds of corruption. It also deals with offenses committed in support of corruption, including obstructing justice (Albanese, 2011).

Corruption and its related crimes occur worldwide and have both domestic and global impact. Transparency International is an organization created to fight corruption in the global arena. Its annual *Global Corruption Barometer* provides data on corruption produced by worldwide public opinion surveys. Respondents are asked to rate, on a scale of 1 (not at all corrupt) to 5 (extremely corrupt), the extent to which they perceive institutions in their country to be affected by corruption. Political parties are the institution deemed most corrupt, with an average rating of 3.8 across all countries (the U.S. rating is 4.1). In some countries, the police (e.g., Bolivia, Ghana, Kenya, Malaysia, Philippines, South Africa, and Venezuela) or the judiciary (e.g., Afghanistan, Albania, Bulgaria, Peru, and Slovakia) was perceived as the most corrupt institution (Transparency International, 2013). Countries where criminal justice institutions are corrupt (or at least perceived to be so by their citizens) may support other transnational crime activities such as drug trafficking, money laundering, or terrorism—or, at best, are not inclined to help thwart it.

DRUG TRAFFICKING   Large-scale drug abuse and its related problems affect much of the world and attempts to control illicit drug trafficking must involve global efforts that match the global reach of the drugs. Since the beginning of the twentieth century, the United Nations and its predecessor, the League of Nations, have collected global data on the illicit drug supply. With its yearly *World Drug Report*, the UNODC provides analysis and statistics on the four major groups of illicit drugs: opiates, cocaine, cannabis, and amphetamine-type stimulates. The information is provided according to the three sectors of production, trafficking, and consumption. As an example of the type of information the data provide, consider the three sectors in terms of the four drug groups overall (United Nations Office on Drugs and Crime, 2016b).

U.S. Immigration and Customs Enforcement (ICE) officers are actively engaged in combating attempts to transport drugs into the United States.

Courtesy of U.S. Immigration and Customs.

- **Production**—The world's most widely cultivated drug crop is cannabis, which was reported by 129 countries over the period 2009–2014. Cannabis production has been stable globally, opium poppy cultivation has been decreasing, whereas coca cultivation has been rising.
- **Trafficking**—Cannabis trafficking tends to be intraregional (locally produced and consumed), but cocaine trafficking is interregional with production being primarily in Colombia, Peru, and Bolivia and consumption occurring in North America and West and Central Europe. Heroin trafficking is both intra- and interregional. For example, heroin produced in Afghanistan is consumed within the region (e.g., Pakistan and Iran) and/or trafficked to Europe. Heroin produced in Mexico and Colombia is typically destined for the United States.
- **Consumption**—Exact numbers are impossible to determine, but UNODC estimates that 1 in 20 adults, or a quarter of a billion people aged 15–64 years, used at least one drug in 2014. Although trends in drug use vary across regions, as does updated reporting on data, the extent of drug use among the world population has remained stable over the past four years. Almost 12 percent of the total number of people who use drugs, or over 29 million people, are estimated to suffer from drug use disorders. As a point of comparison, about 25 percent of the world's adult population (15 years and older) are current tobacco smokers. Overall, men are three times more likely than women to use cannabis, cocaine, or amphetamines, whereas women are more likely than men to engage in the non-medical use of opioids and tranquilizers.

Although production and consumption of the traditional drugs has been steady or even declining, there are other parts of the illicit drug markets where expansion is more apparent. Every year new products are manufactured, and especially rapid growth is found in the case of synthetic drugs. New substances that imitate the pharmacological properties or chemical structures of existing controlled substances enter the market, but since they contain unregulated material they may be sold as "legal highs." Synthetic cannabis ("spice"), for example, has been detected in herbal smoking blends.

Such products contain a very small amount of finely cut plant material to which one or more synthetic cannabinoids have been added. Since they do not contain regulated products, they are often marketed as legal alternatives to cannabis. Countries respond by placing the synthetics among the controlled substances, which lessens the problem until other new drugs emerge. The problem is constant and ever-evolving.

MONEY LAUNDERING   Traditionally, money laundering has referred to the process by which criminals attempt to conceal the illicit origin and ownership of the proceeds from their unlawful activities. However, that link to the proceeds of crime is no longer an essential element in the definition. Joyce (2005) explains that today the concept must include the ways in which money laundering mechanisms are used to finance crimes such as terrorism and corruption.

Money laundering typically takes place in a three-stage process (see Figure 2.2) wherein funds are moved from direct association with the crime (called placement),

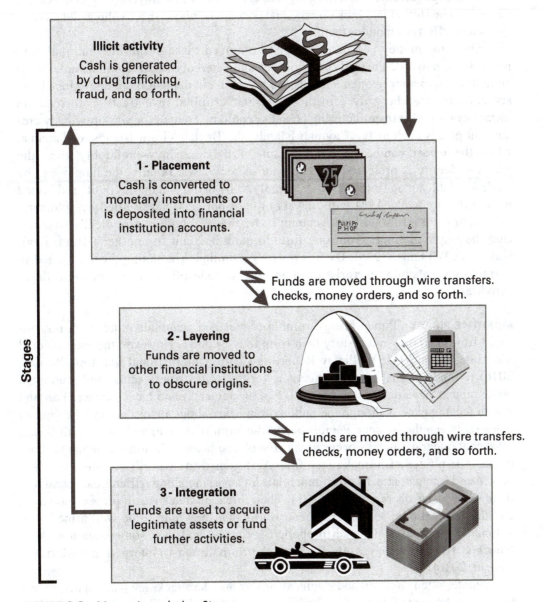

FIGURE 2.2   Money Laundering Stages

Source: U.S. Government Accountability Office. *Money laundering: extent of money laundering through credit cards is unknown* (Figure 1, page 7). Last modified July 22, 2002. http://www.gao.gov/products/GAO-02-670.

hidden in the accounts of a legitimate business (layering), and then made available to the criminal again (integration) as earnings from a business that has a plausible reason for generating that much cash.

In its simplest form, when the sums involved are relatively small, money laundering takes place in the same jurisdiction as the crime. For example, winning tickets at race tracks or from state lotteries can be purchased by the launderer—probably paying the true winner a premium—then presented for payment. The funds are then identified as legitimate earning from gambling. Larger sums typically involve an international dimension and it is at this level that the three stages become more distinct.

The easiest, and most popular, way to move money out of the country of origin (placement) is to carry or ship it out in bulk. One and a half million dollars in $100 bills will fit nicely into two regular size briefcases, or one might choose to carry $1.2 million in a single doctor's bag. Where inspection of hand luggage is tight, bulk cash can be moved through checked personal luggage, especially when traveling by ship. Or the money can be stuffed into bulk commercial containers whose sheer volume defeats any systematic efforts to monitor them.

Once the money is abroad, it must be moved through the international payments system to hide the trail (layering). Despite stereotypes, it would be unwise for an individual to simply open a numbered account and deposit the money since bank secrecy can often be waived in the event of a criminal investigation. Instead, an instant-corporation manufacturing business could be created (or was previously created) in places such as the Cayman Islands, the British Virgin Islands, or Panama, where the deposit can be made in the name of that company—preferably where the owner's identity is protected by corporate secrecy laws. Finally, the money can be made available again (integration) as simply as by using a debit or credit card issued by an offshore bank. ATM withdrawals or card purchases are settled by automatic deduction from a foreign bank account or by the card holder periodically transferring the required funds from one foreign bank account to another (Blum, Levi, Naylor, & Williams, 1998). By this process, criminals (including those engaged in corruption or planning terrorist acts) are able to hide illicit monies or fund illegal activities.

MARITIME PIRACY Piracy brings to mind crimes and criminals more often remembered from literature and history than from today's news. However, the International Maritime Bureau (IMB)'s Piracy Reporting Centre (International Maritime Bureau, 2016) reminds us that piracy remains a very serious crime. Actual and attempted pirate attacks have decreased since 2011 (439 incidents) and have numbered around 250 in recent years. Although the public often hears about attacks around the Gulf of Aden (between the Arabian Peninsula and the Horn of Africa) and the Somali Basin, most contemporary attacks occur in the area of Southeast Asia and the Indian subcontinent. The pirates of Somalia (see Map A.1) gained the world's attention for their brazen and frequent attacks on commercial ships passing along Africa's east coast, but their attacks have decreased since 2011. Their threat of attack is still present, however, and the International Maritime Bureau warns that they tend to be well armed with automatic weapons and rocket-propelled grenades, and they sometimes use skiffs launched from mother vessels far from the Somali coast (International Maritime Bureau, 2016).

Pirates often target oil and chemical tankers and the attacks are particularly violent and highly organized. Ships may be hijacked and forced to sail to unknown locations where the pirates ransack and steal the ship's equipment and cargo. Crew, ship, and cargo can also be held hostage as pirates wait for ransom demands to be met.

WEB PROJECT

Maritime Piracy

Go to the IMB Piracy Reporting Centre at https://icc-ccs. org/piracy-reporting-centre and click on links to "Live Piracy Map" and "Piracy News & Figures." Write a few paragraphs describing the information you find. Include your comments as to how useful you think this information can be.

THEFT OF ART AND CULTURAL OBJECTS   Also called *crimes against cultural heritage*, *patrimonial crimes*, or *illicit antiquities*, these acts violate a country's heritage through the unlawful procurement or acquisition of archaeological and artistic objects that are part of the country's cultural legacy. The black market in works of art is becoming as lucrative as those for drugs, weapons, and counterfeit goods (INTERPOL, 2016c).

According to INTERPOL, countries around the world are affected by this crime—especially in Europe, Latin America, North and Sub-Saharan Africa, and Southeast Asia—but over the past decade there has been an increasing trend of illicit trafficking in cultural objects from countries in the Middle East that are affected by armed conflict. The majority of thefts are carried out from private homes, but museums and places of worship are also among the common targets. Although the type of objects stolen varies from country to country, paintings, sculptures and statues, and religious items are among the more frequent targets. It is important to note, however, that no category is spared, including such diverse items as archaeological pieces, antiquarian books, antique furniture, coins, weapons and firearms, and ancient gold and silverware. INTERPOL collaborates with a variety of agencies to recover stolen antiquities and has a special role at present in helping curb the trade in illicit antiquities from Iraq and Syria.

TRADE IN HUMAN BODY PARTS   In a classic example of supply and demand economics, there is a great global demand for organs suitable for transplant but the number of consensual donors to meet the demand is insufficient. It is exactly this type of situation that appeals to organized crime interests. In the United States alone, more than 120,000 people are awaiting transplants (count kept at http://optn.transplant.hrsa.gov/), but only about 30,000 transplants are performed each year.

There is a legitimate transplant market involving organs from live or deceased donors to needy patients, but the transnational crime version involves black market or underground transactions. The United Nations identifies three broad categories of organ trafficking (Global Initiative to Fight Human Trafficking, 2016):

1. Cases where traffickers force or deceive the victims into giving up an organ
2. Cases where victims formally or informally agree to sell an organ and are cheated because they are not paid for the organ or are paid less than the promised price
3. Vulnerable persons (such as migrant workers, homeless persons, and illiterate persons) are treated for an ailment, which may or may not exist and thereupon organs are removed without the victim's knowledge

The shortage of organs is a universal problem and the disparity between supply and demand allows organized crime to thrive. The activity requires organization because of the number and diversity of people involved. In addition to the buyer and donor/victim, there are recruiters who identify the donors, transporters of both people and organs, hospital/clinic staff, medical professionals, middlemen and contractors, and the banks where organs are stored. Rarely is the entire racket exposed (Global Initiative to Fight Human Trafficking, 2016).

Human trafficking (increasingly referred to as modern-day slavery) occurs when a person has been recruited or is kept by means of force, fraud, or coercion for the purposes of exploitation.

Ximagination/123RF

TRAFFICKING IN PERSONS The United Nations *Protocol to Prevent, Suppress and Punish Trafficking in Persons, Especially Women and Children*, supplementing the United Nations Convention against Transnational Organized Crime, defines human trafficking basically as the acquisition of people by improper means such as force, fraud, or deception, with the aim of exploiting them. A point of confusion is how human trafficking differs from migrant smuggling (see Figure 2.3). An increasingly agreed-upon distinction is that trafficking, but not smuggling, requires deception or coercion. Smuggling typically involves migrants who have consented to the smuggling. Although trafficking victims may have initially consented, that consent is rendered meaningless by the coercive, deceptive, or abusive action of the traffickers. In addition, smuggling is always transnational—one cannot have "domestic smuggling."

Trafficking in persons is a multibillion-dollar form of transnational organized crime, wherein victims are recruited and trafficked within countries or between countries and regions. Estimates of the extent of human trafficking are inexact due to the clandestine nature of the enterprise, but estimates by the International Labour Organization (2016) indicate almost 21 million people are victims of forced labor—22 percent of whom are victims of forced sexual exploitation, 68 percent are victims of

Differences between Human Trafficking and Smuggling*	
Trafficking	**Smuggling**
There must be an element of force, fraud, or coercion (actual, perceived, or implied), unless the victim is under 18 years of age and involved in commercial sex acts.	The person being smuggled is generally cooperating.
Forced labor and/or exploitation.	There is no actual or implied coercion.
Persons trafficked are victims.	Persons smuggled are complicit in the smuggling crime. They are not necessarily victims of the crime of smuggling, although they may become victims depending on the circumstances in which they were smuggled.
Trafficking victims were enslaved, subjected to limited movement or isolation, or had documents confiscated.	Smuggled persons are free to leave, change jobs, etc.
Trafficking need not involve the actual movement of the victim.	Smuggling involves the illegal entry of a person or persons from one country into another.
There is no requirement to cross an international border.	Smuggling always crosses an international border.
Trafficked persons must be involved in labor/services or commercial sex acts. That is, they must be "working".	Smuggled persons must only be in country or attempting entry illegally.

FIGURE 2.3 Trafficking versus Smuggling
*This chart does not provide a precise legal distinction of the differences between smuggling and trafficking. It is designed to illustrate general fact scenarios that are often seen in smuggling or trafficking incidents.

Source: Modified from Human Smuggling and Trafficking Center. (2006). *Fact sheet: Distinctions between human smuggling and human trafficking 2006* (p. 4). Washington, DC: U.S. Department of State. http://www.state.gov/documents/organization/90541.pdf.

forced labor exploitation, and 10 percent are victims of state-imposed forced labor (e.g., in prisons or in work imposed by the state military or rebel armed forces).

The major types of trafficking in persons are sex trafficking and forced labor trafficking (see Figure 2.4). Included in the forced labor category is bonded labor (often called debt bondage), wherein persons are forced to work to pay off their own or even their family members' or ancestors' debts. Another type of forced labor is the involuntary servitude of domestic workers. These are often foreign migrants, usually women, who were recruited from less developed countries to work as domestic servants and caretakers in more developed countries. But, since their workplace is often a private home, authorities cannot provide oversight regarding the work conditions and too often a result is exploitation of the worker. Confined to the home, either because of physical restraint or through confiscation of identity and travel documents, the workers may find it difficult to make others aware of their situation. The U.S. Department of State (2015) and the Organization for Security and Co-operation in Europe (2014) have recently highlighted the problem of domestic servitude in diplomatic households.

Human trafficking has become one of the most recognized types of transnational crime and as such it receives considerable attention at domestic and global levels. That attention has resulted in action by local and national politicians, world leaders, international nongovernmental organizations (NGOs), and supranational organizations such as the United Nations and INTERPOL. It is an especially insidious crime (often called modern-day slavery), and one can only hope that the future will bring increased effectiveness in combating the traffickers and protecting the victims.

FIGURE 2.4 Major Types of Human Trafficking

WEB PROJECT

Trafficking in Persons Report

The U.S. Department of State publishes an annual report on trafficking in persons. Find the most recent report at http://www.state.gov/j/tip/rls/tiprpt/index.htm, then download and read the "Introductory Material." Write a few paragraphs that summarize your understanding of the material (content and/or statistics) covered in that year's report.

TERRORISM   What is terrorism? If you have the answer, many of the experts in the field would like to speak with you. Defining terrorism is not easily accomplished because it takes no single form, and acts considered to be terrorist acts often have few common traits. Most would agree that Timothy McVeigh, who was convicted and executed for his part in the 1995 bombing of the Murrah Federal Building in Oklahoma City that killed 168 people, was a terrorist. His conviction, however, was not for terrorism but for conspiracy to use a weapon of mass destruction, use of a weapon of mass destruction, destruction by explosive, and eight counts of first-degree murder.

If McVeigh's acts were not examples of terrorism as a crime, are the deaths resulting from sniper attacks in the Washington, DC, area in October 2001? The shootings occurred in several jurisdictions in the Washington, DC, area and in Alabama, Georgia, and Louisiana. After John Allen Muhammad and Lee Boyd Malvo's capture, they became suspects in 20 shootings—including 13 deaths—throughout those jurisdictions. Virginia was the first jurisdiction to bring charges against Muhammad and Malvo; and each was charged, in separate counties, with several counts of capital murder including one based on Virginia's new antiterrorism law. That statute makes a murder defendant eligible for capital punishment if the crime was intended to intimidate the public or influence the government (Code of Virginia, § 18.2–31[13]). Juries found both defendants guilty of capital murder, including the terrorism charge. Muhammad was executed in 2009 and Malvo continues serving a life sentence. Are Muhammad and Malvo's acts more like your idea of terrorism than were those of Timothy McVeigh?

Most attempts to define terrorism include an additional note that there is no single, universally accepted definition of terrorism. This seems surprising because a necessary characteristic of criminal law (see Chapter 3) is that a criminal act should be clearly defined so that people will know in advance how they must behave. But—and here's the catch—terrorism is typically not a crime in itself. Consider the following definitions of terrorism:

- The U.S. Code uses the term "terrorism" to mean premeditated, politically motivated violence perpetrated against noncombatant targets by subnational groups or clandestine agents (Title 22, Chapter 38, §2656f[d]).
- The U.S. Department of Defense considers terrorism to be the unlawful use of violence or threat of violence to instill fear and coerce governments or societies. Terrorism is often motivated by religious, political, or other ideological beliefs and committed in the pursuit of goals that are usually political (*Department of Defense Dictionary of Military Terms*).
- In the United Kingdom, the *Terrorism Act of 2000* (amended in 2006, 2008, and 2015) defines terrorism in part as the use or threat of action designed to influence the government or an international governmental organization or to intimidate the public or a section of the public, and the use or threat of action is made for the purpose of advancing a political, religious, racial, or ideological cause (United Kingdom, 2000).

WEB PROJECT

Foreign Terrorist Organizations

Find the Department of State's most current *Country Report on Terrorism* at http://www.state.gov/j/ct/rls/crt/index.htm. Find the chapter on "Foreign Terrorist Organizations" (probably Chapter 6). In that chapter, select any three organizations and read the information provided about each. Write several paragraphs comparing the three in terms of their history, activities, and area of operation.

Violence is a key component in two of the definitions and in one, political motivation specifically is important. The motivation in the other two definitions can be political, but can also be religious or ideological—and even racial in one definition. As you consider the implications of the words that might be used in any definition of terrorism, it becomes easier to understand why international organizations have problems developing an agreed-upon definition. Actions by Palestinians are viewed as acts of terrorism by Israel, but are considered freedom fighting by the Palestinians themselves. Some Japanese may believe it was an act of terrorism to drop atomic bombs on Hiroshima and Nagasaki, but most Americans are likely to disagree. As we consider specific examples of actions that constitute terrorism, we begin to suspect that one reason a universally agreed-upon definition of terrorism has been avoided is because the acts are considered criminal, but the motivation for those acts is often not considered criminal (Duursma, 2008).

Not surprisingly, the difficulties associated with defining terrorism means it is hard to identify terrorist groups and terrorist acts. The groups have been categorized according to such criteria as their motivation (e.g., political or religious), their targets (e.g., persons of a race or ethnicity different from the terrorists), their locus of operation (domestic or international), or on some other basis.

By default, any accounting of terrorist acts is dependent on the definition used by the entity doing the counting. As an example of how terrorist acts are identified, consider the data provided by the U.S. National Counterterrorism Center (Department of State), which uses the definition of terrorism as found in the U.S. Code to decide if something was a terrorist act.

In 2013, 9,707 terrorist attacks occurred worldwide, producing more than 17,800 deaths and more than 32,500 injuries. Furthermore, more than 2,990 people were kidnapped or taken hostage. Terrorist attacks took place in 93 different countries in 2013 but were heavily concentrated geographically. More than half of all attacks (57 percent) and fatalities (66 percent) and nearly three-quarters of all injuries (73 percent) took place in three countries: Iraq, Pakistan, and Afghanistan (see Table 2.2). The highest numbers of attacks, fatalities, and injuries took place in Iraq. The average lethality of attacks in Iraq was nearly 40 percent higher than the global average (1.84 killed per attack) and 33 percent higher than the 2012 average in Iraq (1.92 killed per attack) (National Consortium for the Study of Terrorism and Responses to Terrorism, 2014; National Counterterrorism Center, 2011).

Comparative criminologists are increasingly intrigued with terrorism as a criminal activity and with all of the other transnational crimes reviewed here. We can expect to find more research and theoretical activity on transnational crime as a social phenomenon and as social behavior. Comparative criminal justice scholars will also be interested in the work of comparative criminologists (just as the reverse will also be true) because theory and research are necessary components to the planning and implementation of justice system responses to transnational crime. This final section reviews some of the ways that countries are working together to combat transnational crime.

TABLE 2.2	Ten Countries with the Most Terrorist Attacks, 2013				
Country	Total Attacks	Total Killed	Total Wounded	Average Number Killed per Attack	Average Number Wounded Attack
Iraq	2495	6378	14956	2.56	5.99
Pakistan	1920	2315	4989	1.21	2.60
Afghanistan	1144	3111	3717	2.72	3.25
India	622	405	717	0.65	1.15
Philippines	450	279	413	0.62	0.92
Thailand	332	131	398	0.39	1.20
Nigeria	300	1817	457	6.06	1.52
Yemen	295	291	583	0.99	1.98
Syria*	212	1074	1773	5.07	8.36
Somalia	197	408	485	2.07	2.46

*Given the limitations of media coverage in Syria, the data presented here are conservative estimates of terrorism in Syria in 2013.

Source: National Consortium for the Study of Terrorism and Responses to Terrorism. (2014). *Annex of statistical information. Country reports on terrorism 2013* (Table 2, p. 4). http://www.state.gov/documents/organization/225043.pdf.

RESPONSE TO TRANSNATIONAL CRIME

In facing global crime we are not powerless. The tools to fight it exist; they have to be adapted and applied.

André Bossard, INTERPOL Secretary General, 1978–1985

This quote from Bossard reflects an optimism often found among persons addressing crime at the international level. Despite what might seem to others to be an overwhelming task, persons affiliated with INTERPOL, Europol, the United Nations, and other intergovernmental organizations believe it is possible for nations to work together to reduce crime. Examples of such efforts in regard to transnational crime are found at the national, regional, and international levels.

National Efforts: The United States of America

Every country where transnational crime occurs (which today is essentially all countries) is interested in reducing its impact. There may be a few countries, such as ones where corrupt officials facilitate the illicit drug trade, that are not interested in combating some transnational crimes, but they are certainly, and thankfully, in the minority.

Efforts to combat transnational crime depend to a great extent on a country's ability to combat crime in general. As a result, there is considerable variation in how available and effective are the national laws, agencies, and personnel to respond to transnational crime. The United States reflects some of that variation.

The United States combats transnational crime on several fronts. Its law enforcement agencies abroad have intensified attempts to thwart foreign-based crime before it reaches America's shores. Enhanced inspection, detection, and monitoring at U.S.

YOU SHOULD KNOW!

Why Should You Care about Transnational Crime?

A country's citizens understandably have a tendency to take a narrow view of the crime problem. In other words, their main concern is how safe they feel in their own neighborhoods. The idea that residents of some neighborhoods in other countries may be similarly concerned is only minimally interesting to the average citizen. Even if criminal activities in one country are shown to have a direct effect on crime in another, residents are unlikely to view that information as significant. After all, if governments cannot do much about local crime, why should they be able to do anything about crime originating in some other country?

Dr. Sarah Sewall, Under Secretary for Civilian Security, Democracy, and Human Rights at the U.S. Department of State since 2014, heads a reorganized unit that includes the Bureaus of Counterterrorism and International Narcotics and Law Enforcement, the new Bureau of Conflict and Stabilization Operations, and the Bureaus of Democracy, Human Rights, and Labor and Population, Refugees, and Migration, as well as the offices that work to promote international justice, engage global youth, and combat human trafficking.

In her confirmation speech before the Senate Foreign Relations Committee, she offers a vision for crime control and good governance around the globe and emphasizes its relationship to the safety of Americans at home. She noted that Martin Luther King, Jr, wrote of a single garment of destiny that bound the human race. Sewall said his words are even more true today in our interconnected, hyperlinked world. Americans are safer when the world is safer, and when the world is more prosperous, Americans can be more prosperous. Further, she recalled Secretary of State John Kerry's point that as we strengthen civilian security and good governance abroad, we get an enormous return on investment—not simply in the conflicts we avoid but in the well-being of future generations of American citizens (http://www.foreign.senate.gov/imo/media/doc/Sewall%20.pdf).

Transnational criminals engage in a variety of activities that pose a grave threat to the national security of the United States and the stability and values of the entire world community. The terrorist attacks on September 11, 2001, made this painfully clear, but other types of transnational crime (e.g., illicit traffic in arms, the modern slave trade of trafficking in humans, and the unregulated flow of crime profits) also have a negative impact on the stability of democratic institutions and free market economies around the world.

borders attempt to deny transnational criminals access to the country. An overview of U.S. efforts is best provided with reference to just a few of the many federal agencies whose mission in part is to combat transnational crime.

The Department of Homeland Security (DHS), the Department of Justice (DOJ), the Department of State (DOS), and the Department of Treasury (DOT) are the federal agencies most involved in combating transnational crime. A few examples of the transnational crime reduction responsibilities of each department, by department bureau or agency, include the following:

- DHS—*Bureau of Customs and Border Protection.* Its primary mission is preventing terrorists and terrorist weapons from entering the United States. It is also responsible for apprehending individuals attempting to enter the United States illegally; stemming the flow of illegal drugs and other contraband; protecting agricultural and economic interests from harmful pests and diseases; protecting American businesses from theft of their intellectual property; and regulating and facilitating international trade, collecting import duties, and enforcing U.S. trade laws (U.S. Bureau of Customs and Border Protection, 2016).
- DHS—*U.S. Secret Service.* It investigates violations of laws relating to counterfeiting of obligations and securities of the United States; financial crimes that include, but are not limited to, access device fraud, financial institution fraud, identity theft, and computer fraud; and computer-based attacks on the nation's financial, banking, and telecommunications infrastructure (U.S. Secret Service, 2016).

Along with several other federal agencies, the Federal Bureau of Investigation is responsible for the protection of the United States from terrorist activities.

Courtesy of FBI Headquarters.

- DOJ—*Federal Bureau of Investigation.* Part of its mission is to protect the United States from foreign intelligence and terrorist activities. Other Bureau priorities include protecting the United States from cyber-based attacks and high-technology crimes as well as combating international organized crime (Federal Bureau of Investigation, 2016).
- DOJ—*Organized Crime and Gang Section.* This section coordinates the Department's program to combat organized crime. The principal enforcement efforts are currently directed against transnational organized crime groups, which pose serious threats to the well-being of Americans and the stability of our economy. Transnational organized crime promotes corruption, violence, and other illegal activities; jeopardizes our border security; and causes human misery. It undermines the integrity of our banking and financial systems, commodities and securities markets, healthcare system, and cyberspace (U.S. Department of Justice, 2016).
- DOS—*Office to Monitor and Combat Trafficking in Persons.* Established in 2000 as a result of the Trafficking Victims Protection Act, the Office leads the United States' global engagement on the fight against human trafficking, partnering with foreign governments and civil society to develop and implement effective strategies for confronting modern slavery. The Office has responsibility for bilateral and multilateral diplomacy, targeted foreign assistance, and public engagement on trafficking in persons (U.S. Department of State, 2016a).
- DOS—*Bureau of International Narcotics and Law Enforcement Affairs.* INL counters transnational and international crime, illegal drugs, and instability abroad. INL helps countries strengthen their police, courts, and corrections systems. INL helps foreign countries build strong law enforcement institutions that counter transnational crime—from money laundering, cybercrime, and intellectual property theft to trafficking in goods, people, weapons, drugs, or endangered wildlife (U.S. Department of State, 2016b).

- DOT—*Financial Crimes Enforcement Network*. FinCEN was established in 1990 to provide a government-wide multisource financial intelligence and analysis network. The organization's operation was broadened in 1994 to include regulatory responsibilities for administering the Bank Secrecy Act, one of the nation's most potent weapons for preventing corruption of the U.S. financial system (U.S. Department of Treasury, 2016).

The abundance of agencies dealing with some aspect of transnational crime is not unexpected given the size and complexity of the United States. As noted in Chapter 6, the U.S. tendency for decentralization of law enforcement efforts makes this situation even more understandable. Other countries (Australia and Canada, for example) also have quite a few different agencies responsible for combating transnational crime.

International Efforts

The premier international agencies working to combat transnational crime are INTERPOL and the United Nations. INTERPOL receives additional coverage in Chapter 6, so, after only a brief comment on INTERPOL, this section emphasizes the United Nations.

INTERPOL RESPONDS TO TRANSNATIONAL CRIME INTERPOL, which is the largest international police organization in the world, facilitates cross-border criminal police cooperation among its member countries. It supports all efforts to combat transnational crime. Because INTERPOL has no enforcement authority, its role is as a conduit for intelligence and information among countries for facilitating police cooperation and for providing training and technical assistance. INTERPOL's website (http://www.interpol.int/Crime-areas) has detailed information on the 19 transnational crime areas of importance to the organization.

INTERPOL is mandated to promote police cooperation in all cases of international crime except those of political, military, religious, and racial character. The exceptions set up a potential conundrum because terrorists often claim their acts are justified on ideological, political, or religious grounds. However, INTERPOL responds to the criminal acts of terrorism, regardless of motivation, because those acts—like other transnational crimes—constitute a serious threat to individual lives and freedom.

Terrorism provides a good example of the way INTERPOL exemplifies an international effort to combat transnational crime (INTERPOL, 2016b). INTERPOL's role is first to prevent acts of terrorism and then, if they are carried out, to ensure that the perpetrators are brought to justice. Prevention efforts are accomplished by collecting, storing, and analyzing information and then sharing it among the member countries. The information may have been provided by a member country or identified in public sources. Terrorist-related information is shared with specialized officers working in INTERPOL's Public Safety and Terrorism Branch. Those officers have the task of assessing the threat and issuing alerts and warnings.

When a terrorist act occurs, member countries are required to send INTERPOL all particulars concerning the nature of the act; investigative developments; any individuals suspected, arrested, or charged; and information about organizations on behalf of which the act was conducted. Based on that information, INTERPOL can instantly issue international notices for fugitive terrorists whose arrest is sought by member countries. For example, the acts of September 11, 2001, resulted in investigative leads and evidence spanning the globe. INTERPOL set up the 11 September Task Force at INTERPOL headquarters (Lyon, France) to coordinate and accelerate the information being sent to the INTERPOL National Central Bureau in Washington, DC, which it then forwarded to the FBI.

INTERPOL is also engaged in the investigation and prosecution of genocide, war crimes, and crimes against humanity. It provides operational and investigative support to international criminal tribunals and justice institutions, as well as to war crimes units in its member countries. It has been cooperating with the United Nations International Tribunals for the former Yugoslavia and Rwanda since 1994.

THE UNITED NATIONS RESPONDS TO TRANSNATIONAL CRIME   The United Nations is a very large and complex organization with many branches, agencies, and affiliated organizations. Much—though certainly not all—of the UN crime and justice work is organizationally handled at its International Centre in Vienna, Austria. More specifically, the UNODC serves as the umbrella organization mandated to assist UN countries in their struggle against illicit drugs, crime, and terrorism. For example, the UNODC Crime Programme promotes stable and viable criminal justice systems in UN member countries and works to combat the growing threats of transnational organized crime, corruption, and trafficking in human beings—with specific programs in each of those areas.

Much of the UNODC's work is advisory, educational, and research-oriented as it helps determine and then carry out the crime and justice policies of the United Nations. The policies themselves are often the result of international agreements (e.g., conventions, rules, and protocols) entered into by UN member states.

The agreements can range from ones that encourage certain behavior to others that demand adherence to specific principles and procedures. Generally, treaties and conventions refer to binding documents that require all ratifying countries to abide by the agreements' specified standards. UN member states that do not ratify the agreement are not bound by the treaty or convention. Protocols are agreements that are less formal than treaties or conventions and may serve to amend or better explain the more formal document. Of the many important agreements related to transnational crime, we consider just a few.

The UN Convention against Transnational Organized Crime became effective in 2003 after being ratified by the necessary 40 member states (United Nations Office on Drugs and Crime, 2016a). The United States signed the document in 2000 and ratified it—meaning the United States agrees to abide by its provisions—in 2005. The convention is the first international instrument against transnational organized crime, and those nations that have ratified it agree to take a series of measures against transnational organized crime. These measures include the creation, in those countries where they are not already present, of laws making specific transnational crimes illegal and the adoption of frameworks that allow for mutual legal assistance, extradition, law enforcement cooperation, and technical assistance and training among the parties to the convention. As a result, the countries will be able to rely on one another in investigating, prosecuting, and punishing crimes committed by organized criminal groups when either the crimes or the groups that commit them have some element of transnational involvement. Three protocols (one on trafficking in persons, another on smuggling migrants, and the third on illicit manufacturing and trafficking in firearms) are attached to the convention, and all have entered into force as a result of being ratified by the necessary number of countries.

The transnational crime of terrorism has received particular attention by the United Nations. The Security Council passed resolution 1373 in the aftermath of September 11, 2001, and it clearly notes the international community's rejection of terrorist activities. Twelve universal conventions and protocols against terrorism have been developed under the auspices of the United Nations and its specialized agencies.

The conventions deal with specific crimes such as hijacking airplanes, taking hostages, stealing nuclear material, using explosives in public places, and participating in activities intended to finance terrorists. Most of the conventions are penal in nature and typically define a particular type of terrorist violence as an offense and require that the state parties penalize that activity in their domestic law. The conventions also create an obligation on the country where a terrorist suspect is found to either prosecute or extradite the suspect. This last element is commonly known as the principle of "no safe haven for terrorists" and is considered an essential antiterrorism obligation of the UN member states.

An example of how the United Nations and, more specifically, the UNODC can assist in combating terrorism is the development of model laws that member states can use when drawing up their own domestic law, making terrorist activities criminal. In 2003, the UNODC completed two model laws to help combat terrorism. They are designed to assist governments in bringing their domestic legislation into compliance with the Convention for the Suppression of the Financing of Terrorism and with UN resolutions aimed at ending terrorism.

The examples of cooperative efforts to combat transnational crime exemplify one topic of interest to comparative criminal justice scholars. As the remainder of this book shows, there are many other topics for comparative justice scholars to consider, but the increasing examples of countries coordinating their efforts to combat transnational crime clearly show why the study of comparative justice systems is so important today.

INTERNATIONAL CRIME

Comparative criminologists are increasingly interested in international crime. International crime is that which violates international law. International law encompasses international criminal law, international human rights law, and international humanitarian law. Niemann (2014) differentiates among these three bodies of law, clarifying that all three of them have been or still are an impingement on state sovereignty, but reflect international consensus on what acts are so egregious or unfair that states must be held accountable to the international community. International criminal law is that which establishes definitions and procedures for criminalizing acts internationally, with individual as well as state liability. International human rights law includes acts that are generally considered criminal as well as noncriminal, and generally holds the state accountable. International humanitarian law applies to armed conflict, whether external or internal. It serves to level the playing field for combatants ("Hague law"), as well as to ensure the humanitarian treatment of civilians ("Geneva law"), based on the Geneva conventions.

Types of International Crime

International crimes include genocide, crimes against humanity, and war crimes. Some domestic crimes, as well as transnational crimes, are international in nature when they occur as part of armed conflict or as part of widespread attacks against civilians (mass atrocities). At the beginning of this chapter, we saw an example of rape as a domestic crime as well as an international crime (rape as a crime against humanity and a war crime). Transnational crimes such as enforced disappearance, unlawful deportation, and enslavement can be international crimes if they occur within a context of armed conflict or widespread attacks against civilians. Criminologists have only recently begun to study these crimes, but there is no doubt that they are worthy of study.

It is generally difficult to obtain precise numbers of offenders or victims of international crimes or conduct more than rudimentary criminological research on international crimes. That is because many of these crimes take place under social conditions of extreme disorder in which we could not reasonably expect any quantitative tallying to occur reliably, such as police recorded crime statistics, victimization surveys, or self-report surveys. Also important is that in many cases, those responsible for these crimes are either state actors (government officials) or non-state actors (militias, rebels), which would make us further doubt any official data gathering efforts since these would involve vested interests and perhaps intimidation. Retrospective studies can be done, but imagine trying to get information from populations that are displaced to many different areas, or for which there are virtually no survivors? Many international agencies or humanitarian assistance organizations do provide estimates, of course. The International Criminal Tribunal for Rwanda (ICTR), for example, estimates that 800,000–1,000,000 Rwandans were killed during the 100-day period from April 7 to mid-July 1994. Genocide, crimes against humanity, and war crimes were perpetrated primarily against Tutsi civilians and moderate Hutus—which included killings but also assaults, sexual violence, property crimes, and many others. Those responsible for these crimes were soldiers, gendarmes, politicians, the Interahamwe (Hutu militia), and ordinary citizens (United Nations, 2016). Criminologists are needed to study international crime for a number of reasons: the large scale of numbers of victims and offenders involved, the lack of criminological theorizing about why and how these crimes occur, and the need for evidence to hold perpetrators responsible.

UNODC's new International Classification of Crime for Statistical Purposes includes the count of these kinds of crimes in its classification (United Nations Office on Drugs and Crime, 2015), and thus, in the future we can expect to see an effort to gather data more systematically on international crimes. Comparative criminologist John Hagan has been a pioneer in the empirical criminological study of international crime, and has written extensively on Darfur and the Balkans (Hagan, Kaiser, Rothenberg, Hanson, & Parker, 2012; Hagan & Rymond-Richmond, 2009). Comparative criminologist Nicole Rafter (2016) authored a major treatise entitled *The Crime of All Crimes: Toward a Criminology of Genocide*. These scholars have started a tradition of applying criminological research methods and theories, expanding our discipline's lens to the most atrocious of crimes.

The International Criminal Court

The advent of the International Criminal Court, located in The Hague, the Netherlands, is part of a long tradition in international criminal justice to form courts to prosecute violations of international criminal law. The Nuremberg Tribunals, established after World War II, were the first instance of such courts in the twentieth century, followed by the ad hoc international tribunals established by the United Nations after conflicts in the former Yugoslavia and Rwanda. More tribunals followed that were collaborative between local countries and the United Nations (East Timor, Kosovo, Cambodia, Sierra Leone), and finally, these efforts culminated in the adoption of the Rome Statute in 1998 that created the ICC for what is hoped to be posterity. In 2002, the court came into existence. The ICC prosecutes genocide, crimes against humanity, and war crimes among its states parties (currently it has 139 Signatories and 118 Ratifications) based on the complementarity principle—it only intervenes in such cases when its states parties are unable or unwilling to intervene. The ICC is not part of the United Nations, but it does have a link to the United Nations. The UN Security Council may refer cases to the ICC or ask it to defer investigation or prosecution. The United States has not signed the Rome Statute (Goldstone, 2007).

The ICC functions with an amalgamation of common and civil law principles. Although its structure includes prosecutors, judges, investigators, and other staff, it is a court without an international police system or an international prison system. As such, it depends on its states parties for assistance in detecting and apprehending offenders, as well as for housing those it convicts and sentences. The ICC has over 800 staff members from 100 countries. Its working languages are French and English. It has an annual budget of 139.5 million euros. The work of the court is arduous and painstaking, since the strategy of the court is to prosecute major figures, not minor offenders and the cases undertaken by the court are at the forefront of international politics. Since its inception, ICC judges have issued 29 arrest warrants against 27 suspects. Thanks to cooperation from states, eight persons have been detained in the ICC detention center and have appeared before the Court. Thirteen persons remain at large. Charges have been dropped against three persons due to their deaths. ICC judges have also issued nine summonses to appear. The judges have issued four verdicts: three individuals have been found guilty and one has been acquitted (International Criminal Court, 2016). The court's first landmark decision on rape as a war crime took place in 2016, as mentioned at the beginning of this chapter. The ICC is of interest to comparative criminologists for at least two major reasons: first, because its history and structure are reflective of the history and structure of studies in comparative criminal justice, and second, because the court sets a deterrent example for the entire world in its prosecution of the most heinous offenses known to humankind.

Summary

Comparative criminology and comparative criminal justice are separate fields of study with overlapping interests. This book focuses on comparative criminal justice; therefore, it is especially interested in how the people and agencies in different countries go about accomplishing justice. All justice systems operate in the context of those activities that a government has identified as criminal and those persons who engage in that behavior. Criminology, more so than criminal justice, studies those crimes and criminals. Because criminology and criminal justice have some subject matter in common, it is appropriate for this comparative criminal justice book to pay some attention to issues related to comparative criminology. That is this chapter's goal.

When comparative criminologists look at crime as a social phenomenon, they are trying to identify similarities and differences in crime patterns across countries. They must be very careful when doing this because there are no universally agreed-upon ways to define, report, and record crime. However, with the cautious use of data sets that report crime and victimization rates from many countries, comparative criminologists are able to conduct research that can advance theoretical explanations for criminal behavior. Examples of the explanations offered when comparative criminologists look at crime as social behavior are those categorized as grand theories.

Traditionally, comparative criminologists have studied domestic crime patterns and behavior. The globalization of crime has brought an increased interest in crime that crosses national borders. Comparative criminologists now find themselves studying such transnational crimes as cybercrime, money laundering, piracy, terrorism, and trafficking in persons.

The growth in transnational crime has been accompanied, understandably, by an increase in efforts to combat that crime. The chapter concludes with some examples of such efforts at the national and international levels, and with a discussion of international crime and the International Criminal Court.

Discussion Questions

- Using the homicide rates reported in Table 2.1, suggest reasons that groupings of countries have higher or lower homicide rates.
- Do you agree with the civilization theorists who suggest that crime declined as civility (e.g., eating with a knife and fork, refraining from urinating in public)

increased in a society? Some people argue that contemporary American society is experiencing a decrease in civility (conduct an Internet search on terms such as incivility). If that is true (and you are welcome to argue the point—nicely!), do you think it can or will affect the crime rate?

References

Aebi, M. F. (2008). Measuring the influence of statistical counting rules on cross-national differences in recorded crime. In K. Aromaa & M. Heiskanen (Eds.), *Crime and criminal justice systems in Europe and North America 1995–2004* (pp. 196–214). Helsinki, Finland: European Institute for Crime Prevention and Control.

Albanese, J. S. (2011). *Transnational crime and the 21st century: Criminal enterprise, corruption, and opportunity*. New York, NY: Oxford University Press.

Barberet, R. (2014). *Women, crime and criminal justice: A global enquiry*. London, UK: Routledge.

Beirne, P., & Nelken, D. (Eds.). (1997). *Issues in comparative criminology*. Aldershot, UK: Ashgate.

Bennett, R. R., & Lynch, J. P. (1990). Does a difference make a difference? Comparing cross-national crime indicators. *Criminology, 28*, 153–181.

Blum, J. A., Levi, M., Naylor, R. T., & Williams, P. (1998). Financial havens, banking secrecy and money laundering. International Money Laundering Information Network. Retrieved from http://www.imolin.org/imolin/en/finhaeng.html

Bouley, E. E., & Vaughn, M. S. (1995). Violent crime and modernization in Colombia. *Crime, Law, and Social Change, 23*, 17–40.

Center for Strategic and International Studies (CSIS). (2014). *Net losses: Estimating the global cost of cybercrime.* Retrieved from http://www.mcafee.com/us/resources/reports/rp-economic-impact-cybercrime2.pdf

Chon, D. S. (2016). A spurious relationship of gender equality with female homicide victimization: A cross-national analysis. *Crime & Delinquency, 62*(3), 397–419. doi:10.1177/0011128713492497

Di Nicola, A. (2005). Trafficking in human beings and smuggling of migrants. In P. Reichel (Ed.), *Handbook of transnational crime & justice* (pp. 181–203). Thousand Oaks, CA: Sage.

Duursma, J. (2008, December 20). Definition of terrorism and self-determination. *Harvard International Review.* Retrieved from http://hir.harvard.edu/definition-of-terrorism-and-self-determination

Elias, N. (1982). *The civilizing process: Power and incivility* (Vol. 2). New York: Pantheon Books.

European Institute for Crime Prevention and Control. (2014). European sourcebook of crime and criminal justice statistics 2014. Retrieved from http://www.heuni.fi/material/attachments/heuni/reports/qrMWoCVTF/HEUNI_report_80_European_Sourcebook.pdf

Farrell, G., Tilley, N., Tseloni, A., & Mailley, J. (2008). The crime drop and the security hypothesis. *British Society of Criminology Newsletter, 62*, 17–21. Retrieved from http://www.britsoccrim.org/wp-content/uploads/2016/04/bscn-62-2008-Farrell.pdf

Farrell, G., Tseloni, A., Mailley, J., & Tilley, N. (2011). The crime drop and the security hypothesis. *Journal of Research in Crime and Delinquency, 48*(2), 147–175. doi:10.1177/0022427810391539

Federal Bureau of Investigation. (2016). What we investigate. About us. Retrieved from https://www.fbi.gov/about-us/investigate

Gillis, A. R. (1994). Literacy and the civilization of violence in 19th-century France. *Sociological Forum, 9*, 371–401.

Global Initiative to Fight Human Trafficking. (2016). Trafficking for organ trade. Retrieved from http://www.ungift.org/knowledgehub/en/about/trafficking-for-organ-trade.html

Goldstone, R. (2007). International criminal court and ad hoc tribunals. In T. G. Weiss & S. Daws (Eds.), *The Oxford handbook on the United Nations* (pp. 463–478). Oxford, UK: Oxford University Press.

Hagan, J., Kaiser, J., Rothenberg, D., Hanson, A., & Parker, P. (2012). Atrocity victimization and the costs of economic conflict crimes in the battle for Baghdad and Iraq. *European Journal of Criminology, 9*(5), 481–498.

Hagan, J., & Rymond-Richmond, W. (2009). *Darfur and the crime of genocide*. Cambridge, UK: Cambridge University Press.

Harrendorf, S., Heiskanen, M., & Malby, S. (2010). *International statistics on crime and justice*. Helsinki, Finland: European Institute for Crime Prevention and Control, United Nations Office on Drugs and Control.

Heiland, H.-G., & Shelley, L. I. (1992). Civilization, modernization and the development of crime and control. In H.-G. Heiland, L. I. Shelley, & H. Katoh (Eds.), *Crime and control in comparative perspectives*. Berlin, Germany: Walter de Gruyter.

Howard, G. J., Newman, G., & Pridemore, W. A. (2000). *Theory, method, and data in comparative criminology, Vol. 4: Measurement and analysis of crime and justice. Criminal Justice 2000* (pp. 139–211). Retrieved from https://www.ncjrs.gov/App/publications/Abstract.aspx?id=185540

Hunnicutt, G. (2009). Varieties of patriarchy and violence against women: Resurrecting "patriarchy" as a theoretical tool. *Violence Against Women, 15*(5), 553–573. doi: 10.1177/1077801208331246

International Criminal Court. (2016). Facts and figures. About. Retrieved from https://www.icc-cpi.int/about

International Labour Organization. (2016). Statistics and indicators on forced labour and trafficking. Forced labour, human trafficking and slavery. Retrieved from http://www.ilo.org/global/topics/forced-labour/policy-areas/statistics/lang--en/index.htm

International Maritime Bureau. (2016). *Piracy and armed robbery against ships: Report for the period 1 January–31 December 2015*. Retrieved from https://icc-ccs.org/piracy-reporting-centre/request-piracy-report

INTERPOL. (2016a, June 9). Online sale of fake medicines and products targeted in INTERPOL operation. Retrieved from http://www.interpol.int/News-and-media/News/2016/N2016-076

INTERPOL. (2016b). Terrorism. Crime areas. Retrieved from http://www.interpol.int/Crime-areas/Terrorism/Terrorism

INTERPOL. (2016c). Works of art. Crime areas. Retrieved from http://www.interpol.int/Crime-areas/Works-of-art/Works-of-art

Joyce, E. (2005). Expanding the international regime on money laundering in response to transnational organized crime, terrorism, and corruption. In P. Reichel (Ed.), *Handbook of transnational crime & justice* (pp. 79–97). Thousand Oaks, CA: Sage.

Killias, M., & Lanfranconi, B. (2012). The crime drop discourse—or the illusion of uniform continental trends: Switzerland as a contrasting case. In J. van Dijk, A. Tseloni, & G. Farrell (Eds.), *The international crime drop: New directions in research* (pp. 268–278). Basingstoke, England: Palgrave Macmillan. Koeppel, M. D. H., Rhineberger-Dunn, G. M., & Mack, K. Y. (2015). Cross-national homicide: A review of the current literature. *International Journal of Comparative and Applied Criminal Justice, 39*(1), 47–85. doi:10.1080/01924036.2013.836676

LaFree, G., & Birkbeck, C. (1991). The neglected situation: A cross-national study of the situational characteristics of crime. *Criminology, 29*, 73–98.

Lewis, C. (1999). Police records of crime. In G. Newman (Ed.), *Global report on crime and justice* (pp. 43–64). New York, NY: Oxford University Press.

McLaughlin, A. (2005, December 15). Nigeria cracks down on e-mail scams. *The Christian Science Monitor.* Retrieved from http://www.csmonitor.com/2005/1215/p07s02-woaf.htm

Minder, R. (2013, February 13). Cybercrime network based in Spain is broken up. *The New York Times.* Retrieved from http://www.nytimes.com

National Consortium for the Study of Terrorism and Responses to Terrorism. (2014). *Country reports on terrorism 2013: Annex of statistical information.* Retrieved from http://www.state.gov/documents/organization/225043.pdf

National Counterterrorism Center. (2011). *2010 Report on Terrorism.* Retrieved from http://www.nctc.gov/wits-banner/docs/2010_report_on_terrorism.pdf

Newman, G., & Howard, G. (1999). Introduction: Data sources and their use. In G. Newman (Ed.), *Global report on crime and justice* (pp. 1–23). New York, NY: Oxford University Press.

Newman, G., & Howard, G. (2001). Introduction: Varieties of comparative criminology. In G. J. Howard & G. R. Newman (Eds.), *Varieties of comparative criminology* (pp. 1–8). Leiden, The Netherlands: Brill.

Niemann, G. (2014). International criminal law and international crimes. In P. L. Reichel & J. S. Albanese (Eds.), *Handbook of transnational crime and justice* (2nd ed., pp. 263–280). Los Angeles, CA: Sage.

Oppel, R. A., Jr. (2013, March 17). Ohio teenagers guilty in rape that social media brought to light. *The New York Times.* Retrieved from http://www.nytimes.com

Organization for Security and Co-operation in Europe. (2014). How to protect human trafficking for domestic servitude in diplomatic households and protect private domestic workers. Retrieved from http://www.osce.org/handbook/domesticservitude

Rafter, N. H. (2016). *The crime of all crimes: Toward a criminology of genocide.* New York, NY: New York University Press.

Rantala, R. R. (2005). Cybercrime against businesses (NCJ 221943). Retrieved from https://www.ncjrs.gov/app/publications/abstract.aspx?ID=243834

Rubin, M. M., Culp, R., Mameli, P., & Walker, M. (2008). Using cross-national studies to illuminate the crime problem: One less data source left standing. *Journal of Contemporary Criminal Justice, 24*(1), 50–68. doi:10.1177/1043986207312937

Schichor, D. (1990). Crime patterns and socioeconomic economic development: A cross-national analysis. *Criminal Justice Review, 15*, 64–78.

Shelley, L. I. (1981). *Crime and modernization: The impact of industrialization and urbanization on crime.* Carbondale, IL: Southern Illinois University Press.

Smith, C. J., Zhang, S., & Barberet, R. (Eds.). (2011). *Routledge handbook of international criminology.* London, UK: Routledge.

Stille, A. (2003, May 3). Did knives and forks cut murder? *The New York Times.* Retrieved from http://www.nytimes.com/2003/05/03/arts/did-knives-forks-cut-murders-counting-backward-historians-resurrect-crime.html?pagewanted=all&src=pm

Transparency International. (2013). Global Corruption Barometer 2013. Retrieved from http://www.transparency.org/gcb2013

Tseloni, A., Mailley, J., Farrell, G., & Tilley, N. (2010). Exploring the international decline in crime rates. *European Journal of Criminology, 7*(5), 375–394. doi:10.1177/1477370810367014

U.S. Bureau of Customs and Border Protection. (2016). Stats and summaries. Newsroom. Retrieved from https://www.cbp.gov/newsroom/stats

U.S. Department of Justice, U.S. Attorney's Office. (2015, February 24). Jury finds two more brothers guilty in human trafficking scheme. Retrieved from https://www.justice.gov/usao-edpa/pr/jury-finds-two-more-brothers-guilty-human-trafficking-scheme

U.S. Department of Justice, Organized Crime and Gang Section. (2016). About OCGS. Retrieved from https://www.justice.gov/criminal-ocgs/about-ocgs

U.S. Department of State. (2015). *Trafficking in Persons Report 2015*. Retrieved from http://www.state.gov/j/tip/rls/tiprpt/2015/index.htm

U.S. Department of State, Office to Monitor and Combat Trafficking in Persons. (2016a). About us. Retrieved from http://www.state.gov/j/tip/about/index.htm

U.S. Department of State, Bureau of International Narcotics and Law Enforcement Affairs (INL). (2016b). Retrieved from http://www.state.gov/j/inl/

U.S. Department of Treasury, Financial Crimes Enforcement Network. (2016). What we do. Retrieved from http://www.fincen.gov/about_fincen/wwd/

U.S. Drug Enforcement Administration. (2005, April 20). International Internet drug ring shattered. Retrieved from http://www.justice.gov/dea/pubs/pressrel/pr042005.html

U.S. Secret Service. (2016). About. Retrieved from http://www.secretservice.gov/about/overview/

United Kingdom. (2000). Terrorism Act 2000. Retrieved from http://www.legislation.gov.uk/ukpga/2000/11/section/1

United Nations Mechanism for International Criminal Tribunals. (2016). The ICTR remembers: 20th anniversary of the Rwandan genocide. Retrieved from http://www.unmict.org/specials/ictr-remembers/?q=ictr-remembers/

United Nations Office on Drugs and Crime, Research and Trend Analysis Branch. (2015). International classification of crime for statistical purposes. Retrieved from http://www.unodc.org/documents/data-and-analysis/statistics/crime/ICCS/ICCS_English_2016_web.pdf

United Nations Office on Drugs and Crime. (2016a). Convention against transnational organized crime and its protocols. Retrieved from https://www.unodc.org/unodc/treaties/CTOC/

United Nations Office on Drugs and Crime, Research and Trend Analysis Branch. (2016b). *World Drug Report 2016*. Retrieved from http://www.unodc.org/wdr2016/

van Dijk, J. (2016, June 7–10). *The latest sweeps of the ICVS: Beijing, the Caribbean and Kyrgyzstan*. Paper presented at the 3rd International Conference of Governance, Crime and Justice Statistics, Merida, Mexico. Paper retrieved from http://internet.contenidos.inegi.org.mx/contenidos/egspj/ponencias/D7_CRIME%20STATISTICS-5-UN.pdf

van Dijk, J., & Kangaspunta, K. (2000). Piecing together the cross-national crime puzzle. *National Institute of Justice Journal, 242*, 35–41. Retrieved from http://www.ncjrs.gov/pdffiles1/jr000242f.pdf

van Dijk, J., Tseloni, A., & Farrell, G. (Eds.). (2012). *The international crime drop: New directions in research*. Basingstoke, England: Palgrave Macmillan.

van Dijk, J., van Kesteren, J., & Smit, P. (2007). *Criminal Victimisation in International Perspective: Key findings from the 2004–2005 ICVS and EU ICS*. Retrieved from http://english.wodc.nl/onderzoeksdatabase/icvs-2005-survey.aspx?cp=45&cs=6796

Vinograd, C. (2016, March 21). Jean-Pierre Bemba convicted at ICC of war crimes, crimes against humanity. NBC News. Retrieved from http://www.nbcnews.com/news/world/

von Hofer, H. (2000). Crime statistics as constructs: The case of Swedish rape statistics. *European Journal on Criminal Policy and Research, 8*(1), 77–89. doi: 10.1023/a:1008713631586

Waldrop, M. M. (2016, May). How to hack the hackers: The human side of cybercrime. *Nature, 533*, 164–167.

Yodanis, C. L. (2004). Gender inequality, violence against women, and fear: A cross-national test of the feminist theory of violence against women. *Journal of Interpersonal Violence, 19*(6), 655–675. doi: 10.1177/0886260504263868

An American Perspective on Criminal Law

LEARNING OBJECTIVES

After studying this chapter, you will be able to:

1. Distinguish between substantive law and procedural law.
2. List and explain the general characteristics of substantive criminal law.
3. List and explain the major principles of substantive criminal law.
4. Summarize and compare the crime control and due process models of procedural criminal law.
5. Explain why some sections of the USA PATRIOT Act are controversial.

COUNTRIES IN FOCUS

Canada
Germany
Mexico

Norway
United States

Scott Jackson, a dental student, gave cocaine to his lover with the intent to kill her and the fetus she was carrying. He decapitated what he believed to be her dead body in an attempt to thwart identification of the body. The effort failed (the victim's shoes bore the name of the store that sold them, eventually leading police to Jackson), and medical testimony established that the woman had been alive at the time of the decapitation. For an act to be a crime of first-degree murder, the actor must have intentionally engaged in harmful conduct. Did Jackson commit first-degree murder when he gave his lover the cocaine? How about when he decapitated her?

When lawyers debate questions such as those posed in the Jackson case, they are arguing over issues of substantive law: Just what is required for thoughts and behavior to qualify as a specific type of crime? We come back to the Jackson case in just a few pages, but the broader concern for this chapter is to identify the basic ingredients of any legal system.

ESSENTIAL INGREDIENTS OF JUSTICE SYSTEMS

Two problems need resolving before any society can implement an institutionalized pattern of criminal justice. First, the laws must be delineated. Next, the manner of enforcement must be specified. The way a society resolves these problems involves the essential ingredients of any legal system. These activities are of equal importance and provide a sound basis for diagramming the basic foundation of legal systems. However, simply stating the existence of this foundation is not sufficient. To allow comparison and contrast, it is necessary to examine these ingredients more closely. That examination is aided by identifying key features of each ingredient.

Figures 3.1 and 3.2 illustrate the essential ingredients and their key features in terms of a justice paradigm. As the figures show, an institutionalized pattern of justice rests on the definition of rules (substantive law) and the determination of their enforcement (procedural law). In turn, delineation of rules specifies the requirements to be met for something to qualify as a law and the criteria used in deciding whether a particular behavior is criminal (see Figure 3.1). The first condition, requirements to qualify as a law, can be called the *general characteristics of law*. The second condition, determining whether a particular behavior is criminal, comprises the *major principles of law*. Importantly, both the general characteristics and the major principles are discussed here in terms of law in Western nations. Although it hints of ethnocentrism, such tunnel vision is necessary at this point to ensure that we have a common base from which to view the law and legal systems in other countries.

Just as we can analyze two aspects of the definition of laws, we can also bifurcate the manner in which the rules are implemented (see Figure 3.2). The rules can be activated to emphasize repressing rule violation (crime control model) or to contain the

Substantive Law

General Characteristics

1. Politicality
2. Specificity
3. Uniformity
4. Penal Sanction

Major Principles

1. *Mens rea*
2. *Actus reus*
3. Concurrence
4. Harm
5. Causation
6. Punishment
7. Legality

FIGURE 3.1   Substantive Criminal Law

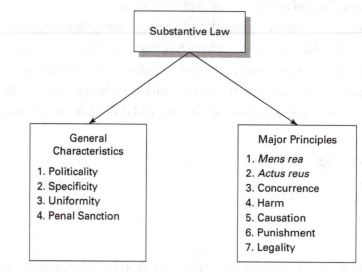

Crime Control Model	Due Process Model
• Assumes freedom is so important that every effort must be made to repress crime. • Seeks to make decisions that will identify factual guilt. • Follows rules that emphasize the repression of criminal activity. • Emphasizes the efficiency of action (i.e., speed and finality). • Requires a high rate of apprehension and conviction by early exclusion of those not likely to be guilty.	• Assumes freedom is so important that every effort must be made to ensure that government intrusion follows legal procedure. • Seeks to make decisions that will identify legal guilt. • Follows rules that emphasize containing the government's level of intrusion into citizens' lives. • Emphasizes the legitimacy of action. • Insists on a formal, adjudicative, adversarial fact-finding process, even though such restraints may keep the process from operating with maximal efficiency.

FIGURE 3.2   Procedural Criminal Law

system's level of intrusion into the citizen's life (due process model). As Packer presents those two models, they are less bound to specific legal systems than are the characteristics and principles of criminal law (Packer, 1968). Therefore, the comments that appear later in the chapter about procedural law are applicable to a wider range of legal systems than is the following analysis of substantive law.

Substantive Criminal Law

An interest in the manner in which definitions of criminal behavior evolve is a concern of substantive law. *Black's Law Dictionary* defines substantive law as "that part of law which creates, defines, and regulates rights." The penal, or criminal, code of each state provides examples of these laws.

The criminal code of Colorado, for example, defines robbery as follows (State of Colorado, 2015):

1. A person who knowingly takes anything of value from the person or presence of another by the use of force, threats, or intimidation commits robbery.
2. Robbery is a class 4 felony.
3. Georgia, on the other hand, has this definition (State of Georgia, 2010):
   a. A person commits the offense of robbery when, with intent to commit theft, he takes property of another from the person or the immediate presence of another:
      1. By use of force;
      2. By intimidation, by the use of threat or coercion, or by placing such person in fear of immediate serious bodily injury to himself or to another; or
      3. By sudden snatching.
   b. A person convicted of the offense of robbery shall be punished by imprisonment for not less than one nor more than 20 years.

Note that in addition to defining (at different lengths) what constitutes the crime of robbery, the statements also specify what punishment will be attached to that crime. A class 4 felony in Colorado requires a sentence of at least 2 but no more than 6 years followed by a 3-year mandatory parole period. Although both states define the crime of robbery, the definitions and punishment vary. Despite the differences, both are examples of substantive law because they each serve two purposes: (1) they define the behavior subject to punishment by the government, and (2) they specify what the punishment will be for those committing that offense.

Substantive law defines a crime and specifies the punishment.

Constantine Panki/Shutterstock

WEB PROJECT

Defining Robbery

Go to the Legal Information Institute's listing of state criminal codes (http://www.law.cornell.edu/wex/table_criminal_code), and click on the criminal code for your state (or another state if you're in Colorado or Georgia). Search for the term *robbery* and then copy and paste the definition to your word processor. Write a paragraph explaining how your state's definition compares with that given in the textbook for either Colorado or Georgia. Do you see any advantages or disadvantages in the way robbery is defined in the two states?

Such definitions are not easily derived. Many criteria must be met before a definition qualifies to be a criminal law. Even more standards are necessary before a specific act is considered to be criminal. Consider, for example, the development of the law of theft. As explained by Hall, the law of theft provides an example of how something comes to be defined as illegal and of how the definition can change over time (Hall, 1952).

Hall notes that prior to the fifteenth century, the crime of theft essentially referred to the taking of property without the owner's consent. Today it has a broader meaning and encompasses acts wherein property was lawfully obtained but then appropriated for the taker's own use (e.g., swindling, embezzlement, and misappropriation). The turning point came in the English Carrier's Case of 1473. The defendant (the carrier) was hired to carry certain bales (probably wool, cloth, or both) to Southampton. Rather than fulfilling his obligation, he carried the goods to another place, where he broke open the bales and took the contents. He was apprehended and charged with a felony.

Today the felony charge of theft seems only reasonable. At that time, however, common law recognized no criminality in a person who came legally into possession of an item and then converted the item to his own use. The reasoning behind such a position was that the owner of transported goods was responsible for protecting himself by employing trustworthy persons. If his trust turned out to be misplaced, it was unfortunate but not illegal. After all, trespass (unlawful interference with a person's property) was an essential part of the definition of theft. It seemed impossible for a person to commit trespass upon items he possessed.

Despite what would appear to be an ironclad defense, the court eventually found the defendant guilty of larceny. The verdict was based on reasoning by Justice Choke (one of three justices hearing the case), who argued, "I think that where a man has goods in his possession by reason of a bailment he cannot take them feloniously, being in possession; but still it seems here that it is felony, for here the things which were within the bales were not bailed to him, only the bales as an entire thing were bailed" (Hall, 1952, p. 9). In other words, the defendant had legal possession of the bales but not of the contents of those bales. The defendant could have sold the bales intact or left the bales unopened in his house, but when he opened them and took the contents, he committed a felony.

Hall suggests that this new interpretation of what constitutes larceny was a result of changing social conditions and pressing social interests. Specifically, Hall notes political and economic conditions that preceded and possibly influenced the outcome of the Carrier's Case. First, consider the political conditions. The king at the time was Edward IV, who, like his predecessor Henry VI, occasionally "consulted" with judges before they handed down a decision. Hall reviews the comments of several chroniclers of the time and concludes that Edward IV was likely to interfere with decisions made at several court levels.

With these political considerations, Hall also emphasizes important economic ones. The Carrier's Case occurred when the economic structure of England was dramatically changing. Alteration of the manorial system and the destruction of serfdom resulted in a situation in which more than 3,000 merchants were engaged in foreign trade as the sixteenth century began. Hall suggests that it would be hard to believe that as the old feudal structure based on agriculture gave way to a new order based on industry and trade, the king would be standing by as a casual observer. Edward IV, supportive of merchants and of trade relations with other countries, was himself a merchant engaged in many private ventures. With this background, and because the merchant "stolen" from was foreign, Hall believes that Edward IV had good reason to use this case as one requiring his "consultation" with the justices. The combination of political and economic conditions brought together the monarchy and the mercantile class and their shared interest in secure transport of wool and cloth. Such new arrangements required a new rule—so the law, which had lagged behind the needs of the times, was brought into a more harmonious relationship with the other institutions by the decision rendered in the Carrier's Case (Hall, 1952, p. 33).

The difficulty in defining something as criminal has led some legal theorists to explain substantive criminal law by reference to its general characteristics and its major principles. A review of those characteristics and principles allows us to appreciate the complexity of our legal system.

GENERAL CHARACTERISTICS OF CRIMINAL LAW   Figure 3.1 showed four general characteristics of Western criminal law (Sutherland & Cressey, 1978):

- Politicality
- Specificity
- Uniformity
- Penal sanction

If any of these four is not present, the activity prohibited or required cannot be called criminal. Politicality refers to the fact that only violations of rules made by a government authority can be crimes. Rules can be made by many groups and individuals. A basketball coach can tell his or her players what time they must be in their dorm room; an employer can tell his or her employee what to wear to work; and a teacher can require students to prepare a paper following a certain typing format. If players, employees, and students violate those rules, they may be subjected to punishment for having done so. They have not, however, committed a crime, because a government authority did not make the rules.

For people to know in advance what particular behavior they must do (e.g., in some states citizens must come to the aid of a police officer upon request) or refrain from doing (e.g., shoplifting), criminal law must be specific. An interesting example is provided in the U.S. Supreme Court case *McBoyle* v. *United States* (283 U.S. 25, 1931), in which the defendant had his conviction for interstate transportation of a stolen airplane set aside. The trial court convicted McBoyle under a statute prohibiting the taking of a motor vehicle or "any other self-propelled vehicle." Because of the airplane's relatively recent invention, the Supreme Court believed such words as "self-propelled vehicle" still brought to many people's minds a picture of vehicles moving on land rather than through the air. Because the legislature had not specifically included airplanes in the statute, their theft was not prohibited. In a 1945 Virginia case, a court set aside a charge of disorderly conduct on a bus because the statute specified only car, train, or caboose (Hall, 1960, p. 39). Although each of these examples may cause some people to wince at the "technicality" of the law, it is important to consider Justice Holmes's remarks in the McBoyle case:

It is reasonable that a fair warning should be given to the world in language that the common world will understand, of what the law intends to do if a certain line is passed. To make the warning fair, so far as possible the line should be clear. (*McBoyle* v. *United States*, 283 U.S. 25, at 27)

Criminal liability should be uniform for all persons despite social background or status. The definition of a crime should not allow one kind of person to commit the act without blame while legally sanctioning a different category of person for the same behavior.

Finally, to qualify as criminal law, there must be some punishment that the government will administer. Without a penal sanction, the rule becomes more of a guideline than a prohibition of crime. It may seem strange that a government would try to make some behavior criminal without providing a punishment for that behavior, but it has happened. For example, some states define adultery as a crime but provide no criminal punishment for its occurrence. Because it can be used in civil court as a basis for divorce, the states believe that it serves a purpose. The following definition of criminal law incorporates each condition:

A body of specific rules regarding human conduct which have been promulgated by political authority, which apply uniformly to all members of the classes to which the rules refer, and which are enforced by punishment administered by the state. (Sutherland & Cressey, 1978, p. 6)

As neat and concise as all that sounds, it is obvious when we look at our criminal laws that the preceding definition is an ideal, relating more generally to Western legal systems and to the American system particularly. There is no requirement that "law" in general needs to be specific or have a sanction before citizens of some society view it as law. Similarly, politicality becomes problematic when, for example, a revolutionary tribunal enforces its decrees. Even uniformity is breached in the United States when we direct laws at specific categories of people, such as prohibiting some citizens from disobeying authority figures, skipping school, or leaving home simply because they are under a certain age.

Despite such problems, these criteria are appropriate and provide a fair description of what constitutes criminal law in much of Western society and in several other places as well. For our purposes, they provide a context and terminology that will be helpful as we look at other legal systems.

MAJOR PRINCIPLES OF CRIMINAL LAW   There are different criteria to be met in deciding whether a particular behavior is criminal. Something that is often hard for the layperson (and even criminal justice employees) to understand is why or how a defendant who seems so obviously guilty can avoid prosecution. At times, an explanation lies in the absence of one or more of the following conditions. Jerome Hall (1960) has suggested seven criteria as constituting the major principles of Western law (see Figure 3.1):

- *Mens rea*
- Act (*actus reus*)
- Concurrence
- Harm
- Causation
- Punishment
- Legality

Mueller (Hall & Mueller, 1965, p. v) summarized these by suggesting that crime refers to legally proscribed (legality) human conduct (act), causative (causation) of a given harm (harm), which conduct coincides (concurrence) with a blameworthy frame of mind (mens rea) and which is subject to punishment (punishment).

The requirement for a guilty act (actus reus) reminds us that having bad intentions is not enough. Behavior is criminal only (with exceptions that are noted shortly) when the individual acts in a prohibited way or fails to act in a required way. In addition, that behavior must be linked in a causal way to some harm considered detrimental to social interests. Consider the following illustration. Suppose that John poisoned Bob with every intent to kill him. Bob is taken to the hospital, where he recovers from the poison but dies of the antidote. Although John's overt act was the necessary first link in the chain of events culminating in Bob's death, it was not John's act that caused the harm (death). Instead, another event (administration of the fatal antidote) intervened between that first link and the final result. John could, of course, still be guilty of several other crimes, such as assault or maybe attempted murder. However, as legal scholars point out, this principle has been the basis for successful appeals in homicide cases in which victims died of negligent medical care instead of the bullet that caused the need for the care in the first place.

The requirement for a guilty mind (mens rea) can be difficult to understand because of confusion between motivation and intent. A young boy may be motivated to take food from a grocery store without paying because his family is starving. Although some see that as an acceptable motivation, the criminal law cares only about the boy's intention. His intent, clearly, was to steal. His motivation may be considered by the store owner, police, prosecutor, and judge as they decide what action to take. Yet, as far as criminal law is concerned, the boy intended to take another person's property without paying and has therefore stolen.

The existence of a harmful act and the presence of mens rea are not enough to show that a crime has occurred. It must also be shown (with exceptions noted as follows) that there was fusion of intent and conduct (i.e., concurrence). Remember the Jackson case that started this chapter? In that 1896 case, a woman died as a result of being decapitated, but interesting legal questions existed. Jackson intended to kill her—and believed he had done so—with cocaine. He then decapitated her—not to kill her but to prevent her identification. So the intent to kill (with cocaine) was not accompanied by the harmful conduct (causing death). Similarly, the harmful conduct (causing death) did not occur with intent (he thought she was already dead). A Kentucky court found Jackson guilty of murder (*Jackson* v. *Commonwealth*, 100 Ky. 239, 1896), but Hall says an argument can be made that the court's decision was wrong because mens rea did not concur with the actual killing (Hall, 1960). At best, Jackson may have committed manslaughter, but the legal ingredients for murder do not seem present—at least for Hall.

As we look over the seven conditions for crime, it becomes easier to appreciate the difficult job that attorneys, judges, and juries sometimes have in determining whether and how these things fit together. As if the task were not difficult enough, there are some exceptions to those conditions that may come into play. For example, we modify the requirement that a harm must be caused by some behavior, so attempts and conspiracy are themselves crimes. Also, the requirement of mens rea is modified in strict liability cases, which consider the individual responsible despite intent. Most strict liability laws concern public welfare offenses (sale of adulterated food, violations of building regulations), but some relate to serious felonies. An example would be the felony-murder rule found in some states. If a death occurs while the offender is committing a felony, that offender may be held criminally responsible for the death even if there was no intent on his part to kill the victim.

Despite those instances of strict liability, intent is an essential part of our legal conception of criminal responsibility. In cases in which intent is absent, the defendant is not criminally responsible for an act that would otherwise be a crime. For example, many of us would not define as criminal a 5-year-old child who opens the mailboxes in his apartment complex and throws his neighbors' mail into his wagon to empty later in the sandbox. We might also question a legal system that brings charges of assault against a woman who caused great physical harm to a man trying to rape her. In each example, our objection seems based on the belief that the child and the woman were not responsible for the acts, though they may have constituted a crime. We may even smile with a sense of self-satisfaction that we live under a system in which such behavior can be excused or justified in appropriate cases. Problems arise, however, when presenting cases not so clear-cut. What would we think if that boy had been 10 instead of 5, or maybe 15? What if the man were unarmed, smaller, and physically weaker than the woman, yet she chose to protect herself by shooting him? The question of responsibility in these situations will not result in as much agreement among us. The *Model Penal Code* notes seven generally recognized defenses based on absence of criminal intent (American Law Institute, 1985). Each state will phrase the defense in its own way and may not even have all seven. One, insanity, is commonly found and provides a good example of one way to approach the question of responsibility.

Under Anglo-Saxon law and well into the thirteenth century, the mentally deranged were treated much like any other criminal. Eventually, "insanity" was accepted as a condition that offers an excuse to what would otherwise be criminal responsibility. Yet deciding what constituted insanity remained a problem. The "wild beast test" developed in the thirteenth century was among the first methods used. It said that a madman was one "who does not know what he is doing, who is lacking in mind and reason, and who is not far removed from the brutes" (Hall, 1960, p. 475).

The first long-lasting criteria for determining insanity came in 1843. In that year, a court found Daniel M'Naghten not guilty of murdering Edward Drummond because M'Naghten was suffering from delusions. Specifically, M'Naghten felt pursued by several enemies, including Sir Robert Peel, who was England's prime minister at the time. M'Naghten killed Drummond while believing that Drummond was actually Peel. The public outcry in response to the acquittal resulted in a request by the House of Lords for the judges of the Queen's Bench to present their views of the insanity defense. Their response, considered by the judges to be a restatement of existing law rather than an innovation, was called the M'Naghten rule (Hall, 1960). They established a "right from wrong" test with the following necessary to show insanity: (1) At the time of the crime, the defendant was operating under a defect of reason so as to be unable to know the nature or quality of the act; or (2) if the defendant was aware of the act's nature, he did not know the act was wrong (Hall, 1960).

From the 1850s to the 1970s, the M'Naghten rule was the primary means for determining insanity in the federal and most state courts in the United States. Some states supplemented M'Naghten with an "irresistible-impulse" test that assumed that people may have known their act was wrong but they could not control the impulse to commit it. Sometimes called the "policeman-at-the-elbow" test, the irresistible-impulse modification accepts the right-versus-wrong concept but presumes that persons may have such a compulsion to commit a crime that they would do so even if they knew the act was wrong and a police officer was present and watching.

Today fewer than half the states still use the M'Naghten rule (with or without the irresistible-impulse modification). Increasingly popular among state legislators is the Model Penal Code definition from the American Law Institute (ALI), which reads:

> A person is not responsible for criminal conduct if at the time of such conduct as a result of mental disease or defect he lacks substantial capacity either to appreciate the criminality [wrongfulness] of his conduct or to conform his conduct to the requirements of law. (American Law Institute, 1985, §401)

Under this standard (also called the Brawner rule from *United States* v. *Brawner*, 471 F.2d 969, 1972), criminal responsibility is linked to "substantial capacity to appreciate" rather than "being unable to know" the wrongfulness of the act.

The difficulty of deciding whether a lack of criminal responsibility is best linked to not knowing right from wrong, to mental disease or defect, or to irresistible impulses is a continuing problem. Since the much criticized verdict finding John Hinckley Jr. not guilty by reason of insanity in the attempted assassination of President Ronald Reagan, the federal government and many states have sought modification and even abolition of insanity defenses. At the federal level, the Insanity Defense Reform Act of 1984 set a new criterion for determining insanity in federal criminal trials. In many ways, it is a return to the M'Naghten rule, because the defendant must be shown to have been unable to appreciate the wrongfulness of his acts. However, it also borrows from the ALI test in linking the inability to appreciate wrongfulness to a severe mental disease or defect. In another important modification of previous standards, the Insanity Defense Reform Act requires that the defense prove insanity. Previously, the burden of proof fell on the state to show that the defendant was sane. Now, in the federal courts, defendants can be required to prove their insanity, thus making such a plea more difficult.

Some states have adopted the new federal guidelines, but others have chosen to make the insanity defense more difficult, or even impossible. In 1982, Idaho provided an example of the latter position when it abolished the insanity defense. Today, three other states (Kansas, Montana, and Utah) have followed Idaho's lead and do not allow the insanity defense. Under the Idaho statute, defendants can be examined before trial to determine whether they are fit to proceed to trial. If not, they are placed in a mental facility until such time that they can adequately participate in their defense. Defendants found fit to go to trial are subject to only two kinds of verdicts: guilty or not guilty. If the defendant is found guilty, his or her mental condition can be considered for sentencing purposes (FindLaw, 2016; Geis & Meier, 1985).

When one country interprets the importance of intent and criminal responsibility in such a variety of ways, we must expect similar variations among nations. Although the substantive law in each country invariably addresses such issues as responsibility, there are differences in how that concept is interpreted and incorporated. If we remember the example of the insanity plea and its variations in the United States, we will be better able to understand differences in issues of substantive law under other legal systems.

YOU SHOULD KNOW!

Guilty but Insane

Because mens rea is an essential element of criminal responsibility, the concept of "guilty but insane" sounds like an oxymoron to some people. After all, if a person is insane at the time of the crime, how could he or she have had the mental state necessary to form criminal intent?

The finding of "guilty but insane"—or, in some states, "guilty but mentally ill"—is usually considered to be a legislative response to public frustration with insanity defenses. Actually, the insanity defense is infrequently used and is seldom successful even when it is used (Callahan, Steadman, McGreevy, & Robbins, 1991). The public perceives the insanity defense as mostly a way for defendants to "get away" with something, so about six states now have laws allowing a person to be held criminally responsible for an act even though he or she may not have had the mental capacity to form mens rea (FindLaw, 2016). As the Alaska law (*Alaska Statutes* §12.47.030) reads: "A defendant found guilty but mentally ill is not relieved of criminal responsibility for criminal conduct."

Procedural Criminal Law

In Figure 3.1, substantive criminal law was conveniently divided into its general characteristics and major principles. Similarly, as Figure 3.2 described, procedural criminal law also has two components. Although general characteristics and major principles theoretically carry equal weight in substantive law, the bifurcation of procedural law results in two components that are unlikely to be found in equal proportion. Instead, procedural criminal law is likely to emphasize one philosophy over the other at any given time.

The due process model and the crime control model were described by Packer as separate value systems competing for priority in the operation of the criminal process (Packer, 1968). Although neither is said to correspond to reality or represent a best approach, they are effectively used to understand the operation of the process. In that manner, the models provide a technique for discussing a variety of criminal justice systems. Because neither model is deemed better than the other, procedural law in different justice systems can be described without making value judgments. Chapter 5 takes exactly that approach. However, as noted earlier, gaining an international perspective is benefited by establishing a parochial base. Therefore, we will see how Packer's models help to understand American procedural law so that we can more fully appreciate the workings of procedural law in other countries. We begin by reviewing aspects of the American Constitution that relate to the criminal process.

CONSTITUTIONAL PROVISIONS FOR THE CRIMINAL PROCESS   After creation of the new Constitution of the United States, some framers expressed concern that the document contained the seeds of a tyranny by government. Discussion focused on adding a bill of rights to restrict the powers of the new federal government. Thomas Jefferson favored such a declaration of rights when he wrote to James Madison:

> Let me add that a bill of rights is what the people are entitled to against every government on earth, general or particular, and what no just government should refuse. (Boyd, 1955)
>
> The inconveniences of the Declaration [of Rights] are that it may cramp government in it's [sic] useful exertions. But the evil of this is short-lived, moderate, and reparable. [The absence, however, of a Declaration is] permanent, afflicting, and irreparable. (Boyd, 1958)

The proponents' voices were so strong that the first Congress to meet following the adoption of the new Constitution submitted 12 amendments for consideration by the states. Ten of those were ratified by 1791, and they have become known as the Bill of Rights. For purposes of criminal law, the Fourth, Fifth, Sixth, and Eighth Amendments have particular relevance. The others are not unconnected to criminal law but typically have a more tangential link. For example, the First Amendment references to restrictions on religion, speech, press, assembly, and petition have been the source of controversy in trial proceedings (conflicts between a free press and a fair trial) and confinement of prisoners (may a Satanist practice his religion while in prison?).

In the interest of focus, we highlight only the Fourth Amendment. The Fifth (protecting, for example, against self-incrimination), the Sixth (providing for such things as the right to a speedy and public trial before an impartial jury and for the assistance of counsel), and the Eighth (prohibiting excessive bail, excessive fines, and cruel and unusual punishment) Amendments are relevant to procedural law but involve topics less appropriate for this book. However, before addressing the Fourth Amendment, there is another amendment to note. When drafted, the U.S. Constitution was not intended to protect individual citizens from the unfair enforcement of state laws. In the spirit of states' rights, and with greater fear of the federal government than of the state government, citizens expressed interest in controlling the closest thing they had to a monarch and Parliament. They did that by having the Bill of Rights limit only the federal government, as was made clear by Chief Justice Marshall in the *Barron* v. *Baltimore* (1833) decision (32 U.S. 243, at 250):

> Had the framers of these amendments intended them to be limitations on the pow-
> ers of the State governments, they would have imitated the framers of the original
> Constitution, and have expressed that intention…. These amendments demanded
> security against the apprehended encroachments of the General Government—not
> against those of the local governments.

That view held until after the Civil War, when protection of citizen rights gained new concern and attention. The Thirteenth Amendment abolished slavery, but in response to continued violation of rights, Congress adopted the Fourteenth Amendment in 1868. The portion of the amendment affecting criminal justice reads, "No State shall … deprive any person of life, liberty, or property, without due process of law…." Since the amendment's adoption, the meaning of the phrase *due process* has been a point of controversy. One resolution rests on the theory that the provisions of the Bill of Rights are incorporated into the due process clause of the Fourteenth Amendment and therefore are applicable to the states as well as the federal government. This legal theory has served as the basis for many U.S. Supreme Court decisions. The Court selectively has made certain Bill of Rights stipulations binding on state governments. In this manner, the U.S. Supreme Court can tell any state how to proceed (due process) when that state seeks to deprive a citizen of life, liberty, or property. Because of the Fourteenth Amendment, the procedural conditions of the Fourth Amendment (and others) must be followed by state governments in criminal proceedings.

The Fourth Amendment states, "The right of the people to be secure in their persons, houses, papers, and effects, against unreasonable searches and seizures, shall not be violated, and no warrants shall issue, but upon probable cause, supported by oath or affirmation, and particularly describing the place to be searched and the persons or things to be seized."

Importantly, this amendment does not prohibit all searches. Only those that are unreasonable are not allowed. The problem becomes one of defining "unreasonable" and, by implication, "reasonable." Since the 1960s, the U.S. Supreme Court has dealt with the question in the context of "searches and seizures" by the police. One type of police procedure governed by the Fourth Amendment would be the stopping and frisking of a citizen. In *Terry* v. *Ohio* (392 U.S. 1, 1968), for example, the U.S. Supreme Court held that police could stop and search three men whom the officer had observed prowling in front of some store windows. The search produced guns on two of the men, and the justices said the search was a reasonable precaution for the officer's safety. Further, after lawfully arresting a person, the police may conduct a "search incident to the arrest" to include the surrounding space in which a suspect could reasonably be expected to obtain a weapon or destroy evidence (see *Chimel* v. *California*, 395 U.S. 752, 1969).

Independent of—yet associated with—the Fourth Amendment is the judicially developed regulation known as the exclusionary rule. In the 1961 case of *Mapp* v. *Ohio* (367 U.S. 643), the U.S. Supreme Court held that state courts must, just as the federal courts had been doing since 1914, exclude from trial any evidence obtained in violation of the privileges guaranteed by the U.S. Constitution. These violations have come to include such things as the absence of a warrant, lack of probable cause to arrest, or use of a defective warrant. In addition, under the "fruits of the poisonous tree" doctrine, evidence generated by or directly obtained from an illegal search also must be excluded.

The primary purpose of the exclusionary rule was to deter police misconduct or, when misconduct has occurred, to return the "case" against a suspect to its position prior to the violation.

It is not comforting to hear about the release of an "obviously guilty" person because the evidence gathered against him could not be used at trial. This is particularly troublesome when the violation is something trivial, such as an incorrect warrant form. One result of efforts to modify the exclusionary rule has been a good-faith exception, which the U.S. Supreme Court put forth in *United States* v. *Leon* (468 U.S. 897, 1984). The Court ruled that evidence obtained through an illegal warrant need not be excluded at trial if the police could show that they got the evidence while reasonably believing they were acting according to the law. The extension of the good-faith exception to include warrantless cases has not been decided by the Court, but in 1988 the House of Representatives added such an exception to the Omnibus Drug Initiative, and at the state level the Wisconsin Supreme Court has applied the good-faith exception for warrantless searches (Ziemer, 2010). Both of these reflect a public desire to continue movement away from a strict application of the exclusionary rule.

Decisions such as those in *Mapp* and *Leon* seem to support a due process model to the extent that they restrict police behavior in favor of protecting citizen rights. The trend toward a more conservative public and U.S. Supreme Court in the 1980s and 1990s brought increased complaints that rights of "criminals" were more protected than were rights of "law-abiding citizens." That opinion reflects a position of the crime control model.

CRIME CONTROL MODEL   Under the authority of the Fourteenth Amendment, the U.S. Supreme Court has tried to stipulate the requirements of due process when government action is taken against a citizen. The result is American procedural law. Analysis of the form that law takes is aided by Packer's (1968) earlier mentioned models. The procedural law can emphasize efficiency of action (crime control model) or legitimacy of action (due process model).

The value system underlying the crime control model assumes that repression of criminal behavior is the most important function performed by the criminal justice process. The primacy of this function is necessary to ensure human freedom and allow citizens to be secure in person and property. The criminal justice process guarantees this goal of social freedom by efficiently operating to screen suspects, determine guilt, and appropriately sanction convicted persons.

To operate successfully, the crime control model requires a high rate of apprehension and conviction following a process that emphasizes speed and finality. Packer compares the model to an assembly-line conveyor belt moving an endless stream of cases to workers standing at fixed stations as they perform their respective operations and thus move the case to a successful resolution. The speed of the conveyor belt is kept high as long as there are no ceremonious rituals cluttering the process and slowing advancement of the case. Speed is also achieved when the cases are handled in a uniform and routine manner. In this sense, the crime control model is appropriately identified as an administrative, almost managerial, model.

An emphasis on finality means reducing chances to challenge the process or the outcome. Borrowing Packer's metaphor, we can point to the problems created when assembly-line workers are constantly subjected to review and second-guessing by supervisors. These interruptions while doing your job are bad enough, but imagine the damage to "finality" when workers are constantly having returned to them products presumably finished several weeks or months earlier. The metaphor is, of course, transparent. An efficient criminal justice process means that as a case proceeds from victim/witness to police, then to prosecutor, each "worker" performs his or her job in a speedy manner without fear of later veto.

A successful conclusion under the crime control model is one that excludes, at an early stage, persons apprehended but not likely to be guilty while securing prompt and lasting conviction of the rest. Packer uses the concept of "presumption of guilt" to describe the orienting attitude toward those not excluded because of probable innocence. The presumption of guilt is important in the crime control model because it allows the system to deal efficiently with large numbers of cases. This model expresses confidence in the screening process used by police and prosecutors when they release the "probably innocent" suspects and sustain action against the "probably guilty" ones. That is, after determining sufficient evidence of guilt to permit further action, all subsequent activity directed toward suspects is based on the view that they are presumed guilty (Packer, 1968).

Packer warns of not thinking of presumption of guilt as the opposite of the presumption of innocence. These concepts are different rather than opposite ideas. Specifically, the presumption of innocence is a concept directing authorities about how they are to proceed—not what they are to believe. That direction includes a warning to ignore their belief (i.e., presumption of guilt) while processing (where they presume innocence) the suspect/defendant. Because the presumption of guilt is simply a prediction of outcome, authorities can believe suspects are "probably guilty" while treating them as if guilt remains an open question.

It is apparent in this review of the crime control model that the early administrative fact-finding stages are of utmost importance. Subsequent stages of adjudication should be as abbreviated as possible to ensure speed and finality.

DUE PROCESS MODEL   If the due process model were put in charge of the assembly-line conveyor belt formerly run by the crime control model, one of the first changes would be an increase in the number and frequency of quality control inspection points. The speed and finality used by the crime control model to achieve its goal are seen by the due process model as inviting abuse of government power. Built upon concepts such as the primacy of the individual and the limitation of official power, the due process model insists on a formal, adjudicative, adversarial fact-finding process. If this means that the process is slowed down and lacks finality, then so be it. As Packer (1968) explains, the criminal process must be subjected to controls preventing it from operating with maximum efficiency precisely because of its capacity to subject the individual to the coercive power of the state.

One way to implement its antiauthoritarian values is with the doctrine of legal guilt. *Legal guilt* can be distinguished from *factual guilt* in the following manner. Police Officer Williams observes Peter Jones run up to Virginia Spry and grab Virginia's purse and then run down the sidewalk. Officer Williams, the fastest runner in the department, catches Jones from behind, places him under arrest, and begins questioning him about the robbery. Jones immediately admits to the criminal act, and, with the corroborating observation by Officer Williams, we can safely say that Jones is in fact guilty of the crime. Under the crime control model, this "presumption of guilt" would result in a rapid and final determination of guilt. However, under the due process model, emphasis is on the manner in which a government official (initially, Officer Williams) used her authority to intrude in the life of Peter Jones. The officer's actions are appropriately reviewed to determine their legality. If it is determined, for example, that Jones's confession was extracted without his being informed of his right to remain silent, the confession cannot be used against him. A result of losing the confession as evidence may mean that the case against Jones is dropped or lost in court. According to the due process model, Jones was not "legally guilty" of the purse snatching because rules designed to protect him and to safeguard the integrity of the process were not in effect. Factual guilt may be apparent or even legitimately known, but legal guilt must be validly decided via the previously determined process.

YOU SHOULD KNOW!

Liberty or Safety?

How would you answer this question?

Some people say that there is a natural tension between protecting individual rights and public safety. In the United States today, does our legal system worry too much about protecting individual rights, too much about public safety, or is the balance about right?

This question was asked by Rasmussen Reports (www.rasmussenreports.com) in a 2013 U.S. national telephone survey of likely voters. The responses showed that 28 percent believe the U.S. legal system worries too much about protecting individual rights at the expense of public safety. Another 24 percent believe the system overemphasizes public safety, whereas about 29 percent think the balance is about right. The remainder are undecided (Rasmussen Reports, 2013).

Using Packer's terms, we might explain these results as indicating that the American public believes the U.S. legal system leans more toward the due process model (protects individual rights) than the crime control model (emphasizes public safety). Do you agree with the public sentiment? Do you think the U.S. legal system has moved further from or closer to the due process model in the twenty-first century?

IMPACT

DUE PROCESS, CRIME CONTROL, AND CORRUPTION

The ability of a country to achieve a reasonable balance of due process and crime control will depend in part on its freedom from corruption. Chapter 2 noted that corruption can encourage transnational crime, but corruption also has a domestic effect that influences how a country's legal system operates and the extent of crime found in that country. Essentially, where corruption is high we might expect neither due process nor security. Where corruption is low, there should be reasonable balance of both due process and crime control. Consider the examples provided by Mexico (see Map A.3) and Canada (see Map A.3).

Transparency International is a nongovernmental organization that seeks to counter corruption at international and national levels. Each year Transparency International releases a corruption perception index (CPI) that reflects the perception of businesspeople, political analysts, and the general public regarding corruption in countries around the world (Transparency International, 2015). The 2015 CPI found Somalia, North Korea, Afghanistan, Sudan, and South Sudan to be perceived as the most corrupt of 168 nations, whereas Denmark, Finland, Sweden, New Zealand, and the Netherlands were perceived as the least corrupt. Canada was perceived as the 9th least corrupt country and Mexico as the 95th—placing Mexico closer to the most corrupt countries than to the least corrupt.

Mexico has ranked in the middle to poor range on the CPI since the mid-1990s. Especially troublesome are Mexico's political parties and legislature, police, and judiciary, which more than 75 percent of Mexicans perceive as their most corrupt institutions (the military and the medical/health services system ranked the least corrupt) (Transparency International, 2013). With corrupt politicians, police, and judges, we cannot expect due process to be very highly valued in the Mexican legal system. But, if public safety is increased as a result of that lack of due process, Mexican citizens could at least have that as a benefit. Unfortunately, there is a comparatively high victimization rate in Mexico and Mexicans report a relatively high fear of crime (Corcoran, 2014; van Dijk, van Kesteren, & Smit, 2007). So, there seems to be neither due process nor public safety in Mexico—and corruption would be a good place to start when assigning blame.

Contrast the situation in Mexico with that in Canada where citizens report high satisfaction with how the police do their job, are likely to report serious crimes to the police, and are satisfied as victims with how the police deal with reported crimes (Cotter, 2015; Perreault, 2015). We would expect those indicators of acceptable due process (views of police) and level of crime (victimization and fear scores) to be matched with a low perception of corruption. And that is indeed what we find, since only 25 percent of Canadian citizens believe their police or judiciary are corrupt (Transparency International, 2013). This absence of perceived corruption in a country where citizens believe due process and crime control are reasonably well balanced highlights the importance of honest and ethical behavior in a country's legal system.

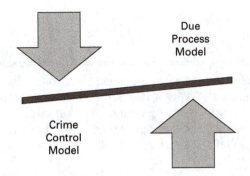

FIGURE 3.3 Balancing Due Process and Crime Control

Ideally, society would balance the dual goals of controlling crime and protecting its citizens' liberties. More realistically, the balance tends to tip in favor of one or the other values.

There is a tendency to suppose that the values of the due process model are opposite those underlying the crime control model. That position would be incorrect because it implies that the due process model is uninterested in repressing crime. Instead, the differences are best seen with reference to procedure rather than outcome. Cole (1986) distinguishes the values of each model in the following manner:

- The crime control model assumes that freedom is so important that every effort must be made to repress crime.
- The due process model assumes that freedom is so important that every effort must be made to ensure that criminal justice decisions are based on reliable information.

Each model seeks to guarantee social freedom. One does so by emphasizing efficient processing of wrongdoers, whereas the other emphasizes effective restrictions on government invasion in the citizen's life.

Who is the greater threat to our freedom? "The criminal trying to harm us or our property," says the crime control model. "The government agents like police officers and prosecutors," argues the due process model. Each position is correct, of course, since both criminals and government agents can invade our interests, take our property, and restrict our freedom of movement. Social freedom requires that the law-abiding citizen be free from unjustifiable intrusion by either criminals or government agents. Unfortunately, it does not appear possible to achieve both goals simultaneously (see Figure 3.3). One is emphasized at the expense of the other, but neither can be identified as qualitatively better. Although we may have an individual preference for one over the other, it would be incorrect to attribute intrinsic superiority to our choice.

LIBERTY, SAFETY, AND FIGHTING TERRORISM

> Those who would give up essential Liberty, to purchase a little temporary Safety, deserve neither Liberty nor Safety.
>
> **Benjamin Franklin**

The difficulty of balancing due process (liberty) and crime control (safety and security) reminds us that good values are—to some degree—always at odds. As Franklin's quote suggests, a loss of liberty does not necessarily bring an equivalent gain in safety. The United States—and the world—was reminded of this conundrum in the aftermath

WEB PROJECT

A Global Counter-Terrorism Strategy

In 2006, the United Nations General Assembly adopted the Global Counter-Terrorism Strategy that provides a global instrument to enhance national, regional, and international efforts to counter terrorism. After visiting https://www.un.org/counterterrorism/ctitf/un-global-counter-terrorism-strategy, list the four pillars of that strategy and then select one pillar to read more about. Write a few paragraphs that identify some of the measures established for that pillar and then give your supported opinion as to the likelihood that the measures can be successfully implemented.

of the 2001 terrorist attacks in the United States and the ensuing "war on terrorism." How does a justice system grounded in principles of due process protect its citizens from terrorism—planned or completed? Is terrorism so different that the traditional criminal justice process cannot be used? If terrorism does require a tilting toward the safety end of the security/liberty seesaw, which liberties should be compromised? It will be no surprise to you that people disagree on the answers to such questions.

Tilting toward Safety and Security

In the wake of the September 11, 2001, terrorist attacks in New York City and Washington, DC, legislators in the United States and other countries took action intended to reduce the likelihood that similar acts would occur again. Many examples of that action involved giving increased surveillance and investigation powers to police authorities. This was accomplished through changes to both substantive and procedural law.

CHANGES IN THE UNITED STATES The Uniting and Strengthening America by Providing Appropriate Tools Required to Intercept and Obstruct Terrorism Act (known, thankfully, by its acronym, the USA PATRIOT Act) was passed by Congress and signed into law by President George W. Bush in the wake of the 9/11 terrorist attacks.

Both the original and reauthorizing versions of the USA PATRIOT Act included provisions designed to more easily identify terrorist suspects, to gather more complete evidence against them, and to increase the likelihood of gaining a conviction against those guilty of planning, assisting, or carrying out terrorist acts. For example, sections of the Act allow for the bulk collection of U.S. phone records by the National Security Agency (Section 215) and for "roving" wiretaps for spy and antiterrorism investigations under the Foreign Intelligence Surveillance Act (Section 206). Such wiretaps are "roving" in the sense that the taps follow the suspect as he or she moves from home to cell phone to cybercafe to pay phone. The court order, in other words, specifies a person (but not necessarily by name) rather than a particular phone line, computer account, or facility to be tapped. Both bulk collection of records and roving wiretaps were criticized as privacy violations, and each was addressed in the USA Freedom Act discussed below.

Some people consider these changes to be sweeping transformations in the American judicial system, whereas others see them as simply giving law enforcement agents the tools needed to fight contemporary crime and criminals. Either way, such changes to substantive law are not without precedent. In fact, the United States and many other democracies have a history of using changes to substantive law when facing traumatic events. Kelman (2003) reminds us of the Alien and Sedition Acts passed in 1798—in the wake of the American Revolution—that undermined free speech and dissent (e.g., publishing false, scandalous, and malicious writing against the government was prohibited). During the Civil War, President Abraham Lincoln suspended the

The increased use of surveillance cameras in countries around the world is seen by some as increasing public safety but by others as an affront to personal liberty.

Dziurek/Shutterstock

writ of habeas corpus (the constitutional provision guaranteeing government will not hold citizens without bringing them to trial) and more than 15,000 people were arrested, many of whom languished in jail during the war. An especially notorious example occurred in 1942 when President Franklin Roosevelt authorized the army to round up more than 110,000 Japanese Americans—the vast majority of whom were U.S. citizens—and place them in concentration camps for the duration of World War II. The explanation given for the internment was disloyalty—something that was not even illegal.

It seems that during times of imminent threat (or at least the perception of an imminent threat) the federal government almost always chooses group security over individual freedoms. At least one lesson to be learned from this is summarized by Kelman in noting that rather than making the PATRIOT Act either right or wrong, these historical precedents simply suggest that the Bill of Rights may be less stable than we might like to imagine (Kelman, 2003).

CHANGES IN OTHER COUNTRIES   Unfortunately, terrorist attacks occur throughout the world and governments from Belgium and India to England and Turkey, like the United States, seek responses that balance security and liberty. Common techniques now found in antiterrorism legislation include extending the length of time that government authorities can detain suspects without charge and restricting access to legal counsel. France, for example, has increased its period of detention without charge for terror suspects from 4 to 6 days and denies uncharged suspects access to a lawyer during the first 3 days. In Spain, suspected terrorists can be held effectively incommunicado up to 13 days (Bennhold, 2006). Sweden's parliament approved laws allowing authorities to scan international calls, faxes, and e-mails—leading some critics to claim it gave Sweden the most far-reaching eavesdropping plan in Europe (BBC News, 2008).

In the face of increased numbers of persons traveling abroad to join terrorist organizations, Germany (see Map A.10) enacted legislation in 2015 making it a crime to travel outside the country with the intent to receive terrorist training and created a national identity card and passport restrictions meant to curtail such travel. The identity card provisions are designed to prevent the travel of foreign terrorist fighters and to make it easier for other countries to identify them. German citizens who constitute a threat to the internal or external security of Germany can have their national identity card and passport revoked and are issued instead a substitute card with the words "not valid for travel outside of Germany" (Law Library of Congress, 2015a).

Canada's Combating Terrorism Act of 2013 expanded investigation powers and increased penalties in terrorism cases. In addition, police can request that the court issue a peace bond for persons the police believe *may* be involved in terrorist activities. In addition to keeping the peace and being on good behavior, a person under a peace bond may have other conditions attached, such as being banned from Internet use or from foreign travel. In this manner, the police are able to monitor individuals suspected of, but not charged with, terrorist activities. Peace bonds are used in a variety of situations in Canada (e.g., domestic violence cases) but critics are concerned about their increased use since 2013 for terrorist suspects and with the severe restrictions that can be placed on a person who has not been charged with a crime. Proponents argue that peace bonds keep terrorist suspects out of the legal system while allowing the police to continue their investigation (Bell, 2016; Khandaker, 2016).

In its attempt to thwart the activities of foreign terrorist fighters, Italy has given the Ministry of the Interior the power to maintain a list of websites used for terrorist recruiting activities and allows authorities to instruct Internet service providers to immediately block access to such websites identified by the authorities. Further, the police are allowed to gather personal data that is directly related to preventing the perpetration of terrorist crimes (Law Library of Congress, 2015b).

Tilting toward Liberty

Much of the antiterrorism legislation in the United States and other countries continues to lean toward security, but there are some tempering examples. In 2015, the USA Freedom Act was passed by Congress and signed by President Obama. The Freedom Act reauthorized parts of the USA PATRIOT Act, but did not include some of its other features. For example, excluded in the Freedom Act is any authorization for the bulk collection of data of Americans' telephone records and Internet metadata. Also, the Freedom Act limits the government from collecting all data pertaining to a particular service provider or to a broad geographical region, such as a city or area code.

Instead of bulk data collection, the Freedom Act allows the government to collect from phone companies the records of persons for whom the government has reasonable suspicion is linked to a terrorist organization, and the records of people who are not suspected terrorists themselves but who have called, or have been called by, suspected terrorists (i.e., "two hops" of call records). However, the authority for roving wiretaps was extended to December 2019 ("USA Freedom Act: What's in, what's out," 2015).

In 2016, the German Federal Constitutional Court ruled as unconstitutional some provisions that dealt with investigative powers to fight international terrorism. Specifically, the legal requirements for carrying out covert surveillance were deemed too broad and unspecific. Protecting Germany and its citizens from international terrorism is not objectionable, the Court said, but the powers delegated to the federal police must be balanced against the fundamental right of individual privacy (Law Library of Congress, 2016).

Whereas legislative and court action in the United States and Germany is more typical of how nations are mitigating some of their antiterrorism actions, Norway (see Map A.10) has taken more unique action. In July 2011, right-wing Christian extremist Anders Behring Breivik killed 77 people in a combined bomb attack (8 dead) and shooting spree (69 dead) in Norway. The assault was, per capita, as significant for Norway as 9/11 was for the United States. What many commentators found interesting about Norway's reaction to this act of terrorism was how different it was from the way other countries have responded to terrorist acts. Media articles with such titles as "Norway Showed Us the Way to Respond to Terrorism" highlighted what many saw as a rather uncharacteristically civilized response from a civilized country (MacWhirter, 2011). The difference in Norway's response (by both politicians and the public) was in the country's hesitancy to turn to increased security measures—or, in this chapter's terminology, to move further toward the crime control end of the teeter-totter. That is, Norway chose to confront terror by reaffirming the values that terrorists want to destroy rather than by violating a democracy's most basic human rights (Egeland, 2011).

For example, after the attacks, surviving victims and the general public were remarkably unanimous in declaring that the best response was to rally around democratic values and the rule of law. There was certainly talk of beefing up security (arming the police, for example), but it was very clear that Norway's reaction would be defined by a belief that pursuing security above all other values, in a quest for absolute safety, is both self-destructive and futile (Egeland, 2011; Greenwald, 2011).

These examples of legislation and court decisions that lean toward either (both, actually) due process or crime control remind us that a country's substantive and procedural laws are the primary means by which law is defined and implemented. The remaining chapters of this book provide specifics regarding the laws, agencies, people, and procedures used in countries not just to combat terrorism, but also for providing criminal justice in general.

Summary

An understanding of basic criminal law concepts is important for appreciating any country's legal system. This chapter highlights terms and concepts that are familiar to most readers but places them in a context that allows us to begin the journey to other countries with familiar baggage. The two essential ingredients to any justice system are substantive law and procedural law. The former concerns the definition of rules, whereas the latter specifies their enforcement. Substantive criminal law is made up of general characteristics that allow identification of some acts as criminal and of major principles that determine whether a particular behavior is criminal. Procedural criminal law is implemented through either a crime control model or a due process model. Although each of these models seeks to ensure the social freedom of citizens, they emphasize different—and often conflicting—ways to achieve that goal.

This chapter emphasized American perspectives, mechanisms, and terminology to provide a common base on which future chapters can build. However, do not confuse the need for a common base with a suggestion that the American way of doing justice is necessarily the best in all instances. As noted in Chapter 1, one of the benefits of taking an international perspective is to identify ways that other countries might handle certain functions more efficiently, effectively, and fairly than do Americans. In the analysis of criminal justice in other countries, it is important to set aside understandable biases that America's way of doing things is the only reasonable or correct way. Such ethnocentrism hinders the ability to understand and appreciate alternative systems.

Discussion Questions

- If you live in a state that allows a finding of "guilty but insane" or "guilty but mentally ill," make an argument for why such a finding should not be allowed. If you live in a state that does not allow such a finding, make an argument for why it should.
- Distinguish between the crime control model and the due process model. If each model represents the ends of a seesaw, toward which end does the United States tilt? Is it possible for any justice system to balance the seesaw?

- Benjamin Franklin's quote, "Those who would give up essential Liberty, to purchase a little temporary Safety, deserve neither Liberty nor Safety," introduced the section titled "Liberty, Safety, and Fighting Terrorism." Do you agree or disagree with the quote? Why?
- Are there any situations in which it might be permissible or even necessary to hold a U.S. citizen in custody without recourse to the judicial system? If so, what are some examples of those situations?

References

American Law Institute. (1985). *Model penal code: Official draft and explanatory notes*. Philadelphia, PA: American Law Institute.

BBC News. (2008, June 19). Sweden approves wiretapping law. Retrieved from http://news.bbc.co.uk

Bell, S. (2016, April 21). Toronto-area men may commit terrorism unless peace bond imposed: RCMP. *The National Post*. Retrieved from http://news.nationalpost.com

Bennhold, K. (2006, April 14). In Europe's terror fight, the rights issue. *The New York Times*. Retrieved from http://www.nytimes.com

Boyd, J. P. (1955). *The papers of Thomas Jefferson* (Vol. 12). Princeton, NJ: Princeton University Press.

Boyd, J. P. (1958). *The papers of Thomas Jefferson* (Vol. 14). Princeton, NJ: Princeton University Press.

Callahan, L. A., Steadman, H. J., McGreevy, M. A., & Robbins, P. C. (1991). The volume and characteristics of insanity defense pleas: An eight-state study. *Journal of the American Academy of Psychiatry and the Law Online*, *19*(4), 331–338.

Cole, G. F. (1986). *The American system of criminal justice*. Monterey, CA: Brooks/Cole.

Corcoran, P. (2014, October 30). Mexico crime survey reveals conflicting trends. InSight Crime. Retrieved from http://www.insightcrime.org/news-analysis/mexico-crime-survey-reveals-conflicting-trends

Cotter, A. (2015, December 7). Public confidence in Canadian institutions. Spotlight on Canadians: Results from the General Social Survey. Retrieved from http://www.statcan.gc.ca/pub/89-652-x/89-652-x2015007-eng.htm

Egeland, J. (2011, September 11). Confronting terrorism. *The New York Times*. Retrieved from http://www.nytimes.com

FindLaw. (2016). The insanity defense among the states. Learn about the law. Retrieved from http://criminal.findlaw.com/crimes/more-criminal-topics/insanity-defense/the-insanity-defense-among-the-states.html

Geis, G., & Meier, R. F. (1985). Abolition of the insanity pleas in Idaho: A case study. *The Annals of the American Academy of Political and Social Science*, *477*, 72–83.

Greenwald, G. (2011, July 28). An un-American response to the Oslo attack. Salon. Retrieved from http://www.salon.com/2011/07/28/norway_4/

Hall, J. (1952). *Theft, law and society*. Indianapolis, IN: Bobbs-Merrill.

Hall, J. (1960). *General principles of criminal law*. Indianapolis, IN: Bobbs-Merrill.

Hall, J., & Mueller, G. (1965). *Cases and readings on criminal law and procedure*. Indianapolis, IN: Bobbs-Merrill.

Kelman, A. (2003, July 6). Civil liberties in the past. *The Denver Post*, p. E1. Retrieved from www.denverpost.com

Khandaker, T. (2016, April 2). When Canadian police can't charge people for terrorism, they use peace bonds. Vice News. Retrieved from http://news.vice.com

Law Library of Congress. (2015a, July 10). Germany: New anti-terrorism legislation entered into force. *Global Legal Monitor*. Retrieved from http://www.loc.gov/law/foreign-news/

Law Library of Congress. (2015b, March 24). Italy: Updated legislation on fight against terrorism. *Global Legal Monitor*. Retrieved from http://www.loc.gov/law/foreign-news/

Law Library of Congress. (2016, May 3). Germany: Federal constitutional court declares terrorism legislation partially unconstitutional. *Global Legal Monitor*. Retrieved from http://www.loc.gov/law/foreign-news/

MacWhirter, I. (2011, July 31). Norway showed us the way to respond to terrorism. *The Herald Scotland*. Retrieved from http://www.heraldscotland.com

Packer, H. L. (1968). *The limits of the criminal sanction*. Stanford, CA: Stanford University Press.

Perreault, S. (2015). Criminal victimization in Canada, 2014. Statistics Canada. Retrieved from http://www.statcan.gc.ca/pub/85-002-x/2015001/article/14241-eng.htm#a10

Rasmussen Reports. (2013, April 28). 24% feel legal system puts public safety ahead of individual rights. Retrieved from www.rasmussenreports.com

State of Colorado. (2015). Colorado Revised Statutes, § 18-4-401, Theft Stat.

State of Georgia. (2010). Official Code of Georgia Annotated, § 16-8-40, Robbery Stat.

Sutherland, E., & Cressey, D. (1978). *Criminology*. Philadelphia, PA: J. B. Lippincott.

Transparency International. (2013). Global Corruption Barometer 2013. Retrieved from http://www.transparency.org/gcb2013

Transparency International. (2015). Corruption perceptions index. Retrieved from http://www.transparency.org/cpi2015

USA Freedom Act: What's in, what's out. (2015, June 2). *The Washington Post*. Retrieved from https://www.washingtonpost.com/graphics/politics/usa-freedom-act/

van Dijk, J., van Kesteren, J., & Smit, P. (2007). Criminal victimisation in international perspective: Key findings from the 2004–2005 ICVS and EU ICS. Retrieved from http://english.wodc.nl/onderzoeksdatabase/icvs-2005-survey.aspx?cp=45&cs=6796

Ziemer, D. (2010, August 23). Good faith exception applies to warrantless searches. *Wisconsin Law Journal*. Retrieved from http://wislawjournal.com/2010/08/23/good-faith-exception-applies-to-warrantless-searches/

Legal Traditions

LEARNING OBJECTIVES

After studying this chapter, you will be able to:

1. Distinguish between legal traditions and legal systems.
2. List the four contemporary legal traditions and summarize the developmental subtraditions of each.
3. Compare the four legal traditions in terms of cultural components.
4. Compare the four legal traditions in terms of substantive components.
5. Compare the four legal traditions in terms of procedural components.

COUNTRIES IN FOCUS

China

England

France

Iran

Japan

North Korea

Saudi Arabia

South Korea

United States

Amina Lawal, a 30-year-old Muslim woman in northern Nigeria, was sentenced to be buried to her neck in sand and stoned to death. She had given birth to a child out of wedlock (having been divorced a few years earlier), and that pregnancy was sufficient evidence to convict her of adultery. The man named as the baby girl's father denied having sex with Lawal, and charges against him were dropped. The sentence was suspended to allow Lawal to nurse her baby until she was weaned. The case received global attention, and many human rights groups took up the cause and provided the assistance of attorneys (she was without a lawyer at her trial) for the appeal of her conviction. Lawal's appeal was before an Islamic appeals court where the prosecutor argued that her pregnancy and divorced status were sufficient evidence of a crime and that no excuse could be acceptable ("Nigerian woman facing death seeks leniency," 2003). One of Lawal's lawyers urged the judges to free her, arguing that an earlier confession was invalid and that some interpretations of Islamic law contend that babies can remain in gestation in their mother's womb for up to 5 years, making it possible under Islam that her former husband could have fathered the child. The appeals court (in a 4 to 1 decision) overturned Lawal's conviction on the basis of trial irregularities (e.g., she had not been allowed to retract her earlier confession and only a single judge presided over the first trial instead of the requisite three). Interestingly, the appeals court also gave some credence to the "sleeping embryo" theory presented by the defense (Sengupta, 2003).

Lawal's case provides an interesting backdrop to this chapter for several reasons, not so much because a death sentence was imposed (death sentences are possible under any of the legal traditions) or even because of the seemingly cruel form the penalty would take (there are arguments that shooting, electrocution, and lethal injection are also cruel). Instead, the Lawal case begins this chapter because it occurs in Nigeria (a secular nation with a judicial system inherited from its period as a British colony), in one of the country's 12 northern states that have adopted versions of Islamic law. As explained in the following paragraphs, it is not possible to draw clear distinctions among the different legal traditions around the world, nor can a country's legal procedures always be clearly categorized as being of a specific type. Nigeria's common law heritage (resulting from being a British colony) is contrasted with its Islamic law heritage (introduced by Arab traders and conquerors), and the country today is trying to accommodate both. Seeing why that is a difficult task requires an understanding of the differences inherent in common, Islamic, and other legal traditions.

LEGAL SYSTEMS AND LEGAL TRADITIONS

The legal systems in today's world can be divided among four families, or traditions. Each legal tradition has unique elements that influenced its development and form. This chapter identifies some of those foundations for each tradition, and then compares them in terms of cultural, substantive, and procedural components.

Because it is obviously impossible to discuss the legal system of every country of the world separately, systems must be grouped according to similarities. The existence of sovereignty and nationalism means that the legal system (i.e., legal institutions, procedures, and rules) in one country is not exactly duplicated in any other, yet certain countries do share "legal traditions" with one another (Merryman, 1985, pp. 1–3). These traditions are the basis for their groupings.

A legal tradition puts the legal system into a cultural perspective. It refers to deeply rooted and historically conditioned attitudes about things such as the nature of law, the role of law in society, how a legal system should be organized and operated, and the way law is or should be made, applied, or perfected (Merryman, 1985). From this perspective, it is possible to analyze the legal systems of a considerable number of countries at one time. In doing so, however, we must not forget the variability of systems within the traditions. England, New Zealand, and New Jersey share a common legal tradition but do not have identical legal systems. Similarly, France, Germany, and Italy have their own legal systems but can be grouped in the same legal tradition along with the separate legal systems of Argentina and Brazil.

Today legal scholars identify three or four legal traditions (some call them legal families). This number has not been consistent throughout history, and some formerly prominent legal traditions no longer even exist. We concentrate on four contemporary traditions but must first mention some historically significant ones.

In 1928, law professor John Henry Wigmore (1928) published a three-volume work on the evolution of the various legal systems. A 1936 version (Wigmore, 1936) not only revised and expanded the information but also incorporated the three previous volumes into one library edition. This prototype of comparative legal studies still sets the standard for comprehensive coverage. Wigmore believed there had been 16 legal systems in the world: Egyptian, Mesopotamian, Chinese, Hindu, Hebrew, Greek, Roman, Maritime, Japanese, Mohammedan, Celtic, Germanic, Slavic, Ecclesiastical, Romanesque, and Anglican. By 1936, Wigmore saw six systems as having completely disappeared as legal structures (Egyptian, Mesopotamian, Hebrew, Greek, Celtic, and Ecclesiastical). Five survived as hybrids (Roman, Germanic, Slavic, Maritime, and Japanese). The Chinese,

Hindu, and Mohammedan systems remained essentially unmixed, and the two newest (Romanesque and Anglican) were hybrids.

A momentary retreat to before the time of Christ will instill an appreciation for the maturity of the idea that law is an instrument for social organization. If, in the process of gaining that appreciation, we gain a sense of humility as well, that is all to the good. After all, in some ways, contemporary legal systems have existed for less time than others have been extinct.

The Egyptian legal system extends back as far as 4000 BCE, but it was especially well organized by the Fourth Dynasty (2900–2750 BCE). By that time, the Egyptian king, or pharaoh, ruled as a theocrat with divine authority coming from the sun god Osiris through his son Horus. In this manner, the source of law and justice was presumed to be divine but was received by way of the pharaoh, who appointed chief judges.

As sole legislator, the pharaoh provided codes that set down the proper behavior of his people. The particular procedures for implementing the codes were more likely handled by the chief judges. Disputing parties brought their case before a judge, who listened to their oral arguments. The trial judge was expected to stay quiet while listening to the petitioner, to not treat him impatiently, and to wait until he has emptied his heart and told his grief.

In its more than 4,000-year existence, the Egyptian legal system obviously passed through many stages and in the process formulated some principles from which Western society could have profited by observing. The discovery of a 250 BCE bail bond for a jail prisoner's release and a recognition of women's independence and equality with men in some legal relations remind us that we more "modern" citizens may be in many respects mere revisors instead of innovators.

In the region between the Euphrates and Tigris rivers (basically Iraq today), the Mesopotamian civilization emerged and fought off successive waves of conquest until the arrival of Persians and Greeks in the centuries before Christ. The legal system developed by these traders emphasized commercial law and has provided reasonable counterparts of today's deeds, partnerships, and other contract forms.

The most notable achievement of the Mesopotamian legal system was the Babylonian law called the Code of Hammurabi. King Hammurabi's (circa 1792–1750 BCE) Code is one of the first-known bodies of law. The laws, engraved on stone tablets, emphasized property rights and spoke to such issues as theft, ownership, and interpersonal violence.

The Hebrew legal system started with Moses receiving the two tablets of stone and the recording of the first five books of the Bible (known as the Torah, or Ancient Law). That first period (about 1200–400 BCE) was followed by the Classic period (300 BCE– 100 CE) in which rabbis developed the law. The Talmudic period (200–500) saw the consolidation of records and was followed by the Medieval period (700–1500) of private codes and commentaries. Finally, in the Modern period (1600–1900), the Hebrew language and legal system were relegated to secondary standing as Jews became more linked to national (territorial) norms. Actually, Wigmore (1936) suggests that the Hebrew system ended as a strictly legal system with the end of the Classical period. After 100 CE, Hebrew law was replaced in Palestine by Roman rule, and since then, Jewish law has operated mainly as local custom and as ceremonial and moral rules.

WEB PROJECT

Aztec Law

Historical accounts of early legal systems often highlight ones in Europe or Asia. Of course, other parts of the world also had important legal traditions that, even if replaced by colonizers or conquerors, probably influenced contemporary legal systems. Visit the site on law in Mexico before the conquest (http://tarlton.law.utexas.edu/exhibits/aztec/), and then write a few paragraphs describing the Aztec courts and the role of attorneys and judges.

With the background provided by Egyptians, Mesopotamians, and Hebrews, we can move to the contemporary arena and begin the journey of understanding one way that today's legal systems can be grouped and categorized. When doing so, it is important to remember that the four categories used here are used for explanatory rather than definitive purposes.

TODAY'S FOUR LEGAL TRADITIONS

As the preceding review suggests, the decision to place the various legal systems into categories is easier than deciding how many categories to use, what to name them, and on what to base them. Bracey (2006) makes a compelling argument for concentrating on three legal traditions based on what its followers believe to be the source of law. The result, for her, are Western law (laws are from humans who are state officials), religious law (law has divine origin), and traditional or customary law (law is as old as the group itself and is proper for the group). Vogler (2005) also sees legal traditions as nicely grouped in three, but for him they are paradigms that may be identified as the inquisitorial, adversarial, and popular justice traditions. In contrast to a tripartite view of the world's legal traditions, Glenn (2014) uses seven categories (chthonic—a bit like Bracey's traditional or customary law and Vogler's popular justice, Talmudic, civil, Islamic, common, Hindu, and Confucian), although he suggests that others also exist.

A key point upon which Bracey, Glenn, and Vogler agree is that any categorization of legal traditions is more provisional than conclusive. Glenn (2010, p. 362) notes that any attempt to isolate one legal tradition from others may be immediately challenged by information that is inconsistent with the separation chosen. Vogler (2005, p. 16) warns that he certainly is not suggesting that any criminal justice system can be characterized as falling wholly or even predominantly within any of his three traditions. And Bracey (2006, p. 30) reminds us that any attempt at grouping legal systems into broader categories of legal traditions results in something reflecting the designer's goals more than any agreed-upon reality. So, why do it? Because, as all three agree, doing so provides some clarity to a very complex situation. Or, as explained in Chapter 1's coverage of the need for classification, it provides a way to order and summarize diversity.

The classification strategy deemed most useful for this text is one using four legal traditions identified as common, civil, religious/philosophical, and hybrid. The religious/philosophical tradition has included such important legal systems as Hindu and Judaic, but the most important contemporary example is the Islamic legal tradition. The hybrid category includes those legal systems drawing from several legal traditions—especially a combination of common and civil but also customary—and legal systems in Asia provide especially good contemporary examples of such combinations. So, for purposes of simplicity and clarity of discussion, the Islamic legal tradition serves as our third category and an Eastern Asia legal tradition as our fourth. It is important to remember, however, that the Islamic and Eastern Asia legal traditions are merely representative of their respective broader categories. Of the four traditions, the American reader is most familiar with the common legal tradition, because the United States falls into that general category. The civil tradition is today's primary competitor with the common legal tradition and can be found in some format throughout the world.

Before embarking on a review of each tradition, it is necessary to note that no legal system is a pure example of a particular legal tradition. As indicated in Figure 4.1, some countries are more accurately described as combining aspects of several traditions. This is especially true in countries colonized by nations that imposed their particular brand of law on an existing indigenous legal system. Further complicating matters are those countries subjected to multiple colonization periods by nations with different legal systems. As a result, the legal systems in countries like some in Africa use combinations of

YOU SHOULD KNOW!

Indigenous Law: The Native American Example

Indigenous law refers to the traditional obligations and prohibitions that a group of people requires its members to follow. Similar terms for these kinds of norms and sanctions include customary law, unwritten law, popular justice, and folk law. Because indigenous law is a culture's original law, it has influenced the development of the four contemporary legal traditions. That point is apparent in this chapter's review of the subtraditions shaping each of the four legal traditions.

Although this book restricts coverage of indigenous law to its role in developing the civil, common, Islamic, and Eastern Asia traditions, the topic has broader importance. Not only are some countries best identified even today as following indigenous law (e.g., the Federated States of Micronesia, the Marshall Islands, and Palau), but also some populations within nations are best understood with reference to their customary procedures. Native American and Alaska Native tribes provide an excellent example because they continue to maintain social order and administer justice in their homelands through the use of ancient laws, traditions, and customs.

The U.S. government recognizes the inherent sovereignty of Indian nations to make and enforce their own laws (see *Williams v. Lee*, 358 U.S. 217, 1958). Because most tribes traditionally responded to criminal activity by consensus rather than through an adversarial system, formal courts are a fairly recent development among Indian tribes. With the 1934 passage of the Indian Reorganization Act, the federal government encouraged tribes to enact their own laws and to establish their own justice system. Today, about 300 Indian nations and Alaska Native villages are thought to have formal tribal court systems (Perry, 2013).

Tribal justice systems are diverse in concept and character. Some are very elaborate with written laws and rules of court procedure, whereas others are adapting modern aspects to their individual nations, but an increasing number of tribes are returning to traditional dispute resolution (Tribal Court Clearinghouse, 2016).

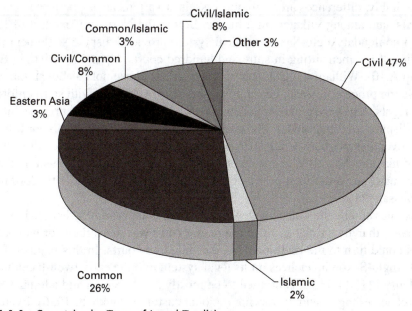

FIGURE 4.1   Countries by Type of Legal Tradition

Type of legal tradition was determined from review of information in *The World Factbook* (https://www.cia.gov/library/publications/the-world-factbook/index.html) and at *Juriglobe* (http://www.juriglobe.ca/eng/index.php).

common and Islamic law, and some in South America were shaped by both civil and common influences. It is appropriate to keep these combined systems in mind as we discuss the four legal traditions—not because they challenge the use of four categories but because they remind us that the categories are artificial groupings that try to bring order to a confusing array of legal systems.

Common Legal Tradition

Although not the oldest, the common legal tradition provides a familiar base for discussing the history and essential features of a legal tradition. After covering that more native material, we can move to less familiar traditions.

The Romans occupied Britain from about 50 CE to the start of the fifth century. At that point, only the groundwork for the Roman law (civil legal tradition) had been laid. By the time the *Corpus Juris Civilis* was published (533 CE), the Romans in Britain had been pushed out by Germanic tribes such as the Saxons and the Angles. St. Augustine's efforts at converting Britain to Christianity (597 CE) provided some Roman influence in terms of church law, but this early period served mainly to provide a base for a separate legal tradition called common law.

The common legal tradition developed from several subtraditions. Those include feudal practices, custom, and equity (see Figure 4.2). An overview of each provides information helpful in understanding the basics of common law.

FEUDAL PRACTICES   The primary political and military system of the Middle Ages (about 500 to 1450) was feudalism. Under this system, a lord provided vassals with land in exchange for military and other services. By the 1200s, when feudalism was in decline, several layers of feudal relations existed. For example, the vassals of an important baron (the vassals lord) were in turn the lord of their own vassals. Obviously, not everyone could be a landholder. Someone had to do the work necessary for keeping the lord (at whatever level) viable. A variety of peasant villagers provided this service in their role as agricultural workers in the lord's estate or manor.

Inevitably, differences arose among vassals at various levels, between vassals and their lords, and among villagers in a manor. Before the Norman Conquest of England (1066), a nonfeudal Anglo-Saxon political system provided dispute settlement through assemblies of freemen sitting in shire and hundred courts. Upon his arrival in England (see Map A.10), William the Conqueror (1066–1087) chose not to abolish the existing Anglo-Saxon process. Instead, he set up an orderly government with stern enforcement of royal rights. A new system of royal courts was developed with the primary interest of settling disputes of landholders. For example, a baron (beholden to his lord the King) presided over disputes between the baron's vassals. In doing so, the baron drew upon the advice of his other vassals (the disputants' peers) in arriving at a judgment. Failure by a vassal to answer an order to appear (summons) in court could result in the lord reclaiming the vassal's land.

Disputes among the villagers were deemed more appropriately handled by the lord of the manor than by a royal court. If the manor court was unavailable or inappropriate, villagers could turn to the traditional shire or hundred courts. In this manner, England retained Anglo-Saxon influences on its legal system into the early twelfth century. Law under Henry I (1100–1135) continued to be mostly Anglo-Saxon and administered at a local level according to widely varying regional custom (Plucknett, 1956). Even so, the administrative machinery, such as royal courts, put into place by William I and Henry I, provided the base for a common law dominating the realm. The realization of a common law occurred with Henry II (1154–1189). We now turn to custom as the next subtradition of common law.

CUSTOM   Henry II saw the reign of his predecessor, Stephen (1135–1154), as a period without law and troubled by civil war. Henry's grandfather, Henry I, on the other hand, ruled over a more orderly kingdom. In addition, in the 100 years since the Norman Conquest, both royal courts and the separate system of church courts had grown and become involved in many jurisdictional disputes. Henry II sought to return order to the kingdom and to solve disputes between state and church courts. One of his efforts resulted in the Constitutions of Clarendon (1164), which listed customs said to be the practice during the reign of Henry I. The 16 articles forming the Constitutions provided custom as a basis for building order and served to declare the proper relation between church and state. The significance of custom must be elaborated.

The principal element in most premodern legal systems was custom. Not surprisingly, custom was an essential aspect of court decisions under Anglo-Saxon law and the English feudal process. Importantly, however, custom was not always consistent by geography or by social standing. Local village customs settled disputes among peasants and other villagers. Occasionally, those customs contradicted those of vassals, lords, and other freemen. Plucknett (1956) notes that village customs in England frequently kept a woman's property free from her husband's control and allowed her to enter into contracts on her own. Bourgeois custom did not allow such behavior by women. This point becomes important because the common legal tradition was built upon only one of these custom types. Specifically, common law was the custom of landholders as accepted and interpreted by the royal courts. It is appropriate to keep this point in mind as we discuss custom's role in the origin of common law.

According to Blackstone's Commentaries (Tucker, 1803) on the Laws of England, legal custom is ancient (no one can remember its beginning), continuous (it has never been abandoned or interrupted), peaceable (it has the common consent of those using it), reasonable (in terms of "legal" reason), certain (ascertainable), compulsory (it is not obeyed at option), and consistent (one custom cannot contradict another). As complete as that definition might sound, we must still consider the question of how custom is determined. One way to decide whether a custom met the criteria for being a good legal custom was the jury system. Presumably, if a freeman's peers settle a dispute by using principles that reflect common and immemorial custom, the decision exemplifies common law. Or, as Blackstone suggested, the only way to prove that a principle is a rule of common law is to show that it has always been the custom to observe it (Tucker, 1803).

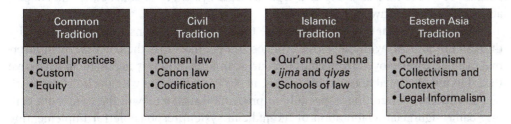

FIGURE 4.2 Developmental Subtraditions in Four Legal Traditions

WEB PROJECT
What is That Country's Legal System?

Categorizing a country's legal system is not easily accomplished because so many countries have had a variety of cultural influences over many decades and even centuries. This book relies primarily on the classification provided by the *World Factbook* and, to a lesser extent, *Juriglobe* (see www.juriglobe.ca/eng/index.php). Go to the *World Factbook* listing of countries at https://www. cia.gov/library/publications/resources/the-world-factbook/, and select at least five countries to view. For each country, click on "Government" and then scroll down to "Legal System." List each country you viewed, identify its legal system, and then write a few comments as to whether the identified legal system was what you expected it to be, or was an unexpected find.

The origin of common law in custom makes precedent a basic concept in the common legal tradition. When stated as a policy, precedent is called *stare decisis*, which means courts are expected to abide by decided cases. However, we must be careful here not to imply that courts before the sixteenth century had anything even resembling the modern principle of precedent or policy of stare decisis. The distinction is best handled by referring to the work of medieval judge Henry de Bracton. Bracton saw the courts of his time (mid-thirteenth century) as foolish and ignorant corruptors of doctrine, deciding cases by whim instead of by rule (Plucknett, 1956). In an attempt to return to the rule of law, Bracton reviewed the original plea rolls (immense in number and without index) from the courts. He used those documents to research legal principles and then to identify cases as historical evidence for the accuracy of his statements.

Note that Bracton's process was different from studying cases and deducing rule of law from them. For Bracton, a case could illustrate a legal principle and provide proof that the principle was once applied, but the case was not in itself a source of law (Plucknett, 1956). In other words, Bracton was searching for evidence of custom, and that custom could be identified through reference to several cases. As a result, court decisions were governed by custom, not by the case or cases cited as proof of that custom.

The movement to citing prior cases as binding (i.e., the movement to precedent in its modern sense) instead of simply showing custom began in the sixteenth century. Still, it was in the seventeenth century that the practice became established. Specifically, decisions of the Exchequer Chamber (where the judges were the state chancellor and the treasurer) were held to be binding on other courts. Even so, the process was not really entrenched until the nineteenth century brought a strengthening of the House of Lords and the organizing of a single court of appeals. Therefore, custom is not only a basic component of common law but also what has allowed precedent and stare decisis to become essential features.

EQUITY   The early history of equity (from the Latin *aequus*, meaning "fair" or "just") links it to the subtraditions of feudal practices and custom, yet it differs from those because of its eventual standing as a separate legal system both conflicting and cooperating with common law.

In the early stages of development, the king was in constant contact (usually through his council) with the various judges and courts across the country. In an informal manner, cases moved from court to court with little difficulty and without excessive regard to jurisdictional boundaries. Judges, in close cooperation with the king's council, had considerable discretion, especially in procedural matters. With the fourteenth century came significant elaboration of the judicial system responsible for implementing the common law. As a result, the contact between monarch and judge became

WEB PROJECT
London's Old Bailey

The Central Criminal Court of London (more commonly, Old Bailey) may be the world's best known criminal court. In a collaborative effort, the University of Sheffield and the University of Hertfordshire and other organizations have created a fully searchable digitized collection of the entire proceedings at Old Bailey from 1674 to 1834. It may be tempting for those of you with British lineage to check for miscreant ancestors in the "search" section (www.oldbaileyonline.org/forms/formMain.jsp), but your assignment instead is to go to the "how to read an Old Bailey trial" section (www.oldbaileyonline.org/static/HowToReadTrial.jsp). Watch the video or read all sections on that page and then write one or two paragraphs that summarize items you found to be different from contemporary trial proceedings.

infrequent, and the court's discretion in handling matters was correspondingly reduced. By the mid-1350s, we find courts refusing to bend procedural rules, even in a sense of "fairness," and instead declaring that judges were bound to custom and to taking a strict definition of statute (Plucknett, 1956).

Not surprisingly, this inflexibility in the royal courts led to unhappy people who were unable to obtain justice. These people turned to the king and asked him to add fairness to the law. The king's agent in such matters was the chancellor, who had responsibility for guiding the king's conscience. Traditionally, the chancellor was also a church official, but with the growth of the office and expansion of responsibilities, laymen came to be appointed as chancellor in the fourteenth century. Simultaneously, then, judges were isolated from the king while another royal office, with direct access to the monarch, was strengthened. The outcome of these events was the institutionalization of equity as an important aspect of law in England.

The chancellors decided conflicts between law and morals based on morality rather than technical law. Therefore, in chancery court, decisions were based on the equity of the case without concern for the procedural necessities (David & Brierley, 1968). By the fifteenth century, the chancellor was essentially an autonomous judge deciding cases in the name of the king. This situation did not always sit well with common law judges. To appease them, the fifteenth- and sixteenth-century chancellors often called upon the judges to explain a point of law.

The cross-pollination of ideas between common law courts and chancery courts benefited both. Common judges learned that technicalities were not an excuse for reaching obviously wrong decisions, and the chancellors came to understand better the law and its application. In addition, chancery courts aided common law courts by providing relief to procedural and substantive defects in the common law system. Plucknett (1956) identifies such faults as slowness, expense, inefficiency, technicality, antiquated methods of proof, and suspicions of volunteer witnesses as particular areas where chancery courts helped common law courts.

Having one court system existing primarily to correct the defects of another court system is not desirable in perpetuity. Something had to give. Over the centuries, the rules of equity became as strict, consistent, and "legal" as those of the common law. The growth and formalization of equity finally provided an opportunity to unite the two legal

YOU SHOULD KNOW!
The Demise of the Socialist Legal Tradition

During the second half of the twentieth century, many scholars identified the socialist legal tradition as an important contemporary legal tradition. Others believed the historical link between civil law and law in socialist countries meant that socialist law was simply a modification of civil law and not deserving of separate status. Earlier versions of this textbook sided with those favoring separate status for a socialist legal tradition and based the argument on the presence of such features as law existing to serve the purposes of the socialist revolution and a hyperinflated public law sector.

Even after the fall of the Soviet Union, arguments were made that a socialist legal tradition continued in the world's remaining socialist countries—and, Partlett and Ip (2016) make a good argument that China (see Map A.7) remains an example of that legal tradition. In the twenty-first century, those arguments were increasingly difficult to justify as countries such as China and Vietnam moved toward versions of free-market economies, private property, and—especially in China—reform of criminal laws and the criminal justice system. The European countries that were previously identified as following a socialist legal tradition are today most accurately placed in the civil legal tradition. Asian countries associated with the socialist legal tradition continue to be led by a communist party, but their version of communism has always been a bit different from European communism. As a result, China and North Korea are now best identified as reflecting an Eastern Asia legal tradition (along with Japan and South Korea) rather than a socialist legal tradition.

systems, and in 1875 a judicature act removed the formal distinction between the two courts. Common law was now complete. From a historical base (feudal practices), the common legal tradition had basic principles (custom) and a sense of fairness (equity).

Civil Legal Tradition

Because the phrase *civil law* is familiar to American readers, it is necessary to distinguish the term's general use from its use in reference to a legal tradition. In its more typical usage in the United States, civil law is set against criminal law because it deals

---

IMPACT

AMERICA'S CIVIL LAW TRADITION

The United States is among the countries identified with the common legal tradition. Yet the lack of surprise with which you read that statement distorts the role played by the civil tradition in America's history. Consider, for example, the role played by Spanish and Mexican civil law in the development of the American West.

Even after receiving statehood (1850), California was feeling the impact of centuries under a civil legal tradition. For example, upon their arrival in California, Americans found Mexican lawmen called *jueces de campo*, or "judges of the plains." In 1851, the California legislature repealed all prior laws but one: the statute relating to judges of the plains (Ruiz, 1974). Mexican law required all cattle runs and drives passing through a city, town, or village to be inspected for brands and ownership by the judges of the plains. Those judges could arrest suspected cattle or horse thieves and take them to the nearest magistrate. In the absence of any English equivalent, the California legislature gave this Mexican law enforcer the same powers as a sheriff, constable, or police officer.

California's use of the judges of the plains exemplifies the necessity of making adjustments in applying English common law to a dramatically different culture. Settlers in the American frontier had to stretch their imagination when applying the ancient customs and traditions of eleventh-century England to the legal problems that arose with the cattle drives and gold rushes of the nineteenth-century West.

The civil law tradition also predisposed some areas to recognize the usefulness of law codes. Miners' codes served as bodies of law in western mining camps from Colorado to California. These rough but workable rules and processes provided a means to record claims, to decide whose claim was first, to settle disputes among claimants, and to enforce decisions of miners' "courts" (Friedman, 1973). Answers to such questions were not easily identified in English common law.

Despite flirtations with codification and the civil tradition, the legacy followed by American legal systems has been that of the common law. Admittedly, Louisiana did more than flirt with civil law. Louisiana codes of 1808, 1825, and 1870 borrowed heavily from the French Code Napoleon. As a result, Louisiana judges decide cases (private more than public law) chiefly on the basis of codes rather than prior decisions. The complicated history of the civil law in Louisiana reminds us that aspects of the civil tradition have helped shape a specifically American legal system.

Undoubtedly, one area in which law in America (and indeed in all common law countries) has become more civil-like is with the increased reliance on statute as an important source for law. Yet, even when the legislature plays a primary lawmaking role, we view the resulting statutes in a special way. As Sereni (1956) explained, statutory provisions are not authoritatively established unless and until they have been interpreted by the courts. For example, the U.S. Congress can pass a law prohibiting the burning of the American flag. In a country where codification prevails, the courts would be obliged to find all flag burners guilty and apply the appropriate punishment. Because of the common legal tradition in the United States, a law prohibiting flag burning is not "authoritatively established" until the courts accept it as such. As this flag burning example shows, then, despite the obvious increase in statutes as a source of law, countries following the common legal tradition are still distinguished from their civil tradition cousins in terms of the power courts have to evaluate the legislature's work.

with private wrongs instead of the social wrongs handled by criminal law. In that manner, civil law deals with such matters as contracts, ownership of property, and payment for personal injury. However, in its original meaning, civil law referred to the code of laws collected by the Roman emperor Justinian. The Corpus Juris Civilis (i.e., the law applicable to all Roman *cives* or citizens) set the stage for subsequent law not only with Justinian's successors but eventually with Napoleon and his *Code Civil* (Code Napoleon) as proclaimed in 1804. The use of civil codes as a legal tradition spread across Europe and to such places as Quebec, Canada, and South America. As a result, in much of the world, the term *civil law* brings to mind a legal tradition based on written codes, not a specific type of law dealing with private wrongs. Because the concern throughout this book is with criminal justice systems, there is no need to use civil law in reference to those laws regulating individual disputes. So when you read about civil law systems and civil legal traditions, place it in the context of a code of laws as first developed for the Roman Empire.

Just as the common legal tradition developed from several basic subtraditions, the civil tradition has its own underpinning (see Figure 4.2). Specifically, we consider the role played by Roman law, canon law, and codification.

ROMAN LAW   Civil law preceded common law chronologically because of its link to Roman law. In turn, Roman law was the result of statutes, edicts of magistrates, and the interpretations of jurists (Kolbert, 1979; Watson, 1970).

Three legislative bodies created Roman law statutes. The *comitia centuriata* and *comitia tributa* enacted statutes known as *lex* (a collection of laws). The *concilium plebis* enacted *plebiscitum*, a law passed by the common people. These laws were binding only on the average citizen unless the Senate made it binding on the nobility and senators. The earliest form of written Roman law dates to 451 and 450 BCE, when a council of 10 men inscribed 12 bronze tablets with specifics concerning the rights of Roman citizens. These Twelve Tables were approved as lex by the *comitia centuriata* in 450 BCE. They provided the basis for private rights of Roman citizens, consisted mainly of ancient custom, and concerned procedure more than substantive law. For example, the opening passage of the Twelve Tables states, "If a man is summoned to appear in court and does not come, let witnesses be heard and then let the plaintiff seize him. If he resists or absconds, the plaintiff can use force. If he is ill or too old, let the plaintiff provide a beast to bring him: but if he declines this offer, the plaintiff need not provide a carriage" (quoted in Kolbert, 1979, p. 13).

Superior magistrates, especially the praetor, of Rome issued edicts that initially identified how magistrates planned to fulfill their duties. Complaints between Roman citizens were taken to the urban praetor, who handled cases of Roman *jus civile* (private law). By issuing edicts at the start of his term, the praetor could identify the principles he would follow during his one year in office. Although the edict was valid only for that praetor's term, a tendency developed for praetors to borrow from their predecessor's edict. This certainly is different from stare decisis in common law, but it does suggest an early means of attaining consistency in procedure (Watson, 1970). A more appropriate link between the praetor and common law refers to a means for attending to fairness. In this manner, the edicts became a body of law known as the *jus honorarium*, which was to Roman law what equity was to common law (Kolbert, 1979). Advance notice of the procedural rules he would follow allowed the praetor to give the process a sense of fairness.

Finally, Roman law was the result of interpretations by jurists. These jurists were statesmen knowledgeable in the law, not lawyers or legal practitioners in the modern sense. The emperor would confer upon certain jurists the right or privilege of giving written opinions on cases. Those opinions would become binding on the parties in the dispute. Because jurists also could write on imaginary cases, there came to be an extensive, and often contradictory, collection of legal opinions on a variety of cases. At this historical point, the emperor Justinian provided one of the most important legal documents in the civil legal tradition.

Justinian became emperor in 527, succeeding his uncle Justin. As one of his first acts, he charged 16 experts with examining the existing juristic writings and refining the massive bulk of material then serving as Roman law. The resulting Corpus Juris Civilis was meant to eliminate incorrect, obscure, and repetitive material. Further, it was to resolve conflicts and doubts while organizing the remaining material into some systematic form (Merryman, 1985). At its completion in 533, the Corpus Juris Civilis stood as the sole authority for the laws and juristic writings.

Interestingly, most of the material in the Corpus Juris Civilis was over 300 years old and, therefore, predated Christianity. Emperor Constantine (275–337) was the first Roman emperor to become Christian, and Theodosius (346–395) made Christianity the sole religion of the empire. Obviously, Justinian's compilers had access to some 200 years of ecclesiastical law that they chose to ignore. Although church law did not have much impact on Roman law, it was an important factor in the development of the civil legal tradition.

CANON LAW The Roman Catholic Church developed canon law to govern the Church and the rights and obligations of its followers. Roman civil law was the universal law of the worldly empire, and canon law was the universal law of the spiritual realm (Merryman, 1985). Civil courts administered Roman civil law, whereas ecclesiastical courts managed the canon law.

The primary source providing the specifics of canon law was the various decretal letters. These decrees were authoritative papal statements concerning controversial points in doctrine or ecclesiastical law. Basically, any matter the papacy considered relevant to the well-being of the whole Christian body public was potential subject matter for a decretal letter. It had official and binding force and in essence was a judicial verdict signifying appropriate behavior and thought.

With the Church claiming jurisdiction over the entire life of Christians, potential conflict with the state was inevitable. In fact, the papacy and the government in Constantinople were in serious conflict from the time of Pope Leo I (440–461) onward. By Pope Gregory's time (590–604), canon law had secured a foothold in the legal system of the empire. Ullman (1975) suggests that an important reason for this ascendancy of canon law was its flexibility. With Gregory, canon law operated as a living law, providing a written system of law for contemporaries. The Roman law, as codified in the Corpus Juris Civilis, stood in stark contrast with its centuries-old standards. Canon law developed from real situations in the current time period and was flexible enough to absorb features of other systems like those of the Germanic tribes.

By the ninth century, both Roman law and canon law had experienced their heyday. Germanic and other invaders provided modifications as the empire collapsed, but by the eleventh century each had reestablished itself as a superior system. Law became a major object of study at Bologna and other Italian universities, and Italy became the legal center of the Western world (Merryman, 1985).

Scholars from many countries came to study the Corpus Juris Civilis, and, as a result, it provided more or less a uniform basis for law throughout continental Europe. This situation prevailed until the fifteenth century when the idea of national sovereignty gave rise to national law. The foundation had been laid, however, and Roman civil law, as well as canon law to a lesser extent, remained a large part of the legal systems in Western Europe.

CODIFICATION The components of the civil legal tradition have relied primarily on written (codified) laws. Though not fully realized until the Corpus Juris Civilis, Roman civil law had a tradition, dating back to the Twelve Tables, of laws being binding because they were authorized and recorded. Canon law supported the codification principle through papal decrees. Codification became so entrenched that in 319 BCE Emperor Constantine could declare, "The authority of custom and long usage is not slight but not to the extent that it will prevail against reason or against statute" (quoted in Kolbert, 1979, p. 13). Roman law and canon law provided a tradition of codification that, in turn, emphasized a revolutionary nature of law and stressed its written form.

When Justinian announced the Corpus Juris Civilis, his goal was to abolish all prior law. When France (see Map A.10) codified its law in the Code Napoleon, all prior law in those areas was repealed. Of course, both Corpus Juris Civilis and the Code Napoleon had principles of prior law incorporated in the new codes. However, in each case, and by implication in all cases of codification, the codes received their validity not from a previous incarnation but from their incorporation and reenactment in the new code (Merryman, 1985; Sereni, 1956).

The relevance of codification's revolutionary nature becomes clearer when contrasted with common law. For example, Merryman (1985) notes that codes exist in common law jurisdictions (e.g., the codes of Louisiana and California), but those codes are not based on the ideology or cultural reality that support French or German codes. Specifically, codes under common law do not abolish all prior law in their field (i.e., they are not revolutionary). Instead, they claim to perfect and supplement it. The view of civil law codes as replacing, instead of extending, prior law more appropriately distinguishes the civil and common traditions than does the presence of codes themselves.

Besides its revolutionary nature, codification is distinguished by its written form. Some people argue that civil law is distinct from common law in that the former is written and the latter is unwritten. This distinction is misleading. Actually, the distinction between written and unwritten law has little to do with whether the law is put in writing (Postema, 1986). Unwritten law exists in the customs of the community and is binding by that fact, regardless of whether someone wrote it down. Written law, on the other hand, exists and is binding because it was enacted by a recognized authority (e.g., a monarch or a legislature) following formal procedures.

Codification gives civil law a revolutionary character and written format that adds to its separate identity among legal families. Upon combining those features with the historical links to Roman and canon law, we have the basic ingredients of the civil legal tradition.

Islamic (Religious/Philosophical) Legal Tradition

The next legal tradition covered here is the religious/philosophical tradition. Although it has included such important legal systems as the Hindu and Judaic ones, its primary contemporary example is Islamic law.

With more than 1.6 billion followers, Muslims represent about 23 percent of the world's population. Christianity is the world's largest religion with an estimated 2.2 billion adherents (31 percent of the global population) but projections by the Pew Research Center indicate that by 2050 Muslims and Christians will each account for about 30 percent of the global population. Muslims live all around the world but a majority live in the Asia-Pacific region (62 percent) and about 20 percent are in the Middle East–North Africa region (Lipka, 2015; Pew Research Center, 2015).

Along with Christians and Jews, Muslims believe in one God, whom they call Allah. Allah's messenger was the Prophet Muhammad (570–632), who had been preceded by Jesus and the Old Testament prophets. The religion preached by Muhammad is Islam (Arabic for "submission"), and its followers are "those who submit to Allah" (Muslims).

Compared with the other three legal traditions, Islamic law is uncommon in its singularity of purpose. Islam recognizes no distinction between a legal system and other controls on a person's behavior. In fact, Islam is said to provide all answers to questions about appropriate behavior in any sphere of life. As a legal tradition, Islam is unique among the four discussed here. Although each of the other three took some principles and techniques from religion, the traditions themselves remained distinct and separate from religion. Islamic law, however, is intrinsic to Islamic faith and life in Islamic countries.

Before Muhammad, Arabic tribes operated under customary law, of which blood revenge was a major tenet. After the angel Gabriel called Muhammad to be a prophet, Muhammad preached about the need to replace old tribal loyalty with equality and brotherhood among all Muslims. In 622 CE, he fled from harassment in Mecca to greater appreciation in the city of Medina. As his prophet status spread, Muhammad was asked to judge disputes between Muslims. Generally, he followed the customary law of the town (to the extent that it was consistent with Islamic principles), but in cases where that law was lacking, he turned to Allah for direction.

Muhammad provided no tables, commandments, codes, or digests. Instead, Allah's revelations and Muhammad's own behavior provided answers to the quarrels and questions of the townsfolk. In time, these events comprised the primary ingredients of Islamic law—the Shari'a, "the path to follow." In its purest form, it consists of the writings in the *Qur'an* (the holy book of Islam) and the Sunna (the statements and deeds of the Prophet).[1] However, even taken together, these two elements do not make up a comprehensive code of law. In fact, they hardly constitute the bare skeleton of a legal system (Coulson, 1969). Therefore, added to the primary sources were two secondary sources of law: consensus by jurists (*ijma*), and analogical reasoning (*qiyas*). Both those primary (Qur'an and Sunna) and secondary (ijma and qiyas) subtraditions of Islamic law were, and are, influenced by differences among schools of thought. Those schools are discussed as the third subtradition of Islamic law (see Figure 4.2).

THE QUR'AN AND SUNNA   The primary subtraditions of Islamic law, or Shari'a, are the Qur'an and the Sunna. The Qur'an, the holy book for Muslims, was recorded by scribes and edited by scholars. It contains rules that God laid down and revealed to the Prophet Muhammad for governing human behavior. As noted earlier, Islam provides rules for all aspects of a Muslim's life. Whereas followers of some religions may turn to articles of faith for guidance in areas of social relations and prayer but not personal hygiene, others may turn to their religion for guidance in the areas of diet and sexual conduct but not business transactions. For Muslims, there is no distinction among rules for different segments of life.

The Qur'an contains rules for the religious, personal, social, economic, and all other aspects of Muslims' lives. There actually is little material dealing with legal issues in the strict sense of the term, but provisions identifying crimes and punishments are included and are considered by Muslims to provide a divinely ordained legal system (Lippman, McConville, & Yerushalmi, 1988).

The Holy Qur'an, along with the Sunna, provides the basic sources for Islamic law, or Shari'a.

Getideaka/Shutterstock

---

[1] Because of differences in the Arabic and Roman alphabets, there is not an agreed-upon standard for writing Arabic words in English text. The spelling of such words as Muhammad, Qur'an, and Shari'a used here are legitimately found as Mohammad, Koran, and Shariah (and other variants as well) elsewhere.

Because Islamic law's basic source is a religious text, it is sometimes portrayed as a harsh and inflexible system that is inappropriate in today's world. Certainly criminals have been amputated, beheaded, and stoned under Qur'anic provisions. However, there have also been criminals whose punishment has been set aside because of their victim's forgiveness. In fact, the Qur'an encourages forgiveness with the same vigor that it advocates retaliation. That point, which becomes clearer throughout this book, is good to keep in mind so that preconceived notions of Islamic law do not prevent a more dispassionate understanding of its operation.

The second basic source of Shari'a is the Sunna, which refers to the way the Prophet Muhammad lived his life. The Sunna is reported in *hadiths*, which are statements providing a narration about the life of the Prophet in terms of what he said, did, or approved. The hadiths have been passed on in a continuous and reliable chain of transmission from Muhammad and his companions to later adherents. A hadith contains three important parts: the statement itself; an indication of its authority by reference to the chain of reporters (i.e., A heard it from B, who heard it from C, who heard it from a companion of Muhammad); and a comment regarding the report as being something Muhammad did, said, or approved. For example, in the area of substantive criminal law, the Sunna advises:

> The Apostle of Allah (peace_be_upon_him) said: There are three [classes of offender who are not to be punished]: a sleeper till he awakes, an idiot till he is restored to reason, and a boy till he reaches puberty. (*Sunan Abu-Dawud*; Book 38, Number 4384: Narrated Aisha, Ummul Mu'minin)

That hadith, explains the Center for Muslim–Jewish Engagement (n.d.) at the University of Southern California, was recorded by Abu-Dawud, who lived a couple of centuries after the Prophet's death. Each report in his collection was checked for compatibility with the Qur'an, and the veracity of the chain of reporters (Aisha, Ummul Mu'minin in this example) was painstakingly established. Abu-Dawud's collection is recognized by the overwhelming majority of the Muslim world to be one of the most authentic collections of the Sunna of the Prophet.

Both the Qur'an and the Sunna are indispensable, and one cannot practice Islam without consulting both of them. The Sunna helps to explain, clarify, and amplify the Qur'an.

IJMA AND QIYAS In applying the Qur'an and Sunna, some Muslims came to take a strict interpretation and believed that every rule of law must be derived from the Qur'an or the Sunna. Others believed that human reason and personal opinion should be used to elaborate the law. In the early ninth century, the jurist Shafi'a proposed a compromise that some authors claim earned him the title "father of Muslim jurisprudence" (Coulson, 1969). Basically, Shafi'a sided with the strict interpreters but also acknowledged gaps that human reason was helpful in filling. Human reasoning, he believed, had to be subordinate to principles established by divine revelation in order to make sure it did not result in human legislative authority. Cases not seemingly answered by the Qur'an or Sunna were to be handled through a consensus of legal authorities (ijma) and by a process of reasoning by analogy, or qiyas.

Ijma is the process wherein qualified legal scholars of the Muslim community reach agreement (consensus) regarding a complex matter or event.[2] Following Muhammad's death, the caliphs (leaders of the Muslim community) used consultants to help in the proper interpretation of the Qur'an and Sunna for situations where judgment

---

[2] Sunni, but not Shi'a, recognize ijma (Kamali, 2008).

YOU SHOULD KNOW!

An Islamic Country Doesn't Necessarily Mean Islamic Law

The degree to which Islam affects law in Muslim societies is not the same across the countries where Islamic law is present. At one end of the spectrum is Saudi Arabia (see Map A.2), where the Qur'an and Sunna are considered the nation's constitution. At the other end is Turkey, where the law is secular, despite a population that is 99 percent Muslim. In between are countries where Islam plays an important, but not sole, role. In some of those countries, Islamic punishments apply only to Muslims. In others, Shari'a is applied only in personal-status matters (e.g., marriage, divorce, and inheritance) but not for crimes. Variation within countries is also found with some allowing Shari'a as a local (e.g., Indonesia) or state (e.g., Nigeria) option.

Saudi Arabia and Iran (see Map A.2) claim to fully implement Shari'a in all areas of law, including the criminal law, whereas such countries as Jordan, Kuwait, and Pakistan have some criminal laws reflecting traditional Islamic practices (e.g., banning Muslims from drinking alcohol) but others that are more secular in nature or involve modern interpretations of Shari'a (Johnson & Sergie, 2014; Otto, 2010).

To show some of the variation, Otto (2010) and Rhode (2005) provide information that allows us to group some predominantly Muslim countries according to the degree to which their legal system has been affected by Shari'a. The first group includes countries where classical Shari'a law affects most areas of law. A second group contains mixed systems wherein Shari'a-based law has no overall dominance, but has a significant role in one or more areas of law. The final category is for secular legal systems in which Shari'a has no role at all in the country's legal system.

- **Classical Systems**: Saudi Arabia and Iran are in this category, but Saudi Arabia has the more puritan version. The penal law of Saudi Arabia is entirely based on Shari'a, so hudud (see Chapter 5) offenses are recognized and corporal punishments can be applied. Iran's new (2013) penal code continues to recognize hudud offenses and, although it is no longer a punishment for adultery, stoning remains the punishment for apostasy. Corporal punishment, including amputation and flogging, may still be applied (Human Rights Watch, 2012).
- **Mixed Systems**: The majority of Muslim countries fall in this category. Some of these countries (e.g., Afghanistan, Pakistan, and Sudan) lean toward the classical group, but others (e.g., Indonesia, Malaysia, and Morocco) are clearly examples of mixed legal systems. For example, Pakistani criminal law is based on legal codes introduced during the colonial period by Britain, but amendments have incorporated Islamic law such as the recognition of hudud offenses. Moroccan criminal law, on the other hand, is influenced by Shari'a in a very limited way. For example, Muslims disrespecting Ramadan can be punished with a fine or detention and the code forbids attempts to convert a Muslim to another religion.
- **Secular Systems**: Turkey is the sole example for this category. Turkey's constitution protects religious freedom and the penal code is broadly consistent with the laws of the European Union. There has been no direct or indirect reference to Shari'a law in Turkish criminal legislation since the 1930s.

was unclear or hard to reach (Souryal, 2004). Not surprisingly, some scholars became more prominent than others did, and each had supporters for his interpretations. Schools of legal thought developed (see section "Schools of Law") around five particular jurists (Hafafi, Maliki, Shafi'i, Hanbali, and Ja'afari). By the end of the ninth century, the five schools had developed documents telling how their school interpreted questions or solved unique cases. When qualified jurists agreed on a given point, their opinion was considered binding and having absolute authority (i.e., ijma was achieved). Because there was consensus among jurists about how to resolve a unique problem, that opinion was accepted as law (Kamali, 2008).

In addition to relying on ijma for resolving questions of proper application of the Qur'an and Sunna, reasoning by analogy also came to play an important role. Souryal (2004) compares this use of analogy (qiyas) to the rule of precedent or stare decisis in the common legal tradition. That is, judgment is rendered in a new case by using a previous solution found in the Qur'an or the Sunna to resolve a similar case. For example, Lippman et al. (1988) note that some judges have sentenced persons who committed sodomy (not mentioned in the Qur'an or Sunna) to the same penalty the Qur'an provides for adultery by reasoning that sodomy and adultery are similar offenses.

With the Qur'an and Sunna serving as primary sources, and qiyas and ijma as secondary, the Shari'a had its basic sources. Not surprisingly, however, those sources were not understood or applied in a similar manner throughout Islamic countries any more than civil, common, or Eastern Asia law is consistent across nations following those traditions. The best way to understand the variation is with reference to the schools of law that developed as Shari'a spread.

SCHOOLS OF LAW Differences among Muslims in how Islam is interpreted and applied are linked first to one of two sects in Islam (Sunni and Shi'a) and then to the school of law to which particular Muslims adhere. These schools of law (*madhahib*, or, singular, *madhhab*) originally numbered in the hundreds but today have narrowed to five major ones: Hanafi, Maliki, Shafi'i, Hanbali, and Ja'afari. The first four are linked to Sunni Islam and the last to Shi'a Islam. We begin by reviewing the two sects.

The division between the Sunnis and the Shi'a (also known as Shiites) dates to the death of Muhammad and the resolution as to who should succeed as the leader (not prophet—only Muhammad was considered a prophet) of the Islamic world. One group of Muslims elected Abu Bakr (a close companion of Muhammad) as the next caliph, and he was duly appointed to that position. A smaller group—believing leadership of Muslims should continue in Muhammad's family line—wanted Ali, Muhammad's cousin and son-in-law, to become the caliph. Those believing Abu Bakr should become the successor have come to be known as Sunni, and those favoring Ali are called Shi'a (also Shiite) Muslims. Table 4.1 shows some of the differences in each school's understanding of Islam.

Sunni Islam started as the larger group and continued to be politically stronger. Today, estimates are that 85 to 90 percent of the world's Muslims are Sunni. In five countries—Iran, Azerbaijan, Bahrain, Iraq, and Lebanon—at least half the Muslim population is Shi'a. In the United States, 65 percent identify as Sunni and 11 percent as Shi'a—the remainder with neither group or simply as Muslim (Lipka, 2014, 2015). As we review differences in Sunni and Shi'a understanding of Islam, it is important to keep in mind that—despite the differences in opinion and practice—Shi'a and Sunni Muslims share the main articles of Islamic belief. Many Muslims do not distinguish themselves by claiming membership in any particular group; however, current global political conditions mean there has been a degree of polarization and hostility in many Muslim societies (BBC, 2009).

When discussing the schools of law in Islam, Glenn (2014) makes a comparison to law in the United States. For both U.S. law and Islamic law, one must know which state law or which school of law is applicable. That is, which state law is pertinent, and which Islamic school of thought is relevant? A key difference, of course, is that state law has geographic boundaries whereas a preferred school of thought indicates personal preference (unless a country or region has legislated adherence to a single school). Briefly, the five madhahib, which are named for their greatest teachers, are (summarized from Glenn, 2014; Schirrmacher, 1994; Shaukat, 2014; University of Cumbria, n.d.):

- **Hanafi:** This is the oldest of the schools and has the largest number of adherents. It recognizes the four basic sources of Islamic law, which are the Qur'an, the Sunna, qiyas, and ijma (see the first and second subtraditions covered earlier in this chapter). In addition to those four, the Hanafi school accepts personal reasoning and local custom to solve a problem. These additions make the Hanafi school the most liberal of all schools of law. Followers of the Hanafi school are found most frequently today in the areas known today as Israel, Syria, Lebanon, Jordan, Turkey, Iraq, Afghanistan, and among the Muslim population located southwest of

TABLE 4.1	Comparison of Sunni and Shi'a Islam*	
	Sunni Islam	**Shi'a Islam**
About	Originated with the teachings of Prophet Muhammad. Sunnis believe that Muhammad's close friend Abu Bakr was his successor.	Originated with the teachings of Prophet Muhammad. Shiites believe that Muhammad's son-in-law, Ali, was his successor.
Proportion of Muslims	85–90%	10–15%
Prophets	Muhammad, Jesus, Moses, and Abraham.	Muhammad, Jesus, Moses, and Abraham.
Primary geographic presence	Spread across the world and comprise the majority of Muslims in most Muslim countries.	Spread across the world, but comprise the majority of Muslims in Azerbaijan, Bahrain, Iran, Iraq, Lebanon, and Yemen.
Current leaders	Imams, who are considered human leaders.	Imams, who are considered infallible and perfect interpreters of the Qur'an.
Religious authority other than the Qur'an	Ijma (consensus) of the Muslim community.	Infallible imams.
Summary of differences and similarities	Distinctions between Sunni and Shi'a Islam began as political (different views regarding the true successor to the Prophet Muhammad and the nature of religious authority) but gradually became more theological. Importantly, however, both hold the same fundamental beliefs and many Muslims do not distinguish themselves as being anything more specific than Muslim.	

*Table created from information provided at (1) Diffen. Shia vs Sunni. Category: Islam. http://www.diffen.com/difference/Shiites_vs_Sunni (Accessed July 10, 2016); (2) FindTheData. Compare Sunni Islam vs Shia Islam. Society: Religions. http://religions.findthedata.org/compare/15-17/Sunni-Islam-vs-Shia-Islam (Accessed July 10, 2016); and (3) ReligionFacts. Comparison of Sunni and Shia Islam. Islam. http://www.religionfacts.com/islam/comparison_charts/islamic_sects.htm (Accessed July 10, 2016).

the former Soviet Union, and in India and Pakistan. It is also present in Sudan and East Africa.

- **Maliki:** As the Hanafi school was spreading north and east from Islam's geographic origins around the cities of Medina (western Saudi Arabia) and Kufa (central Iraq), the Maliki school went west and is prevalent today in Northern and Western Africa and northern Nigeria. Under the Maliki doctrine, the four basic sources of Shari'a are recognized. The Malikis' concept of ijma originally was more restrictive than that of the Hanafis, but over time the Malikis broadened their acceptance of the legal scholars they recognized as authorities.

- **Shafi'i:** Taking a position between the more liberal Hanafi and more conservative Maliki schools was the Shafi'i. The most distinguishing feature of the Shafi'i school is that it recognizes only the four basic sources of Shari'a—with the Qur'an and the Sunna being paramount and qiyas and ijma secondary. The Shafi'i school spread farther east than the Malikis and prevails today in Islamic communities throughout Southeast Asia and in Egypt, where al-Shafi'i died.

- **Hanbali:** The Hanbali school is found today mostly in Saudi Arabia, Qatar, and the United Arab Emirates. Similar to the Shafi'i school, Hanbali adherents recognize the four basic sources of Shari'a and place the Qur'an and the Sunna above qiyas and ijma in authority. Even as secondary sources, qiyas and ijma are restricted. For example, Hanbalis accept as authoritative only an opinion given by a companion of Muhammad, providing there is no disagreement with another companion. If there is disagreement, the opinion that is nearest to that of the Qur'an and the Sunna prevails.

- **Ja'afari:** The most important Shi'a school of law is the Ja'afari. Shi'a Islam differs from Sunni Islam in its belief of the "Imamate." This means that, after the prophet, the only true leader of the Muslims at any given time is an Imam who is descendent from Muhammad's family and is appointed by Allah. The last such Imam for the main Shi'a group (the Twelvers) was Muhammad Mehdi. He disappeared at age 9 in CE 878 and is believed by the Twelvers to be still alive and in hiding. He will reappear near Judgment Day to establish the Kingdom of Allah, to fill the world with equality and justice, and to bring about the victory of the Shi'a faith. Shi'a Islam regards the Imam to be an independent source of religious behavior with the same standing as the Qur'an and the Sunna. His rulings should be obeyed in the same way as those primary sources of Shari'a hadith and must therefore be obeyed the same way. The Shi'a school of law can be found in Iran, Pakistan, India, Iraq, Lebanon, Bahrain, and Azerbaijan.

The geographical distribution of these five schools provides variation in how Islamic law is applied from one country to another—and even within a country. It is important to remember that the Shari'a is not necessarily the sole basis for all law in every Islamic (or predominantly Muslim) country—nor do Muslims necessarily want Shari'a law to be the official law of the land in their home country. A Pew Research Center survey (Lipka, 2015) of Muslims in 39 countries found that nearly all Muslims in Afghanistan (99 percent) and most in Iraq (91 percent) support Shari'a law as official law, but in other countries—especially Southeastern Europe and Central Asia—relatively few favor the implementation of Shari'a law (e.g., Turkey, 12 percent; Albania, 12 percent; Kazakhstan, 8 percent).

Countries such as Jordan and Kuwait have both civil and Islamic aspects in their legal systems, whereas other nations combine Islamic and common traditions (e.g., Kenya and Nigeria). Muslim countries providing the clearest examples of widespread use of Islamic law as official law include Iran, Pakistan, Saudi Arabia, Sudan, and Syria.

The Islamic legal tradition encompasses diverse legal systems and undoubtedly is influenced by civil, common, and socialist countries. Nevertheless, it gives all appearances of maintaining its footing in its subtraditions of the Qur'an, the Sunna, ijma, and qiyas.

Eastern Asia (Hybrid) Legal Tradition

Hybrid legal traditions are those that consist of elements found in some or all of the other main legal traditions. In Figure 4.1, these would include those systems identified as Civil/Common, Civil/Islamic, Common/Islamic, and Other. But beyond that, hybrid legal traditions could also include aspects of traditional or customary law.

Designating one of the four contemporary legal traditions as "hybrid" is more accurate than helpful. There is no question that many countries have legal systems that draw from more than one legal tradition. In fact, an argument could be made that such adaptation is true of all legal systems. But trying to describe and analyze a legal tradition that incorporates aspects of other traditions will not be very practical. For example, each of the three legal traditions discussed so far has been identified by specific developmental subtraditions. For a hybrid tradition, does one simply lump together all the subtraditions from the other three legal families in order to explain how hybrid legal traditions came about? A more practical approach seems to be one that selects a specific example of the hybrid tradition to represent the broader hybrid category. This is similar to using the Islamic legal tradition to represent the broad religious/philosophical category. The specific hybrid example used here is an Eastern Asia legal tradition.

Asia, of course, encompasses an extremely large area that includes remarkably diverse cultures. For our purposes, the specific area termed "Eastern Asia" by the United Nations Statistics Division (2013) identifies the countries said to be following an Eastern Asia legal tradition. Specifically, those countries are China (including the special administrative regions of Hong Kong and Macao), Japan, Mongolia, and both North and South Korea (see Maps A.7 and A.8).

As the Eastern Asia legal tradition is described and explained, the influence of both civil and common legal traditions will become apparent. However, the countries used to show an Eastern Asia tradition (China especially, but Japan as well) have enough unique characteristics that the result is clearly a hybrid that blends those Western influences with more clearly Asian traits. Those traits to be highlighted here are linked to the ethical and philosophical teachings of Confucius with their emphasis on collectivism and a preference for legal informalism.

CONFUCIANISM   Confucius (the Latin name for the Chinese philosopher K'ung-fu-tzu) was a fifth-century BCE teacher whose philosophy had great influence in China, Korea, and Japan. Rather than a religion, Confucianism is best viewed as a moral and ethical system developed from the teachings of Confucius. It is considered to be the most important single source of an Eastern Asia legal tradition (Glenn, 2014; Liu & Palermo, 2009).

More generally, the countries in Eastern Asia have been influenced by Confucianism because, compared with the West, they all emphasize family- or group-based collectivism, hierarchy, harmony, and informal control mechanisms (Jiang, 2014). For our purposes, the essential principles of Confucianism lie in the concepts of *li* and *fa*. Li has many meanings but mostly it refers to moral and social rules of conduct that are shared and internalized by individuals. At a very basic level, it has been defined as etiquette or propriety, but it is more than that. Li is a way of life—or, at least a way of living one's life—that includes adherence to the specific legal code, but even more importantly it presumes conforming to the broader moral code. In this sense, there is a similarity between li and Islam's perspective of Shari'a as encompassing all aspects of the devout Muslim's life—not just one's legal obligations.

The essence of li is maintenance of an orderly society with harmonious social relationships among people. This harmonious society is the result of rulers who govern in moral and virtuous ways and thereby set examples for everyone else. As moral and virtuous behavior trickles down to the public (and is supported with moral and virtuous examples from family, teachers, and others), people internalize virtue as simply the way to behave rather than the way others are forcing them to behave. China's leader, Xi Jinping, made this point (quoting Confucius) when he said that he who rules by virtue is like the North Star—it maintains its position and the other stars pay their respect (Buckley, 2014). In other words, li means that social order is self-imposed rather than externally dictated (Bracey, 2006; Glenn, 2014; Liu & Palermo, 2009).

Contrasted with li is the concept of fa—formal law and sanctions or, for our purposes, criminal law and punishment. When li is successfully implemented in society, there is no need to call upon fa. Unfortunately, li is not always able to prevent misbehavior and fa must step in to maintain social order.

Confucianism, with its belief that humans are teachable and improvable, is most obviously found in li, but it is also seen in fa. This is important since formal law is clearly present in Eastern Asia legal systems. If principles of Confucianism were not found in the formal legal codes of China and other Eastern Asia countries, it would be difficult to argue that an Eastern Asia legal tradition exists. More on that point later, but here the idea is simply that Confucius did not deny the utility of formal law and punishment, but he did stress the superiority and effectiveness of li (Liu & Palermo, 2009).

An example of fa influenced by Confucianism would be formal codes that present models for behavior rather than specifying particular rules. Similarly, teaching would be preferred over punishment as the response to violation of the legal code. We will see examples of both of these later in this chapter and in other chapters as well.

If the moral philosophy of Confucianism were the only aspect of an Eastern Asia legal tradition, it would be better to simply present that tradition as an example of the religious/philosophical family rather than setting it apart as a key example of a hybrid legal tradition. But the moral preference for persuasion over punishment is not the only unique aspect of the Eastern Asia legal tradition. Also important are collectivism, context, and informalism.

The teachings of Confucius, and especially the concepts of *li* and *fa*, are important to the understanding of the Eastern Asia legal tradition.

Philip Lange/Shutterstock.

COLLECTIVISM AND CONTEXT   In Chapter 10's discussion of Japan, collectivism and context are separately highlighted as key cultural patterns when trying to understand Japan's legal system. The two characteristics are discussed together in this section because of their shared importance in the development of an Eastern Asia legal tradition.

One's sense of self can be described in either individual or collectivist terms. The family and group orientation of such Eastern Asia cultures as China, Japan, and Korea results in a sense of self-worth and identity that is linked to the groups to which one belongs. One's individual nature is understood in the context of that person's relationships. The point can be made no clearer than by Nisbett and Masuda's (2003) observation that if an important person is removed from an individual's social network, that individual actually becomes a different person.

Contrast that view of self with the Western view of the person as an individual, different from others, rebellious even. Such training starts early with Western babies often sleeping in a different bed (even a different room) than their parents—a rare situation for Asian babies. While Asian children are learning the proverb about the nail that sticks out getting hammered down, the Western child is learning about rugged individualism. These differences are seen when comparing self-descriptions of North Americans with those of Asians. For example, Americans and Canadians typically describe themselves in terms of personality traits and attitudes more so than do Japanese. Similarly, North Americans overestimate their distinctiveness and prefer uniqueness in themselves. In one interesting study, Koreans and Americans were given a choice among different colored pens to have as a gift. Americans chose the rarest color, whereas Koreans chose the most common color (Nisbett & Masuda, 2003).

Linked to this collectivist sense of self is an appreciation for the importance of context and relationships. Again, psychologists help us understand this. When shown animated vignettes of underwater scenes, Japanese and American participants were asked to report what they had seen. The American participants concentrated on specific characteristics (a large fish, a brightly colored fish, a faster moving fish) but the Japanese participants more frequently described a holistic picture that included the environment in which the fish were swimming and the relations between objects in the scene (Nisbett & Masuda, 2003).

A sense of collectivism and greater attention to field or context by Asians helps explain aspects of the Eastern Asia legal tradition that emphasizes the group over the individual and encourages interest in the context surrounding the act more so than the act itself (Bracey, 2006). This means, for example, that an instance of burglary must be considered in light of such things as the time of the burglary, the location of the place burglarized, the financial situation of the offender, the offender's relationship with his or her family and work colleagues, and so on. To consider only the act without regard to the context in which the act was committed is impractical. In order to consider this broader context, a legal system that allows some informality is more desirable than is a very formal legal system.

LEGAL INFORMALISM Informal justice relies on legal institutions that are mostly non-bureaucratic, minimize the use of professionals, and prefer substantive and procedural norms that are vague and flexible (Abel, 1982). Under such a model, reconciliation, restitution, and reintegration become more important than punishment and retribution (Bracey, 2006).

This preference for legal informalism is seen in several Eastern Asia legal system-sand is highlighted with examples from China throughout this book and from Japan in Chapter 10. For example, we will see in Chapter 7 that many disputes in China are handled at the grassroots level by a people's mediation committee. Mediation is, of course, an attractive way to respond to criminal acts informally. During the mediation process, the context within which the act was committed can be given due attention and the information gained can be used to determine the appropriate penalty. Further, Chinese law permits some criminal offenses to be handled by informal procedures and for others allows criminal punishment to be replaced by noncriminal punishment (e.g., apologies or promises to repent).

A preference for vague and flexible substantive and procedural norms is less apparent in the legal system of some Eastern Asia countries than in others. Japan, for example, seems not to have this characteristic as much as does China, although Chapter 10 describes a bureaucratic informalism in Japan that includes flexibility in procedural norms. Laws in China, on the other hand, do seem to be vague and flexible at times, as described in Chapter 5 under the heading "Substantive Law in the Eastern Asia Legal Tradition."

We must be careful not to deemphasize the increasingly important role of formal law in Eastern Asia legal systems. For example, several authors note how China's legal system has been fundamentally transformed since 1978 and that China today has sophisticated legal institutions, a large number of lawyers, and a commitment to the rule of law (Liebman, 2009). In addition, law is increasingly used as a tool by ordinary people to resolve disputes and challenge what they perceive to be unjust decisions. But the continuing preference for li over fa and for legal informalism suggests that Confucianism remains an important backdrop to the Eastern Asia legal tradition and that it deserves continued recognition as a contemporary legal tradition.

COMPARISON OF THE LEGAL TRADITIONS

Because a goal of this text is to use classification strategies to provide a sense of order to diverse institutions and procedures, it is appropriate to identify more carefully the similarities and differences among the four legal traditions (common, civil, Islamic, and Eastern Asia). Our classification strategy choices, you will recall, are either synthetic or authentic in nature. The former, resulting in artificial groups, requires knowledge of only one or two aspects of the groups being classified. The latter, which provides natural groups, depends on extensive investigation of the objects.

Many legal scholars and comparative criminal justicians have written about legal traditions (Dammer & Albanese, 2014; Glenn, 2014; Vogler, 2005), but not as many have attempted a comprehensive analysis comparing the traditions based on some common criteria (Ehrmann, 1976; Ingraham, 1987). The shortage of detailed information means that any current classification of legal traditions is most accurately described as synthetic rather than authentic. This means that the categories of common, civil, Islamic, and Eastern Asia should be seen as artificial groups arrived at based on one or two criteria of interest to the scientist.

Predictivity is the main quality lacking in synthetic versus authentic classification. With the natural groups resulting from authentic classification, we could be told that a country's legal system falls in the civil legal tradition and immediately predict characteristics of that system. With synthetic groups, though, the best we can do is assume that the country has cultural similarities or links to Western Europe and speculate that the country's system might therefore share ideas with Western Europe about such things as the appropriate source of law and the proper role of judges. The great variability of systems within each tradition means that we cannot yet (and maybe never will) achieve an authentic classification of legal families. A much more extensive investigation of the various systems and a clearer understanding of their characteristics must precede any progress toward identifying natural groups of law systems. Until then, we must rely on artificial groups such as the four presented here.

Because artificial groups depend on the criteria chosen by the person doing the classification, the resulting categories reflect his or her interests. My interests are threefold: the values and attitudes supporting legal systems (the cultural component), the characteristics of law in each system (substantive law), and procedures by which each system enforces the law (procedural law).

Chapter 3 explained that two essential ingredients of any justice system are substantive law and procedural law. With these components, law is delineated (substantive law) and the manner of enforcement is specified (procedural law). The cultural component is also important, because it often provides the key ingredient distinguishing legal systems between, and even within, legal traditions. For example, the state of Louisiana has specific substantive and procedural elements linking it to the civil legal tradition. However, the cultural elements of law in Louisiana are undoubtedly closer to those of Arkansas and Texas than to France.

In this chapter, certain aspects of each legal tradition have already been identified. Several of these speak of cultural elements relevant to the historical development of that legal tradition. Yet so far, the discussion has not addressed specific areas of substantive and procedural law. To place comments about the four traditions in a broader context, I now compare and contrast each in terms of cultural, substantive, and procedural aspects. Because remaining chapters provide country-specific information, this chapter continues its general discussion of the four traditions and saves individual treatment for later chapters.

Cultural Component

Although the role of culture is often noted to be indispensable to understanding a country's legal system, it remains one of the least researched areas (Bracey, 2006; Merryman, 1985; Rosen, 1989). Custom in common law, codification in civil law, the integration of religion and criminal justice in Islam, and a preference in some Asian countries for persuasion over punishment are examples of cultural elements that help us appreciate each legal tradition. Sometimes the cultural differences hide similarities among the traditions.

For example, Lippman et al. (1988) suggest that the Islamic restrictions on what evidence is allowable show a shared belief with the common law principle that it is better to release a guilty person than to punish one who is innocent.

Similarly, some traditions are culturally alike in certain ways but have very different operations as a result. For example, the civil law tradition and the Islamic tradition share a religious heritage but with greatly disparate impact. Canon law under the civil tradition operated in a highly civilized world where law enjoyed great prestige. Christianity lacked interest in the actual organization of society, so there was no need to have church law replace, for example, Roman law. Thus, Roman law spread throughout the West without conflicting with the Christian religion (David & Brierley, 1968). The same was not true for Islamic law. By its very nature, Islam is all-encompassing. Its relevance to all aspects of the individual's life includes the organization of society, the role of social institutions, and the norms appropriate for human behavior. Islamic law had to replace any existing legal system as it spread from Medina.

An important cultural component to consider when discussing an Eastern Asia legal tradition is the role played by socialism generally and the Communist Party more specifically—especially when China is used as an example of an Eastern Asia legal tradition. Some aspects of socialism were easily incorporated into an Eastern Asia legal tradition—for example, a socialist belief that law should be used to educate people about proper behavior. Even as contemporary China moves toward a market economy and increasingly shows examples of providing (or, at least proposing) increased civil rights, the influence of socialism is apparent. Importantly, Confucianism has become an ally in communist efforts to generate loyalty and in how legal institutions are structured and operate (for more complete arguments see Glenn, 2014; Liebman, 2009). The cultural influence of socialism, and certainly its political and economic authority as well, must be considered in any discussion of China's example of an Eastern Asia legal tradition.

By drawing attention to points such as these, the comparative justice scholar seeks to identify similarities and differences among legal traditions. As examples, we briefly consider the cultural components concerning "public and private law" and the "balance/separation of powers" (see Table 4.2).

TABLE 4.2	Some Cultural Components of Legal Traditions			
	Common Tradition	**Civil Tradition**	**Islamic Tradition**	**Eastern Asia Tradition**
Do legal rights and obligations lie with the individual (private law) or the state (public law)?	Public law, with both the individual and the state having a legal personality.	Public law when concern is with the state's legal personality; private law when concern is with the individual's legal personality.	Private law because the concern always centers on the individual's legal personality.	Legal rights and obligations simultaneously have both private and public aspects.
What is the position of the judiciary in relation to other government branches?	Courts share in balancing power.	Courts have equal but separate power.	Courts and other government branches are subordinate to the Shari'a.	Courts are subordinate to the legislature in some countries (China and North Korea), share in balancing power in others (South Korea), and have equal but separate power in still others (Japan).

PRIVATE AND PUBLIC LAW   The concepts of private law and public law provide a useful distinction in comparing legal systems. In the sense used here, the terms refer to a "legal personality." That is, where do legal rights and obligations lie? Under civil law, the question requires two answers. Some matters are the sole concern of the individuals involved. Those individuals come as equals before the judge, who serves as referee in the matter. The legal rights and interests lie with the private individuals, and, in its truest form, the right to sanction rests with the individual as well. Public law in the civil tradition refers to rules governing activities of the state or of persons acting in the public interest. A separate system of laws, of courts to hear such cases, and of procedures regulating the whole process is a feature of the civil tradition.

Under common law, the distinction between public and private law is not so clear. Common law does not provide separate systems for handling private and public disputes. Both types of questions go before the same courts of law, are heard by the same judges, and are governed by similar rules. Cases involving state action are placed in the same position as those involving the action of ordinary citizens (Schwartz, 1956).

The absence of a distinction between public and private law in the common tradition is historically based. Essentially, English common law is predominantly public law because the courts were justified in settling disputes only because of the lord's (finally, the Crown's) interest in the case. In this manner, the public or state was given a legal personality. In the capacity of a "personality," the state could bring claims against an individual. Civil law also recognized a legal personality of the state, but claims initiated by that "personality" progressed through the separate legal system set up for that purpose.

The idea of the state having a legal personality is not present under the Islamic tradition. The Shari'a took no steps to define the interests of the community or public. Consistent with the Arabic emphasis on the individual, the Islamic legal tradition gives primacy to private law (Lippman et al., 1988). The Shari'a exists to orient the private lives of Muslims and their relations with each other. As in the common tradition, a single legal system appropriately hears all types of disputes. However, instead of justifying this as resulting from a widespread interest by the state, Muslims justify it as a general concern with the individual.

Describing Islamic law as emphasizing private law should not be understood as saying that state officials cannot initiate action against suspected offenders. Chapter 5 explains the three categories of criminal acts recognized in the Islamic legal tradition (*hudud*, *qisas*, and *tazir*), and we will see that the first are considered acts against God. Acting as God's agent, the state initiates action against persons accused of committing hudud crimes; however, in doing so, the state is still protecting an entity (albeit an omnipresent one in this case). Similarly, the state may initiate action (rather than waiting for the victim to bring action) against offenders in the other two crime categories as well. In doing so, the state acts to maintain public order among citizens rather than acting in response to behavior that has harmed society as a whole. The offenses are considered to have been private wrongs rather than public wrongs, and it is, therefore, the individual's legal personality that is emphasized—although the state may act to protect the individual.

Hybrid systems, by definition, have characteristics from several of the other legal traditions. As such, it is not surprising that legal personality in the Eastern Asia tradition has aspects of both civil and common traditions. However, one must also consider the notions of li and fa as expressed in Confucianism. When that is done, the distinction between public and private law becomes cloudy.

A society based on li is orderly and harmonious because everyone has internalized the moral and virtuous ways exemplified by those in authority. Proper behavior is the result of internal rather than external forces, so the obligation to behave is "private" in the sense that it reflects individual obligations. Since an entirely li-based society is utopian, the Eastern Asia legal tradition came to rely also on formal law and sanctions (fa) wherein the state came to have a legal obligation to enforce proper behavior. However, the state role is tempered by a preference to rely on li. The result is a view of legal rights and obligations as simultaneously having both private and public aspects. For example, when misbehavior occurs the preference is to handle the matter informally between the parties involved—even if that misbehavior is criminal. That informal response may not even involve a criminal justice agency, but even when the police or courts are involved the response may be informal in nature. When a formal response is required, the established legal institutions are used and the state, in its legal personality, takes action against the wrongdoer. The result is a coinciding of public and private law—at least as we are using the terms.

BALANCE/SEPARATION OF POWERS   Some of the more important cultural changes in modern times were the eighteenth-century political and intellectual revolutions in most Western nations. Especially significant were documents such as the American Declaration of Independence and the French Declaration of the Rights of Man and of the Citizen, which offered ideas about human equality and the relationship between state and citizen. We quickly notice political, economic, and intellectual aspects of the revolutions, but there were important legal ramifications as well. Consider first the impact that these events had on the civil and common law countries.

Members of the French judicial aristocracy were targets of the French Revolution because of their tendency to identify with the landholders. Repeated efforts toward reform had been obstructed by courts' refusing to apply new laws, interpreting them contrary to their intent, or hindering attempts of officials to administer them (Merryman, 1985). The situation differed from the one found in England (and America), where judges had more often been on the side of the individual against a power-wielding ruler. English citizens did not have the French fear of judicial lawmaking and of judicial interference in administration.

Another reason for targeting French judges was their failure to distinguish clearly between applying law and making law. Montesquieu and Rousseau had argued for the importance of establishing and maintaining a separation of governmental powers. Especially important was a clear distinction between legislative and executive duties on the one hand and the duties of the judiciary on the other. In the French Revolution, this emphasis on separation of powers led to a system designed to keep the judiciary from intruding into areas reserved for the other two powers: lawmaking and execution of the laws. Again, this situation differed from that found in the American colonies. The system of checks and balances developed in the United States does not try to isolate the judiciary, nor does it try to approximate the sharp division of powers typically encountered in civil law countries. Essentially, the judiciary was not a target of the American Revolution the way it was a decade later in France (Merryman, 1985).

Following the French lead, European countries moved to separate the three governmental powers so that the judiciary could be isolated. In America and England, a system of checks and balances was used without any particular interest in isolating the judiciary.

Although the common law tradition operated with a judiciary that balanced the power of the legislature and the executive, the civil tradition functioned with a judiciary separated from the other two branches of government. This separation of powers is one explanation for the development of a separate legal system for public law. It also, of course, reflects a greater suspicion of the judiciary under the civil tradition than was present in the common legal tradition (Merryman, 1985).

Despite the different paths taken, both civil and common law traditions rely on each government part as a source of law. As is explained later, there are important differences with regard to which government area is emphasized as the primary source of law, but for now we need only point to the expectation that each part has a role to play.

Islamic courts do not operate as a counterbalance to the legislature and executive. Instead, consistent with its emphasis on private law, the Islamic court serves as a stabilizing device among contending persons (Rosen, 1989). Actually, under classic Islamic theory, neither the state nor the courts were instruments for the application of law. Instead, each was to focus on the individual and perform its respective duties in a way that allowed individuals to carry on with their own affairs.

More so than for other topics, discussion of balance and separation of powers in the Eastern Asia legal tradition requires us to make a political distinction. Contemporary China and North Korea operate under the political leadership of their respective communist party. Japan and South Korea are democracies with multiparty systems. Socialism's influence on both China and North Korea is seen in both countries' rejection of the separation of powers principle and instead in the fact that all power is invested in the hands of the legislature (e.g., the National People's Congress in China). As a result, courts in China and North Korea are not the equal of the legislature, either by isolation from that branch or by serving as a check and balance to that branch. The judiciary in Japan, on the other hand, reflects a civil legal tradition by having complete independence and autonomy from the other two branches of government. South Korea's judiciary is better described as sharing in the balancing of power as is done in the common legal tradition.

There are other intriguing and important issues about the cultural component of legal traditions. It would be good to know such things as the attitude of people toward their courts, what type of people and cases go to court, the extent to which courts are used or avoided, and so on. Yet such issues still await an interested scientist. Preliminary information on cultural views, like the role of the state in human affairs and the positioning of various parts of government, is sufficient at least to propose a rudimentary design for the structure of each legal tradition. The cultural suspicion of the judiciary in many pre–French Revolution civil law countries has already helped explain the civil tradition's preference for separate public and private law systems. Similarly, the lack of distrust of common law judges explains that tradition's satisfaction with a single system hearing both public and private disputes. The trust/distrust distinction also suggests that the common law may be more willing to provide judges with lawmaking powers.

Substantive Component

In its broadest sense, substantive law concerns where laws come from (see Table 4.3) and how they are defined. More specifically, as explained in Chapter 3, substantive law is composed of internal and external characteristics. Chapter 5 provides detailed information about the internal and external characteristics of criminal law in several countries, so here we can concentrate on a broader question of substantive law: Where do the laws come from?

TABLE 4.3	A Substantive Component of Legal Traditions: Where Does the Law Come from?			
	Common Tradition	**Civil Tradition**	**Islamic Tradition**	**Eastern Asia Tradition**
The primary source of law is	Custom	Codification	Divine revelation	Principles of Confucianism
	Law expresses entrenched visions of right and wrong.	Written code provided by rulers or legislators.	Law has the authority of God rather than tradition or directive.	Ideally the "source" is within each individual but realistically lies in codes presenting models for behavior.

Any legal tradition must consider the role local custom plays as a source of law. The Qur'anic part of Islamic law is supposed to be of divine origin, but, besides its divine inspiration, the Sunna certainly reflects Muhammad's understanding of local custom. In the civil legal tradition, codes substituted for prior custom. Under common law, decisions by judges reflected custom and provided it with legitimacy. The Eastern Asia tradition was heavily influenced by the concepts of li and fa as understood by the public. Unfortunately, a summary such as this is misleading. Custom played a role in all four traditions, but the actual source of law in each does not equally reflect custom.

PRIMARY SOURCE OF COMMON LAW   For the common legal tradition, the primary source of law is custom. Law is a public expression of society's entrenched vision of right and wrong, or good and bad (Postema, 1986). Like the civil law, common law rests on certain principles. The difference between the two is that for common law, the principles exist as generally accepted tradition instead of through writing. Writing them down reveals, not creates, the principles. Because the traditional way of identifying custom was through the court rather than legislative process, judges came to play a pivotal role in common law. A decision by a judge was accepted as legal recognition of a custom. In this sense, the judge "made law" by accepting the custom as binding in a particular case. The absence of a cultural suspicion about judicial actions and the tradition of accepting principles other than those specifically written by rulers and legislators gave the common law judge lawmaking and law-applying authority.

PRIMARY SOURCE OF CIVIL LAW   The primary source of law in the civil tradition is the written code. The code, which is complete and self-sufficient, is provided by the ruler or the legislature. Of course, completeness is a problem because the codes would become unreasonably extensive if they anticipated all possible acts and the specifics of every case. Instead of offering direct and specific solutions to particular problems, codes supply general principles from which logical deduction provides a resolution in each case (Sereni, 1956). In this manner, civil judges need only identify the applicable code principle to decide a particular case. The solution is expected to be reached through an independent process of legal reasoning that the judge can identify and explain. This process allows the judge to apply the law but not to make it—exactly what the cultural tradition of separation of powers had in mind. Therefore, under the civil legal tradition, the solution to each case is to be found in the provisions of the written law, and the judge must show that the decision is based on those provisions.

PRIMARY SOURCE OF ISLAMIC LAW   Islamic law is presumed to be of divine origin. Its primary sources, the Qur'an and the Sunna, specify the legal principles linked to right and wrong behavior. Its authority is based on God's commands instead of long-held traditions or directives issued under the auspices of state power. In fact, its divine nature means that no worldly authority can supplement it, let alone change it. So, like civil law judges, Islamic qadi (i.e., judges) must turn to written documents for solutions to disputes. Also like their civil counterparts, qadi cannot do more than identify the correct principle for use in a particular case. The difference lies in the source of that principle.

PRIMARY SOURCE OF EASTERN ASIA LAW   Preferably, for the Eastern Asia tradition, formal law is not even needed, so no "source" can be identified. When moral virtue has been internalized (i.e., when li is dominant), law's "source" is within each individual. Realistically, if disappointingly, formal law (fa) is required in modern societies, but that formal law can still reflect aspects of Confucianism. Legal codes (in the civil legal tradition sense) are necessary for maintaining social order in modern society, but those codes can be based in Confucianism to the extent that they present models for behavior rather than specifying particular rules. Further, when enforcement of those codes relies on informal more than formal procedures, there are aspects of li in the law's enforcement. This is the approach taken by the Eastern Asia tradition, so the primary source of law is identified by the principles of Confucianism.

Procedural Component

If law under each tradition really came only from the source identified in the preceding paragraphs, few legal systems of any type could remain effective. The belief that state authorities anticipate every nuance of each potential dispute is just as unreasonable as trusting that ancient custom provides useful guidelines for contemporary behavior. Similarly, believing that God's pronouncements for appropriate behavior today are the same as those provided in the sixth century requires as much faith as accepting utopian theories of a fifth-century BCE philosopher. Obviously, each system had to provide ways to update, modify, fill in the gaps, and supplement the various sources of law in their respective legal traditions. The ways in which that was done bring us to the final topic for this chapter: the procedures for solving problems of flexibility (see Table 4.4).

FLEXIBILITY IN COMMON LAW   The concept of stare decisis has the potential to tie common law to the vestiges of the past. When judges are expected to decide the present case similarly to the way like cases were decided in the past, it seems unlikely that much change can occur. Perhaps even more important, what happens when the court is presented a case that seems very dissimilar to preceding ones? Luckily for the judge and, therefore, for nations under this tradition, common law provides for flexibility by empowering judges to develop solutions to unique cases by "making law" (Postema, 1986). The only restraint requires the solution to be built from a base of existing law. The result is law established by judicial decision and precedent rather than issuing from statutes, codes, or divine proclamation.

Another technique to achieve flexibility under common law is the practice of particularization. A review of U.S. Supreme Court holdings in any subject area quickly exemplifies this point. The common legal tradition limits court decisions to very particular facts. Two cases may involve stopping a suspect and searching the suspect's person and surrounding area. However, in case A, the suspect was walking away from the reported scene of the crime while in case B the suspect was running away. The particular behavior of the suspect may well make the cases different in the court's eyes. As a result, the judge in case B may decide that the decision in case A did not set a precedent for the situation now before her. So the case B judge has the flexibility to make law for this "unique" case.

TABLE 4.4	A Procedural Component of Legal Traditions: How Does Law Keep Pace with Changing Society?			
	Common Tradition	**Civil Tradition**	**Islamic Tradition**	**Eastern Asia Tradition**
How is flexibility provided?	Judge-made law and particularization.	Variation in reasoning and definition, and identification of issues as either questions of law or questions of fact.	*Fatwa* (legal opinion or ruling) and the process of *ijtihad* (independent reasoning).	The reliance on informal procedure and, for China and North Korea, on vagueness in how the law is written.

FLEXIBILITY IN CIVIL LAW   The civil legal tradition faces a similar problem but for different reasons. The idea of a state authority (e.g., legislature, parliament, and the like) reducing to writing all the necessary components of substantive and procedural law cannot be seriously proposed, yet that is the objective under civil law. Ideally, the civil law judge simply extracts the facts in the case, finds the appropriate provision from the legislature, and applies it to the problem. As Merryman (1985) explains, if a relevant provision is not found, the fault is assumed to lie with either the judge (who obviously cannot follow clear instructions) or the legislator (who failed to draft clearly stated and clearly applicable legislation). Unfortunately, the ideal is, like most ideals, unrealistic. Relevant provisions often cannot be found, so where is the flexibility needed to handle those situations?

One way to provide flexibility in civil law is to recognize that deducing a solution from a necessarily general legislative provision may lead judges to different conclusions. That is, different judges will often employ different reasoning, which will lead to different results (Sereni, 1956). As long as the judge shows how the decision proceeds logically from the rule stated by the legislature, the solution should be regarded as acceptable. Similarly, the civil tradition allows for changes in meaning over time. Earlier civil courts may have correctly ruled in their time, but subsequent modification in the meanings attached to words in the written law allows and requires contemporary courts to arrive at different findings with reasoning as sound as that of their predecessors.

The civil legal tradition gains flexibility by giving judges authority to characterize issues as either problems of law or problems of fact. Particularization in common law and the characterization of judicial precedents as law have resulted in more law in common law countries than in civil law countries (Sereni, 1956). The result is the designation of many issues as points of "law" instead of simply issues of "fact." This is an important distinction because a legal issue, once recognized as such, must be followed. A factual issue is presented at face value and without authoritative connotation.

While common law requires many issues to be considered questions of law, civil law provides courts with the discretion to view those same issues as questions of fact. Consider, for example, issues about evidence and testimony. A civil court judge may find it strange to keep an important piece of evidence or relevant testimony out of court, yet for that judge these are issues of fact: Did this person commit this offense? For the common law judge, the same issues may be legal ones: Was this evidence or testimony gathered in the appropriate (legal) manner? Obviously, providing the civil court judge discretion to decide whether an issue is a factual or legal question gives that tradition a degree of flexibility not found under common law.

FLEXIBILITY IN ISLAMIC LAW   Ijma provides a process by which religious scholars can ensure the continuity of law and the ability to adapt to change, and qiyas allows decisions in unique cases to be resolved with the help of analogy. As a result, Shari'a has some basic features of flexibility. In addition to ijma and qiyas, flexibility is provided in the Islamic tradition by *fatwa* and by the process of *ijtihad*.

Generally, a fatwa (literally, a "response") is a legal opinion issued by a recognized Islamic law specialist on a specific issue. Islam has no centralized hierarchy, so there is no controlling authority stipulating who can issue a valid fatwa. However, the person doing so should be an Islamic scholar or jurist who arrived at the opinion or ruling through a deep understanding of Islamic law and following the correct procedures. Persons meeting the criteria are known as ulama (foqaha in the Shi'a tradition) and some who are given the specialist task of issuing fatwas have the title of mufti (ayatollah in the Shi'a tradition).

Many non-Muslims know the word "fatwa," but probably as a result of media coverage reporting on fatwas that are sensational (e.g., the banning of yoga), noteworthy (e.g., the destruction of Buddhist statues), or that reflect a cultural clash with Western values (e.g., prohibiting women from driving cars). But for Muslims, fatwas are mostly a positive and integral component of Islamic law that provides guidance on what is permitted and what is forbidden. Fatwas are also important for Muslims living in non-Muslim countries since they can provide guidance through the challenge of adhering to two sets of laws: those of Islam and the enacted national laws—with the recognition that the country's national laws take precedence (Black, Esmaeili, & Hosen, 2013).

A fatwa is issued in reply to a question asked by a person (e.g., individual, judge, government official) or an entity (e.g., corporation, institution, organization). Traditionally, fatwas are nonbinding with compliance being voluntary, although in a few countries they can be given legal force when issued by state jurists (e.g., in Saudi Arabia) or by sanctioning the enforcement of those that are published in an official journal (e.g., in Malaysia).

Fatwas provide flexibility in Islamic law in terms of contemporary social and economic practices. Since many modern topics are not addressed in the Qur'an, fatwas provide a means by which those problems can be addressed. For example, in 1727 a fatwa authorized the printing of nonreligious books and in 1845 a fatwa declared vaccination to be legitimate (Black et al., 2013). Importantly, fatwas not only provide a mechanism for growth and change in Islamic law, the fatwas themselves are adaptable and can be revised when they are deemed no longer suitable to the situation to be contrary to the Qur'an, the Sunna, or consensus (ijma). Thus, fatwa makes Islamic law adaptable to social change (Black et al., 2013; Kamali, 2008).

Kamali (2008, p. 25) explains that since divine revelation came to an end with the demise of the Prophet, ijtihad is the primary mechanism for interpreting the divine message and relating it to changing conditions. Essentially, decisions on facts and disputes are to be based first on the Qur'an and Sunna, but if the answer cannot be found in either, a Muslim scholar may use independent reasoning (ijtihad) to determine the solution.

During the first several centuries of its growth, Islamic law allowed jurists to interpret independently the Qur'an and Sunna when deliberating a case. This process provided significant flexibility, because each judge could arrive at a decision based on his understanding of the law as it related to the current case. By the tenth century, it was determined that sufficient opinions had been written regarding interpretation of the Qur'an and Sunna. The door of ijtihad was closed, and future generations of jurists were denied the right of independent inquiry. Instead, jurists had to follow the doctrine of their predecessors.

Since the late nineteenth century, a new ijtihad is considered by some to be relevant (e.g., see Black et al., 2013, p. 19). According to the new ijtihad, Muslim scholars believe that regarding legal matters (but not devotional), the Prophet Muhammad urged Muslims to follow his principles in establishing their own system of rules within the general spirit of Islam. Similarly, there are arguments that for ijtihad to be viable today, it must be a collective endeavor—although ijtihad by individual scholars would not be discontinued (Black et al., 2013; Kamali, 2008). Collective ijtihad allows modern, contemporary, and complex problems to be resolved by involving Muslim scholars from different schools of law to perform ijtihad cooperatively. Black et al. (2013, p. 20) and Kamali (2008, p. 166) view the process of ijtihad to be the most important mechanism by which the Qur'an and Sunna are related to societal change and for Islamic law reform.

FLEXIBILITY IN EASTERN ASIA LAW   As we have seen, law in the Eastern Asia tradition must be considered in both its li and fa aspects. The flexibility of li is best understood by emphasizing its preference for maintaining harmony. When confronted with misbehavior, the primary goal must be to achieve harmony and restore peace. This is best accomplished by applying wisdom and common sense rather than relying on some written rule (Bracey, 2006, p. 71). Since no two instances of misbehavior are identical, society's response to any particular misbehavior must be flexible enough to account for the peculiarities of that specific instance. This is best accomplished by handling misbehavior informally, so a reliance on informal sanctions is a key aspect of flexibility in the Eastern Asia tradition.

Even when li is put in written form and its enforcement assigned to formal institutions—that is, when fa takes precedence—flexibility is possible. As Glenn (2010, p. 328) explains, even in its written form, li can be flexibly interpreted so that harmony in society is preserved through mutual reinforcement of norms rather than fighting over their content. It is, in other words, more important to maintain harmony than to get hung up on the literal meaning of the law. A flexible understanding of the law isn't just allowed, it is expected.

Another source of flexibility in Eastern Asia laws—especially in China—is the lack of specificity in those laws. Outside pressures, such as Party–state goals, sometimes require that formal rules yield to concerns for stability. Even as China moves toward more professionalism and formality in its criminal justice system, there are concerns among Party officials that professionalism and formality is not gained at the expense of flexibility (Liebman, 2009, p. 30).

Summary

Four legal traditions are identifiable today. Although there is considerable variety of legal systems within each tradition, it is possible to distinguish a common heritage making up each legal family. The common legal tradition is familiar to American students because it developed in England and had significant impact on the legal system of the United States. Important aspects of its development include feudal practices, the importance of custom, and the concept of equity. The civil legal tradition is the oldest of the four contemporary families; its roots extend back to Roman law and canon law as it emphasizes codification. The Islamic legal tradition, the Shari'a, has a divine source in the Qur'an and the Sunna, as well as from secondary sources: the doctrine of consensus (ijma) and reasoning by analogy (qiyas). However, application of Shari'a is influenced by the tradition of schools of law in Islam and that results in variation in how Islamic law is applied around the world. Among the hybrid traditions, the Eastern Asia legal tradition provides an interesting example since it draws on the principles of Confucianism but adds intriguing aspects of collectivism, context, and informalism.

Attempts to compare the four traditions are most appropriately handled by considering certain cultural, substantive, and procedural components. In that manner, we can identify how law is emphasized as either public or private, what the relationship is between the judiciary and other organs of government, what the primary source of law is, and how each tradition responds to the problem of flexibility. With this basic understanding of four categories of legal traditions, you are ready to tackle more specific topics concerning particular countries.

Discussion Questions

- In the chapter discussion of "custom," it is noted that both precedent and stare decisis became essential features of the common law tradition because of custom. Explain what that means.
- Although religion played a key role in the development of both the civil and Islamic legal traditions, only the Islamic tradition continues to rely heavily on religion. Suggest a scenario in which canon law came to have a continued and deciding role in how the civil legal tradition developed. What might be some key features of a contemporary civil legal tradition that relies heavily on canon law?
- Use information about the schools of law in Islam to explain how persons claiming to be devout Muslims can have very different views on such issues as terrorism.

References

Abel, R. L. (1982). Introduction. In R. L. Abel (Ed.), *The politics of informal justice*, Vol. 1: *The American experience* (pp. 1–13). New York, NY: Academic Press.

BBC. (2009, August 18). Sunni and Shi'a Religions. Retrieved from http://www.bbc.co.uk/religion/religions/islam/subdivisions/sunnishia_1.shtml

Black, A., Esmaeili, H., & Hosen, N. (2013). *Modern perspectives on Islamic law*. Northampton, MA: Edward Elgar.

Bracey, D. H. (2006). *Exploring law and culture*. Long Grove, IL: Waveland Press.

Buckley, C. (2014, October 11). Leader taps into Chinese classics in seeking to cement power. *The New York Times*. Retrieved from http://www.nytimes.com

Center for Muslim–Jewish Engagement. (n.d.). Partial translation of Sunan Abu-Dawud. Religious texts. Retrieved from http://www.usc.edu/org/cmje/religious-texts/hadith/abudawud/

Coulson, N. J. (1969). *Conflicts and tensions in Islamic jurisprudence*. Chicago, IL: University of Chicago Press.

Dammer, H. R., & Albanese, J. S. (2014). *Comparative criminal justice systems* (5th ed.). Belmont, CA: Wadsworth Cengage Learning.

David, R., & Brierley, J. E. C. (1968). *Major legal systems of the world today*. London, UK: Collier-Macmillan Ltd.

Ehrmann, H. W. (1976). *Comparative legal cultures*. Englewood Cliffs, NJ: Prentice Hall.

Friedman, L. M. (1973). *A history of American law*. New York, NY: Simon & Schuster.

Glenn, H. P. (2010). *Legal traditions of the world: Sustainable diversity in law* (4th ed.). New York, NY: Oxford University Press.

Glenn, H. P. (2014). *Legal traditions of the world: Sustainable diversity in law* (5th ed.). Oxford, UK: Oxford University Press.

Human Rights Watch. (2012). Codifying repression: An assessment of Iran's new penal code. Retrieved from https://www.hrw.org/report/2012/08/28/codifying-repression/assessment-irans-new-penal-code

Ingraham, B. L. (1987). *The structure of criminal procedure: Laws and practice of France, the Soviet Union, China, and the United States*. New York, NY: Greenwood Press.

Jiang, S. (2014). Corrections in Asia: An introduction. *The Prison Journal, 94*(1), 3–6. doi:10.1177/0032885513511939

Johnson, T., & Sergie, M. A. (2014, July 25). Islam: Governing under Sharia. CFR Backgrounders. Retrieved from http://www.cfr.org/religion/islam-governing-under-sharia/p8034#1

Kamali, M. H. (2008). *Shari'ah law: An introduction*. Oxford, UK: Oneworld Publications.

Kolbert, C. F. (1979). *The digest of Roman law*. New York, NY: Viking Penguin.

Liebman, B. L. (2009). Assessing China's legal reforms. *Columbia Journal of Asian Law, 23*(1), 17–33.

Lipka, M. (2014, June 18). The Sunni–Shia divide: Where they live, what they believe and how they view each other. Pew Research Center. Retrieved from http://www.pewresearch.org/fact-tank/2014/06/18/the-sunni-shia-divide-where-they-live-what-they-believe-and-how-they-view-each-other/

Lipka, M. (2015, December 7). Muslims and Islam: Key findings in the U.S. and around the world. Pew Research Center. Retrieved from http://www.pewresearch.org/fact-tank/2015/12/07/muslims-and-islam-key-findings-in-the-u-s-and-around-the-world/

Lippman, M. R., McConville, S., & Yerushalmi, M. (1988). *Islamic criminal law and procedure: An introduction*. New York, NY: Praeger.

Liu, J., & Palermo, G. B. (2009). Restorative justice and Chinese traditional legal culture in the context of contemporary Chinese criminal justice reform. *Asia Pacific Journal of Police & Criminal Justice, 7*(1), 49–68. Retrieved from http://www.aaps.or.kr/Issues/2009volum7_number1_/3.pdf

Merryman, J. H. (1985). *The civil law tradition* (2nd ed.). Stanford, CA: Stanford University Press.

Nigerian woman facing death seeks leniency. (2003, August 28). *The New York Times*. Retrieved from www.nytimes.com

Nisbett, R. E., & Masuda, T. (2003). Culture and point of view. *Proceedings of the National Academy of Sciences, 100*(19), 11163–11170. Retrieved from http://www.pnas.org/content/100/19/11163

Otto, J. M. (2010). *Sharia incorporated: A comparative overview of the legal systems of twelve Muslim countries in past and present*. Leiden, The Netherlands: Leiden University Press.

Partlett, W., & Ip, E. C. (2016). Is socialist law really dead? *Journal of International Law & Politics, 48*(2), 463–511.

Perry, S. W. (2013). Tribal crime data collection activities, 2013 (NCJ 242584). Retrieved from http://www.bjs.gov/index.cfm?ty=pbdetail&iid=4758

Pew Research Center. (2015). The future of world religions: Population growth projections, 2010–2050. Demographic study. Retrieved from http://www.pewforum.org/2015/04/02/religious-projections-2010-2050/

Plucknett, T. F. T. (1956). *A concise history of the common law*. Boston, MA: Little Brown and Company.

Postema, G. J. (1986). *Bentham and the common law tradition*. Oxford, UK: Clarendon Press.

Rhode, D. (2005, March 13). The world: A world of ways to say "Islamic law". *The New York Times*. Retrieved from http://www.nytimes.com

Rosen, L. (1989). *The anthropology of justice: Law as culture in Islamic society*. Cambridge, UK: Cambridge University Press.

Ruiz, M., Jr. (1974). *Mexican American legal heritage in the Southwest* (2nd ed.). Los Angeles, CA: Author.

Schirrmacher, C. (1994). Islamic jurisprudence and its sources. Retrieved from http://web.archive.org/web/20060721124621/http://www.ishr.org/activities/campaigns/stoning/background.htm

Schwartz, B. (1956). The code and public law. In B. Schwartz (Ed.), *The Code Napoleon and the common-law world* (pp. 247–266). Westport, CT: Greenwood Press.

Sengupta, S. (2003, September 26). Facing death for adultery, Nigerian woman is acquitted. *The New York Times*. Retrieved from www.nytimes.com

Sereni, A. P. (1956). The code and the case law. In B. Schwartz (Ed.), *The Code Napoleon and the common-law world* (pp. 55–79). Westport, CT: Greenwood Press.

Shaukat, K. (2014, December 16). Chronology of early scholars of Islam. Moonsighting Committee Worldwide. Retrieved from http://moonsighting.com/chronology.html

Souryal, S. S. (2004). *Islam, Islamic law, and the turn to violence.* Huntsville, TX: Office of International Criminal Justice.

Tribal Court Clearinghouse, Tribal Law and Policy Institute. (2016). Tribal courts. Retrieved from http://www.tribal-institute.org/lists/justice.htm

Tucker, S. G. (1803). Blackstone's commentaries on the laws of England: Book I, Section III. Retrieved from http://www.constitution.org/tb/tb-0000.htm

Ullman, W. (1975). *Law and politics in the Middle Ages.* Ithaca, NY: Cornell University Press.

United Nations Statistics Division. (2013, October 31). Composition of macro geographical (continental) regions, geographical sub-regions, and selected economic and other groupings. Retrieved from http://unstats.un.org/unsd/methods/m49/m49regin.htm

University of Cumbria. (n.d.). Sunni tradition: Schools. PHILTAR overview of world religions (Islam). Retrieved from http://www.philtar.ac.uk/encyclopedia/islam/sunni/sunni.html

Vogler, R. (2005). *A world view of criminal justice.* Burlington, VT: Ashgate.

Watson, A. (1970). *The law of the ancient Romans.* Dallas, TX: Southern Methodist University Press.

Wigmore, J. H. (1928). *A panorama of the world's legal systems* (Vol. 1). Saint Paul, MN: West.

Wigmore, J. H. (1936). *A panorama of the world's legal systems* (Vol. library edition). Washington, DC: Washington Law Book Company.

5

Substantive Law and Procedural Law in the Four Legal Traditions

LEARNING OBJECTIVES

After studying this chapter, you will be able to:

1. List and describe the general characteristics and major principles of substantive criminal law.

2. Summarize and compare substantive criminal law as it is found in each of the four legal traditions.

3. Compare and contrast the adversarial and inquisitorial processes as they operate in the procedural criminal law of the common and civil legal traditions.

4. Describe procedural criminal law in the Islamic and Eastern Asia legal traditions.

5. Explain the concept and three models of judicial review.

COUNTRIES IN FOCUS

Argentina	Japan
Austria	Mexico
Brazil	Nigeria
China	Portugal
England	Scotland
France	United States
Germany	Venezuela
Italy	

In Saudi Arabia, criminal responsibility is linked to the onset of puberty. In Argentina, the police are not allowed to interrogate suspects. The United States is unique in having pretrial motions. Laypersons are used in German trials, but they make up part of the judicial bench rather than sitting as a jury. In South Africa, a judge's decision to impose a prison sentence of more than 3 months is forwarded on automatic appeal if that magistrate has less than 7 years of experience on the bench.

Although such "factoids" may not come up in a trivia contest, they do show some of the variety existing in substantive and procedural law around the world. This chapter takes a closer look at that variety by applying concepts introduced in Chapter 3 to examples of particular countries.

SUBSTANTIVE CRIMINAL LAW

You will recall that substantive law deals with defining criminal behavior. With its general characteristics, substantive law provides citizens with information about what behavior is required or prohibited (specificity) and explains what may happen to people who misbehave (penal sanction). Further, substantive law assures citizens that the law comes from a legitimate authority (politicality) and will be applied by that authority in an unbiased manner (uniformity).

These four general characteristics of substantive criminal law—specificity, penal sanction, politicality, and uniformity—reflect a Western bias. Similarly, the seven major principles of criminal law—mens rea, actus reus, concurrence, harm, causation, punishment, and legality—are criteria linked to Western law. There is a danger in applying these general characteristics and major principles to non-Western systems if we insist that they are in any way superior to other legal standards. However, if they serve merely as a point of contrast, the characteristics and principles can provide a useful comparative technique. Therefore, as an aid to comparison, we use traditionally Western aspects of substantive criminal law to describe law in other legal traditions.

General Characteristics and Major Principles

Every legal system relies on some version of politicality to create and define criminal behavior. The authority may take forms such as a tribal chief, a monarch, a supernatural force, a court official, or an elected body of citizen representatives. Whatever its form, it has the authority (either granted by the citizens or taken by force) to make laws. Similarly, every legal system provides some type of punishment, or penal sanction, to people who misbehave. Sanctions may range from a required apology to execution of the offender, but in each instance the offenders should understand that they have misbehaved and must suffer the consequences.

Providing citizens with specific information (specificity) about their obligations is difficult but remains a universal ideal. American vagrancy laws and laws related to European football hooliganism are examples of laws lacking specificity. Although the intent of laws without specificity is not to trick the citizen, sometimes that is the result. Political authorities agree that specificity is a desirable attribute of criminal law. It is also, however, difficult to achieve.

Citizens in virtually all countries are aware of laws being applied with prejudice. Some citizens seem above the law, whereas others have the law applied to them with obvious vigor. Such absence of uniformity does not mean that citizens and authorities see uniformity as an undesirable characteristic of law; rather, uniformity is an ideal we are striving for (or at least want to give the appearance of doing so) despite falling short at times.

Extensive discussion of how different legal traditions or systems view the four general characteristics of substantive law is unnecessary because they are widely accepted as appropriate ideals. What country would not describe its laws as demonstrating, or striving for, politicality, specificity, uniformity, and penal sanction? We must find more debatable and identifiable aspects of criminal law if we wish to distinguish among legal traditions or systems.

The major principles of substantive law also present ideals, but the seven internal requirements have the advantage of being more often applied than their four philosophical cousins of general characteristics. Mens rea, actus reus, concurrence, harm, causation, punishment, and legality are used to identify a particular behavior as criminal. As such, they can provide a mechanism to compare legal systems on points such as the requirements each uses to show criminality. We provide a brief example of how a few countries deal with the idea of criminal responsibility, because that concept incorporates several of the principles.

Germany's criminal code assigns criminal responsibility to persons acting intentionally (mens rea and actus reus) to violate a criminal statute, but Germans do not assign criminal capacity to anyone under age 14. Further, if the act is the result of a mistake of fact or necessity, the actor is not criminally responsible. Similarly, persons acting in self-defense do not act unlawfully (Federal Republic of Germany, 1971). Those modifications of criminal responsibility by defenses and justifications should look familiar to Americans.

In a comparable manner, the Italian Penal Code says that no one may be punished for an offense unless at the time it was committed the actor was responsible. For the Italians, one is "responsible if he has the capacity to understand and to will" (*The Italian penal code*, 1978). As do the Germans, the Italians require a person to be age 14 before criminal responsibility is attributed. The Italians further specify that offenders from ages 14 through 17 shall be responsible but subject to reduced punishment if the person had capacity to understand and to will. Other justifications and excuses for criminal responsibility in Italy include accidents, physical compulsion (similar to duress in American jurisdictions), self-defense, and necessity.

Islamic law requires the presence of both criminal conduct and criminal intent to show criminal responsibility. As part of criminal conduct, Muslim jurists say that criminal responsibility also demands causation. However, recall the example in Chapter 3 in which Bob, having been poisoned by John—who had intended to kill Bob—dies from the poison's antidote rather than from the poison. Because Bob's death was not the direct cause of the poison administered by John, John cannot legally be charged with murder. Had the Bob and John story occurred in an Islamic law jurisdiction, the outcome could be quite different. Sanad (1991, p. 86) points out that under Islamic law, a person is considered criminally responsible as long as any intervening factors are insufficient to have brought about the result by themselves and do not break the causal relationship between result and the act or omission—which remains the principal cause. Criminal intent, as Islam's second requirement for criminal responsibility, is taken to mean an evil state of mind (i.e., mens rea). Muslim scholars distinguish between general and specific criminal intent by viewing the former as inferred whenever someone voluntarily participates in criminal conduct, but general intent is not always sufficient to show criminal responsibility. There are times when specific intent must be proved. In this sense, specific intent seems to refer to the need to prove that the person intended to commit the particular act under question and did so without justification or excuse. Because Islamic law will withhold criminal responsibility in such circumstances as coercion and necessity, it is possible for a person to have committed an illegal act with general intent (e.g., he knowingly hit another person) but without specific intent (e.g., he did so only to protect himself from the assailant).

Some of the Islamic reasons for withholding responsibility add an interesting twist to similar ones found in other countries. For example, infancy is a defense to crime under Islamic law, but some Muslim schools believe that criminal capacity increases with age. As a result, criminal capacity is not possible until age 7 is reached because younger children are not viewed as able to reason. Children between age 7 and the onset of puberty have partial criminal capacity and therefore have some criminal responsibility—though not for hudud or qisas crimes (discussed later in this chapter). After the onset of puberty, a person can be held fully criminally responsible as long as he or she is of sound mind. Because puberty plays such an important role in assigning responsibility, we might expect it to be well defined by Muslim jurists. However, Sanad (1991) reports considerable disagreement. Some scholars say that responsibility is determined by age (either 11 or 12, depending on the scholar), whereas others say it varies in males and females, and still others argue that some signs of puberty should be used in making the judgment.

This brief review of how some countries view criminal responsibility reminds us that the similarity among countries can be just as interesting as the differences. As a final example, before moving to a discussion of substantive law in each legal tradition, we look at how Germany (see Map A.10), France (see Map A.10), and Nigeria (see Map A.1)

WEB PROJECT

Criminal Responsibility in Iran

Go to http://www.iranhrdc.org/english/ and enter in the search box: penal code. From the search results, find and click on "English Translation of Books I & II of the New Islamic Penal Code." From that page, scroll down and click on "Part Four—Conditions and Obstacles of Criminal Responsibility." Read through the various conditions (Articles 140–145) and obstacles of criminal responsibility (Articles 146–159). Write a few paragraphs in which you provide examples of criminal responsibility in Iran and provide your reaction to any similarities and differences that you find for Iran in comparison with your own state/province/country.

handle the insanity defense. As Chapter 3 pointed out, the insanity defense has generated considerable debate in the United States as to what the most appropriate phrasing should be. Do you suppose other countries have come up with better wording?

Section 20 of Germany's criminal code (Federal Republic of Germany, 1971) excuses those suffering from a mental disorder as follows:

> Any person who at the time of the commission of the offense is incapable of appreciating the unlawfulness of their actions or of acting in accordance with any such appreciation due to a pathological mental disorder, a profound consciousness disorder, debility or any other serious mental abnormality, shall be deemed to act without guilt.

The German code continues, in Section 21, to also excuse persons of "diminished capacity." Here, if the perpetrator's ability either to understand the wrongfulness of his conduct or to act in accordance with that understanding is substantially diminished (rather than "absent" as in Section 20), he is still criminally responsible but subject to a reduced penalty.

The French penal code (French Republic, 1995) specifies that

> A person is not criminally liable who, when the act was committed, was suffering from a psychological or neuropsychological disorder which destroyed his discernment or his ability to control his actions. (Article 122-1)

Similar to the Germans, the French go on to provide for those having diminished capacity by noting that they are still subject to punishment but their condition will be considered by the court when deciding the penalty (Article 122-2).

Nigeria's penal code (Federal Republic of Nigeria, 1916) holds that

> A person is not criminally responsible for an act or omission if at the time of doing the act or making the omission he is in such a state of mental disease or natural mental infirmity as to deprive him of capacity to understand what he is doing, or of capacity to control his actions, or of capacity to know that he ought not to do the act or make the omission. (Chapter 5, Section 28)

An interesting addition to that statement explains that a person who is affected by delusions regarding some specific matter—but is not otherwise entitled to the benefit of the first part of Section 28—is criminally responsible only to the extent that he or she would be had the real state of things been as he or she was deluded to believe they were. That seems to suggest, for example, that a person under a delusion that his or her life was in danger (when in fact it was not) may not be criminally responsible (i.e., acted in self-defense) even though the person did not otherwise qualify as insane.

The variety expressed in these codes emphasizes the difficulty of attempts to be fair when assigning criminal responsibility. Such issues in the area of substantive criminal law present worldwide problems. Although specific examples like those just given are useful in showing both similarity and difference, it is necessary to move to a more general discussion as we consider substantive law in the four legal traditions.

Substantive Law in the Common Legal Tradition

As the historical home of common law, England (see Map A.10) presents an excellent example of that tradition's substantive law. Because common law was unwritten law, there was no source to which one could turn and read a list of crimes and their punishments. Identifying what was criminal relied on earlier decisions by judges and through reference to community folkways. As a result, the earliest common law offenses, called felonies, included crimes such as murder, robbery, rape, arson, and larceny. These serious transgressions were punishable by death or mutilation and by loss of property. The judiciary could also identify other offenses, called misdemeanors, which were deemed less serious.

It seems that crimes under common law were essentially "pulled out of a hat" held by the judge. Even if the judge was a political authority applying penal sanction in a uniform manner, where was the specificity? If the judge got to decide what was criminal, how could citizens have any advance warning? The answer relies on the concept of immemorial custom. The "hat" from which a judge pulled the crimes included the norms guiding people in that community. Because everyone presumably shared these norms, everyone well knew what behavior was acceptable. Custom provided specificity.

Scotland (see Map A.10) provides a good contemporary example of substantive criminal law in the common legal tradition. Along with England, Wales, and Northern Ireland, Scotland comprises the United Kingdom. These four countries operate under a single government but have three separate legal systems. The systems of England, Wales, and Scotland have more in common with one another than they do with that of Northern Ireland, but even the Scottish system differs from that of England and Wales. At this point, our general discussion need only note that Scotland is considered a member of the common legal family. More particularly, Scottish courts continue to take an active role in judge-made substantive law.

Although most common law countries view legislation as the appropriate task for lawmakers (as discussed later), Scotland continues the common law traditions of judge-made law in addition to legislation-based law. This position may be related to the absence, until 1999, of a specifically Scottish parliament. Prior to the reestablishment of a parliament separate from that of the United Kingdom, the Scots relied on their representatives in the Parliament at Westminster to provide necessary laws. That body never showed much interest in the substantive criminal law of Scotland (Jones, 1990). As a result, the traditional flexibility that common law allows the court is embraced by the Scots as a strength of the system.

The High Court of Justiciary has a "declaratory power" that allows the court to declare behavior that it considers morally wrong to be a criminal offense—even though the behavior was not punished in the past. That power has not been explicitly used since 1838. However, in cases that are closely analogous to existing crimes, the High Court continues to create new crimes—but without citing its declaratory power as authority. The cases of *Khaliq* v. *H. M. Advocate* (1983) and *Strathern* v. *Seaforth* (1926) are typically offered as examples where the High Court invoked the power (Jones, 1990; White & Willock, 2007). The latter case, although older, provides the better example of this technique.

In the *Strathern* v. *Seaforth* case, the accused had used another person's automobile without permission. However, he had no intention of permanently depriving the owner of his property; hence, there was no intent to "steal" under existing Scottish law. Nevertheless, the High Court decided it was wrong to secretly take and use any property belonging to another. With that phraseology, the court created a new crime.

In addition to creating new crimes, the Scottish judiciary can also decide whether an old crime has simply been perpetrated in a new way. This is done in the court's role of applying common law principles to new circumstances. In common law, malicious mischief identifies acts that involve serious and willful damage to another's property. All relevant precedents before 1983 involved physical damage to the property in question. However, in *H. M. Advocate* v. *Wilson* (1983), Scotland's High Court extended the crime of malicious mischief to cover economic loss as well as property damage. The court did not intend to create a new crime; it was simply applying existing law to new circumstances (Jones, 1990).

The perseverance with which Scotland holds to the tradition of judge-made substantive law is not repeated in most other common law countries. With expanding populations and increased heterogeneity, common law countries found it increasingly difficult to rely on custom to inform citizens of their obligations. The problem was intensified in colonies, where the ancient ways of English villages provided little support for handling unique problems in the new surroundings. In America, for example, criminal law became essentially a matter of statute. By 1900, most states technically recognized the possibility of common law crime, but other states had specifically abolished the concept (Friedman, 1973). In the latter states, statutes said all crimes were listed in the penal code. If the code did not require or prohibit the behavior, it was not a crime—even if a judge believed such behavior was customarily abhorred.

YOU SHOULD KNOW!

How Can Courts Change or Make Law?

Laws in Scotland are made primarily by legislators, but also by the Scottish courts. Legislative lawmaking is deliberately and formally created, whereas lawmaking by the courts is created incidentally when judging disputes where no legislation exists (Shelter Scotland, 2016; White & Willock, 2007, p. 163). Judge-made law is accomplished through the principle of precedent wherein a specific case, dealing with specific facts, is decided on the basis of inferred rules that are believed to express timeless principles (custom). Although judge-made law does not happen very often, when it does occur it is usually at the appellate court level. Examples of situations where Scottish courts change the existing law or make new laws include decisions that (Shelter Scotland, 2016; White & Willock, 2007, pp. 297–300, 441, 445):

- *Clarify what the law says where the legislation isn't clear.* For example, what does a phrase such as "in charge of a motor vehicle" actually mean? Is a person alone in the front seat without the car keys "in charge"? How about a person in the back seat with the keys? When the legislation leaves key terms undefined, the judge must provide clarity.
- *Redefine or reformulate the law so that it has a new meaning.* For example, in 1989 a Scottish court decided that a wife has not surrendered herself to her husband's sexual demands simply by being his wife. Husband and wife were equal partners, the judges said, and he can be charged with raping her just as any other person—thus reformulating the legislative law to include spousal rape.
- *Expand or extend the law to apply to new situations.* For example, judges expanded the law of theft to include situations where property is simply retained rather than actually removed (wheel-clamping a vehicle without removing it was held to be theft).

In this manner, Scotland retains an aspect of common law wherein judges have an active role in making substantive law.

Substantive Law in the Civil Legal Tradition

It may surprise you to learn that some people, mostly in civil law countries, find the common law to be crude, unorganized, and culturally inferior to civil law. In fact, Merryman (1985) suggests that the civil law lawyer's attitude of superiority over common law lawyers has become part of the civil law tradition. As he puts it, a lawyer from a relatively undeveloped Central American country may recognize the advanced economic development and standard of living of the United States but will find comfort in thinking of our legal system as undeveloped and of common law lawyers as relatively uncultured people.

One basis for the civil lawyer's lack of appreciation for the common law concerns the substantive law. Even though common law jurisdictions have moved more toward statutory crimes and procedures, the civil law holds much more closely to the principle that every crime and every penalty must be embodied in a statute enacted by the legislature. The civil lawyer sees common law courts violating this principle every time people are convicted of common law crimes and every time judges prohibit relevant evidence and make rules regarding criminal procedure.

As we saw in Chapter 4, an early emphasis on the idea that crime existed only through statute enacted by a legitimate authority was a prime characteristic of the civil legal tradition. Add to that the belief that average citizens should be able to easily find, read, and understand the law, and you have the reasoning behind codification. The French saw this point as especially true in the areas of criminal law and procedure. In fact, a criminal code was the first object of codification in revolutionary France.

Just as England is home to common law, France can argue for a similar heritage regarding civil law. France, like most civil law countries, has divided its various laws into public law and private law. The criminal laws are in the public law category, and, as expected in a civil law system, they are the result of specific legislation resulting in a written document. The two primary documents are the *Code of Criminal Procedure* and the *Penal Code*. The former specifies how to investigate a case and how to try a person charged with a criminal offense. Substantive law is prescribed in the *Penal Code*, which identifies the types of offenses and their respective punishments. There are other sources of substantive law, but a written law defines all criminal offenses.

The French penal code (French Republic, 1995) has five books relevant to our discussion:

- Book I includes general provisions applicable to all offenses (e.g., stipulations regarding criminal liability and responsibility).
- Book II describes felonies and misdemeanors against the person (ranging from the broad "person" category of humanity to the very individual category of "personality") and specifies the applicable penalties.
- Book III describes felonies and misdemeanors against property (ranging from traditional larceny provisions to the newer category of money laundering) and specifies the applicable penalties.
- Book IV describes felonies and misdemeanors against the nation, state, and the public peace (e.g., treason, terrorism, and corruption) and specifies the applicable penalties.
- Book V describes other felonies and misdemeanors (e.g., public health offenses and cruelty toward animals) and specifies the applicable penalties.

Although the words misdemeanors and felonies are used in translations, criminal offenses in France are actually divided into the three categories of *crimes* (serious felonies), *délits* (misdemeanors), and *contraventions* (petty offenses). These distinctions not only refer to the seriousness of the offenses but also indicate which court will hear the case (see Chapter 7).

Such organization of crimes and jurisdiction is exactly what proponents argue is the advantage of codification over common law. The presumption is that criminal codes under civil law are clear, have no conflicting provisions, and are without gaps. With those features, citizens can know their rights and obligations and judges can simply apply the appropriate provision of the code as cases come before the court. One result of this approach is an extremely comprehensive code book that tries to anticipate all possible actions to prohibit. Another approach is to develop codes that express general principles to guide judges when they try cases.

Common law jurisdictions have increasingly relied on statutes (i.e., codes) to express substantive law. As a result, there are fewer differences today between the ways common and civil law countries define crime and prescribe punishment. However, some illustrations may still prove instructive. Consider, for example, how the State of Colorado and the countries of Germany and France define the crime of theft.

As an example of a common law jurisdiction, the State of Colorado (2015) provides a standard definition of theft:

> (1) A person commits theft when he knowingly obtains or exercises control over anything of value of another without authorization, or by threat or deception, and:
>
> (a) Intends to deprive the other person permanently of the use or benefit of the thing of value; or
>
> (b) Knowingly uses, conceals, or abandons the thing of value in such manner as to deprive the other person permanently of its use or benefit; or
>
> (c) Uses, conceals, or abandons the thing of value intending that such use, concealment, or abandonment will deprive the other person permanently of its use and benefit; or
>
> (d) Demands any consideration to which he is not legally entitled as a condition of restoring the thing of value to the other person.
>
> (1.5) For the purposes of this section, a thing of value is that of "another" if anyone other than the defendant has a possessory or proprietary interest therein.

The statute then specifies theft as either a misdemeanor or a felony (hence subject to the appropriate punishment) depending on the value of the thing involved.

It seems unlikely that theft codes under a civil legal tradition could be more complete or precise than they are in Colorado. In fact, as noted earlier, codification either can be very comprehensive or can rely on general principles. Although Colorado legislators seem to prefer a code that tries to anticipate most contingencies, some countries of the civil legal tradition are more comfortable with providing guiding standards rather than specifics. As a result, their codes are comparatively short.

The German criminal code (Federal Republic of Germany, 1971, §242) has two subsections:

> 1. Whosoever takes chattels belonging to another away from another with the intention of unlawfully appropriating them for himself or a third person shall be liable to imprisonment of not more than five years or a fine.
> 2. The attempt shall be punishable.

Two other sections of the German code define the related crimes of especially serious cases of theft, armed theft, and gang theft, but in each instance the code explains what constitutes *serious*, *armed*, and *gang* rather than modifying or elaborating the term *theft*.

The French are even more succinct:

> Article 311-1: Theft is the fraudulent appropriation of a thing belonging to another person. (French Republic, 1995)

Both the German and French codes are relatively concise. In both examples, it is apparent that these countries of the civil legal tradition do not see the goal of codes to be that of providing specific solutions to particular problems. Instead, codes are meant to supply general principles from which logical deduction provides a resolution in each case. Therefore, as described in Chapter 4, civil judges need only identify the applicable code principle to decide a particular case. The principle expressed regarding theft in Germany and France seems to be the idea that it is illegal to take something that doesn't belong to you. When a theft case is brought to court, German and French judges are expected to use logical deduction to determine whether the circumstances of the case show that the defendant did indeed take something that didn't belong to him or her.

Interestingly, it is the code (statute) from the common legal tradition that provides greater detail and specificity. Are Colorado legislators trying to limit judicial discretion by providing such detail that the law is not open to interpretation by the judge? More likely, Colorado is simply following the common law concept of judicial precedent and, in doing so, must provide more elaboration to incorporate the various case laws relating to theft. Such issues as these are intriguing but lie outside the scope of our present discussion. Instead, the statute and codes relating to theft merely provide examples of substantive law in both the common and civil legal traditions. With that background, we are ready to look at substantive law in the Islamic and Eastern Asia traditions.

Substantive Law in the Islamic Legal Tradition

Substantive law in the Shari'a identifies three categories of crime: hudud (plural of *hadd*), qisas, and tazir. The first category, hudud, is considered the most serious because hudud are specifically mentioned in the Qur'an and Sunna and are considered offenses against God. Qisas crimes are also serious but because of their harm to the individual rather than to God. The tazir category includes offenses not fitting into the hudud or qisas categories. Because the crime categories are important for understanding Islamic law, they are considered more closely.

HUDUD CRIMES   There is disagreement among religious scholars and schools of law as to the exact number of hudud offenses. Schacht (1964) finds five (adultery, false accusation of adultery, using alcohol, theft, and highway robbery), whereas Lippman, McConville, and Yerushalmi (1988), Sanad (1991), and Souryal (2004) suggest seven (adultery, false accusation of adultery, using alcohol, theft, highway robbery, apostasy, and rebellion).

El-Awa (1982), Hakeem (2003), and Kamali (2008) argue that there are but four hudud. They make the argument on the understanding that to be a hadd, not only must an offense be mentioned in the Qur'an and hadith (a point upon which all agree), but those sources must also provide a fixed penalty. The four offenses meeting that criterion are adultery, false accusation of adultery, theft, and highway robbery. The other three, using alcohol, apostasy, and rebellion, do not have a strictly defined punishment in the Qur'an and hadith.

The argument for only four hudud seems especially convincing, but for our purposes we briefly identify six in order to err on the side of more completeness (Black, Esmaeili, & Hosen, 2013; Hakeem, 2003; Kamali, 2008):

- **Adultery (*zina*):** Adultery, taken to include fornication, is forbidden under Islamic law because it could disrupt the social fabric of the community if left unchecked. Offspring may not know who their natural parents are and family units may disintegrate. Punishment (depending on the school of law followed) must be stoning to death (the same punishment for adultery as prescribed in the Torah), banishment, or flogging.

- **Unsupported accusation of adultery (*qadhf*):** Also referred to as defamation or slander, this hadd is restricted to a false (or at least unsupported) accusation that another has committed adultery. A person guilty of qadhf is punished with 80 lashes.
- **Use of intoxicants (*shurb al-khamr*):** This hadd is typically listed as "using alcohol," but Souryal's (2004) explanation and Asad's (2003) translation of the Qur'an make excellent arguments for using the broader term intoxicant when reading Surah 5:91 in the Qur'an. Lippman et al. (1988) note that the Hanafi school (see Chapter 4) allows the consumption of alcohol until inebriation. That is based on an understanding of the hadd as punishing for being drunk—not for drinking. The punishment (whipping) for this hadd is found in the hadith but not the Qur'an—supporting the argument of those who exclude it from among the hudud.
- **Theft (*sariqa*):** The Qur'an (Surah 5:38) says: "Now as for the man who steals and the woman who steals, cut off the hand of either of them in requital for what they have wrought, as a deterrent ordained by God." Muslim jurists agree that "theft" refers to taking another's property by stealth, but there is no agreement as to what value the property must have, what actually counts as custody, and how the hand is to be cut off. More on this follows.
- **Highway robbery (*hiraba*):** This hadd is distinguished from (and more serious than) theft because it is committed with force (e.g., armed robbery or murder during robbery). Possible punishments for hiraba (depending on the school) include execution by the sword, crucifixion, cross-amputation (cutting off the hand and foot on opposite sides), or banishment.
- **Apostasy (*ridda*):** Apostasy is the rejection or abandonment of Islam by one who once embraced it or was born to Muslim parents. It is forbidden as an example of bearing false witness to God and mentioned in many Qur'anic verses with reference to the awful doom in the hereafter awaiting those committing this crime. Although there is no specific punishment in the Qur'an (again, supporting the reasoning for omitting this crime from the hudud), the Sunna provides the earthly punishment of death.

Because hudud crimes are decreed by Allah, they are absolute, universal, and cannot be subjected to interpretation by judges or government officials (Souryal, Potts, & Alobied, 1994). In addition, the punishment for a hadd must be harsh and swift because such an act violates the sanctity of God and threatens the integrity of society. The harshness of Islamic punishment is often noted by Westerners, who highlight punishments of beheading, stoning, whipping, and amputation. Too often ignored by those same Westerners is an equally important aspect of Shari'a—rigorous rules of evidence. We use the crime of theft to understand better the hudud crimes and their punishments.

As noted earlier, the Qur'an (Surah 5:38) requires that men or women who steal must have their hands cut off. This harsh penalty reflects the belief that theft not only deprives the owner of property but also creates fear, distrust, and apprehension in the community. For a society to be truly Islamic, all men and women have the right to protection of their spiritual, intellectual, and physical needs. This right is attached to a corresponding duty that requires each person to respect the person and property of everyone else or be punished for failing to show such respect (Lippman et al., 1988).

Importantly, the Shari'a realizes that such a harsh penalty as amputation must be applied only when there is no doubt about the nature of the act and about the offender's guilt. The first point, the nature of the act, is important because the act is theft for hadd purposes only when (1) the item was taken by stealth, (2) it had some value, and (3) it was taken from a secure location. Regarding the "taking by stealth," Black et al. (2013) explain that property taken by force in front of other people does not qualify for amputation since the owner could have asked for help to stop the thief. Various schools of

Islamic thought agree that stolen property must have value—both in a financial sense and in importance. The item's monetary value must exceed a certain limit, but its importance provides the more interesting criterion (Çiğdem, 2007; Souryal, 2004). Items not worth guarding—that is, without value—include dry wood, hay, game, fish, and other things that are found in great quantity in the land. Similarly, there is no amputation for stealing items such as milk and fruit, which quickly spoil, or for theft of prohibited items (e.g., alcohol) because the offender need only claim that his intent was to destroy the harmful item (Siddiqi, 1985).

The requirement that the item of value be taken from a secure location in a clandestine manner takes us to the second point that must be addressed before the hadd penalty is applied: proof of the offender's guilt. This is where the rules of evidence serve to control the inappropriate application of the penalty. The victim has the responsibility to show that a hadd offense has occurred. The hadd of theft cannot be established, and therefore the amputation punishment cannot be imposed, unless the victim is shown to have exercised reasonable care in safekeeping the property. Because the judge, using ethical reasoning, determines whether the stolen property had been kept in a safe place, it is not surprising that interesting differences arise. Çiğdem (2007), for example, explains that in the Hanafi school of thought, drilling a hole in the wall of a house in order to take out a valuable item does not mean that the item has been taken from a secure place, so it is not a hadd theft. However, the same act is considered a hadd offense in the Shafi'i and Hanbali schools. In addition to the victim showing that the theft qualified as a hadd offense, the rules of evidence require that the theft be proven either by the testimony of two qualified witnesses or by the confession (twice) of the thief (Black et al., 2013). Clearly, harsh penalties for hadd offenses are handed down in those countries using Shari'a criminal law, but just as clearly those punishments are given only when very strict rules of evidence have been met.

QISAS CRIMES Offenses understood in Western penal codes as "crimes against the person" are examples of qisas crimes (Souryal, 2004). More specifically, they include murder (intentional and unintentional killing) and assault (intentional and unintentional bodily injury). Qisas, which is translated as "the equivalent" or "equitable retribution," is the infliction upon the offender of a harm equivalent to what the offender inflicted upon the victim. Qisas crimes are, therefore, offenses requiring equivalent retaliation by the victim or the victim's family.

Some observers may think that Islamic law has less appreciation for the seriousness of murder (a qisas crime) than for theft or drinking alcohol, which are among the higher-category hudud offenses. That would be an inaccurate assumption because when a murder has occurred, it was not God's rights that were violated (a requirement for a hadd offense) but the right of a human being. Further, through qisas offenses Shari'a law attempts to satisfy the human tendency to retaliate. In placing murder and other bodily injury crimes (but excluding crimes such as arson and even theft) in the category of offenses for which personal retaliation is appropriate (even required), the law hopes to avoid escalation of violence (Black et al., 2013; Schirrmacher, 1994; Souryal, 2004).

Retaliation for a qisas offense may be in an "eye for an eye" sense (inflicted only by someone with the competence to do so correctly—which may be a professional acting on behalf of the victim) or by financial compensation. This is because the Qur'an clearly prescribes retaliation for qisas offenses but just as clearly encourages forgiveness. The expression of that forgiveness is found in the use of *diyya*, which is defined as money paid to a harmed person or his heir in compensation for a felony committed against him (Al-Saagheer, 1994; Black et al., 2013).

When diyya can be paid (normally it is assigned to unintentional crimes such as those a Western code might call involuntary manslaughter), the amount paid and the recipient of payment are all covered by specific rules. For example, the standard during the times of the Prophet was 100 cattle, which today would be close to $7,000 (Souryal, 2004, p. 113). Payment is typically made by the offender or the offender's blood relatives to the victim or the victim's family. We return to diyya in Chapter 8's coverage of compensation.

TAZIR CRIMES   Tazir offenses are harmful acts that are not specifically mentioned in the Qur'an or Sunna—but are understood to be included among actions the Shari'a calls *transgressions*. Since they are not specifically mentioned, their punishment is unspecified and at the discretion of the government or the court. When the court has determined that the conduct is indeed a transgression as understood in Shari'a—and that the offense has been proved through legally required evidence—the judge imposes a punishment that is proportionate to the offense and is consistent with the goal of protecting the common good (Black et al., 2013; Kamali, 2008).

Tazir crimes include—but are not limited to, because new crimes can be added—such offenses as those violating proper Muslim conduct (e.g., obscenity, provocative dress, eating pork) and ones necessary for an orderly society (e.g., traffic violations, fraud, embezzlement, corruption). Importantly, the tazir category also includes acts from the hudud crimes that, for some legal reason or technicality, cannot be handled as a hadd crime. Examples might include petty theft, attempted adultery, homosexuality, and cases supported by doubtful evidence (Kamali, 2008; Souryal, 2004).

Any imposed punishment for tazir offenses should be educational, rehabilitative, and have a deterrent effect. As such, the sanctions can range from long-term imprisonment or light corporal punishment to counseling and payment of restitution (Black et al., 2013; Wiechman, Kendall, & Azarian, 1996). When deciding the appropriate punishment, judges are encouraged to be flexible and choose a punishment they believe will help the offender and deter others from committing the same crime.

Substantive Law in the Eastern Asia Legal Tradition

As noted in Chapter 4, a developmental subtradition and key feature of the Eastern Asia legal tradition is a preference for legal informalism. That informal justice works best when substantive and procedural norms are somewhat vague and flexible. North Korea, for example, has charged people simply (and broadly) with committing "hostile acts" (Rastogi, 2009). Both of our primary examples of the Eastern Asia tradition (Japan and China) reflect aspects of this ambiguity in their substantive criminal law.

THE JAPAN EXAMPLE   Japan's (see Map A.8) criminal law consists of the *Penal Code*, the *Code of Criminal Procedure*, and the *Prison Law*. Crimes and punishments are defined in the *Penal Code*, so it provides the substantive criminal law. Two parts comprise the *Penal Code*, with Part 1 covering general provisions and Part 2 dealing with crimes (Japan Ministry of Justice, 1907). One example of the law's lack of specificity is seen in the recognized defenses to crime. For example, the code notes that "An act of insanity is not punishable," and that "An act of diminished capacity shall lead to the punishment being reduced" (Article 39). No further details are provided regarding what might constitute insanity or diminished capacity. Similarly, some of the crimes seem to lack specificity in their definition. Homicide, for example, involves "a person who kills another" (Article 199). Other definitions are more specific—a person who "through assault or intimidation, forcibly commits sexual intercourse with a female of not less than thirteen years of age commits the crime of rape" (Article 177).

Notable in its absence from the definitions of crime is any formal distinction regarding levels of culpability. That is, there is no division between first- and second-degree murder or manslaughter—to use terms familiar to American readers. Nor is there even any broader separation among crime categories. Rather than identifying something equivalent to felonies and misdemeanors as done in the United States, or the French distinction among crimes, délits, and contraventions, Japan has no gradation of offenses. Instead, degrees of seriousness are made with reference to punishments. For example, the Penal Code notes that

> The principal punishments are categorized as the death penalty, imprisonment with work, imprisonment without work, fine, misdemeanor imprisonment without work and petty fine, with confiscation as a supplementary punishment. (Article 9)

The next section then explains that "The order of gravity of the principal punishments shall be according to the order in which they are provided for in the preceding Article" (Article 10). Thus, one knows that setting fire to a building used as a dwelling is a more serious offense than is doing the same act through gross negligence because the former can be punished by the death penalty or imprisonment with work for life or for a definite term of not less than 5 years, whereas the latter is punished by imprisonment without work for no more than 3 years (Articles 108 and 117-2).

But this still gives the judge considerable discretion regarding the actual penalty to impose. Presumably, this is where attention to culpability and malice occurs. For example, whereas rape is defined as using assault or intimidation to forcibly commit sexual intercourse, "quasi" rape occurs when a person commits sexual intercourse with a female "by taking advantage of a loss of consciousness or inability to resist, or by causing a loss of consciousness or inability to resist" (Article 178). Both rape and quasi rape are punishable by imprisonment with work for a definite term of not less than 3 years. Whether the crime of rape is more or less serious than the crime of quasi rape cannot be determined from the Penal Code. However, "seriousness"—or, at least the sentencing judge's perception of seriousness—may be implied from the sentences given to each offender. Possibly, the quasi rapist is sentenced to 4 years of imprisonment with work whereas the rapist is given 7 years. Impressions of each offender's evil intent may have influenced the sentence imposed.

THE CHINA EXAMPLE Japan's substantive criminal law provides some examples of vagueness, but such ambiguity is even more clearly found in China's (see Map A.7) criminal code. Consider, for example, how crime is defined in China:

> A crime refers to an act that endangers the sovereignty, territorial integrity and security of the State, splits the State, subverts the State power of the people's democratic dictatorship and overthrows the socialist system, undermines public and economic order, violates State-owned property, property collectively owned by the working people, or property privately owned by citizens, infringes on the citizens' rights of the person, their democratic or other rights, and any other act that endangers society and is subject to punishment according to law. However, if the circumstances are obviously minor and the harm done is not serious, the act shall not be considered a crime. (People's Republic of China, 1979a, Article 13)

Some of that vagueness is explained by the influence of Soviet law that often provided that crime be defined as any socially dangerous act that threatened the foundations of the Soviet structure. But the lack of specificity also expresses a preference for justice without laws (the li of Confucianism).

Under communism, the indigenous preference for laws that are somewhat vague in order to allow for flexibility in their enforcement results in Chinese criminal law that is so broad and vague regarding the conduct prohibited and punishment prescribed that critics suggest that justice without law is replaced by laws without justice (Glenn, 2014, p. 353). Increasingly, there are examples of Chinese laws with greater specificity, but by keeping the idea of criminal behavior as something that "endangers society," they are able to allow some flexibility.

Consider, for example, Article 264 of the code (People's Republic of China, 1979a):

Whoever steals a relatively large amount of public or private property, commits thefts many times, commits a burglary or carries a lethal weapon to steal or pick pockets shall be sentenced to imprisonment of not more than 3 years, criminal detention or control and/or a fine; if the amount involved is huge or there is any other serious circumstance, shall be sentenced to imprisonment of not less than 3 years but not more than 10 years and a fine; or if the amount involved is especially huge or there is any other especially serious circumstance, shall be sentenced to imprisonment of not less than 10 years or life imprisonment and a fine or forfeiture of property.

Determining whether the amount of property stolen was "relatively large," "huge," or "especially huge" certainly reflects ambiguity and allows for considerable flexibility. One result is a procedural law that includes, encourages even, informal response to criminal behavior. This is discussed later in the chapter under the heading "Procedural Law in the Eastern Asia Legal Tradition."

PROCEDURAL CRIMINAL LAW

As you can see, issues of substantive law do not vary much among the four legal traditions. Each considers similar acts to be criminal, and they all debate questions such as criminal intent and responsibility while struggling with defenses to crime. The real differences among the traditions fall in the area of criminal procedure.

Chapter 3 presented Packer's (1968) two models of procedural law: one of due process and another of crime control. Because neither model corresponds to reality nor represents an ideal, both are offered simply as techniques to understand how the legal process operates. Each model seeks to guarantee social freedom, but the crime control version does so by emphasizing efficient processing of wrongdoers whereas the due process model emphasizes restrictions on government invasion into citizens' lives.

To exemplify this point, we reconsider the topic of public law versus private law (first covered in Chapter 4) in terms of the crime control and due process models. Whereas the civil legal tradition distinguishes between private and public law, the other three traditions do not. The division between public and private law presents interesting problems when the civil legal tradition deals with criminal matters. Private law, which deals with disputes between individual citizens, has been the

WEB PROJECT
Criminal Procedure in Italy

Go to http://www.avvocatoadriani.com/index.php/en/a-brief-introduction-to-italian-criminal-procedure and read through the overview of criminal procedure in Italy (see Map A.10) as provided by avvocato (attorney) Adriani. Concentrating on "3. The preliminary investigations phase" and "5. Arrest and confinement as a provisional measure by the police," write a few paragraphs that describe some similarities and differences you find with how Italy handles these issues compared with your understanding of how they are handled in your home state, province, or country.

primary concern of civil law since Roman times. Public law under the civil legal tradition deals with relations between citizens and public officials or agencies. Its focus on public matters makes it more administrative than legal in nature. It provides a way for citizens to complain about the way social institutions and officials are acting.

Distinguishing between public and private law presents a problem when criminal law is categorized. Originally, crime was considered the concern of private law because the wronged person was expected to initiate action against the offender. When crimes came to be seen as also affecting the whole society, the public began to share an interest in what had been a solely private area. As the state (public) developed a legal personality (recall Table 4.2 in Chapter 4), criminal law came to have a public component with two aspects. First, in addition to the victim, the public at large was harmed and had the right to sanction the wrongdoer. Second, the state took from the wronged citizen the obligation to investigate, prosecute, and punish the offender. That development was not a problem under common law because the same courts handled both public and private law. However, civil law countries were presented the dilemma of leaving crimes a matter of private law or switching them to the jurisdiction of public law courts.

The dilemma was resolved by keeping crimes in the private law domain. However, that solution meant that the officials in private law courts were asked to judge the actions of government officials (e.g., police officers and prosecutors), a matter more comfortably handled by the administrative judges hearing public law complaints. This positioning of criminal law as part of public law but managed by the regular (i.e., private law) courts helps explain why civil law systems seem to emphasize the crime control model.

The French, for example, do not view public law as law in the strict sense. Instead, public law is essentially administrative law, useful to help keep society operating. The "true" law for French citizens concerns relations between individuals, for which the state simply serves as an impartial arbitrator. The public and administrative aspect of criminal law requires the state to play a more active role. French citizens allow their government a degree of discretion and even arbitrariness, because society's interest is directly involved in catching and punishing the criminal. The general attitude is that as long as officials such as police and prosecutors act in a spirit respecting the liberty and equality of citizens, it is not so important whether the law is strictly followed. The result, to return to the metaphor in Chapter 3, is an assembly line where workers are able to complete their task with minimal interference from suspicious supervisors concerned with the ways in which workers do their job.

There are many aspects of procedural law and unlimited points to use for comparing legal systems. We concentrate on just two general topics: the adjudicatory process and judicial review. In each instance, you will find examples of legal systems following what seems to be one or the other of Packer's models. Just remember that Packer presents the two models as being different without labeling one as better than the other. We should view them the same way.

WEB PROJECT

"Miranda Rights" in Other Countries

Go to www.lawprofessor.com/miranda-rights/miranda-rights-outside-of-the-us/ and read about the procedures used in other countries to inform people about their rights pertaining to arrest. Write a few paragraphs summarizing the approach taken by other countries and then explain which country's procedure you find most appropriate.

Adjudicatory Processes

The process of adjudication is typically either adversarial (also called accusatorial) or inquisitorial in nature (see Table 5.1). Both systems have the finding of truth as a fundamental aim, and each is guided by the principle that the guilty should be punished and the innocent left alone. The differences between the two are in their assumptions about the best way to find the truth.

The adversarial system is often considered the successor to private vengeance. As societies evolve, the power to initiate action first lies with the wronged person (the accuser). That power eventually extends to relatives of the "victim," then to all members of the person's group, and finally to the government responsible for the well-being of the person. In time, then, the accuser moves from being the individual to being the state (as in *State of Texas* v. *Jones*). The setting for the accusation is before an impartial official serving as referee (judge). Because the disputing parties (the state and the accused) behave in a manner similar to a contest, they are considered adversaries.

The inquisitorial process also shows societal evolution but along a different path. Here the wronged person is eliminated as private accuser and replaced with a public official. Unlike the adversarial process, the inquisitorial process does not keep the public official in the role of accuser. Instead of accusation, there is now investigation. Because the parties are not engaged in a contest, a referee is not necessary. Instead, the impartial official (judge) serves as an inquisitor actively seeking to determine what transpired.

In broad terms, the common legal tradition uses the adversarial process, whereas the civil legal tradition follows one of inquisition (although see the section "Merging Adversarial and Inquisitorial Processes" later in this chapter). The Islamic and Eastern Asia legal traditions offer a unique combination of adversarial and inquisitorial processes. Because these distinctions provide one of the most common comparisons of legal systems, we should consider them in greater depth.

INQUISITORIAL PROCESS One of the first things necessary for an understanding of the inquisitorial process is to separate it from the term inquisition. The Spanish Inquisition of the late fifteenth century was notorious for its use of torture to compel cooperation in

TABLE 5.1 The Adjudicatory Process

	Adversarial Systems	**Inquisitorial Systems**
Who plays the role of the accuser?	Role of accuser moves from the individual to the state in an evolutionary continuation of private vengeance.	The state as accuser replaces the individual in a developmental substitution for private vengeance.
How is truth determined?	Truth is said to arise from competition between opposing sides, so the emphasis is on the trial phase.	Truth is said to arise from a continuing investigation, so the emphasis is on the screening process.
Where does power lie?	Power is shared by the prosecutor, defense, judge, and jury, so the judge exerts influence indirectly in the role of referee.	Power is concentrated more in the judge, so the judge exerts influence directly in the role of investigator.
What level of cooperation is expected of the defendant?	Defendant is neither expected nor required to cooperate with the investigation or court officials.	Defendant is expected, but not required, to cooperate with investigation (including court) officials.

its religious investigations. The only thing it had in common with today's inquisitorial process was the prominent role given to the judges. The judge is at the center of the fact-gathering process in the inquisitorial system, but torture is not.

The inquisitorial process dates at least to the thirteenth century, but its contemporary version is found in Napoleon's code of 1808 that, among other things, removed torture as a preliminary stage of the criminal process (Spencer, 2016). In its initial version, the inquisitorial process had a single judge investigate the case and decide guilt or innocence. With Napoleon's revision, a new judicial officer, the *juge d'instruction* (the investigating judge), questioned defendants and witnesses in private, recorded their statements in writing, and prepared a dossier that formed the basis for the case against the defendant. Then, a different judge (or, several judges in serious cases) sitting with laypeople decided guilt or innocence at a public trial (Spencer, 2016; Terrill, 2016). During the Napoleonic Wars (1803–1815), the French spread the use of the Code Napoleon to much of Continental Europe. After Napoleon was defeated, the Code continued to be in force not only in France, but also in what are today Spain, Portugal, Italy, the Netherlands, Belgium, and Poland, and influenced German, Austrian, and Swiss procedural law.

Rather than a competition between opposing sides, a trial under the inquisitorial system is more like a continuing investigation. The parties in the case must provide all relevant evidence to the court. The judges, not the attorneys for the plaintiff or defendant, then call and actively examine witnesses. In this way, the inquisitorial system assumes that truth can be—in fact, must be—discovered in an investigative procedure. Because parties on either side may have an interest in hiding the truth, the state must be involved early and continually in the investigation.

There is no civil law equivalent to the American model of plea bargaining whereby a defendant enters a guilty plea in court in exchange for a stipulated bargain. In fact, since finding the truth is an objective goal and not subject to the interests of either defense or prosecution, a plea bargain in the sense of an overt agreement between the defendant and the prosecutor as to the charges is neither theoretically possible nor practicably advisable (Rauxloh, 2011). Specifically, a plea bargain would violate the principle of legality that requires civil law prosecutors to bring charges for what the suspect is alleged to have committed, not for what he or she is willing to admit to. And, as a practical matter, the reality of day-to-day prosecutorial work does not include opportunities for negotiation between prosecutor and the defendant or defense counsel. However, and increasingly, there are examples of negotiations at various stages of the criminal process in several civil legal tradition countries that seem comparable to plea bargaining in the common legal tradition. For example, France does not have a system whereby the defendant enters a plea in court. Instead, as in most inquisitorial proceedings, the defendant's confession (about as close to a guilty plea as a French defendant comes) is technically considered as merely another piece of evidence. However, Hodgson (2005, 2015) explains that a 2004 legislation in France introduced a system of plea bargaining wherein the accused (in the presence of counsel) is offered a lower sentence by the prosecutor in exchange for an admission to the charges. The procedure only applies to cases with a maximum sentence of 5 years' imprisonment—but that covers more than half the cases handled by the criminal courts. Prosecutors may propose a prison sentence of up to 1 year or half of the maximum penalty for the charged offense. The offer, if accepted by the accused, must also be accepted by a judge in open court. The judge must either accept or reject (i.e., cannot modify) the proposed sentence. If rejected, the normal trial procedures come into play.

Although, as noted above, there is no exact parallel to plea bargaining in most European trial systems, the fiscal realities of all Western countries—even those following the civil legal tradition—dictate the use of "incentive mechanisms" that allow a case

YOU SHOULD KNOW!

Proof and Truth

In Chapter 3's discussion of the due process model, a distinction was drawn between legal guilt and factual guilt. That was a useful way to explain how the due process model (in which legal guilt is emphasized) is distinguished from the crime control model (emphasizing factual guilt). The contrast is useful in this chapter as well, because adversarial and inquisitorial proceedings have also been distinguished as emphasizing either due process and legal guilt (adversarial) or crime control and factual guilt (inquisitorial).

That distinction, which has been characterized by some as "proof" (adversarial) or "truth" (inquisitorial), highlights the greater time spent on the trial in the adversarial process compared with the time spent on investigation under inquisitorial proceedings. A concern that all procedures are followed, as government officials

take action against a citizen, requires a lengthy trial in which challenges to the government's actions are heard. If the defense can show that the defendant's due process rights were violated, it may mean that the defendant (who actually committed the crime) cannot legally (i.e., under the rules of criminal procedure) be found guilty. This situation describes a due process model of criminal justice wherein an adversarial proceeding emphasizes the government's ability to prove (i.e., requires "proof") the defendant is guilty while following required procedures (i.e., is "legally guilty"). Contrasted with that is the crime control model wherein inquisitorial proceedings require the government officials to spend considerable time investigating the crime until they are satisfied that the defendant did in fact commit the offense (i.e., "factual guilt" and "truth").

resolution without requiring a full-blown trial (Frommann, 2009; Pizzi, 1999; Rauxloh, 2011). For example, Section 153a of the German criminal procedure code assumes that public interest in prosecution can be satisfied by having the offender make a payment or perform some action that will benefit the public (Federal Republic of Germany, 1987). Under that section, misdemeanor offenders can avoid a criminal trial and a conviction by paying a sum of money to the victim, a charitable organization, or the state, or by performing some act of public service. Because the payment or action precedes conviction, the offender must consent to the "provisional termination," which seems to give this sanction a "bargained" aspect.

Although the inquisitorial process may be implemented, in slightly different ways among various countries, common features include a pretrial investigative stage wherein both condemning and exonerating evidence is gathered and a trial stage at which the gathered evidence is presented in its written form rather than orally by witnesses present in court. In addition, the trial itself has a procedurally active judge and rather passive lawyers. This situation is nearly the opposite of that in the adversarial process, which has a procedurally passive judge and rather active advocates who present evidence via the oral testimony of witnesses in open court.

ADVERSARIAL PROCESS   The adversarial process assumes that truth will arise from a free and open competition over who has the correct facts. The struggle is between the state on one side and the defendant on the other. This "sporting" or "fighting" system of justice developed from the trial by ordeal in the tenth to thirteenth centuries, wherein a battle settled disputes between parties. The victor was assumed to have "truth" on his side, so a triumphant accused was cleared of the charges whereas a defeated one was deemed guilty.

As trial by combat grew in popularity, procedures for conducting the ordeal received increased attention. The language setting forth the rules of the proceeding and the language used in that proceeding became very exacting. Procedure became so important that, some authors believe, the adversarial process became a system emphasizing procedure over substance. As a result, each side plays a game in which the players use the law (especially procedural rules and rights) to gain an advantage or act as a bargaining chip (Ingraham, 1987).

Waldron (1989) identifies two safeguards of the adversary system. First, it uses cross-examination (in place of swords) to challenge or destroy a witness's testimony. Each side has a chance to question the honesty of witnesses, search for biases, and figure out what witnesses actually know instead of what they think they know. Second, instead of power being granted to a single position, the prosecution, defense, judge, and jury share it. The prosecutor represents the state in trying to prove the defendant's guilt. The defense attorney argues the client's innocence and ensures that the accused has all the legal protection possible. The judge serves as the referee in this contest and guarantees that the players abide by the rules. This system of checks and balances differs from the inquisitorial process, which concentrates more power in the judge's position.

Importantly, just as variation exists among countries using the inquisitorial system, the adversarial process is not the same in all common legal traditions. Some of the clearest examples of such differences are the ways in which American and British defense counsels approach a jury trial. Americans who are used to hearing emotional and dramatic orations by a lawyer on behalf of the client would be quite surprised at the apparent detachment, lack of interest, and absence of aggressiveness displayed by an English solicitor or barrister.

When representing the client, English barristers do not see their function as obtaining an acquittal by using procedural rules in the hope that the prosecution will stumble. Of course, it is not fair to say that American defense attorneys see their duty as constantly erecting procedural barriers. However, one does not have to be especially cynical to believe that such action occurs in the American courtroom—and some are convinced that it occurs much more frequently than in the British courtroom (Graham, 1983).

The English barrister tends to approach a trial as something to be decided on the basis of contested facts. The jury should inflict punishment on the defendant only if the jury is sure that the prosecution's story is true. But because the barrister has an attitude of acceptance toward punishment applied to a defendant who is proved guilty, some (especially Americans) may see the barrister as detached and uncommitted to the defense of the client.

Graham (1983) speculated on the reason that English barristers do not become more aggressive during the trial. He decided that the barrister's working conditions are the main reason. Unlike the American defense counsel (especially a privately hired one working in a large law firm), barristers usually work alone. They prepare much of their own cases and appear in court with the frequency of an American public defender in a large city. Such factors make it difficult to maintain an aggressive posture with each new case. As a result, the appearance of the adversarial process looks rather different in these two common law countries. Nevertheless, the contrast between the adversarial and inquisitorial methods is still more pronounced than are any differences between the American and British versions of the adversarial process.

CONTRASTING ADVERSARIAL AND INQUISITORIAL PROCESSES Ingraham developed an intriguing and helpful model of criminal procedure that allows us to compare and contrast procedures in a variety of nations (Ingraham, 1987, p. 121). The application of his model to procedural criminal law resulted in the identification of four areas in which inquisitorial and adversarial procedures differ:

1. The inquisitorial systems emphasize the screening phase of the criminal process with the idea that a careful investigation will determine factual guilt. The adversarial systems emphasize the trial phase, in which the idea is that complex rules of evidence to produce substantive results will ensure the defendant a fair trial.
2. The adversarial systems are much more likely to restrict the involvement of the judiciary in both the investigatory and adjudicatory processes. The direct involvement of a judicial officer in inquisitorial systems contrasts with his or her more indirect involvement in adversarial systems.

3. Because the inquisitorial system assumes that all involved persons are seeking the truth, the defendant is expected (though not required) to be cooperative. That cooperation includes supplying information to investigators and answering questions at trial. The adversarial systems, on the other hand, neither expect nor require the defendant to assist investigators.

4. The role of the judge in adversarial proceedings is primarily one of referee. The attorneys develop and present their respective cases, and then a jury decides between the two versions of the facts. The court in an inquisitorial system is another investigator with the added power of being able to decide the case. The judges ask most of the questions and develop the facts while the attorneys exist more to argue the interpretation that the court should give those facts.

Ingraham believes that the main objectives of the inquisitorial system are a search for truth and the achievement of procedural justice. Are these objectives different from those of the adversarial system? The adversarial approach differs in the sense that the quest for truth and justice officially begins at the trial stage because information from the investigation is not considered until presented in court. Then each side presents its own private version of the truth, and the judge or jurors must decide who is the most convincing. As a result, the importance of how a person is adjudicated seems a more important objective in the adversarial process than determining whether the accused actually committed the crime. This point is similar to the distinction made in Chapter 3 in terms of legal guilt versus factual guilt. One may argue that although each system seeks to determine both types of guilt, the inquisitorial system emphasizes the latter (factual guilt) while the adversarial system highlights the former (legal guilt).

MERGING ADVERSARIAL AND INQUISITORIAL PROCESSES   Despite the distinctions identified in the previous section, there has been a noticeable merging of procedures in countries around the world. There are examples of adversarial countries adapting inquisitorial aspects but more frequently the inquisitorial countries are incorporating adversarial and accusatorial measures.

Looking first at a few examples of inquisitorial procedures influencing the process in primarily adversarial countries, Turner (2016) points to U.S. jurisdictions that are adopting the inquisitorial practice of early and broad disclosure of prosecutorial evidence. Noting that although many U.S. jurisdictions require certain evidence to be disclosed prior to trial, such disclosure is not as often required prior to a guilty plea. Even potentially exculpatory evidence may be withheld from defendants before they plead guilty. This lack of disclosure can be seen as problematic to the extent that it hinders fair and informed guilty pleas. Liberal pre-plea disclosure (as is often found with inquisitorial proceedings), on the other hand, enables defense counsel to provide more effective advice to their clients and—since defense can respond to charges early on—gives prosecutors a better understanding of weaknesses in their case. Turner (2016) uses Germany as an example of a country requiring early and extensive disclosure and shows that the German experience supports arguments for early and broad discovery as a central feature in a fair criminal process.

Another example of the adversarial process being influenced by inquisitorial proceedings is the increased emphasis on the pretrial stage in adversarial proceedings. As common legal tradition countries continue to rely heavily on plea negotiations, actual trials make up a very small percentage of criminal case resolutions. The point made earlier that truth is determined under adversarial systems by emphasizing the trial phase is rightly questioned when the majority of cases never reach trial. U.S. jurisdictions make very frequent use of plea negotiation—more than 90 percent of time (*Missouri* v. *Frye*, 566 US _, 2012)—but the practice is also frequent in the common law countries

IMPACT

SOCCER VERSUS FOOTBALL

Pizzi (1999) has an especially interesting way to contrast the adversarial and inquisitorial systems. He uses a sports analogy of American football versus European soccer. A notable difference between these two sports—and between the adversarial and inquisitorial justice systems—is in the way rules are applied. In the European trial system and the popular European sport of soccer, rules are relatively few in number and rather easy to express. In the American trial system and the more popular (among Americans) sport of football, rules are numerous and complex.

- The rules of soccer are expressed rather easily with statements such as "A player cannot intentionally trip someone or push someone off the ball or engage in dangerous play."
- In football, the rules are often made complicated by the exceptions: (1) certain players on the offense may move (but only in certain directions) before the ball is snapped, but other players may not even flinch; and (2) the defense can block offensive players but only certain ones and—for some—only within a specified distance from the scrimmage line.

In addition to a different emphasis on rules, the sports also differ on how those rules are enforced:

- In soccer, one referee on a large playing field has sole responsibility for controlling play among the players as they move quickly about the entire field. Two assistant referees follow the play from the sidelines to help with decisions in locations where the referee may not be well positioned. But only the referee has a whistle, and only the referee can stop play.
- A football game, which is played on a smaller field, requires six to eight officials and many whistles. Any of those officials can stop play whenever they believe a rule infraction has occurred—which, given the extensive and complex rules, can be quite often.

One effect of the different rules and their enforcement is that soccer is played with minimal interruption and a tendency to let the players play. Minor infractions may be ignored, and the referee stays in the background as much as possible. In football, on the other hand, nonenforcement of the rules simply to avoid interrupting the flow of the game would be shocking to players and fans alike.

Throughout his intriguing book, Pizzi uses this soccer/football analogy to distinguish the inquisitorial and adversarial trial systems. The Europeans seem to have reflected a similar spirit in both their trials and their sport. Like a soccer game, the inquisitorial system has rather clearly expressed rules of procedure that are relatively few in number. And, as we see more clearly in Chapter 7, overseeing the process is a primary official who tends to stay in the background and let the courtroom players play. A few assistants (two or three citizens serving as lay judges) help the professional official (the judge) make decisions.

The trial system preferred by rule-obsessed Americans, the argument goes, reflects a football game with many complex rules that provide any courtroom official (e.g., judge, prosecutor, defense counsel) with an opportunity to stop play and get a ruling on whether an infraction has occurred. Both soccer and football games eventually end, and each provides a clear outcome. Trials following either an inquisitorial or adversarial process also end—but the outcome may not always be clear. Was the accused really guilty? Does a heavy reliance on procedural rules prevent the players from playing? Are outcomes of either sporting events or trials influenced by the degree to which play is controlled and how often it is interrupted? Would sports fans resent game outcomes that proclaimed winners on the basis of who best followed the rules (a "legal win") regardless of who scored the most points (a "factual win")?

of Australia, Canada, England, and New Zealand (Brook et al., 2016). A result of plea negotiation is that appearance in the courtroom for case disposition is not for purposes of a trial but rather for the judge to review and rule on written evidence and pretrial investigation rather than on oral testimony in open court. And that emphasis on the pretrial stage is, of course, a hallmark of the inquisitorial process rather than the adversarial one (see Spencer, 2016, pp. 606–607).

Examples of adversarial proceeding being adapted to the inquisitorial process are more frequently found. One of the more notable is Italy's 1988 Criminal Procedure Code, which made several modifications that are adversarial in nature. For example, written statements taken from witnesses during the investigation cannot be treated as evidence by the trial court—directly contradicting the more traditional inquisitorial process (Spencer, 2016).

Another change concerns guilty pleas. As noted earlier, an admission of guilt has little bearing on inquisitorial proceedings. That admission is simply accepted by the court as another piece of evidence—which can be contradicted by conflicting evidence. However, Spencer (2016) and Hodgson (2015) point out that in the face of increased caseloads some inquisitorial countries are introducing versions of the guilty plea (e.g., in Italy as part of the 1988 reform, and in France, in 2004, with a guilty plea equivalent).

You will recall that the investigating judge was a key feature in the inquisitorial process as it developed in France. Its abolition in many countries can be linked to an increased use of adversarial roles—specifically putting the prosecutor in charge of the preliminary investigation (although judges continue to authorize arrests, seizures, searches, etc.). This has occurred in Germany (1974), Italy (1988), Venezuela (1988), and other Latin American countries in the 1990s. In Spain (1995), the investigating magistrate is now a more neutral pretrial judge who investigates only in response to a request by the prosecution, defense, or victim (through a private prosecutor). The demise of the investigating judge is attributed mostly to the position being deemed redundant to the work of police and prosecutors. In fact, the relevance of the position is even being questioned in France where a 2014 law (as yet to be implemented due to its financial implications) will transfer the investigating function from a single judge to a group of judges (Spencer, 2016; Thaman, 2015).

Finally, not only is the role of the investigating judge being reconsidered, there is also a decrease in the trial judges' active involvement. Traditionally, the inquisitorial trial judge (and other judges when additional ones were used) is actively involved in deciding which witnesses would be called and what questions they would be asked during trial. Examination of the witnesses and the defendant was influenced by the information provided to the judge in the dossier. The prosecution and defense could submit questions for the judge to ask, but the judge could allow the questions or not. This system continues in France, Germany, the Netherlands, Belgium, and other countries, but Thaman (2015) explains that it is gradually being replaced (e.g., Italy and Spain) with the adversarial practice wherein prosecution and defense have responsibility for preparing and presenting the evidence and witnesses, including expert witnesses. The judge takes a more passive role, deciding on admissibility of evidence and assuring balance in the presentation of each side's case.

As we move to procedural law in the remaining legal traditions, we will see other examples of how adversarial and inquisitorial procedures are mixed. This section and the next make it clear that it is increasingly difficult to find countries today that are clearly or wholly accusatorial or inquisitorial. However, it remains important to understand the traditional differences between the models if for no other reason than to have points of comparison among even mixed systems.

PROCEDURAL LAW IN THE ISLAMIC LEGAL TRADITION Islamic procedural law is a mixed system combining adversarial and inquisitorial aspects. Because the Shari'a is a religious law based on divine command and revelation, it did not develop through judicial precedent or legislative codification. Furthermore, it does not require the administration of justice to be a combined office (e.g., the inquisitorial judge) or divided into many (e.g., the adversarial attorneys, judge, and jury). Identifying Islamic procedural law is not so easy. Though the sacred law prescribes penalties for criminal acts, it does not specify the means used to apprehend the offender and bring him to justice. The matter is left to the discretion of the state (Awad, 1982).

Because of this discretion, Islamic law has features of both procedural types. The inquisitorial process seems to predominate, because historically there has been little division between the judge and the investigator. In addition, the defense attorney's role is not so much adversarial as it is one of presenting favorable evidence and safeguarding against improper incrimination. Simultaneously, such adversarial provisions as the right to confront accusers, the right to maintain silence, and a modified presumption of innocence reflect adversarial interests.

The mechanism for administration of Islamic law is the qadi's court. The qadi (an Islamic judge) is appointed by the ruler and must be a male Muslim (some schools of law allow females to serve as qadis in limited circumstances) of recognized intelligence, religious piety, and knowledgeable in Shari'a (Lippman et al., 1988). Criminal procedure under Shari'a presumes the accused is innocent until proven guilty. The burden of proof lies with the accuser, and when doubt exists the case is resolved in favor of the defendant. On this last point—nullification of penalty by doubt—Souryal (2004) explains that the Sunna requires that punishment be prevented in case of doubt because it is better to be wrong in forgiving than wrong in punishing.

Criminal convictions, then, are to be based on assertion and certainty. That is accomplished in Islamic law with three forms of criminal evidence: testimony, religious oath, and confession. Because those forms of evidence can help us understand aspects of Islamic procedural law, we consider them briefly.

The testimony of witnesses has been a hallmark of Islamic law since its earliest development. You will recall from Chapter 4 that the hadiths in the Sunna were validated by naming the line of respected men through whom the stories about the Prophet had passed. In other words, a recollection about Muhammad's statements or actions was considered true because trusted and reliable men passed the recollection from generation to generation. The tradition of Islamic law, then, is to seek truth through statements made by reliable people.

A criminal case is brought before the qadi by the victim, the victim's family, or the state's prosecutor. Consequently, upon being assaulted or stolen from, for example, it becomes your responsibility to bring a complaint against the offender. You show the truthfulness of your complaint (i.e., prove your case) by presenting witnesses on your behalf and/or taking appropriate oaths. The Qur'an and Sunna set down the number of witnesses and type of oath required. For example, proof of adultery requires four witnesses, whereas theft can be proved with just two (see Lippman et al., 1988, p. 42).

Accusers must always shoulder the burden of proof. They do this by calling witnesses who give oral testimony to the truth of the accusers' claims. Generally, the witnesses must be male adult Muslims (some qadi allow two women to count as one man) of high moral character who are able to speak clearly, possess a good memory, and be of sound mind (for variation among schools of law, see Çiğdem, 2007, p. 26; Souryal, 2004, pp. 148–149). The witnesses must testify directly about their personal knowledge of the truth. Testimony from family members (either for or against another family member) or from persons determined to be biased in favor or against the defendant is not accepted. Hearsay evidence is not admissible, but circumstantial evidence may be considered when it is so strong as to be considered conclusive. The primary way to ensure that the witnesses are testifying truthfully is through the oath.

Because it is not always possible to produce the required number of witnesses, the qadi is often presented with only partial evidence against a defendant. At this point, the tradition of oath taking enters the court procedures. As Rosen describes its operation, the oath under Shari'a is very different from its quaint ritual status in Western jurisprudence (Rosen, 1989). Under Islamic law, witnesses are not sworn before testifying, nor is there any punishment for perjury. In fact, given the nature of the proceeding, the law assumes that a person may well make statements that do not bear on the truth. Rosen compares the process to bartering in the marketplace. Statements are tossed out in court to get a reaction in the same manner that one tosses out a price at the bazaar just to see how the merchant responds. In the courtroom, witnesses speak freely and judges inquire cleverly, but no one is held to the implications of truth until truth is attached via an oath.

There is no established form for the oath, and some hadiths (Center for Muslim–Jewish Engagement, 2011) suggest that it is incumbent upon the defendant to take a holy oath denying the allegations (e.g., Sahih Bukhari, Book 48, Number 835), whereas others indicate lots should be drawn to determine who takes an oath first (e.g., Sahih Bukhari, Book 48, Number 480).

Kamali (2008) points out that the presumption of innocence is not overruled by a mere accusation, and the principle of legality entitles the accused to defend himself. So, absent evidence supporting the claim (with supporting evidence, the court would have ruled in favor of the plaintiff), the accuser can ask the court to put the defendant on oath. If the defendant takes a solemn oath affirming that he is telling the truth (i.e., he denies the plaintiff's accusation), the case is dismissed. In Saudi Arabia, the defendant can decline to take the oath and require instead that his accuser take an oath (Kingdom of Saudi Arabia, 2000, Article 109; Lippman et al., 1988, p. 71; Schacht, 1964, p. 190).

The oath works under Shari'a because it is believed that false swearers will suffer the consequences on judgment day. The seriousness with which Muslims approach oath taking is shown by many cases in which persons have maintained their testimony right up to the moment of oath taking only to stop, refuse the oath, and surrender the case.

A confession is a type of evidence that may be used for all categories of crime. A confession is considered to have been provided when the accused voluntarily admits to the charge or charges facing him or her. There are, however, certain requirements to be met before a confession is admissible. The confessor should be a mature person capable of understanding the nature and legal consequences of the confession. It should be rendered voluntarily and be explicit and clear regarding the act.

YOU SHOULD KNOW!
Oaths and Evidence in Islamic Law

A very controversial trial in Pakistan provides some insight into the use of oaths and evidence under Islamic law (Dahlburg, 1995; Rashid, n.d.). Two Christians were convicted of blasphemy against Islam (a crime that carries mandatory death) after being accused of scrawling anti-Islamic slogans on a mosque wall. The conviction was interesting because it was based on oaths rather than evidence.

The offending words had been immediately washed off the walls, so there was no evidence supporting the accusations. There was not even testimony as to the nature of the writing because witnesses who had seen them refused to repeat the words in court. They were too offensive for devout Muslims to say aloud, the witnesses said. The defense attorneys argued that there was no evidence against their clients, but the trial judge disagreed and found the two men guilty. The judge reasoned that the allegations were so serious that no faithful Muslim would falsely make them.

The idea that an accusation must be true or the accuser would not make it seems unusual to many observers. In fact, a Pakistani appeals court agreed that there was no evidence on which to base guilt and the convictions were overturned. Regardless of the appellate ruling, the lower court's decision is instructive because it highlights the importance some judges place on oral statements given by devout Muslims. In the absence of evidence, oral testimony and oaths are considered effective ways to determine truth under Islamic law.

If the evidence produced is deemed conclusive (guilt is clear and explicit), the defendant is convicted. Evidence failing to meet this standard requires finding in favor of the defendant. The intent of these procedures, as noted earlier, is to ensure that any error that may occur will result in acquittal of a guilty person rather than conviction of an innocent one.

PROCEDURAL LAW IN THE EASTERN ASIA LEGAL TRADITION   Formal procedural law in the Eastern Asia tradition has a mixture of both inquisitorial and adversarial aspects. In Japan, especially with the move to a quasi-jury system (see the discussion in Chapter 10), adversarial features are increasingly present. However, access to legal counsel for defense and the role of defense counsel in court are less clearly linked to more fully adversarial procedures.

Formal procedures in China have more inquisitorial than adversarial aspects, but it would still be difficult to argue that China's is an inquisitorial process. That is primarily because the three stages of the criminal process are completely separate and independent from each other. The police have complete control over the investigation, the prosecutors over the charging decision, and the courts over adjudication (Belkin, 2007, p. 92). The institutional independence of these stages means that, at a minimum, the inquisitorial view of the criminal process as a continuing investigation wherein police, prosecution, and courts work together to determine what happened is absent in China. As such, it would be inappropriate to describe the formal Chinese process as clearly adversarial or inquisitorial.

Whereas formal procedural law in the Eastern Asia legal tradition is not easily categorized as either adversarial or inquisitorial, the informal procedural law can be more clearly explained. As noted earlier when discussing substantive law, the importance of legal informalism in the Eastern Asia tradition means it is not surprising that Japan and especially China have some vagueness in their respective criminal codes. That vagueness allows for flexibility when responding to suspects, defendants, and offenders. For Japan, that flexibility receives considerable attention in Chapter 10 under the heading "Law by Bureaucratic Informalism." Here we can consider a few examples from China.

Ambiguity in the law and flexibility in its application allows Chinese officials to follow informal procedures and use informal sanctions. Consider Article 37 of the criminal law:

> If the circumstances of a person's crime are minor and do not require criminal punishment, he may be exempted from it; however, he may, depending on the different circumstances of the case, be reprimanded or ordered to make a statement of repentance, offer an apology or pay compensation for the losses, or be subjected to administrative penalty or administrative sanctions by the competent department. (People's Republic of China, 1979a)

Fu (2011) discusses this proclivity for handling minor offenses without involving prosecutors and the courts as an example of "extra-law," which he explains is a use of power that is not subject to independent oversight (judicial or otherwise). Although China's legal reform during the past 30 years shows a slow transition from extra-law to law, the size of extra-law remains significant in the area of criminal law. As explained by Fu (2011), some 100,000 criminal cases go through the formal criminal process each year, but millions of offenses are dealt with administratively by the police under the name of punishment, treatment, or rehabilitation. Prostitutes, drug addicts, and a wide range of minor offenders are especially likely to be handled in this manner. In doing so, those people are being sanctioned without representation or due process and under uncertain legislative authority.

In January 2013, an amended version of China's 1979 Criminal Procedure Law came into effect (People's Republic of China, 1979b). It was the first extensive revision since 1996. Some of the key features (as identified by the National People's Congress) include (People's Republic of China, 1979b; Zeldin, 2012):

- Inclusion of the phrase "respect and protect human rights" as a general principle of the Law (Article 2).
- Strengthened protection of suspect and defendant rights by specifying when a "defender" (guardian, close relative, or lawyer) can be retained and requiring that the suspect or defendant be informed of the right to retain a defender (Article 33).
- Allowing indigent suspects and defendants to apply to a legal aid organization to have a lawyer appointed for their defense (Article 34).
- Detailing when defense lawyers may meet and communicate with detained suspects and defendants (Article 37).
- The exclusion of evidence gathered by the use of torture or other illegal means and the exclusion of witness testimony or victim statements gathered by the use of such illegal methods as violence or threats (Article 54).

Whereas the changes are widely considered to be appropriate and beneficial, there are concerns about key rights that are not included, such as requiring authorities to produce a detention warrant or to provide the location where suspects and defendants are being detained (Zeldin, 2012). Regardless, the revised law should be considered at least a tentative step toward increased protection of individuals against arbitrary state power.

As these examples from adversarial, inquisitorial, and mixed systems show, there is greater diversity among nations in terms of procedural criminal law than we found on issues of substantive criminal law. However, this focus on the adjudicatory process may lead us to believe that procedural law issues are essentially differentiated on the basis of which legal tradition a country follows. That assumption would be incorrect because there are differences in procedural law both among and between the legal traditions. One area of variation is linked to the concept of judicial review. As we consider that topic, we will see that procedural criminal law shows variation beyond that which is explained by legal tradition affiliation.

Judicial Review

The phrase "laws change but the Law must remain" is commonly used to express the concept of the rule of law. That point reduces to the question of whether a country views its law or its government as supreme. A Soviet journalist expressed it by writing that when the English king put people to death, the king broke the law, but when the Russian Tsar put people to death, he created the law (Feofanov, 1990/1991).

WEB PROJECT

Excluding Evidence

To encourage the police to abide by procedural law when gathering evidence against a suspect, the United States relies on the exclusionary rule wherein evidence illegally obtained must be excluded from the trial. The United States is the world's only country to take the position that some police misconduct must automatically result in the suppression of physical evidence. Read the article at www.nytimes.com/2008/07/19/us/19exclude.html?ref=americanexception on how the U.S. approach compares with that of other countries. Write a few paragraphs describing how other countries handle police misconduct and then provide your opinion as to whether the U.S. approach is appropriate or outdated.

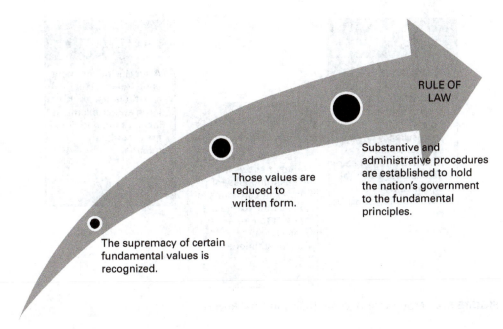

RULE OF LAW

Substantive and administrative procedures are established to hold the nation's government to the fundamental principles.

Those values are reduced to written form.

The supremacy of certain fundamental values is recognized.

FIGURE 5.1 Flowchart for Achieving Rule of Law

As Figure 5.1 shows, reaching a position wherein rule of law is established requires a nation to first recognize the supremacy of certain fundamental values. Those values may have either secular or divine origin as long as they are understood to reflect basic and ultimate principles. After being recognized, the fundamental values must be reduced to written form. A country's constitution often accomplishes this task. Finally, the trip to rule of law requires a nation to provide procedures that hold its government to the tenets of this higher law. If citizens cannot challenge laws made by the country's legislature or ruler, the concept of a higher law is lost. For example, say that the legislature in a country whose constitution ensures freedom of religion passes a law prohibiting Muslims from operating a place of worship. If citizens cannot challenge the substance of such a law as violating fundamental values (recorded in the constitution), the concept of rule of law is emasculated.

The procedures supporting the rule of law need to be of two types: those related to questions of substance and those related to questions of administration. Questions of substance are similar to the example of the Muslims prohibited from worshipping in a country guaranteeing freedom of religion. Questions of administration, on the other hand, deal with how the government enforces its statutes and is itself subject to the law. Consider, for example, a case of pretrial detention in the former Soviet Union—a country without the rule of law.

A Soviet journalist became aware of a defendant who had been kept in prison for 5 years and 11 months while awaiting his trial (Feofanov, 1990/1991). The journalist asked the USSR Procuracy (prosecutor) if such action was consistent with the principles of law and justice. The response was basically one of surprise that someone believed that a thief should be set free just because the term of pretrial confinement was violated. The government official explained that the defendant was accused of a crime that warrants a 15-year sentence. From the official's point of view, if the person is eventually convicted and 6 years are subtracted from that sentence, nothing so terrible has happened. The situation was worsened, in Western eyes, by the fact that the Procuracy was the very agency that the Soviets used to monitor such behavior. When the law is deemed inapplicable to certain citizens or agencies, it cannot have an independent value and there is no rule of law.

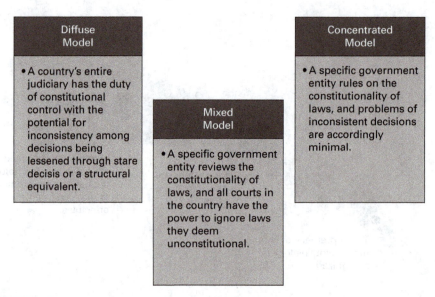

FIGURE 5.2   Models for Accomplishing Judicial Review

Of the three steps to a rule of law (i.e., recognizing supremacy of certain values, reducing them to writing, and providing a way to hold the government to those laws), the third is particularly interesting. The first two steps are rather well accomplished today and show little differentiation—at least in the common, civil, and in Japan's version of the Eastern Asia legal traditions. A rule of law, if it exists in the Islamic tradition and in China, must be approached differently. Consequently, we review ways to hold the government accountable in common and civil legal families and then turn to the question of rule of law under Islamic law and in China.

The process by which governments are held accountable to the law is called judicial review. The term refers to the power of a court to hold unconstitutional (hence, unenforceable) any law, any official action based on a law, or any other action by a public official that the courts deem in conflict with the country's basic law. One of two models can be used to accomplish judicial review (Brewer-Carías, 1989; Cappelletti, 1989). The diffuse model is decentralized and allows a wide variety and large number of courts in the country to rule on issues of constitutionality of laws. The concentrated model is centralized by restricting issues of the constitutionality of laws to a specific state agency (see Figure 5.2).

The diffuse model had its origin in the United States and is now found primarily in Britain's former colonies (e.g., Canada, Australia, and India). It is not, however, confined to countries following the common legal tradition. European countries such as Norway, Denmark, and Sweden have procedures that are very similar to the American prototype, as do the Latin American countries of Argentina and Mexico.

The concentrated model was first established in Austria in 1920 and then spread to such European countries as Germany, Italy, and Spain. Not surprisingly, some countries fail to fit neatly into one of these two models. These mixed model countries (e.g., Venezuela, Colombia, Brazil, and Switzerland) offer interesting variations of judicial review. As a result, they also warrant our attention (see Figure 5.2).

DIFFUSE MODEL FOR JUDICIAL REVIEW   The diffuse model gives a country's entire judiciary the duty of constitutional control. This approach follows the assumption that the judiciary functions to interpret the laws in order to apply them in concrete cases. When two laws conflict, the judge must determine which of the two prevails and then apply it. In countries with a rigid constitution, the judge is expected to decide by deferring to the higher law because a constitutional norm prevails over an ordinary legislative norm. Therefore, in countries following a diffuse model of judicial review, any judge having to decide a case in which an applicable legislative norm conflicts with the constitution must disregard the former and apply the latter. As a result, even low-level courts can rule a statute unconstitutional or declare police action as violating a suspect's fundamental rights.

Providing all judges and courts the general power to act as constitutional judges is a consequence of the principle of the supremacy of the constitution. For example, the Constitution of the United States includes a Supremacy Clause that makes clear the link between the principle and the diffuse model. A clause in Article 6, Section 2, states:

> This Constitution, and the Laws of the United States which shall be made in Pursuance thereof; and all Treaties made, or which shall be made, under the Authority of the United States, shall be the supreme Law of the Land; and the Judges in every State shall be bound thereby, any Thing in the Constitution or Laws of any State to the Contrary notwithstanding.

After establishing the constitution as supreme and empowering judges at all levels to act as a constitutional court, the diffuse-model countries are left with a potential problem. Because judges at all court levels and regions can rule on constitutionality, the potential for conflicting opinions and rulings is great. How does a system of diffuse judicial review respond to the danger of different judges reaching inconsistent results on close questions? Countries in the common legal tradition respond to that problem with the aid of stare decisis.

An emphasis on stare decisis reduces the danger of inconsistent rulings by requiring judges to follow their own prior decisions and the precedents of higher courts. In the United States, the presence of a single national Supreme Court and the requirement that lower courts follow its superior precedents ensure the uniformity of constitutional adjudication. The civil legal tradition countries using a diffuse system of judicial review cannot, customarily, rely on stare decisis. Instead, as we will see, they use related concepts, set up special procedures, or establish special courts. In such ways, countries with a civil legal tradition and a diffuse system of judicial review are able to resolve problems of uncertainty and conflict arising when numerous judges make decisions on constitutionality of laws (Brewer-Carías, 1989). An overview of judicial review in two countries will highlight these modifications while elaborating on the system of diffuse judicial review.

Like many other Latin American countries, Argentina (see Map A.4) and Mexico (see Map A.3) were influenced by the constitutional system of the United States. This presented some problems in the area of the judiciary because those same countries had modeled their legal system after the civil legal tradition of European countries. In the area of judicial review, many Latin American countries eventually moved from the American diffuse system to a mixed system combining this common law feature with their civil law system. Argentina and Mexico, however, remained faithful to the American system (Brewer-Carías, 1989). Understandably, each country also added its own modifications, but the two clearly follow a diffuse model of judicial review.

Section 31 of Argentina's constitution states, in part, that the constitution and the laws passed by Congress are "the supreme law of the Nation" (Argentine Republic, 2008). Furthermore, Section 116 makes the Supreme Court and the various lower courts competent to hear cases related to the Constitution and congressional laws. As in the United States, therefore, all Argentinean courts can declare legislative acts, as well as executive and administrative acts and judicial decisions, to be unconstitutional.

In its appellate jurisdiction, the Argentinean Supreme Court of Justice hears two kinds of appeal. For ordinary appeals, the Supreme Court reviews particular decisions made by the National Chamber of Appeals and serves as a court of last resort for such matters. It is the second type of appellate jurisdiction, extraordinary appeals, that provides Argentina's special procedure for judicial review.

Any party having direct interest in a case decided at the provincial superior court or at the National Chambers of Appeals level can bring the case before the Supreme Court of Justice. The primary restriction for such access is that the case must involve a constitutional issue. In this manner, the Supreme Court provides final interpretation of the Constitution. For that reason, extraordinary appeal is the most important means for judicial review of state acts.

Judicial review in Mexico is directly linked to the *juicio de amparo* (trial for protection), which in turn comes from the Mexican Constitution. The *amparo* proceedings (constitutional protection lawsuit) can be used for five different purposes: (1) protection of fundamental constitutional rights, (2) against unconstitutional laws, (3) reviews on the constitutionality of legislation, (4) judicial review of administrative action, and (5) protection of communal agrarian rights. Legislation in 2013 provides for the Supreme Court of Justice of the Nation to remove and prosecute any authority that does not comply with an amparo judgment (Brewer-Carías, 2009; Gutierrez, 2013).

In addition to covering similar topics, Mexican and American judicial reviews share an appreciation for the concept of judicial precedent. As noted earlier, the absence of stare decisis in civil law countries makes it difficult for them to use a diffuse system of judicial review. Mexico integrated diffuse judicial review into its civil legal tradition by developing *jurisprudencia* as a procedure similar to stare decisis.

In cases in which the law of amparo is at issue, precedents from previous federal court decisions are considered binding for lower courts. This process is similar to stare decisis in common law but differs in an important respect. Whereas stare decisis relies on a single decision, Mexican jurisprudencia (precedents from previous decisions) require five consecutive decisions to the same effect (Brewer-Carías, 1989, 2009).

These similarities with judicial review in the United States are balanced by other aspects that set the Mexican system apart. Possibly most important is the restriction of amparo jurisdiction to federal level courts. Therefore, judicial review is not a power of all courts in Mexico as it is in America.

CONCENTRATED MODEL FOR JUDICIAL REVIEW   The alternative to diffuse judicial review is a concentrated approach. The distinguishing feature of the concentrated system of judicial review is the use of a single state organ to act as a country's constitutional judge. That entity can be the Supreme Court of Justice, acting as the highest court in the judicial hierarchy, or a specialized court organized outside the ordinary court hierarchy. In either situation, the country's constitution expressly creates and regulates the agency responsible for upholding the supremacy of that constitution.

The idea that a constitution should create and specify the process of judicial review is a distinguishing feature between the diffuse and concentrated models. For example, neither the U.S. Constitution nor Argentina's Constitution (as examples of the diffuse models) conferred judicial review power on the courts. Instead, both constitutions simply note their supremacy and the duty of all courts to make decisions consistent with their contents. By default, not by decree, all courts in the United States and Argentina are constitutional courts. In the concentrated model of judicial review, there is no doubt concerning which agency decides constitutional questions. That duty falls to a very specific state organ, identified in the country's constitution itself.

Most adherents of this position are civil law countries. The archetype is Austria (see Map A.10), but the concentrated model was also adopted by Italy, Cyprus, and the

Russian Federation. The countries following this model tend to believe more strongly in the separation of powers (rather than simply checks and balances) and the supremacy of statutory law. The concentrated model refuses to grant judicial review power to the judiciary generally. The ordinary judge must accept and apply the law as he or she finds it; judicial review is undertaken by a specialized court or tribunal.

Austria provided the model for concentrated judicial review when its 1920 constitution created a constitutional tribunal (*Verfassungsgerichtshof*). This 14-person court was reinstituted in 1945. Members are appointed by the president of the republic after recommendations from the Parliament. They have life tenure and possess the power to review the constitutionality of legislation and decide jurisdictional disputes (Abraham, 1998). Since 1920, Austrian citizens have been able to file complaints when they feel their constitutional rights have been violated by an act of administration. Since 1975, complaints have also been allowed regarding a violation of rights by an act of legislation.

Italy's constitutional court (*Corte Costituzionale*) was established in 1948 and began functioning in 1956. This 15-member body is staffed with distinguished persons having at least 20 years' experience as practicing lawyers, experienced judges, or professors of law. The judges are appointed for staggered 9-year terms with five selected by the president of the republic, five by three-fifths vote of Parliament, and five by the ordinary and administrative judiciary. The Corte Costituzionale is the final interpreter of the constitution and has the power to declare both national and regional laws unconstitutional.

With constitutional courts like those in Austria and Italy, the concentrated model of judicial review achieves the same goal as the diffuse model: to provide procedures for holding the government to certain fundamental values.

MIXED MODEL FOR JUDICIAL REVIEW   Because the concentrated and diffuse systems of judicial review can exist in countries with either a common or civil legal tradition, it is not surprising that mixed systems of judicial review sometimes occur. Brewer-Carías (2009) believes that countries such as Portugal (see Map A.10) and Venezuela (see Map A.4) exemplify mixed systems.

The Portuguese constitution of 1976 and its 1982 revision established a complete system of judicial review, which has elements of concentrated and diffuse models. The Constitutional Court, created by the constitution as part of the judicial hierarchy, represents the concentrated aspect. Along with the establishment of the Constitutional Court, the Portuguese constitution authorizes all courts in the country to avoid implementing any law deemed by the Court to be unconstitutional. This rule, of course, agrees with the diffuse model. Similarly, building on a 100-year tradition, Venezuela's 1961 constitution established the Supreme Court of Justice as competent to review the constitutionality of laws. Simultaneously, the Code of Civil Procedure allows all courts in Venezuela to declare inapplicable laws that the court deems unconstitutional. These combinations of diffuse and concentrated systems of judicial review provide Venezuela and Portugal with two of the most extensive systems of judicial review in the world.

Brazil's (see Map A.4) constitution places it among countries with mixed systems of judicial review (Brewer-Carías, 2009). Although Brazil originally followed the United States and used a diffuse model, constitutional reforms over the years kept adding aspects of a concentrated model. As a result, any Brazilian judge at any court level today can ignore law that he or she considers unconstitutional for the current case. In addition, the Supreme Federal Court of Brazil not only rules on the constitutionality of laws related to the case immediately before it but also can declare unconstitutional any action initiated by the office of the attorney general of the republic.

JUDICIAL REVIEW IN THE ISLAMIC LEGAL TRADITION AND IN CHINA As noted earlier, discussion of a rule of law in the Islamic tradition and in China differs slightly from its discussion under common and civil legal traditions. Countries in the common and civil families usually follow one of two judicial-review models to hold their governments accountable to fundamental values. In all cases, those values have been reduced to written form through a constitution. Under Islamic law, the fundamental values are presented in the Qur'an and Sunna, and in China the fundamental values do not really support a rule of law.

Islam very clearly accepts the supremacy of fundamental values or laws. Those laws preceded the state, and the state exists solely to maintain and enforce them. The Shari'a records the fundamental values, so Islamic law meets the first two criteria for achieving a rule of law: recognition of the supremacy of fundamental values and reduction of those values to written form. For those viewing the rule of law as desirable, the problem with the Islamic tradition is that it goes no further than the first two steps.

The Shari'a does not visualize any conflict between the interests of the ruler and those of the citizen. As a result, there are no procedures (judicial or otherwise) to review the actions of government. Substantive questions cannot be brought by citizens because the law is considered to be of divine origin and valid for all time. To question the legitimacy of a law would mean that a Muslim is questioning Allah. Similarly, questions regarding the procedures used to enforce the law are inappropriate because Muslims are told to give allegiance to the existing authority, regardless of the nature of that authority. Unjust rulers and their inappropriate procedures will be punished by Allah in the next world.

The lack of any system to provide a remedy against the abuse of individual rights by government agents means that Islamic law does not completely operate under a rule of law. The recognition and written account of fundamental values are not backed up with formal procedures by which citizens can hold their government accountable to those values. Instead, the Islamic tradition simply counsels against abuse and relies on faith that rulers will hold themselves answerable.

In terms of achieving a rule of law, Islamic law is similar to the common and civil legal traditions in recognizing and reducing to writing certain fundamental values. It differs from the other two by having incomplete mechanisms for judicial review to force the government to abide by the same values it requires of the citizens.

The rule of law is viewed by Western legal traditions as unequivocally a desirable societal value. Confucianism was not so sure about that. Bracey notes that until the end of the nineteenth century, "rule of law" actually had a negative connotation in China. Confucius had argued that rulers should govern by behaving correctly themselves, thus setting a good example for others. Lower government officials would follow that example, as would village officials, then family heads, and finally the members of households. Supporting these examples would be the study—early on and throughout life—of Confucian principles of virtue. Engrossed in the principles of correct behavior and surrounded by people who practiced them, children would grow into adults who had internalized virtue, morality, and proper behavior, not because they were forced to, but because it was the right thing to do. Law, with its detailed rules and punishment for misbehavior, meant that the nation's rulers were no longer setting a good example or that the education system had failed (Bracey, 2006).

Given that background, it may be less surprising that China—regardless of its communist central government—has been slow to accept the idea that rule of law is desirable. China's constitution (People's Republic of China, 1982) includes rule of law language—affairs will be handled in accordance with the law (Article 2) and no organization or person is above the law (Article 5)—but critics find the practical effect of these words to be rather small. An important obstacle to attaining rule of law is the absence of judicial review. China is a unitary state with all power flowing from the central government. There is neither horizontal nor vertical separation of powers and the Supreme People's Court cannot rule on the constitutionality of laws. The rule of law in China remains a target more than a reality.

Summary

Every legal system must address issues of substantive and procedural law, but each system may approach the terms differently. This chapter takes the admittedly Western-linked perspective on substantive and procedural law as first presented in Chapter 3 and uses these concepts as a comparative aid in discussing legal systems.

Looking at substantive law in each of the four legal traditions, we found that defining what was criminal and specifying the punishment included reliance on judges (common legal tradition), legislators (civil and Eastern Asia legal traditions), and God (Islamic legal tradition). Regardless of who or what is doing the defining, it is apparent that each legal tradition has some difficulty with several or all of the general characteristics and major principles associated with substantive law.

Procedural law was addressed with specific attention to the issues of the adjudicatory process and judicial review. Adjudication typically follows either an adversarial or inquisitorial model. Both models seek the truth in claims made by the state against an individual. The inquisitorial process (civil law systems) seems like a continuing investigation with all parties cooperating to determine what happened. The adversarial process (common law systems), on the other hand, is more obviously a contest between competing sides, where truth is said to lie with the victor. Importantly, the chapter notes that it is increasingly difficult to find countries that are wholly adversarial or inquisitorial. Instead, we find some adversarial countries incorporating inquisitorial methods and, even more so, inquisitorial countries adapting adversarial proceedings. Adjudication under Islamic procedural law is a particular combination of the inquisitorial and adversarial models. Japan's example of the Eastern Asia tradition also has both inquisitorial and adversarial aspects, but China does not clearly reflect either.

The procedure of judicial review was introduced as an important way to ensure that a government abides by the fundamental values of a nation. In this way, a rule of law can be achieved because the government, like its citizens, is made accountable. One model of judicial review is the diffuse design, wherein all courts in a country have authority to find laws unconstitutional. This decentralized model is used in the United States and in some civil law countries, so it is not attached to particular legal traditions. The concentrated model for judicial review follows a centralized design and invests all constitutional review power in a single state organ. Some countries have successfully adopted aspects of both diffuse and concentrated models and, as a result, are said to have a mixed model for judicial review. Still other countries (e.g., some under the Islamic tradition and in China) do not seem to operate under a rule of law and as such have incomplete or nonexistent procedures for judicial review.

Discussion Questions

- During the discussion of hudud and qisas crimes, it was noted that by having a category of crimes that require retaliation (i.e., qiyas offenses), Shari'a law is attempting to satisfy the human tendency to retaliate. Do you agree that there is such a human tendency? If so, does the American system of justice provide any mechanism to accommodate that tendency?
- The "You Should Know!" box titled "Proof and Truth" suggests that adversarial proceedings can be distinguished as relying more on the government's ability to prove (following specific rules of criminal procedure) the defendant's guilt whereas the inquisitorial process spends more time on investigations to determine whether the defendant truly committed the crime. Do you think that is a fair distinction? Include in your response reference to the additional identifiers noted in the box (e.g., legal guilt versus factual guilt and due process versus crime control).

References

Abraham, H. J. (1998). *The judicial process: An introductory analysis of the courts of the United States, England, and France* (7th ed.). New York, NY: Oxford University Press.

Al-Saagheer, M. F. (1994). Diyya legislation in Islamic Shari'a and its application in the United Kingdom of Saudi Arabia. In U. Zvekic (Ed.), *Alternatives to imprisonment in contemporary perspective* (pp. 80–91). Chicago, IL: Nelson-Hall.

Argentine Republic. (2008, July 26). National Constitution of the Argentine Republic. Political Database of the Americas. Retrieved from http://pdba.georgetown.edu/Constitutions/Argentina/argen94_e.html

Asad, M. (2003). *The message of the Qur'an: The full account of the revealed Arabic text accompanied by parallel transliteration.* Bitton, UK: The Book Foundation.

Awad, A. M. (1982). The rights of the accused under Islamic criminal procedure. In M. C. Bassiouni (Ed.), *The Islamic criminal justice system* (pp. 91–107). London, UK: Oceana.

Belkin, I. (2007). China. In C. M. Bradley (Ed.), *Criminal procedure: A worldwide study* (2nd ed., pp. 91–106). Durham, NC: Carolina Academic Press.

Black, A., Esmaeili, H., & Hosen, N. (2013). *Modern perspectives on Islamic law.* Northampton, MA: Edward Elgar.

Bracey, D. H. (2006). *Exploring law and culture.* Long Grove, IL: Waveland Press.

Brewer-Carías, A. R. (1989). *Judicial review in comparative law.* Cambridge, UK: Cambridge University Press.

Brewer-Carías, A. R. (2009). *Constitutional protection of human rights in Latin America: A comparative study of amparo proceedings.* New York, NY: Cambridge University Press.

Brook, C. A., Fiannaca, B., Harvey, D., Marcus, P., McEwan, J., & Pomerance, R. (2016). A comparative look at plea bargaining in Australia, Canada, England, New Zealand, and the United States. *William & Mary Law Review, 57*(4), 1147–1224.

Cappelletti, M. (1989). *The judicial process in comparative perspective.* Oxford, UK: Clarendon Press.

Center for Muslim–Jewish Engagement. (2011). Translation of Sahih Bukhari, Book 48. Religious texts. Retrieved from http://www.usc.edu/org/cmje/religious-texts/hadith/bukhari/

Çiğdem, R. (2007). Corporal punishment (amputation of a hand): The concept of sariqa (theft) in theory and in practice. *Ankara Law Review, 4*(1), 25–41.

Dahlburg, J.-T. (1995, February 24). Pakistani court acquits Christians. *The Denver Post,* p. 16A.

El-Awa, M. S. (1982). *Punishment in Islamic law: A comparative study.* Indianapolis, IN: American Trust Publishers.

Federal Republic of Germany. (1971). The German Criminal Code (amended version of 2013). Gesetze im Internet. Retrieved from http://www.gesetze-im-internet.de/englisch_stgb/index.html

Federal Republic of Germany. (1987). The German Code of Criminal Procedure (amended version of 2014). Gesetze im Internet. Retrieved from http://www.gesetze-im-internet.de/englisch_stpo/index.html

Federal Republic of Nigeria. (1916). Criminal Code Act (amended version of 1990). Refworld. Retrieved from http://www.refworld.org/docid/49997ade1a.html

Feofanov, I. (1990/1991). A return to origins: Reflections on power and law. *Soviet Law and Government, 29*(3), 15–52.

French Republic. (1995). Penal code (amended version of 2005). Legifrance Translations. Retrieved from https://www.legifrance.gouv.fr/Traductions/en-English/Legifrance-translations

Friedman, L. M. (1973). *A history of American law.* New York, NY: Simon & Schuster.

Frommann, M. (2009). Regulating plea-bargaining in Germany: Can the Italian approach serve as a model to guarantee the independence of German judges? *Hanse Law Review, 5*(2), 197–220.

Fu, H. (2011, June 28). The varieties of law. *Chinese Law Prof Blog,* Retrieved from http://lawprofessors.typepad.com/china_law_prof_blog/2011/06/fu-hualing-on-the-varieties-of-law.html

Glenn, H. P. (2014). *Legal traditions of the world: Sustainable diversity in law* (5th ed.). Oxford, UK: Oxford University Press.

Graham, M. M. (1983). *Tightening the reins of justice in America.* Westport, CT: Greenwood Press.

Gutierrez, N. (2013, April 30). Mexico: New amparo law is enacted. *Global Legal Monitor.* Retrieved from http://www.loc.gov/law/foreign-news

Hakeem, F. B. (2003). Alternative perspectives on penalty under Sharia: A review essay. *International Journal of Comparative and Applied Criminal Justice, 27*(1), 85–105.

Hodgson, J. (2005). *French criminal justice: A comparative account of the investigation and prosecution of crime in France.* Portland, OR: Hart.

Hodgson, J. (2015). Plea bargaining: A comparative analysis. In J. D. Wright (Ed.), *International encyclopedia of the social & behavioral sciences* (2nd ed., pp. 226–231). Oxford, UK: Elsevier.

Ingraham, B. L. (1987). *The structure of criminal procedure: Laws and practice of France, the Soviet Union, China, and the United States.* New York, NY: Greenwood Press.

The Italian penal code. (1978). (E. M. Wise & A. Maitlin, Trans.). Littleton, CO: F. B. Rothman.

Japan Ministry of Justice. (1907). Penal Code of Japan (amended version of 2007). Japanese Law Translation. Retrieved from http://www.japaneselawtranslation. go.jp/law/detail/?id=1960&vm=02&re=02

Jones, T. H. (1990). Common law and criminal law: The Scottish example. *The Criminal Law Review*, 292–301.

Kamali, M. H. (2008). *Shari'ah law: An introduction*. Oxford, UK: Oneworld Publications.

Kingdom of Saudi Arabia. (2000). The law of procedure before Shari'ah courts. About Saudi Arabia. Retrieved from http://www.saudiembassy.net/about/country-information/laws/Law_of_Procedure_before_Shariah_Courts.aspx

Lippman, M. R., McConville, S., & Yerushalmi, M. (1988). *Islamic criminal law and procedure: An introduction*. New York, NY: Praeger.

Merryman, J. H. (1985). *The civil law tradition* (2nd ed.). Stanford, CA: Stanford University Press.

Packer, H. L. (1968). *The limits of the criminal sanction*. Stanford, CA: Stanford University Press.

People's Republic of China, Congressional-Executive Commission on China. (1979a). Criminal Law of the People's Republic of China (amended version of 2011). Retrieved from http://www.cecc.gov/resources/legal-provisions/criminal-law-of-the-peoples-republic-of-china

People's Republic of China. (1979b). Criminal Procedure Law of the People's Republic of China (amended version of 2012). China Law Translate. Retrieved from http://chinalawtranslate.com/criminal-procedure-law/?lang=en

People's Republic of China, Congressional-Executive Commission on China. (1982). Constitution of the People's Republic of China (amended version of 2004). Retrieved from http://www.cecc.gov/resources/legal-provisions/constitution-of-the-peoples-republic-of-china

Pizzi, W. T. (1999). *Trials without truth*. New York, NY: New York University Press.

Rashid, A. (n. d.). Cleric drops blasphemy case against Christians. *The Electronic Telegraph*. Retrieved from http://www.telegraph.co.uk

Rastogi, N. (2009, May 14). Objection, dear leader! How do court trials work in North Korea? *Slate*. Retrieved from http://www.slate.com/articles/news_and_politics/explainer/2009/05/objection_dear_leader.html

Rauxloh, R. E. (2011). Formalization of plea bargaining in Germany: Will the new legislation be able to square the circle? *Fordham International Law Journal, 34*, 296–331.

Rosen, L. (1989). *The anthropology of justice: Law as culture in Islamic society*. Cambridge, UK: Cambridge University Press.

Sanad, N. (1991). *The theory of crime and criminal responsibility in Islamic law: Shari'a*. Chicago, IL: Office of International Criminal Justice.

Schacht, J. (1964). *An introduction to Islamic law*. Oxford, UK: Oxford University Press.

Schirrmacher, C. (1994). Islamic jurisprudence and its sources. Retrieved from http://web.archive.org/web/20060721124621/http://www.ishr.org/activities/campaigns/stoning/background.htm

Shelter Scotland. (2016). How Scots law is made. The legal system. Retrieved from http://scotland.shelter.org.uk/get_advice/advice_topics/complaints_and_court_action/structure_of_the_scottish_legal_system/how_scots_law_is_made

Siddiqi, M. I. (1985). *The penal law of Islam*. Lahore, Pakistan: Kazi Publications.

Souryal, S. S. (2004). *Islam, Islamic law, and the turn to violence*. Huntsville, TX: Office of International Criminal Justice.

Souryal, S. S., Potts, D. W., & Alobied, A. I. (1994). The penalty of hand amputation for theft in Islamic justice. *Journal of Criminal Justice, 22*, 249–265.

Spencer, J. R. (2016). Adversarial vs inquisitorial systems: Is there still such a difference? *The International Journal of Human Rights, 20*(5), 601–616. doi:10.1080/13642987.2016.1162408

State of Colorado. (2015). Colorado Revised Statutes, § 18-4-401, Theft Stat.

Terrill, R. J. (2016). *World criminal justice systems: A comparative survey* (9th ed.). New York, NY: Routledge.

Thaman, S. C. (2015). Criminal procedure: Adversarial and inquisitorial legal systems. In J. D. Wright (Ed.), *International encyclopedia of the social & behavioral sciences* (2nd ed., pp. 227–231). Oxford, UK: Elsevier.

Turner, J. I. (2016). Plea bargaining and disclosure in Germany and the United States: Comparative lessons. *William & Mary Law Review, 57*(4), 1549–1596.

Waldron, R. J. (1989). *The criminal justice system: An introduction* (4th ed.). New York, NY: Harper & Row.

White, R. M., & Willock, I. D. (2007). *The Scottish legal system* (4th ed.). Haywards Heath, UK: Tottel Publishing.

Wiechman, D. J., Kendall, J. D., & Azarian, M. K. (1996). Islamic law: Myths and realities. *C. J. International, 12*(3), 13–19.

Zeldin, W. (2012, April 9). China: Amendment of criminal procedure law. *Global Legal Monitor*. Retrieved from http://www.loc.gov/law/foreign-news

6

An International Perspective on Policing

LEARNING OBJECTIVES

After studying this chapter, you will be able to:

1. Explain Bayley's typology of police structures and provide examples of countries exemplifying each type.

2. Compare police misconduct in the United States to police misconduct in other countries.

3. Give both international and regional examples of police cooperation in fighting transnational crime.

COUNTRIES IN FOCUS

Canada	Italy
China	Japan
France	Mexico
Germany	Spain
Ghana	United States

In Japan, Seicho Matsumoto's fictional Inspector Imanishi travels throughout the nation to investigate a case. No one seems to mind the fact that Imanishi-san is with the Tokyo Metropolitan Police Force yet is interviewing witnesses, asking questions of local police officers, and apparently having the run of the country with no regard for jurisdictional boundaries. A continent away, Georges Simenon has his French inspector Maigret investigate crime scenes under the watchful eye of deputy public prosecutors and upstart examining magistrates. Meanwhile, farther north in the Netherlands, police Commissaris Van der Valk (courtesy of Nicholas Freeling) must deal with an Officer of Justice who operates as an amalgam of a French public prosecutor and examining magistrate. Also in the Netherlands but operating at lower ranks, Detective Adjutant Grijpstra and Sergeant de Gier (from the pen of Janwillem van de Wetering) work the Amsterdam streets, making decisions on such matters as the distance between a prostitute and the bar down the street. Because prostitution is illegal within 200 feet of a public place selling alcohol, police (who may actually be looking for drugs) may want to stop and question the streetwalker.

Police-procedure novels showing officers with nationwide jurisdiction, having to work under the direction of an examining magistrate, reporting to a combination prosecutor-judge, or dealing with laws that allow prostitution only on certain parts of the street may raise questions of credibility from American readers. However, upon realizing that the U.S. police structure and organization, as well as procedures followed, are just one of several models available, American readers may find such novels to be doubly intriguing.

WEB PROJECT

Enforcing Religious Norms

This chapter focuses on public policing of government laws. In a few countries around the world, there are police agencies that enforce religious norms. Go to the Pew Research Center at http://www.pewresearch.org/fact-tank/2014/03/19/religious-police-found-in-nearly-one-in-ten-countries-worldwide/ and read the article on religious police. Write a few paragraphs that summarize the findings reported in the article. Read some of the comments at the end of the article that were left by other readers. Why do you think there is disagreement, at least as indicated in some of the comments, regarding the presence of religious police in some countries?

In fact, the American model of policing is more unusual than common. A basic principle of the American republic was the notion that the states and federal government would share power. In terms of maintaining law and order, the power was to be primarily at the state level. As if to emphasize the point, the U.S. Constitution mentions only two crimes (counterfeiting and treason) and avoids any mention of a national police force to protect federal property and enforce federal laws. Taking their cue from the federal government, the states avoided direct involvement in law enforcement and delegated such duties to the local communities. This seemed appropriate, because crime was a local phenomenon and thus local authorities were presumed to know best how to respond to violators.

A result of this assignment of responsibilities was an absence of federal and state law enforcement agencies in accordance with a general decentralization of policing throughout the country and within each state. Even when the federal government increased its involvement in law enforcement, Congress, instead of investing all authority in one agency, divided enforcement responsibilities so that each federal department has investigative units responsible for enforcing laws relevant to that department's jurisdiction. The result ranges from U.S. Department of Agriculture agents enforcing specific legislation such as food stamp regulations to the Federal Bureau of Investigation (Department of Justice) investigating over 200 different types of cases (e.g., terrorism, robbery of federally insured banks, interstate racketeering, and transporting stolen property across state lines).

This chapter focuses on the various ways policing is structured around the world. You should bear in mind that this is only one of many ways policing may be presented in a comparative book. Comparison of police duties, training of officers, how police handle human rights issues, procedural law and the police, and the presence and nature of specialized units are also appropriate topics. Because one chapter does not provide an opportunity for a great variety of issues, only two other points are presented here: police misconduct and the growth of international cooperation in law enforcement. However, we begin with the structure of police departments.

CLASSIFICATION OF POLICE STRUCTURES

The way in which a country organizes its police is often considered a key issue for such central values as human rights and political freedom. Before dismissing such claims as grandiose, consider your reaction to a proposal that U.S. jurisdictions replace all local police departments with a single federal police agency having authority to enforce national and state laws across the country. Tampering with the structure of decentralized American policing in this manner would be viewed by some as tantamount to tampering with the Constitution itself.

Arguing that the topic of police organization is important is easier than deciding how it should be presented. Should all countries with a single national police force be compared before moving to a comparison of countries with both state and federal agencies? Do countries with several national police forces present different issues that benefit from separate comparison? Grieve, Harfield, and MacVean (2007) wonder if comparison should be structured on the basis of the differences in procedural power—that is, the different relationships police agencies have with other criminal justice agencies. Others have considered whether a country's policing is fragmented, centralized, or integrated (Hunter, 1990) and have evaluated the interplay of structure, function, and legitimacy (Mawby, 1990, 2003). Jiao (1997) suggests making distinctions on the basis of police professionalism, community policing, problem-oriented policing, and a security orientation. Wright (2002) prefers to distinguish depending on the relationship between the police, the state, and the military. There are, clearly, a variety of ways by which comparison of police forces can be approached.

David Bayley (1985, 1992) suggests a categorization on the basis of dispersal of command and number of forces. It is Bayley's scheme that directs our review. Here the concepts of centralization/decentralization and single/multiple forces serve as a base for a typology of worldwide police structures. Because multiple forces, either centralized or decentralized, can work together (coordinated) or at cross-purposes (uncoordinated), the result is the six-cell matrix found in Table 6.1. The following analysis and discussion borrow heavily from Bayley's work.

Bayley's criterion for identifying a system as either centralized or decentralized is the stated locus of control. The emphasis is on "stated" because it is possible for a system to be one way in principle but another in actuality, meaning that the resulting categorization may not always reflect the actual condition. France, for example, has multiple police forces for which the day-to-day operations are decided at the unit level. Structurally, the command is from Paris, but it is seldom applied. Using the criterion of stated locus of control, France has a centralized police command. Bayley (1985) realizes that this criterion is deceptively simple because it ignores the reality of informal command relationships. It may be that more comparative studies will suggest some refinements to Bayley's work, but for our purposes it provides a sensible option.

Bayley's typology is especially helpful for understanding relationships among the countries in a particular cell and between countries in different cells. It also provides a

TABLE 6.1	Types of Police Structure	
Number of Forces	**Dispersal of Command**	
	Centralized	**Decentralized**
Single	Ireland Ghana Nigeria Poland Saudi Arabia	Japan
Multiple coordinated	Austria England and Wales France	Australia Canada Germany India
Multiple uncoordinated	Belgium Italy Spain Switzerland	Mexico United States

Note: Based on *Patterns of Policing* by D. H. Bayley. Copyright © 1985 by Rutgers, the State University of New Jersey. Additional information from "Comparative Organization of the Police in English-Speaking Countries," by D. H. Bayley, 1992, *Crime and Justice, 21*, pp. 509–545.

concise way to describe policing in many different countries by emphasizing the similarities rather than allowing superficial differences to confuse the analysis. In other words, like all good classification schemes, Bayley's typology of police structures summarizes and makes sense of diversity.

Upon understanding the characteristics of each category for police structures, you can assign immediately a new structure to the appropriate category. For example, Kurian (2006b) says that in Mexico the structure of police organizations is complex, and organization changes frequently. Police forces exist at the federal, state, and municipal levels through many overlapping layers of authority. We also know that Mexico has a main federal police; that each state and the federal district has its own police force; and that police delegations, headed by a commandant, operate in large urban areas. Applying Bayley's classification scheme to these characteristics should result in your assignment of Mexico to the cell containing "decentralized" (a different authority supervises the force at each level), "multiple" (there are at least three types of police), and "uncoordinated" (there are apparently overlapping layers of authority) police structures.

With the aid of Bayley's categorization, we now move to a description of one police system falling into each major type found in Table 6.1. Because the United States uses a police system that is less often found, it seems fitting that we better understand what most countries are doing. We do that by describing the police systems in countries that fall into each of six cells in Bayley's typology. The six countries representing each cell are Ghana (centralized single), Japan (decentralized single), France (centralized multiple coordinated), Germany (decentralized multiple coordinated), Spain (centralized multiple uncoordinated), and Mexico (decentralized multiple uncoordinated).

Centralized Single Systems: Ghana

The idea of one national police force responsible for enforcing a single set of laws throughout an entire country sounds strange to Americans. However, as Table 6.1 shows, that system is perfectly acceptable to the citizens of many countries. Nations as geographically and culturally diverse as Cambodia (Cambodian National Police), Denmark (Danish National Police), Israel (the Israel Police), New Zealand (the New Zealand Police), Scotland (Police Scotland), and Singapore (Singapore Police Force) find it possible to operate effective governments with a single national police force.

National police forces are also found throughout the African continent, with countries from Angola to Zimbabwe using this single centralized police structure. We look at the Ghana Police Service as an example of this type (Browne-Marshall, 2005; Ebbe, 1993; Gariba, 2014; Ghana Police Service, 2016; Kurian, 2006a; Odo, 2006).

Ghana (see Map A.1), which is in West Africa, gained its independence from the British in 1957. In 1960, the Ghana Police Force, which had operated under British rule, became the Ghana Police Service (GPS). As an agency operating under Ghana's Ministry of the Interior, the GPS is an autonomous organization whose director (the Inspector-General of Police) is appointed by the president acting in consultation with Ghana's Council of State (a small body of prominent citizens, analogous to the Council of Elders in the traditional political system, which advises the president on national issues).

The GPS is organized into two main groupings under the Inspector-General of Police (IGP): administration and operations (see Figure 6.1). The Deputy IGP for Administration has responsibility for four "schedules" (similar to departments) that range from police recruitment and training to budget and financial matters. The Deputy IGP for Operations oversees four schedules as well, including the criminal investigations division, operations (e.g., traffic and antiterrorism), and the legal unit. The ninth schedule, police intelligence and professional standards, reports directly to the IGP.

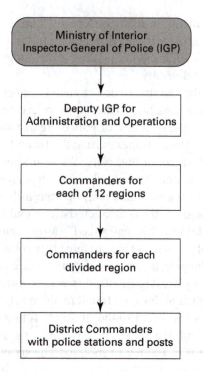

FIGURE 6.1 Ghana's Police Organization

Actual implementation of policing duties is provided under a regional command structure with Ghana being divided into 12 police regions. Under each region's Regional Commander (except the undivided regions of Tema, Upper West, and Upper East) are Divisional Commanders, and they, in turn, have their division divided into districts with District Commanders. It is at this district level where police stations, posts, and officers are found.

The Domestic Violence and Victim Support Unit (DOVVSU) is an interesting specialized unit within the GPS. It was established in 1988 (and formerly called the Women and Juvenile Unit) in response to an increased number of cases of abuse and violence against women and children. In addition to investigating all female- and children-related crimes, the DOVVSU handles domestic violence cases and cases of child abuse. Due to the specialist nature of the DOVVSU's work, the Unit does not function as a regular police station. Instead, it operates in conjunction with other agencies such as nongovernmental organizations (NGOs) that support the Unit by providing office space and access to counselors and social workers.

Private security businesses are allowed to perform guard duties for banks, offices, recreational facilities, and other businesses but must do so under the supervision of police and only after obtaining the necessary training to be registered and licensed.

The centralized single police forces of countries such as Poland, Saudi Arabia, Israel, and Nigeria show us just one way of providing law enforcement in a country. The fact that these countries vary considerably in size (Israel is slightly larger than New Jersey whereas Saudi Arabia is one-third the size of the United States) and population density (Nigeria has 322 people per square mile and Saudi Arabia 15) suggests that geography alone is not a likely variable to explain the existence of this type of police structure. Nor does government type seem to predict a single centralized police force because even these few examples include a democratic state (Poland); a monarchy with a council of ministers (Saudi Arabia); a parliamentary republic (Israel); and a federal republic under, until recently, a military leadership (Nigeria).

A country's preferred police structure is not easily explained as the result of one or two clearly identifiable features. A people's history, culture, traditions, and links to other people are only some of the topics to be considered in trying to understand a country's social institutions. Such disciplines as political science, history, sociology, psychology, and anthropology are among those that may provide answers. For our purposes, we must be content with appreciating the variety and forgoing the analysis. In presenting the other examples of police structures, we continue to rely on descriptive accounts rather than analyzing the reasons that various countries share a similar police structure.

Decentralized Single Systems: Japan

Japan (see Map A.8) is offered as the sole example in Table 6.1 of a single police force under decentralized command. Not only are examples scarce for this category, but also there is disagreement even about Japan's placement in that cell. However, to understand the disagreement, it is necessary first to examine the structure of Japanese policing—so we begin at that point.

A combination of pre–World War II reliance on centralization and the remnant of a decentralized format imposed by occupation forces after the war helps explain Japanese policing as an example of a single force under decentralized command. The Tokugawa shogunate (1600–1868) provided for law enforcement through an elaborate system wherein town magistrates (or their delegates) served in roles we would today call police chief, prosecutor, and judge. Average citizens also played an important part because they were grouped into organizations and made mutually responsible and collectively liable for any crimes or disorder caused by each other (Ames, 1983). The shogun provided a central authority over this policing arrangement through his links to town magistrates and the citizen organizations.

With the Meiji Restoration (1868–1912), Japan began gathering ideas about policing from the West. When Kawaji Toshiyoshi was sent to Europe in 1872, he was charged with investigating the police structures in several countries. Upon his return to Japan later that same year, Kawaji recommended police reorganization along the lines of France (Westney, 1987). The result was the 1873 establishment of the Home Ministry, which provided direct control over prefectural administration. The Police Bureau, within the Home Ministry, allowed the ministry to control police activities throughout Japan. It was centralization such as this that the Allied occupation forces found potentially destructive to the newly established peace. As a result, as was correspondingly done in post–World War II Germany, Allied occupation forces in Japan decided to decentralize the nation's police.

Ames (1983) and Chwialkowski (1998) describe how the American advisers made suggestions for a reorganized Japanese police that would closely follow the American model. With the new Police Law of 1947, the Home Ministry was abolished, police were relieved of administrative duties (e.g., issuing permits and regulating public health, construction, and similar businesses), and autonomous police units were established.

WEB PROJECT

Comparing Police

Go to the OSCE-POLIS member country page at http://polis.osce.org/countries/ and select two of the hyperlinked countries for a closer look. You will find that for each country there is information about that country's police. Although specific information will vary according to what the country has provided, there will often be material on the topics of "function and missions," "structure and organization," and "education/training." Write a few paragraphs that compare the two countries on the topic (or topics) you have chosen.

All cities and towns with populations of 5,000 and over were told to establish a police force, and, as a result, some 1,600 independent municipal police departments were organized. The smaller towns and villages were policed by a new National Rural Police, which was organized at the prefecture level with very limited national level involvement.

Like the citizens of the new West Germany, which we discuss shortly, the Japanese had immediate problems with these structures imposed by the occupation forces. Difficulties in providing financial support for the local police and the presence of undesirable influence from politicians and gangsters were of particular concern. Finally, in June 1951, the Police Law was amended to allow smaller communities to merge their police forces with the National Rural Police. Eighty percent of the communities with autonomous police forces quickly disbanded their independent forces and joined with the rural police.

In 1954, a new Police Law abolished the dual system of municipal and rural police and integrated the two types into prefectural police forces, which provided the base for today's structure (Terrill, 2016; Yuki, 2005).

Japan now has three main law enforcement organizations (see Figure 6.2). The National Public Safety Commission, under the direct authority of the prime minister, is responsible for all police operations and activities in Japan. This remnant from decentralization times is a relatively ineffective approach to maintaining public control of the police. The typically elderly and conservative men serving on the commission almost

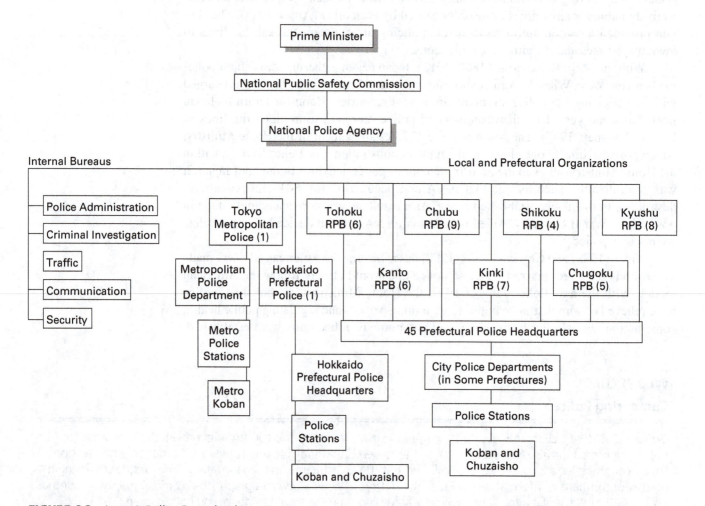

FIGURE 6.2 Japan's Police Organization

always defer to police decisions. As a result, the police are independent of effective formal external checks on their power and operation.

The National Police Agency (NPA), the second of the three main organizations, serves as a central supervisory agency for the Japanese police system. The NPA is not a separate police force, and its officers perform strictly supervisory duties. This agency compiles crime statistics, furnishes criminal identification services, procures police equipment, supervises police education and training, and is authorized to take command of prefecture police forces in a national emergency or large-scale disaster (Ames, 1983; Terrill, 2016; Yuki, 2005). The NPA is headed by a commissioner-general and consists of five bureaus: Police Administration, Criminal Investigation, Traffic, Communications, and Security.

Providing a step toward decentralized command are seven regional police bureaus (RPBs), which serve as a liaison with the prefectural police. In addition to the seven RPBs, two police communications divisions also operate under the NPA (see Figure 6.2). These divisions provide structural integration of the country's largest city police force (Tokyo Metropolitan Police Communications Division) and for Japan's only region that is also a prefecture (Hokkaido Prefectural Police Communications Division).

The only agencies to perform actual police work in Japan are the local and prefectural organizations. That may seem to make Japan an example of a centralized (command is from a common national agency) multiple (there are different local forces) police structure. However, this is where Japan offers a singular example to Table 6.1. Japan is divided into 47 prefectures, which are similar in concept to American states and in size to large American counties. The organizational chart in Figure 6.2 indicates (in parentheses) the number of prefectures in each of Japan's regions (e.g., the Tohoku region has six). Each prefecture has one police headquarters from which chiefs and assistant chiefs control everyday police operations.

It is at the prefecture level that confusion arises about whether Japan has single or multiple forces and whether it is a centralized or decentralized structure. The highest-level officials at prefectural police headquarters (e.g., chief and senior police superintendents) are employees of the NPA. That fact would suggest a single force rather than multiple forces. All other officers (e.g., police superintendent, police inspector, police sergeant, and policeman) are employed by the prefecture and at the prefecture's expense. The prefecture-employed police are primarily found at the organizational levels below prefectural police headquarters—suggesting multiple rather than single forces. Based on Figure 6.2, an assumption that police in the police station and *koban* and *chuzaisho* levels are prefectural employees would be correct in most cases. Furthermore, each prefectural police department is supervised by the prefectural public safety commission under the prefectural governor's jurisdiction.

Koban

Koban vary in size and shape from kiosk-like structures at busy street intersections to a quaint house on the bank of a canal. Between these extremes are koban operating from a thin, two-story building crammed among tall office buildings or a room sandwiched between the bar below and a restaurant above.

Courtesy of Dorling Kindersley.

The 47 prefectures are themselves divided into districts. Each district has its own police station area under the direct control of prefectural police headquarters. Some of the police station boundaries correspond to city boundaries, but larger cities often have several police stations (Ames, 1983). Officers start their shift by reporting to the police station headquarters and are then deployed throughout the station boundaries. Because the NPA supervises and trains both its employees (the highest level officials at prefectural headquarters) and the prefecture employees (the regular police officers) and is the administrative unit for all police operations, Japan seems to have a single police force. Yet, that single force clearly operates under a dispersal of command to the prefectural level. That means we have the unusual situation of a single force with decentralized command (Bayley, 1992).

The area covered by a police station further divides into small jurisdictions linked to police boxes called koban and chuzaisho. Koban, which are located in urban areas, are staffed by 2–12 officers in a single shift. The specific number varies according to the area covered by the koban. Ames (1983), Bayley (1991), and Parker (1984, 2013) provide interesting descriptions of koban based on their individual experiences in Japan.

Chuzaisho are the koban of rural areas. These police boxes are more typically built like the houses of their village. The chuzaisho includes a living area for the assigned police officer and his or her family. Parker (1984) highlights the close ties that develop between an officer and the community by noting that the chuzaisan ranks with the village headman and school principal as top town officials.

YOU SHOULD KNOW!

Policing in the People's Republic of China

Policing in China (see Map A.7) is clearly centralized and multiple. A lack of research and available information makes it difficult to determine whether it is coordinated or uncoordinated. But, whether coordinated or uncoordinated, it is certainly flexible.

In its 1995 Police Law, China identified four police types: the Public Security Police (under the Ministry of Public Security), the State Security Police (under the Ministry of State Security), the Prison Police (under the Ministry of Justice), and the judicial police (operating under various levels of People's Courts and levels of People's Procurators). However, in addition to those four, Sun and Wu (2006) make a good argument for including the People's Armed Police (PAP) in the list of Chinese police agencies.

The Public Security Police agency is the largest, oldest, and primary component of Chinese policing (Ma, 2005). This agency, which is responsible for day-to-day policing activities, includes the railway police, transportation police, civil aviation police, and forest police. The State Security Police (protect against foreign espionage, sabotage, and conspiracies) also have general policing duties, but the Prison Police (supervise convicted offenders in prisons) and the judicial police (maintain security and order in courts, and escort suspects) are much more specialized.

What makes the PAP interesting as possible additions to the more typically cited examples of Chinese policing is their shared command between the Ministry of Public Security (China's main civilian administrative body) and the Central Military Committee (China's main military administrative body). Sun and Wu (2006) believe this agency deserves more attention than it receives (it was not mentioned in the 1995 Police Law) because the Central Military Committee has made it clear that the PAP will be the first to be mobilized in situations of social disorder. In that sense, the PAP becomes China's main force in charge of domestic security and social stability. This paramilitary force is apparently authorized to stop and question suspicious persons, to search people and their property, and to seize objects and contraband. Although the PAP do not seem to have arrest and detain powers (they must be assisted by regular police), the research by Sun and Wu suggests that the PAP may take suspects into custody and take them to local police for disposition or further investigation. On that basis, the PAP deserves consideration when police forces in China are explained.

Centralized Multiple Coordinated Systems: France

Bayley (1985) distinguishes between multiple coordinated and multiple uncoordinated systems to demarcate situations in which several forces operate within defined jurisdictions from those in which several forces have overlapping authority. He reminds us, however, that all national governments create police agencies with authority for areas that transcend the concerns of subordinate government units. Examples include the FBI in the United States and Canada's Royal Canadian Mounted Police. So, technically, all multiple-force countries have uncoordinated systems because there is inevitably a national-level agency with overlapping authority.

Bayley (1985) assigns a country to a coordinated or uncoordinated cell according to his judgment about the level of importance attached to the central government's responsibilities in the total view of policing. In a coordinated police system, enforcement by the central government is deemed relatively unimportant. Central authority is curtailed by such techniques as limiting its jurisdictional area and allowing it to intervene only at the request of local authorities. Alternatively, uncoordinated forces are independently active, have responsibility for many offenses, and can act without prior approval of local authorities. Although recognizing that multiple-force countries are necessarily uncoordinated, we follow Bayley's lead and, for purposes of description and education, distinguish some as coordinated.

Table 6.1 places countries such as Austria and England and Wales among the centralized multiple coordinated types. The England and Wales placement would likely irritate some British observers and, therefore, deserves brief justification. There are 43 police forces in England and Wales. Forty-one are provincial forces and two serve the London area: the London Metropolitan Police (with Scotland Yard being its Criminal Investigation Department) and the City of London Police. The Home Office (i.e., the central government) has indirect supervision over all the police forces. The controversy about England and Wales being an example of a centralized police command is based on how "indirect" the Home Office supervision is over the police forces.

The argument for England and Wales being described as having decentralized policing is supported by an organizational structure that allows responsibilities to be shared by local police and crime commissioners (elected by the people living in the community), the chief constable responsible for each police force, and by the Home Secretary (representing the central government). The police and the crime commissioners, as community representatives, are expected to influence priorities for local policing since they understand the problems affecting their specific community (Terrill, 2016). The commissioners also establish the budget for the police force and have the authority to hire and fire the chief constable. Because of these local influences, British citizens and politicians cringe at the suggestion that they have a national police force with multiple agencies.

Although the role of local police authorities seems to be a good criterion for a decentralized system, persons arguing for England and Wales as a centralized system point out that the central government (along with grants from local government and a locally-levied property tax) provides the police funding, approves the appointment of the chief and assistant constables, and supervises (through Her Majesty's Inspectorate of Constabulary) annual inspections of each department. As a result, many authors believe that centralization is a fact that is becoming increasingly apparent. So, with no intent to offend British feelings, England and Wales are included here among the centralized multiple coordinated police types.

A less controversial example of centralized multiple coordinated police structures is France (see Map A.10), to which we now turn our attention. French policing dates back at least to 1666 and Louis XIV's creation of a Lieutenant-General of Police for Paris. The holder of that position had both administrative and judicial tasks ranging from controlling prices, weights and measures, and inspecting markets to apprehending criminals and developing surveillance of suspected traitors. This office was abolished after the French Revolution, and Napoleon appointed a Minister of Police, who initially focused on information gathering and state security.

In 1941, the Vichy government established the basic structure of French policing with the Gendarmerie Nationale policing the rural areas and the Police Nationale having responsibility for urban policing. In this manner, French policing reflects the multiple coordinated type because each force has separate jurisdictions.

Prior to 2002, each force not only had separate jurisdictions but also reported to separate ministries within the central government. The director of the Gendarmerie Nationale reported to the Minister of Defense (reflecting the gendarmes' military affiliation), whereas the director of the Police Nationale reported to the Minister of the Interior. That forked version of centralization is described by Stead (1983) as a conspicuous strategy to avoid the concentration of force in the hands of a single person. That began changing in 2002 when a decree gave the Ministry of the Interior responsibility for the Gendarmerie when the gendarmes are fulfilling their policing (but not their military) duties. This organizational change has resulted in the gendarmes being teamed with the civil police in several parts of France to help distribute police services more evenly across the country and to make more effective use of resources and intelligence (OSCE POLIS, 2010; Terrill, 2016).

GENDARMERIE NATIONALE   The French Gendarmerie is the older of the two police forces. It is responsible for enforcing the law in the rural areas of France and in communities that typically have fewer than 20,000 people. The fact that there are few densely populated metropolitan areas means that 90 percent of French territory and nearly half its population are the gendarmes' responsibility (OSCE POLIS, 2010).

A director-general—responsible to the Minister of the Interior for policing duties and to the Minister of Defense for military duties—controls the Gendarmerie (see Figure 6.3). The military linkages should not, however, detract attention from the Gendarmerie's sophisticated and highly successful style as they conduct typical civilian policing duties of patrol, surveillance, maintaining public order, and criminal investigation. The policing of France's road traffic and smaller towns is carried out by personnel meeting high recruitment and training standards using quality equipment that would be the envy of most police forces.

The Gendarmerie has two significant subdivisions. The first, the Departmental Gendarmerie, is divided into brigades and includes specialized units for such tasks as criminal investigation; prevention of juvenile delinquency; and the patrolling of roads, mountains, and air traffic. The other subdivision is the Gendarmerie Mobile, which is a public-order force with semi-military training. The mobile Gendarmerie units are housed in barracks and are distributed throughout the country. Their principal mission is the maintenance or reestablishment of order, so the units can be deployed on short notice at the government's request. The squadrons are mobile through their armored vehicles, light tanks, and helicopters (Horton, 1995; OSCE POLIS, 2010).

POLICE NATIONALE   Stead (1983) points out that most foreigners seem to assume that all French police are gendarmes. The high visibility of gendarmes (constantly in uniform and on patrol throughout the country) makes the assumption understandable. The Police Nationale, however, is the larger of the two forces, with about 150,000 police officers and administrative employees compared with 100,000 Gendarmerie officers and staff. Operating primarily in urban centers of more than 16,000 in population, the

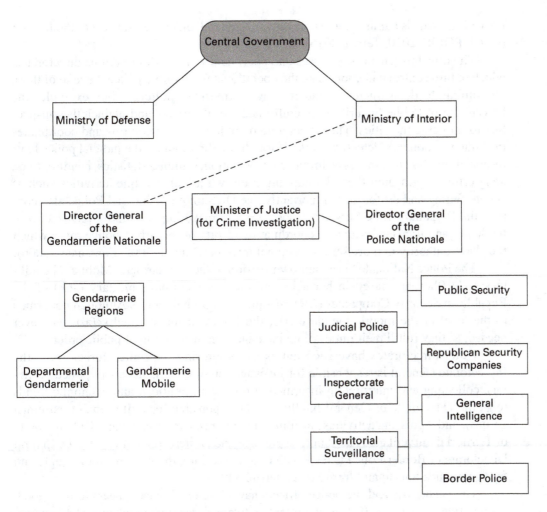

FIGURE 6.3 France's Police Organization

The French Gendarmerie has been among the fastest-expanding security force in France over the last several decades—playing an increasingly prominent role in counterterrorism activities (Lutterbeck, 2013). Over the same period, it has been increasingly demilitarized (civilianized). That began in 2002, when authority over the Gendarmerie's civil policing duties was transferred to the Ministry of Interior (with its military duties remaining under the Defense Ministry). To strengthen cooperation between the Gendarmerie and the Police Nationale, regional intervention brigades were created to link officers of both forces and persons from other enforcement agencies. These brigades combat violent crime, illegal trafficking, and the illegal economy generally—meaning that the gendarmes are directly involved in prominent policing action.

In 2009, the Interior Ministry's powers over the Gendarmerie were further strengthened by placing essentially all nonmilitary aspects of the Gendarmerie's control, function, and budget under the Interior Ministry. Since 2011, gendarmes and certain police officers have been able to request a temporary transfer to the other force while remaining at the equivalent rank—and officers from both forces have requested such a transfer.

Despite a clear trend toward the demilitarization of the French Gendarmerie (in terms of transfer of control to the Interior Ministry and increased interaction with civilian law enforcement), the formal military status of the Gendarmerie has been maintained. Lutterbeck (2013) suggests that the formal military status is likely to remain since that status means the officers are always available (military officers cannot strike nor can they form unions) and the military's strict sense of discipline are viewed as important assets that would be lost with further civilianization.

Police Nationale is administrated by a director-general under the Ministry of the Interior (OSCE POLIS, 2010; Terrill, 2016).

The director-general supervises and coordinates the work of various directorates, which in turn control and coordinate the operational work of the police. Several of these are similar to departments found in Anglo-American policing. For example, the Directorate of Public Security uses uniformed patrol officers and plainclothes inspectors for policing the cities. The Directorate of Judicial Police controls and coordinates the Police Nationale's detective work. Through sub directorates, the judicial police have responsibility for such things as forensic investigation, criminal statistics, banditry (e.g., gang crime, aggravated theft, kidnapping), and white-collar crime activities such as counterfeiting and art forgery. Importantly, the Directorate of Judicial Police also controls the Regional Crime Services. These services make inquiries into organized, professional, and transient crime by coordinating efforts of the urban police, over which they have authority in more serious criminal matters (Dupont, 2005; Fontanaud, 2006).

The Police Nationale have their own version of the Gendarmerie Mobile. The military style (they are based in barracks and their officers have military rank) of the Republican Security Companies (CRS) disguises their civil nature. Although not armed to the level of the mobile Gendarmerie, the CRS can move equally fast, wherever needed, as they fulfill their duties of maintenance and restoration of public order.

Other directorates have such duties as monitoring the police forces (e.g., the Inspectorate General is responsible for investigation of complaints about police behavior), collecting and interpreting information on social, political, and economic trends (e.g., the Directorate of General Intelligence is responsible for infiltration of extremist groups), and repressing activities harmful to the interests of France (e.g., the Directorate of Territorial Surveillance has counterespionage and antiterrorist duties, and the Central Directorate of Border Police is responsible for controlling the movement of people and foreign publications to and from French territory).

The gendarmes and the police officers have developed what appears to be a good, cooperative, and respectful arrangement between large independent police forces. Americans are more used to seeing police agencies at odds with one another than engaging in a spirit of cooperation. The local police complain that the FBI takes credit for breaking a case, or a city police department withholds evidence from the sheriff's department in the hope of making its own unaided arrest. Those examples seem more typical of America's version of interagency cooperation. But we should not be too quick to assume that France avoids similar problems (Hodgson, 2005; Horton, 1995). As Stead (1983) points out, police everywhere and throughout time have been reluctant to share their hard-won criminal intelligence, so it is not surprising that two different organizations with different traditions will encounter competition and rivalry as they pursue the same ends. Hodgson (2005) reports that gendarmes and police she interviewed showed a degree of mutual distrust and even resentment between the two forces. As an example, she notes that the gendarmes complained about the difficulty they have when wanting to work as plainclothes officers compared with the ease of doing so for the Police Nationale. The police, on the other hand, resented the greater powers gendarmes have to carry firearms. It appears that despite the tranquility of force coordination on paper, there is less harmony in practice.

POLICE MUNICIPAL Further indication that the French system is not as synchronized as the French would like is suggested by a January 1983 law authorizing locally controlled police. Today, there are about 20,000 municipal police officers and agents responsible for daily urban policing. These municipal police officers are employed, managed, and paid for at the local level and are accountable to the mayor (Hodgson, 2005; OSCE POLIS, 2010). Their existence could present a problem for our placement of France with the police systems under a centralized command because they are under local rather than central authority. At this time, however, there are several reasons to downplay the importance of the mayors' police and to keep France among the countries with a centralized police system. These reasons include the municipal police forces' typical size, duties, and authority.

Police Municipale units are usually small and the officers lack the power of the national police. Because the mayors have considerable latitude in developing their police agencies (including whether or not they should be armed), substantial variation exists in the duties given to each force. In towns with significant tourist traffic, the Police Municipale are primarily order-maintenance personnel. In other cities, they are weapons-carrying, crime-fighting, traditional cops. In both instances, however, these municipales are supplements to—not replacements of—the Police Nationale and the Gendarmerie. The municipal police have only limited enforcement powers and no general investigative powers. In cases of serious crime and for criminal investigations, they are expected to call the judicial police, the Gendarmerie, or the Police Nationale.

In recent years, the municipal police have become more professional and now wear unique uniforms and have cars that distinguish them from the national police and the gendarmerie. However, despite an increasingly unique look, they still tend to follow national police procedures and act primarily to complement and reinforce the work of the national police. For these reasons, and because most French cities have not formed municipal police units, it seems appropriate to retain France among the countries operating a centralized multiple coordinated police structure.

Decentralized Multiple Coordinated Systems: Germany

Quite a variety of countries have police systems that are composed of several forces under the command of different government levels. Table 6.1 suggests that Australia, Canada, and India are examples of such police systems. Each of Australia's six states and two territories has its own police force with jurisdiction defined by the state and territorial boundaries. An exception is the Australian Federal Police, which enforces federal statutes throughout the country (compare it to the FBI in the United States) and has responsibility for the Australian Capital Territory. India has 25 state forces plus national units stationed in seven Union Territories. Canada, which receives closer attention in this chapter's "Impact" box, has police forces at the municipal, provincial, and federal levels. A common trait among these countries is the coordination each has been able to achieve among its multiple and decentralized police forces. Germany (see Map A.10), the example provided here, shows similar characteristics.

The occupation of Germany by Allied forces after World War II provides a relevant recent history for German policing. The Potsdam Agreement of 1945 provided the Allies with the task of decentralizing, democratizing, and demilitarizing areas of public life in each defeated country's zone of occupation. Although there was agreement on the need to decentralize the police, the Allies had different ideas about what decentralization was, and the goal was approached differently by the British, French, and Americans (Fairchild, 1988; Thomaneck, 1985).

To the British, decentralization meant regionally organized police under the watchful eye of civilian police authorities. The system the British established in Germany was remarkably similar to that found in Great Britain. Also, as in Britain, the police function in this occupation zone was limited to the maintenance of law and order and the detection of crime. This meant that the traditional administrative functions of German police (e.g., registration of all residents, environmental health, building permits and regulations, road supervision) were transferred to other administrative departments.

The police administrative functions were retained in the French zone. Also, the French saw nothing inherently bad in centralized control of the police, so that structure

YOU SHOULD KNOW!

Was That a Mountie?

Canada (see Map A.3) falls among the decentralized multiple coordinated police systems. There are three levels of Canadian law enforcement (federal, provincial, and municipal), with control and supervision decentralized to the government at each level. Yet, the differences are not always apparent. For example, during a visit to North Vancouver, you will find Royal Canadian Mounted Police (RCMP) officers providing police services to that city. Should you need a police officer as you leave North Vancouver and travel across the rural parts of British Columbia, you will be directed to the provincial police, whom you will easily recognize because they are still the RCMP. Of course, if the federal police stop you anywhere in the province, you will again see the now familiar RCMP uniform.

Just as you think you have this system figured out, you fly from Vancouver to Toronto. After renting a car at the airport, you drive to your hotel and pass a police car with "Metro Toronto Police" painted on the door. Inside the car is a police officer wearing a non-Mountie uniform. The next day you decide to drive to Ottawa. With

a concern for the provincial police, whom you correctly assume to be responsible for catching speeders on the highway, you look for officers like the ones you saw in British Columbia. Unfortunately, while concentrating on remembering the Mountie uniform, you are pulled over by a police officer wearing an Ontario Provincial Police uniform.

Canada's police structure is not as strange as your visit may lead you to believe. In fact, it is very straightforward. As has been noted, there are three distinct levels operating under the supervision of federal, provincial, and municipal authorities. The different experiences in British Columbia and Ontario are simply the result of Canada's provision for contract policing. The province of British Columbia and its city of North Vancouver have contracted with the RCMP (the federal agency) to provide the province and some cities with police services. The province of Ontario and its city of Toronto have chosen to provide their own provincial and local law enforcement. See this chapter's "Impact" box for more on the idea of contracting for police services.

was essentially retained, with a concession to decentralization being the granting of some police functions to small-town mayors. Again, the similarity to the structure of policing at home—in this case, France—was not well hidden.

Americans retained central police control as an organizational principle but only in communities with fewer than 5,000 inhabitants. Larger communities had locally controlled communal police in much the same way that American cities have their own local police. This plan represented the greatest difference from the traditional German organization. In the American zone, mayors were made responsible for setting up police forces and providing for weapons, clothes, and supervision.

Not surprisingly, Germans found the mixture of police structures to be inconvenient, inappropriate, and ineffective. In 1949, German officials complained that communal police forces in small towns were impractical. In 1950, the Allied High Command decided that each state government (in then West Germany) could centralize its police at the state level. Gradually, cities gave up their local police force until each state passed police laws regulating the activities and organization of the newly centralized police. By 1955, all northern German states had completed the reconstruction of their police. In 1975, Munich disbanded its communal police force, and the reconstruction was finally complete for all West Germany.

Today, the day-to-day operations of German policing are decentralized to the state (Länder) level (see Figure 6.4). Federal forces exist, but policing is essentially a state matter. The two primary federal agencies are the Federal Criminal Police (Bundeskriminalamt—BKA) and, since 2005, the Federal Police (Bundespolizei—BPOL). The BKA, which is modeled on the FBI, has a broad range of federal and international duties and operates under the Federal Ministry of the Interior. It serves as the central headquarters for law enforcement in Germany and is the conduit for electronic data interchange between the federal and the state police. The BPOL, also under the Federal Ministry of the Interior, patrols the borders and railways and protects most of

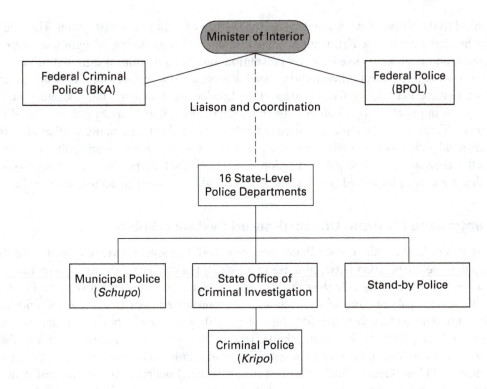

FIGURE 6.4 Germany's Police Organization

the major airports. In addition, the BPOL has responsibility for preventing illegal immigration and is increasingly involved in police missions abroad.

Each of Germany's 16 states controls its own police force, with the federal government acting as a liaison and coordinating agent. Despite the potential for great divergence, there is considerable similarity among the various state police. The glue providing the similarity arises from tradition and from the fact that the laws enforced in each Land are rather standard. As a result, one hardly notices any difference among the police from one state to another. The trend is toward even greater similarity. For example, before 1976 the police in each state wore different uniforms. In that year, a standard forest green uniform (with different state sleeve patches, cap emblem, and rank insignia) was introduced and in 1980 made mandatory. After unification of Germany in 1990, the five states of former East Germany also adopted the standard uniform. In an effort to conform to EU standards, the German police have gradually been converting from their traditional uniform to a dark blue color. By 2009, most state police agencies had converted to blue uniforms, but the states of Bavaria and Saarland have not joined in the conversion and continue to use the traditional green color for the police (Banninga, 2016).

The typical structure of policing in the Länder involves a three-part division (Feltes, 2005, 2006; Harnischmacher, 2006; OSCE POLIS, 2006). The Schutzpolizei (typically shortened to Schupo) are the uniform-wearing police and have the highest visibility and broadest range of duties. They are the first to arrive on the scene of all types of crimes and are initially responsible for all aspects of enforcement and investigation. Patrol is mostly by car, but the Schupo also have mounted police units, canine units, and armed police officers working in helicopters.

Soon after the Schupo have determined that a crime has occurred or have identified a suspect, the criminal police or Kriminalpolizei (Kripo) are called in—unless it was a minor, open-and-shut case, which the Schupo is likely to handle. The Kripo are plainclothes officers similar to detectives in the United States. They have the authority to search and seize and are responsible for developing a case and initiating charges against suspects.

Linked to the Kripo in every Länder is a State Office of Criminal Investigation. This central headquarters for the Kriminalpolizei is responsible for gathering all significant information and documents used for the prevention and investigation of criminal offenses. Personnel at this central crime-fighting headquarters analyze information, conduct crime lab activities, and notify police throughout the Länder about the current crime situation.

The third police organization is the Bereitschaftspolizei, or "standby police." The officers in this paramilitary force are quartered in barracks and act only in units rather than as individual police. Traditionally, their function has been the training of young police officers. As the name suggests, their public function is to support the Schupo when large numbers of police are needed for crowd control, emergency activities, serious accidents, and the like.

Centralized Multiple Uncoordinated Systems: Spain

Any rivalry between the French Police Nationale and the Gendarmerie may lead some to question the cooperation between those two French police forces. However, a review of uncoordinated forces quickly shows us that any problems encountered between the French police groups pale in comparison to those in uncoordinated systems such as the ones in Belgium, Italy, and Switzerland. Italy (see Map A.10), for example, has six national police forces (Carrer, 2006) with general (the Polizia di Stato—the State Police Force, and the Carabinieri—military police force) or specific (Finance Police, Penitentiary Police, Forestry Police, and Coast Guard) duties. The first two, as general police, have the broadest duties and are the ones that best typify the lack of coordination (Bjorken, 2005). As with the French system, Italy sets one police force under its Ministry of Defense (the Carabinieri) with a focus on—but is not restricted to—rural law enforcement. The other force, the Polizia di Stato, operates under the Ministry of Interior and is responsible for law enforcement throughout the country. Problems arise because the Carabinieri, when engaged in police duties, is supposed to follow directions from the Interior Ministry. However, institutional rivalry, competition, and a somewhat high degree of animosity between the two police forces persuade the Carabinieri to be more responsive to orders from the Ministry of Defense. The result is a centralized system with multiple yet uncoordinated policing (Barbagli & Sartori, 2004). Similar problems confront Spain's (see Map A.10) police system.

Italian Carabinieri
Italy's Carabinieri is the largest gendarmerie-type force in Western Europe. Although the Carabinieri are responsible for policing Italy's rural areas (and the State Police the cities), in practice the division is not strictly followed—as suggested by this Carabinieri patrol in Venice.
Philip L. Reichel

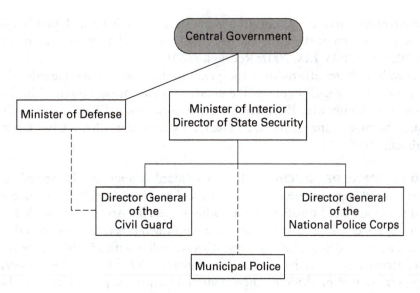

FIGURE 6.5 Spain's Police Organization

Spanish police forces can trace their history to the twelfth century, but the first modern versions were formed in 1829 with the Carabineros and in 1844 with the Guardia Civil. Today Spain has three major law enforcement systems: the Cuerpo Nacional de Policia (National Police Corps), the Guardia Civil (Civil Guard), and the Policia Municipal (Municipal Police). In addition, there are three regional police forces sharing some law enforcement tasks with the state forces in Spain's three autonomous regions: Basque Country, Catalonia, and Navarre (Onieal, 2005). The system is considered centralized because all forces operate under the authority of the national government. The Minister of the Interior has responsibility for policing in Spain, but within the ministry the task specifically falls to the Director of State Security. Even the Municipal Police are ultimately linked to the central government because those local forces are governed by the same 1986 law that regulates the two national forces (see Figure 6.5).

GUARDIA CIVIL   The oldest national police force in Spain is the Guardia Civil (Civil Guard). This force was patterned after the French Gendarmerie but since the 1970s has not been formally a part of the armed forces. It is more accurately described as an armed institution of military nature. The Guardia Civil appears in the Defense Ministry organizational chart, but only with an indirect link that restricts the military's role mostly to issues of recruitment, careers, and discipline (Lutterbeck, 2013). The Director General of the Civil Guard, who has almost always been a civilian, reports to both the defense and interior ministries, but the role of the Interior Ministry is clearly stronger.

The Guardia Civil operates primarily in rural areas where it covers all aspects of policing and law enforcement. It also has exclusive authority over weapons and explosives control and the monitoring of sea and land borders and generally takes the lead in

WEB PROJECT

Inside Spain's Civil Guard

Read the article about Spain's Civil Guard at http://elpais.com/elpais/2014/10/20/inenglish/1413807111_949949.html and then write a few paragraphs that describe some items you found especially interesting. Do you get the impression that the Civil Guard will continue to be linked with the military?

counterterrorism activities. About 40 percent of the Spanish population live in areas under the jurisdiction of the Civil Guard (Canabata & Dulin, 2006; Lutterbeck, 2013; Onieal, 2005; OSCE POLIS, 2007; Rodríguez, 2014).

There have been efforts over the years to demilitarize the Guardia Civil and there have even been calls to merge the guard with the national police. This is similar to the move to demilitarize the French Gendarmerie, but a difference in Spain is that there may be more support for such change by members of the Civil Guard itself (Lutterbeck, 2013).

CUERPO NACIONAL DE POLICIA   If the Civil Guard is a symbol of Spain's past, the National Police Corps represents a new order and provides a symbol of democracy. The national police are a combination of two earlier forces: the Armed and Traffic Police and the Superior Police Corps. The former was a uniformed urban force under military control. The latter served as plainclothes investigative police with a highly political purpose and was accused of repressive tactics (Macdonald, 1987; Morn & Toro, 1989). When the two were united in 1986, the new National Police Corps took responsibility for policing Spain's urban areas. Today, the National Police Corps (with the Superior Corps as its detective component) operates in all provincial capitals and in municipalities with over 20,000 residents—covering about 60 percent of the Spanish population. Its responsibilities include maintaining and restoring public order and security, issuing identity cards and passports, supervising private security forces, and enforcing gambling and drug laws (Canabata & Dulin, 2006; Onieal, 2005; OSCE POLIS, 2007).

The National Police Corps is headed by a director-general of the police who reports to the Minister of the Interior through the Director of State Security. The separate and distinct nature of the two police forces before their combination has caused some turmoil as Spain tries to improve police efficiency and eliminate rivalry between the previously divided units. Attempts to reduce such problems have included the institution of common training and entrance procedures along with a clean break with any military links to the Armed and Traffic Police.

POLICIA MUNICIPAL   Municipal Police officers are recruited locally and are responsible to the mayor and town hall in each city. They are considered ambassadors for their town and are likely to assist tourists but also devote much time to local traffic control and parking violations (Onieal, 2005). Because every municipality, from the largest cities to those under 100 people, is authorized to create its own police force, these units would seem to make Spain's system decentralized. However, as mentioned earlier, the Municipal Police are regulated by the same 1986 law that governs the National Police and the Civil Guard. That law restricts the Municipal Police duties to protecting city buildings, traffic control, and assisting other police forces in such tasks as crowd control.

UNCOORDINATED POLICING   Spain's 1986 law attempted to improve police efficiency by eliminating parallel structures, dual command systems, and intercorps rivalry (Onieal, 2005). The endeavor was successful to a great extent, but Spain's police system remains correctly classified as uncoordinated rather than coordinated. Macdonald (1987) identifies several areas of conflict among the three law enforcement units. First, both the National Police Corps and the Civil Guard have some authority to operate anywhere in the nation despite the presumed urban/rural jurisdictional division. The National Police can go anywhere their criminal investigation and intelligence operations take them, and the Civil Guard can follow any lead their inquiries may present. That national authority becomes especially troublesome when the crime areas for each police force overlap. For example, drug trafficking falls in the National Police Corps' concern with drug crime but is also linked to the Civil Guard's charge to protect ports and airports and to halt smuggling operations. When both national police forces investigate the same criminal activity and can conduct that investigation throughout the country, the potential for confusion is considerable.

The lack of coordination is not just between the two national forces. Under the Spanish system, every member of any police force is automatically a member of the Judicial Police (Canabata & Dulin, 2006). In that role, the police assist the judges and prosecutors as they investigate a crime. Prior to 1986, this provision caused some problems because the police often took a leadership role in investigations whereas the court personnel simply followed. The 1986 law reasserts judicial power and makes units of Judicial Police functionally responsible to the courts although still administratively linked to the Ministry of the Interior. Because Municipal Police officers can act as Judicial Police when necessary, criminal investigation under court direction may at times rely on police from three different forces. Again, the possibility of confusion and working at cross-purposes is increased by such an arrangement.

The 1986 law takes specific interest in trying to avoid disorder and create cooperation among the police forces. The law stipulates that police units must act in accordance with the principle of reciprocal cooperation and even sets penalties of dismissal or suspension for officers not so behaving (Macdonald, 1987). If both national forces find themselves involved in the same action, the first force committed is to continue its operation until the Civil Governor or the Ministry of the Interior rules on jurisdiction. The fact that the law must include these provisions reinforces the characterization of Spain's policing system as involving a centralized command with multiple uncoordinated forces. It is now time to see how decentralized policing handles the problem of supervising its multiple forces.

Decentralized Multiple Uncoordinated Systems: Mexico

The United States, with more separate police forces than any country in the world, is easily the most extreme case of a decentralized multiple uncoordinated system. There are about 18,000 federal, state, and local law enforcement agencies in the United States ranging from single-officer police departments to those with more than 30,000 officers (Banks, Hendrix, Hickman, & Kyckelhahn, 2016). As if that multiplicity of effort were not enough, there are times when the jurisdictions of these agencies overlap. The result is an uncoordinated system that deserves brief elaboration before considering the example of Mexico (see Map A.3).

Both city and county forces are usually considered local policing in the United States. Although city police chiefs typically owe their position to a mayor or city council, the sheriff is an elected official responsible for policing the unincorporated areas of a county. Local police officers enforce the laws of their state and the laws and ordinances passed by the city and county governments. As a county force, sheriff's deputies have authority throughout the county, including the ability to enforce state and county laws being violated in towns and cities. As a courtesy, sheriff's deputies are unlikely to operate in a municipal police jurisdiction without being invited by the police chief.

Because the primary enforcement of state laws is the responsibility of local police, the police agencies at the state level tend to have specific duties. For example, states may have police agencies responsible for patrolling the highways in the state, providing police services to state colleges and universities, enforcing state regulations of items such as alcohol, and policing the state's parks and recreation areas. In many states, these duties are divided among several agencies with names such as Highway Patrol, University Police, Public Safety Officers, Bureau of Investigation Agents, and Park

WOULD CANADA'S SYSTEM WORK IN THE UNITED STATES?

As this chapter points out, police systems are either centralized or decentralized (although Japan presents a unique combination). The U.S. version of extreme decentralization not only places us in the minority among nations but also attracts criticism as being too complex, inefficient, and expensive. Is it possible that other countries use a police structure that we should consider? If so, an intriguing alternative is provided by our neighbor to the north.

The Royal Canadian Mounted Police (RCMP) is a force as familiar to Canadians as the FBI is to U.S. citizens. Like its American counterpart, the RCMP is a federal agency dedicated to the enforcement of federal statutes and executive orders. In addition to federal-level policing, Canada also provides territorial, provincial, and local policing. Although the responsibility for administration of justice actually lies with the provinces, a province can fulfill that duty by contracting with the federal government to provide policing services. Eight of Canada's 10 provinces, all 3 of the territories, and some 150 municipalities have chosen to contract with the federal government and have the RCMP operate as the provincial police (Royal Canadian Mounted Police, 2013). In these cases, the RCMP is under the direction of the provincial attorney general while being under administrative control from the Ottawa headquarters. The exceptions to federal contract policing for the province are Ontario and Quebec. In those provinces, the Ontario Provincial Police and the Quebec Police Force provide law enforcement.

Municipal police forces include those in cities, towns, villages, and townships. Like their counterparts in the United States, these local police departments, when grouped together, make up the country's largest body of police. As the "street cops," they handle most of the crime and are the primary enforcers of the law. The Canadian municipal forces differ from their American neighbors in two important ways:

1. The local Canadian officer may actually be a member of the RCMP with which the city has contracted for policing.
2. The local Canadian officers have the authority to enforce all laws in their jurisdiction—including certain federal statutes, the criminal code and the statutes of their province, and municipal bylaws. Local police officers in the United States enforce city codes and state laws but do not have the authority to enforce federal statutes.

Municipal contracting for police services is done with the province. Because the RCMP serves as the provincial police for eight provinces, the local police officer ends up being an RCMP officer if the municipality contracts with the province to provide police services. Quebec lacks a legal provision for contracting with its municipalities to provide policing, so Ontario is the only province where non-RCMP provincial police do contract policing for municipalities (although the Royal Newfoundland Constabulary provides policing in four Newfoundland municipalities).

The contracting system is very cost-effective for both provinces and municipalities. The procedure began for economic reasons during the 1930s and continues today for similar reasons. The province is charged a percentage of the actual per capita cost for RCMP expenses. That charge is low enough that provinces and municipalities can maintain a highly efficient police system for a reasonable cost (Clarke, 2005; Murray, 2006).

Canada's system of contracting for police services may be appealing to Americans because we already contract for things such as defense counsel and correctional services, and some communities contract with their state police/patrol for law enforcement. Expansion of this option for police services would not violate the American preference for decentralization but would require greater coordination of effort and may mean giving up some local control.

If increased contracting occurs, who will be the contractor? Would local governments contract with each other but not with the state level? Would any state be willing to contract with the federal government for very specific services? Or, would local and state governments contract with private companies? Private security companies may be able to provide traditional police services for some communities. Maybe the future structure of American policing will include a variety of both private and public police forces under command structures that are centralized in one case (e.g., a national private police corporation) and decentralized in the other (e.g., traditional city, state, and federal agencies). Even if that would be too extreme, can you think of alternatives or modifications that could use private policing in the traditionally public arena?

Rangers. In other states, many tasks are consolidated and assigned to one agency, often called the State Police, who provide services ranging from highway patrol to criminal investigations.

Even federal-level law enforcement reflects America's commitment to decentralization of policing. Command authority in federal law enforcement is split two ways. First, policing divides between military and civilian agencies. Their authority is further apportioned within the military and civilian agencies themselves. Military law enforcement, for example, typically rests with traditional police-type agencies such as the Military Police and three investigative agencies: the Naval Criminal Investigative Service, the Air Force Office of Special Investigations, and the Army Criminal Investigation Command. These agencies are responsible for the investigation of crimes committed against U.S. military personnel or property and crimes committed by military personnel. Command authority within federal civil law enforcement is divided among various federal departments, agencies, and bureaus but rests primarily with the Department of the Treasury and the Department of Justice. In the spirit of decentralization, division of authority does not even stop at the department level.

A result of this proliferation of agencies is an occasional overlapping of jurisdictions. State police jurisdictions tend to be large but confined to unincorporated areas and highways. County police (sheriffs) usually share authority with state and municipal forces. Although their jurisdiction may be geographically small in comparison, municipal forces have been known to find themselves working on cases that state and even federal agencies have laid claim to. Our neighbor to the south is faced with a similar situation.

Kurian (2006b) describes Mexico's police system as imitating the American system by having forces at the federal, state, and municipal levels with many overlapping layers of authority. Adding to the confusion, there is very limited public access to information regarding the internal workings of Mexican law enforcement (Vargas, 2006). As a result, descriptive summaries that explain the characteristics of the thousands of federal, state, and municipal police agencies in Mexico are not easily prepared. We rely here on an approach that combines jurisdictional descriptions (e.g., federal, state, municipal) and police function. Reames (2005) explains that police in Mexico have either a preventive function (uniformed, order controlling) or judicial function (typically plainclothes, investigators). To explain policing in Mexico, we use the jurisdictional categories with reference to the different functions (see Figure 6.6).

FEDERAL POLICING Prior to reforms initiated in 2008, policing at the federal level was accomplished by the Federal Preventive Police (Policía Federal Preventiva—PFP) and the Federal Agency of Investigation (Agencia Federal de Investigaciones—AFI). Those agencies typified the separation of functions wherein one agency was tasked with maintaining order and deterring crime through a visible public presence (the PFP) and a separate agency (the AFI) had responsibility for preserving crime scenes and investigating a crime that had been committed (Olson, 2009).

Today, Mexico is moving toward a more collaborative process wherein the preventive police have increased responsibility for crime investigation, securing crime scenes, executing arrest warrants, and other functions that previously fell to the AFI. In 2009, the AFI was effectively dissolved and a new Federal Ministerial Police (Policía Federal Ministerial—PFM) was created. Also, the PFP became the Federal Police (Policía Federal—PF), with the new name reflecting an expansion beyond a solely preventive mandate. As a result, the PF and the PFM work together on investigation—although the protocols to manage this collaboration had yet to be made clear by 2010 (Ingram & Shirk, 2010).

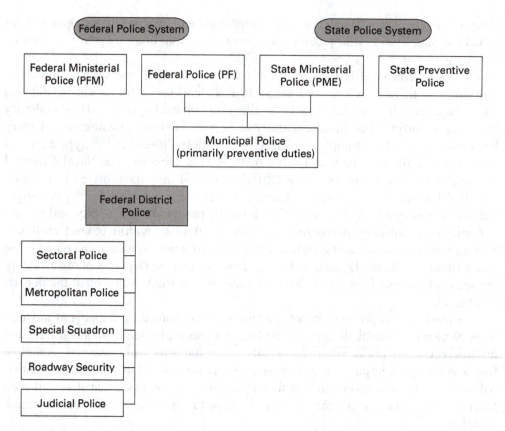

FIGURE 6.6   Mexico's Police Organization

STATE POLICING   Each of Mexico's 31 states has both preventive and investigative police forces, although the actual structure of policing may vary from state to state. Generally, however, there is a judicial police organization (the State Ministerial Police or Policía Ministerial Estatal—PME) that is charged with crime investigation and executing arrest warrants and state-level preventive police with primary responsibilities for order maintenance. The vast majority of police investigations are handled by the state prosecutors and their PME, whereas the state preventive police operate much like the municipal police in Mexico in the sense of being responsible for patrols and responding to calls for service. Should a crime require an investigation, the case is handled by either the PME or a federal agency.

MUNICIPAL POLICING   Mexico's municipio government level is similar to counties in the United States and may contain many smaller towns and cities. Although each municipio may have its own police force, this must be of the preventive force type. All investigations will be handled by the state PME or the federal PF. There are nearly 2,400 municipios in Mexico and some 2,060 of them have a police force (Reames, 2005). The majority of municipios with a police force (2,000 of them) have fewer than 100 officers. Rather than providing much in the way of service to community members, it appears that most of the municipal police officers' time is spent on pedestrian and vehicular patrols. Brown and his colleagues explain this as resulting from the lack of confidence that many citizens have in the municipal police (Brown, Benedict, & Wilkinson, 2006). Some may even fear being victimized by the officers who respond.

FEDERAL DISTRICT POLICING   A fourth jurisdiction is the Federal District. Much like the District of Columbia in the United States, the Distrito Federal (DF) contains the heart of Mexico City and is the seat of the federal government. The area has Mexico's highest crime rate and a very large preventive police force working for the DF's Secretary of

Public Security. Most of the DF preventive police are assigned to the Sectoral Police (Policía Sectoral), and those remaining are distributed among such divisions as the Metropolitan Police (e.g., public transit, mounted, emergency rescue), the Special Squadron (e.g., helicopter, motorcycles, terrorist threats), and Roadway Security. The DF judicial police function is the responsibility of the Judicial Police of the Federal District.

REFORM ATTEMPTS   Since 2000, Mexico's presidents have struggled to achieve reform of the police and other aspects of the justice system. Success has remained elusive, however. By 2010, persistent patterns of corruption, abuse, and ineffectiveness at all levels of policing were openly acknowledged and police reform was at the top of the national agenda (Sabet, 2010). An important result of this failure by civilian police forces to provide basic public security was an increased reliance on the Mexican military to provide domestic security. Interestingly, whereas the police are viewed as ineffective and severely corrupted, the Mexican military enjoys a high degree of public confidence (Donnelly & Shirk, 2010).

In 2012, a National Gendarmerie, modeled after the gendarmeries in France and Spain, was proposed by Mexico's President Nieto. The initial plan was for a paramilitary force under the authority of the secretary of the interior with personnel drawn from the army, marines, and navy. The unit was to be led by a civilian, but operate under military/naval command. The gendarmes would have responsibility for rural municipalities, ports, airports, and borders, and be instrumental in fighting drug cartels (Chalk, 2013). By the time of its eventual implementation in 2014, the plans had been scaled back considerably and the new gendarmerie was responsible for protecting industries likely to be threatened by organized crime (e.g., the harvesting, transport, and sale of crops).

Operating as a division of the Policía Federal, the gendarmes have both police and military training but they are all civilians. They are deployed throughout the country so that they can operate where needed at the time. They are not the type of force initially envisioned, but that is not necessarily bad. After all, as first conceived, it would have added another layer of complexity to an already highly convoluted law enforcement community (Chalk, 2013).

A more promising reform may be the system known as the Mando Unico (implemented in 2014, around the same time as the National Gendarmerie), which would replace locally controlled municipal police with state-led forces. Should it be fully implemented in line with the original plan, Mexico's 1,800 municipal police units would be replaced with 32 centralized state departments. By 2016, only about 20 percent of municipalities were covered under the model, and efforts were seen as having stalled (InSight Crime, 2016; "Why Mexican security is a work in progress," 2016).

The military has in practice had the primary public security role in Mexico since 2006 and it continues to target criminal groups and to conduct public security operations in areas where local authorities are simply too corrupt or ineffective to provide policing (LaSusa, 2016; "Why Mexican security is a work in progress," 2016). Although the military may provide a temporary fix for public security in Mexico, the longer-term solution depends, in part, on addressing corruption in the domestic police forces. However, concerns about police corruption are not limited to Mexico. Unfortunately, corruption and misconduct in law enforcement seems to be a worldwide problem. It is not so much a question of whether such corruption and misconduct exist in law enforcement in an individual country, as how much corruption and misconduct there is.

POLICING ISSUES: POLICE MISCONDUCT

Police misconduct may range from accepting gifts and free meals to protecting the illegal activity of others or committing crimes directly. An even broader definition may include actions that violate citizens' and suspects' procedural rights or exhibit discriminatory behavior toward minority group members. Although there may be disagreement among police and citizens regarding the evil attributed to such low-range versions of misconduct as accepting gifts and free meals, it is safe to assume that behavior at the other extreme (e.g., committing crimes, excessive use of force, unequal treatment based on race) is universally despised.

U.S. citizens are constantly reminded of police misconduct by a seemingly never-ending thread of media reports about graft, corruption, shootings, beatings, and criminal activity. It is clearly an important problem and one that courts, commissions, talk show hosts, editorial writers, average citizens, and police officers themselves have addressed with great seriousness and concern. For many decades, the misconduct was explained by police officials as instances of a "few bad apples" misbehaving and giving the rest of the barrel a bad name (Glazer, 1995). More recently, some criminologists are suggesting the "barrel" itself may be rotten. That is, police work may actually breed misconduct by perpetuating a culture that encourages or at least tolerates police misbehavior. Comparative studies may help answer such questions by finding similarities and contrasts in the occurrence of police misconduct in different countries.

Bracey (1995) notes that until the mid-1970s studies of police corruption tended to focus on the United States. That began changing as media reports about police misbehavior in other countries became more widespread and as surveys such as the *Global Corruption Index* began asking about corruption in various social institutions—including the police. According to Transparency International (2013), the perception of police corruption is found around the world—but it does vary considerably from country to country. For example, the police in Sierra Leone, Nigeria, and Indonesia are perceived to be among the national institutions most affected by corruption, whereas the police in Australia, Finland, and Japan are perceived to be among those least affected by corruption. Police corruption is not restricted by geography or legal tradition.

Certainly, one can argue that levels and types of police misconduct vary by time and country, but keep the big picture in mind for a moment: Police misconduct is undeniably pervasive. How should we interpret this pervasiveness in terms of causes and solutions? Are certain "personality types" attracted to police work in all countries? If police misconduct flourishes only when it is tacitly supported by upper command, why do commanders worldwide seem to approach their supervisory duties so similarly? Does power corrupt? When any society gives some of its citizens the authority to control the behavior of other citizens, will that power inevitably corrupt the controllers?

This book is not an appropriate place to discuss at any length the proposed theories of corruption. Certainly, such features as cultural mores, police management, police–community relations, and many other factors are at play. However, the idea that police

WEB PROJECT

When the Police Shoot

The Guardian (https://www.theguardian.com/us-news/2015/jun/09/the-counted-police-killings-us-vs-other-countries), the *Christian Science Monitor* (http://www.csmonitor.com/World/2015/0628/Why-police-don-t-pull-guns-in-many-countries), and *The Huffington Post* (http://www.huffingtonpost.com/entry/american-cops-lethal_us_565cde59e4b079b2818b8870) are among the media sources writing news stories that compare shootings by police officers in countries around the world. Read at least two of the articles and then write a few paragraphs that summarize points raised in the article and provide your opinion about the article's apparent accuracy, fairness, and the reasonableness of any suggestions in the article for change in the United States.

work itself may breed misconduct is intriguing because of its comparative implications. In other words, if police misconduct results from the occupation itself, we should expect to find misconduct by police officers everywhere. Evidence thus far suggests there may be some truth to this occupational explanation of police misconduct. Confirmation awaits the interested researcher.

POLICING ISSUES: GLOBAL COOPERATION

Both crime and criminals increasingly ignore national boundaries. Because transnational crime and the reaction to it have significant consequences for citizens of every country, the second policing issue considered here is the international response to transnational crime.

Much of the international cooperation in law enforcement is linked to specific crimes. For example, the World Customs Organization (http://www.wcoomd.org) is an international association of national customs agencies that tries to combat transnational crimes such as drug smuggling, money laundering, and the theft of art and cultural objects. The Financial Action Task Force on Money Laundering (http://www.fatf-gafi. org) is an intergovernmental body that focuses on the development and promotion of national and international policies to combat money laundering and terrorist financing. In addition, the United Nations Office on Drugs and Crime (http://www.unodc.org) operates the Joint Programme on Drug Dependence Treatment and Care, the Global Programme against Money-Laundering, and the United Nations Global Initiative to Fight Human Trafficking (UN.GIFT). All of these efforts are especially important in the fight against transnational crime, but there are three other examples used here to show cross-national cooperation in policing: (1) the International Criminal Police Organization (INTERPOL), (2) the European Police Organization (Europol), and (3) the South Asian Association for Regional Cooperation (SAARC). INTERPOL truly reflects global cooperation, while the other two are examples of regional efforts. Discussion here concentrates on these three structures.

International Criminal Police Organization (ICPO)—INTERPOL

The idea of international cooperation in police activities was first introduced in 1914 (with the French as primary advocates), but the onset of World War I postponed action. Attempts were again made in 1923 (Austrian instigation this time), and headquarters for the International Criminal Police Commission (ICPC) were established in Vienna until World War II caused suspension of activities. After the end of the war, in 1946 the French offered a building near Paris for the reestablishment of the headquarters. The ICPC continued to grow, and in 1956 was renamed the International Criminal Police Organization (ICPO–INTERPOL). In 1966, INTERPOL moved to Saint Cloud (outside Paris) and in 1989, having outgrown its Saint Cloud building, moved to new facilities in Lyon, France.

One of the most curious aspects of INTERPOL's status is the organization's legal basis. It is not based on an international treaty, convention, or any similar document. The multinational group of police officers who drew up its constitution never submitted it to their respective governments for approval, authorization, or ratification. Yet INTERPOL is treated as a legitimate organization by most governments of the world. Nations must apply for membership, appoint delegates, pay dues, and abide by the organization's rules. With recognition now from and working relations with such prestigious organizations as the United Nations, the Council of Europe, the World Health Organization, and the World Customs Organization, INTERPOL remains a legal curiosity but stands on firm ground.

Today, INTERPOL is the largest international police organization with 190 member countries. It operates with two interrelated governing bodies: the General Assembly and the Executive Committee. These are decision-making bodies with

YOU SHOULD KNOW!

INTERPOL FAQs

Is INTERPOL an International Police Force?

- No. INTERPOL is an international organization that has coordinated police international cooperation among its member nations since 1923.

Does INTERPOL Actually Investigate Cases?

- No. Investigations are conducted by the national police forces of member nations under their own sovereign laws. INTERPOL's role is to supply criminal information of a transnational nature to these national police forces.

How Does INTERPOL Communicate?

- Each member country establishes a National Central Bureau (NCB) staffed by its own police force. Communication between an NCB and INTERPOL, and among NCBs is via a global communications system that enables police in all member countries to request, submit, and access vital data instantly in a secure environment. The system provides a secure and rapid means of communication using encryption.

Does INTERPOL Collect Information on International Criminals?

- Yes. INTERPOL manages several databases that contain such critical information on criminals as their photographs, fingerprints, or DNA profiles.

How Is an Internationally Wanted Criminal Traced?

- At the request of a member country, the General Secretariat issues a "Red Notice" to all members. That notice contains sufficient details of the case, description, personal details, criminal history, photograph, and fingerprints of an internationally wanted criminal. Member nations use that information to locate, arrest, and detain the suspect pending an extradition application.

supervisory powers. Charged with implementing the decisions and recommendations adopted by the two governing organs is the General Secretariat, which operates continuously in Lyon and through seven regional offices around the world (INTERPOL, 2016).

Three factors have hampered international cooperation over the years:

- The different structures of police forces around the world make it difficult for officials in one country to know which department in another country has authority to deal with a case or supply information.
- The use of different languages can become a barrier to communication and may discourage or even interfere with communication.
- Differences among legal systems may present problems ranging from frustration to inability to cooperate.

To overcome these potential problems, INTERPOL established National Central Bureaus (NCBs) in each of INTERPOL's member states. Each country provides space, supplies, and personnel to serve as a liaison for INTERPOL communication and to handle requests from other member countries. Because each country controls its own NCB, they differ widely in size, personnel, and level of activity. However, each NCB has three responsibilities: (1) maintain open channels to all police units in its own country; (2) maintain connections with the NCBs of all other member countries; and (3) maintain liaison with the General Secretariat. In this manner, the NCBs provide a contact point in each member nation to allow the coordination of international criminal investigation.

So INTERPOL is not a force of international detectives with worldwide jurisdiction; it instead serves as a global conduit for communication and data sharing for member nations. Operating through the NCB network, any police officer or agency in a member country has access to global policing services when faced with a problem involving a foreign jurisdiction.

WEB PROJECT

Interactive INTERPOL

Go to INTERPOL's interactive educational website at http://www.interpol.int/ipsgapp/educational/index.html and play the game that has you in the role of an INTERPOL Junior Officer. Write a paragraph or two describing what you learned about INTERPOL's work.

Determining the appropriate police agency to serve as a country's NCB is not difficult in countries with centralized systems. With greater decentralization, though, the difficulty increases. In the extremely decentralized United States, it would be practically and politically unsuitable to name a state or local police department as the country's representative to INTERPOL. Instead, the NCB of the United States is in Washington, DC, where it operates under the Department of Justice in conjunction with the Treasury Department.

The U.S. commitment to INTERPOL increased dramatically in the 1970s and 1980s and remains strong today. The need for such a system is the result of increasing internationalization of crime with Americans committing crimes abroad—or committing crimes in the United States and then fleeing abroad—and foreign nationals committing crimes in the United States and then returning home or coming to the United States after committing crimes abroad. To respond to these situations, it is increasingly apparent that even local police need an international channel of communication available at their level. As a result, even the decentralized police system in America is participating at a local level in a multinational effort in policing.

European Police Office—Europol

Europol, the European law enforcement cooperation organization, was made possible in 1992 with the Maastricht Treaty of the European Union (EU) and, since 2010, is a full EU agency. After ratification by the member nations and the passage of some needed legal statutes, Europol was able to take up full operation in 1999. From its headquarters in The Hague, the Netherlands, Europol operates under a mandate for preventing and combating criminal activities ranging from those that are widely known (e.g., illicit drug trafficking, trafficking in human beings, terrorism, and money laundering) to ones that are less familiar (e.g., tobacco smuggling, VAT fraud, and outlaw motorcycle gangs). As that list suggests, initial efforts at cooperative policing are directed toward criminal activities that require an organized crime structure and that typically involve operations in several countries. That is exactly the kind of criminal activity that calls for a multinational cooperative response because the criminals do not confine their activities to a single country's border.

Europol supports crime prevention and combating duties by facilitating the exchange of both personal and nonpersonal data among the Europol liaison officers who represent the various law enforcement agencies. In addition, Europol provides member countries with strategic reports and crime analysis based on information supplied by member nations or generated by Europol itself and other agencies. Finally, Europol provides expertise and technical support for operations and investigations engaged in by member nations and plays an important role in training and capacity building (Europol, 2016).

You will note from the review of Europol activities that there is no separate Europol police agency with law enforcement authority across the European Union. This is an important point because it is not often clear to laypeople that Europol is a framework to facilitate cooperative efforts among different countries, not a freestanding police agency that engages in independent investigations and makes arrests. And, of course, it is just that type of facilitative arrangement that fits in with contemporary versions of multinational police cooperation. The idea of a "Supranational Bureau of Investigation" with agents assigned throughout the European Union, charged with enforcing laws applicable to all citizens in each member nation, seems a bit far-fetched today. Far more reasonable and workable in preventing and combating cross-border crimes is an agency like Europol that can coordinate the efforts of different policing systems rather than imposing yet another police agency upon each member country.

South Asian Association for Regional Cooperation—SAARC

In 1985, the governments of Bangladesh, Bhutan, India, Maldives, Nepal, Pakistan, and Sri Lanka formed the South Asian Association for Regional Cooperation (SAARC, 2016) as an intergovernmental organization that would encourage and facilitate cooperation among the member countries on a variety of issues ranging from agriculture and rural development to tourism. Afghanistan joined in 2007 to bring SAARC membership to eight countries.

Regional security is one of the cooperation areas, with SAARC being particularly involved in activities related to drugs and terrorism. Conferences on cooperation in police matters have been held intermittently since 1996 and police authorities from the member nations have shared ideas and information about preventing and combating organized crimes such as corruption, drug abuse, drug trafficking, and money laundering. There has even been discussion of establishing SAARCPOL—which, presumably, would be an information and intelligence sharing organization in the manner of INTERPOL and Europol.

Two SAARC initiatives are instructive regarding regional cooperation in combating crime. The SAARC Drug Offenses Monitoring Desk (SDOMD) was established 1992 to collate, analyze, and disseminate information on drug-related offenses in the region, and the Terrorist Offenses Monitoring Desk (STOMD) was established in 1995 to do the same for terrorist offenses, tactics, strategies, and methods. The drug monitoring desk has facilitated training courses and programs for member nations and urges its members to share information about best practices for drug abuse prevention, drug demand reduction, and drug supply strategies. The desk on terrorism is trying to identify the best way to share information in real time and to assure secure data exchange among police authorities in the member countries (SAARC, 2016).

The efforts of SAARC seem to be progressing more slowly than those of INTERPOL and Europol, but in many ways that helps to highlight both the need for regional cooperation and the difficulty in bringing it to fruition. Increasingly, countries are finding that effective measures against transnational crime and criminals require quick action based on accurate and reliable intelligence. INTERPOL is likely to continue its predominant role in accomplishing that task, but there is certainly room for, and a need for, similar efforts at the regional level.

Summary

This chapter was organized around the concept of variation in police structure. Building from Bayley's classification scheme, we categorized police structures according to their type of supervision or command (centralized or decentralized) and the number of forces being supervised (singular or multiple). When multiple forces are supervised, Bayley noted that some work well together (coordinated) while others seem to operate at cross-purposes (uncoordinated). Upon putting these conditions together, a typology was created yielding six possible cells, each containing a different police structure.

Countries such as Ghana, Ireland, Israel, Poland, and Saudi Arabia have a single police force reporting to a centralized command. Japan presents a unique combination of a single police force with command decentralized to the prefecture level. The simplicity of a single police structure has not, however, made it a worldwide favorite. Other countries accept the central government as appropriate for supervision purposes but show a preference for having multiple police forces to report to that central authority. France was highlighted as a country falling into this division, because both its Gendarmerie and Police Nationale report to ministries of the central government. Although some conflict exists between the French forces, they are considered coordinated because they basically respect their assigned jurisdictions. In Spain, on the other hand, the multiple forces of Cuerpo Nacional de Policia, Guardia Civil, and Policia Municipal have overlapping responsibilities and jurisdiction. The result is an uncoordinated system.

Countries that have decentralized police services also provide examples of both coordinated and uncoordinated efforts. Germany was highlighted as a coordinated multiple police system because its different state police forces are coordinated by the federal government serving as a liaison and coordinating agent. The United States presents the most extreme form of decentralized multiple uncoordinated policing, but Mexico was highlighted to provide the international perspective.

Finally, the chapter included a brief look at two of the many important issues that can be addressed regarding policing around the world. After a review of police misconduct in a variety of countries, we were left with questions about the effect of police work on police officers and the type of person that may be attracted to police work. The chapter ended with discussion of important ways that countries have tried to work together to combat the ever-increasing cross-national nature of both crime and criminals.

Discussion Questions

- The text uses a scheme that categorizes the world's police forces based on the basis of dispersal of command (centralized or decentralized) and number of forces (single or multiple). What other type of categorization scheme could be used to make sense of the various ways in which police are organized?
- Ghana has a specialized Domestic Violence and Victim Support Unit that investigates cases involving women, children, and juveniles. Do you believe such a specialized unit (staffed by both men and women, in Ghana) is an appropriate way to organize a police force? What social, cultural, or economic factors existing in a country may encourage you to take a different perspective?
- In both Japan and Germany, the police forces were reorganized by victorious countries following a war. In each case, the resulting policing structure varied from what the conquered country had prior to the war. When one country comes to have control over another (whether by war or colonization), what factors should be considered when the conquering country goes about establishing internal security in the conquered country?
- This chapter's "Impact" feature asks whether Canada's system of contracting police services could work on a large scale in the United States. How do you respond?
- Although the chapter was not able to take the space to discuss explanations for the pervasiveness of police misconduct, you certainly can explore this subject on your own. Is police misconduct indicative of something about the people choosing police work (in all countries), the result of doing police work over time (regardless of country), or maybe the management tactics typically used (again, around the world) by supervisors?

References

Ames, W. L. (1983). Police system. *Encyclopedia of Japan* (Vol. 6, pp. 198–201). Tokyo: Kodansha.

Banks, D., Hendrix, J., Hickman, M. J., & Kyckelhahn, T. (2016). National sources of law enforcement employment data (NCJ 249681). Bureau of Justice Statistics. Retrieved from http://www.bjs.gov/content/pub/pdf/nsleed.pdf

Banninga, C. (2016). The police. The German Way & More. Retrieved from http://www.german-way.com/history-and-culture/germany/the-police/

Barbagli, M., & Sartori, L. (2004). Law enforcement activities in Italy. *Journal of Modern Italian Studies, 9*(2), 161–185.

Bayley, D. H. (1985). *Patterns of policing: A comparative international analysis.* New Brunswick, NJ: Rutgers University Press.

Bayley, D. H. (1991). *Forces of order: Policing modern Japan.* Berkeley, CA: University of California Press.

Bayley, D. H. (1992). Comparative organization of the police in English-speaking countries. In M. Tonry & N. Morris (Eds.), *Crime and justice: A review of research* (Vol. 21, pp. 509–545). Chicago, IL: University of Chicago Press.

Bjorken, J. (2005). Italy. In L. E. Sullivan & M. R. Haberfeld (Eds.), *Encyclopedia of law enforcement, Vol. 3: International* (pp. 1134–1140). Thousand Oaks, CA: Sage.

Bracey, D. H. (1995). Police corruption. In W. G. Bailey (Ed.), *The encyclopedia of police science*. New York, NY: Garland.

Brown, B., Benedict, W. R., & Wilkinson, W. V. (2006). Public perceptions of the police in Mexico: A case study. *Policing: An International Journal of Police Strategies and Management, 29*(1), 158–175.

Browne-Marshall, G. J. (2005). Ghana. In L. E. Sullivan & M. R. Haberfeld (Eds.), *Encyclopedia of law enforcement, Vol. 3: International* (pp. 1078–1080). Thousand Oaks, CA: Sage.

Canabata, J., & Dulin, A. (2006). Spain. In G. T. Kurian (Ed.), *World encyclopedia of police forces and correctional systems* (2nd ed., Vol. 2, pp. 846–849). Detroit, MI: Thomson Gale.

Carrer, F. (2006). Italian police forces and the internal security system. *Crime & Justice International, 22*, 11–17.

Chalk, P. (2013). Mexico's new strategy to combat drug cartels: Evaluating the National Gendarmerie. *CTC Sentinel, 6*(5), 16–18.

Chwialkowski, P. (1998). Japanese policing—An American invention. *Policing: An International Journal of Policing Strategies & Management, 21*(4), 720–730.

Clarke, C. (2005). Canada. In L. E. Sullivan & M. R. Haberfeld (Eds.), *Encyclopedia of law enforcement, Vol. 3: International* (pp. 992–999). Thousand Oaks, CA: Sage.

Donnelly, R. A., & Shirk, D. A. (2010). Introduction. In R. A. Donnelly & D. A. Shirk (Eds.), *Police and public security in Mexico* (pp. 1–37). San Diego, CA: Trans-Border Institute.

Dupont, B. (2005). France. In L. E. Sullivan & M. R. Haberfeld (Eds.), *Encyclopedia of law enforcement, Vol. 3: International* (pp. 1065–1070). Thousand Oaks, CA: Sage.

Ebbe, O. N. I. (1993). Ghana. *The world factbook of criminal justice systems*. Retrieved from http://www.bjs.gov/content/pub/html/wfcj.cfm

Europol. (2016). About Europol. Retrieved from https://www.europol.europa.eu/content/page/about-us

Fairchild, E. S. (1988). *German policing*. Springfield, IL: Charles C. Thomas.

Feltes, T. (2005). Germany. In L. E. Sullivan & M. R. Haberfeld (Eds.), *Encyclopedia of law enforcement, Vol. 3: International* (pp. 1073–1078). Thousand Oaks, CA: Sage.

Feltes, T. (2006). Germany. In G. T. Kurian (Ed.), *World encyclopedia of police forces and correctional systems* (2nd ed., Vol. 1, pp. 423–430). Detroit, MI: Thomson Gale.

Fontanaud, D. (2006). France. In D. K. Das (Ed.), *World police encyclopedia* (Vol. 1, pp. 295–303). New York, NY: Routledge.

Gariba, S. P. (2014). *Police professionalism: To what extent can recruitment and training practices impact on police professionalism in Ghana?* (Doctoral dissertation.)

University of Leicester. Retrieved from https://lra.le.ac.uk/handle/2381/31391

Ghana Police Service. (2016). Home page. Retrieved from http://www.police.gov.gh/Home.aspx

Glazer, S. (1995). Police corruption. *The CQ Researcher, 5*(44), 1043–1063.

Grieve, J., Harfield, C., & MacVean, A. (2007). *Policing*. London, UK: Sage.

Harnischmacher, R. F. J. (2006). Germany. In D. K. Das (Ed.), *World police encyclopedia* (Vol. 1, pp. 314–323). New York, NY: Routledge.

Hodgson, J. (2005). *French criminal justice: A comparative account of the investigation and prosecution of crime in France*. Portland, OR: Hart.

Horton, C. (1995). *Policing policy in France*. London, UK: Policy Studies Institute.

Hunter, R. D. (1990). Three models of policing. *Police Studies, 13*(3), 118–124.

Ingram, M., & Shirk, D. A. (2010). Judicial reform in Mexico: Toward a new criminal justice system. Trans-Border Institute. Retrieved from http://catcher.sandiego.edu/items/peacestudies/2010-IngraShirk-JRM%20%282%29.pdf

InSight Crime. (2016, January 11). Implementation of "Mando Unico" moves slowly in Mexico. Investigation and analysis of organized crime. Retrieved from http://www.insightcrime.org/news-briefs/implementation-of-mando-unico-moves-slowly-in-mexico

INTERPOL. (2016). About INTERPOL. Retrieved from http://www.interpol.int/About-INTERPOL/Overview

Jiao, A. Y. (1997). Factoring policing models. *Policing: An International Journal of Policing Strategies & Management, 20*(3), 454–472.

Kurian, G. T. (2006a). Ghana. In G. T. Kurian (Ed.), *World encyclopedia of police forces and correctional systems* (2nd ed., Vol. 1, pp. 431–435). Detroit, MI: Thomson Gale.

Kurian, G. T. (2006b). Mexico. In G. T. Kurian (Ed.), *World encyclopedia of police forces and correctional systems* (2nd ed., Vol. 2, pp. 643–647). Detroit, MI: Thomson Gale.

LaSusa, M. (2016, May 26). Mexico official signals shift away from militarized security strategy. InSight Crime. Retrieved from http://www.insightcrime.org/news-briefs/mexico-official-signals-shift-away-from-current-security-strategy

Lutterbeck, D. (2013). The paradox of gendarmeries: Between expansion, demilitarization and dissolution (Paper 8). *SSR Papers*. Retrieved from http://www.dcaf.ch/Publications/The-Paradox-of-Gendarmeries-Between-Expansion-Demilitarization-and-Dissolution

Ma, Y. (2005). China. In L. E. Sullivan & M. R. Haberfeld (Eds.), *Encyclopedia of law enforcement, Vol. 3: International* (pp. 1004–1011). Thousand Oaks, CA: Sage.

Macdonald, I. (1987). Spain's 1986 police law: Transition from dictatorship to democracy. *Police Studies, 10,* 16–22.

Mawby, R. I. (1990). *Comparative policing issues: The British and American experience.* London: Unwin Hyman Ltd.

Mawby, R. I. (2003). Models of policing. In T. Newburn (Ed.), *Handbook of policing* (pp. xxxvi, 757). Cullompton, UK: Willan.

Morn, F., & Toro, M. (1989). From dictatorship to democracy: Crime and policing in contemporary Spain. *International Journal of Comparative and Applied Criminal Justice, 13,* 53–64.

Murray, T. (2006). Canada. In D. K. Das (Ed.), *World police encyclopedia* (Vol. 1, pp. 155–162). New York, NY: Routledge.

Odo, J. C. (2006). Ghana. In D. K. Das (Ed.), *World police encyclopedia* (Vol. 1, pp. 323–329). New York, NY: Routledge.

Olson, E. L. (2009). Police reform and modernization in Mexico, 2009. Retrieved from http://www.wilsoncenter. org/news/docs/Brief%20on%20Police%20Reform% 20and%20Modernization.pdf

Onieal, B. (2005). Spain. In L. E. Sullivan & M. R. Haberfeld (Eds.), *Encyclopedia of law enforcement, Vol. 3: International* (pp. 1310–1314). Thousand Oaks, CA: Sage.

OSCE POLIS. (2006). Germany: General information. Policing profiles of participating and partner states. Retrieved from http://polis.osce.org/countries/ details?item_id=17

OSCE POLIS. (2007). Spain: General information. Policing profiles of participating and partner states. Retrieved from http://polis.osce.org/countries/details?item_id=36

OSCE POLIS. (2010). France: General information. Policing profiles of participating and partner states. Retrieved from http://polis.osce.org/countries/details?item_id=24&lang=en

Parker, L. C. (2013). *Crime and justice in Japan and China: A comparative view.* Durham, NC: Carolina Academic Press.

Parker, L. C., Jr. (1984). *A Japanese police system today: An American perspective.* Tokyo: Kodansha.

Reames, B. (2005). Mexico. In L. E. Sullivan & M. R. Haberfeld (Eds.), *Encyclopedia of law enforcement, Vol. 3: International* (pp. 1186–1193). Thousand Oaks, CA: Sage.

Rodríguez, J. (2014). Inside Spain's Civil Guard. El País. Retrieved from http://elpais.com/elpais/2014/10/20/ inenglish/1413807111_949949.html

Royal Canadian Mounted Police. (2013). Contract policing. Retrieved from http://www.rcmp-grc.gc.ca/ccaps-spcca/contract-eng.htm

SAARC. (2016). Areas of cooperation: Security aspects. Retrieved from http://www.saarc-sec.org/areaofcooperation/cat-detail.php?cat_id=59

Sabet, D. (2010). Police reform in Mexico: Advances and persistent obstacles. In E. L. Olson, D. A. Shirk, & A. Selee (Eds.), *Shared responsibility: U.S.–Mexico policy options for confronting organized crime.* Washington, DC: Mexico Institute at the Woodrow Wilson Center. Retrieved from http://wilsoncenter.org/ topics/pubs/Sabet.pdf.

Stead, P. J. (1983). *The police of France.* New York, NY: Macmillan.

Sun, I. Y., & Wu, Y. (2006). *The role of the People's Armed Police in Chinese policing.* Paper presented at the Annual Meeting of the Academy of Criminal Justice Sciences, Baltimore, MD.

Terrill, R. J. (2016). *World criminal justice systems: A comparative survey* (9th ed.). New York, NY: Routledge.

Thomaneck, J. (1985). Police and public order in the Federal Republic of Germany. In J. Roach & J. Thomaneck (Eds.), *Police and public order in Europe.* London, UK: Croom Helm.

Transparency International. (2013). Global Corruption Barometer 2013. Retrieved from http://www.transparency.org/gcb2013

Vargas, E. L. P. (2006). Mexico. In D. K. Das (Ed.), *World police encyclopedia* (Vol. 2, pp. 552–557). New York, NY: Routledge.

Westney, D. E. (1987). *Imitation and innovation: The transfer of western organizational patterns to Meiji Japan.* Cambridge, MA: Harvard University Press.

Why Mexican security is a work in progress. (2016, January 26). Stratfor. Retrieved from http://www.stratfor.com

Wright, A. (2002). *Policing: An introduction to concepts and practice.* Devon, UK: Willan.

Yuki, H. (2005). Japan. In L. E. Sullivan & M. R. Haberfeld (Eds.), *Encyclopedia of law enforcement, Vol. 3: International* (pp. 1144–1147). Thousand Oaks, CA: Sage.

An International Perspective on Courts

LEARNING OBJECTIVES

After studying this chapter, you will be able to:

1. Distinguish between legal professions that are unified and those that are specialized.

2. Compare and give examples of the various ways prosecution of criminal cases can be accomplished.

3. Compare and give examples of the various ways a defense against criminal prosecution can be provided.

4. Explain and give examples of the different ways in which professional judges and laypeople can be involved in the adjudication process.

5. Describe and compare how criminal courts are organized in China, England, France, Nigeria, and Saudi Arabia.

COUNTRIES IN FOCUS

China
England
Finland
France

Germany
Nigeria
Saudi Arabia

In November 2007, British exchange student Meredith Kercher was found semi-naked with her throat slit in the house she shared with American exchange student Amanda Knox in Perugia, Italy. The investigation eventually led Italian prosecutors to charge Knox and two others in the killing of Meredith Kercher. The trial garnered international media attention with a particular focus on Knox who was alternately depicted as an innocent American caught up in the unpredictable Italian justice system and as a pot-smoking wild child capable of committing murder in the heat of a sex game (Donadio, 2009). In 2009, Knox was convicted of murder and sentenced to 26 years. In 2011, the appeals court overturned the murder conviction. Then, in 2013, the conviction was reinstated by the appeals court and Knox was ordered to be retried for murder. In 2014, she was found guilty by the appeals court. Finally, in 2015, Knox was definitively acquitted at the appeals level (Krol, 2015; Povoledo, 2011a).

In addition to being an 8-year process, the case had many interesting aspects for those who followed the proceedings since they often involved roles and procedures that were unfamiliar to an American audience. It was not uncommon to read comments in social media that in Italy a person was considered guilty until proven innocent. Such comments emphasize the importance of understanding better the criminal justice system of other countries so that misunderstandings such as the one by that blogger are not perpetuated. For example, as a member of the European Union, Italy subscribes to Article 48 of the

Charter of Fundamental Rights, which says "Everyone who has been charged shall be presumed innocent until proved guilty according to law" (European Parliament, 2012). Further, Article 533 of the Italian Code of Criminal Procedure stipulates that conviction requires the accused to be proven guilty beyond a reasonable doubt (Italian Republic, 2014). However, although defendants in Italy are not presumed guilty, there are important differences in how investigations occur and how trials proceed. For example,

- In Italy, a judicial official, rather than a police official, directs and coordinates the investigating team that includes police and other magistrates. A formal prosecution case is prepared and presented in court.
- U.S. prosecutors have discretion over the decision to seek charges against an individual, but in Italy there is a constitutional principle of mandatory prosecution requiring prosecution when there is sufficient evidence to build a case (Vogt, 2009).
- One of the initial defendants asked for a "fast-track trial," in which evidence is presented in document form and no witnesses testify. It can lead to a lesser sentence if the suspect is convicted and that defendant's 30-year sentence was, in fact, reduced on appeal to 24 years and then cut by one-third to 16 years, as is the custom when defendants opt for a fast-track trial (Kington, 2009).
- Once in court, the case is heard by a panel of two professional judges (one, the presiding judge) and six lay judges. The lay judges (mistakenly referred to as "jurors" by most of the Western press) participate in the trial proceeding and in determining the verdict.
- The panel of professional and lay judges is never sequestered and, in a system where trials can last more than a year—as this one did, Italians believe it would be inappropriate to do so (Krings, 2015; Poggioli, 2009). As a result, there was considerable criticism in the American press that the panel members were influenced by the negative press coverage Knox received in the Italian media.
- Unlike in the American system, in which appeals center on issues of law, not fact, in the Italian system, appeals are automatic and defendants can ask to retry the entire case in a first round of appeals. The initial appeal trial in 2011 included a request by defense lawyers that the DNA evidence used to convict Knox and Sollecito be re-examined (Donadio, 2009; Povoledo, 2011b). That evidence was indeed re-examined and deemed questionable by independent experts who were highly critical of the police's handling and analysis of the materials. But, also unlike the American system, the prosecution can appeal in Italy (and in many other countries, actually). As explained above, during the appeals process Knox had her conviction overturned, then was ordered to be retried, found guilty again, and then was definitively acquitted (Povoledo, 2011a).

The concern of this chapter is with the institutions that different countries establish to bring a defendant to justice. Of course, when looking at particular social institutions, we also must consider the people who work there. Recall that Chapter 1 distinguished between a functions/procedures strategy and an institutions/actors one. The former highlights the similarities among legal systems but in doing so masks their differences. In several ways, Chapters 3 through 5 followed a functions/procedures approach because they presented general material about legal systems according to separate traditions. As a result, you now have general information about the function of law in four legal families and some specific information about legal procedures in countries representing each family. You do not, however, have much understanding of who carries out those functions and procedures or in what setting they work. That information is what the actors/institutions strategy provides. Of course, it is not possible to speak of the "who" and

WEB PROJECT

Difference between Italian and American Trials

Some interesting and informative comparisons have been made between trials in Italy and the United States using the Knox trial as an example. Visit http://inns.innsofcourt. org/ and search for: trial of Amanda Knox, then select the article *highlighting differences*. Also visit http://law. ku.edu/sites/law.ku.edu/files/docs/comparative-criminal-procedure-essay-john-head.pdf, where you will find an article by law professor John Head that considers various aspects of the Knox trial. After reading both items, write a few paragraphs that highlight some of the main differences between the trial process in Italy and the United States. Are there any aspects of the Italian process that you believe are preferable to that in the United States?

"where" without occasional reference to the "what." Therefore, as we learn about the actors and institutions in various countries, we must be intermittently reminded of the functions and procedures.

We approach these topics by looking first at the actors Americans know as the prosecutor and defense counsel. We then turn to the players responsible for deciding the outcome of a case. These adjudicators can be either professionals or laypersons. Finally, we consider the stage upon which these performers carry out their duties.

PROFESSIONAL ACTORS IN THE JUDICIARY

The primary actors in the criminal process are the advocates (prosecutor and defense counsel) and the judge. These three positions indicate possible career tracks in the legal profession. Other choices may include legal scholar, corporate attorney, notary, or other forms of public and private legal work. The ease with which a law school graduate can move among these occupational areas helps show whether a country has a unified or specialized legal profession. In the former, all legal professionals are considered to have the basic knowledge and training to participate in any of the fields. In the latter, each field has distinct entrance requirements that restrict horizontal movement by the legal professionals. Part of the difference results from how a country educates its law students.

Variation in Legal Training

Americans tend to associate legal education with graduate work undertaken after the student has completed a general college or university education. This process is actually uncommon from the world perspective because civil law countries—and even legal studies in England—provide training in law at the undergraduate level. The law degree, offered at the undergraduate level, is essentially under the control of the universities rather than the legal profession itself. The members of the legal profession are primarily state employees with a status similar to that of other civil servants.

As with college training almost everywhere, the study of law under the civil law tradition is typically general and interdisciplinary rather than professional. As a result, civil law graduates are not trained to begin the practice of law immediately. Instead, those wishing to enter a legal profession need further practical training. The American law school graduate, on the other hand, is expected to be prepared to do any type of legal work with only a minimal apprenticeship.

The type and duration of training in the civil law vary by country and also according to the kind of legal career the new graduate wants to pursue. Shortly after receiving the university degree in law, new civil lawyers are given the option of being a private lawyer, a judge, a government lawyer (basically a public administrator), or a legal scholar. Entrance into each legal profession typically depends on the applicant successfully passing an exam and completing a period of apprenticeship. With different educational backgrounds, occupational choices, and career entrance requirements, it is not surprising that countries vary regarding the role and social position of their legal professionals.

Lawyers in America often find themselves in the peculiar position of being in a prestigious occupation while also serving as the butt of many jokes. Actually, jokes and negative comments about lawyers have been around since the late sixteenth century. Shakespeare's Dick the butcher said, "The first thing we do, let's kill all the lawyers" (King Henry VI, Part II), as he was making suggestions in support of Jack Cade's promise of a better society. In colonial America, outright belligerence often took the form of hostile legislation. McDonald reminds us of the pre-Revolutionary dictum that it was not deemed necessary, or even advisable, to have judges learned in law (McDonald, 1983). The hostility came primarily from the landed gentry and the clergy, both of whom feared the loss of their power and status to a lawyering class. The role of lawyers in England and the United States continues to occasion feelings of contempt as well as respect among the citizens.

Lawyers in civil law countries seem to fare better in some respects. Certainly, they are not the catalyst for jokes as much as are the lawyers in common law countries. Part of the public perception of civil law attorneys results from the variety of distinct professional careers from which they choose. Graduates not wanting to become judges can follow a path leading to positions such as public prosecutor, government lawyer, defense advocate, or private attorney. The specific career decision is made early and places the young graduate on a rather precise path.

The distinctions among the various legal careers in civil law countries may seem unusual to Americans. In the United States, the legal profession is more unified and allows lateral movement by lawyers from one type of position to another. For example, recent law school graduates may initially serve in a district attorney's office or as a public defender to get some experience and a reasonable starting salary. After a few years in that field, they may then set up an independent practice in which criminal law plays only an insignificant role.

The legal fields in civil law countries are much less unified. Civil lawyers often develop separate skills, images, and professional associations as they follow their chosen legal paths. This process results in knowledgeable and rather efficient personnel, but it also causes some problems. Results of the early career decision and separation of professions include isolation, inflexibility, professional rivalries, jurisdictional problems, and communication difficulties (Merryman, 1985). In an attempt to lessen the chances that a new university graduate will make an uninformed career choice, some countries (e.g., Germany) require law graduates to engage in a period of practical training. Over a period of many months or several years, the "interns" experience the work of judges, government lawyers, and private attorneys. Drawing on those experiences, the still rather recent graduate can choose a legal profession with a better idea of what the career will involve.

England (see Map A.10) presents an interesting departure from the common law practice of a unified legal profession. The positions of barrister and solicitor provide the basis for a bifurcated system of

Barrister
British advocates are either solicitors or barristers, with the latter being more specialized practitioners making oral arguments in the higher courts.

Lisa F. Young/Shutterstock

advocates in England. The distinction between the two professions is often made as being similar to medical professionals who are general practitioners (solicitors) and those who are specialized surgeons (barristers). When members of the public need general legal advice or assistance they usually turn to a solicitor, whereas more complex legal problems require the assistance of a barrister.

Barristers can make arguments before higher-level courts to which solicitors have restricted access. The solicitor's right to full audience in lower courts but only limited hearing in higher courts means that after preparing a case for the higher level, the solicitor must employ a barrister to make the arguments. The British legal system relies on the presenting of oral arguments, so his or her verbal skills and specialized talents make the barrister a respected figure in that system.

General comments about Islamic advocates are difficult to make. Because the trial proceeding is as much a mediation process as one of adjudication, the parties in legal disputes do not necessarily need the representation of counsel. Although nothing in Islamic law prevents the accused from being represented by an attorney, the tendency is to represent oneself in criminal matters (Glenn, 2014, p. 188; Souryal, 2004, p. 128). In Saudi Arabia, for example, Article 1 of the *Code of Law Practice* specifically notes that any person may litigate for himself (Kingdom of Saudi Arabia, 2001). Lawyers are, however, available for both criminal and civil purposes. In Saudi Arabia, persons wishing positions as lawyers must hold a degree from a Shari'a college or from one of the Kingdom's universities (or equivalent degrees from abroad) and must practice the profession in accordance with the Shari'a and the laws in force. In addition, persons wishing to qualify as a practicing lawyer must have their application approved by the Lawyers Registration and Admission Committee, which will ensure that the applicant meets the basic educational requirements and all other criteria (e.g., 3 years of practical legal experience, be of good conduct, must not—within the previous 5 years—have been subjected to any hadd or other sentence that impugns integrity).

Variation in Prosecution

Prosecution of criminal cases is accomplished through either private or public prosecutors (see Figure 7.1). The oldest process (private prosecution) allows the victim or victim's relatives to initiate action against the offender. Where private prosecution is retained today, it is typically alongside public prosecution rather than standing as a country's sole system.

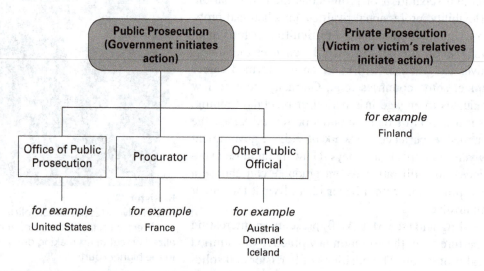

FIGURE 7.1 Variation in Prosecution

However, it can still be an important and effective procedure even if it is not the only or even primary means of prosecution. For example, Dr. Matti Joutsen with Finland's Ministry of Justice (personal communication, August 2016) explains that in some civil law jurisdictions victims can (and in some jurisdictions, only the victim can) prosecute for certain categories of offenses, such as trespass or libel. In several jurisdictions (e.g., Austria and Germany), victims can serve as "subsidiary prosecutors" in that they have rights of presenting evidence, requesting that certain witnesses be called, commenting on evidence, and otherwise addressing the court. In some jurisdictions (e.g., Austria, Germany, and Sweden), the victim can prosecute if the public prosecutor refuses to do so (Foster, 2003, p. 93).

Finland (see Map A.10) provides a particularly interesting continuation of private prosecution by granting the victim a secondary right of prosecution. If the prosecutor decides not to prosecute, or if the investigation authority or prosecutor decides a criminal investigation will not be conducted or will be interrupted or concluded, the victim is entitled to bring charges and to have the case considered by a court (Republic of Finland, 1997, Chapter 1, Section 14). Before taking such action, the victim is advised to read carefully the prosecutor's statement of the reasons for not prosecuting so that the victim understands any difficulties associated with prosecuting the case. Typically, the victims defer to the prosecutor's decision, but even if it is not often used, the existence of the provision certainly gives victims in Finland a prosecutorial power not frequently found today. Instead, prosecution in countries around the world tends to be initiated by the government (i.e., public prosecution) rather than the individual (i.e., private prosecution). For that reason, we focus on variations in the way public prosecution is managed.

Public prosecution can be conducted by an office of public prosecution, by a procurator, or by the other officials (again, see Figure 7.1). To exemplify each type, we look at the United States, France, and a few countries that rely in part on persons other than public prosecutors.

UNITED STATES As noted earlier, colonial Americans were not keen on the idea of lawyers. Because of that, private prosecution rather than public prosecution by a government attorney dominated the colonial system of criminal justice. For example, in colonial Pennsylvania, victims with a criminal complaint against another person were responsible for initiating action against that person. The victim informed the justice of the peace (whose fees the victim would pay) about the charge. The victim then attended pretrial hearings, ensured the appearance of witnesses, and hired an attorney to plead the case if the victim did not wish to argue it himself (Steinberg, 1984). It was the private citizen who pursued the case to its conclusion.

Public prosecutors did exist during this period, but prior to 1850 the official title for such persons was "deputy attorney general" and they had responsibility for prosecuting serious offenses or "great public wrongs." However, because most cases were minor offenses that were fully resolved by the aldermen (similar to councilmen today), the public prosecutor was seldom called upon.

The public prosecutor's role began changing as the private citizen's role in law enforcement began to decline. During the 1840s and 1850s, the problem of public order reached crisis proportions. Philadelphia responded to these problems by increasing its police watch in 1850 and then consolidating the police force in 1854. Also, in 1854, the prosecuting attorney's title was changed to district attorney, the position was made elective, and the officer was required for the first time to act in the name of the commonwealth (Steinberg, 1984).

The discretionary power of the district attorney increased slightly over the next 25 years, but private prosecution remained popular and served to limit that discretion. The end of this situation was in sight, however. Complaints grew about private settlements between aldermen and the parties, about the failure of private prosecutors to appear before grand or petit jurors, and about the petty content of the cases themselves. Finally, in 1874, Pennsylvania set in motion changes that effectively altered the relationship between citizens, police, and the courts. The main characters in the criminal justice system became officers of the state (police and public prosecutors) instead of private citizens. Equally important, neither police officers nor prosecutors were officers of the court. Instead, they were independent law enforcement agencies whose purpose was to channel some cases into the courts while resolving others in alternative ways. The effect of the change occurred almost immediately. The percentage of felonies heard by the courts rose, and conviction rates increased, whereas the number of dismissed cases declined dramatically. This shift from a criminal justice process relying upon citizen initiation to one dominated by state initiation provided the power and discretion now housed in the office of public prosecutor.

It is important to note that private prosecution has not been completely abandoned in the United States. Although the practice is no longer as widespread as it was in the first two centuries of the nation's development, some jurisdictions permit crime victims to conduct a private prosecution when the public prosecutor will not. Often there are restrictions placed on private prosecution that may require the private citizen to get approval from the public prosecutor or that restrict private prosecutions to specific offense types such as those for which a fine is the maximum punishment (Fairfax, 2009; Followill, 2016). Despite those jurisdictions holding to the private prosecution concept, public prosecution is well entrenched in the American system of justice. The result is a person, the prosecutor, said at the least to have broad discretionary power and at the extreme to be the most influential person in America in terms of the power he or she has over the lives of citizens.

FRANCE Discussing public prosecution in countries of the common legal tradition is fairly straightforward—you describe the office of public prosecutor. When attention turns to prosecution in countries of the civil tradition, discussion becomes a bit more complicated. The main reason for that is the civil tradition's (more accurately, the inquisitorial process's) emphasis on the investigative stage and the office of procurator. The *procurator* is a person acting in the place of someone else. In this case, a government attorney takes action for a private citizen who has been wronged. Importantly, procurators act for society and are not simply out to defend state interests. This means that procurators do not so much have the duty of securing a conviction as they have the duty to ensure that justice is done and society's interests are served (Terrill, 2016, p. 169). France (see Map A.10) provides a good example of the prosecutorial role under a civil legal tradition, so we briefly describe prosecution in that country.

The *magistrature* is the career judiciary in France. As noted earlier in this chapter, a career judiciary is rather common in many countries but usually it consists of only those persons who have chosen to be judges. The French career judiciary (the magistrature) includes the public prosecutor (the *procureur*), the investigating judge (the *juge d'instruction*), and the trial judge—and all are *magistrats* (Hodgson, 2005). This differs, for example, from Germany where the trial judges (the *Richterschaft*) and the public prosecution service (the *Staatsanwaltschaft*) are separate career structures.

Recall from Chapter 5, the discussion of the inquisitorial procedure that the trial is essentially a continuation of the investigatory process. This becomes clear as we consider how the magistrature takes part in everything from the crime's investigation to decisions regarding prosecution and overseeing the eventual trial. The juge d'instruction is especially interesting in this context since he or she is responsible for investigating more serious and complex criminal cases. Although the need for this position is being questioned (as mentioned in Chapter 5), it will be retained for the time being (Spencer, 2016). The magistrat conducts a neutral and wide-ranging investigation of the crime, reviews and evaluates the case against the suspect, and determines whether the evidence and charges are well founded. However, the investigating judge also has responsibility for protecting the rights and liberties of the suspect in deciding whether coercive powers (e.g., wiretaps) may be used in the investigation—a distinct judicial responsibility in the more adversarial proceeding of countries such as England and the United States (Hodgson, 2005).

This overlap of investigative and judicial functions has been criticized by some in France. In response, the juge d'instruction has lost some responsibilities (e.g., he or she no longer determines whether a suspect will be released on bail or detained in custody), but the position remains one that combines investigative and judicial responsibilities in a way that seems unusual to persons more familiar with the adversarial process. However, because the inquisitorial process considers the criminal trial to be, essentially, the final stage of the investigation, an overlap is inevitable—even expected. Keeping this point in mind, let's briefly follow the steps of a criminal investigation and prosecution in France.

As explained in Chapter 6, France has two police forces, the police nationale and the Gendarmerie. In addition, each force has two distinct roles, one administrative and the other judicial. The administrative role is one of prevention and order maintenance, whereas the judicial role concerns the investigation of a specific crime (Horton, 1995). Although duties that begin as administrative may move to judicial (e.g., while maintaining order at a public demonstration, an officer observes a crime being committed), the distinction is more problematic than simply "changing hats." Only specific police officers can perform the judicial or investigative function. These *police judiciaire* (or judicial police) are plainclothes officers in the police nationale or the Gendarmerie (members of which are always in uniform) and are part of specific units.

Supervision of the judicial police takes us back to the discussion of magistrats and prosecution. The *procureurs général* (prosecutors general) have authority over prosecution in their jurisdiction and are responsible for supervising the judicial police of that district. More specifically, supervision of the judicial police falls to the district prosecutor (*le procureur de la République*)—similar to the American public prosecutor or district attorney—operating under the prosecutor general. The French *Code of Criminal Procedure* (Articles 41–44) authorizes the district prosecutor to have the judicial police and law enforcement agencies collect any information the prosecutor considers useful for the proper administration of justice (French Republic, 1995a).

Examples of investigations at this level include those for flagrant offenses, which are defined as those in the process of being committed or have recently been committed. They also include situations in which the person suspected is found in the possession of articles or has on or about him any items that give reason to believe he has taken part in the felony or misdemeanor (Article 53). In such cases, the judicial police—under the supervision of district prosecutors—are given extensive search, seizure, and detention authority. There are procedural safeguards over that authority (e.g., under Article 57 of the *Code of Criminal Procedure*, house searches must be witnessed by persons independent of the searching authorities), but there are no legal standards similar to probable cause under common law regarding, for example, where police may look for evidence. Decisions as to what follows these investigations are left to the district prosecutor who may dismiss a case or bring formal charges. For the less serious crimes, the prosecutor even has the discretion to suspend prosecution and impose conditions such as payment of a fine or surrender of a driver's license (Frase, 2007; French Republic, 1995a).

When the case involves serious crimes, the district prosecutor is required to pass the case to the juge d'instruction for formal judicial investigation. For less serious crimes, the judicial investigation process is optional for the procureur. Under judicial investigation, Article 81 of the *Code of Criminal Procedure* directs the juge d'instruction to undertake any investigative steps deemed necessary for the discovery of the truth and to seek out evidence of innocence as well as guilt. During this process, the investigating judge can issue arrest warrants and detention orders and can initiate interrogations of the accused and questions for the victim. When the judicial investigation is deemed complete, the accused is either released or formally charged.

Later in this chapter, the French court system is described and reference is again made to the procureur. At that point, you will be reminded that the prosecutor has a rather limited role in the actual conduct of the trial. Despite differences in the role of procureur as compared to the U.S. prosecutor, we must remember that both exemplify public prosecution. That is a key point, because the existence of public rather than only private prosecutors reaffirms the idea that "crime" is a public wrong.

PROSECUTION BY OTHERS   In several European countries, persons other than the public prosecutor can perform tasks similar to the prosecutor. In Austria, for example, the *Bezirksgericht* courts (similar to a municipal court) rely on an agent (the *Bezirksanwalt*) who acts on behalf of the public prosecutor's office. These employees need not be lawyers but they do have specialized training that allows them to perform prosecutorial tasks under the supervision of a public prosecutor. They are not, however, considered to be public prosecutors (Council of Europe, 2000; Foster, 2003).

In other countries (e.g., Denmark, Greece, Malta, and Norway), police officers have duties similar to public prosecutors or actually act as the prosecutor in lower-level courts. In Denmark, for example, attorneys (called police prosecutors) are employed by both the national police and the prosecution service. They are considered part of the Danish prosecution service and they act as the prosecuting authority before the district courts—which are the lower-level courts in Denmark (Danish National Police, 2015).

Iceland presents another example of police prosecution (National Commissioner of the Icelandic Police, 2005). The regional Commissioners of Police, who are in charge of the police forces in their jurisdiction, have prosecution powers in a majority of offenses coming before the country's district courts. The Director of Public Prosecutions, who has overall command of police investigations, supervises how the police commissioners exercise their prosecution authority, but in less serious cases, prosecution is basically in the hands of the police commissioner.

Variation in Defense

Variation in the way nations go about prosecuting cases is continued in the procedures that countries develop to defend those citizens being prosecuted (see Figure 7.2). In the Shari'a courts of Saudi Arabia and other Islamic countries, professionally trained lawyers do not

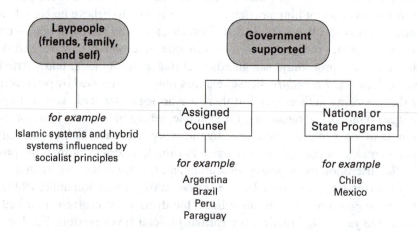

Keep in mind that variation exists within as well as among countries. The countries identified as exemplifying each general type may be accurately placed under another type as well. For example, Mexico also has an Assigned Counsel government-support system, and some hybrid systems influenced by socialist principles also provide legally trained defense counsel.

FIGURE 7.2   Variation in Defense

have a monopoly on legal representation. In fact, Muslims have traditionally acted for themselves or nominated others, relatives or character witnesses, to act for them. In Saudi Arabia, legal counsel—chosen by either the defendant or the accuser (there is no prosecutor either)—is actually regarded as an assistant to the judge because this person helps the judge reach an equitable verdict (Kingdom of Saudi Arabia, 2009).

The former Soviet Union provided an active role for nonprofessionals in the prosecution and defense of criminal defendants. If a person were accused of a crime, coworkers could secure a colleague of the accused to go to court as a "social defender" to testify about the defendant's good moral character and work habits. On the other hand, if the accused's work habits and other characteristics were not appreciated, colleagues could send a "social accuser" to speak against the defendant. In this manner, the public's interests were represented in court on a level equal to those of the defendant.

Despite these examples of laypeople helping in the defense of an accused, most countries rely on legally trained professionals to help defendants present their case. Before the mid-nineteenth century, legal protection for people unable to hire an attorney was primarily the result of charitable acts. Men such as Saint Yves of Brittany—"'a lawyer and yet not a thief, to the wonder of the people'—were canonized for their work in representing the impoverished" (Cappelletti & Gordley, 1978, p. 516). Even the more organized programs faded in and out of use with changes in monarchs. When legal assistance programs were in use, it was not always clear just who benefited from the assistance, under which circumstances it would be provided, and by what process the assistance would be carried out.

More modern programs in the West began in 1851 with French legislation designed to remove financial barriers that the poor encountered during litigation. A 1901 act established a national system of bureaus to determine eligibility in that program. Italy (in 1865) and Germany (in 1877) also initiated programs that allowed judges to appoint lawyers, serving without pay, to assist in the defense of an impoverished defendant (Cappelletti & Gordley, 1978).

In the twentieth and twenty-first centuries, provisions for the defense of poor people around the world continued to improve but not always quickly. A 1972 French reform substituted a system of aid paid by the state for the previous "charity" with unpaid lawyers providing legal assistance to the poor. Even today, however, many French lawyers find that when they are assigned to an indigent client, the meager fee received for expenses (there is no compensation for service) means they are still performing charity. Italian law allows defendants to choose no more than two attorneys of their choice or to have one appointed from a list compiled by a local bar association. A 1990 law provides that the state will pay for the legal defense of any indigent regardless of whether the counsel is selected by the defendant or appointed by the court (Van Cleave, 2007).

Latin American countries offer examples of some recent developments in providing legal assistance to poor defendants. In many of these countries, it has only been in this century that formal defense systems have been provided. Throughout most of the twentieth century, defense was provided by the judge or some other entity appointing a lawyer from a list of practicing attorneys—giving those attorneys a chance to fulfill their charitable obligations since they typically served without pay. For example, Belize still relies on private attorneys appointed by the Supreme Court's Records Office to provide legal assistance to the indigent (Justice Studies Center of the Americas, 2007).

However, many Latin American countries have established national public defense offices. For example, the Dominican Republic has created a public defender's office charged with providing legal defense and counsel for low-income defendants. These public defenders, who are charged with reaching the most favorable solution for the defendant, must have at least 2 years in legal practice and undergo merit-based completion in order to be accepted in the public defender's office. Similar entities exist in

Panama (where the public defenders are appointed by the Supreme Court) and Argentina (where, interestingly, the Public Defender's Office exists as a dual entity with the Public Prosecutor's Office in Argentina's Public Ministry). Chile and Guatemala represent a somewhat different system, wherein defense services are provided by a mix of both public defenders and private attorneys (Justice Studies Center of the Americas, 2007).

General comments about the legal assistance systems in continental and Latin American countries provide the necessary overview of worldwide options. Even in these brief remarks, you should see similarities with the primary legal assistance procedures in the United States. We have government-supported programs as well as programs that depend on judges to assign counsel from lists of available attorneys. American states also have jurisdictions in which defense attorneys are full-time government employees. A review of defense systems on other continents would reveal few variations from these themes, yet it is still instructive to highlight the defense system of a particular country.

THE ADJUDICATORS

Journalist Iurii Feofanov (1990/1991) relates an Eastern parable as he reflects on the idea of a state governed by law. He explains that a young man spent 10 years studying law with a sheik known for his wisdom. The youth spent his time writing down on scrolls the pronouncements of the holy sheik. When he returned to his homeland as a mature man, he brought with him an ass loaded down with the scrolls of wisdom. The man began judging his countrymen by listening to their problems, unfolding a scroll, and reading off a dictum. People marveled at his learning, but they didn't understand what they were to do, so they would ask him again only to receive a new dictum, even wiser than the first. Once the man went to the mountains to teach the people about the laws but when crossing a stream, the ass sunk under its load of scrolls. The wise man, not knowing how he could now pronounce judgments, began for the first time to ask the people who came to him: "What did you say your problem was?" When he looked into the matter carefully, he remembered what he had been taught and told the people what had to be done. He spoke clearly and wisely and his fame spread. The people would say about him: "Earlier, a wise ass would teach us, now it is the wise man himself."

From the perspective of the common legal tradition, that parable may be interpreted as criticizing the civil tradition's reliance on codes (the scrolls carried by the ass) for dispensing justice. However, Feofanov used the parable to support the civil legal tradition's belief that law is best envisioned as general principles instead of specific rules. He interprets the parable as showing that even though the ass with the "scrolls of laws" sank in the mountain stream, the principles of law remained in their original sense within the memory of the wise man and judge (Feofanov, 1990/1991). In this manner, the common legal tradition is disparaged as being loaded down with so many specific rules covering every individual problem that the legal system sinks from its own weight.

A distinguishing feature between the civil and common legal traditions is the former's preference for codes that clearly set forth general principles for judges to follow as they dispense justice. The latter's preference is for judges to follow specific guidelines as set down in similar cases handled by the same or other judges. A goal of both traditions is to provide uniformity of justice. The common tradition sees that as best achieved when judges follow decisions in similar cases, whereas the civil tradition finds that the goal is reached by judges following the same general principles. In either case, achieving the goal is linked to the behavior of an adjudicator.

In a sense, the adjudication process is the raison d'être for a justice system. Citizens and agencies of the government use the justice system when they seek resolution of some dispute. Whether the dispute concerns a private or public wrong, some process for adjudication must be part of the resolution. The preceding parable highlights the role that a judge plays in the decision, but in some justice systems, others are recruited to assist the judge.

Plato was among the first to champion a role for laypersons in the criminal process. He believed that the people must participate when offenses against the state are being judged since a wrong against the state is a wrong against everyone (Ehrmann, 1976, p. 95).

Today, the United States is among the countries that are putting Plato's suggestion in practice. Although a jury is used very infrequently in criminal cases, when it is used, Americans are relying on laypeople to decide the defendant's guilt or innocence while a judge, separate from those laypeople, controls the proceedings. The seriousness of the task before these members of the public, acting without legal training, is highlighted daily by judges across the country. Although a fictional account, the words of Judge Larren L. Lyttle in Scott Turow's best-selling novel, *Presumed Innocent*, give a feel for the role and mission of American jurors.

In the novel, murder defendant Rusty Sabich watches as the prospective jurors for his case are brought into the courtroom. Of the 75 people, 12 will be chosen to decide his fate. As a former prosecutor, Sabich knows that most jurors are going to begin the trial with a pro-prosecution bias. After all, jurors usually tell themselves, the police and prosecutor think the guy is guilty, so who am I, a mere citizen off the street, to say he isn't guilty? The only way Sabich can maintain hope is his knowledge that Judge Lyttle has a reputation for emphatically explaining to the jury such concepts as the presumption of innocence. Sabich listens carefully as the judge begins by telling the potential jurors what the case is about (Turow, 1987, pp. 234–235).

> [Judge Lyttle] has probably seen a thousand juries chosen during his career. His rapport is instantaneous: this big, good-looking black man, kind of funny, kind of smart. . . . He is skilled in addressing juries, canny in divining hidden motivation, and committed to the foundation of his soul to the fundamental notions. The defendant is presumed innocent. Innocent. As you sit here you have gotta be thinking Mr. Sabich didn't do it.
>
> "I'm sorry, sir. In the first row, what is your name?"
>
> "Mahalovich."
>
> "Mr. Mahalovich. Did Mr. Sabich commit the crime that he is charged with?"
>
> Mahalovich, a stout middle-aged man who has his paper folded in his lap, shrugs.
>
> "I wouldn't know, Judge."
>
> "Mr. Mahalovich, you are excused. Ladies and gentlemen, let me tell you what you are to presume. Mr. Sabich is innocent. I am the judge. I am tellin' you that. Presume he is innocent. When you sit there, I want you to look over and say to yourself, There sits an innocent man."

The parable of the "wise ass/wise man" and the story of Judge Lyttle's speech to potential jurors suggest extremes in the assignment of people to adjudicate a dispute. At one extreme is a trained judge with sole responsibility for hearing the dispute, determining guilt or innocence, and assigning appropriate sanctions. At the other extreme, carrying out the same duties, is a panel of citizens, minimally knowledgeable in the law. Using these extremes as ideal types for purposes of analysis suggests the continuum in Figure 7.3.

Note that we are referring only to decisions of fact (i.e., did the accused commit the offense?) when speaking of the adjudication process. Courts will often decide questions of law as well as ones of fact. In those instances, the court will rule on such things

| Heavy Reliance on Professional Judges | Mixed Reliance | Heavy Reliance on Laypeople |

for example
Saudi Arabia

for example
Germany

for example
England

FIGURE 7.3 Variation in Adjudication—an Adjudication Continuum

as the legality of police procedures in the arrest or the constitutionality of the law that the accused supposedly violated. When dealing with questions of law, courts typically rely only on professional judges. Those judges may be at the mercy of political or religious leaders when making their decisions, but the decision is given by the judge. For questions of fact (and even questions of law in some jurisdictions), however, several countries provide for input from laypeople. It is to this process we refer when speaking of the adjudication continuum. After considering the issue of presumption of innocence, we will deal with players at the continuum's ends and middle and then look at country-specific examples along that continuum.

Presumption of Innocence

We covered the distinction between presumption of guilt and presumption of innocence in Chapter 3, but a brief review is in order because this issue relates to the mindset of adjudicators as they consider a case. To the extent that civil law systems follow a crime control model, one could argue that they presume the guilt of a defendant. Or, as Packer (1968) might put it, the investigation by civil law system officials is assumed to identify any accused person who is probably innocent. Similarly, people whom the investigation does not exclude are probably guilty. Therefore, subsequent action against those people proceeds under a presumption of guilt. Conversely, one could argue that common law systems emphasizing a due process model presume the innocence of a defendant. Proponents of this system may argue that the assumption of innocence is necessary because the investigatory stage is neither as complete nor as intensive as it is under civil law. As a result, common law officials cannot be so sure they have already excluded the "probably innocent."

Maybe instead of trying to view one legal system as presuming guilt, another presuming innocence, and a third as presuming nothing, it is best to try to appreciate how a country's legal system tries to avoid prosecution of probably innocent people. Some choose to weed out the innocent in the early stages with intensive investigation of suspects, whereas others believe that the procedures themselves can be used to do the weeding as the suspect/defendant moves through the system.

WEB PROJECT

The Scottish Verdict of "Not Proven"

In Scotland, a jury can return one of three verdicts: guilty, not guilty, or not proven. The "not proven" verdict, which is likely unique to Scotland, has the same impact as a verdict of not guilty. Presumably, in returning a not proven verdict, the jurors may be sending a message that they feel the accused did indeed commit the crime, but that there was insufficient evidence to justify a conviction.

Go to http://www.bbc.com/news/uk-scotland-scotland-politics-35659541 and read the article, and then scroll down and start with the material under the heading "What is the not proven verdict?" Write a few paragraphs on whether you think the not proven verdict is appropriate and useful. Should the Scots keep it? Should other countries consider it?

It is difficult not to ask which system is more just. Merryman (1985) tells of a comparative scholar who said that if he were innocent, he would prefer to be tried in a civil law court, but if he were guilty, he would rather be tried by a common law court. Merryman believes that comment considers criminal procedure in civil law to be more likely to distinguish accurately between guilty and innocent. But whichever system—and whatever the presumption—the adjudication process relies on people to make that distinction. It is to those people that we turn our attention.

Professional Judges

At the start of the twenty-first century, at least 315 jurists worldwide suffered reprisals for carrying out their professional duties. Included in that number, according to the International Commission of Jurists, were 39 who were killed and 5 who disappeared (Seiderman, 2002).

Harassment and persecution of judicial officials is of greater concern than just a humanitarian interest in the well-being of these people. When the judiciary does not feel free to function, the law cannot operate. The problem is not equally severe in all countries, but a judiciary subject to manipulation by others is a well-recognized problem. We will take a look at procedures used in various countries to ensure their judiciary is able to act independently.

AN INDEPENDENT JUDICIARY In 1986, the General Assembly of the United Nations passed a resolution on the Basic Principles on the Independence of the Judiciary. Those principles emphasize that the independence of the judiciary should be guaranteed by the state and enshrined in the constitution or law of each country. This position was taken in the belief that an independent judiciary is indispensable for implementing everyone's right to a fair and public hearing before a competent and impartial tribunal (United Nations, 1988).

It is difficult to imagine that any country would take a stand against an independent judiciary. In fact, most governments claim that the UN Basic Principles are already embodied in the constitution or laws of their countries. Yet, after seeking information from nongovernment agencies, the United Nations found that the basic principles were not always fully respected despite the public stance taken by government officials.

A country's judiciary can deal with all crimes (including abuse of power by government agents) only when it exists separate and independent from the legislative and executive branches. How do countries seeking an independent judiciary go about finding people to serve as judges? Strange as it may seem, some countries rely on the legislative and executive branches. Other nations use committee recommendations, and still others hold public elections. Of course, various combinations of these approaches are also possible. Some countries seek a more clear-cut separation of government powers and have made the judicial service a bureaucratic career that can be chosen by persons formally educated in the law.

The various ways in which judges arrive at their positions deserve closer attention. After all, every country's goal (or at least the publicly stated one) is to provide citizens with an independent judiciary. Only in this way can judges be free to decide in an impartial manner the disputes brought forward by citizens and government officials.

BECOMING A JUDGE The people who adjudicate legal disputes typically come to their position in one of two ways: selection by others or self-selection. When the selection of judges is by others, it takes the form of either appointment or election. The people chosen usually have already gained experience as attorneys and, especially when chosen for higher courts, might have attained a certain level of distinction in the legal profession.

Appointment to the magistracy can be by the executive or by a special committee. For example, the president of the United States appoints (with the consent of the Senate) federal judges, and in Argentina judges are appointed for life by the executive branch with the consent of the Senate (for federal judges) or the state legislators (for state judges). Special committees sometimes appoint judges through recommendations to the executive (e.g., Israel) or a member of the executive's cabinet (e.g., Germany). In some Latin American countries (e.g., Bolivia, Honduras, and El Salvador), judges of the highest court appoint members of the lower courts (Carrió & Garro, 2007; Harnon & Stein, 2007; Hitchner & Levine, 1981).

Election of judges by the people is not frequently found in countries of the world. The United States provides an exception; the majority of American states select judges through some form of popular election. Even in the United States, several states are moving toward a combination appointment/election process.

Judges also can be elected by a country's legislature. This process is used to free judges from executive control (e.g., some Central American states), to ensure political reliability (e.g., China), or to provide appropriate distribution of desirable characteristics (e.g., judges on the Swiss Federal Court must reflect the German-, French-, and Italian-speaking aspects of Swiss culture) (Congressional-Executive Commission on China, 2016; Hitchner & Levine, 1981).

In the self-selection process, judicial service is chosen as a career after the completion of one's formal legal education. In countries with this process, graduates with law degrees choose among such careers as prosecutor, defense counsel, private attorney, or judge. When choosing a judicial career, the aspirant typically takes a state examination and, if successful, begins serving as an adjudicator. In some countries, the new judge will attend a special school but more often will immediately be sent to a remote part of the country to begin service at the lowest-level courts (Merryman, 1985). Promotion in the court hierarchy and transfer to more desirable locations result from some combination of seniority and proven ability.

Self-selected judges are most often found in countries following the civil legal tradition, but the process is also found in Islamic countries (e.g., Saudi Arabia). Because civil law judges have the duty of applying rather than making law, their function is essentially a mechanical one. Judges in the common law tradition are more involved in lawmaking and are often expected to be knowledgeable enough in the law to render creative decisions. One result of this distinction is the perception that common law requires experienced and renowned persons to serve as judges, whereas the civil law operates well with a civil servant or expert clerk. After all, the judicial process in civil law should be a fairly routine activity (Merryman, 1985). The judge is presented with a fact situation, and his or her duty is merely to link that situation with the appropriate legislative provision and then to pronounce the solution that the union automatically produces. That process, one could argue, can as easily be completed by a young law school graduate as by a celebrated lawyer with many years of legal experience.

Jurors and Lay Judges

When Americans think of laypeople participating in the court process, they typically picture 12 citizens sitting off to one side of the courtroom. The right to a trial by jury has been cherished for quite some time in America's history. Thomas Jefferson provided the reasoning for such a procedure when he wrote that should he be asked to decide whether to omit the people from the legislative or the judicial arena, he would leave them out of the legislative since, for him, the execution of the law is more important than making it (Moore, 1973, p. 159).

Participation of laypeople as jury members is only one way that citizens take part in the adjudication process. An alternative is the use of lay judges (also called lay assessors or citizen judges). A basic, if imprecise, distinction is that jurors decide—without a professional judge voting—whether the defendant is guilty, whereas lay judges vote together with one or more professional judges. These two means of participation (juror or lay judge) identify the primary ways in which citizens provide a judiciary with input from the common folk. After an overview of each strategy, we will look at country-specific examples of how these techniques operate.

JURIES Although similar assemblies existed in continental Europe before the eleventh century (Moore, 1973), and at least one author suggests the Islamic *Lafif* (developing between the eighth and eleventh centuries) had many similarities (Makdisi, 1999), England is considered the birthplace of the jury. The first type of jury, as it developed after 1066 in England, decided whether an accusation against a person was well founded. Sometimes, that accusatory jury determined guilt or innocence. Yet, eventually two types of juries were established, with the accusatory one called the grand jury and the verdict one becoming the petit or trial jury.

The early trial juries assembled and stated what they knew about a particular crime or were told to go into the countryside and establish facts about the alleged crime. To accomplish that duty, the jurors talked to neighbors, picked up hearsay information and rumors, and spoke with the accused and the accuser. After gathering their evidence, they would reassemble and draw a conclusion about guilt or innocence (Stuckey, 1986). If the accused was found guilty, he or she was given the punishment prescribed for the crime. Soon not only the jurors expressed what they had learned about the crime, but witnesses might even have appeared before the jury and related what they knew about the accusation.

The witnesses' knowledge, like that of the jurors, was often no more than rumor or hearsay, so the jury might have given little weight to their testimony. This was particularly true if the witnesses portrayed the accused as innocent. The reason for discounting witness testimony and deciding contrary to what appeared to be the facts rested in the jurors' fear of the king (Stuckey, 1986). The jurors knew that the king's justices often had advance information about a crime because of reports from the sheriffs and the coroners. If the justices believed that the jurors had presented a false verdict, the jurors would be required to make atonement (a payment of property or money) or be punished.

The bias toward conviction in a trial by jury meant that many accused preferred other systems for exoneration. For example, before its abolishment in 1215, many an accused opted for trial by ordeal. Here, the accused had to do some physical feat as a call to the Deity for help in determining guilt or innocence. It was presumed that God would enable the innocent to do the required ordeal, while the guilty would fail in the performance. Such required feats included holding a red-hot iron or removing a large rock from a boiling pot of water. After the test, the accused's hand was wrapped; then 3 days later he appeared before a priest who unwrapped the wound and determined whether it had healed. A healed hand showed innocence, an unhealed one guilt.

Trial by compurgation was another alternative. This system used "character witnesses" for both the accused and the accuser to take oaths asserting the truthfulness of their respective statements. The technical language of the required oath (an error when repeating it meant guilt) and the general unreliability of the oath helpers (compurgators) did not make this option especially popular. The remaining choice was trial by battle. The accused and the accuser would go into actual combat with each other, usually using battle-axes. Like trial by ordeal, the "winner" in the battle was said to have had the assistance of God and therefore must be innocent (Stuckey, 1986).

Jury

Jury trials can be used in countries following any of the legal traditions, but seem to be more frequently found in the common legal tradition and where adversarial proceedings are followed.

Bikeriderlondon/Shutterstock

Efforts to "encourage" the accused to submit to trial by jury included the placing of weights on his or her chest in increasing amounts until they submitted to a jury trial. Even then, the accused often preferred being crushed to death in an effort to save their possessions for their family rather than having them confiscated by the king after being convicted by the jury.

As time passed, the king could no longer confiscate property as payment for crimes. Equally important, jurors were no longer punished or required to make atonement for possible erroneous verdicts, and the testimony of witnesses received greater consideration. It was this newer concept of the jury trial that the colonists brought with them to America. By 1673, trial by jury had become an important procedure in Virginia, the Massachusetts Bay Colony, New York, and Pennsylvania (Moore, 1973). Jury trials continued to play a major role in the development of the American republic as the colonists prepared for the Revolution. The Declaration of Rights of the First Continental Congress (1774) included trial by peers as a "great and inestimable privilege." In the Declaration of Causes and Necessity of Taking Up Arms (1775), the colonists claimed that they had been deprived of "the accustomed and inestimable privilege of trial by jury in cases affecting both life and property." And the Declaration of Independence (1776) gave as one reason requiring separation "for depriving us, in many cases, of the benefits of Trial by Jury." The place of honor American revolutionaries gave jury trials continues today in the hearts of Americans, although very few cases ever get to the jury stage.

LAY JUDGES The enthusiasm that American revolutionaries had for jury trials was repeated by revolutionaries in the French Revolution and the nineteenth-century bourgeois European revolutions. The rising middle classes saw participation in criminal proceedings as a weapon in the fight against aristocracy, the professional judiciary, and overpowering monarchs (Ehrmann, 1976). The idea caught on in France and spread to most civil law countries, but it proved a disappointing experiment.

The Europeans tried to incorporate the common legal tradition of a jury into their civil legal tradition system without otherwise modifying their system. The inquisitorial trial format, the importance of the investigatory stage, and the active role of the judge made it difficult for jurors to follow the evidence presented under civil legal procedure. In their confusion regarding their role, European jurors often asked the judge for advice. The advice was provided in forms that would be inadmissible in an Anglo-American jury trial (Ehrmann, 1976).

Today, the classical jury system is primarily a common law tradition. Some civil law country examples exist, but typically for serious crimes only and with a variety of modifications. For example, the jury of 12 in Belgium needs only 8 votes for conviction and Norway's juries encourage gender parity by drawing names from separate lists of males and females. Spain's jury system uses nine jurors in a court presided over by one professional judge to hear cases in 12 specific offense categories (e.g., murder, arson, bribery). Potential jurors are chosen from voter registration lists and are subject to peremptory challenges (four each for the prosecution and the defense) and to challenge for cause (Jimeno-Bulnes, 2004; Thaman, 2000; Vidmar, 2000).

Despite the presence of juries in some civil legal tradition countries, research by Jackson and Kovalev (2016) found a general decline across Europe in the use of the traditional jury since 2005. A 2005 survey identified nine countries in continental Europe as having a traditional jury system (Austria, Belgium, Denmark, Malta, Norway, Russia, Spain, Sweden, and some of the Swiss cantons). By 2012, a new survey found that the list no longer included Denmark and Switzerland, and Norway was seriously considering abolishing the jury system in favor of a mixed panel. Further, some of the remaining jury systems had been curtailed (e.g., Russia and Sweden).

Both versions of lay participation have their supporters and detractors. Lay participation is praised as providing a rigorous fact-finding process, reducing opportunities for corruption, representing the community in the courtroom, legitimizing the justice system, and increasing civic engagement. Detractors argue that jury verdicts sometimes appear inconsistent with the evidence and that lay judges are little more than puppets nodding in agreement with the professional judges (Hans, 2008; Machura, 2001; Thaman, 2007). But proponents are prevailing as more countries seek ways to incorporate citizens into the adjudication process.

Japan's lay judge system (discussed more fully in Chapter 10) adds citizen judges to Japan's courts and similar changes have occurred elsewhere in East Asia, including South Korea and Taiwan. In 2013, South Korea's National Assembly gave official status to an advisory jury system that had been in an experimental stage since 2008. When the defendant agrees to this procedural addition, randomly selected civilian participants hear testimony and then deliberate on their own before consulting with professional judges regarding guilt and, as necessary, punishment (Kim, Park, Park, & Eom, 2013; Lee, 2009, 2010). Similarly, Taiwan is considering a proposal wherein a group of five randomly chosen citizens would sit with and advise three professional judges in serious criminal trials (Huang & Lin, 2013, 2014).

The use of lay judges is exemplified below in the discussion of Germany. When used as intended, the lay judges provide an intriguing alternative to the jury system as a means of providing citizen input to the trial process. They stand as a contrast to the law systems that prefer to rely almost totally on professional judges and avoid any active participation by laypeople. That point brings us back to the adjudication continuum (see Figure 7.3).

Examples along the Adjudication Continuum

Before we consider country-specific examples of the continuum types, it is important to emphasize the continuum's analytic purpose. As with all ideal-type constructs, the extremes are not represented by any real-life example. Still, for purposes of analysis, we can identify examples that are closer to one end or the other. Similarly, whenever you have two ends, there must be a middle; that is, there should be mid-range examples that serve

WEB PROJECT

Lay Judges in Finland

As in many countries, Finland relies on average citizens to participate in criminal trials—not as jurors but as lay judges. Visit http://www.oikeus.fi/tuomioistuimet/karajaoikeudet/en/index/layjudges.html and read about the lay judge's roles, responsibilities, and eligibility. Write a few paragraphs summarizing how the lay judge system operates in Finland.

as a balance between the two extremes. Below the continuum line in Figure 7.3 are names of countries that arguably exhibit characteristics running from one ideal type to the other. To provide structure for our discussion of adjudicators, we consider these countries as they relate to a heavy reliance either on judges or on laypeople in the adjudicating process. To set the boundaries, we will look at the extremes and then move toward the middle.

SAUDI ARABIA It may seem strange to have Saudi Arabia (see Map A.2) toward the "judge-heavy" end of an adjudication continuum. During the discussion of judicial review (Chapter 5), this same country exemplified the absence of complete judicial review, and that may imply the absence of judicial power. However, we must remember that judicial review concerns the ability of the judiciary to rule on actions of the legislature and the executive. For purposes of an adjudication continuum, we are looking only at the more traditional role of the judge as he or she decides disputes between citizens or between the government and a citizen. In other words, does the adjudication process rely more heavily on a single judge or a group of laypeople in deciding the question of guilt?

Adjudication in a *qadi* court relies on that judge's ability to direct independently the activities of the accused, the defendant, and any witnesses. Granted, the qadi is in turn directed by the Qur'an and Sunna, which stipulate the number of witnesses and types of oaths necessary for conviction of hudud and qisas offenses. Yet it is still the qadi, without the assistance of any laypeople, who decides if the evidence is acceptable as he seeks to resolve disputes in accordance with Shari'a. The qadi may not have judicial independence and may lack the power of judicial review, but in the courtroom he, and he alone, adjudicates the cases brought before him.

The Kingdom of Saudi Arabia describes the procedure in its Shari'a courts as very straightforward, informal, and heavily reliant on oral testimony (Kingdom of Saudi Arabia, 2001). In fact, the judge's findings must be based solely on the oral proceedings conducted during the hearing. That means all motions, pleas, and evidence are presented orally in the presence of the opposing parties and the judge—with opposing parties given the opportunity to challenge. When it is necessary to base trial proceedings on written documentation, it must be done in a manner that it is heard by all persons present. The oral nature of proceedings is said to allow judges opportunities to question the parties and hear details of their pleas. In doing so, the impartiality of the proceedings is more apparent.

After questioning the accuser regarding the claim, the qadi demands an immediate reply from the defendant—which may be delayed to provide the defendant time to check or secure records. The judge may then question other witnesses (including expert witnesses) before making a decision in the case.

Proceedings are expected to be heard promptly, examined carefully, and resolved rapidly (Kingdom of Saudi Arabia, 2009). Upon passing judgment against the defendant, the qadi must specify the reasons upon which it is based. The judge does not have to follow precedent, not even his own previous rulings, but the decision must have support in the Qur'an, Sunna, and ijma (Kingdom of Saudi Arabia, 2001).

The heavy reliance on a judge for adjudication purposes is consistent with how Shari'a sees a just and impartial trial. Under Islam, there is no need to have laypeople involved in adjudication because judges are assumed to be unbiased. This assumption is more than just a "hope" because it has its base in Islam itself. Sanad (1991) explains that Muhammad commanded judges to be just in their judgments and is reported to have made his point as follows:

> The judges are of three kinds, two of them go to Hell and one to Heaven. A judge aware of the right and ruled in accordance with it, then he goes to Heaven, and a judge ruled by ignorance he is in Hell; and a judge who knew the right but deviated from it, he is in Hell too. (p. 83)

Because, from the Muslims' perspective, judges want to go to Heaven, they will rule fairly and do not need to be monitored by laypeople. A judge-heavy adjudication process is the result.

ENGLAND   Figure 7.3 places England at the "heavy reliance on laypeople" end of the adjudication continuum. Actually, English courtroom policy allows a much more active role for the judge than does American procedure. In the English tradition, the court often questions witnesses and takes a rather active role in the proceedings. At the conclusion of prosecution and defense presentations, the judge may deliver a summary and instructions to the jury. Those comments may include the judge's opinions on witness credibility and may express a particular view of the case.

Judges must be careful with this opportunity to influence the jury via the summary because the defense could appeal on the grounds the judge went too far in trying to persuade the jury. However, Zander believes that judges can normally make the summing up "appeal proof" while at the same time indicating (e.g., through body language) their true opinion of the facts (Zander, 1989). Because the judge in criminal cases knows of any criminal record the accused may have (a fact the jurors may not know), there is likely a temptation to exert improper influence on the jury. In the United States, such a temptation is avoided by having judges sum up only on the law, not on the facts. Complaints that English judges abuse their power have certainly been made, and there is support for such complaints in those cases that resulted in a retrial or even a not-guilty verdict on appeal because a judge was deemed to have misdirected the jury (Lloyd-Bostock & Thomas, 2000; Scott, n.d.). One critic suggests that biased summing up is rarer than it used to be—possibly because it tends to be counterproductive. When a jury realizes that the presumably neutral judge is in fact biased toward one side, the jury may do precisely the opposite of what the judge is urging (Scott, n.d.).

Although judges have a fairly involved role, it remains for the English jury to adjudicate questions of fact. On that basis, England is correctly placed on the continuum, because laypeople have an active role as jurors. Additionally, as discussed later in this chapter, laypeople in England are used as magistrates and in that capacity have an even more active role in the justice process.

While the English jury trial would look more familiar to Americans than would the process in countries outside the common legal tradition, it still seems unusual. A first impression would likely be surprise at the placement of the key courtroom actors. In the English courtroom, the opposing barristers sit next to each other and wear identical wigs and robes. Instead of being at his or her barrister's side, the accused sits in the dock at the rear of the courtroom. The jury never sees the defendant talk directly with the defense counsel (Graham, 1983).

Before 1972, English jurors were selected from a group of persons occupying a dwelling with a certain taxable value. This procedure did not provide much of a cross section of the population and tended to exclude women and low-income people. Today, Acts of Parliament require jury panels to be chosen at random from all those on the electoral register (i.e., voter registration list) who are between 18 and 70 years old and have lived in the United Kingdom for at least 5 consecutive years since age 13. The changes seem to have worked because research shows that today's juries are much younger and less middle class, although women and ethnic minorities remain underrepresented (BBC News, 2008; Lloyd-Bostock & Thomas, 2000).

Randomness is also believed to be achieved in selecting British juries by avoiding, as much as possible, the American practice of voir dire. In that procedure, the American adversaries question potential jurors to identify possible biases for or against the defendant. However, in some exceptional cases (e.g., national security issues), the potential British jurors may be subjected to a vetting process that checks their suitability in relation to the trial. The vetting will include a routine police check as well as a background check to include political affiliations (In Brief, 2016).

During the voir dire process in the American trial, prosecution and defense have an allotted number of "challenges," by which the attorneys can have some jurors they believe are most likely to favor the opposing side excluded from service. English jurors, on the other hand, arrive at their position without having to suffer such questioning by prosecutor and defense counsel. The result, some cynics have suggested, is a situation in which English trials start once the jury selection ends, while American trials are essentially over after the jurors have been "picked." Actually, challenges to particular jurors are possible in the British system. It does not happen often, but either the prosecution or the defense may challenge a potential juror. The challenges are of two types. A challenge to the array challenges the entire jury on the basis that it was chosen in an unrepresentative or biased way. A challenge for cause, as in an American courtroom, must be for a particular reason. An example of a good reason would be that one of the lawyers knows the potential juror, as would an argument that the potential juror has a criminal record or is biased. The judge determines whether the challenge will be allowed. Not available to the British attorneys is a peremptory challenge, which American advocates can use to remove a potential juror without having to give a reason.

Following closing speeches by prosecuting and defense counsel (defense always having the last word), the British judge, as noted earlier, summarizes the evidence for the jury. Basically, the judge is allowed to express an opinion about the defense as long as questions of fact are left to the jurors. Such action by the judge would be

YOU SHOULD KNOW!
Should Jurors Be Allowed to Ask Questions during a Trial?

When laypeople serve as lay judges in many civil law countries, they are full participants in the trial process and are often allowed to ask questions of the witnesses. Even in some jury systems—in England, for example—the jurors are able to propose questions to the judge that the judge may or may not ask of the witness. In fact, the practice of allowing jurors to submit questions for witnesses is possible in most American jurisdictions, but jurors are seldom told of the possibility. American jurors are generally expected to remain silent.

According to a survey conducted by the National Center for State Courts (Mize, Hannaford-Agor, & Waters, 2007), the practice of allowing juror to submit written questions to be asked of witnesses during criminal trials is mandatory in some states (e.g., Arizona, Colorado, and Indiana), prohibited in others (e.g., Georgia, Minnesota, Mississippi, Nebraska, and Texas), and left to the discretion of the judge in the rest. In most states and in federal courts, some form of juror-posed questioning is allowed. Even where it is allowed, however, it is rarely encouraged. Traditional arguments against juror participation in the questioning of witnesses have included beliefs that jurors will be unable to keep an open mind until all evidence has been presented, that the questions are disruptive, and that the questions are more likely to benefit the prosecution. On the other hand, proponents suggest that allowing jurors to ask questions is a way to keep the jury more engaged and to help clarify witness testimony and could increase juror confidence in the verdict. What do you think? Can American jurors be trusted as active participants in trials?

distressing to American defense counsels, who are given considerably more leeway in their attempts to win over the jury with emotion and oratory when the facts of the case may not be enough.

GERMANY Despite the examples of several civil law countries using aspects of the classic jury system, many civil law countries use laypeople in a somewhat different manner. Instead of using laypeople who independently and bindingly determine guilt or innocence, countries of the civil legal tradition are more likely to use a "mixed bench," wherein two or three laypeople work with professional judges to adjudicate criminal cases. This approach seems better suited to the inquisitorial process because the laypeople and professional judges are expected to work together toward sound verdicts and sentences. Germany (see Map A.10) provides a particularly good example of the mixed-bench approach.

The German people used the jury system in the 1840s and briefly in Bavaria after World War II. For the most part, however, recent German history has involved the use of citizens as lay judges rather than as jurors. Specifically, the community chooses citizens to serve on the bench with professional judges. These lay judges have full powers of interrogation, deliberation, voting, and sentencing.

Lay judges serving in German criminal courts are called *Schöffen*. They serve in courts of limited jurisdiction and in the higher-level courts with general jurisdiction. An accused criminal will be tried in a court with professional and lay judges if imprisonment between 2 and 4 years is possible or in certain cases requiring at least 1 year in prison. For cases where the punishment is not likely to be more than 2 years' imprisonment, the case is heard by a single professional judge (Aronowitz, 1993; Jehle, 2015; Wolfe, 1996).

There are two types of mixed trial courts, the *Schöffengericht*, a lower-level court of limited jurisdiction (one professional and two lay judges), and the *Grosse Strafkammer* (with three professional and two lay judges). When the Grosse Strafkammer is hearing a very serious crime (murder, manslaughter, etc.), the court is referred to as a *Schwurgericht*. Decisions of the lower-level courts, with and without lay judges, can be appealed to another mixed court, the *Kleine Strafkammer* (with one professional and two lay judges). All of the more serious cases can be appealed only on points of law and only to a purely professional court.

The lay judges are assigned to sessions over a period of 4 years. Usually they serve an average of 1 day per month. If their service ever exceeds 24 days in 1 year, they can ask to be stricken from the list of lay judges. Because a defendant lacks choice between a bench or jury trial, it is easier than it would be in the United States to figure out the number of lay judges needed over a 4-year period. In addition, the date and length of a German trial are more predictable. This is so because the judge in the inquisitorial system determines the evidence to introduce, the witnesses to summon, and the general nature of the proceedings. As a result, German trials tend not to be as long as those in America. There are other time-savers as well. Because there is no jury, the rules of evidence are uncomplicated and there is never a need to remove a jury while attorneys make motions and arguments the jurors should not hear. Finally, "hung juries" are eliminated because decisions on guilt can be made with less than a unanimous vote.

As in the United States, the participation of the lay public is the result of efforts to ensure representation of the average citizen. Selection of the Schöffen varies by region because there is no federal standard. In some parts of Germany (e.g., the rather small Bremen), the names are hand-picked by the political parties. In other parts (e.g., the very big Nordrhein-Westfalen), the Schöffen list is drawn from the population registers. Schöffen may repeat their service as long as it has been at least 8 years since they last served. The state courts determine via formula the number of citizens required and call the necessary principal lay judges (*Hauptschöffen*) and a number of alternates (*Hilfschöffen*).

IMPACT

CONCURRENT CONSIDERATION OF GUILT AND SENTENCE

Under the American system of justice, sentencing hearings typically follow trials—sometimes by as much as several weeks. One reason for this procedure is to provide time to gather information about the defendant for the judge to use in determining the appropriate sentence. The probation department, for example, needs time to complete a presentence investigation. Because determination of guilt and determination of sentence are separate procedures, the rules governing trials in the United States differ greatly from those controlling sentencing hearings. Consider the law of evidence. In the United States, it limits the nature and sources of information to be considered during the guilt phase of a trial, but there are few such limits at the time of sentencing. And the restriction on evidence about the defendant's prior criminality vanishes after conviction. As a result, few evidentiary or other restraints are placed on the court during the sentencing phase.

In many countries, especially some in the civil legal tradition, there is no separation of the guilt-finding and sentencing functions. In Germany and Italy, for example, at the completion of the trial, the professional judges and lay judges immediately meet to deliberate and vote as to whether or not guilt has been proven (Federal Republic of Germany, 1987, Sections 260 and 268; Italian Republic, 2014, Article 525). When the verdict is guilty, the judges also determine and announce the sentence—all as part of the same proceeding. The same was true in France until reform of the penal code in 2014. Now, courts are allowed to pronounce a sentence in a separate session from the one in which the defendant's guilt was decided (Boring, 2014). This was done to allow the court time to examine the defendant's personality and situation so that the most appropriate sentence can be imposed.

The standards used in Germany to collect evidence about guilt and sentencing are deemed sufficient for both purposes. The Code of Criminal Procedure (Federal Republic of Germany, 1987) stipulates that the taking of evidence shall extend to all facts and means of proof relevant to the decision (Section 244). The rules may, however, seem rather loose to many Americans. For example, hearsay evidence may be introduced, and the closest thing to an exclusionary rule is the barring of evidence gathered in such extreme situations as torment, deception, or hypnosis (Section 136a). Evidence about the defendant's character, including prior convictions, can also be introduced (Weigend, 1983).

Germans do not view the unified trial (i.e., simultaneous determination of guilt and sentence) and the unstructured manner of gathering evidence as unjust. Their confidence in the fairness of the procedures is based on at least three points:

1. The absence of an unsupervised lay fact-finder (an American jury).
2. A tradition of the inquisitorial procedure.
3. Because the sentence is based largely on the offense and not the offender, for most cases the sentence awaiting the convicted offender is quite predictable as to type and length (M. Joutsen, personal communication, July 2016).

Together, these features result in a different approach to truth-seeking. First, the German court system does not have to control the deliberations of lay jurors through complicated rules of evidence. The lay judges discuss and decide cases with the professional judge and are under that judge's continuous guidance and advice. The German system relies on the professional judge's ability to explain to the lay judges the relevance and weight of the evidence. Professional judges, because of their training and experience, are presumed to know how to assess evidence properly without the guidance of formal rules (Weigend, 1983).

Consideration of this different way of conducting a trial highlights distinctions between the inquisitorial and adversarial systems. In America, truth emerges in an indirect fashion from a contest between the people involved. Therefore, as in any other "competition," procedural rules to guide and regulate the contest are of foremost importance. In Germany, the truth comes directly to the court through questioning of persons most likely to know it. That does not mean that the truth can be sought at any cost, but the German system does put less emphasis on formality and rules of evidence. The difference is made clear in Weigend's (1983) comment that a German judge would think it absurd to limit testimony from a witness who is about to convey useful information on the defendant's need for rehabilitation simply because the witness was called to testify about the offense. The loss of truth would be regarded as much more harmful than upsetting the sequence of taking proof.

Notably absent from this process is a procedure similar to American voir dire, where either prosecution or defense challenges lay judges. But even though there is no German counterpart to the voir dire process, it is possible to challenge the persons on the nomination list and the chosen lay judges. Moreover, lay judges chosen for a particular trial can be challenged for bias—as can the professional judges. Nevertheless, such challenges are rare. The presiding judge has responsibility for the composition of the court, but a Schöffe must inform the judge if he or she does not feel completely free in considering the case.

We now have a better understanding of the actors involved in the judicial process of different countries of the world. It is time to move on to the second part of the actors/institutions strategy and consider the stage on which these actors play: the courts.

VARIATION IN COURT ORGANIZATION

A review of court organizations around the world reveals a strange combination of similarity and uniqueness. The similarity comes from the seemingly universal use of a basic organizational structure composed of lowest-level, mid-level, and highest-level courts. We find uniqueness when we look more closely and see many possible variations on that basic theme. Attempts to classify the various organizations into only a few categories would be fruitless. In some countries, a dual system operates with courts at the state or province level coexisting with courts at the federal level. In other countries, the system is so centralized that one simple three-tiered structure handles criminal, civil, and administrative cases in the same courts with the same judges. Criminal, civil, and administrative disputes may be under the jurisdiction of three separate court hierarchies in other countries. Some countries include a system of religious courts with an autonomous system of secular courts.

Obviously, finding three or four common variables to use in categorizing the systems is an unwieldy assignment. The most reasonable approach for handling the profusion of organizations is simply to describe some variations to show the different ways in which a basic theme can be played. In the absence of a reasonable classification scheme, we simply consider examples from some countries covered in other chapters and a few new nations to ensure a broad-based representation.

France

The courts of France are organized into two major systems: the ordinary, or regular, courts and the administrative courts. The simplicity of the French system stops at this point, however, because each system has separate and distinct hierarchies that even the French authorities consider quite complex. Confusion regarding court jurisdiction required the creation of the eight-member *Tribunal des Conflits*. This tribunal, presided over ex officio by the Minister of Justice, makes unappealable decisions regarding the system to which a case will be assigned.

Because the ordinary courts handle both civil and criminal cases, our discussion is restricted to that area. Furthermore, as seen in Figure 7.4, there are different lower- and intermediate-level courts for civil and criminal cases. We follow the hierarchy for criminal cases. Because there are some common features of trials at each court level, an overview of court procedures will be helpful before we tackle the inevitable differences.

In the most general sense, French defendants do not enter pleas in their courts. In principle, all cases go to trial, and whether the accused agrees with or fights the charges is simply another piece of evidence for the court to consider. Obviously, a full-fledged trial in all instances would be too burdensome for almost any country, especially an industrialized nation such as France. As a result, several procedures and practices (especially at the lower-level courts) are designed to save time and discourage unnecessary litigation (Frase, 2007). At the lowest tier (police court), trials can be completely avoided

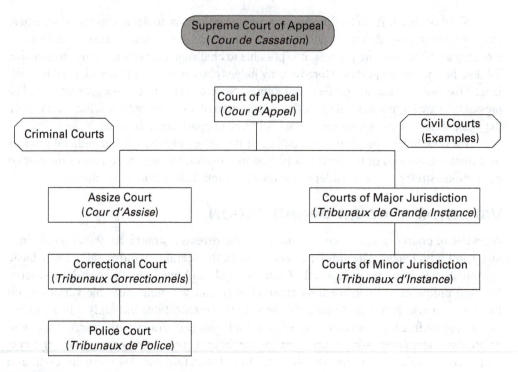

FIGURE 7.4   Ordinary Courts of France

through trial substitutes. At the next higher tier (correctional court), there are several ways (see the following discussion) to condense the process.

The trial is conducted by the presiding judge at each court level. The accused is given an opportunity to provide a statement to the court, after which the attorneys can pose questions (usually through the judge) to the defendant. The accused, who is not put under oath, is not required to answer any of the questions, but the court is not prohibited from drawing unfavorable conclusions from that silence. After interrogating the accused, the court calls in the witnesses, places them under oath, and asks them to provide information that they have regarding the offense and the accused. The presiding judge may interrupt the witnesses' narrative to clarify ambiguities and encourage relevance. The attorneys can also question the witnesses, but they do so under restricting guidelines. Following the last witness, the prosecution and the defense attorneys (always in that order) make their closing arguments. With that brief overview in mind, let us look more closely at the different types of French courts.

TRIAL LEVEL: POLICE COURT   The basic tribunal for petty offenses subject to a fine of up to €1,500 (up to €3,000 for a persistent offender) is the police court (*tribunal de police*). Additional penalties such as suspension of a driver's license, immobilizing the offender's vehicle, confiscation of weapons, and restrictions on writing checks may also be imposed. These courts are spread throughout the country and are presided over by justices of the peace (a lay or professional judge), who are required to live in the tribunal's jurisdictional area. Although several judges may be assigned to the court, a single judge makes the decision (French Ministry of Justice, 2012; French Republic, 1995b, Article 131).

When trials occur in police court, they are invariably brief and simple. Even more likely, the court will follow simplified procedures that take place away from the actual courtroom and involve no trial. Instead, the prosecutor sends the case file and supporting documents to the police court judge, who reviews the material and then dismisses the case or imposes a fine—along with supplementary penalties if deemed appropriate. The judge could also decide that the case needs a formal hearing and simply return the file to the prosecutor for prosecution. The court notifies the prosecutor of the judge's order, and the prosecutor has 10 days to file paperwork to set aside the order. If no request to set the order aside is filed, the accused is notified of the order and he or she has 30 days to either pay or object. An objection means formal proceedings in police court will be followed (French Republic, 1995a, Articles 524–528).

TRIAL LEVEL: CORRECTIONAL COURTS   Correctional courts (*tribunal correctionnel*)—also translated as criminal courts—are above the police courts in the hierarchy. These courts (typically composed of three judges, one of whom may be a lay judge) have jurisdiction over less serious criminal offenses (misdemeanors) and can assign penalties of up to 10 years' imprisonment (20 years for repeat offenders) as well as such penalties as a fine, community service, and other less severe penalties (French Ministry of Justice, 2012; French Republic, 1995b).

The accused appearing before this court has the right to counsel (either retained or appointed), but counsel is not required unless the accused suffers from some disorder that could compromise the defense (French Republic, 1995a, Article 417). Because witnesses are allowed, the trial process would be rather time-consuming if not for the fact that both defense and prosecution typically rely on pretrial statements and information from any judicial investigation instead of bothering with witnesses.

The proceedings are further consolidated by having rather permissive rules of evidence. As Article 427 of the Code of Criminal Procedure states, "Except where the law otherwise provides, offenses may be proved by any mode of evidence and the judge decides according to his inner-most conviction." Being able to use "any mode of evidence" to find the accused guilty (or not guilty) means the proceedings are not prolonged by many questions of law. Although it could be delayed upon the presiding judge's announcement, it is expected that the verdict and sentence will be announced immediately after closing arguments.

TRIAL LEVEL: ASSIZE COURT   The assize court (*cour d'assises*) has original jurisdiction in serious felony cases and can assign penalties ranging from fines to life imprisonment. It is comprised of three judges—a president or presiding judge, who is always a member of the *cour d'appel* (the next higher-level court), and two magistrates who may come from the cour d'appel or a local lower court. As indicated by the word *assize*, this court meets only periodically, but in a specific location—one is found in each French department (similar to a U.S. county). Typically, it meets every three months for about two weeks (French Ministry of Justice, 2012; French Republic, 1995a, Articles 243–253).

In Chapter 5 and earlier in this chapter as well, we learned that a trial under the inquisitorial process is more like a continuation of the investigation than a completely separate step. Activities at the assize court provide a good opportunity to explain more about this important difference between adversarial and inquisitorial proceedings. For example, the distinction between an active inquisitorial judge and a more passive adversarial judge is seen in the authority given to the president of the assize court. The Code of Criminal Procedure gives the presiding judge the power to "take any measure he believes useful for the discovery of the truth" (Article 310). The judge may, for example, summon (using an arrest warrant if necessary) any person the judge feels will help in discovering the truth. Similarly, the judge can have brought before the court any new element that, as the hearing develops, the judge deems relevant.

Lay jurors, who are used only at this court level, are also part of the assize court. Potential jurors must be French citizens over age 23 who can read and write in French. They are chosen by lot from a list of potential jurors based on voter rolls. However, the French version seems unusual to those familiar with the English and American juries because the nine French jurors join the three professional judges on whom the jurors depend for explanations of both law and facts. Even though the jurors are chosen by lot

Assises
The Cour d'Assises is the primary criminal court in France with original jurisdiction for serious felony cases. Each French department (similar to a U.S. county) has Cour d'Assises.

Philip L. Reichel

from all those called for that term of court, Article 298 of the criminal procedure code makes them subject to peremptory challenges by the prosecution (four such challenges) and the defense (with five challenges).

During the trial and with the presiding judge's approval, the jurors and two magistrates can question the accused and the witnesses (Article 311). Also, subject to the presiding judge's mandate to maintain an orderly courtroom and proceeding (Article 309), the prosecution and defense may directly question anyone called to testify or may submit questions for the presiding judge to ask (Article 312).

After hearing the last witness and the closing statements, the presiding judge instructs the jurors on their duty to determine the accused's guilt or innocence. Rather than a standard of proof such as "beyond a reasonable doubt," the presiding judge reads specific instructions to the judges and jurors that explain the law and ask them a single question (Article 353): "Are you inwardly convinced?" The law does not ask them how they became convinced but instead requires them to ask themselves what impression the evidence and the defense made on their reason. If those impressions "inwardly convinced" (translated by Frase (2007) as "thoroughly convinced") the juror or judge that the accused is guilty, then he or she is obligated to vote accordingly.

Voting by judges and jurors is by secret ballot, with conviction requiring at least 8 of the 12 members. A vote for conviction is immediately followed by a vote on the penalty. From the possible penalties, the sentence imposed is one reached by an absolute majority of voters, except that maximum custodial sentences require a majority of at least eight votes.

APPELLATE LEVEL: COURTS OF APPEAL Criminal cases from correctional courts or police courts are heard on appeal by courts of appeal (cour d'appel). There is limited appeal for police courts' decisions (e.g., if the penalty was a driver's license suspension), but decisions on guilt, innocence, dismissal, or sentence from correctional courts may be appealed by the accused or by the prosecuting attorney (and a few other officials).

The appeal is heard before three judges, and the appeals court's judgment may not be one that is less favorable than that imposed at the trial level (Frase, 2007).

APPELLATE LEVEL: SUPREME COURT OF APPEAL The court of last resort in the French hierarchy is the Supreme Court of Appeal (*Cour de Cassation*). This highest-level court has five civil chambers; only one chamber hears criminal cases. The court, which lacks original jurisdiction, is headed by a president and must have seven judges (from a total of 15) present to hear a case.

The term "cassation" derives from the French *casser*, which means "to break" or "to smash." The term is appropriate for this tribunal because the court's power is limited to voiding the legal point of a case. When the Cour de Cassation decides that the lower court inappropriately applied a point of law, the case is returned for retrial to a different court at the same rank and of similar category. However, if the new court disagrees with the Cour de Cassation's position (and the new court has the right to do that), the case goes once again before the Cour de Cassation (Council of Europe, 2000). At this second appearance, the full court hears the case. This opinion, now considered an authoritative interpretation on the point of law, must be followed by the lower tribunal.

England and Wales

The Courts Act 2003 brought important changes to the structure and organization of courts in England and Wales—which share a common criminal justice system (United Kingdom Parliament, 2003). Most relevant for our discussion are the reform of the Lord Chancellor's position, the move to create a supreme court for the United Kingdom, a new process for selecting judges, and the unification of magistrates' courts and crown courts under a single administrative unit. These are described in detail as follows under the appropriate subheading as we review the structure and organization of criminal courts in England and Wales.

HER MAJESTY'S COURTS SERVICE Her Majesty's Courts and Tribunals Service (HMCTS) is an agency of the Ministry of Justice charged with providing for a fair, efficient, and effective justice system delivered by an independent judiciary (United Kingdom Ministry of Justice, 2016). The agency is responsible for the administration of the criminal, civil, and family courts and tribunals in England and Wales. The courts for which the HMCTS has administrative responsibilities include the magistrates' courts, the County Court, the Family Court, the Crown Court, and the Royal Courts of Justice. The tribunals, which decide disputes in a particular area of law (e.g., consumer credit, mental health, and immigration), are less important for criminal justice purposes and are not covered here.

Most minor criminal cases, called summary cases, are heard in local magistrates' courts, whereas the most serious offenses (indictable-only offenses) are passed on by the magistrates' courts to the Crown Court. Some cases fall in between, called either-way cases, and they may be heard in either court.

TRIAL LEVEL: MAGISTRATES' COURT At the lowest level of the criminal court hierarchy (see Figure 7.5) are magistrates' courts. Unpaid lay magistrates (also called justices of the peace or JPs) preside over these highly visible tribunals that Edward II (1307–1327) established near the end of his reign. More than 20,000 JPs work in magistrates' courts throughout the country. They are assigned to a Local Justice Area and are appointed by the Secretary of State and the Lord Chancellor from people recommended by a local advisory committee (GOV.UK, 2015; Judiciary of England and Wales, 2016b).

In certain areas, especially larger cities, district judges (known as stipendiary magistrates prior to 2000) are more likely than JPs to be found at the helm of the magistrates' courts. The approximately 140 district judges are part of the professional judiciary.

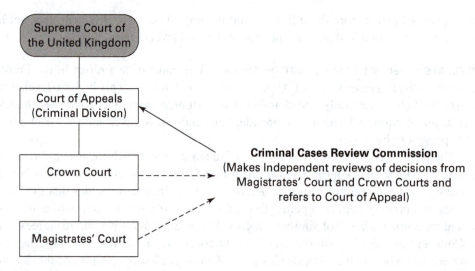

FIGURE 7.5 English Court Organization

Unlike the JPs, they must be legally qualified and they receive a salary. They are required to have at least 7 years' experience as a Barrister or Solicitor and 2 years' experience as a Deputy District Judge, and they deal with more complex or sensitive cases (e.g., cases arising from the Extradition Act or the Fugitive Offenders Act).

The magistrates' courts serve as the workhorse for the English criminal jurisdictions with virtually all criminal cases beginning here and more than 95 percent completed at this level. The trials at this lowest level court are conducted without a jury and before at least two but usually three JPs—including one who is trained to act as chairperson. When a district judge heads the court, he or she hears the case alone.

Defendants before the magistrates' court are typically unrepresented by counsel and find themselves subjected to proceedings that are conducted at a dazzling speed. The rapid action is surprising because the JPs are lay magistrates, both in the sense of being unpaid (although they claim expenses and an allowance for loss of earnings) and in terms of not needing a legal background. It may be expected that such a person would run a rather deliberate and time-consuming courtroom. Luckily, because magistrates' courts have such a heavy workload, that situation does not occur. The court's efficiency may come in part from the presence of lawyers volunteering as magistrates (there is no prohibition against legally trained people becoming JPs) but is more clearly the result of the management by the court's clerk.

The magistrates' clerks often are but are not required to be legally trained. They are assigned to the magistrates' courts, where their duties range from helping unrepresented defendants to advising the magistrates on points of law or procedure, though not on the decision. The clerk provides advice when asked by the magistrates but may also offer advice even if unasked. Although the JPs receive basic legal training, they are typically pleased to accept their clerk's advice on matters of law.

Sentencing options available to the magistrates include the imposition of fines, community service orders, and probation orders or a custody sentence of up to 6 months (or 12 months for multiple offenses). In cases triable either way (in either the magistrates' court or the Crown Court), the offender may be committed by the magistrates to the Crown Court for sentencing if a more severe sentence is thought necessary (GOV. UK, 2015; Judiciary of England and Wales, 2016b).

TRIAL LEVEL: CROWN COURT   Immediately above the magistrates' court level is the Crown Court. This court has both appellate and original jurisdiction and is the first level at which an accused is entitled to a trial by jury. The Crown Court, which is based at 77 centers across England and Wales, is presided over by a High Court judge for Class 1 offenses (e.g., treason or murder) and by a Circuit Judge for Class 2 offenses (e.g., rape and other serious crimes). Class 3 offenses (e.g., robbery, burglary, and grievous bodily harm) are usually tried by a Circuit Judge or Recorder. A Recorder is a part-time or fee-paid judge who has been selected from solicitors or barristers with at least 10 years' experience and has agreed to be available on a part-time basis to hear cases. A Circuit Judge must also have at least 10 years' experience and have served either as a Recorder on criminal cases or as District Judge on civil cases (Judiciary of England and Wales, 2016a).

The Crown Court carries out its duties with great pageantry and fanfare. All contested trials take place before a jury of 12. In such cases, the jury alone decides whether the defendant is guilty or not guilty. Verdicts are to be unanimous; however, the Juries Act of 1974 allows a majority verdict (for both conviction and acquittal) when there are only 10 or 11 jurors (e.g., from the original panel one or two were excused due to illness). In such cases, a verdict of 10-1 or 9-1 is allowed (United Kingdom Parliament, 1974, Section 17).

APPELLATE LEVEL: COURT OF APPEAL AND THE CRIMINAL CASES REVIEW COMMISSION
The Court of Appeal is divided into two divisions, criminal and civil. The Criminal Division hears appeals in criminal matters from the Crown Court. The prosecution cannot appeal a verdict of acquittal. Sitting without a jury, this court hears appeals based on the transcripts of the evidence taken at the trial.

Several high-profile cases involving the miscarriage of justice in the 1980s and 1990s (e.g., the Guildford Four and the Birmingham Six) caught the attention of the British media and public. In a 1993 report to Parliament, a Royal Commission on Criminal Justice recommended that an independent body be established to consider suspected miscarriages of justice and, when appropriate, to arrange for their investigation. When the investigation reveals matters that should be considered further by the courts, the case is referred to the Court of Appeal. As a result of this recommendation, the Criminal Appeal Act of 1995 was passed, and the Criminal Cases Review Commission (CCRC) was established as an independent body responsible for investigating suspected miscarriages of justice in any Crown Court or magistrates' court in England, Wales, and Northern Ireland.

The CCRC started handling casework in 1997, and now receives about 1,500 applications each year. Around 30 cases have been referred to the appeals courts each year. Decisions about whether a case should be referred to the Court of Appeal are made after a review by case review managers determines that pertinent evidence or arguments were not considered at the original trial or appeal. Upon passing case review, the final decision on referring a case is made by a committee of at least three Commission Members. Of those cases referred to the appeals courts, about 60 percent have resulted in convictions being quashed or sentences varied (Criminal Cases Review Commission, 2014).

APPELLATE LEVEL: SUPREME COURT OF THE UNITED KINGDOM   The Constitutional Reform Act 2005 created a new Supreme Court for the United Kingdom. In October 2009, the new Court opened for business and 12 Supreme Court justices officially replaced the House of Lords as the final court of appeal for all UK civil cases, and criminal cases from England,

WEB PROJECT
You Be the Judge

The website for the Judiciary of England and Wales provides an interesting interactive page at http://www.ybtj.justice.gov.uk/. At that page, watch the video on the case and then write down what you think should be the appropriate sentence. Write a paragraph or two that compare your sentence to the one actually imposed. Explain why you think there were differences or similarities in the sentences.

Wales, and Northern Ireland. Despite the similar court name, there are a few important differences between the supreme courts of the United Kingdom and the United States. First, the process for appointing justices to the UK Supreme Court is conducted in private by a selection committee convened by the Lord Chancellor in contrast to the very public American process that includes questioning by U.S. Senators. An even greater difference is that the U.S. Supreme Court can effectively strike down laws passed by the U.S. Congress, but the UK Supreme Court does not have the power to overturn acts of Parliament. Instead, its role is to interpret and clarify the law, not to make it. As a result, the UK Parliament remains supreme (United Kingdom Supreme Court, 2016).

Nigeria

Nigeria (see Map A.1) is located on the West African coast near its namesake river, the Niger. As they did in several other parts of Africa, the British began colonizing important areas of Nigeria in the late 1800s. The important port of Lagos was taken as a British colony in 1861 and then incorporated with the rest of southern Nigeria in 1906 as the Colony and Protectorate of Southern Nigeria. The country won independence in 1960, but in 1966 the fairly new Federal Republic of Nigeria was placed under a federal military government that held all executive and legislative power. In 1989, the military lifted a ban on political activity, and in 1999 a civilian government was reestablished.

Nigeria's Constitution provides for courts at both the federal and state levels and includes traditional courts as well (see Figure 7.6). At the federal level, the highest court is the Supreme Court of Nigeria. According to the Constitution (Section 230), the Supreme Court consists of the chief justice and a number of associate justices (not exceeding 21) as may be prescribed by federal legislation. The justices are appointed by the president upon the recommendation of the National Judicial Council (Federal Republic of Nigeria, 1999).

Beneath the Supreme Court is the Court of Appeal (Section 237), which consists of a president and a number of justices as prescribed by legislation, but not fewer than 49. At least three of the justices must be knowledgeable in Islamic law and another three in customary law. The Islamic and customary knowledge requirement is present because the Court of Appeal hears appeals from the federal high court, the state high courts, Shari'a courts of appeal, customary courts of appeal, and other courts that may be established by law (Section 239).

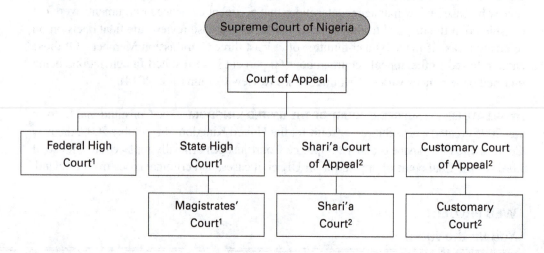

[1]These courts are part of Nigeria's modern court system.

[2]These courts are part of Nigeria's traditional court system.

FIGURE 7.6 Nigeria's Modern and Traditional Courts

The courts from which the Court of Appeal receives appeals are placed in Figure 7.6 on a tier of "high courts" that include the Federal High Court and the State High Courts (Dina & Akintayo, 2013). The Federal High Court handles mostly civil cases related to issues such as taxation and immigration and is not of importance for our purposes. The other courts at that tier reflect part of Nigeria's modern court system (the State High Courts) as well as its traditional court system (the Shari'a Court of Appeal and the Customary Court of Appeal).

Each of Nigeria's 36 states has a State High Court that serves as the state's trial court of general jurisdiction. Each court is headed by a chief judge, appointed by the state governor and supported by such number of judges as is prescribed by state law— also appointed by the governor but upon advice by a judicial commission. This court hears and decides any civil and criminal case involving state law.

The court structure at this level is complicated by the inclusion of customary courts providing for traditional law (mostly in Nigeria's southern region) and by the declaration of several states (all in the north) to implement Islamic law throughout the state. The constitution provides for a Customary Court of Appeal (headed by a president appointed by the state governor) and a Shari'a Court of Appeal (headed by a Grandi Kadi appointed by the state governor) for any state requiring either type of court.

Below the tier of high courts are various inferior courts (e.g., magistrates' courts under the modern court system and Shari'a courts or customary courts under the traditional system) that are established by state laws (Dina & Akintayo, 2013). The magistrates' courts, which are the workhouses of Nigeria's modern court system, handle about 90 percent of all criminal cases. Nigerian customary courts dispose of cases by reference to established customs, beliefs, and values. In the northern states, with a primarily Muslim population, Shari'a courts give these Nigerians a means to decide personal law cases (e.g., marriage, divorce, inheritance, guardianship) on the basis of Islamic law.

Problems with the operation of magistrates' courts provide one reason for the desire by many Nigerians to have more traditional courts resolve disputes. These courts continue to exist because the modern courts are considered ineffective for many issues, irrelevant for others, and lacking credibility on issues where they could be relevant. For example, most felony cases are tried in the magistrates' courts, so it is this court that provides the average Nigerians with most of their knowledge about how modern courts operate.

A hesitancy to use formal courts is actually rather widespread in sub-Saharan Africa according to a Gallup poll (Loschky, 2016). More than half of adults in those countries reported that they would turn to a traditional justice system or to religious leaders rather than use their government's judicial system and courts. Access to the government legal system may require a long trip to the regional capital, whereas a tribal chief or religious leader may be just steps away. Gallup found that older and less educated sub-Saharan Africans are least likely to settle a legal dispute with government courts, but the decision to refer a legal dispute to a religious leader was equally likely among Christians or Muslims. Nigeria was among the countries where religious leaders were likely to be used to settle disputes, and that point returns us to Nigeria's customary courts.

The attraction of Shari'a law has received considerable attention as increasing numbers of Nigerian states use Islamic law for criminal cases. Prior to 2000, Shari'a law was used primarily for land disputes and family squabbles, but 12 predominantly Muslim states in northern Nigeria are now using Shari'a penalties such as flogging (for drinking alcohol), amputation (for theft), and stoning (for adultery). The attraction of Shari'a to Nigerian Muslims is certainly linked to religious principles but seems also to be a reaction to the negative opinions held about the secular courts. In addition to the poorly financed and cumbersome procedures present in the magistrates' courts, the underpaid police officers and judges often accept bribes to pervert the course of justice

("The attractions of sharia," 2002). Shari'a courts, in contrast, settle disputes without strict adherence to written procedural rules and judge cases according to local custom and Islamic beliefs. Legal fees are saved because most people choose to represent themselves, and the resultant justice—although certainly harsh—is quick.

China

As noted in Chapter 4, China (see Map A.7) provides a good example of an Eastern Asia legal tradition with influences from Confucianism, an appreciation for collectivism and context, and a preference for informal justice when possible. It is that last characteristic of legal informalism that we consider more closely in this section.

Victor Li titled his book comparing law in China and the United States *Law Without Lawyers* (Li, 1978). The title nicely characterizes the informal justice structure that some consider the lowest tier of China's criminal justice system (Rojek, 1985). A main benefit of the informal system is the absence of lawyers, law being an occupation that the Chinese have never awarded much prestige. Although lawyers are becoming more prominent in today's China, it remains to be seen whether they will become more acceptable to the public. There is, after all, a well-entrenched dislike for attorneys dating at least to Imperial China, when one could receive a 3-year sentence for helping litigants prepare documents (McCabe, 1989). An 1820 Imperial edict referred to lawyers as "litigation tricksters" and "rascally fellows (who will) entrap people for the sake of profit" (Li, 1983, p. 103).

In the absence of reliance on legally trained professionals to handle disputes, Chinese citizens turned to each other (Clark, 1989; Li, 1978; Situ & Liu, 2000). The foundation for the resulting informal justice structure is the people's mediation committee (PMC), composed of 10–20 people elected by the people to a 3-year term. These committees are authorized by Article 111 of China's constitution, which stipulates that "the residents' and villagers' committees establish committees for people's mediation, public security, public health and other matters in order to manage public affairs and social services in their areas . . . ." (People's Republic of China, 1982). The "residents' committees" are neighborhood committees in urban areas whereas the "villagers' committees" are in the rural areas. The resulting peer pressure from these constant companions provides the glue holding together an informal sanctioning process.

In the tradition of socialist legality, China believes that education must play a primary role in the justice system. The PMCs have historical ties to Confucianism and are based on the belief that moral education through mediation is the best way for communities to resolve conflict. The education role is made clear in Article 5 of the regulations for the PMCs, which explains their mission as being to "mediate civil disputes and, through such mediation, publicize laws, regulations, rules and policies and educate citizens to abide by laws and respect universally accepted morals" (China Internet Information Center, n.d.).

The PMCs serve as a conduit for the norms and values that upper levels of government believe are appropriate. Government officials use the mass media to spread such information as legal norms, and then the PMCs furnish a setting to discuss and enforce those norms. Importantly, the norms provided by the central government are simply general policies indicating priorities and directions. Actual application of those general principles is, government officials believe, more appropriately done at the local level. One obvious result is that different local groups will interpret the general principles differently. Such variation is not considered bad. Central authorities issue a single general policy, and then local units adapt that policy to suit local needs and conditions (Li, 1978). Consistency with socialist principles in this hybrid tradition is ensured by having the PMCs operate under the guidance of local governments and the local people's courts.

Members of the PMCs serve as volunteers and must be adults who are impartial, close to the people, enthusiastic about mediation, and knowledgeable about legal and policy issues (China Internet Information Center, n.d.).

Through a process of discussion and persuasion, the small groups respond to everything from misbehavior and outright deviance to questions of health care and family planning. Justice is provided in this informal way without the use of lawyers or courtrooms. However, because the utopian ideal of pure Communism has not been achieved in China or anywhere else, there is also the need for a more formal justice system.

In 2013, the Supreme People's Court announced plans to reform China's court system and in 2016 it issued a report on Judicial Reform of Chinese Courts (People's Republic of China, 2016). The report details extensive reforms that could have significant impact on such areas as judicial transparency and protection of human rights. Some of the planned reforms include no longer requiring defendants in criminal court to wear prison uniforms, strengthening the rights of criminal lawyers to review case files and to apply for exclusion of illegally obtained evidence, and reforming the organization and administration of the court system (Lubman, 2016).

The outline for reforming China's courts is not especially clear, but is generally viewed as intended to change some of the old patterns of authoritarian control and to give greater autonomy to a more professional judiciary (Finder, 2015; Lubman, 2016). Key to this court reform is the plan to reduce control by local party and government officials and shifting control to the province level. Such a change will, reformers believe, reduce protectionism at the local level where local officials often interfere in court cases.

Although critics, including some in China, believe many major issues remain unaddressed (see Lubman, 2016 for examples of reforms the Deputy Director of the All China Lawyers Association thinks are still needed), most observers find the planned reforms to be both welcome and needed. As Finder (2015) explains, some of the changes are easily accomplished but the most difficult challenges lie ahead as the broad principles provided in the plan are converted to workable systems and institutions. And, equally important, over many decades there have been shifts in behavior and institutional culture. Absent clear descriptions of how the court system's organization and administration will be reformed, this chapter continues with a description of the system as it exists until the reforms are fully implemented.

China's formal justice system uses four layers of courts, organized along territorial lines (see Figure 7.7). The Supreme People's Court serves as the highest tribunal in the country. Below it in the hierarchy are the higher people's courts, intermediate people's courts, and the basic people's courts. Court officials at each level are elected and recalled by the people's congress relevant to each court level. The courts are essentially agencies of the central government and do not have judicial independence in a manner similar to courts in Western countries (McCabe, 1989). Central government supervision is not direct but is routed through judicial committees appointed by the various people's congresses. The judicial committees review court activities, discuss major difficult cases, and concern themselves with other court-related issues.

WEB PROJECT
Trials in China

China's trial system is described in detail at http://www.china.org.cn/english/Judiciary/31280.htm. Visit this website and scroll down to the section titled "The Fundamentals of China's Judicial System" where you will find information about open trials and, just below that section, the defense system. Write a paragraph explaining the types of cases that are not open to the public and another paragraph that explains who is eligible to defend the accused.

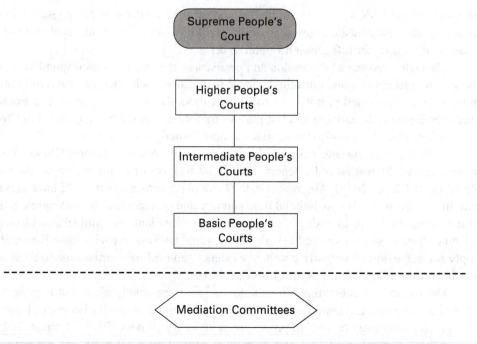

FIGURE 7.7   China's Court Organization

The Supreme People's Court, which is made up of several subcourts or branches, handles cases affecting the entire country. According to the constitution, the Supreme People's Court supervises the administration of justice by the local people's courts at different levels and by the special people's courts (People's Republic of China, 1982, Section 7).

It interprets statutes and provides explanations and advisory opinion to the lower courts. Because the interpretations, explanations, and advice provided by the court must be consistent with socialist principles, the Supreme People's Court is responsible to and supervised by the National People's Congress—that is, the Communist Party. The Supreme People's Court must also approve all death sentences imposed by intermediate or higher people's courts.

The higher people's courts are found at the province and autonomous region levels and in autonomous cities (Beijing, Tianjin, and Shanghai). These courts try criminal, civil, and administrative cases of a serious or complicated nature (often transferred by a lower court) and, under specified conditions, cases that have been submitted by prosecutors. The higher courts also supervise trials by lower courts and provide the first stop for approval of death penalty cases (China Internet Information Center, n.d.).

The intermediate people's courts handle cases similar to those at the higher people's court level, but they perform their duties at the municipal or prefecture level. These courts hear appeals from lower-level courts—which they also supervise—and provide a first hearing for cases such as those involving national security, criminal cases involving life imprisonment or the death penalty, and criminal cases committed by foreigners. They also hear major crime cases such as murder, rape, robbery, bombing, arson, and grand larceny (China Internet Information Center, n.d.; Davidson & Wang, 2000).

The workhorses in China's formal court system are the basic people's courts (sometimes called the grassroots courts). Operating at the rural county level and the urban district level, these courts have original trial jurisdiction over ordinary criminal and civil cases. District courts in larger cities such as Beijing and Tianjin have also established neighborhood-based courts to help relieve the district court's caseload (Davidson & Wang, 2000). Discussion of the basic people's court activities gives us a chance to look more closely at some of the players and procedures in Chinese courts.

As a hybrid system, China follows the inquisitorial process often found in countries of the civil legal tradition. As such, a Chinese trial is essentially a continuation of the investigation that was started by the procurator before the trial. Following the Soviet model of the 1950s, China developed a national procuracy responsible for investigating and prosecuting cases at each government level. When the court has decided to open the court session and adjudicate the case, it must first determine the adjudicators. In each type of court, the adjudicators are a collegial panel of judges and laypersons (called people's assessors). Article 178 of the People's Republic of China's Criminal Procedure Law (1979) specifies that in the basic people's court and the intermediate people's court, the panel will consist of three judges or a combination of a total of three judges and people's assessors. If a case in either the basic or intermediate court is considered suitable for "simplified procedures" (e.g., cases in which defendant can be sentenced to less than 3 years' imprisonment and where the facts of the crime are clear and the evidence sufficient), it may be adjudicated by a single judge.

For cases of first instance in the higher people's court or the Supreme People's Court, the panel has three to seven judges (but always an odd number) or a combined total of three to seven judges and people's assessors. Other key participants in the trial are the defendant, procurator, defenders (a lawyer, relative, or lay advocate), victims, witnesses, and interpreters (all defendants have the right to use their own spoken and written language in court proceedings).

The trial proceeds through defined steps, which can be summarized as including the following:

- Court is called to order, and the judge introduces all the participants.
- The charges are read and the defendant advised of his or her rights.
- The judge and people's assessors question the defendant.
- The procurator makes a statement, questions the defendant, and verifies evidence.
- The defender makes a statement and questions the defendant.
- The procurator and defender present their arguments.
- The defendant, if he or she so chooses, makes a statement.
- After a brief recess allowing the panel to deliberate, court is reconvened.
- Defendants found innocent are dismissed. Those found guilty are told the crime for which they have been found guilty and the criminal punishment (if any) that will be applied (Davidson & Wang, 2000).

Saudi Arabia

In 2007, new laws regulating Saudi Arabia's judiciary came into force. The new system divides the courts of general jurisdiction into three categories—from high to low: the High Court, the Courts of Appeal, and First-Degree Courts (see Figure 7.8).

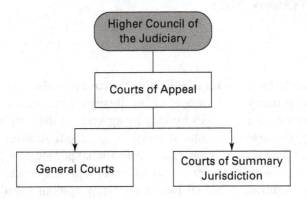

FIGURE 7.8 Saudi Arabia's Courts

WEB PROJECT

A Saudi Court for Terrorism

The new Saudi court system includes the possibility of establishing specialized courts subject to the King's approval. In 2009, a specialized criminal court was established to try suspects in cases involving terrorism and national security. Go to http://www.nyulawglobal.org/ globalex/Saudi_Arabia1.html and scroll down to the section 3.3.3.1 Specialized Criminal Court. Read the material in that section and write a few paragraphs that describe how this new Saudi court operates.

Prior to the 2007 reform, the Supreme Judicial Council served as the highest court. Under the new laws, it continues to oversee administrative aspects of the judiciary (e.g., establish, merge, or abolish courts, and issue rules regarding how judges are selected) but its position as the Kingdom's highest court has been replaced with the High Court.

First-Degree Courts are of several types (e.g., labor courts, commercial courts, personal status courts), including the criminal courts. These courts operate as three-judge benches and deal with all criminal cases at provincial and regional levels. The plan is to have 18 criminal courts and 25 criminal circuits in general courts distributed around the Kingdom (Ansary, 2015). Recall from Chapter 5 that Islamic substantive law is built around the type of punishment to be applied for various offenses. To that end, the criminal courts have specialized panels dealing with qisas and hudud penalties, other panels for discretionary punishments (ta'zir), and panels for juveniles (Ansary, 2015).

The Courts of Appeal are also of specialized types, including the criminal division. There is at least one appeals court in each province and this court is charged with looking at judgments issued by the first-degree criminal courts. All judgments issued by the first-degree court are appealable (except petty cases) and even some of the appeals court's own judgment can be appealed under particular circumstances (e.g., the judgment was based on evidence later found to be fraudulent).

The High Court (sometimes translated as Supreme Court) is the Kingdom's highest authority in the new judicial system. It consists of a President (appointed by the King) and a "sufficient" number of Appellate Justices—also appointed by the King but on recommendation of the Supreme Judicial Council (Ansary, 2015). The High Court's criminal division sits as a five-judge panel and reviews judgments in certain cases involving Shari'a penalties as well as rulings issued or upheld by the Courts of Appeal.

The Saudi judiciary is in a transitional period as new courts are being built, judges undergo training, and the judicial sector undergoes a revamping process that is not yet fully implemented. A goal of these reforms is to provide Saudi society with opportunities to respond to social and economic changes in a way that safeguards the independence and impartiality of the Saudi judicial system while ensuring the highest possible fair trial standards (Ansary, 2015).

Summary

This chapter looked at the judiciary from an institutions/actors perspective. Beginning with how the primary actors in a judicial system arrive at their positions, we considered various processes of legal training. Because every system has some type of prosecutor and defense attorney, we then looked at the different ways those positions are implemented. In addition to prosecution and defense, each legal system has actors responsible for adjudicating the case brought to court. An adjudication continuum illustrated the variation in adjudicator types by identifying systems that rely heavily on a professional judge (e.g., Saudi Arabia) and others that emphasize a role for laypeople (e.g., England). Still other countries prefer a mixed bench, wherein professional judges and laypeople sit together to judge the facts of a case (e.g., Germany).

Because these actors must have a setting for their performance, we next looked at different ways courts can be structured. Because the diversity here does not lend itself to easy classification into types, we simply looked at examples from several countries to show the variation. The formal structure was typically emphasized, although the informal justice system in some countries (e.g., China and Nigeria) was pertinent to a more complete understanding of that country's judiciary.

Discussion Questions

- This chapter describes legal training for lawyers and judges as being either unified or specialized. For example, in the United States, law school graduates may practice any type of law without additional training, whereas law graduates in many European countries must choose a specific area of law—including the judiciary—in which they will specialize and receive additional training. Would the American criminal justice system benefit from the more specialized training approach to becoming a prosecutor, defense attorney, or judge?
- While discussing the concept of presumption of innocence, note was made of a comparative scholar reportedly saying that if he were innocent, he would prefer to be tried in a civil law court, but if he were guilty, he would rather be tried by a common law court. On what basis could someone make such a statement? Do you agree or disagree that the civil legal tradition protects the innocent more whereas the common legal tradition provides more protection to the guilty?
- After reading the "You Should Know!" feature titled "Should Jurors Be Allowed to Ask Questions?" respond to the questions posed at the end of that box.

References

Ansary, A. F. (2015). UPDATE: A brief overview of the Saudi Arabian legal system. Retrieved from http://www.nyulawglobal.org/globalex/Saudi_Arabia1.html

Aronowitz, A. A. (1993). Germany. The world factbook of criminal justice systems. Retrieved from http://www.bjs.gov/content/pub/html/wfcj.cfm

The attractions of sharia. (2002, September 5). *The Economist*, 44.

BBC News. (2008, January 14). How is a jury selected? The Magazine answers. . . . Retrieved from http://news.bbc.co.uk/2/hi/uk_news/magazine/7180764.stm

Boring, N. (2014, September 2). France: Major reform of penal code. *Global Legal Monitor*. Retrieved from http://www.loc.gov/law/foreign-news/

Cappelletti, M., & Gordley, J. (1978). Legal aid: Modern themes and variations. In J. H. Merryman & D. S. Clark (Eds.), *Comparative law: Western European and Latin American legal systems*. Indianapolis, IN: Bobbs-Merrill.

Carrió, A. D., & Garro, A. (2007). Argentina. In C. M. Bradley (Ed.), *Criminal procedure: A worldwide study* (2nd ed., pp. 3–55). Durham, NC: Carolina Academic Press.

China Internet Information Center. (n.d.). China's judiciary. Retrieved from http://www.china.org.cn/english/Judiciary/25025.htm

Clark, J. P. (1989). Conflict management outside the courtrooms of China. In R. J. Troyer, J. P. Clark, & D. G. Rojek (Eds.), *Social control in the People's Republic of China*. New York, NY: Praeger.

Congressional-Executive Commission on China. (2016). Judicial independence in the PRC. Retrieved from http://www.cecc.gov/judicial-independence-in-the-prc

Council of Europe. (2000). France. *Judicial organisation in Europe* (pp. 119–132). Strasbourg, France: Council of Europe Publishing.

Criminal Cases Review Commission. (2014). CCRC Annual Report and Accounts 2013/14. Retrieved from http://www.ccrc.gov.uk/publications/corporate-publications/

Danish National Police. (2015). The prosecution service. About the police. Retrieved from https://www.politi.dk/en/About_the_police/prosecution_service

Davidson, R., & Wang, Z. (2000). The court system in the People's Republic of China with a case study of a criminal trial. In O. N. I. Ebbe (Ed.), *Comparative and international criminal justice systems: Policing, judiciary and corrections* (2nd ed., pp. 205–218). Boston, MA: Butterworth–Heinemann.

Dina, Y., & Akintayo, J. (2013, March). Update: Guide to Nigerian legal information. *GlobaLex*. Retrieved from http://www.nyulawglobal.org/globalex/Nigeria1.html

Donadio, R. (2009, December 5). Verdict in Italy, but American's case isn't over. *The New York Times*. Retrieved from http://www.nytimes.com

Ehrmann, H. W. (1976). *Comparative legal cultures*. Englewood Cliffs, NJ: Prentice Hall.

European Parliament. (2012). Charter of fundamental rights of the European Union. Retrieved from http://eur-lex.europa.eu/legal-content/EN/TXT/?uri=CELEX:12012P/TXT

Fairfax, R. A., Jr. (2009). Delegation of the criminal prosecution function to private actors. *UC Davis Law Review*, *43*, 411–456.

Federal Republic of Germany. (1987). The German code of criminal procedure (amended version of 2014). Gesetze im Internet. Retrieved from http://www.gesetze-im-internet.de/englisch_stpo/index.html

Federal Republic of Nigeria. (1999). Constitution of the Federal Republic of Nigeria, 1999. Retrieved from http://www.nigeria-law.org/ConstitutionOfTheFederalRepublicOfNigeria.htm

Feofanov, I. (1990/1991). A return to origins: Reflections on power and law. *Soviet Law and Government, 29*(3), 15–52.

Finder, S. (2015, March 26). China's master plan for remaking its courts. *The Diplomat*. Retrieved from http://thediplomat.com/2015/03/chinas-master-plan-for-remaking-its-courts/

Followill, P. (2016). Filing a criminal complaint. Criminal Defense Lawyer. Retrieved from http://www.criminaldefenselawyer.com/resources/criminal-defense/criminal-offense/filing-a-criminal-complaint.htm

Foster, N. G. (2003). *Austrian legal system & laws*. Portland, OR: Cavendish Publishing.

Frase, R. S. (2007). France. In C. M. Bradley (Ed.), *Criminal procedure: A worldwide study* (2nd ed., pp. 201–242). Durham, NC: Carolina Academic Press.

French Ministry of Justice. (2012). The French legal system. Retrieved from http://www.justice.gouv.fr/art_pix/french_legal_system.pdf

French Republic. (1995a). Code of criminal procedure (amended version of 2005). Legifrance translations. Retrieved from https://www.legifrance.gouv.fr/Traductions/en-English/Legifrance-translations

French Republic. (1995b). Penal code (amended version of 2005). Legifrance translations. Retrieved from https://www.legifrance.gouv.fr/Traductions/en-English/Legifrance-translations

Glenn, H. P. (2014). *Legal traditions of the world: Sustainable diversity in law* (5th ed.). Oxford, UK: Oxford University Press.

GOV.UK. (2015, October 9). Magistrates' courts. Criminal courts. Retrieved from https://www.gov.uk/courts/magistrates-courts

Graham, M. M. (1983). *Tightening the reins of justice in America*. Westport, CT: Greenwood Press.

Hans, V. P. (2008). Jury systems around the world (Paper 305). Cornell Law Faculty Publications. Retrieved from Cornell University Law Library website: http://scholarship.law.cornell.edu/facpub/305

Harnon, E., & Stein, A. (2007). Israel. In C. M. Bradley (Ed.), *Criminal procedure: A worldwide study* (2nd ed., pp. 273–302). Durham, NC: Carolina Academic Press.

Hitchner, D. G., & Levine, C. (1981). *Comparative government and politics* (2nd ed.). New York, NY: Harper & Row.

Hodgson, J. (2005). *French criminal justice: A comparative account of the investigation and prosecution of crime in France*. Portland, OR: Hart.

Horton, C. (1995). *Policing policy in France*. London, UK: Policy Studies Institute.

Huang, K.-C., & Lin, C.-C. (2013). Rescuing confidence in the judicial system: Introducing lay participation in Taiwan. *Journal of Empirical Legal Studies*, *10*(3), 542–569. doi:10.1111/jels.12019

Huang, K.-C., & Lin, C.-C. (2014). Mock jury trials in Taiwan—Paving the ground for introducing lay participation. *Law and Human Behavior*, *38*(4), 367–377. doi:10.1037/lhb0000080

In Brief. (2016). The selection process. How is a jury selected? Retrieved from http://www.inbrief.co.uk/legal-system/jury-selection-process/

Italian Republic. (2014). The Italian code of criminal procedure (amended version of 2013). In M. Gialuz, L. Lupária, & F. Scarpa (Eds.), *The Italian code of criminal procedure: Critical essays and English translation* (pp. 81–499). Italy: Wolters Kluwer Italia.

Jackson, J. D., & Kovalev, N. P. (2016). Lay adjudication in Europe: The rise and fall of the traditional jury. *Oñati Socio-Legal Series*, *6*(2). Retrieved from http://ssrn.com/abstract=2782413

Jehle, J.-M. (2015). Criminal justice in Germany: Facts and figures. Retrieved from http://www.bmjv.de/SharedDocs/Downloads/DE/Statistiken/Download/Criminal_Justice_Germany_Facts_Figures.html

Jimeno-Bulnes, M. (2004). Lay participation in Spain: The jury system. *International Criminal Justice Review*, *14*, 164–185.

Judiciary of England and Wales. (2016a). Crown court. You and the judiciary: Going to court. Retrieved from https://www.judiciary.gov.uk/you-and-the-judiciary/going-to-court/crown-court/

Judiciary of England and Wales. (2016b). Magistrates' court. You and the judiciary: Going to court. Retrieved from https://www.judiciary.gov.uk/you-and-the-judiciary/going-to-court/magistrates-court/

Justice Studies Center of the Americas. (2007). *Report on judicial systems in the Americas, 2006–2007* (3rd ed.). Santiago, Chili: Author.

Kim, S., Park, J., Park, K., & Eom, J.-S. (2013). Judge–jury agreement in criminal cases: The first three years of the Korean jury system. *Journal of Empirical Legal Studies*, *10*(1), 35–53. doi:10.1111/jels.12001

Kingdom of Saudi Arabia. (2001). The code of law practice. About Saudi Arabia. Retrieved from http://www.saudiembassy.net/about/country-information/laws/CodePractice01.aspx

Kingdom of Saudi Arabia. (2009, May 12). Protection of human rights in criminal procedure and in the organization of the judicial system. Ministry of Foreign Affairs. Retrieved from Web archive website: http://web.archive.org/web/20090512153134/http://www.saudiembassy.net/Issues/HRights/hr-judicial-1-menu.html

Kington, T. (2009, December 22). Court cuts Rudy Guede's sentence for Meredith Kercher murder. *The Guardian*.

Retrieved from https://www.theguardian.com/world/2009/dec/22/rudy-guede-sentence-kercher-murder

Krings, M. (2015, February 4). Professor: Amanda Knox trial shows problems with comparing legal systems. *KU Today*. Retrieved from https://today.ku.edu/2015/01/28/law-professors-article-argues-amanda-knox-trial-showed-lack-understanding-problems

Krol, C. (2015, March 28). Amanda Knox acquitted: 'I'm incredibly grateful'. *The Telegraph*. Retrieved from http://www.telegraph.co.uk/

Lee, J.-H. (2009). Getting citizens involved: Civil participation in judicial decision-making in Korea. *East Asia Law Review*, 4(Fall), 177–207.

Lee, J.-H. (2010). Korean jury trial: Has the new system brought about changes? *Asian–Pacific Law and Policy Journal*, 12(1), 58–71.

Li, V. H. (1978). *Law without lawyers: A comparative view of law in China and the United States*. Boulder, CO: Westview Press.

Li, V. H. (1983). Introductory note on China and the role of law in China. In J. H. Barton, J. L. Gibbs, Jr., & J. H. Merryman (Eds.), *Law in radically different cultures* (pp. 102–136). St. Paul, MN: West.

Lloyd-Bostock, S., & Thomas, C. (2000). The continuing decline of the English jury. In N. Vidmar (Ed.), *World jury systems* (pp. 53–91). Oxford, UK: Oxford University Press.

Loschky, J. (2016, March 25). Majority in sub-Saharan Africa wouldn't use formal courts. Gallup. Retrieved from http://www.gallup.com/poll/190310/majority-sub-saharan-africa-wouldn-formal-courts.aspx

Lubman, S. (2016, March 11). China's highest court eyes judicial reform, while a lawyer criticizes TV confessions. *The Wall Street Journal*. Retrieved from http://blogs.wsj.com/chinarealtime/2016/03/11/chinas-highest-court-eyes-judicial-reform-while-a-lawyer-criticizes-tv-confessions/

Machura, S. (2001). Interaction between lay assessors and professional judges in German mixed courts. *Revue internationale de droit pénal*, 72(1), 451–479.

Makdisi, J. A. (1999). The Islamic origins of the common law. *North Carolina Law Review*, 77(5), 1635–1739.

McCabe, E. J. (1989). Structural elements of contemporary criminal justice in the People's Republic of China. In R. J. Troyer, J. P. Clark, & D. G. Rojek (Eds.), *Social control in the People's Republic of China* (pp. 115–129). New York, NY: Praeger.

McDonald, W. F. (1983). In defense of inequality: The legal profession and criminal defense. In W. F. McDonald (Ed.), *The defense counsel* (pp. 13–38). Beverly Hills, CA: Sage.

Merryman, J. H. (1985). *The civil law tradition* (2nd ed.). Stanford, CA: Stanford University Press.

Mize, G., Hannaford-Agor, P., & Waters, N. (2007). The state-of-the-states survey of jury improvement efforts: A compendium report. Retrieved from http://www.ncsc-jurystudies.org/state-of-the-states-survey.aspx

Moore, L. (1973). *The jury: Tool of kings, palladium of liberty*. Cincinnati, OH: W. H. Anderson.

National Commissioner of the Icelandic Police. (2005). The Icelandic police and the justice system: A short introduction. Retrieved from http://www.logreglan.is/displayer.asp?cat_id=215

Packer, H. L. (1968). *The limits of the criminal sanction*. Stanford, CA: Stanford University Press.

People's Republic of China. (1979). Criminal procedure law of the People's Republic of China (amended version of 2012). China Law Translate. Retrieved from http://chinalawtranslate.com/criminal-procedure-law/?lang=en

People's Republic of China. (1982). Constitution of the People's Republic of China (amended version of 2004). Congressional-Executive Commission on China Retrieved from http://www.cecc.gov/resources/legal-provisions/constitution-of-the-peoples-republic-of-china

People's Republic of China. (2016). Judicial reform of Chinese courts. The Supreme People's Court. Retrieved from http://english.court.gov.cn/2016-03/03/content_23724636.htm

Poggioli, S. (2009, December 13). Amanda Knox trial a tangle of cultural tensions. *Weekend Edition Sunday*. Retrieved from http://www.npr.org/templates/story/story.php?storyId=121388806

Povoledo, E. (2011a, October 3). Amanda Knox freed after appeal in Italian court. *The New York Times*. Retrieved from http://www.nytimes.com

Povoledo, E. (2011b, June 27). Amanda Knox's murder conviction appeal begins in Italy. *The New York Times*. Retrieved from http://www.nytimes.com

Republic of Finland. (1997). Criminal procedure act (amended version of 2015). Finlex translations of Finnish acts and decrees. Retrieved from http://www.finlex.fi/en/laki/kaannokset/1997/en19970689

Rojek, D. G. (1985). The criminal process in the People's Republic of China. *Justice Quarterly*, 2, 117–125.

Sanad, N. (1991). *The theory of crime and criminal responsibility in Islamic law: Shari'a*. Chicago, IL: Office of International Criminal Justice.

Scott, M. (n.d.). Summing up—A precis or chance to show bias? BarristerBlogger. Retrieved from http://barristerblogger.com/published-articles-3/summing-up-a-precis-or-chance-to-show-bias/

Seiderman, I. D. (Ed.). (2002). *Attacks on justice: A global report on the independence of judges and lawyers* (11th ed.). Geneva, Switzerland: Centre for the Independence of Judges and Lawyers of the International Commission of Jurists.

Situ, Y., & Liu, W. (2000). The criminal justice system of China. In O. N. I. Ebbe (Ed.), *Comparative and international criminal justice systems: Policing, judiciary and corrections* (2nd ed., pp. 129–142). Boston, MA: Butterworth–Heinemann.

Souryal, S. S. (2004). *Islam, Islamic law, and the turn to violence*. Huntsville, TX: Office of International Criminal Justice.

Spencer, J. R. (2016). Adversarial vs inquisitorial systems: Is there still such a difference? *The International Journal of Human Rights, 20*(5), 601–616. doi:10.1080/13642987.2016.1162408

Steinberg, A. (1984). From private prosecutor to plea bargaining: Criminal prosecution, the district attorney, and American legal history. *Crime and Delinquency, 30,* 568–592.

Stuckey, G. (1986). *Procedures in the justice system* (3rd ed.). Columbus, OH: Charles E. Merrill Publishing.

Terrill, R. J. (2016). *World criminal justice systems: A comparative survey* (9th ed.). New York, NY: Routledge.

Thaman, S. C. (2000). Europe's new jury systems: The cases of Spain and Russia. In N. Vidmar (Ed.), *World jury systems* (pp. 319–351). Oxford, UK: Oxford University Press.

Thaman, S. C. (2007). The nullification of the Russian jury: Lessons for jury-inspired reform in Eurasia and beyond. *Cornell International Law Journal, 40*(2), 355–781.

Turow, S. (1987). *Presumed innocent.* New York, NY: Farrar, Straus and Giroux.

United Kingdom Ministry of Justice. (2016). About us. Her Majesty's Courts and Tribunals Service. Retrieved from https://www.gov.uk/government/organisations/hm-courts-and-tribunals-service/about

United Kingdom Parliament. (1974). Juries act 1974 (amended version of 2015). Retrieved from http://www.legislation.gov.uk/ukpga/1974/23/section/17

United Kingdom Parliament. (2003). Courts act 2003. Retrieved from http://www.legislation.gov.uk/ukpga/2003/39/contents

United Kingdom Supreme Court. (2016). About the Supreme Court. Retrieved from https://www.supremecourt.uk/about/index.html

United Nations. (1988). *Basic principles on the independence of the judiciary.* New York, NY: U.N. Department of Public Information.

Van Cleave, R. A. (2007). Italy. In C. M. Bradley (Ed.), *Criminal procedure: A worldwide study* (2nd ed., pp. 303–349). Durham, NC: Carolina Academic Press.

Vidmar, N. (2000). The jury elsewhere in the world. In N. Vidmar (Ed.), *World jury systems* (pp. 421–447). Oxford, UK: Oxford University Press.

Vogt, A. (2009, November 29). Computer and crucifix: Amanda Knox's guilt will be judged in a system that is a mix of old and new. Seattlepi. Retrieved from http://www.seattlepi.com/local/412696_knox30.html

Weigend, T. (1983). Sentencing in West Germany. *Maryland Law Review, 42,* 37–89.

Wolfe, N. T. (1996). An alternative form of lay participation in criminal adjudication: Lay judge courts in the Federal Republic of Germany. In C. B. Fields & R. H. J. Moore (Eds.), *Comparative criminal justice.* Prospect Heights, IL: Waveland.

Zander, M. (1989). *A matter of justice.* Oxford, UK: Oxford University Press.

8

An International Perspective on Corrections

LEARNING OBJECTIVES

After studying this chapter, you will be able to:

1. Explain two classification schemes that can be used to show the variation among countries in how convicted offenders are sanctioned.

2. Name and describe the four classic justifications and goals for punishment.

3. Explain and provide several examples of financial penalties as they are implemented around the world.

4. Describe how corporal punishment is applied in some of the world's countries and place its use in the context of international standards.

5. Describe how capital punishment is applied in some of the world's countries and place its use in the context of international standards.

6. Summarize how probation is an example of a noncustodial sanction and list three responsibilities of probation agencies.

7. Compare the prison systems of Brazil, Australia, and India.

8. Summarize the issues facing women, foreign national, and minority prisoners throughout the world.

COUNTRIES IN FOCUS

Australia
Brazil
China
France
Germany

India
Saudi Arabia
Sweden
United States

People have different ideas about the sentence that should be given to offenders. Take, for example, the case of a 21-year-old man who is found guilty of burglary for the second time. This time he has taken a television set. Which of the following sentences do you consider the most appropriate for such a case?

- Fine
- Prison
- Community service
- Suspended sentence
- Any other sentence

That question (somewhat modified here) was asked in the International Crime Victim Survey of people in more than 30 countries around the world (van Dijk, van Kesteren, & Smit, 2007). The most frequently chosen sentences were community service and prison. Figure 8.1 shows that respondents from the United States were among those where a prison sentence was more likely to be selected, although not with as much vigor as in Mexico or Japan. A community service order was considered the most appropriate sentence in such countries as Luxembourg, Portugal, France, and Switzerland. As we see later in this chapter, the American public's preference for imprisonment is consistent with the country's actual practices because incarceration rates in the United States are the highest in the world. Why are Americans choosing imprisonment as the appropriate sanction for a repeat burglar when people in many other countries are choosing noncustodial sentences? Intriguing as that question is,

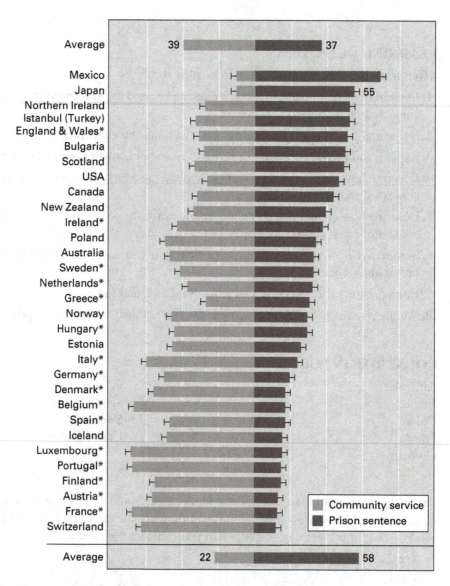

FIGURE 8.1   Preferred Sentence for a Young Recidivist Burglar

Source: van Dijk, J., van Kesteren, J., & Smit, P. (2007). Criminal victimisation in international perspective: Key findings from the 2004–2005 ICVS and EU ICS (criminal victimisation). The Hague, The Netherlands: Boom Juridische uitgevers. Retrieved from http://english.wodc.nl/onderzoeksdatabase/icvs-2005-survey.aspx?cp=45&cs=6796. Used with permission.

we cannot answer it directly in this chapter. However, possible explanations may result from our review of popular reasons for punishment and the variety of sentences that are available around the world.

COMPARATIVE PENOLOGY

In Chapter 2, a distinction was made between comparative criminology and comparative criminal justice. Another area of comparative studies, comparative penology, is linked to each of those. Persons interested in comparative penology compare and contrast the practical differences among countries on topics such as the varying use of imprisonment but also on the more elusive concept of variation in the harshness, or punitiveness, of penal sanctions.

Cavadino and Dignan (2006, pp. 4–5), although appreciating the problems of doing so, suggest those topics can be combined by using imprisonment rate statistics as at least a rough estimate of a country's punitiveness. Later in this chapter, we use imprisonment rate statistics for comparison purposes, but we begin this chapter with a broader look at options available for comparing countries in terms of their penal sanctions.

Typologies for Comparative Penology

As explained in Chapter 1, this book relies on classification as an effective way to summarize and make sense of the diversity found in criminal justice systems around the world. From types of legal systems to categories of police structures and through ways in which criminal defendants are adjudicated, we have used classification schemes to help visualize and conceptualize the material. What, then, might be an appropriate way to approach the variation in how convicted offenders are sanctioned? Actually, several interesting approaches have been used.

In their book comparing penal systems around the world, Cavadino and Dignan (2006) propose a typology wherein countries are grouped according to similarities in social and economic organization, as well as cultural and ideological compatibility. The resulting typology identifies four "family models" of contemporary capitalist society: neo-liberalism, conservative corporatism, social democratic corporatism, and oriental corporatism.

At the risk of oversimplifying the well-developed and explained argument made by Cavadino and Dignan (2006), we only note here that when 12 countries are compared on the basis of their use of imprisonment, the neo-liberal countries (e.g., Australia, England and Wales, New Zealand, South Africa, and the United States) have the highest imprisonment rate, followed by conservative corporatist countries (France, Germany, Italy, and the Netherlands), then the social democracies (Sweden and Finland), and, finally, Japan—the sole example of oriental corporatism. When presented in the more complete context of their book, this is an intriguing way to compare penal systems. However, doing so in this chapter would require more space than is available.

Another option for developing a useful classification scheme is presented by Ruddell and Urbina (2004)—although doing so was not their intent. These researchers were interested in how countries whose population is very homogeneous (i.e., of similar race and ethnicity) compare with countries that are heterogeneous (i.e., culturally, ethnically, and racially different) in terms of punitiveness (measured by presence of the death penalty and by imprisonment rate). Upon comparing 140 countries on indicators of homogeneity and punitiveness, they found that the more diverse nations were also more punitive. These findings suggest that it may be appropriate and useful to compare and contrast penal systems among countries based on a classification scheme that groups nations according to degrees of heterogeneity.

YOU SHOULD KNOW!

Australia and Transportation

Australia is the only continent settled as a penal colony. In January 1788, after 8 months at sea, 11 British ships landed in Sydney Cove. Of the more than 1,000 people going ashore, nearly 750 were prisoners being transported from England as punishment for a variety of offenses. From that date until 1840, English prisoners were continually transported to New South Wales, and until 1867, to other parts of Australia. They represented both men and women who had been convicted of a wide range of offenses. The typical transportee was sentenced for theft, had been a propertyless laborer, and was 26 years of age. In all, about 160,000 prisoners were transported to Australia.

With a lingering death from 1841 to 1868, the system provided convict labor primarily to Van Diemen's Land (now known as Tasmania). When that reception point dried up in 1853, a last dribble of convicts was sent to Western Australia to help colonists settle that difficult part of the continent. By 1868, transportation ended (Hughes, 1987; O'Brien & Ward, 1970).

The work of scholars such as Cavadino, Dignan, Ruddell, and Urbina is important for a complete understanding of the nature of punishment and to help determine the potential of comparative penology. However, for our purposes we rely on a much less sophisticated categorization tool to show the diversity of penal sanctions—sentence types.

Sentences are attached to particular crimes as a result of statutory law (see Chapter 3). Creative sentencing (e.g., requiring persons convicted of drunk driving to place bumper stickers on their cars so that other drivers are forewarned of the drivers' past behavior) is possible, but judges generally impose traditional sentences as provided in statute. The variety of sentencing types found around the world is reflected in the range shown by assessment of fines to execution for murder. Falling between those extremes are sentences to community service, imprisonment, and amputation.

For this chapter's categorization scheme, sentences are grouped into four broad categories: financial penalties, corporal and capital punishment, noncustodial sanctions, and custodial sentences. Within each category, practices in several countries are presented and, when appropriate, contrast with American practices is noted. In order to have a context for the discussion of sentence types, we begin with a review of the broad concept of punishment.

PUNISHMENT

Attempts to maintain social order require governments to identify, capture, process, and punish persons who violate the law. The "punish" aspect, which is of concern here, should reflect the reasons or justifications society has for carrying out the punishment and then should provide a sufficient variety of punishment types to reflect those justifications.

Justifications for Punishment

The classic justifications and goals for punishment are retribution, deterrence, rehabilitation, and incapacitation. Retribution, possibly the oldest of these, is considered by some to reflect a basic human tendency toward vengeance. The argument for retribution is that punishment is a necessary and natural response to persons violating social norms. Its most explicit depiction is in the "eye for an eye, tooth for a tooth" dictum of biblical times. A goal of retribution is to retaliate for the wrong done in such a way that the nature of the punishment reflects the nature of the offense. For example, the Germanic tribes in northern Europe of the Middle Ages were very protective of their forests. In fact, the penalty for illegally cutting down trees was execution. In an effort to have the "punishment fit the crime," the offender was executed in a manner that would reflect the crime itself. So persons taking the life of a tree by cutting off its top were buried in the ground from the shoulders down. A plow was then taken across the offender's head and his life was lost by topping, just as the tree had been topped.

The deterrence fork has two prongs: specific and general deterrence. Specific deterrence means that the offender is punished for the express purpose of deterring his or her personal acts of future wickedness. General deterrence means that the offender is punished in the belief that the penalty will prevent other people from committing a similar crime.

Rehabilitation was recognized as a legitimate goal of punishment as early as the eighteenth century when the Quakers encouraged the reforming of offenders into productive members of society. During its peaks and valleys of acceptance over the last several centuries, rehabilitation has taken a variety of forms. In one version, it follows a medical model wherein the offender (or patient) is classified (or diagnosed) according to his or her problems (or illness). The classification committee (or physicians and pathologists), composed of psychologists, social workers, clergy, health workers, educators, and the like, discuss the offender's needs and develop a treatment plan. Successful completion of the treatment plan is expected to make the offender better able to operate as a law-abiding member of society.

Incapacitation as a punishment goal refers, in its most general sense, to restricting an offender's freedom of movement. Presumably, society is protected when the offender cannot move freely about in the community. Historically, incapacitation was achieved almost solely through incarceration in jails and prisons. Incapacitation of the future is likely to rely on technology to restrict the offender's movement. The increased popularity of electronic monitoring devices probably foretells gadgets that will allow constant monitoring of a person's movement and immediate analysis of blood and urine samples.

Retribution, deterrence, rehabilitation, and incapacitation are not always mutually exclusive, but it is often difficult for several of them to operate together. Although a penal system may be effectively based on a combination of retribution and deterrence, it is more difficult to merge, for example, rehabilitation with retribution. Also, the location where the punishment is administered may affect the ability to realize each goal. General deterrence is possible only in an open society in which the public is kept informed of the application of punishments. Movement is more easily restricted in a prison than in an open community. Rehabilitation that may be achieved in a community setting may be impossible in the confines of a secure prison.

Justice systems seldom follow a single punishment philosophy when creating and implementing sentences, nor is there any reason that they should. Public opinion, media attention, seriousness of the crime, and offender characteristics are only some of the factors that may result in a country using sentences to rehabilitate one moment and to incapacitate another. So, just as there are several justifications for punishment, there are also a variety of sentencing types.

The different reasons for punishing offenders and the assortment of sentencing types suggest that many combinations of sentences and justification are possible. That diversity can result in punishments that some may regard as ineffectively undemanding and others that may be considered inappropriately harsh. Attempts to provide a reasonable level of civility to penal sanctions have led some national and international organizations to provide standards that can be used to gauge how a country's sentence types and procedures compare with generally agreed-upon criteria.

International Standards for Corrections

Sentencing types—despite great variety within type—can generally be placed into four basic categories. As this chapter reviews each type, comments are made regarding international standards appropriate for each sentence category.

INTERNATIONAL AGREEMENTS ON CORRECTIONS Agreements between and among countries interested in cooperating on issues of mutual concern can take many forms. Bilateral agreements are made between two countries, and multilateral agreements are among three or more countries. Agreements that are truly international—in the sense that all the world's countries have joined in—remain only theoretically possible. However, the concept of international agreements is typically accepted as referring to those involving a large number of countries from all political, cultural, and economic situations. Such agreements typically result from activities by the United Nations, which serves as the world's primary international organization. Our review of corrections-related agreements is restricted to those at the international level and conducted under the auspices of the United Nations.

When we think of international agreements in the broadest sense, we can include actions by any of the six principal organs of the United Nations (General Assembly, Security Council, Economic and Social Council, Trusteeship Council, International Court of Justice, and Secretariat) or from one of its many offices, commissions, or agencies. For example, resolutions from the General Assembly relate to a wide variety of topics concerning the international community. Agreements from the U.N. Commission on Human Rights are more specifically focused on human rights topics, and those from the International Center for the Prevention of Crime or the Commission on Crime Prevention and Criminal Justice deal specifically with criminal justice issues. A review of agreements from these sources results in many documents on issues ranging from the use of force and firearms by law enforcement officials to protection of prisoners against torture. The following agreements are especially relevant for our discussion. The full text of each is available from the Office of the High Commissioner for Human Rights (United Nations, 2016).

- United Nations Standard Minimum Rules for Noncustodial Measures (the Tokyo Rules)
- Standard Minimum Rules for the Treatment of Prisoners (the Nelson Mandela Rules)
- Basic Principles for the Treatment of Prisoners
- Convention against Torture and Other Cruel, Inhuman or Degrading Treatment or Punishment
- Optional Protocol to the Convention against Torture and Other Cruel, Inhuman or Degrading Treatment or Punishment
- International Covenant on Civil and Political Rights
- The Second Optional Protocol to the International Covenant on Civil and Political Rights, aiming at the abolition of the death penalty

As can be seen, international agreements have been given a variety of titles. Terms such as standard minimum rules, basic principles, and protocols are mixed with agreements called conventions and covenants. This diversity of terminology means there is no precise nomenclature for these agreements. Similarly, the agreements can range from ones that encourage certain behavior to others that demand adherence to specific principles and procedures.

Generally, conventions and covenants refer to binding documents that require all ratifying countries to abide by the agreement's specified standards. Rules and principles are typically nonbinding agreements that encourage specified procedures and policies by signers of the agreement. Protocols, which are usually called optional protocols in U.N. agreements, are linked to a prior agreement and are designed to provide procedures related to that agreement or to address a substantive area related to the agreement. The preceding list has four binding (conventions, covenants, and protocols) and three nonbinding (rules and principles) agreements. Each is discussed as we review sentence types within the sentence categories except for the category of financial penalties for which no international agreements apply.

FINANCIAL PENALTIES

The idea of punishing offenders financially predates the Code of Hammurabi and remains popular today in many countries. In fact, the fine appears to be the most frequently used noncustodial sanction in the world, ranging from 95 percent of noncustodial sanctions in Japan through more than 70 percent in Western European countries to much lower percentages in the developing world (Zvekic, 1997). That popularity is understandable when we consider the advantages that fines have over other sentencing types. For example, financial penalties are relatively inexpensive to administer, they do not damage the offender's ties with family and community in the same way that incarceration might, and they can be combined with other sanctions when multiple sentencing goals are sought. Two types of financial penalties are considered here: fines and compensation to victims and community.

Fines

Fines in U.S. jurisdictions are used primarily for traffic offenses and less serious high-volume crimes such as misdemeanors and ordinance violations. Because these types of offenses are so numerous throughout the United States, fines are actually the most frequently used sanction in America. The key is that fines are viewed as appropriate for the high-volume inconsequential offenses, not for felony-level crimes. Morris and Tonry (1990) find it ironic that a country relying so heavily on financial incentives in its social philosophy and economic practice is reluctant to use the financial disincentive as a punishment for crime. Other countries consider financial penalties to be quite appropriate for more serious crimes as well.

DAY FINES The primary example of fines as a penalty for more serious crimes is the European day fine. This system is based on the idea that monetary punishment should be proportionate to the seriousness of the crime and have a roughly similar financial sting on persons with differing financial resources. Fines in the United States, on the other hand, are typically the tariff or fixed-fine type that presume that the same or similar fine amounts should be imposed on all defendants convicted on a particular offense, regardless of the offender's financial resources. Since the tariff or fixed-fine system is based on the severity of the offense without concern for the offender's ability to pay, it is understandable that judges and the public look skeptically on the fine as a penalty for crime. Setting a fixed amount that is high enough to deter financially secure offenders will result in an amount so high that poor offenders cannot reasonably receive the penalty. On the other hand, setting a fixed amount that is within the financial ability of poorer offenders will be little more than a slap on the wrist for criminals with greater financial resources.

If fines are linked to a person's ability to pay, it seems reasonable to assume that fines could better meet their punitive and deterrent goals. Variable fining systems are not a new concept; they date at least to thirteenth-century England, but their most recent version was proposed by a Scandinavian criminologist. Called day fines, this variable fining idea was implemented in Finland in 1921, Sweden in 1931, Cuba in 1936,

Day Fine

Financial penalties, especially in the form of day fines, are used extensively in several countries as a way to set a punishment that reflects both the seriousness of the crime and the offender's ability to pay.

Lisa S/Shutterstock

Denmark in 1939, and West Germany and Austria in 1975 (Hillsman, 1990; Zedlewski, 2010). Because the day-fine procedures in Sweden and Germany have received the most attention in recent years, we concentrate on them here.

EXAMPLES FROM SWEDEN AND GERMANY The basic idea behind day fines is to separate the calculation of the fine penalty into two components. In the first, the fine amount is linked to the severity of the crime. In the second, the fine is adjusted to the offender's financial circumstances. In this manner, more serious offenses warrant higher fines, but what is "high" depends on the offender's finances. Judges decide how much punishment an offender deserves for a particular crime by identifying the offense as requiring a certain number of punishment units. Those punishment units are translated into monetary terms by, for example, making one punishment unit equal to 1 day's pay. So, a sentence of 10 punishment units, or 10 days' pay, results in a large day fine for high-income offenders and a smaller amount for lower-income people. Despite the differing amounts, the penalty should weigh equally on both offenders.

Sweden (see Map A.10) and Germany (see Map A.10) take this basic approach and modify it to suit particular objectives. In Sweden, the day fine is seen primarily as a more equitable way to impose an economic sanction when a jail sentence would not normally be used. The Germans, on the other hand, see day fines as a replacement for short-term imprisonment and therefore use them even for serious offenses such as burglary or aggravated assault (Subramanian & Shames, 2015; Vera Institute of Justice, 1996).

Under the German system, day-fine units are valued at or near the offender's net daily take-home pay with no deductions for financial responsibilities. A person may, for example, be fined the equivalent of his net daily income (e.g., €30) times 50 daily units, resulting in a fine of €1500. In this way, daily income reflects the individual's ability to pay and the daily units reflect the degree of guilt. This straightforward calculation emphasizes the idea that offenders are avoiding jail for a day by paying a day's wages. The fine can be paid at a future date or over time, but failure to pay the fine results in imprisonment (one daily unit equals one day in prison) or, when the jurisdiction permits, community service (Jehle, 2015).

Because Swedish day fines are primarily intended for less serious offenses, the financial impact is less burdensome for the offender. The punishment units (e.g., 20 days) are converted to a monetary unit by subtracting business expenses, maintenance, or living expenses from a person's gross annual income. The resulting figure is a quantity equal to about one-fourth of the offender's daily income (Vera Institute of Justice, 1996).

Both Sweden and Germany make significant use of their day fines. About half of all property and violent crime convictions in Sweden result in day fines. In Germany, day fines are the primary sanction in about 80 percent of the criminal cases (Hillsman, 1990; Subramanian & Shames, 2015). Obviously, both countries are pleased with the day fine as a criminal penalty.

Compensation to Victims and Community

In addition to fines, other forms of financial compensation continue to be popular in countries around the world. Some of these are based on traditional justice systems (as in the following Saudi Arabian example) in which the victim is compensated directly;

others are an important part of contemporary sanctions that compensate the community (as in the following example from Germany).

DIYYA IN SAUDI ARABIA   Recall from Chapters 4 and 5 that under Islamic law the state does not have a separate legal personality, so wrongs are actions against the individual rather than against the government. Obviously, this view of crime sets the stage for a very victim-oriented legal system, as seen in Saudi Arabia (see Map A.2).

Because the state has not replaced the individual as the victim of criminal acts in Islamic society, the Shari'a allows and even encourages nonlegalistic response to misbehavior. Criminal complaints are often resolved through arbitration even before a police record is made. Even such serious crimes as homicide may never be brought to formal trial because the Qur'an condones at least two types of responses that do not involve the court system: retaliation and compensation.

Retaliation—in the sense of "just retribution" as distinguished in Asad's (2003) translation and explanation of the Qur'an—by a victim's family is an accepted response to murder under Islamic law. The Qur'an explains that "Just retribution is ordained for you in cases of killing: the free for the free, and the slave for the slave, and the female for the female" (Surah 2:178). Similarly, any intentional, serious, but nonlethal harm inflicted on a human body can also be responded to with just retribution. The Qur'an repeats the Torah's version of retaliation in noting that "a life for a life, and an eye for an eye, and a nose for a nose, and an ear for an ear, and a tooth for a tooth, and a [similar] retribution for wounds" (Surah 5:45). An important distinction between Islam's version of retaliation and a pure *lex talionis* is that the Qur'an clearly tempers retaliation by encouraging forgiveness. For example, the "life for life" verse continues by noting that "he who shall forego it out of charity will atone thereby for some of his past sins" (Surah 5:45). Expression of that charity or forgiveness is found in the concept of compensation in the form of *diyya*.

When just retribution for an offense takes the form of forgiveness by the victim or victim's family, it is called diyya, or blood money. Diyya is a possible punishment only for qisas offenses, which you will recall from Chapter 5 are roughly equivalent to crimes against persons. Although diyya may have a deterrent function, it is considered a way to rid society, including the victims and their families, of any grudges toward the offender. It attempts, in other words, to make the victim and the community whole again.

The concept of diyya may sound familiar to you because it is similar to the old Anglo-Saxon process of wergild (literally, man-gold, but also translated as man-price) that demanded monetary compensation by a murderer to the relatives of the victim. The price paid was often determined by the victim's rank or social status (e.g., royalty required a larger payment than nonroyalty). Similarly, diyya payments are influenced by such considerations as whether the victim was Muslim (requiring greater compensation than a non-Muslim) or male (requiring greater compensation than a female), or may vary based on the victim's age or nationality (U.S. Department of State, 2009). In moderate Islamic states today, diyya payments are being made more equitable—especially in terms of gender (Souryal, 2004).

DONATION PENALTIES IN GERMANY   Direct compensation to victims is certainly found in the sanctioning options of other countries, but increasingly common are financial sanctions that compensate the broader community as seen in Germany's use of a donation sanction. Since 1975, prosecutors in Germany can use an interesting alternative to the formal criminal processing of misdemeanor offenders. For example, Section 153a of the German Code of Criminal Procedure is based on the idea that the public interest in prosecution can be satisfied by having the offender make a payment or perform another action that will benefit the public. Under Section 153a, misdemeanor offenders can avoid a criminal trial and a conviction, thereby avoiding a criminal record, by paying a sum of money to the victim, a

YOU SHOULD KNOW!

Diyya and the U.S. Military

As early as 2003, the U.S. Army was making condolence payments to Iraqi and Afghan civilians for loss of life resulting from combat actions by U.S. and coalition forces. Payments for other personal injury or property damage are also possible (Brown, 2008; Pincus, 2007). These payments, called "solatia" payments by the U.S. government, are not admissions of legal liability or fault, but are instead expressions of sympathy.

Solatia payments are of interest here because they are used under military doctrine as payments—made in accordance with local custom—to express remorse or sympathy. The "local custom" of relevance in Iraq and Afghanistan is diyya. Brown (2008) explains that direct comparison of the military condolence payments with the concept of diyya is not quite accurate since diyya assumes an equal relationship between giver and receiver. Because the U.S. government is always the giver and never the recipient with solatia payments, the payments could be perceived as attempts to "buy off" relatives. Although military commanders have discretion when determining the appropriate payment amount, the average for loss of life has been $2,500 and up to $1,500 for serious injury and a general ceiling of $5,000 (Currier, 2015; Government Accountability Office, 2007).

charitable organization, or the state (Federal Republic of Germany, 1987). By compensating the victim or by giving to charity, the defendant acknowledges responsibility for the offense and shows a willingness to act in a socially commendable way.

This procedure may look like a fine, but the German statute very carefully avoids any such reference because linking the compensatory payment to a fine would present serious legal problems. The payment under Section 153a precedes conviction, so imposing a fine (i.e., a sentence) before conviction would clearly violate the presumption of innocence and have prosecutors rather than judges setting sentences. To avoid such complications, payments under Section 153a require the prior consent of the defendant and are therefore considered voluntary, unlike a fine sentence, which does not require or seek the offender's consent.

Weigend (1993) explains that either prosecution or defense can initiate the conditional dismissal under Section 153a. Most often it is the prosecutor who proposes dismissal (with a judge's approval in more serious cases) and suggests an appropriate amount to be paid, although the defendant can make a counteroffer. The victim need not be consulted before dismissal is offered to the defendant. The defendant is not required to confess guilt but only to agree to the proposed disposition. When the defendant submits proof that the required payment has been made or work assignment fulfilled, the prosecutor dismisses the case and no criminal record is made of the incident.

Conditional dismissals have been given for personal, property, and financial offenses. Because Americans often view misdemeanors as involving trivial matters, it is important to note that German law categorizes actions such as aggravated assault, most drug offenses, and larceny in this less serious crime category (Dubber, 1997).

German critics of conditional dismissal are bothered by the increased discretion Section 153a gives to prosecutors and by the haggling over how much the dismissal will cost. This would be less of a concern in the United States, where there is a long tradition of unlimited prosecutorial discretion and of bartering on both charges and sentences. Another argument of the critics is not so easily dismissed in either Germany or the United States. Because the conditional dismissal allows defendants to avoid possible conviction and any criminal record of the event, there is a question regarding how voluntary the consent to make payments can be. The prosecutor's offer to dismiss in exchange for payments may be an offer the accused cannot refuse, even if he or she is innocent or otherwise unconvictable. While these criticisms are important considerations, proponents argue that when properly limited to appropriate offenses, conditional dismissal, also called prosecutorial diversion, is a sensible solution with obvious advantages for all concerned.

CORPORAL AND CAPITAL PUNISHMENT

Most people consider even significant financial penalties to be clearly at one end of a continuum and purposeful damage to the offender's body or the offender's execution at the continuum's other end. Although they are becoming increasingly rare on the world stage, examples of an offender being sentenced to punishment of, or inflicted on, his or her body (corporal punishment) and to death (capital punishment) continue to exist.

International Standards

The U.N. Convention against Torture and Other Cruel, Inhuman or Degrading Treatment or Punishment (CAT) considers torture to be the intentional infliction of physical or mental pain or suffering to obtain information or confession or as punishment (United Nations, 1984a). The CAT became effective in 1987, and the United States ratified it in 1990. The CAT essentially bans torture under all circumstances and establishes the U.N. Committee against Torture to monitor convention compliance. Countries that have ratified the CAT are required to make torture illegal and to provide appropriate punishment for those engaging in torture. Many activities of the Committee against Torture are directed toward claims of torture used as an interrogation technique rather than as punishment. Our concern in this chapter is with the possibility that corporal punishment may be considered torture or cruel punishment under the CAT.

Unlike the very clear stance taken to ban torture, international organizations have been hesitant to require that nations abandon the death penalty. Zimring (2003) notes that until the 1970s no international organization of consequence had even become involved in death penalty debates. In 1977, Amnesty International expressed concern that the death penalty was often used for political ends, but only recently has capital punishment been criticized as a violation of one's "right to life." In fact, early statements on right to life (e.g., the European Convention on Human Rights, adopted in 1950) specifically excluded one's right to life upon conviction of a crime for which the penalty is execution. Even the more recent (1966) U.N. International Covenant on Civil and Political Rights (ICCPR) exempted executions from the protected scope of a right to life.

Instead of demanding that member nations abolish their death penalty statutes, the United Nations has proposed an optional protocol to the ICCPR that aims at the abolition of the death penalty and has issued safeguards to be followed by nations that continue to use the death penalty. The Second Optional Protocol to the ICCPR (effective in 1991) has been ratified by 81 countries—the United States is not one of them (United Nations, 1989). That protocol prohibits ratifying countries from conducting an execution and requires them to take all necessary measures to abolish the death penalty. The Safeguards Guaranteeing Protection of the Rights of Those Facing the Death Penalty was adopted by the U.N. Economic and Social Council in 1984 (United Nations, 1984b). Those safeguards suggest, for example, that countries still using the death penalty impose it only for the most serious crimes for which guilt is determined by clear and convincing evidence and when the execution can be carried out with the minimum possible suffering. In addition, it should not be applied to persons under 18 years of age, pregnant women or new mothers, or insane persons.

Keeping in mind those international standards for corporal and capital punishment, we now turn our attention to where and how such penalties are still used.

Corporal Punishment

Corporal punishment (more accurately, judicial corporal punishment because it is applied as a sentence) refers to any kind of punishment of, or inflicted on, the body. Although this means that imprisonment is technically an example of corporal punishment, the term more often brings to mind actions such as whipping, amputation, and branding. Similarly, execution is certainly a punishment inflicted on the body, but as the ultimate sanction, it has its own identity as capital punishment.

Self-reports by countries using judicial corporal punishment are not very frequent. In the Seventh United Nations Crime Trends Survey (United Nations Office on Drugs and Crime, 2004), only five countries reported having used corporal punishment (usually flogging) as a punishment sanction (Qatar, Singapore, Swaziland, Zambia, and Zimbabwe). As a result, most of the information about the application of corporal punishment as a criminal sanction comes from human rights organizations such as Amnesty International and Human Rights Watch.

Mutilation, including amputation, is a form of corporal punishment that is still used in several countries and is considered contrary to international standards prohibiting torture and other cruel punishment. In Saudi Arabia, in 2000, Amnesty International recorded at least 21 amputations, with seven of them being cross-amputations (right hand and left foot, the penalty for highway robbery). Saudi Arabia ratified the CAT in 1997, but Amnesty International (among others) questions the country's compliance with its provisions. In 2010, cross-amputation was still being handed down in Somalia and carried out, although most often by rebel Islamist groups rather than by a country's legitimate government (Rice, 2010). In 2015, Amnesty International reported that authorities at the Central Prison in Mashhad, Iran, amputated four fingers from the right hands of two men sentenced for theft, apparently without anesthetic. Also in Iran, a man was deliberately blinded in his left eye after a court sentenced him to "retribution-in-kind" for throwing acid into another man's face (Amnesty International, 2016b).

Corporal punishment in other countries is more likely to take the form of whipping than of amputation. Sentences to flogging or caning are given for a variety of offenses in such countries as Brunei Darussalam, Iran, Libya, Malaysia, the Maldives, Qatar, Saudi Arabia, Singapore, Somalia, Sudan, and Yemen. More than 30 different crimes have mandatory caning sentences in Singapore and flogging is a punishment for alcohol-related crimes and for sexual offenses in Qatar and Yemen. Examples of recent flogging sentences include the arrest, trial, and conviction of more than 400 people in Iran for publicly breaking their fast during Ramadan. Most received flogging sentences to be administered by the Office for Implementation of Sentences and some of these were carried out in public (Amnesty International, 2016b).

In addition to the notoriety that many Islamic countries receive regarding their use of amputation, citizens of other countries are also appalled, delighted, or at least intrigued by their methods of execution. Beheading is a common technique, but Islamic law also proscribes stoning as the means of carrying out a death penalty. The extent to which stoning is used to execute a condemned prisoner is difficult to verify, but Rejali (1994) suggests that, at least in Iran, the percentage of executions by stoning is a small proportion of all executions. This discussion is shifting our focus from corporal punishment to capital punishment, which requires a more specific introduction.

WEB PROJECT

Judicial Corporal Punishment

Visit the World Corporal Punishment Research website at http://www.corpun.com/ and look at the material in a few of the links (e.g., What's new). Eventually, visit the Country Files link at http://www.corpun.com/rules.htm and choose three or four countries that currently have judicial corporal punishment. Write a few paragraphs describing how judicial corporal punishment is being used in those countries, and then present your opinion about whether such punishments provide a reasonable or desirable sanction for adoption in American jurisdictions.

Capital Punishment

Records are not complete for all countries, but Amnesty International reports that at least 1,634 executions were carried out in 25 countries around the world in 2015. That does not include the thousands of executions believed to have been carried out in China (see Map A.7) that year. Almost 90 percent of all known executions (excluding China) took place in Iran (more than 977), Pakistan (326), and Saudi Arabia (more than 158). Although beheading was the execution method in Saudi Arabia (along with shooting), the more typical methods were hanging (e.g., Afghanistan, Egypt, India, Iran, Iraq, Japan, Pakistan, and Singapore), lethal injection (e.g., China, the United States, and Vietnam), and shooting (e.g., China, Indonesia, North Korea, Taiwan, and Yemen). In recent years, sentences to death by stoning have been handed down in Iran, the Maldives, Nigeria, Pakistan, and Saudi Arabia, but there have been no reports of judicial executions by stoning actually carried out for several years (Amnesty International, 2016a). When death by stoning has been carried out in recent years, it is more likely to be the work of extra judicial groups such as the Taliban or the Islamic State of Iraq and Syria.

RETENTION AND ABOLITION AROUND THE WORLD   Amnesty International (2016a) reports that more than two-thirds of the world's countries have abolished the death penalty in law or in practice. Figure 8.2 shows that the abolitionist category includes those countries that have abolished the death penalty for all crimes, those where it has been abolished only for ordinary crimes (meaning execution is still possible for unusual crimes such as those committed under military law or crimes committed in exceptional circumstances), and those where the death penalty has been abolished in practice (i.e., it is a legally possible sentence but no one has been executed in the past 10 years).

Most European countries (and all European Union countries) are abolitionist. Many countries in South and Central America are abolitionist in full or in practice. The death penalty is retained in much of the Caribbean, but the region has been execution-free for several years. In North America, Canada and Mexico have abolished the death penalty for all crimes but in the United States death penalty statutes vary by jurisdiction with 31 states, the federal government, and the U.S. military authorizing the death penalty.

Countries in the Middle East and North Africa generally retain the death penalty as an important sanction under Shari'a. In the African regions south of the Sahara, capital punishment has been abolished in practice in many of the countries. Much of the

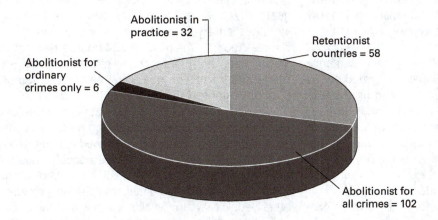

FIGURE 8.2   Abolitionist and Retentionist Countries

Source: Based on Chart prepared from information provided by Amnesty International (2016, p. 65). "Death Sentences and Executions in 2015." Index number: ACT 50/3487/2016. Retrieved from https://www.amnesty.org/en/documents/act50/3487/2016/en/.

Asia-Pacific region retains the death penalty, with China being the greatest proponent, but executions have also been conducted in Afghanistan, Bangladesh, India, Japan, Malaysia, North Korea, Singapore, Taiwan, and Vietnam.

WHY THE VARIATION IN ACCEPTANCE?   Capital punishment has a history of use across the ages and around the world. Anthropologist Keith Otterbein actually considers capital punishment to be a universal cultural trait in a manner similar to the universal presence of religion and the family. He attributes its universality to a notion common among cultures that dangerous people must be disposed of through the use of the death penalty. Otterbein's (1986) research led him to make four generalizations about capital punishment:

- Capital punishment is a cross-cultural universal; although exceptions may exist, the evidence shows that most, if not all, societies at one time or another will use the death penalty.
- Capital crimes are most likely to be offenses that directly threaten people: homicide, stealing, violations of community religious norms, and sexual offenses.
- Disposal of the wrongdoer is the reason most frequently found for executing a community member.
- In the vast majority of cultures, most members of the community accept capital punishment as an appropriate sanction.

YOU SHOULD KNOW!
Secret Executions in Japan

One criticism of capital punishment, at least as carried out in U.S. jurisdictions, is its planned and purposeful nature. The condemned is given a specific time and date on which he or she will die, and, although the prisoner can hope for a last-minute reprieve, he or she essentially spends the last weeks knowing that death awaits. Is it crueler to know exactly when you will die and be forced to sit idly by until the moment arrives or to know you are scheduled to die but not whether it will be this afternoon or 10 years from now?

Amnesty International (2016a) reports that in several countries—including Belarus and Japan—death row inmates are not told of their forthcoming execution, nor are their families or lawyers.

In 2016, at least 143 people were under sentence of death in Japan. Executions in Japan are carried out by hanging at a secret time and location and on a seemingly arbitrary basis. Prisoners are given less than 2 hours' warning that their execution time has arrived, and there is no notification at all to the families or lawyers. In fact, only recently has there been minimal confirmation of who was hanged and when the execution took place (Amnesty International, 1995, 2006, 2009, 2015).

The decision about when a prisoner is to be executed is made by Japan's Minister of Justice. Amnesty International found the selection for execution to be apparently random, with no clear reason why a particular prisoner is chosen to die. Some were under sentence of death for 30 years, and several of them are over age 70. The secret executions also affect the condemned's family as related in a 1995 case wherein a mother went to visit her condemned son only to be told that visiting hours were very busy and she should return at noon. Upon her return, she was asked if she wanted to take her son's body away for burial (Amnesty International, 2006).

In addition to expressing concern about an execution process that is conducted in secret and applied at random, Amnesty International and other human rights groups are also disturbed about the conditions of Japan's death row, which, the groups claim, are making the inmates mentally ill. Lights are never switched off, video cameras monitor the prisoners 24 hours a day, and strict rules require those sentenced to death to do things such as sit in the middle of the cell in one of three authorized positions (Amnesty International, 1995, 2002).

A new law governing the treatment of prisoners in Japan was enacted in May 2005, and presumably there is now a broader range of visitors allowed to meet detainees awaiting execution (e.g., all relatives, people "necessary" to deal with important matters, and those who contribute to the mental stability of detainees). The law provides that other people may also be allowed to visit at the discretion of the head of the detention center (Amnesty International, 2006). Nevertheless, the secrecy surrounding the executions continues and is justified as necessary to avoid disturbing the prisoner's emotional state.

Where capital punishment is not used, Otterbein argues, the community members must find an alternative method to dispose of individuals who threaten the community. The communities most likely to accept alternatives to capital punishment are those where citizens have stable, mature governments in which crime and fear of crime are not the major concerns. Presumably, where crime and the fear of crime become major concerns, even mature, stable communities may turn to capital punishment as the ultimate protection against threatening individuals.

THE ROLE OF PUBLIC OPINION   Hood (2002) reminds us that public opinion is often cited as a major factor in whether a country has abolished or retained the death penalty. After all, one could argue that it would be undemocratic for legislators to pass laws that are in direct conflict with strong public sentiment. United States courts seems to have taken

IMPACT

FOREIGN NATIONALS AND THE DEATH PENALTY

If you had the misfortune of being arrested while on vacation in a foreign country, do you think the local authorities should have to notify the American consulate about your arrest if you ask them to do so? Should you be allowed to communicate with the consulate? Should the consular have access to you while you are being detained? Should foreigners arrested in the United States have the same rights regarding their consulate?

Article 36 of the Vienna Convention on Consular Relations provides that at a national's request, local authorities must notify the consulate of the national's arrest "without delay." Further, detained foreigners must be informed (also, "without delay") of their right to have their consulate informed of their detention (United Nations, 1963). The United States and more than 170 other countries have ratified the Vienna Convention. Of course, having a right is sometimes more clearly recognized than is getting it enforced. To assist in ensuring that these rights are truly provided by the countries ratifying the treaty, an Optional Protocol was established that gave the International Court of Justice (ICJ) the final decision as to whether a national's right to see a home-country diplomat had been violated. The United States ratified the Optional Protocol and was actually the first country to invoke it when the United States successfully sued Iran for taking 52 Americans hostage in Tehran in 1979.

This seemingly agreeable arrangement among most of the world's countries began unraveling in 1999 when the ICJ started hearing complaints that U.S. jurisdictions had violated the Vienna Convention in cases of foreigners who had not been informed of their right to contact their consulate. The cases chosen for the suits were particularly serious ones wherein the foreigners had eventually been sentenced to death.

In 2004, the ICJ ruled that the United States had violated the rights of 51 Mexicans (on death row in eight states) to receive diplomatic assistance, and ordered the federal government to review the cases. The response by the Bush administration was to send U.N. Secretary General Kofi Annan a letter stating that the United States was withdrawing from the Optional Protocol to the Vienna Convention (Lane, 2005). Withdrawal from the Optional Protocol only means the United States does not accept the ICJ as the final arbitrator in cases involving the Vienna Convention. The United States remains a signatory to the convention itself and the requirement that foreign nationals be advised of their right to access their consulate. However, the U.S. Supreme Court ruled in 2008 (*Medellin* v. *Texas*, 552 U.S. 491) that the Vienna Convention was not binding domestic law and Congress must pass legislation in order for the ICJ decision to be enforced at the state level. Attempts to pass such a bill have not been successful, but the U.S. Department of State has actively encouraged local law enforcement authorities to comply with consular notification requirements on their own initiative. The Bureau of Consular Affairs (2016) provides information on when and how a detained foreign national's consulate should be notified, offers training on consular notification, and distributes posters in several languages that can be used in detention facilities.

this position in some corporal and capital punishment cases when decisions are based on what the court views as evolving standards of decency. For example, in *Jackson* v. *Bishop*, the U.S. Court of Appeals found whipping prisoners to be unconstitutional because it "offends contemporary concepts of decency" (404 F.2d at 580). Similarly, in forbidding the execution of offenders who were under the age of 18 when their crimes were committed (*Roper* v. *Simmons*, 543 U.S. 551, 2005) and of persons who are mentally retarded (*Atkins* v. *Virginia*, 536 U.S. 304, 2002), the U.S. Supreme Court noted that evolving standards of decency no longer supported such punishment.

Presumably, one reason the death penalty itself has not been ruled unconstitutional in the United States is because the Supreme Court does not believe it violates standards of decency in contemporary American society. Support for that position is found not only in the 34 states where death sentences may be imposed but also in public opinion polls. The Gallup Organization, which, in the 1930s, began asking Americans if they are "in favor of the death penalty for a person convicted of murder," reports public support at its lowest in 1966 (42 percent favoring) and its highest in 1994 (80 percent favoring). The percentage favoring the death penalty has not been below 50 percent since the early 1970s and has stayed around 60–65 percent during the twenty-first century (Dugan, 2015).

As reasonable as the "express the will of the people" argument seems, it is not always persuasive. The death penalty was abolished in Canada, France, Germany, and the United Kingdom at times when a majority of their respective citizens favored its use (Hood, 2002). Even years after it has been abolished, public opinion in many countries may support the death penalty—however, differences in the way survey questions are framed present problems when trying to compare opinions across countries. European polls, for example, sometimes ask the question in terms of the death penalty for terrorism, genocide, depraved sexual crimes, and so forth. But, even if the question is asked in a more restricted manner than it is in many American polls, there are few European countries where the public clearly opposes it—and some countries where support is strong.

Gallup Polls (Moore, 2006) taken in Canada, Great Britain, and the United States found Americans to be more supportive of the death penalty for persons convicted of murder (64 percent favoring) than either Canadians (44 percent favoring) or the British (49 percent favoring). However, more recent surveys (with different question phrasing) found that 63 percent of Canadians and 65 percent of Britons support reinstating capital punishment for murder (Angus Reid Institute, 2011, 2013). In 1997, Russia imposed a moratorium, which continues today, on the use of the death penalty, but 44 percent of Russians believe capital punishment should be fully reinstated and applied (Angus Reid Institute, 2010).

Interesting as a discussion about the role of public opinion on court decisions may be, it is one that some see as misplaced. Determining the current state of an evolving standard of decency does not, for example, rely on public opinion polls—even though such polls may be useful in identifying that standard. Writing in dissent of the

WEB PROJECT

Death Penalty: Your Questions Answered

Visit Amnesty International's page on the death penalty at https://www.amnesty.org/en/what-we-do/death-penalty/death-penalty-your-questions-answered/ and read all the questions and answers provided. Write a few paragraphs describing some of the questions and answers mentioned. For purposes of discussion, and regardless of your personal opinion on the death penalty itself, comment on which questions and answers you found particularly interesting.

Furman v. *Georgia* (408 U.S. 238 1972) decision, Justice Powell explained that regardless of how one may assess the changing public opinion on the death penalty, the relevance of those attitudes is "at the periphery—not the core—of the judicial process in constitutional cases. The assessment of popular opinion is essentially a legislative, not a judicial, function" (408 U.S. at 443).

In a 1995 decision by the South African Constitutional Court, Arthur Chaskalson took a similar position to that of Justice Powell, wherein he agreed that the majority of South African citizens believe the death penalty should be imposed in extreme cases of murder and that it is not cruel, inhuman, or degrading. However, he explained, "The question before us is not what the majority of South Africans believe a proper sentence for murder should be. It is whether the Constitution allows the sentence" (*State* v. *Makwanyane*, Case No. CCT/3/94 at para. 87). He continues by noting that public opinion may have some relevance to the question, but it cannot substitute for the Court's duty to interpret and uphold the Constitution. The constitutionality of sentences must be decided through judicial review of legislation because that is the process designed to protect the rights of minorities and others who are unable to adequately protect their rights through the democratic process. As he concludes, "It is only if there is a willingness to protect the worst and the weakest amongst us, that all of us can be secure that our own rights will be protected" (at para. 88).

THE DEATH PENALTY IN CHINA   China presents an interesting country for closer consideration of the death penalty because Amnesty International consistently believes it to have the highest number of executions each year. Executions, by shooting or lethal injection, are authorized for drug offenses and violent crimes as well as for nonviolent crimes such as tax fraud and embezzlement. After many years of trying to estimate the number of executions in China, Amnesty International in 2010 decided to no longer publish a minimum figure. Instead, Chinese authorities were challenged to publish figures for the number of people sentenced to death and executed each year as a way for them to confirm Chinese claims that there has been a reduction in the country's use of the death penalty (Amnesty International, 2016a).

Recall Otterbein's conclusion that countries most likely to retain, or return to, capital punishment for protection against threatening individuals are those in which crime and the fear of crime are major concerns. To the extent that is true, it may help explain increased use of capital punishment in some U.S. jurisdictions, the reintroduction of death penalty statutes in jurisdictions that had previously abolished it, and the occasional calls for its reinstatement in jurisdictions currently without it. Until an interested researcher tests correlations among variables such as a country's crime rate, citizen perception of crime as a problem, dates of abolishment and reintroduction, and legislative attempts at reinstatement, we can only wonder about Otterbein's conclusion. To the extent that it appears crime rates are increasing or the perception of crime as a major problem is increasing in places where the death penalty has been reintroduced or has received more discussion, it seems at least reasonable to suggest the link is an appropriate area for research. This is not the place to undertake such a study, but as anecdotal support for Otterbein's position we can look at the Chinese example.

Lepp (1990) explains that during the late 1970s China experienced a significant jump in its crime rate, and Chinese leaders began using the death penalty more frequently. Crime continued to rise; with the launching of an anticrime campaign in the early 1980s, China resorted to the death penalty even more frequently. Foreign press estimates suggest that between 1983 and 1986, anywhere from 7,000 to 14,000 executions were carried out. In early 1987, Chinese officials announced there had been a substantial drop in the number of crimes in the first half of 1986. The anticrime campaign had struck a "ruthless blow," Communist Party officials said, and in response, the campaign's intensity was reduced throughout 1987. Serious crime increased again in 1988, and the government returned to the frequent use of the death penalty. The correspondence of ups and downs in the crime rate with increased and decreased use of capital punishment seems to support Otterbein's contention that the death penalty is linked to actual or perceived levels of crime. Because crime statistics in the People's Republic of China are suspect—mostly because they are not made available to researchers for analysis and because government policy, Communist or otherwise, does not necessarily reflect public opinion—it is inappropriate to draw conclusions from the Chinese example. The Chinese experience certainly presents food for thought among those interested in possible relationships between a country's use of capital punishment and the actual or perceived rate of serious crime in that country.

Linked to Otterbein's conclusion that the death penalty is retained or reinstated when citizens fear serious crime is the broader issue of deterrence. Noting the Chinese saying that one should "kill the chicken to frighten the monkey," Lepp (1990) believes the expression reflects a traditional faith in the power of punishment as a deterrent. The practical application of this belief is found in the Chinese custom of using degrees of punishment to achieve degrees of deterrence. The centuries-old "five punishments," which basically remain today, started with five degrees of beating with a light stick (ranging from 10 to 50 blows) and increased in severity to two degrees of death (strangulation or decapitation). Two degrees of a death punishment were seen as possible because strangulation, although it was the more prolonged and painful death, was considered less severe than decapitation. That perception was based on social and religious views of the body, which saw decapitation as being disrespectful to one's parents. By the early eighteenth century, a sentence of strangulation was usually commuted to exile, but the term *strangulation* was still used, presumably for deterrent effect.

The tradition of harsh punishment to achieve general deterrence remained after the Communist Party took control in 1949 and declared the People's Republic of China. Following the preferred tradition in other socialist countries, Chinese officials turned to a single pistol shot to the back of the head as the method of execution. To emphasize the deterrent goal of the executions, China has made sure that executions are well publicized and accompanied with appropriate propaganda. As expressed by one Chinese court official, "by killing one we educate one hundred" (quoted in Lepp, 1990, p. 1015). News of executions is spread throughout the country with the aid of television, radio, and the press, and occasionally an execution is carried out in public or a corpse may remain exposed after the punishment.

Although deterrence seems to be the primary justification for capital punishment in China, retribution also has an important role. The highly publicized process of punishment—sometimes including the public parading of condemned prisoners with head bowed and placards hung from their neck to announce their crime—is as much an outlet for vengeance and outrage as it is a means of deterrence. Evidence of such

WEB PROJECT

Death Penalty Database

Go to Cornell Law School's death penalty database at https://www.deathpenaltyworldwide.org/search.cfm and read about how to use the "filter search" option. After you are comfortable with how it works and what variables are available, form two or three questions (e.g., "Which countries authorize stoning as a method of execution?" and "In which countries can one be executed for burglary?") and conduct a search. Write a few paragraphs in which you state the question asked, the results, and your reaction to what you found.

feelings is often found in the pronouncement of death sentences that include a declaration by the court that "the people are extremely indignant." In other sentences, in which the punishment is life or long imprisonment, the court may simply announce that the people are only "very indignant" (quoted in Lepp, 1990, p. 1022).

In 2005, the Chinese press reported on several miscarriages of justice in death penalty cases and there was widespread suspicion that too many innocent people are being sentenced to death (Yardley, 2005). Reforming capital punishment became a government priority, and a particularly well-publicized procedural change was the transfer of power to approve death sentences from the local courts to the Supreme People's Court. The local courts, it was believed, were less likely to provide a safeguard against unfair proceedings. In addition, the death penalty is now imposed for fewer crimes than in the past. In 2011, 13 economy-related nonviolent crimes (e.g., smuggling cultural relics, gold, and silver) were removed from the death penalty eligible list, and another 9 crimes (e.g., smuggling weapons, raising funds by means of fraud, arranging for or forcing another person to engage in prostitution, and counterfeiting currency) were removed in 2015 ("China ends death penalty for 9 crimes," 2015).

In addition to reducing the number of crimes for which the death penalty can be imposed, reforms in the use of capital punishment are found in an increased use of China's policy of *sihuan zhidu*, or suspended death sentence. In an interesting twist to what appears to be a harsh and vengeful system, Chinese law permits suspension of the death sentence in certain situations. The Chinese criminal law says that "If the immediate execution of a criminal punishable by death is not deemed necessary, a two-year suspension of execution may be pronounced simultaneously with the imposition of the death sentence" (People's Republic of China, 1979, Article 48). Even more interesting is the fact that during this period of suspension, offenders who do not intentionally commit another crime are to have the sentence reduced to life imprisonment. If the court determines that the offender has demonstrated meritorious service, the sentence should be reduced to not less than 15 years and no more than 20 years. Where, at the end of the 2-year suspension, if there is verified evidence that the condemned person has intentionally committed another crime, the death penalty is to be carried out (People's Republic of China, 1979, Article 50).

The suspended death sentence policy was used in the past primarily for political prisoners, young offenders, and pregnant women (Lepp, 1990). More recently, it has become a useful alternative to execution and has played a significant role in downsizing the volume of capital sentences during the past decade. Although there are clear benefits in having an alternative to the death penalty, Miao (2016) warns that uncritical acceptance and unrestrained expansion of the suspended death sentences could lead to inconsistency, justify miscarriage of justice, and violate prisoners' basic rights. These concerns are especially relevant given the new and harsher forms of suspended death sentences that provide for restricted commutation and that allow the suspension without the possibility of commutation and parole.

NONCUSTODIAL SANCTIONS

Corporal and capital punishments receive considerable attention when discussing sentence types, but in most countries the more typical sentences are ones served at liberty in the community. Probation, for example, is commonly known and is a frequently used sanction in many countries. However, other noncustodial sanctions are also found. Our discussion emphasizes probation around the world after noting a few of those other community sentences.

International Standards

The U.N. Standard Minimum Rules for Noncustodial Measures (the Tokyo Rules) were adopted by the General Assembly in 1990 and provide the primary international standards for community sanctions (United Nations, 1990b). The rules are designed to promote the use of noncustodial sentences and to provide minimum safeguards to persons subject to prison alternatives. The Tokyo Rules (after the city where the rules were adopted) are meant to identify generally accepted good principles and practices for imposing and implementing noncustodial sentences. They have application for both community corrections in general and probation more specifically, as the following sections indicate.

Community Corrections

The Tokyo Rules identify noncustodial sentences as including furloughs, halfway houses, work or education release, parole, remission (reprieve), and pardon. The guiding principle is to provide a wide range of alternatives to prison and to encourage the early release and reintegration into society of those who were sent to prison. An especially popular example of such sanctions is community service orders.

Poland's Criminal Code provides for a number of prison alternatives, including the "restriction of liberty." Under this sanction, the offender is not placed in prison but instead must remain at a specified residence and must complete unpaid work as determined by the court. The penalty, which is imposed in months, will be for at least 1 month but no more than 12 months. The work is performed at a charitable or nonprofit organization and is likely to involve between 20 and 40 hours per month (Republic of Poland, 1997; Rudnev, n.d.). In the Czech Republic, the court may impose community service as a prison alternative when a sentence of up to 5 years is applicable. The community service sentence, which may be in conjunction with other sentences such as a fine, can include 50–400 hours of compulsory work in the local community or for the general interests of society. The work is to be performed without pay during the offender's otherwise free time. Failure to complete the community service obligation may cause the court to replace the work obligation with a prison sentence at a rate of 1 day of imprisonment for 2 hours of community service (Penal Reform International, n.d.).

In South Australia, community service is also a court-ordered sentence; it can be for up to 320 hours (40 days) over a maximum period of 18 months (Department for Correctional Services, 2011). Offenders sentenced to community service clean waterways, build boat ramps, restore historical sites, and clean litter from roadsides. In France, community service is imposed as the main sentence (e.g., 200 hours to be performed within 6 months) or in combination with a suspended sentence (e.g., 3 months' suspended sentence with the requirement to perform 200 hours of community service within 6 months). Should the offender fail to complete the required work, a prison sentence or fine may be imposed (if the community service sentence was of the first type) or the suspended sentence (the second type) may be totally or partially revoked (Durnescu, 2014; Picquart, 2005).

Growing in popularity, first in North America and Britain and then more recently in Western Europe, Australasia, and Singapore, is the use of electronic monitoring (called electronic tagging in some countries) as an alternative to pretrial detention, a condition of community release, as an actual sentence in lieu of serving a short prison term, and as a condition for early release (Cavadino & Dignan, 2006; Durnescu, 2014; Stacey, 2006). The addition of a surveillance component emphasized a more punitive than rehabilitative aspect of community corrections, and this approach was found throughout Europe and the United States in the late 1980s and the 1990s. Classifying and treating offenders according to the level of risk the offenders presented was the orienting philosophy and a result that continues today are community sanctions that are more clearly alternatives to prison (Durnescu, 2014).

This brief review of community service sentences indicates the typical community service sanctions in general. The number of hours may vary quite a bit, but there is agreement that the type of work completed should be unpaid and of benefit to the general community.

Probation

Students of criminology and criminal justice are familiar with the work of Boston shoemaker John Augustus in establishing a basis for probation as a sentence for criminal offenders. Resulting in part from his efforts, the first law actually providing for paid probation officers supervising both children and adults was enacted by the Massachusetts legislature on April 26, 1878. Those same students are often less familiar with the role played by Matthew Hill in England toward the use of probation in Europe.

Probation in England actually developed in a manner similar to its progression in the United States. In early 1841, the same year John Augustus began his volunteer probation work, Matthew Hill, a court recorder in Birmingham, added supervision by relatives or volunteers to the existing practice of releasing offenders to their parents or trade master after 1 day's imprisonment. In his book about his experiences, Hill explains that beginning in 1841 he would identify juvenile offenders who were not wholly corrupt and hand them over to persons willing to act as guardians (Timasheff, 1941).

Probation continued to develop in England at a pace similar to its growth in Massachusetts. Massachusetts made probation formal with legislation in 1878, and an English statute followed in 1879. There was, however, an important difference between the two jurisdictions' use of probation. The Massachusetts law provided for paid probation officers, but the English model avoided the use of organized supervision and the assignment of officials specifically responsible for probation. Instead, English magistrates, police officers, and volunteers were expected to watch over the cases. Not until 1907 did the English Parliament pass a bill providing for appointment of paid probation officers to supervise those offenders placed on probation.

The use of organized supervision in Massachusetts and the preference for unorganized supervision in England provided two models for other countries to consider as the concept of probation grew. A brief review of probation's development in other countries shows some of the different directions the American and English innovation took.

PROBATION'S HISTORY AROUND THE WORLD   Probation in continental Europe lagged behind its development in Massachusetts by some 40 years. The reasons for this delay were the severing of ties to historical institutions and procedures (e.g., benefit of clergy and recognizance) that had given common law countries an important base from which to work. Further, the civil legal tradition's predominance in continental Europe meant judges had less freedom to experiment with punishment and sentences than did their counterparts in the common legal tradition (Timasheff, 1941). Thus, the introduction of probation could come about only through legislation in countries with a civil legal tradition.

France (see Map A.10) was among the first European countries to enact a law containing aspects of probation (in 1891), but not until 1958 did French law allow for a formal sentence to supervised probation. France's 1891 legislation was influenced by the English law of 1879 and had been under discussion by the French Parliament since 1884 when Berenger introduced it in continental Europe. In its final form, French "probation" was used for persons who had not previously been sentenced to prison for either a misdemeanor or felony but in the current case had received a prison sentence or a fine.

This probation, therefore, was of the "suspended execution of sentence" type. The suspension term was 5 years (the longest sentence mid-level courts could impose) and could result in placing offenders in prison if they committed another offense. This is not, however, a true example of probation because the law did not provide for supervision of the probationer's behavior. When supervised probation was implemented in 1958, France finally had a formal probation procedure.

Other countries adopted procedures reminiscent of American probation's origin but without the supervision aspect. Belgium's 1888 law called for probation through suspension of sentencing rather than France's suspension of execution; parts of Switzerland passed laws in 1891 that directed benevolent societies to help the offenders find jobs, a nod toward supervision; in Germany, probation took a form more accurately seen as conditional pardon. Eventually the American model—that is, probation with organized supervision—grew in popularity. Countries such as Denmark (in 1905) were placing offenders under the supervision of the Prisoner's Aid Society, and Hungary (in 1908) used either salaried officers or volunteers to supervise behavior. The aspect of supervision took strong hold in Europe; by 1940, only Finland, Estonia, and Romania had failed to include provisions in their criminal law for care and guidance of probationers (Timasheff, 1941).

Because of their historical and legal ties to continental Europe, Latin American countries first followed a similar path that built on the use of suspended execution of sentence and only later incorporated supervision. The penal codes of Costa Rica (1924), Mexico (1921), and Colombia (1936) provided for supervision by authority, but that authority was essentially a kind of police surveillance rather than guidance by a probation officer. Countries of Asia and Africa often had probation enforced during colonization (e.g., French and Dutch colonies emphasized the suspended sentence aspect) or by nations keeping the country in semi-independent status (e.g., in the 1930s probation in the Philippine Islands incorporated the American use of supervision). Asian and African countries having independent status in the first several decades of the twentieth century showed variation in probation as diverse as that found on the European continent. In Egypt, probation was possible only to those who had never been imprisoned for more than 1 week and had never before received probation. In both Japan and China, a person could receive probation multiple times as long as he or she had never been sent to prison. The Chinese law of 1912 allowed for supervision by the police, charitable organizations, government officials, members of the public, or even the offender's relatives (Timasheff, 1941).

By the mid-twentieth century, it was obvious that the idea of probation was one whose time had come. It was equally obvious, however, that there would be variations on the basic theme as different countries and different sections of a single country modified the Massachusetts and English models.

PROBATION TODAY   A defining characteristic of contemporary probation practices around the world is that they attempt to reintegrate the offender into the society. In doing so, the offender is making a symbolic apology, and the community is offering symbolic forgiveness. The balance is the key! The probation service must not come to be seen as more concerned with the offender's needs than with those of the community (nor would the reverse be desirable) because both sets of concerns are important and must be addressed in balance. Of course, as with so many things that must be balanced, achieving and maintaining that equilibrium are not easily accomplished. As a result, probation is provided in a variety of ways among the world's countries and even by jurisdictions within countries.

In most jurisdictions where it is an established sanction, probation agencies are responsible for the following:

- Providing information to other criminal justice agencies (e.g., presentence reports that assist the judge in determining an appropriate sentence)

- Case supervision (e.g., assisting the reintegration process and monitoring offender compliance)
- Enforcement (e.g., initiating revocation proceedings when the offender violates conditions of probation)

Klaus (1998) provides a complete review of these (and a few other) responsibilities for probation and notes that each is accomplished to a different extent and in varying ways by probation agencies around the world. For example, probation officers in some systems become involved very early in the judicial process (e.g., providing bail assessment and bail supervision), but in other systems they participate in the process only after a person has pled or been found guilty. Case supervision under some systems is limited to persons who have been sentenced to noncustodial supervision; in other systems, the service extends to persons being released from custody (using terms familiar to Americans, probation and parole are combined under some systems and distinct under others). Enforcement responsibilities vary from systems that allow only the judiciary to modify (e.g., add conditions, add other sanctions, or revoke probation) the probation sentence to systems in which the probation service itself (or a quasi-judicial body such as a probation board) can make changes or impose disciplinary measures.

Probation is typically provided by a government agency, but in a few countries private organizations take the lead (van Kalmthout & Durnescu, 2008). Probation in the Netherlands, for example, is a private initiative and in Austria probation services are provided by a private organization that falls under the jurisdiction of the federal government.

CUSTODIAL SANCTIONS

As with the variation in noncustodial sanctions around the world, there are also differences among countries in the use of custodial sanctions. Essentially, all countries use imprisonment (often called deprivation of liberty) as a sentence type, but there is considerable disparity in its frequency of use. Some countries use custodial sentences almost exclusively, whereas others use them very seldom. A country's preference for custodial over noncustodial sentences may be the result of a specific policy (e.g., the lawmakers set imprisonment as the only or primary punishment for crimes), court predilections (e.g., judges have other options but consistently choose imprisonment), or system infrastructure (e.g., prison alternatives are authorized but have not been sufficiently developed).

This section reviews the use of imprisonment around the world by comparing prison populations, providing a description of imprisonment in a few countries, and considering the particular issues of women and minorities in prison. We begin by noting some of the international standards by which a country's prison system may be gauged.

International Standards

The U.N. Convention against Torture and Other Cruel, Inhuman or Degrading Treatment or Punishment (discussed earlier with corporal and capital punishment) is certainly applicable to prison conditions and the treatment of prisoners, but our discussion here concentrates on the U.N. Standard Minimum Rules for the Treatment of Prisoners. The original version of those rules was first adopted in 1957, but in 2015 those rules were revised and adopted as the Nelson Mandela Rules to honor the legacy of the late President of South Africa who spent 27 years in prison during his struggle for global human rights (United Nations, 2015).

Robben Island, SA
South Africa's Robben Island prison is where Nelson Mandela spent most of his 27 years of imprisonment and is now a world heritage site and a South African national monument.
Darrenp/Shutterstock

The rules are in two parts. Part I (rules 1–85) covers the general management of institutions and is applicable to all categories of prisoners (e.g., criminal or civil, untried or convicted). Part II (rules 86–122) has rules applicable to special categories of prisoners, such as those under sentence, those awaiting trial, the mentally ill, or civil prisoners. The latter category, which occurs only seldom around the world, refers to persons who are imprisoned for nonpayment of a debt or who are sent to prison by a judicial authority other than a criminal court. Examples of Part I rules can be summarized as follows:

- There shall be no discrimination based on sex, race, ethnicity, religion, and so on although individual religious beliefs and moral precepts should be respected.
- Men and women should be kept in separate facilities or, if in the same facility, in separate locations within the facility. There should be similar separation of young offenders from adults and of civil offenders from criminals.
- Prisoners awaiting trial should be kept separate from convicted prisoners. (This rule seems odd to American readers until we note that most countries do not have both jails for persons awaiting trial and prisons for those convicted. Instead, a single facility may hold both types of prisoners.)
- Prisoners should receive appropriate nutrition, exercise, medical attention, clothing, and bedding and be allowed to maintain personal cleanliness.
- Prison staff are encouraged to use conflict prevention and alternative dispute resolution techniques to prevent disciplinary offenses and to resolve conflicts.
- Solitary confinement should be used only in exceptional cases and even then as a last resort. It should not be used at all for prisoners with mental or physical disabilities that could be exacerbated by that confinement.

Part II rules cover the following:

- All appropriate means should be used (e.g., academic and vocational training, casework, employment counseling, and religious care) to provide treatment that leads to law-abiding and self-supporting lives after the prisoner's release.

- Sufficient work of a useful nature (preferably one providing marketable skills after release) shall be provided to keep prisoners actively employed for a normal working day.
- As soon after admission to prison as possible, each inmate should undergo a classification process designed to determine a treatment program appropriate to his or her individual needs, capacities, and disposition.
- Persons who have severe mental disabilities shall not be detained in prisons, and arrangements shall be made to remove them to mental health facility as soon as possible. Prisoners suffering from other mental diseases or abnormalities shall be observed and treated in specialized institutions under medical management.

There are also the Basic Principles for the Treatment of Prisoners (adopted by the General Assembly in 1990) that were developed to assist in implementing the standard rules, but they are simply more concise statements of the standard minimum rules and provide no additional standards (United Nations, 1990a).

Prison Populations

A popular way to compare the use of imprisonment by country is to measure their respective incarceration rates with a basic formula to determine each country's rate of imprisonment (Ir).

$$Ir = \frac{\text{Number of Persons Held in Custody}}{\text{Total Population of Country}} \times 100{,}000$$

Applying that formula to the United States results in an incarceration rate (i.e., total number of persons held in state and federal prisons and in local jails) of 690 per 100,000 residents (Kaeble, Glaze, Tsoutis, & Minton, 2015). But, the ease with which this has been calculated is deceiving.

We encounter definitional and methodological problems when we figure incarceration rates in this manner. Definition problems come from differences about what counts as a prison and who counts as a prisoner. For example, some countries count the people in prisons, jails, and residential community corrections facilities. Others may count only persons in prisons and jails. A similar problem is posed by the question of whether juvenile facilities are counted as prisons and whether countries that send mentally ill criminals to hospitals include those hospitals among their prison count. In the United States, the Bureau of Justice Statistics distinguishes between the incarceration rate (the population in prison or jail) and the imprisonment rate (essentially, the prison population only).

Besides the problem of deciding what constitutes a prison, there is the additional problem of deciding who is a prisoner. In some countries, pretrial detainees spend months or years awaiting trial. In other countries, the average stay in an unconvicted status is comparatively short and may not count as prisoner status. Some persons may be in prison for civil rather than criminal offenses. Is it appropriate to count persons serving time for nonpayment of fines with others who are truly criminal offenders? Because neither the facility (i.e., the prison) nor the unit (i.e., the prisoner) of count is universally defined, any comparison of countries concerning prison population is problematic (Rahim, 1986).

Methodological problems in calculating incarceration rates also exist. First, the numerator and denominator may not correspond. For example, the numerator comes from the adult population (where juveniles are not counted as prisoners) of a country, but the denominator includes persons of all ages living in that country. The result, therefore, reflects a downward bias because a country with a high proportion of juveniles shows a low incarceration rate even with a high prison population. In the United States, for example, the stated incarceration rate of 690 is based on the entire U.S. resident population. If the population of U.S. residents age 18 or older is used, the incarceration rate is 900 (Kaeble et al., 2015). Countries wishing to use incarceration rates as a political or public relations tool can conveniently manipulate both numerator and denominator when presenting information on their use of imprisonment.

Another problem with the denominator in the traditional *Ir* formula is its implication that everyone in a particular country has a random chance of being imprisoned. That, of course, is not true. Instead of reflecting a random selection process, a country's imprisonment rate may be more correctly given per 100,000 arrests, crimes, prosecutions, or convictions (Buck & Pease, 1993; Lynch, 1988; Rahim, 1986). Other problems come from using the number of persons in prison on a specific date rather than the number of admissions to prison over a certain time. Lynch calls the former figure "stock design" and notes that the likelihood of an offender's being in prison on a given day is a function of sentence length. Therefore, stock designs overrepresent more serious offenders with longer sentences. Lynch prefers the "flow design" because it uses the number of admissions over time and thereby separates the tendency to incarcerate from the length of sentence served. The flow design has its disadvantage, too, in that it risks double counting inmates who may be released and then returned during the time period for technical reasons rather than for having committed a new crime.

A variety of alternative formulas to find a country's use of imprisonment have been offered. Rahim (1986) believes that the rate should be the number of persons sentenced to prison divided by the number of persons convicted during the same year. Lynch (1988) suggests dividing the number of persons admitted to prison by the number of arrests made during the same year. Buck and Pease (1993), expanding on both Rahim and Lynch, applied this reasoning to their analysis of European imprisonment rates from 1985 by expressing the number of prisoners in relation to recorded crime rather than to total population. Because some countries may record quite trivial crimes compared to those recorded in other countries, Buck and Pease suggested that it is even more appropriate to compare the prison population to the number of prosecutions in a country. Of course, there is then the problem that some countries prosecute more trivial offenses than do other countries. Well, then, how about a formula that takes offense seriousness into account?

When Buck and Pease performed the calculations, they found that England and Wales (typically high in comparison with other European countries when the traditional *Ir* formula is used) did indeed have a higher prison population per conviction of the most serious offenses but a much lower population per conviction of the least serious offenses. The point that England and Wales are harsh (i.e., likely to imprison) to the most serious offenders but lenient (i.e., unlikely to imprison) to the less serious is hidden when the traditional *Ir* formula is used.

Despite the appropriate criticism offered by Buck and Pease, Lynch, and Rahim, we will still use the traditional method to find incarceration rates because of a lack of the necessary numbers to compute rates as suggested by critics of the traditional method. Although much easier than a decade ago, obtaining incarceration rates in a consistent manner remains difficult. Further, when they are available, it is most often in the "total prisoners divided by total population" method. Therefore, despite its problems, the traditional incarceration rate is best for comparing the largest number of countries and, as such, becomes the means for our categorization of countries. We will heed the warnings of the critics and proceed cautiously in applying the results of these calculations.

Prison Systems

Figure 8.3 orders selected countries around the world from high to low rates of imprisonment. Note that there appears to be no pattern based on the legal tradition to which the country belongs. Countries from all regions and each legal tradition are well dispersed throughout the list. It would be difficult to argue that use of imprisonment is a function of a country's legal family or geographical location.

Given the definitional and methodological problems just noted, it seems unwise to try to distinguish among countries with somewhat similar rates. It probably is not safe, for example, to claim that South Africa uses imprisonment less than does Brazil or more than does Taiwan. The rates in the three countries are just too close together to discuss reasons for differences that may not exist or may exist in a different order if measured otherwise. On the other hand, it seems unlikely that definitional and methodological problems account for the standing of New Zealand in comparison with that of Finland. A difference of almost 150 suggests, at the very least, that one country imprisons its citizens more than the other country does. Similarly, statistics for England and Wales—falling around the middle of the chart—probably really does provide a middle example.

To get an idea of incarceration across the extremes, we take a brief look at the prison system in three countries that represent the high, middle, and low sections of Figure 8.3: Brazil, Australia, and India.

BRAZIL For decades, Brazil's (see Map A.4) prisons have been identified as essentially inhumane, corrupt, and degrading. In their various reports on human rights conditions,

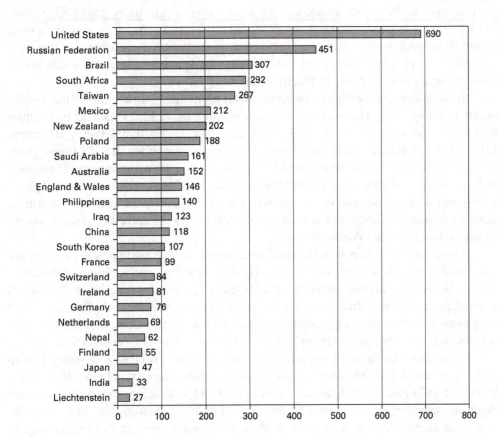

FIGURE 8.3 Imprisonment Rates per 100,000 Population for Selected Countries

Source: Based on World Prison Brief, Institute for Criminal Policy Research (August, 2016). Data available from http://www.prisonstudies.org/highest-tolowest/prison-population-total.

YOU SHOULD KNOW!

World Prison Populations

Drawing on data from several sources, Walmsley (2016) provides a number of interesting key points regarding the world's prison population:

- More than 10.35 million people are held in penal institutions throughout the world, more than half of them in Brazil, China, Russia, or the United States.
- Most of the world's countries (55 percent) have incarceration rates below 150 per 100,000 population.
- Prison populations vary considerably by regions and within continents:
  - The median rate in western African countries is 52 but is 188 in southern African countries.
  - The median rate for South American countries is 252 but is 347 in Caribbean countries.
  - The median rate for south central Asian countries (essentially the Indian subcontinent) is 74 but is 166 in the central Asian countries.
  - The median rate for Western European countries is 84 but is 236 for countries spanning Europe and Asia (e.g., Russia and Turkey).
  - In Oceania (including Australia and New Zealand), the median rate is 155.
- The total of female prisoners has increased proportionately more than the male total in every continent, with the result being the proportion of women and girls now being almost 7 percent of the world prison population compared with about 5 percent in 2000.

Walmsley notes that the use of median rates for world regions helps minimize the effect of countries with untypically high or low rates when comparing prison populations.

Human Rights Watch has consistently condemned Brazil for severe prison overcrowding and horrendous detention conditions that range from the presence of rats and diseased pigeons to the use of torture and the domination of prisons by gangs. That situation led Human Rights Watch to identify Brazil's prisons as one of the country's main human rights problems—noting that national and international sources agree that prisons and other places of detention hold inmates in scandalously abusive conditions (Human Rights Watch, 1998, 2008, 2016a, 2016b).

Brazil has one of the highest incarceration rates in the world and one of the world's largest penal systems. The prison population of more that 622,000 is held in facilities with an official capacity of about 372,000 (Institute for Criminal Policy Research, 2016). That 157 percent occupancy level is clearly one reason for Brazil's prison problems. An indication of how those crowded conditions impact prisoners' health is found in the prevalence of HIV infection (60 times greater in prison than for the overall population) and tuberculosis (40 times greater in prison). Inadequate medical screening, along with poor sanitation and ventilation, contributes to the spread of disease among inmates (Human Rights Watch, 2016a).

Prison administration is at the state level, so the nearly 1,400 prison facilities are distributed across 26 state prison systems. There is, however, one additional prison system for the federal district—which includes the administrative region of Brasilia. A national penal law specifies how all prisons should be managed and what rights and obligations are afforded to all prisoners and prison staff. However, those rules are regularly and consistently ignored (Human Rights Watch, 1998; Lemgruber, 2005).

Upon arrest, in the ideal anyway, the criminal suspect is taken to a police lockup for booking and initial detention. If not released within a few days, he or she is transferred to a jail or house of detention to await trial and sentencing. Convicted prisoners should be transferred to a prison facility, possibly after spending the first weeks or months in an observation center where trained personnel study (using interviews and testing) his or her behavior and attitude. The resulting information, along with such factors as sentence length, perceived dangerousness, and type of crime, should be used to determine which prison or other penal facility is best equipped to reform his or her criminal tendencies. Ideally, persons beginning their sentence in a prison should eventually be transferred to less-secure facilities (e.g., halfway houses) in order to allow greater freedom and gain useful skills prior to return to the community.

In reality, that progression rarely occurs because the country's penal system lacks the physical infrastructure needed to follow this ideal. In many states, for example, halfway houses simply do not exist (Human Rights Watch, 1998). Where such facilities do exist, they lack sufficient capacity to handle the inmate numbers. Problems begin at the police lockup level where 25 percent of Brazil's prison population is found. Lemgruber, a former director of one of the state prison systems, explains that such a high percentage of prisoners in a facility that by law is to be used only to hold persons giving testimony, being screened, or having their fingerprints taken is inappropriate at best and illegal at worst. Nationwide, nearly 40 percent of the persons in police lockups have already been sentenced (and therefore should be transferred to a prison or other penal facility), and in many states convicted prisoners serve their entire sentence in these lockups.

The demographics of Brazil's inmate population is similar to most everywhere else. More than half of the prisoners are between 18 and 29 years old, and the vast majority are poor, male, and have not completed first grade. Many of the young men are in prison for carrying small amounts of drugs and they often remain in prison for 5 to 15 years. In rural locations, men and women sometimes share cells (Human Rights Watch, 1998; Lemgruber, 2005; McLoughlin, 2016).

Explanations for Brazil's crowded prisons are often linked to soaring crime rates that were responded to with "get tough" measures putting more offenders in prison for longer periods of time. Rather than using the limited prison capacity for violent offenders, some 30 percent of sentenced offenders (and at least that percentage of pretrial detainees) committed crimes identified as drug related, theft, or "other."

Internal efforts at improving Brazil's prison situation have been generally ineffective. Not surprisingly, suggestions are made increasingly by external sources. Human Rights Watch, for example, encourages changes in many areas (e.g., decreasing instances of abuse and brutality by police and guards, limiting police lockups to persons in short-term detention, improving physical conditions and health care), but consider the ones related to overcrowding. Those suggestions include expanding the possibilities of pretrial release, establishing the full array of prison facilities identified in the national prison law, and encouraging judges to make greater use of noncustodial sanctions in appropriate cases.

One change is showing good potential, however. Beginning in 2014, Brazil's states have started to bring detainees before a judge promptly after arrest for custody hearings. At those hearings, judges determine whether pretrial detention is warranted and may be able to detect whether the detainee had been subjected to torture or mistreatment—a major problem in Brazil. Data from one state where custody hearings are used show that in 50 percent of the hearings the judges determined that pretrial detention was not warranted and pretrial release was ordered—compared with only 10 percent of the cases receiving pretrial release when a custody hearing was not used (Human Rights Watch, 2016a). Having fewer people under pretrial detention is considered by many to be an important step for relieving Brazil's crowded prisons and some of the problems related to that crowding.

AUSTRALIA Each of Australia's (see Map A.6) six states and two territories has responsibility for the operation and management of prison facilities in their jurisdiction. There are no federal prisons, and federal prisoners (persons charged and sentenced under a Commonwealth statute or transferred from another country) serve their sentence in a state or territory facility. There are more than 111 institutions across the country, with

85 being government operated, 9 privately operated, and the remainder being local court or detention centers (Australian Bureau of Statistics, 2016; Institute for Criminal Policy Research, 2016).

There are about 38,000 persons in full-time custody across Australia, with more than half being in New South Wales (33 percent of the prisoners) and Queensland (20 percent). Prisoners held in medium- or maximum-security facilities (79 percent of all prisoners) are confined by a secure physical barrier, whereas 21 percent of prisoners are in open custody (minimum-security) facilities that do not require confinement to a secure perimeter—even though a physical barrier might exist (Australian Bureau of Statistics, 2016).

Aboriginal and Torres Strait Islander prisoners comprise the main minority categories and, although they are about 2 percent of the total Australian population age 18 and over, they represent 28 percent of the adult prisoner population (Australian Bureau of Statistics, 2016).

Although overcrowding is not to the extent as that found in Brazil, some commentators are expressing concern that Australia is becoming a nation of captives with ever growing numbers of prisoners (Bagaric, 2015; Rubinsztein-Dunlop, 2014). The number of prisoners nationwide (the highest ever in Australia) is seen as a result of a tough on crime policy that is providing unprecedented growth in the prison population—approaching capacity in some jurisdictions. For example, the situation got so severe in Victoria that the state government began placing prisoners in shipping containers in 2014 (Rubinsztein-Dunlop, 2014). Women, especially indigenous women, are the fastest rising group of prisoners—nearly doubling over a decade.

Because New South Wales holds one-third of Australia's prisoners and operates the country's largest prison system, we will take a brief look at that state's system as an example of prisons in Australia. Corrective Services New South Wales (CSNSW) is responsible for the management of offenders in custody and in the community throughout the state. There are 35 correctional facilities at all security levels in NSW and more than 11,000 inmates in custody. Rehabilitation is a priority, and more than 40 evidence-based rehabilitation programs are designed to address criminal behavior traits. Offenders with the highest risk of reoffending are targeted. Specific programs include ones directed toward aggressive and violent behavior, addiction, and reintegration to the community (New South Wales Government, 2016).

Real work experience and vocational training for inmates is provided by Corrective Services Industries (CSI), which operates workshops and factories in prisons. The products and services under CSI include furniture, printing, agriculture, food services, and a sawmill. About 80 percent of eligible inmates were employed by CSI and were able to receive training and attitude development that can enhance their employability upon release to the community. The inmates working under CSI receive weekly wages ranging from about 25 to 70 Australian dollars for a 5-day 30-hour workweek. The money earned can be used to purchase grocery and other items available to inmates, assist with their family responsibilities by sending some money home, make contributions to victims' compensation, and save money for their release (New South Wales Government, 2016).

Students familiar with the U.S. prison system will find many similarities to the description of prisons in NSW. An additional similarity is a turn toward the use of private prisons. Just as some U.S. states and the federal government are contracting prison services to private companies, so too are Australian states and territories. In 2016, the NSW government was taking bids to let private operators run a medium-security jail near Sydney. And, the government warned that other public prisons that don't reduce reoffending rates will also be put up for bid. The NSW prison system is operating at 112 percent capacity and a turn toward the private sector is viewed as both a cost-cutting measure and a way to improve performance of the facility (Code, 2016).

INDIA There are 29 states in India (see Map A.9) and 7 union territories (UTs). The administration for each of these jurisdictions has responsibility for the operation of all prisons/jails in its territory. Unlike the United States—but consistent with Brazil and many other countries around the world—India houses persons awaiting trial (called undertrials in India) and convicted prisoners in the same facility. As a result, the terms *jail* and *prison* are interchangeable when referring to India's detention/imprisonment facilities.

Three categories of prisoners are housed in India's jails. Persons convicted and serving a sentence comprise about 31 percent of the total prisoner population. Most of these convicts (61 percent) were sentenced on murder charges. Most of the prisoner population is made up of the undertrial category (about 68 percent) and about 1 percent of them have been in that category of pretrial detainee for more than 5 years (National Crime Records Bureau, 2015). The remaining category (making up about 1 percent of the total population) includes the mentally ill persons, the elusive "other" grouping, and an interesting category of detenues—neither a convict nor an undertrial but rather a person who has been placed in preventive custody in the interest of preserving public order (Chakraborty & Okita, 2004). Certain officials have the authority to place individuals designated as a detenue in jail on a temporary basis and subject them to review by judicial or quasi-judicial authorities. This version of preventive detention has been criticized by some in India as a violation of human rights (Rahman, 2004).

Although variation exists within and among the states and UTs, many jurisdictions will have central jails, district jails, and subjails. Where one of those facility types is missing, another will take its role. For example, states and UTs with central jails use those facilities to house persons sentenced to death or for more than 2 years' imprisonment. District jails in that jurisdiction will house other categories of prisoners. Should a state or UT not have one or the other type, the remaining type holds all categories of offenders. Offenders sentenced to short-term imprisonment (up to about 3 months) will stay in a subjail. These subjails, which are about 55 percent of all the jail facilities in India, have a rather small capacity and are subordinate to a district or central jail (Chakraborty & Okita, 2004; National Crime Records Bureau, 2015).

In addition to the central, district, and subjails, a jurisdiction may have separate facilities for women, juveniles, habitual offenders, or trustees. Most young offenders (12–18 years old) are kept in Borstal schools (reformatories) in order to prevent contact with and exploitation by adult offenders (Chakraborty & Okita, 2004). Only a few states have coed Borstals (none of the UTs currently have Borstals), so the typical Borstal school has only young males. In those jurisdictions, young females are kept in children's homes (as are young male offenders in states without any Borstal). Unfortunately, the Borstals and children's homes have been subject to criticism that they are typically of substandard condition and provide little treatment (National Crime Records Bureau, 2015; Zalkind & Simon, 2004).

Other facility types include minimum security "open jails" for inmates exhibiting good behavior, temporary detention cells (lockups) in police stations, and jails for housing specific categories of detainees or prisoners (e.g., those violating prison regulations, persons exhibiting violent or aggressive tendencies, or others presenting particular difficulties to officials).

As shown in Figure 8.3, India has a low imprisonment rate in comparison with other countries. With a total population of more than 1 billion, there are fewer than 420,000 inmates. However, as with so many countries, India is experiencing prison overcrowding. The stated capacity of its nearly 1,400 jails is about 357,000, so it has an occupancy level at about 117 percent—with some prison operating at more than 200 percent occupancy (National Crime Records Bureau, 2015).

As with Brazil, overcrowding in India's prisons results in apparent human rights abuses. The U.S. Department of State (2015) reports that the crowded conditions present inadequate food, medical care, and sanitation circumstances, and that prison conditions in India are frequently life-threatening and fail to meet international standards. Persistent inefficiencies in the judicial system result in many instances wherein detainees spent more time in jail under pretrial detention than they would have if found guilty and sentenced to the longest possible term.

Proposed solutions, or at least responses, to prison overcrowding in India have included calls to reduce the undertrial population (e.g., speed up the trial process), make greater use of community sanctions (house arrest, electronic monitoring, and probation are often mentioned), and have a greater number of medium- and minimum-security prisons.

Our review of prison systems in countries falling at three different places in Figure 8.3's incarceration rate rankings has resulted in identification of both similarities and differences. There is one other area that these countries (and most others) have in common—an increase in the number of women prisoners.

Women in Prison

There are few constants around the world when it comes to issues of criminal justice, but here is clearly one: Women offenders everywhere have been, are being, and seemingly will be treated poorly in relation to their male counterparts. In countries in which prison conditions and treatment programs for men are reasonable, they are merely acceptable for women prisoners. In countries in which prison conditions and treatment programs for men are unsatisfactory, for women they are abysmal. Many examples indicate the extremes, but consider these for purposes of illustration:

- During his 2014 visit to prisons in Mexico, the United Nations Special Rapporteur noted that in Santa Martha prison, inmates, including mothers, are living in overcrowded conditions, must share mattresses, and have limited access to water and suitable food. More than 60 percent of women prisoners in Mexico are in mixed facilities where they tend to be held in confined areas and share common areas with male prisoners. The Special Rapporteur also observed a lack of specialized gynecological and psychological care, as well as a lack of attention to women's hygienic and biological needs. Further, there is a lack of rehabilitation programs with a gender approach (United Nations, 2014).
- At Bredtveit women's prison in Norway, inmates don't wear uniforms and guards aren't armed. Each inmate has her own room (one that looks more like a bedroom than a cell), and is allowed personal belongings including jewelry and CDs. The four-story building has common areas, a kitchen, sofas, and a television. Israel's only prison for women, Neve Tirza, is equipped with a petting zoo, a meditation room, and glow-in-the-dark fish tanks. There are conjugal visits and vacation programs where eligible prisoners can get three-day furloughs. The prison made international headlines, in 2014, when it hosted its first fashion show, complete with gowns, hairdressers, intricate makeup, and a runway (Blakinger, 2016).

The extremes presented by the conditions for women prisoners in Mexico and those in Norway and Israel highlight differences in prison systems as much as differences in the way women prisoners specifically are treated. In fact, the similarities in the way women prisoners are responded to around the world may be more striking than the differences. Much of the similarity is explained as resulting from the consistently small percentage of female inmates in all countries, the worldwide tendency to imprison drug offenders, and the general similarity of needs and problems among women prisoners.

THE SMALL NUMBERS OF WOMEN PRISONERS Explanations for a country's lack of attention or concern for its women offenders are invariably based on their small percentage of the country's inmate population. Walmsley (2015) summarizes what we know about women prisons as follows:

- Female prisoners generally comprise between 2 percent and 9 percent of a country's prison population, with the world median being 4.4 percent. Notable exceptions include Hong Kong (19 percent), Myanmar (16 percent), Bolivia (15 percent), Thailand (15 percent), and Vietnam (14 percent).
- About 700,000 women and girls are imprisoned throughout the world, and more than half of them are in the United States, China, and Russia.
- The lowest proportion of women and girls within the total prison population is in African countries (median level is about 3 percent) and the highest is in Asian countries (6 percent).
- The number of females in the world's prison has increased about 50 percent since 2000, but that increase cannot be explained simply by population growth, which rose by 18 percent during that period.

The most frequently stated problems attributed to the low numbers of women prisoners in comparison with the number of men prisoners are linked to the condition and location of the facilities for those women. As noted earlier, the Standard Minimum Rules for the Treatment of Prisoners indicate that women prisoners should be housed in separate facilities or at least in separate parts of men's prisons. That standard seems well accepted in most countries, but the small number of women offenders often makes it financially difficult to provide clearly separate prisons or even annexes.

Despite the presumption that separation by sex is desirable, few countries are responding to the problems of building and maintaining separate facilities for women prisoners by integrating women in prisons for men instead. Sweden provides an especially good example in its use of neighborhood prisons that are mixed-gender facilities. About 80 percent of the female prisoners are housed in the neighborhood, where they take part in prison activities with male prisoners. Both men and women prisoners have an opportunity for contact with the local community, and in that manner a degree of equity may be achieved that cannot be realized in large central or regional prisons (Bishop, 1991; von Hofer & Marvin, 2001).

THE IMPACT OF IMPRISONING DRUG OFFENDERS Another common theme among women prisoners around the world is their link to drug offenses. Several commentators have noted

YOU SHOULD KNOW!

Rules for Women Offenders

In December 2010, the General Assembly adopted the United Nations Rules for the Treatment of Women Prisoners and Non-custodial Measures for Women Offenders. These rules—to be known as the Bangkok Rules for the city where they were drafted—will supplement the Standard Minimum Rules for the Treatment of Prisoners (SMR) that were adopted in 1955. The Bangkok Rules recognize that female prisoners have significantly different needs than their male counterparts and encourage UN member states to take into consideration the specific needs and realities of women as prisoners when developing relevant legislation, procedures, policies, and action plans and to draw, as appropriate, on the Bangkok Rules (United Nations, 2010).

The Bangkok Rules cover such issues as the implementation of gender-sensitive prisoner classification and security risk assessments, the provision of gender-specific health care services, and the development of pre- and post-release programs that take into consideration the stigmatization and discrimination faced by women upon release from prison.

that much of the increase of women in American prisons is the result of mandatory prison sentences for drug offenders. Some have even suggested that the "war on drugs" has translated into a war on women (Chesney-Lind & Pollock, 1995; Joseph, 2006). The same may be said of drug policy in other parts of the world. For example, a repressive drug policy in most of Western Europe has caused persons sentenced for drug law violations to make up an increasing percentage of the prison population (Dünkel & van Zyl Smit, 2001).

Because of the link between many female offenders and drug use, many countries have experienced a growth in the proportion of women in their prisons. Joseph makes the point in her analysis of drug offenses in England and Wales, where she finds that (as in the United States) women are imprisoned in much greater numbers, proportionally, for drug-related crimes than for any other offense (Joseph, 2006).

The increased number of men and women being sent to prison as the world gets tough on drugs has also resulted in deteriorating prison conditions and the facilities that are pushed beyond capacity. In Mexico, more than 50 percent of sentenced federal prisoners are drug offenders (that is also true for the United States) and in Thailand the percentage is almost 60 percent (Bewley-Taylor, Hallam, & Allen, 2009). Especially important here is that in most countries women are overrepresented among drug offenders in prison. For example, drug offenders are about 22 percent of Japan's male prison population but 35 percent of its female prison population. In the Argentine federal prison system, 12 percent of the prisoners are women, but 60 percent of those women prisoners are there for drug offenses (Bewley-Taylor et al., 2009).

NEEDS AND PROBLEMS OF WOMEN PRISONERS   A final common theme to mention here is an example of the needs and problems that are more relevant to women than men prisoners. Specifically, there is a universal concern about how the relationship between an inmate mother and her child is affected by the prison sentence. There are always arguments about the desirability of caring for infants in a prison setting. In many countries, women rarely receive adequate ante- and postnatal care in prison and prison health care services in most countries are underresourced and understaffed. As a result, especially in low-income countries, a policy allowing newborns to stay with incarcerated mothers may result in children with lifelong physical and mental health problems. On the other hand, the separation of women from their children—especially in the formative years—is likely to have a traumatic and long-term effect on both mother and child. It seems like a no-win situation.

In most of the world's countries, mothers can keep their babies with them in prison up to a certain age. The age differs from country to country and typically ranges from the age of 1 to 6—sometimes even longer (United Nations, 2008). Some prison systems allow small children, whether or not they were born in prison, to live with their inmate mothers. The laggard in this area is the United States, where the federal prison system and most state prisons do not allow newborns to stay with their mothers for any length of time. A notable exception is New York, where state law provides that mothers be allowed to keep their infants until the baby is 1 year old.

WEB PROJECT
Babies in Prison

Although it is unusual in most American prisons for inmate mothers to have their newborn children with them in prison, it is rather typical in other countries. Visit the National Resource Center for Permanency and Family Connections page at http://www.hunter.cuny.edu/socwork/ nrcfcpp/info_services/children-of-incarcerated-parents.html and open a few of the documents with titles you find interesting. Write a few paragraphs explaining what the item was about and note how the information influenced your opinion regarding babies in prison.

There have clearly been improvements in the way women prisoners are treated in prisons around the world. Just as clearly, there is room for more improvement. The following recommendations for revising the way a society responds to its female offenders seem applicable to just about any country:

- The geographic dislocation of many women from their families and from community resources must be reduced.
- Programs must be specifically designed to (1) address needs such as maintaining mother–child relations, (2) treat substance abuse problems, and (3) consider the results of victimization by sexual and physical abuse.
- Educational and vocational opportunities must be provided to increase the female offender's acceptance of nontraditional work areas and increase her chances to find employment that allows independent living.
- Serious consideration should be given to achieve the preceding recommendations by significantly decreasing the use of imprisonment for female offenders and by significantly increasing the use of community-based corrections.

Minorities in Prison

Disproportionate representation of racial and ethnic minorities in American prisons is a consistent and embarrassing problem. Explanations for the disparity include the emphasis on increased involvement of minorities in criminal behavior and individual and systemic discrimination in the justice process. Whichever explanation is more accurate, the relevant point for current discussion is that the disparity exists and affects the system's structure and operation. Noting, as we do here, that racial and ethnic minorities are consistently overrepresented in prisons around the world does not suggest the problem is inevitable or unsolvable. Instead, the global nature of difficulties faced by minorities everywhere should highlight the seriousness and complexity of the problem. Unfortunately, in many of the world's countries, members of ethnic and racial minorities are significantly overrepresented in the criminal justice system generally and the prison system more specifically.

DISPARITY AROUND THE WORLD Although making up only 13 percent and 17 percent of the nation's total population, American blacks and Hispanics, respectively, account for about 37 percent and 22 percent of America's state and federal prison population (Carson, 2015). In the federal system, noncitizens comprise about 22 percent of the total prison population (Bureau of Prisons, 2016).

WEB PROJECT
Women and Foreign Prisoners Around the World

Visit the World Prison Brief page at http://www.prisonstudies.org/highest-to-lowest/prison-population-total, where you can select from several options for ranking countries by area and category. Select "Female prisoners" from the category dropdown box and press GO, then select "Entire World" for area. Click "Apply" and view the results. Write a paragraph describing your impression of the ranking. Comparing the countries at 10 percent and more with those at 3 percent and less, can you identify any common characteristic of countries in each grouping? Return to the starting page and now select "Foreign prisoners" from the category dropdown box and use "Entire World" again for area. Looking at the countries ranking in the top 15, write a paragraph suggesting reasons for why these countries might imprison such a high percentage of foreigners.

Based on her research of women prisoners, Joseph (2006) concludes that foreign nationals of ethnic minority background, primarily blacks, are overrepresented in prison in England and Wales. Unfortunately, similar disparity is found in both custodial and noncustodial arenas of other countries where minorities and noncitizens are often found in numbers disproportionate to their presence in the country's total population (Hammond, 2005).

Many countries do not keep statistics specifically on ethnic minorities. In France, for example, a 1978 law specifically bans the collection and computerized storage of race- or ethnicity-based data and as a result there is no official data on the race or ethnicity of French citizens (Bleich, 2001). The countries providing that data show disproportions similar to those in the United States. For example, in Canada, Aboriginals are about 4 percent of the general population but about 25 percent of the prison population (CBC News, 2016). In Hungary, the Roma population (estimated at between 5 percent and 8 percent) is more than 40 percent of the prison population (Nagy, 2001). More typical than statistics on ethnicity are data on foreign nationals.

Foreign prisoners have become a greater problem for many European countries since the opening of country borders in the early 1990s. Survey results from the Council of Europe (2003) indicate that reporting countries have a mean average of about 17 percent foreign prisoners. The range went from highs of 83 percent of Andorra's prison population and 71 percent of Switzerland's to lows (all less than 1 percent) in Albania, Armenia, Latvia, Romania, and San Marino. Countries outside of Europe with high percentages of foreign prisoners (Institute for Criminal Policy Research, 2016) include the United Arab Emirates (92 percent), Saudi Arabia (92 percent), and Gambia (67 percent).

A country's demographic statistics typically do not often indicate a country's percentage of foreigners (the closest is often a count of "foreign-born" who may, of course, be citizens), so it is not assumed that a high percentage of foreigners in the total prison population is actually disproportionate to the percentage of foreigners in the total population. However, it seems unlikely that the total population of any country is comprised of more than 50 percent foreigners. On that assumption, we may conclude that at least countries with prison populations exceeding 50 percent foreigners (e.g., Austria, Gambia, Israel, Qatar, Switzerland, United Arab Emirates) have disparity. But it seems reasonable to also suspect disparity in other countries with high percentages of foreign prisoners (e.g., Belgium—45 percent, Norway—35 percent, and Italy—34 percent).

Some authors suggest that a disproportionate representation of ethnic minorities in these countries may be the result of selective criminalization practices and/or selective prosecution of certain ethnic group minorities (Dünkel & van Zyl Smit, 2001). Others believe it is not so much a discriminatory justice system that gets a person to prison as it is the typically poor social and economic status that foreigners and ethnic minorities have in many countries (Ruggiero, 1995). Both explanations are similar to ones debated in the United States, and it is increasingly obvious that each country's minority groups present similar problems and concerns to each country.

It is difficult to find a country anywhere in the world at which charges of institutionalized racism and discrimination are not levied—blacks in South Africa; Turks in Austria; Koreans and Burakumin in Japan; Finns in Sweden; Moroccans in the Netherlands; Latinos, African Americans, and Native Americans in the United States; and the list, unfortunately, goes on.

Summary

No part of the criminal justice system is easily described in a short chapter of a single book, but that point seems even more true for the corrections aspect. After reviewing the main justifications for punishment, this chapter identified four sentence types on which to concentrate: financial penalties, corporal and capital punishment, noncustodial sanctions, and custodial sanctions.

In the process of discussing each sentence type, comments were made regarding the international standards that attempt to guide nations as they implement various sanctions. Also, under each sentence type were comments that compared American practices to those in other countries. The chapter concluded with attention to the problems confronted globally by women prisoners and by prisoners who are racial and ethnic minorities.

Discussion Questions

- Research by Ruddell and Urbina (2004; see the review at the chapter's start) suggests that countries made up of people who are culturally, racially, and ethnically similar may have less harsh punishments than do countries that are more diverse. Does this seem reasonable to you? Why or why not?
- During the war in Iraq, the American military paid millions of dollars in "condolence payments" to family members of noncombatant Iraqis killed or injured during the fighting. A *New York Times* article (June 10, 2006; "The Struggle for Iraq: Civilian Losses; Compensation Payments Rising, Especially by Marines") reported that the payments were not an admission of guilt by American forces but were in keeping with Iraqi custom and meant to lessen ill will toward Americans. As discussed in this chapter, diyya payments are also meant to lessen ill will between the offender and the victim. How are "condolence payments" made by the American military similar to or different from the diyya payments made by individuals?
- Which is more humane—telling a condemned prisoner the exact day and time he or she will be executed or "surprising" the condemned on the morning of the execution?
- Many U.S. jurisdictions responded to increasing numbers of prisoners by building more prisons. Would that be a good tactic for countries such as South Africa, Brazil, and India to use in response to their overcrowding? Why or why not?

References

Amnesty International. (1995, May 3). Japan prisoners on death row wait for secret random executions. Research, Index number: ASA 22/006/1995. Retrieved from http://www.amnesty.org/en/library/info/ASA22/006/1995/en

Amnesty International. (2002, November 9). Japan: Cease all executions. Research, Index number: ASA 22/010/2002. Retrieved from http://www.amnesty.org/en/library/info/ASA22/010/2002/en

Amnesty International. (2006, July 6). Will this day be my last? The death penalty in Japan. Research, Index number: ASA 22/006/2006. Retrieved from https://www.amnesty.org/en/documents/asa22/006/2006/en/

Amnesty International. (2009, September 10). Hanging by a thread: Mental health and the death penalty in Japan. Research, Index number: ASA 22/005/2009. Retrieved from https://www.amnesty.org/documents/asa22/005/2009/en

Amnesty International. (2015, June 25). Japan: Authorities deceiving the public by resuming executions. Asia and the Pacific. Retrieved from https://www.amnesty.org/en/latest/news/2015/06/japan-authorities-deceiving-the-public-by-resuming-executions/

Amnesty International. (2016a). Death sentences and executions in 2015. Retrieved from https://www.amnesty.org/en/latest/research/2016/04/death-sentences-executions-2015/

Amnesty International. (2016b, February 23). The state of the world's human rights. Amnesty International Report, Index number: POL 10/2552/2016. Retrieved from https://www.amnesty.org/en/documents/pol10/2552/2016/en/

Angus Reid Institute. (2010, January). Two-in-five Russians would rely on death penalty. *Angus Reid Global Monitor*. Retrieved from http://angusreid.org/two_in_five_russians_would_rely_on_death_penalty/

Angus Reid Institute. (2011, August 23). Most Britons support reinstating the death penalty for murder. *Angus Reid Public Opinion*. Retrieved from http://angusreid.org/most-britons-support-reinstating-the-death-penalty-for-murder/

Angus Reid Institute. (2013, March 20). Three-in-five Canadians would bring back death penalty. *Angus Reid Public Opinion.* Retrieved from http://angusreid.org/three-in-five-canadians-would-bring-back-death-penalty/

Asad, M. (2003). *The message of the Qur'an: The full account of the revealed Arabic text accompanied by parallel transliteration.* Bitton, England: The Book Foundation.

Australian Bureau of Statistics. (2016, September 6). Summary of findings: Persons in corrective services. Corrective Services, Australia, March Quarter. Retrieved from http://www.abs.gov.au/ausstats/abs@.nsf/mf/4512.0

Bagaric, M. (2015, April 9). Prisons policy is turning Australia into the second nation of captives. *The Conversation.* Retrieved from http://theconversation.com/prisons-policy-is-turning-australia-into-the-second-nation-of-captives-38842

Bewley-Taylor, D., Hallam, C., & Allen, R. (2009). *The incarceration of drug offenders: An overview.* Report 16. Retrieved from http://www.beckleyfoundation.org/pdf/BF_Report_16.pdf

Bishop, N. (1991). Sweden. In D. van Zyl Smit & F. Dünkel (Eds.), *Imprisonment today and tomorrow* (pp. 599–631). Deventer, The Netherlands: Kluwer Law International.

Blakinger, K. (2016, January 22). From fashion shows in Israeli lockup to 'tiger chairs' in China, a look at women's prisons around the world. *Daily News.* Retrieved from http://www.nydailynews.com/news/world/women-prisons-world-article-1.2505704

Bleich, E. (2001, May 21). Race policy in France. *Brookings.* Retrieved from https://www.brookings.edu/articles/race-policy-in-france/

Brown, K. (2008). 'All they understand is force': Debating culture in operation Iraqi freedom. *American Anthropologist, 110*(4), 443–453. doi: 10.1111/j.1548-1433.2008.00077.x

Buck, W., & Pease, K. (1993). Cross-national incarceration comparisons inherently misleading. *Overcrowded Times, 4*(1), 5–6, 17.

Bureau of Consular Affairs. (2016). Consular notification and access. Department of State. Retrieved from https://travel.state.gov/content/travel/en/consularnotification.html

Bureau of Prisons. (2016, June 25). Inmate citizenship. Federal Bureau of Prisons Statistics. Retrieved from https://www.bop.gov/about/statistics/statistics_inmate_citizenship.jsp

Carson, E. A. (2015). Prisoners in 2014 (NCJ 248955). Retrieved from http://www.bjs.gov/index.cfm?ty=pbdetail&iid=5387

Cavadino, M., & Dignan, J. (2006). *Penal systems: A comparative approach.* London, UK: Sage.

CBC News. (2016). Prison watchdog says more than a quarter of federal inmates are aboriginal people. Retrieved from http://www.cbc.ca/news/aboriginal/aboriginal-inmates-1.3403647

Chakraborty, T., & Okita, K. (2004). Adult corrections in India. In J. A. Winterdyk (Ed.), *Adult corrections: International systems and perspectives* (pp. 159–197). Monsey, NY: Criminal Justice Press.

Chesney-Lind, M., & Pollock, J. (1995). Women's prisons: Equality with a vengeance. In A. Merlo & J. Pollock (Eds.), *Women, law, and social control* (pp. 155–175). Boston, MA: Allyn & Bacon.

China ends death penalty for 9 crimes. (2015, September 1). *The Straits Times.* Retrieved from http://www.straitstimes.com/asia/east-asia/china-ends-death-penalty-for-9-crimes

Code, B. (2016, March 19). Private prisons: NSW government announces plans to let private operators tender for jail at Windsor. *ABC News.* Retrieved from http://www.abc.net.au/news/2016-03-20/nsw-jails-private-prison-operators-ohn-morony-windsor/7261300

Council of Europe. (2003). *Penological information bulletin.* Strasbourg, France: Council of Europe Publishing.

Currier, C. (2015, March 4). Newly released records show US paid $6 million for civilian harm in Afghanistan. *The Intercept.* Retrieved from https://theintercept.com/2015/03/04/newly-released-records-show-us-paid-6-million-afghan-civilian-harm/

Department for Correctional Services. (2011, August 11). About community corrections. Community Corrections. Retrieved from https://web.archive.org/web/20110813143210/http://www.corrections.sa.gov.au/community%5Fcorrections/

Dubber, M. D. (1997). American plea bargains, German lay judges, and the crisis of criminal procedure. *Stanford Law Review, 49*(3), 547–605.

Dugan, A. (2015, October 15). Solid majority continue to support death penalty. *Gallup.* Retrieved from www.gallup.com/poll/186218/solid-majority-continue-support-death-penalty.aspx

Dünkel, F., & van Zyl Smit, D. (2001). Conclusion. In D. van Zyl Smit & F. Dünkel (Eds.), *Imprisonment today and tomorrow* (2nd ed., pp. 796–859). The Hague, The Netherlands: Kluwer Law International.

Durnescu, I. (2014). Community sanctions. In S. Body-Gendrot, M. Hough, K. Kerezsi, R. Levy, & S. Snacken (Eds.), *The Routledge handbook of European criminology* (pp. 409–421). New York, NY: Routledge.

Federal Republic of Germany. (1987). The German code of criminal procedure (amended version of 2014). Gesetze im Internet. Retrieved from http://www.gesetze-im-internet.de/englisch_stpo/index.html

Government Accountability Office. (2007, May 31). The Department of Defense's use of solatia and condolence payments in Iraq and Afghanistan. Military Operations, GAO-07-699. Retrieved from http://www.gao.gov/products/GAO-07-699

Hammond, N. (2005, December). Foreign national offenders and victims: Meeting the challenge to work effectively and equitably. *Probation in Europe*, (35). Retrieved from http://www.cepprobation.org/uploaded_files/december%202005%20Bulletin%2035%20-%20E.pdf

Hillsman, S. T. (1990). Fines and day fines. In M. Tonry & N. Morris (Eds.), *Crime and justice: A review of research* (Vol. 12, pp. 49–98). Chicago, IL: University of Chicago Press.

Hood, R. G. (2002). *The death penalty: A worldwide perspective* (3rd ed.). Oxford, UK: Oxford University Press.

Hughes, R. (1987). *The fatal shore*. New York, NY: Alfred A. Knopf.

Human Rights Watch. (1998, November 30). Behind bars in Brazil. Americas, Brazil. Retrieved from http://www.hrw.org/en/news/1998/11/30/behind-bars-brazil

Human Rights Watch. (2008, April 6). Universal periodic review of Brazil. Human Rights Watch's submission to the Human Rights Council. Retrieved from http://www.hrw.org/news/2008/04/06/universal-periodic-review-brazil

Human Rights Watch. (2016a). Brazil: Events of 2015. *World Report 2016* (prison conditions). Retrieved from https://www.hrw.org/world-report/2016/country-chapters/brazil#3159b0

Human Rights Watch. (2016b). *World Report 2016*. Retrieved from https://www.hrw.org/world-report/2016

Institute for Criminal Policy Research. (2016). *World Prison Brief*. Institute for Criminal Policy Research. Retrieved from http://www.prisonstudies.org/world-prison-brief

Jehle, J.-M. (2015). *Criminal justice in Germany: Facts and figures*. Retrieved from http://www.bmjv.de/SharedDocs/Downloads/DE/Statistiken/Download/Criminal_Justice_Germany_Facts_Figures.html

Joseph, J. (2006). Drug offenses, gender, ethnicity, and nationality. *The Prison Journal*, *86*(1), 140–157.

Kaeble, D., Glaze, L., Tsoutis, A., & Minton, T. (2015). Correctional populations in the United States, 2014 (NCJ 249513). Revised January 21, 2016. Retrieved from http://www.bjs.gov/index.cfm?ty=pbdetail&iid=5519

Klaus, J. F. (1998). *Handbook on probation services: Guidelines for probation practitioners and managers*. Rome, Italy: United Nations Interregional Crime & Justice Research Institute.

Lane, C. (2005, March 10). U.S. quits pact used in capital cases; foes of death penalty cite access to envoys. *Washington Post*. Retrieved from http://www.washingtonpost.com

Lemgruber, J. (2005, February 15). *The Brazilian prison system: A brief diagnosis*. Paper presented at the Woodrow Wilson International Center for Scholars (Panel on Prisons in Crisis), Washington, DC.

Lepp, A. W. (1990). Note, the death penalty in late imperial, modern, and post-Tiananmen China. *Michigan Journal of International Law*, *11*(1990), 987–1038.

Lynch, J. P. (1988). A comparison of prison use in England, Canada, West Germany, and the United States. *Journal of Criminal Law and Criminology*, *79*(1), 180–217.

McLoughlin, B. (2016, August 2). Behind the Olympics: Brazil's dirty incarceration secret. *OZY*. Retrieved from http://www.ozy.com/rising-stars/behind-the-olympics-brazils-dirty-incarceration-secret/70060

Miao, M. (2016). Two years between life and death: A critical analysis of the suspended death penalty in China. *International Journal of Law, Crime and Justice*, *45*, 26–43. doi: http://dx.doi.org/10.1016/j.ijlcj.2015.10.003

Moore, D. W. (2006, February 20). Death penalty gets less support from Britons, Canadians than Americans. *Gallup*. Retrieved from http://www.gallup.com/poll/21544/Death-Penalty-Gets-Less-Support-From-Britons-Canadians-Than-Americans.aspx

Morris, N., & Tonry, M. H. (1990). *Between prison and probation: Intermediate punishments in a rational sentencing system*. New York, NY: Oxford University Press.

Nagy, F. (2001). Hungary. In D. van Zyl Smit & F. Dünkel (Eds.), *Imprisonment today and tomorrow* (2nd ed., pp. 351–372). The Hague, The Netherlands: Kluwer Law International.

National Crime Records Bureau. (2015). *Prison statistics India 2014*. Retrieved from http://ncrb.gov.in/StatPublications/PSI/Prison2014/Full/PSI-2014.pdf

New South Wales Government. (2016). CNSW fact sheets. Corrective Services. Retrieved from http://www.correctiveservices.justice.nsw.gov.au/Pages/CorrectiveServices/csnsw-fact-sheets.aspx

O'Brien, E., & Ward, J. (1970). *The foundation of Australia*. Westport, CT: Greenwood Press.

Otterbein, K. F. (1986). *The ultimate coercive sanction: A cross-cultural study of capital punishment*. New Haven, CT: HRAF Press.

Penal Reform International. (n.d.). *The probation service in the Czech Republic*. Retrieved from http://web.archive.org/web/20051223183323/http://www.penalreform.org/english/altern_czechproba.htm

People's Republic of China. (1979). Criminal law of the People's Republic of China (amended version of 2011). Congressional-Executive Commission on China. Retrieved from http://www.cecc.gov/resources/legal-provisions/criminal-law-of-the-peoples-republic-of-china

Picquart, J.-M. (2005, August 31). Community service, the French experience. Penal Reform International. Retrieved from http://web.archive.org/web/20050831224545/http://www.penalreform.org/english/altern_csfrance.htm

Pincus, W. (2007, June 18). The measure of a life, in dollars and cents. *Washington Post*. Retrieved from http://www.washingtonpost.com

Rahim, M. A. (1986). *On the issues of international comparison of "prison population" and "use of imprisonment."* Ottawa, Canada: Ministry of the Solicitor General.

Rahman, A. F. (2004, September 7). Preventive detention an anachronism. *The Hindu.* Retrieved from http://www.hindu.com/op/2004/09/07/stories/2004090700101500.html

Rejali, D. M. (1994). *Torture & modernity: Self, society, and state in modern Iran.* Boulder, CO: Westview Press.

Republic of Poland. (1997). Criminal code (amended version of 2012). *Legislationline.* Retrieved from http://www.legislationline.org/documents/section/criminal-codes/country/10

Rice, X. (2010, October 20). Somali schoolboy tells of how Islamists cut off his leg and hand. *The Guardian.* Retrieved from http://www.guardian.co.uk/world/2010/oct/20/somali-islamists-schoolboy-amputation-ordeal

Rubinsztein-Dunlop, S. (2014, July 2). Australia's prison system overcrowded to bursting point with more than 33,000 people in jail. *ABC News.* Retrieved from http://www.abc.net.au/news/2014-07-02/austrlaian-prison-overcrowding-female-populations-growing/5567610

Ruddell, R., & Urbina, M. G. (2004). Minority threat and punishment: A cross-national analysis. *Justice Quarterly, 21*(4), 903–931.

Rudnev, V. I. (n.d.). Criminal sentencing measures as alternatives to imprisonment. Penal Reform International. Retrieved from http://web.archive.org/web/20051223200657/http://www.penalreform.org/english/altern_crimsent.htm

Ruggiero, V. (1995). Flexibility and intermittent emergency in the Italian penal system. In V. Ruggiero, M. Ryan, & J. Sim (Eds.), *Western European penal systems: A critical anatomy* (pp. 46–70). Thousand Oaks, CA: Sage.

Souryal, S. S. (2004). *Islam, Islamic law, and the turn to violence.* Huntsville, TX: Office of International Criminal Justice.

Stacey, T. (2006). Electronic tagging of offenders: A global view. *International Review of Law, Computers & Technology, 20*(1–2), 117–121. doi: 10.1080/13600860600775401

Subramanian, R., & Shames, A. (2015, October). Sentencing and prison practices in Germany and the Netherlands: Implications for the United States. Vera Institute of Justice. Retrieved from https://www.vera.org/publications/sentencing-and-prison-practices-in-germany-and-the-netherlands-implications-for-the-united-states

Timasheff, N. S. (1941). *One hundred years of probation, 1841–1941—Parts 1 & 2.* New York, NY: Fordham University Press.

United Nations. (1963). Vienna Convention on Consular Relations. Retrieved from http://legal.un.org/avl/ha/vccr/vccr.html

United Nations. (1984a). Convention against Torture and Other Cruel, Inhuman or Degrading Treatment or Punishment. Office of the High Commissioner for Human Rights. Retrieved from http://www.ohchr.org/EN/ProfessionalInterest/Pages/CAT.aspx

United Nations. (1984b). Safeguards Guaranteeing Protection of the Rights of Those Facing the Death Penalty. Office of the High Commissioner for Human Rights. Retrieved from http://www.ohchr.org/EN/ProfessionalInterest/Pages/DeathPenalty.aspx

United Nations. (1989). Second Optional Protocol to the International Covenant on Civil and Political Rights, aiming at the abolition of the death penalty. Office of the High Commissioner for Human Rights. Retrieved from http://www.ohchr.org/EN/ProfessionalInterest/Pages/2ndOPCCPR.aspx

United Nations. (1990a). Basic Principles for the Treatment of Prisoners. Office of the High Commissioner for Human Rights. Retrieved from http://www.ohchr.org/EN/ProfessionalInterest/Pages/BasicPrinciplesTreatmentOfPrisoners.aspx

United Nations. (1990b). Standard Minimum Rules for Non-custodial Measures. Office of the High Commissioner for Human Rights. Retrieved from http://www.ohchr.org/EN/ProfessionalInterest/Pages/TokyoRules.aspx

United Nations. (2008). *Handbook for prison managers and policymakers on women and imprisonment.* Retrieved from http://www.unodc.org/documents/justice-and-prison-reform/women-and-imprisonment.pdf

United Nations. (2010). United Nations Rules for the Treatment of Women Prisoners and Non-Custodial Measures for Women Offenders (the Bangkok Rules). Office of the High Commissioner for Human Rights (A/RES/65/229). Retrieved from http://www.ohchr.org/Documents/ProfessionalInterest/BangkokRules.pdf

United Nations. (2014, December 29). Report of the Special Rapporteur on torture and other cruel, inhuman or degrading treatment or punishment, Juan E. Méndez. Human Rights Council, A/HRC/28/68/Add.3. Retrieved from www.insightcrime.org/images/PDFs/UNMexicoTorture.pdf

United Nations. (2015). Standard Minimum Rules for the Treatment of Prisoners (the Nelson Mandela Rules). Office of the High Commissioner for Human Rights. Retrieved from http://www.ohchr.org/Documents/ProfessionalInterest/NelsonMandelaRules.pdf

United Nations. (2016). Universal Human Rights Instruments. Office of the High Commissioner for Human Rights. Retrieved from http://www.ohchr.org/EN/ProfessionalInterest/Pages/UniversalHumanRightsInstruments.aspx

United Nations Office on Drugs and Crime. (2004). The Seventh United Nations Survey on Crime Trends and the Operations of Criminal Justice Systems (2001–2002). Retrieved from http://www.unodc.org/unodc/en/data-and-analysis/Seventh-United-Nations-Survey-on-Crime-Trends-and-the-Operations-of-Criminal-Justice-Systems.html

U.S. Department of State. (2009, February 25). 2008 Human Rights Report: Saudi Arabia. *2008 Country Reports on Human Rights Practices*. Retrieved from http://www.state.gov/j/drl/rls/hrrpt/2008/nea/119126.htm

U.S. Department of State. (2015). India. *Country Reports on Human Rights Practices for 2015*. Retrieved from http://www.state.gov/j/drl/rls/hrrpt/humanrightsreport/index.htm?year=2015&dlid=252963

van Dijk, J., van Kesteren, J., & Smit, P. (2007). Criminal victimisation in international perspective: Key findings from the 2004–2005 ICVS and EU ICS. Retrieved from http://english.wodc.nl/onderzoeksdatabase/icvs-2005-survey.aspx?cp=45&cs=6796

van Kalmthout, A. M., & Durnescu, I. (Eds.). (2008). *Probation in Europe*. Nijmeger, The Netherlands: Wolf Legal Publishers.

Vera Institute of Justice. (1996). How to use structured fines (day fines) as an intermediate sanction (NCJ 156242). Retrieved from https://www.ncjrs.gov/pdffiles/156242.pdf

von Hofer, H., & Marvin, R. (2001). Sweden. In D. van Zyl Smit & F. Dünkel (Eds.), *Imprisonment today and tomorrow* (2nd ed., pp. 634–652). The Hague, The Netherlands: Kluwer Law International.

Walmsley, R. (2015). *World female imprisonment list* (3rd ed.). Retrieved from http://www.prisonstudies.org/sites/default/files/resources/downloads/world_female_imprisonment_list_third_edition_0.pdf

Walmsley, R. (2016). *World prison population list* (11th ed.). Retrieved from http://www.prisonstudies.org/sites/default/files/resources/downloads/world_prison_population_list_11th_edition.pdf

Weigend, T. (1993). In Germany, fines often imposed in lieu of prosecution. *Overcrowded Times, 4*(1), 15–16.

Yardley, J. (2005, December 31). In worker's death, view of China's harsh justice. *The New York Times*. Retrieved from http://www.nytimes.com

Zalkind, P., & Simon, R. J. (2004). *Global perspectives on social issues: Juvenile justice systems*. Lanham, MD: Lexington.

Zedlewski, E. W. (2010). Alternatives to custodial supervision: The day fine (NCJ 210296). Retrieved from http://www.ncjrs.gov/App/Publications/abstract.aspx?ID=252434

Zimring, F. E. (2003). *The contradictions of American capital punishment*. Oxford, UK: Oxford University Press.

Zvekic, U. (1997). International trends in non-custodial sanctions. In R. Villé, U. Zvekic, & J. F. Klaus (Eds.), *Promoting probation internationally* (pp. 21–45). Rome, Italy: United Nations Interregional Crime and Justice Research Institute.

9

An International Perspective on Juvenile Justice

LEARNING OBJECTIVES

After studying this chapter, you will be able to:

1. Describe some similarities and differences in delinquency among the various regions of the world.

2. Explain the problems faced by the United Nations in trying to define a minimum age of criminal responsibility or the ages to which their juvenile justice standards should apply.

3. Compare the welfare and justice models of juvenile justice.

4. Describe characteristics of the juvenile justice system in New Zealand and Italy and explain why they are considered examples of the welfare model.

5. Describe characteristics of the juvenile justice system in China and in England and Wales and explain why they are considered examples of the justice model.

COUNTRIES IN FOCUS

China   Italy
England and Wales   New Zealand

On November 12, 1934, Charles Maddox was born out of wedlock to 16-year-old Kathleen Maddox in Cincinnati, Ohio. For the first several years of Charles's life, Kathleen disappeared for days and weeks at a time. Charles would ricochet between the homes of his grandmother and aunt. In 1939, Kathleen received a 5-year penitentiary sentence after she and her brother were arrested for armed robbery in West Virginia. While his mom was "away," Charles stayed with an aunt and uncle until Kathleen's release. Then, back with his mother, Charles lived in run-down hotel rooms visited by a long line of "uncles" who, like his mother, drank heavily.

After a year with foster parents, Charles was sent for by Kathleen, who had moved to Indianapolis. Again, he received minimal attention and his mother continued to receive visits from a number of "uncles." In 1947, Kathleen tried unsuccessfully to place Charles with foster parents. Instead, Charles became a ward of the county and was sent to the Gibault Home for Boys in Terre Haute, Indiana. His stay at the home was not beneficial as his record showed poor institutional adjustment, only a fair attitude toward school, moodiness, and a persecution complex. After 10 months, Charles ran away to his mother, but she rejected him.

Burglary and theft became part of Charles's life, and eventually he was sent to the Juvenile Center. After escaping and then being recaptured, he was placed at Father Flanagan's Boys Town. After only 4 days there, he stole a car and made it to Johnsonville, Iowa, with stops for two armed robberies along the way. After "training" from a friend's uncle, Charles tried burglary but was arrested in his second attempt.

Now age 13, Charles went to the Indiana Boys School, where he ran away 18 times during his 3-year stay. His 19th attempt was successful, but it was not escape from his final prison (Wooden, 1976).

Charles's story highlights the classic conflict confronting society's response to juveniles. With its inception in 1899, the juvenile court in America reflected a concern for the care, protection, and treatment of children. Eventually, citizens expressed concern about the informal juvenile court as a violator of due process and called for greater attention to legal procedure. More recently, the philosophy of "just deserts" questions the basic concept of a juvenile justice system geared toward treatment instead of punishment. Juveniles like Charles were sent, presumably with good intentions, to institutions that responded to youths who had been neglected (Charles at the time of his first stay) and delinquent (Charles at the time of his later stays).

One question Charles's case brings up is whether a social welfare or treatment orientation is the most desirable societal response to neglected or misbehaving children. Perhaps a more compassionate societal response would have prevented Charles from falling into a pattern of delinquent and criminal behavior. Accordingly, some would argue that the justice system should have the welfare and protection of the juvenile foremost in its process. On the other hand, there is the argument that the welfare and protection of society must be of predominant concern in the juvenile justice system. Hence, even kids like Charles, who have endured unfortunate circumstances, should be treated the same as any other offender when their behavior threatens society.

Both positions are reasonably argued. Sometimes a spectacular case influences a preference for one position. One fact not mentioned in the foregoing account of Charles is that several years after his birth, his mother married William Manson, who adopted Charles and gave him his last name. The idea that the juvenile justice system should have expressed more concern about the care and protection of Charles Manson than about the welfare of society as a whole is likely to send shivers up the back of people who remember the gruesome murders committed by Manson's "family" in 1969. It is just this type of philosophical difference that is now discussed throughout the world. What is the best way to respond to the "problem youth" of society? An attempt at answering that question is provided later in this chapter, but it is important that we first understand the problem that juvenile offenders present throughout the world.

DELINQUENCY AS A WORLDWIDE PROBLEM

In its report on juvenile justice around the world, the International Child Development Centre noted the difficulty in determining the extent of law violations by young people (International Child Development Centre, 1998). Problems are presented by differing definitions of the ages that represent a juvenile, the variation in record keeping by countries, and differences in the types of acts counted as offenses. Despite such complications, reports suggest that delinquency is considered a problem—and often a growing problem—in most regions of the world. In a world report, the United Nations summarized findings on delinquency in this manner (United Nations, 2011):

- Youth are disproportionately represented in statistics on crime and violence, both as victims and as offenders. In many developed countries, violent crimes are being committed at younger ages than in the past.
- Statistical data suggest that delinquency is largely a group phenomenon with the majority of offenses committed by young people who are committed members of gangs or groups. Even youth who commit offenses alone are likely to be associated with groups.

- Poverty and unemployment are not, by themselves, causes of violence. However, they become important factors when coupled with other triggers such as lack of opportunity, inequality, exclusion, the availability of drugs and firearms, and restricted access to education.
- Whereas adolescence can be an age of "breaking rules," evidence shows that most first-time offenders do not reoffend, and that diversion and other community-based measures are the best responses to offenses committed by young people.
- Crime committed by young people is mainly an urban phenomenon. Evidence shows that the probability of being a victim of crime and violence is substantially higher in urban areas than in rural areas.

The seemingly universal nature of delinquency has been commented on by Hartjen and Kethineni (1996), who suggest that current data support a position that young people around the world engage in comparable behavior with great demographic similarities. A 12-country study of self-reported delinquency also found remarkable similarity among the countries leading to at least the suspicion that committing delinquent acts seems to simply be part of growing up for children in the West (Junger-Tas, 1996).

Although crime by young people presents similar problems for countries throughout the world, the response by justice agencies varies significantly, with each country's response reflecting the history and culture of its citizens. Nevertheless, one consistent feature is the idea that young people should be responded to differently than adults. Perhaps the earliest recognition of this point was a thirteenth-century Norwegian penal code specifying that adult thieves should lose both hands but children only one (International Child Development Centre, 1998). Country differences appear in the identification and processing of young offenders in different legal systems. We should first consider some attempts to provide standards toward which any country should strive.

Setting International Standards

More than 1 million children worldwide are in detention facilities after having come into conflict with their country's laws (Musiani, 2006). Sometimes that confinement is the result of legitimate procedures but too often it occurs without a fair judicial process. The United Nations has been at the forefront in developing rules for the administration of juvenile justice and there are now several documents to assist and encourage countries to respond to young offenders in a humanitarian manner. Four instruments are especially relevant:

- United Nations Standard Minimum Rules for the Administration of Juvenile Justice—1985 (commonly the Beijing Rules, after the location at which the rules were developed)
- United Nations Convention on the Rights of the Child—1989 (commonly the CRC)
- United Nations Guidelines for the Prevention of Juvenile Delinquency—1990 (commonly the Riyadh Guidelines)
- United Nations Rules for the Protection of Juveniles Deprived of their Liberty—1990 (commonly JDLs)

These rules and guidelines set minimum standards for juvenile justice by providing fair trial guarantees and basic procedural safeguards (e.g., presumption of innocence, right to notification of charges, and right to legal representation) and by promoting the desirability for rehabilitation and reintegration of the young person. Unfortunately, successful implementation of the standards into some national legal and judicial systems has not been fully achieved, but progress is apparent.

YOU SHOULD KNOW!

Delinquency Around the World

Two International Self-Report Delinquency Studies (ISRD) have been completed and a third is ongoing in 2016. The results provide interesting information about delinquency around the world. Some findings from both ISRD-1 and ISRD-2 include the following (Junger-Tas, 1996; Junger-Tas et al., 2010; Musiani, 2006):

- Juvenile delinquency mostly involves minor offenses with only a small proportion of offenders committing serious offenses (ISRD-2).
- Boys, in all countries, are more likely than girls to commit violent and serious offenses (ISRD-1 and ISRD-2).
- The peak ages for committing particular crimes are similar in most countries, for example, 14–15 for vandalism, 16–17 for property crimes, and 18–20 for violent crimes (ISRD-1).

- Property offenses, especially shoplifting, are more prevalent in cities of Central and Eastern Europe than in cities of Western Europe and Anglo-Saxon countries (ISRD-2).
- There is a correlation between self-reported delinquency and peer group activities with youths being most likely to misbehave when they are with their peers (ISRD-2).
- Parental supervision is a powerful predictor of delinquency in all the countries—the less supervision, the more delinquent behavior (ISRD-1).

Check the ISRD website at http://www.northeastern.edu/isrd/ for news about the third survey.

The Beijing Rules, the JDLs, and the Riyadh Guidelines are nonbinding instruments that do not carry any formal obligations for their implementation by countries. The CRC, like all U.N. conventions, is a binding document that requires all signing countries to abide by its standards in its national laws, procedures, and policies. It has become the most universally approved treaty in the world, with only two countries—Somalia and the United States—refusing to ratify it. The U.S. Senate has not ratified, and presumably will not ratify, the convention because some individuals and groups believe the convention will undermine parental authority, interfere with parents' ability to raise and discipline their children, and could even elevate the rights of children above the rights of parents.

When agreeing to the CRC, countries are allowed to note reservations they have regarding any of the provisions. This procedure provides countries an opportunity to avoid abiding by certain provisions as long as a majority of the other signing nations make no objection to the reservations. For example, Australia, Canada, and several other countries registered reservations regarding separation of detained children from adults. Those countries generally accept the principle involved but maintain there are situations when separation is not feasible or could even be inappropriate. Several countries following Islamic law have made reservations regarding the application of the CRC when its articles conflict with the provisions of Shari'a. Germany and the Netherlands noted that minor offenses could be tried without legal assistance (International Child Development Centre, 1998). Despite the occasional reservation, however, the CRC stands as an important international document that provides minimum standards for handling young offenders and has encouraged countries around the world to recognize and respect the rights of children.

Determining Who Are Juveniles

One area of historical and cultural differences that makes it difficult to compare how countries respond to juvenile offenders lies in the definitions related to the term *juvenile*. Americans can appreciate the problem of varying definitions for the minimum age of criminal responsibility because each of the 50 states can choose its own age limits. Actually, most states use 18 as the cutoff, so there is at least consensus if not uniformity.

WEB PROJECT

At What Age Does Criminal Responsibility Begin?

The Child Rights International Network provides a helpful database on minimum ages of criminal responsibility. From https://www.crin.org/en/home/ages, select two or three regions then read about the age at which a person can be held criminally responsible in at least two countries from each region. Write a few paragraphs that explain your findings and add your comments about why there might be such variation and what you believe is an appropriate age for someone to be considered criminally responsible.

Of course, what appears to be agreement on that point conceals the dissension on other points. For example, there is considerable variation in how the states define the circumstances under which a juvenile's case can be heard in adult court. In some jurisdictions, transfer to adult court is possible between the ages of 14 and 17, but in a few states a child of any age can be processed by the criminal courts. In other jurisdictions, the determining factor is the type of crime being charged, with more serious offenses being excluded from juvenile court jurisdiction.

The variation we see in how American states handle juveniles is a microcosm of the variation found in countries of the world. Table 9.1 shows the variation in what is considered the minimum age for criminal responsibility in all U.N. member states. In more than 25 countries, children risk being sanctioned for criminal acts at the age of 7, but in other countries the person could be as old as 16. Still others provide no clear indicator as to the age at which criminal responsibility begins (Cipriani, 2009).

Given such variation, it is understandable that the United Nations has been frustrated in its effort to define either a minimum age of criminal responsibility or the ages to which the juvenile justice standards should apply. Because some legal systems do not even recognize the concept of the age of criminal responsibility, the United Nations has settled for broad statements and general guidelines. Rule 4.1 of the Beijing Rules states

> In those legal systems recognizing the concept of the age of criminal responsibility for juveniles, the beginning of that age shall not be fixed at too low an age level, bearing in mind the facts of emotional, mental and intellectual maturity (United Nations, 1985).

One intention of this rule was to encourage countries where the age reached down to the level of infancy to raise that age so that the notion of responsibility would have more meaning.

Similar generalities are used in reference to the ages comprising "juveniles" or "children." Rule 2.2(a) of the Beijing Rules states, a "juvenile is a child or young person who, under the respective legal systems, may be dealt with for an offense in a manner which is different from an adult" (United Nations, 1985). That is not a particularly helpful description, but it serves the United Nations' goal of inclusion by making sure that a broad collection of countries will determine it is possible for them to abide by the standards regardless of a country's specific definition for juvenile.

Determining the Process

The variation among countries regarding what age distinction will orient the justice system is repeated when attention turns to the procedures used to handle juveniles. The various international standards and guidelines are purposely imprecise when describing the appropriate philosophy or rationale that should direct a country's juvenile justice system.

TABLE 9.1	Minimum Age of Criminal Responsibility Around the World		
Puberty	**No Minimum Age**	**Age 7**	**Age 8**
In some countries where Shari'a law is imposed, criminal responsibility is assigned upon puberty. This includes certain offenses in Malaysia, Nigeria, Pakistan, Saudi Arabia, and Sudan.	More than 20 countries are considered to have no clear lower age limit below which criminal responsibility is ruled out in all cases. This includes such countries as France and the United States (where more than 30 states either have no minimum age for adjudicating children delinquent or have no minimum age for adult criminal court jurisdiction).	More than 25 countries assign criminal responsibility at age 7. Those countries include Egypt, India, Kuwait, South Africa, and Thailand.	About 10 countries, including Botswana, Indonesia, and Kenya, have criminal responsibility starting at age 8.
Age 9	**Age 10**	**Age 11**	**Age 12**
Fewer than 10 countries identify age 9 as the start of criminal responsibility. Examples include Bangladesh, Ethiopia, and Malta.	Criminal responsibility begins at age 10 in fewer than 20 countries, including Australia, England and Wales, Ireland, and New Zealand.	Barbados and Japan are two of only a few countries where the age of criminal responsibility begins at 11.	More than 25 countries assign criminal responsibility at age 12. Those countries include Afghanistan, Belgium, Brazil, Canada, Israel, and Mexico.
Age 13	**Age 14**	**Age 15**	**Age 16**
Criminal responsibility begins at 13 in Algeria, Chad, Dominican Republic, Haiti, Monaco, and about 20 other countries.	With almost 40 countries included in this grouping, 14 is the most frequently used age of criminal responsibility. Countries include Austria, Chile, China, Germany, Italy, Peru, Russia, and Spain.	Fewer than 10 countries identify age 15 as the start of criminal responsibility. Examples include Denmark, Finland, Iceland, and Norway.	Few countries wait until age 16 to hold persons criminally responsible. Argentina, Cape Verde, and Timor-Leste are among them.

Source: Based on Cipriani, D. (2009). *Children's rights and the minimum age of criminal responsibility: A global perspective.* Table 5.1 (pp. 98–108). Burlington, VT: Ashgate; and Child Rights International Network. (2016). *Minimum ages of criminal responsibility around the world.* Retrieved from https://www.crin.org/en/home/ages.

The provisions do agree that rehabilitation and reintegration of the juvenile should be given greater weight than punishment. Consistent with that philosophy, the CRC and the Beijing Rules include specific restrictions (e.g., offenders who committed their crime while a child cannot be sentenced to death) and requirements (e.g., detention and imprisonment of a child shall occur only as a last resort and even then should be for the shortest appropriate time).

The Beijing Rules encourage the use of diversion from the formal court system for all but the most serious of young offenders. The Riyadh Guidelines consider much of youthful offending to be simply part of the maturation process and as such to require a supportive response by society that encourages behavioral change and fosters reintegration in the community. These responses suggest—even if they don't require— a particular type of juvenile justice system, and that point brings us back to the models of juvenile justice noted earlier in the chapter.

MODELS OF JUVENILE JUSTICE

It is reasonable to suspect that the four major legal traditions would each produce a subsystem for handling juvenile offenders. Things are not that simple. In fact, there is often considerable variation among countries in the same legal family regarding their response to and even definition of delinquents. In the common legal tradition alone, we find countries emphasizing either treatment (e.g., Australia) or justice (e.g., Ireland). It is also important to note that juvenile justice models, like the legal traditions themselves, undergo change over the years. A country's preference for a treatment approach to juveniles may be exchanged for a "get-tough" approach if citizens start demanding that change. As a result, developing a classification scheme to describe variation in juvenile justice systems is at least as difficult to accomplish as is preparing one for adult justice systems.

Distinguishing among juvenile justice systems is often based on a dichotomy that contrasts those systems taking a paternalistic and protectionist approach that emphasizes treatment against those viewing juveniles as rational beings who must be held accountable for their behavior. More succinctly, the contrast is between a welfare (paternalistic) model and a justice (accountability) model.

Misbehaving Youth

Deciding how to best handle misbehaving young people is a concern in all countries. The selected response tends to fall toward either a welfare or justice model.

Lisa F. Young/Shutterstock

These welfare and justice models are, of course, ideal types for which no specific country will be an exact match. However, as ideal types are designed to do, they provide end points along a continuum on which countries can be placed. Hazel makes the continuum point by noting that all identifiable models of juvenile justice are essentially variations of either the welfare or the justice ideals (Hazel, 2008). Also, the concept of a continuum fits nicely with the point made earlier that countries fluctuate between a treatment and a "get-tough" approach to juvenile misbehavior. Describing a country today as being toward one end of the continuum allows for the possibility that tomorrow that country may be moving toward the other end.

With the ends of the continuum set, we turn our attention to where various justice systems fall between the extremes. Following that lead, Figure 9.1 presents a continuum

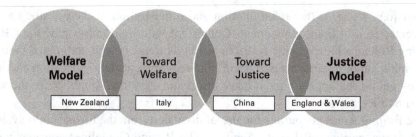

Welfare Model | Toward Welfare | Toward Justice | Justice Model

New Zealand | Italy | China | England & Wales

Emphasizes paternalism with a typical result being treatment rather than formal justice and punishment

Emphasizes ideas of judicial rights and accountability with a result being formal justice and proportionality in sentencing

FIGURE 9.1 A Continuum of Juvenile Justice Models

with the ideal types of welfare model and justice model at each end. It is tempting to provide names for various models falling between those ideal types, and many authors choose to do exactly that. Winterdyk (2002), for example, proposes nine juvenile justice models and Cavadino and Dignan (2006) identify five. Obviously, the points along the continuum can get quite crowded if as many as nine specific models are identified. For some purposes, that specificity may be necessary—but not for our discussion.

The preference for this chapter is to avoid naming the variants and instead let the concept of continuum allow discussion of juvenile justice systems that "lean" toward one ideal type or the other. For our purposes, the result is a discussion of two systems that are more toward the welfare end—with New Zealand being closer than is Italy— and two other systems leaning toward the justice end—with England and Wales being closer than is China.

The Welfare Model of New Zealand

The development of America's juvenile justice system was built on the doctrine of *parens patriae*, meaning that the state is obliged to serve as guardian over children who are in such adverse conditions that their health and/or basic law-abiding nature may be in jeopardy. Because of this welfare model of juvenile justice, the juvenile court had jurisdiction over young people who were dependent or neglected (protection of the juvenile's health) or who had violated the penal code (protection of the juvenile's law-abiding nature). This emphasis on the child's general well-being has been an important characteristic of most all juvenile justice systems but continues to be especially descriptive of such systems as in New Zealand and Italy.

Prior to colonization by the British, New Zealand's (see Map A.6) indigenous population (the Maori) had a justice system that approached problem youth very differently than did the imposed British system. The same could be said for most any indigenous group that was subjected to colonization, but the point is especially relevant here because aspects of the indigenous system have returned to play a key role in the contemporary system. As Cavadino and Dignan (2006) explain, criticisms of the imposed juvenile justice system as it was operating in the mid-1970s and early 1980s included complaints that it was culturally inappropriate to the extent of being racist in how it dealt with young indigenous offenders. In response to that criticism and in reaction to other political and social forces, New Zealand modified the procedures used in responding to youths in a way that stresses the well-being of children and the empowerment of families. The result is an interesting combination of the welfare model's focus on a juvenile's "needs" rather than "deeds" and a restorative justice model (drawing from Maori culture) focusing on reintegration of the offender into the community by involving offender, victims, and community members in the process.

In 1989, New Zealand enacted Children, Young Persons and their Families Act (CYPF Act) that dramatically altered the way it responded to youth crime—which, in New Zealand, refers to persons under age 17. Generally, the act encourages diversion; specifically, it establishes the family, including extended family members, as the locus for authority and expertise on matters of juvenile delinquency. The philosophy orienting the legislation is clearly restorative in nature because it emphasizes young offenders paying for their wrongdoing in an appropriate way. In addition, it involves families of both offenders and victims in a decision-making process resulting in solutions that help restore the lost balance. The specific format used to implement the philosophy is the family group conference (FGC), which is used with both offenders and young people in need of care and protection.

The path through New Zealand's youth justice system depends, in part, on the youth's age, whether the youth has been arrested, and whether those arrested admit to the charges. As a result, the key points in the process are how the police respond (arrest or no arrest), the FGC (not arrested but charged, or arrested and admit), and the Youth Court (arrested and deny charges). We consider each of these key points below, but must first address the issue of age.

New Zealand distinguishes between the age of criminal responsibility (10) and the age of prosecution (14). It also distinguishes between children (those under age 14) and young persons (those at least 14 but less than 17). Procedures differ for these two groups when they are believed to have committed an offense. Children who commit offenses are dealt with under care and protection provisions, whereas young persons who offend are dealt with under the youth justice provisions. We are concerned with the young persons (juveniles age 14, 15, and 16), but it is important to note that children (those age 10 through 13) who have committed an offense or offenses that give rise to concern for their well-being can experience the same type of intervention as do young persons. The difference is that for children the system's focus is intended to be the child's welfare rather than the child's accountability, which is the focus for young persons (Morris, 2004; New Zealand Ministry of Social Development, 2016b).

POLICE RESPONSE   The diversionary principles of the CYPF Act begin with the goal of using police-organized alternative responses rather than charging young offenders. Upon believing that a crime has been committed and that they have identified a young person as the offender, the police have several options.

Typically, the expectation is that persons committing minor offenses will be diverted from prosecution with an immediate warning to not reoffend by the street level police officer. If the police believe further action is needed, or in cases of more serious or persistent offending, they can refer the juvenile to the Police Youth Aid section, which is a unit made up of highly specialized and well-trained members of the national police force. Examples of actions that might be taken by the Police Youth Aid section include issuing a warning to the youth in the presence of his or her parents, requiring an apology to the victim, or directing the juvenile to complete some work in the community. Youth Aid will either deal with the matter through alternative action or, if there is an intention to place charges, refer it to the Department of Child, Youth and Family Services (DCYFS) for a Family Group Conference. If there has been an arrest, the police will submit a charge directly in the Youth Court (New Zealand Ministry of Justice, 2016; Walker, 2015).

The importance of the police role in how juveniles are handled is clear upon looking at statistics showing that approximately 80 percent of all youth offending is dealt with through prompt, community-based alternative intervention (Walker, 2015). The involvement of the Youth Aid officer is key to the alternative action, since it is the officer who decides on a plan of action after talking to the young person and visiting with their family and the victim. As Walker (2015) explains, the plan options are limited only by the imagination of the people involved and the best Youth Aid officers spend considerable time and effort tailoring solutions that will prevent reoffending and reintegrate young people into their community.

FAMILY GROUP CONFERENCE   The FGC is a meeting that involves a child or young person, their family, and the victim. It is a fundamental part of the process in situations where a charge is formally laid in the Youth Court, or when the police have stated an intention to charge. About one-fourth of all youth justice cases fall in these categories. As explained later, cases in which an arrest was made and the young person does not deny the charges are also referred to an FGC. In addition, cases in which the charges were denied but the Youth Court found the young person responsible are referred to an FGC as well. In both cases in which the young person has been to Youth Court, the FGC stage is done in order to provide the Youth Court judge with sentencing recommendations (New Zealand Ministry of Justice, 2016; Walker, 2015).

Essentially, the FGC operates both as an alternative to courts (i.e., a pre-charge mechanism for young people who have not been arrested) and as a post-charge mechanism for making recommendations to judges before sentencing (for young people who have been arrested).

Participants in an FGC include the young person, members of his or her immediate and extended family, and whomever they invite (e.g., friends, teachers, and youth club organizers). In addition, the victim or victims (or their representative), victims' support persons, the police, the young person's lawyer (usually only in court-referred cases), and, sometimes, a social worker are present.

The FGC is facilitated by a youth justice coordinator (YJC) who, mostly, is a social worker linked to the DCYFS. Even before an FGC is convened, the coordinators are involved by exploring other alternatives or, when alternatives are not deemed appropriate, preparing the parties for the FGC (New Zealand Ministry of Social Development, 2016a).

The actual procedures for each FGC are up to the participants, but the process typically begins with introductions of those in attendance and an explanation of the procedures to be followed. The police summarize the offense facts and the juvenile is given an opportunity to comment on the accuracy of the police statement. The juvenile provides a formal admission of his or her involvement, the victims (or representatives) present their views, and a general discussion of possible outcomes ensues. Eventually, a formal plan is developed and agreed upon by the participants.

Importantly, the professionals have a low-key role in the conference. The YJC is simply a facilitator and the police role is usually limited to describing the offense and, when neither victim nor their representative is present, how the offense affected the victim. A youth advocate, if one is present, advises on legal issues and protects the young person's rights. They may also express an opinion about the proposed penalties if they seem excessive. A social worker if present will normally only provide background information on the young person and participate in supporting the plans of the family and the young person for the future.

Unless the plan is so extreme or so lenient as to be out of line with how similar offenses are handled, the plan will almost always be accepted by the Youth Court judge (or the police, in police-referred cases). Even when accepting the plan, the judge has the discretion to impose additional requirements (e.g., a fine or community service) as necessary. In this way, the Youth Court retains an important supervisory and monitoring role in respect of plans.

For the small group who do come to the Youth Court, the mandatory FGC is both a diversionary tool to avoid charging and the main decision-making mechanism for all charges that were not denied or that were subsequently proved. The FGC allows authorities to rely less on judicial decision making and instead places families, victims, and the community at the heart of the decision-making process. A consensus-based plan is created to hold the young people accountable for their behavior while addressing the

WEB PROJECT

Juvenile Justice in European Union Countries

Visit the European Commission site at http://www.childreninjudicialproceedings.eu/Criminal/ and select "National & International Data." Click on the flag icon for at least two different EU countries. You will see a variety of information and opportunities for additional links. Feel free to wander around the page, but at some point click on the file icon for "Contextual Overview." Read the PDF that opens for each country and write a few paragraphs that compare aspects you find interesting about the juvenile justice proceedings for the two countries you chose.

underlying causes of offending. Once the young person's future interests have been balanced against the protection of public interest, the successful completion of an FGC plan is usually rewarded with an absolute discharge (Walker, 2015).

FGCs have been quite successful at diverting young people from courts, custody, and confinement facilities. In addition, they have been reasonably successful at involving offenders, victims, and their families in key decisions about the best way to deal with offending in a way that holds the young person accountable and enables victims to put the matter behind them. Although there is criticism (e.g., victims are not as involved as had been hoped for), it is still possible to view the FGC process as an innovative approach to youth justice.

YOUTH COURT The majority of youth offending cases do not result in a formal charge in the Youth Court. In fact, the CYPF Act stipulates that criminal proceedings should not be instigated against a child or young person unless the public interest requires it and alternative methods are not appropriate. The Youth Court deals with young people 14, 15, and 16 years old who have been arrested or who have been at an FGC that decided a charge should be made. Young people who do not have their own attorney will have a youth advocate appointed to help them understand the court process and available options, and to ensure that the judge understands the young person's point of view. If the young person admits to the charges, referral is made to an FGC. When the charges are denied, the case remains in Youth Court (Bradley, Tauri, & Walters, 2006).

Youth Court is actually part of the adult court system, but its procedures, practices, and jargon are modified. At the Youth Court, the judge may gather information from such sources as the police, medical and mental health personnel, social workers, the youth's family members, and, of course, the youths themselves. To avoid stigmatization, charges are either "proved" or "not proved" rather than the juvenile being found guilty or not guilty. When charges have been proved, the offender is given a court order rather than a sentence.

Outcomes of cases that have gone to Youth Court include withdrawal of the charges, a warning to stay out of trouble, a conditional discharge (penalties follow if the law is broken again), an order to make reparation or restitution, community work for up to 200 hours, being put under DCYFS for supervision, or placement in a DCYFS facility for up to 6 months. For the most serious crimes, the case is transferred to adult court (Bradley et al., 2006; Walker, 2015).

As we see from police action through Youth Court procedures, New Zealand's approach to youth offending attempts to deal with children and young people who commit offenses in a way that acknowledges their needs and enhances their development. Such an approach is the hallmark of the welfare model and also incorporates aspects of restorative justice that are increasingly appealing to other countries as they consider ways to provide for victims and family members in the youth justice process.

Italy: More Welfare than Justice Model

Italy (see Map A.10) was among the last of the Western European nations to set up a juvenile court. This 1934 formal achievement was preceded by developments such as the 1929 creation of special sections in the courts of appeal that provided prosecutors instruction and judgment on juvenile cases. In 1930, a penal code revision raised the age of minimum responsibility from 9 to 14 while lowering the age of full responsibility from 21 to 18. The 1934 law solidified these prior actions and gave the new juvenile court jurisdiction over youths who were shown to have strayed and be in need of correction. Additional changes made in 1977 gave local authorities more control over the way juveniles were treated by the system, prompting increased use of community intervention and small group homes. The current system operates under modifications implemented under the 1988 Code of Criminal Procedure (Canetta, 2014; Cavadino & Dignan, 2006).

Today, Italy's juvenile justice system has a reputation for being rather tolerant and lenient. Although those terms can be confusing when used in a comparative context, they seem relevant when considering the various options available to divert juvenile offenders from the formal court process. The need for diversion results primarily from a legal requirement that prison be avoided as much as possible for youths aged 14–18. Care is to be taken in juvenile court to not interrupt the normal process of education and growing up—and imprisonment would certainly be a prime example of such interruption (Nelken, 2006).

For those 14- to 18-year-old offenders, the court must determine intent and capacity to understand—both of which must also be considered with respect to the alleged offense, the circumstances in which it took place, and the minor's personality. Once a judge has decided that a juvenile has the capacity to be legally responsible for his or her actions, the judicial proceedings move to a pretrial stage. From there, some will progress to trial.

PRETRIAL STAGE Many cases are disposed of at this pretrial stage. When the pretrial preliminary hearing indicates to the judge that conditions for a conviction exist, the court may hand the juvenile over for trial or the accused is allowed to have the preliminary hearing regarded as the final step in the process—called an abbreviated trial (Gatti & Verde, 2016). In the context of the preliminary hearing, the judge can decide to issue a judicial pardon, dismiss the charges as being insufficiently serious, or impose a pretrial measure. For cases in which the offender's responsibility for the act has been established during the preliminary hearing, the judge—taking into consideration the nature and gravity of the offense—may determine that the defendant is unlikely to commit other deviant acts. If so, and in the interest of aiding the maturation process, a judicial pardon may be issued, although this can be granted only once (Canetta, 2014).

Cases dismissed as insufficiently serious (acquittal for criminal irrelevance) are done so under a specific provision of the juvenile criminal law. After a thorough examination of the case—and after consulting with the offender, the victim, the offender's parents, and lawyers for each party—the judges may determine the case to be too trivial to prosecute (Cavadino & Dignan, 2006; Scalia, 2005). Three conditions must be satisfied for this option to be available: (1) the offense must be minor, (2) the conduct of the child must be of an occasional nature, and (3) continuing prosecution would interfere with the juvenile's education (Canetta, 2014).

When deciding to order a pretrial measure, the judge must take into account the child's educational needs and must determine whether the sanction is appropriate given the circumstances and the seriousness of the offense. Typical pretrial measures include the imposition of specific treatments that relate to education, work, or other activities useful to the child's education. A directive of home confinement is also possible, wherein the child is confined to the family home or other private residence and under the supervision of his or her parents. This sanction can also include limits on persons (other than those who are also in the home) with whom the child can communicate. With the court's permission, the child can leave home for school, work, or other appropriate activities. A third pretrial measure is placement in an educational community where the child must follow specific school and educational activities (Canetta, 2014).

TRIAL AND SENTENCING Cases going to trial are held in juvenile criminal court before a panel of four judges (two professional and two lay). When a trial occurs, the case is prosecuted by the public prosecutor attached to the juvenile court and is held, usually in private, in the juvenile court setting. The accused is questioned directly by the magistrate and, to avoid upsetting the minor, no cross-examination takes place. The procedures require that specific rules be followed in juvenile court and that the court must explain to every young defendant the significance of the proceedings and the content and grounds for the court's decision.

Both noncustodial and custodial sanctions are available to the judges when a juvenile is convicted. Just as during the pretrial stage, the sentencing stage is focused on the promotion of education and the development of a sense of responsibility in the juvenile. An example of noncustodial sanction that follows these principles includes the suspension of trial with probation. Under this procedure, the trial is suspended by placing the young person on probation with community supervision for a maximum period of 1 year (3 years in the case of serious offenses). During the period of trial suspension, the juveniles engage in educational and work projects that are designed to support them as their behavior is assessed. At the end of the 1-year (or 3-year) period, the judge determines if probation was successfully completed and, if it was, the original crime goes unrecorded (Canetta, 2014; Cavadino & Dignan, 2006; Nelken, 2006; Scalia, 2005).

Custodial sentences are considered to be a measure of last resort to be imposed only when the child poses a threat to society. When a deprivation of liberty sentence is given to persons between 14 and 21 years of age, it is to a penal facility for children (prison schools). Those institutions operate in cooperation with the other juvenile justice services to ensure that the educational aim of the penalty is guaranteed. Upon turning 21, young detainees are transferred to detention centers for adults. The sentence given is typically one-third of what an adult would receive for the same offense, and the juvenile may be conditionally released prior to completing the sentence (Canetta, 2014; Gatti & Verde, 2016).

China: More Justice than Welfare Model

As we move toward the justice model end of the continuum, we expect to find juvenile justice systems that consider children and youngsters to be rational individuals who are responsible for their actions. When juveniles are viewed in this way, the welfare model's focus on treatment and the underlying causes of delinquency is seen as misplaced. Instead, the justice model argues that misbehaving juveniles must be held accountable for their acts—using a procedure that gives them their rights of due process—and be punished in accordance with the seriousness of the offense. China (see Map A.7) provides an example to the responsibility/accountability aspect of the justice model—but the relative absence of due process keeps China from moving further toward the justice end of the continuum.

China has no special substantive or procedural law dealing with juvenile delinquency. As a result, juvenile court proceeding in China can be considered essentially to be criminal proceedings (Zhao, Zhang, & Liu, 2014). The Chinese Criminal Code provides that persons who have reached 16 years of age shall bear criminal responsibility for their acts. However, persons between ages 14 and 16 who commit crimes of murder, serious injury, rape, robbery, drug trafficking, arson, explosion, or poisoning also bear criminal responsibility. Persons between ages 14 and 18 who commit crimes are to be given a lighter or mitigated punishment and it is this age group for which the juvenile courts have jurisdiction (People's Republic of China, 1979, Article 17). As an interesting aside, China also stipulates a different response at the other end of the age spectrum. According to Article 17a, people age 75 and more may be given a lighter or mitigated penalty if they commit an intentional or a negligent crime.

In addition to the criminal responsibility provisions of the Criminal Code, two other laws serve to establish China's juvenile justice system. The Law on Protection of Minors (People's Republic of China, 1991) includes social, welfare, and legal protections but does not provide specific rights of due process and correctional treatment. The Law on Delinquency Prevention (People's Republic of China, 1999) serves to legalize and define the juvenile justice system and focuses on the education and correction responsibilities that family, school, and community have in relation to juveniles involved in delinquent behavior (Shen, 2016; Zhang, 2008; Zhang & Jianhong, 2007).

The Law on Delinquency Prevention classifies juvenile offenses into three categories: juvenile misbehavior (sometimes translated from the Chinese as unhealthy behavior), serious juvenile misbehavior (seriously unhealthy behavior), and juvenile criminal law violations. Because the law includes the countermeasures to be used for each type, the three categories provide an appropriate way to explain the Chinese system of juvenile justice.

JUVENILE MISBEHAVIOR Examples of misbehaviors include truancy, staying away from home overnight, fighting, carrying controlled weapons, stealing, begging with force, gambling, watching or reading pornographic material, and other serious violations of social norms (Shen, 2016; Yisheng & Yijun, 2006). Responses to these misbehaviors often fall to the police, who have the authority to reprimand parents or other guardians of the juveniles and order them to discipline the juveniles (Wang, 2006).

Hangzhou Police

Police in China, such as those at this station in Hangzhou, have the authority to reprimand parents and order them to discipline their misbehaving children.

Courtesy of Philip L. Reichel

SERIOUS JUVENILE MISBEHAVIOR Misbehavior of the serious type includes wrong-doings that cause serious harm to society, but do not amount to criminal behavior deserving criminal sanctions. Those acts include repeatedly carrying prohibited weapons, beating up other people, disseminating pornographic material, repeated theft and gambling, using drugs, groups of people gathering to disturb the public order, and other serious behaviors that endanger social norms (Shen, 2016; Yisheng & Yijun, 2006).

A primary response to serious misbehavior is sending the juvenile to work and study school for a period of 2–3 years. School-age juveniles (typically those from age 13 up to age 18) may be sent to these special schools where rigid discipline and special education programs are designed for rehabilitation rather than punishment. The work–study schools are often boarding schools and some allow students to go home on weekends and school holidays, whereas others hold tighter control over the students' movements. Placement in these schools requires an application from either the school or the juvenile's parents and actual assignment requires the agreement of the student, parents, and the school (Shen, 2016).

Since the mid-1990s, "work" has been deemphasized as an element in the work–study school. A variety of hobby classes are offered, but the clear emphasis is providing a specialized education for juveniles who are unable to continue study in ordinary schools due to their disorderly, impulsive, and nuisance behaviors. Academic performance is important, but the goal is for the students to gain knowledge, experience, and skills through participation in student-centered and classroom-based group activities (Shen, 2016).

JUVENILE CRIMINAL LAW VIOLATIONS If responses to the misbehavior and the serious misbehavior categories are more welfare in nature, the responses to this "crimes committed by minors" category are more justice oriented. Since China has no special procedural law for juveniles, those who are charged with crimes have the protections provided in the Criminal Procedure Law. There are often special sections in police departments that handle cases of juvenile delinquency (i.e., violations that would be criminal if committed by a person age 18 or older) and it is also typical to have special sections in the procurators' office to handle delinquency cases. But despite those special sections, the rules guiding the police and procurator actions are those established in the Criminal Procedure Law. This point is one of the reasons China is placed toward the justice model end of the continuum.

When delinquency cases are handled formally, they appear before a juvenile court—or, more correctly, the adult intermediate people's court, with some "special case" modifications. The first of these juvenile tribunals was in Shanghai in 1984, and today there are about 1,800 tribunals and some 420 mixed courts that try both adult and juvenile criminals (Jou, Chang, & Hebenton, 2014). As a result, the formal procedures are similar to those described in Chapter 7 and need not be repeated here. However, the sanctions applied to juvenile offenders vary from those for adults. Two important ones are rehabilitation through labor at a Juvenile Rehabilitation Camp and placement in a Juvenile Reformatory.

Rehabilitation through labor is for persons committing minor offenses such as prostitution, theft, drug abuse, disturbing the public order, or preventing public officials from carrying out their duties. This sanction, which can be used for adult offenders as well, is imposed for a period of 1–3 years and involves placement in a residential facility (the Juvenile Rehabilitation Camp) that emphasizes work and education as well as mandatory labor. Juvenile offenders typically work (but not at heavy manual labor) for half of the workday, then study for the other half, followed by time for rest and sleep. The work is believed to have a positive influence on these juveniles since they are considered to be rather lazy and to lack family supervision—both of which are considered major causes of delinquent behavior. Unlike the work–study schools, the education programs in juvenile rehabilitation centers include ideological, cultural, and technical education designed to provide a moral base that will tie individuals to society (Jou et al., 2014). The Juvenile Reformatory is essentially a prison for juveniles aged 14–18 who have been sentenced to a fixed term of imprisonment—or even life imprisonment. When they reach age 18, they will be sent to an adult prison (Wong, 2001; Yisheng & Yijun, 2006).

The philosophical base upon which China's juvenile justice system operates has aspects of both welfare and justice models—hence its placement on the continuum. The justice component comes from the Confucian perspective that humans are basically good and act only after thinking (i.e., humans are rational). Because they are rational, they are also responsible and must be held accountable. However, the principle of "Educate, Reform, Rescue, and Redeem" is the orienting philosophy when Chinese authorities respond to juvenile crime. Under that principle, education is the primary measure and punishment only supplemental. Even when punishment is used, the goal is rehabilitation in the sense of teaching children their legal responsibilities so that they will know from a very young age what is wrong and what is right (Wang, 2006).

The Justice Model of England and Wales

For much of the twentieth century, England and Wales (see Map A.10) fell toward the welfare end of the juvenile justice continuum. By the 1960s that approach received increased criticism as stigmatizing, dehumanizing, and criminogenic rather than being rehabilitative and therapeutic as claimed. By the 1980s, civil libertarians were arguing that welfare-based procedures did little more than provide spurious justification for placing restriction on individual liberty that were disproportionate to the seriousness of the offense or the needs of the juvenile. In the wake of such criticism, England and Wales moved toward the justice end of the continuum with goals of proportional punishment and protection of rights through due process (Muncie & Goldson, 2006). The focus moved from punishing the person to punishing the crime, and it is considered by some to be the most punitive juvenile justice system in Europe (Tonry & Chambers, 2012).

As the twentieth century was ending, responsibility and accountability were added to the mix of proportional punishment and due process. The result was a clearer positioning of England and Wales at the justice end of the continuum and an interest in seeing that juveniles got their just deserts—but only after following due process.

The Crime and Disorder Act 1998 (CDA) provides the current structure for juvenile justice in England and Wales (United Kingdom Parliament, 1998). Although some modifications were made as a result of the Criminal Justice Act 2003 (United Kingdom Parliament, 2003), the CDA still provides the basic structure for responding to young offenders in England and Wales.

A primary change accomplished by the CDA is the abolition of a three-category division for handling minors. Prior to the CDA, minors under age 10 were considered incapable of committing a criminal act; those at ages 10–13 were not regarded as criminally responsible if it could be proved that they were psychologically not an adult in their criminal act; and those older than age 13 were considered fully liable but subject to different procedures and punishment. With the implementation of the CDA, a person is considered criminally responsible from age 10 onward. There is no longer any "maybe" stage in which minors ages 10–13 could be found to lack criminal responsibility.

Although people from age 10 through age 17 now have responsibility for their acts, the justice system still provides special procedures and penalties for offenders in that age category. We consider these procedures and penalties by reviewing first the key agencies involved, then the stages of diversion, courts, and custody.

KEY AGENCIES   Overseeing the youth justice system in England and Wales is the Youth Justice Board (YJB). Its mission is to prevent offending and reoffending by children and young people under age 18. The YJB also has responsibility for ensuring that custody for those children and young people is safe, secure, and addresses the causes of their offending behavior (GOV.UK, 2016). The YJB has been controversial in recent years, but survived a 2010 bid to abolish it in part by promising to handle complaints more fairly and effectively and to improve access to helping services for those young people in facilities under YJB control (BBC News, 2011; Letters, 2016).

A principal aim for the entire youth justice system is to prevent offending by children and young persons. To help accomplish that goal, local government authorities (similar to US counties) have established multiagency Youth Offending Teams (YOTs) that are responsible for coordinating and providing youth justice services at the local authority level (Cavadino & Dignan, 2006; GOV.UK, 2015c). The YOT has, at a minimum, a social worker, a probation officer, a police officer, an education officer, and a health official. When appropriate, people from other agencies may also be included.

IMPACT

PUNISHING PARENTS

Have you ever wondered why parents are not punished for their misbehaving children? Actually, there have been occasions when juvenile court judges have imposed sanctions on parents, but such actions are unusual in American juvenile courts. It was also unusual in British youth courts until the advent of Parenting Contracts and Parenting Orders (both implemented in the early 2000s).

Parenting Contracts, which are often used alongside with Acceptable Behavior Contracts, provide an option to Youth Offending Teams (YOT) in situations where parents are not cooperating with the YOT in providing an effective response to the parents' misbehaving child. The contracts are designed to provide a formal structure for working with the parents on a voluntary basis.

The contract specifies conditions designed to help the parents stop the child from getting in trouble. For example, the contract might require the parents to:

- make sure their child is at home at night
- make sure they go to school
- attend a parenting program

Parenting Contracts are voluntary and there is no penalty for the parent who refuses to enter or comply with the contract. However, refusing to enter into a contract or complying with one can be used as evidence to support an application for a Parenting Order.

Parenting Orders provide a way to sanction parents and guardians of misbehaving young people. They are likely to be used in cases where a Parenting Contract has not produced desired results and when the child is constantly truant, has been suspended from school, is convicted of a crime, or has been given an Anti-Social Behaviour Order (ASBO), a Child Safety Order, or a Sex Offender Order (Tameside Metropolitan Borough, 2013; Youth Justice Board, 2014).

The ASBO, which can be used even for adults, is given for behaving in a manner that causes distress or harassment to someone. The Child Safety Order is applied to a child under 10 years of age who has committed an offense, broken a curfew, or caused others distress or alarm. Both the ASBO and the Child Safety Order are pre-trial diversion orders. A Sex Offender Order (issued, for example, to a young person who admitted to a sex

Coordination of the YOTs at a national level is accomplished by the YJB, but management is at the local authority level. Local decisions are made on issues such as arranging for and appointing a YOT manager, developing a youth justice plan appropriate for the local area, and arranging for resources available to the YOT. The YOT is responsible for providing pre-court and court services, as well as community supervision related to any type of community sanction.

Because the YOT incorporates representatives from a wide range of service agencies, it can respond to the needs of young offenders in a comprehensive way. Those needs are identified with the use of an assessment instrument (similar to a risk/needs scale with which you may be familiar from courses on the correctional system) that identifies the specific problems making the young person offend—as well as measuring the risk they pose to others. This enables the YOT to identify suitable programs to address the needs of the young persons with the intention of preventing further offending (GOV.UK, 2015c).

DIVERSION OPTIONS A variety of alternatives to judicial proceedings are available for children who are behaving in an antisocial manner, including committing minor offenses. The type of response is determined by such factors as the severity and impact of the offense, any pervious offenses the child may have, how well the child complied with any previous interventions, and the child's willingness to accept responsibility (Altan, 2014).

offense and received a reprimand or warning from the police) prohibits the person from doing anything that may cause the public serious harm.

The Parenting Order has two elements. First, the parent is required to attend counseling or guidance sessions for up to 3 months and not more than once per week in which they receive help in dealing with their children. They may learn, for example, about setting and enforcing consistent standards of behavior for their children. Second, the court may require the parents or guardians to exercise a measure of control over their child (e.g., ensuring the child attends school or avoids certain people or places) for a period up to 12 months. The order is supervised by YOT workers, and failure to comply with its terms could result in the parent being fined up to £1,000 (about $1,600). Bottoms and Dignan note that parenting orders were inspired by the connection found in criminological research studies between poor parenting skills and the development of criminal careers (Bottoms & Dignan, 2004). Preliminary research on the parenting program conducted by Ghate and Ramella allowed the researchers to conclude that it was clearly successful in terms of having a positive impact on parents—according to both parents and staff (Ghate & Ramella, 2002). Participation, at least in the short term, was associated with positive improvements in parenting skills and parent–child relationships.

The positive perception by parents was not matched to the same extent by their children, who showed only mild (statistically nonsignificant) indications of any improvement in the way they perceived their relationships with their parents. However, in the year after their parents left the parenting program, the reconviction rates of the young people had been reduced by nearly one-third, offending had dropped by more than 50 percent, and the average number of offenses per young person had dropped by half.

Bottoms and Dignan (2004) note—and Ghate and Ramella (2002) would certainly agree—that although these findings have been heralded by the Youth Justice Board as evidence that parenting orders can reduce short-term reconviction rates, they should be interpreted with great caution. The most obvious reason for caution is the absence of a control group, which makes it impossible to say whether the changes in offending rates before and after the program would have been different in the absence of a parenting program. Additional research is certainly needed, but these preliminary results indicate that efforts at reinforcing and supporting parental responsibility certainly do not hurt and may be quite beneficial.

Young people committing minor offenses may be given an out-of-court youth caution by the police if they admit the offense, there is sufficient evidence to presume a conviction, and it is not in the public interest to prosecute. A youth conditional caution is possible under similar conditions plus a belief that the public interest can be served by having the child comply with specific conditions as to their behavior.

More formal action for behavior falling short of a criminal offense includes the issuing of an Acceptable Behaviour Contract (ABC), which are agreements between the child and the police or local authorities. Actions for which an ABC might be appropriate include smoking or drinking while under age, begging, or harassment of passersby. The child agrees to either engage or not engage in certain actions under a written ABC. The agreement is not legally binding and violation of an ABC does not result in a criminal record, but it can be used as a reason to issue an Anti-Social Behaviour Order (ASBO).

An ASBO can be given to anyone over age 10, and is used for young people and adults as well as for children. The ASBOs are civil orders designed to protect the public from behavior that causes harassment, alarm, or distress (e.g., drunken or threatening behavior, vandalism, graffiti, and excessive noise—especially at night). Typical conditions in an ASBO are requirements to refrain from certain acts and for avoiding interaction with specific people (Altan, 2014; Youth Justice Board, 2003).

YOUTH COURT If the case goes to court, it is heard by a magistrates' court (see Chapter 7) sitting as a youth court. That means the regular magistrates' court is configured to three (sometimes two) magistrates hearing the case and deciding guilt or innocence of persons between ages 10 and 17. When sitting as a youth court, the magistrates' court is closed to the public. Children under age 16 must be accompanied by their parent or guardian, and parents/guardians of those age 16 or 17 should attend—and must attend if they have received a court order. The young person may also have a lawyer present to either defend the case or make explanations to the court. Other people present in court may include victims or members of the YOT (GOV.UK, 2015b).

Placement of England and Wales toward the justice end of the continuum is done in part because of the formal rights afforded to juveniles during court proceedings. Children essentially have the same right to be heard and participate in court as do adult defendants. As with adult defendants, children have the right to legal counsel (including free legal assistance when their circumstances require that). Further, if convicted, the child has the same rights of appeal as do adult defendants (Altan, 2014).

Sentencing options available to the youth court include a range of community sentences and a custody sentence (see Table 9.2). The custody sentence, a Detention and Training Order, is served in one of three types of facilities (GOV.UK, 2015a):

- **Secure children's home:** These are for the youngest offenders (aged between 10 and 14), and those who may have been in care or have mental health problems. These facilities vary in size from ones holding as few as 8 children to those holding up to 40. The residents attend classes following a school day timetable and receive a lot of individual attention and support since typically there is one staff member for every two young people.
- **Secure training centre:** These centers, which hold between 50 and 80 young people in separate units of 5–8 people, are for offenders up to the age of 17. Residents receive up to 30 hours of education and training every week, following a school day timetable. Individual attention is not as great as in a secure children's home since here ratio of staff to young person is about 3:8.
- **Young offender institution:** These facilities are run by the Prison Service and by private companies. They hold 15- to 21-year-olds, but those under 18 are held in

TABLE 9.2	Sentence Options Available to the Youth Court

Community Sentences

Referral Orders

When a young offender pleads guilty to a first offense, a referral order is a typical sanction. This order sends the young person to a youth offender panel that decides on a sentence designed to keep the juvenile from reoffending. The panel is made up of two volunteers from the offender's local community and a member of the youth offending team. Both youth and parents are involved in agreeing to the sentence and, when appropriate, the victim may also be involved. The sentence will last between 3 and 12 months.

Reparation Orders

The reparation order is designed to tackle youth offending through positive intervention and in accordance with the principles of restorative justice. As such, the order can relate to the victim, another person affected by the act, or the entire community. The goal is to have the juvenile in some way make up for the harm caused by the act. Under a reparation order, the young offender may be required to repair any damage to the victim's property (with the victim's agreement), remove graffiti from public buildings, or take part in mediation sessions with the victim where the offender meets the victim and apologizes. A reparation order is typically completed in about 24 hours spread over several days.

Youth Rehabilitation Order

A Youth Rehabilitation Order, which can last up to 3 years, includes both "must do" and "must not do" items. Each order is different so that it can reflect the type of crime committed and any particular needs of the offender—such as helping with a health problem. Examples of requirements in a rehabilitation order are:

- be at home by a certain time each day (a "curfew")
- stay away from specific places ("exclusion")
- be tested for drugs regularly
- get treatment for a drug addiction

Violating the requirements of a Youth Rehabilitation Order may result in a custody sentence.

Custodial Sentence

Detention and Training Order

Young offenders aged 12–17 can be given a Detention and Training Order (DTO). The length of the sentence can be between 4 months and 2 years. The DTO is served in two parts with the first half served in custody and the second under supervision in the community. A DTO is only given to young people who represent a high level of risk, have a significant offending history, or are persistent offenders and where no other sentence will manage their risks effectively.

Source: Developed from information available at GOV.UK. (2014, November 12). *Sentences for young people. Types of prison sentences.* Retrieved from https://www.gov.uk/types-of-prison-sentence/sentences-for-young-people; GOV.UK. (2015, October 5). *Community sentences if you are under 18. Community sentences.* Retrieved from https://www.gov.uk/community-sentences/community-sentences-if-you-are-under-18; and Sentencing Council. (2016). *Types of sentences for young people. Young people and sentencing.* Retrieved from https://www.sentencingcouncil.org.uk/about-sentencing/young-people-and-sentencing/types-of-sentences-for-young-people/.

different buildings from those over 18. Some of the institutions share a site with an adult prison, and others are by themselves. The institutions vary in size with some holding about 60 people and others housing more than 400—although most of the larger facilities are split into wings holding 30–60 young people. These residents receive up to 25 hours of education, skills, and other activities every week, including treatment programs. There is little individual attention in these facilities, with one staff member for every 10 young people.

In 2015, there were about 1,800 children and young people held in all three facility types in England and Wales—down considerably from more than 3,300 in the early 2000s. However, any encouraging news from the decline in numbers of young people in custody is offset by an increase in the percentage of black and ethnic minorities in custody.

About 40 percent of prisoners under 18 years old are from black, Asian, mixed race, or "other" ethnicity backgrounds. Of the factors that might explain the phenomenon, one may be the re-offense rate of young Muslims (four in five reoffend), who lack community and family support upon their release from custody, but others may be differential treatment by police and prosecutors (Sloan & Allison, 2015). As officials have noted, the government must commit to providing a criminal justice system that promotes equality and does not discriminate against anyone because of race. Progress has been made, but there is clearly more to do (Puffett, 2010; Sloan & Allison, 2015). That, of course, is a goal of juvenile justice systems regardless of which end of the continuum they fall.

Summary

This chapter began with a sketch of how juvenile justice agencies in America responded to Charles Manson, eventually the instigator of at least eight murders. The dilemma facing juvenile justice agencies around the world is the same regardless of the legal tradition to which the system is linked. There is, on the one hand, an interest in doing what is best for the child and, on the other hand, a need to respond in a way that protects society. These goals are not necessarily mutually exclusive, but it seems difficult to give each equal weight simultaneously.

Some response to misbehaving young people is necessary because delinquency is a worldwide problem. United Nations data were used to show how all regions of the world report problems with misbehaving youth. Nations do not agree, however, on what constitutes delinquency, who is a "juvenile," or what is the appropriate way to respond to juvenile offenders.

Given the difficulty in finding agreement on such seemingly simple things such as deciding who is included in the category of "juvenile" and what acts are "delinquent," it is not surprising that a variety of systems have developed to respond to misbehaving youth. Distinguishing among those systems is often accomplished by referring to whether a system tends to emphasize the protection and treatment of the young person or views juveniles as rational and culpable beings who must be held accountable for their behavior. We presented this dichotomy as a continuum with the ideal type of "welfare model" at one end and of "justice model" at the other end.

The emphasis in England and Wales on juveniles as rational and culpable people who should be held accountable for their actions through procedures that protect their due process rights explains their placement at the justice end of the continuum. That perspective contrasts with New Zealand's paternalistic approach where the focus is on the misbehaving juvenile more so than his or her actions and society's response is primarily through the family and community rather than government officials.

Falling between the systems of New Zealand and England and Wales are the systems of Italy and China. Italy's system seems closer to the New Zealand model since it specifies formal procedures but takes a rather tolerant approach toward the juvenile by emphasizing diversion from those formal procedures. China, on the other hand, seems more appropriately placed near England and Wales and views juveniles as rational and responsible for their actions, but considers the best response to be one of education and reliance on family and community.

Discussion Questions

- Can family group conferences truly have a positive impact on juvenile offenders and their victims, or are they more likely to be simply a way that the offenders can "get off easy"?
- Should American jurisdictions follow the example of Britain's "parenting orders" (this chapter's "Impact" section) and provide juvenile courts with legal options for both holding parents responsible for their children's behavior and providing parents with opportunities to improve their parenting skills? What are some pros and cons of doing so?
- Identify at least one positive and one negative aspect of the juvenile justice system from each of the four countries reviewed in this chapter.

References

Altan, L. (2014). Study on children's involvement in judicial proceedings: Contextual overview for the criminal justice phase—England, Wales and Northern Ireland. Retrieved from http://bookshop.europa.eu/

BBC News. (2011, March 28). Lords reject government bid to bin Youth Justice Board. Politics. Retrieved from http://www.bbc.co.uk/news/uk-politics-12887855

Bottoms, A., & Dignan, J. (2004). Youth justice in Great Britain. In M. Tonry & A. N. Doob (Eds.), *Crime and justice: A review of research* (Vol. 31, pp. 21–184). Chicago, IL: University of Chicago Press.

Bradley, T., Tauri, J., & Walters, R. (2006). Demythologizing youth justice in Aotearoa/New Zealand. In J. Muncie & B. Goldson (Eds.), *Comparative youth justice: Critical issues* (pp. 79–95). Thousand Oaks, CA: Sage.

Canetta, E. (2014). Study on children's involvement in judicial proceedings: Contextual overview for the criminal justice phase—Italy. Retrieved from http://bookshop.europa.eu/

Cavadino, M., & Dignan, J. (2006). *Penal systems: A comparative approach.* London, UK: Sage.

Cipriani, D. (2009). *Children's rights and the minimum age of criminal responsibility: A global perspective.* Burlington, VT: Ashgate.

Gatti, U., & Verde, A. (2016). Juvenile justice in Italy. Retrieved from http://www.oxfordhandbooks.com doi:10.1093/oxfordhb/9780199935383.013.66

Ghate, D., & Ramella, M. (2002). Positive parenting: The national evaluation of the Youth Justice Board's Parenting Programme. Retrieved from http://webarchive.nationalarchives.gov.uk/+/http://www.yjb.gov.uk/Publications/Resources/Downloads/PositiveParenting.pdf

GOV.UK. (2015a, August 12). What custody is like for young people. Young people in custody. Retrieved from https://www.gov.uk/young-people-in-custody/what-custody-is-like-for-young-people

GOV.UK. (2015b, October 9). Youth courts. Criminal courts. Retrieved from https://www.gov.uk/courts/youth-courts

GOV.UK. (2015c, August 12). Youth offending teams. Young people and the law. Retrieved from https://www.gov.uk/youth-offending-team

GOV.UK. (2016). Youth Justice Board. Retrieved from https://www.gov.uk/government/organisations/youth-justice-board-for-england-and-wales

Hartjen, C. A., & Kethineni, S. (1996). *Comparative delinquency: India and the United States.* New York, NY: Garland.

Hazel, N. (2008). Cross-national comparison of youth justice. Youth Justice Board. Retrieved from http://www.academia.edu/1621782/Cross-national_comparison_of_youth_justice

International Child Development Centre. (1998). Juvenile justice. *Innocenti Digest, 3.* Retrieved from http://www.unicef-irc.org/publications/105

Jou, S., Chang, L., & Hebenton, B. (2014). Youth justice in China. Oxford Handbooks Online. doi: 10.1093/oxfordhb/9780199935383.013.72. Retrieved from http://www.oxfordhandbooks.com/

Junger-Tas, J. (1996). Delinquency similar in western countries. *Overcrowded Times, 7*(1), 1, 10–13.

Junger-Tas, J., Marshall, I.-H., Enzmann, D., Killias, M., Steketee, M., & Gruszczynska, B. (2010). Chapter 30: Synthesis and outlook. *Juvenile delinquency in Europe and beyond: Results of the Second International Self-Report Delinquency Study* (pp. 423–427). New York, NY: Springer.

Letters. (2016, May 22). Youth justice board's record under scrutiny. *The Guardian.* Retrieved from https://www.theguardian.com/society/2016/may/22/youth-justice-board-record-under-scrutiny

Morris, A. (2004). Youth justice in New Zealand. In M. Tonry & A. N. Doob (Eds.), *Crime and justice: A review of research* (Vol. 31, pp. 243–292). Chicago, IL: University of Chicago Press.

Muncie, J., & Goldson, B. (2006). England and Wales: The new correctionalism. In J. Muncie & B. Goldson (Eds.), *Comparative youth justice: Critical issues* (pp. 35–47). Thousand Oaks, CA: Sage.

Musiani, F. (2006). Prison is not for kids: Children in conflict with the law. *UN Chronicle, XLIII*(4), 38–39.

Nelken, D. (2006). Italy: A lesson in tolerance? In J. Muncie & B. Goldson (Eds.), *Comparative youth justice: Critical issues* (pp. 159–175). Thousand Oaks, CA: Sage.

New Zealand Ministry of Justice. (2016, February 16). Overview of youth justice principles and processes. About the Youth Court. Retrieved from https://web.archive.org/web/20160216161115/http://www.justice.govt.nz/courts/youth/about-the-youth-court/overview-of-principles-and-process

New Zealand Ministry of Social Development. (2016a). Family group conferences. Child, Youth and Family. Retrieved from http://www.cyf.govt.nz/youth-justice/family-group-conferences.html

New Zealand Ministry of Social Development. (2016b). Youth justice. Child, Youth and Family. Retrieved from http://www.cyf.govt.nz/youth-justice/index.html

People's Republic of China. (1979). Criminal law of the People's Republic of China (amended version of 2011). Congressional-Executive Commission on China. Retrieved from http://www.cecc.gov/resources/legal-provisions/criminal-law-of-the-peoples-republic-of-china

People's Republic of China. (1991). Law on protection of minors. Retrieved from http://www.china.org.cn/english/government/207411.htm

People's Republic of China. (1999). Law on prevention of juvenile delinquency. Retrieved from http://www.npc.gov.cn/englishnpc/Law/2007-12/11/content_1383561.htm

Puffett, N. (2010, March 8). Rise in proportion of ethnic minorities in custody. Children & Young People Now. Retrieved from http://www.cypnow.co.uk/cyp/news/1042726/rise-proportion-ethnic-minorities-custody

Scalia, V. (2005). A lesson in tolerance? Juvenile justice in Italy. *Youth Justice, 5*(1), 33–44.

Shen, A. (2016). The role of the study–work school: A Chinese case study on early intervention and child-centred juvenile justice. *Youth Justice, 16*(2), 95–112. doi:10.1177/1473225415601250

Sloan, A., & Allison, E. (2015, June 24). Sharp rise in the proportion of young black and ethnic minority prisoners. *The Guardian.* Retrieved from http://www.theguardian.com

Tameside Metropolitan Borough. (2013, January 30). The parenting order. Tameside Youth Offending Team. Retrieved from http://www.tameside.gov.uk/yot/parentingorder

Tonry, M., & Chambers, C. (2012). Juvenile justice cross-nationally considered. In B. C. Feld & D. M. Bishop (Eds.), *The Oxford handbook of juvenile crime and juvenile justice* (pp. 871–897). New York, NY: Oxford University Press.

United Kingdom Parliament. (1998). Crime and Disorder Act 1998. Retrieved from http://www.legislation.gov.uk/ukpga/1998/37/contents

United Kingdom Parliament. (2003). Criminal Justice Act 2003. Retrieved from http://www.legislation.gov.uk/ukpga/2003/44/contents

United Nations. (1985). Standard Minimum Rules for the Administration of Juvenile Justice (the Beijing Rules). Office of the High Commissioner for Human Rights. Retrieved from http://www.ohchr.org/Documents/ProfessionalInterest/beijingrules.pdf

United Nations. (2011). Fact sheet on juvenile justice. Retrieved from http://www.un.org/esa/socdev/unyin/documents/wyr11/FactSheetonYouthandJuvenileJustice.pdf

Walker, J. (2015). Diversion from court proceedings: The New Zealand youth justice experience. Retrieved from http://www.oijj.org/en/docs/general/diversion-from-court-proceedings-the-new-zealand-youth-justice-experience

Wang, D. (2006). The study of juvenile delinquency and juvenile protection in the People's Republic of China. *Crime & Justice International, 22*(94), 4–13.

Winterdyk, J. (2002). Introduction. In J. Winterdyk (Ed.), *Juvenile justice systems: International perspectives* (2nd ed., pp. xi–xl). Toronto, Canada: Canadian Scholars' Press.

Wong, D. S. W. (2001). Changes in juvenile justice in China. *Youth & Society, 32*(4), 492–509. doi:10.1177/0044118x01032004005

Wooden, K. (1976). *Weeping in the playtime of others.* New York, NY: McGraw-Hill.

Yisheng, D., & Yijun, P. (2006). An introduction to the juvenile justice system in China: Traditional crime control meets the challenges of modernization. In P. C. Friday & X. Ren (Eds.), *Delinquency and juvenile justice systems in the non-Western world* (pp. 191–210). Monsey, NY: Criminal Justice Press.

Youth Justice Board. (2003). A guide to anti-social behaviour orders and acceptable behaviour contracts. Retrieved from https://www.gov.uk/government/uploads/system/uploads/attachment_data/file/219663/asbos9.pdf

Youth Justice Board. (2014). Support parents of young offenders: Section 9 case management guidance. Retrieved from https://www.gov.uk/government/publications/support-parents-of-young-offenders/support-parents-of-young-offenders-section-9-case-management-guidance

Zhang, L. (2008). Juvenile delinquency and justice in contemporary China: A critical review of the literature over 15 years. *Crime, Law and Social Change, 50*(3), 149–160. doi:10.1007/s10611-008-9137-1

Zhang, L., & Jianhong, L. (2007). China's Juvenile Delinquency Prevention Law. *International Journal of Offender Therapy and Comparative Criminology, 51*(5), 541–554. doi:10.1177/0306624x06292675

Zhao, R., Zhang, H., & Liu, J. (2014). China's juvenile justice: A system in transition. In J. Winterdyk (Ed.), *Juvenile justice: International perspectives, models, and trends* (pp. 137–162). Boca Raton, FL: CRC Press.

10

Japan: Examples of Effectiveness and Borrowing

LEARNING OBJECTIVES

After studying this chapter, you will be able to:

1. Identify two reasons why Japan provides an appropriate case study for highlighting the benefits of comparative study.

2. Summarize and explain four broad cultural patterns that may be helpful in understanding the relative success of Japan's social control model.

3. Explain the concept of bureaucratic informalism in the context of Japan's criminal justice system.

4. List and explain three aspects of Japanese policing that may help explain the police role in Japan's comparatively low crime rate.

5. Explain how the Japanese preference for compromise and conciliation and the importance of apology affect how the country's judiciary operates.

6. Describe how probation and parole operate in Japan.

COUNTRIES IN FOCUS

Japan   United States

Japan (see Map A.8) offers an excellent opportunity to highlight the benefits of comparative study. Its example is so perfect because much of Japan's criminal justice system is borrowed, yet the adaptation was made in the context of Japan's cultural heritage and the Eastern Asia legal tradition. The Japanese have a long history of identifying key elements of the social institutions in other countries and modifying those ingredients so that they become workable in Japan. This is an important point to remember as we conclude this tour of comparative criminal justice. Just because something works well in one country does not mean that it is appropriate for other countries. However, the procedures and experiences a country has with the components of its justice system may suggest useful modifications for the systems of other countries. As long as the receiving country remembers to adapt rather than adopt the idea, comparative studies will benefit individual countries and the world.

This concluding chapter on the criminal justice system of Japan drives home that point. After showing why Japan is an appropriate example for such concentrated attention, we review its history as a borrower of ideas; identify some relevant cultural patterns important in specific ideas that were adapted and how they were adapted; and then describe Japan's criminal justice system through review of its criminal law, police, courts, and corrections.

WHY STUDY JAPAN?

Japan is an island nation perceived by many people (the Japanese included) to be quite small—although size is a relative matter. Japan is admittedly dwarfed by such neighbors as China to its immediate west, Australia to the south, and the United States and Canada to its far east on the globe. A more accurate perspective is to compare Japan to some of the European countries: Japan's nearly 146,000 square miles of land area is considerably larger than Italy (116,000 square miles) and half again the size of the United Kingdom (94,000 square miles). If it were superimposed on a map of the United States, Japan's northern island of Hokkaido would begin just north of New York State (almost to Montreal, Canada), and the other main islands (Honshu, Shikoku, and Kyushu) would extend south into the Florida panhandle. Similar latitudes on America's West Coast would take Japan from Oregon's border with Washington to California's border with Mexico.

Since the post–World War II era, Japan has operated as a parliamentary-cabinet system. The National Diet (parliament) serves as the sole law-making organ of the state, whereas the Cabinet (the Prime Minister and other ministers of state) operates as the government's executive branch. The majority of Cabinet ministers are Diet members, serving simultaneously as heads of government departments and directors of civil servants. The Cabinet, then, combines politics (the Diet) with administration (government departments). Japan's constitution identifies the emperor as the symbol of the state and of the unity of the people, but his position does not include powers related to government.

Japan provides an appropriate case study for our purposes because (1) its criminal justice system seems to provide an effective response to the crime problem and (2) its effective criminal justice system owes much to the policies and procedures of criminal justice systems in other countries.

Japan's Effective Criminal Justice System

From the 1960s to the early 1990s, Japan's crime rate remained rather stable and low in comparison with other industrialized countries. Crime began increasing in the mid-1990s as Japan experienced an economic recession and Asia in general suffered a financial crisis. After peaking in the mid-2000s, Japan's crime rate has declined, and is now back to levels seen in the 1970s. As shown in Figure 10.1, Japan's imprisonment rate tracks rather closely to the crime rate. As crime increased from 1995 to 2005, so too did the imprisonment rate. Then as crime declined during the last decade to levels in the 1970s, the imprisonment rate also fell, but now actually remains relatively high when compared with earlier imprisonment rates. A similar "low crime/high imprisonment" situation in the United States led some experts to suggest that fewer crimes are committed when the criminals are in prison—although most experts believe the explanation is much more complex (Dewan, 2009; Wilson, 2011).

Even at its highest point since, Japan's crime rate remains among the lowest of all industrialized countries. When crime does occur and the police catch the offender, the Japanese criminal justice system continues to stand apart from those of other nations. More than 96 percent of the offenders eventually coming before a judge are convicted. Furthermore, nearly 99 percent of those convicted are sentenced to prison. As this chapter shows, such statistics are potentially misleading because informal control mechanisms are used at each stage regardless of the formal terminology. A conviction rate greater than 96 percent hides the fact that the vast majority of these cases are not contested by the defendant. Moreover, saying that 99 percent of those convicted receive a prison sentence seems impressive until we realize that over half of those prison sentences are suspended and, in most of those cases, the offender is not even placed under supervision in the community. However, even this significant use of informal sanctioning separates the Japanese system from most others in the industrialized world.

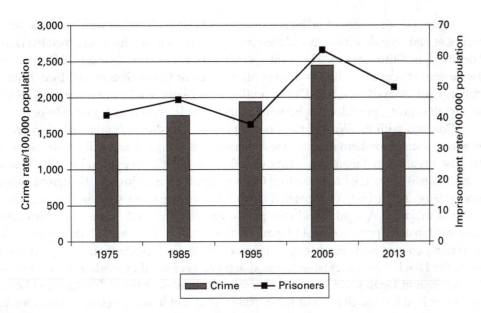

FIGURE 10.1 Crime and Inmate Trends in Japan

Source: Based on *White paper on crime 2014* (Part1/Chapter1/Section1 and Part2/Chapter4/Section1/1). Retrieved from http://hakusyo1.moj.go.jp/en/63/nfm/mokuji.html.

As a comparatively safe industrialized urban society, Japan has attracted much scholarly attention. Some studies have emphasized the police role (Bayley, 1991; Parker, 1984), others the law or the courts (Castberg, 1990; Johnson, 2002; Upham, 1987), and still others the corrections systems (Johnson, 2000; Parker, 1986). A common theme, at least among those scholars who actually visited Japan for their research, is an appreciation for the apparent absence of crime and the perception of safety that is produced. Bayley (1991) presents the feeling most succinctly by titling his first chapter "Heaven for a Cop." He also wonders, as have many other researchers and authors, how Japan's justice system operates, why it is so effective and efficient, and whether some of its features are transferable to other countries. In this chapter, we examine some scholars' attempts to answer these questions.

Borrowing in a Cross-Cultural Context

Diffusion is a classic way by which innovation is shared. This is true in the broad areas of science and humanities, as well as specific areas such as systems of justice. The way modern policing operated in early nineteenth-century America was heavily influenced by happenings and experiences in other countries. Prison construction in European countries was influenced by America's experiment with the Pennsylvania system. Roman law had specific and long-lasting impact on the legal systems of countries ranging from Europe to South America. Sometimes the influence of one country is imposed on another, but there are also occasions when ideas are freely and willingly imitated. Japan's system of criminal justice, as well as many of its other social institutions, has both imposed and imitated aspects.

In a fascinating manner, Westney (1987) provides detailed information on how Japan's Meiji Era transformation (1868–1912) relied on the deliberate emulation of Western organizations. The Japanese navy was modeled on the British; the army on the French and then on the German; the educational system on the French, the American, and the German; and the banking system on the American. This nineteenth-century willingness to look beyond its own boundaries was simply a continuation of an earlier disposition to view foreign ideas with favor.

Japan's first sources of influence (around 300 BCE–500 CE) were from the Asian continent and included important developments such as agriculture and metalworking. The fourth and fifth centuries brought specific influences from China (via Korea), and the Japanese became familiar with the philosophies of Confucianism and Buddhism as well as Chinese written script. China continued to play the role of primary model into the eighth century, providing Japan with a link to the Eastern Asia legal tradition.

Contacts with the West did not occur until 1543, when a Portuguese ship drifted ashore on a small southern island in the Japanese archipelago. These sailors, who brought the first firearms to Japan, were followed 6 years later by the arrival of the Spanish Jesuit, Francis Xavier, who introduced Christianity. By the 1630s, the Tokugawa shogunate became increasingly concerned that Christian missionaries were intent on political conquest of Japan. A rigid isolationist policy was adopted, and Portuguese ships could not enter Japanese ports nor could Japanese people take trips abroad. The only countries continuing contact with Japan were China and Holland. Despite their European placement, the Dutch were acceptable to the shogunate because they made it very clear that their interest in Japan was financial rather than spiritual or political. Through the Dutch, Japan received information about the outside world, but in many respects Japan missed the scientific and industrial revolutions of the eighteenth century.

By the early nineteenth century, Japan was confronted with internal pressure for political reform and external pressure for economic contacts. Russian and British ships made occasional approaches, but the real breakthrough came in 1853 when Commodore Matthew Perry and his fleet of ships forced the Japanese government to accept a letter from the president of the United States. The Tokugawa shogunate realized that the opening of Japan was inevitable, so treaties of friendship and commerce were initiated with Western countries.

Japan's period of modern history begins in 1868 when control of the government moved from the shogunate back to the emperor. This Meiji (after the reign name of the emperor) Restoration and the resulting Meiji Era (1868–1912) brought dramatic political, economic, and cultural changes to Japan. Things Western came to be defined as good, and the Japanese once again turned to other countries for ideas. Among the more important innovations was the 1890 establishment of a constitutional government modeled in the European tradition. The U.S. government structure was not deemed suitable to the Japanese because it did not provide for an emperor. Germany and Prussia, on the other hand, operated with a kaiser, and this provided a version of parliamentary government more appealing to Japan.

Over the centuries, Japan has been remarkably skillful in its borrowing practices. Whether it was religion from China or a political structure from Germany, the Japanese took to heart Sakuma Shozan's (a Tokugawa reformer) phrase "Eastern morals, Western science" (Upham, 1987). It was desirable to import and adapt Western learning but only while protecting the Japanese spirit. That philosophy continues today and provides the heart of this chapter's argument: Countries can and should learn from each other, but things borrowed must be adapted rather than adopted. To best understand the application of this argument, we must appreciate aspects of the "Japanese spirit" that have influenced the development of Japan's justice system.

JAPANESE CULTURAL PATTERNS

With Japan's increased economic prowess in the 1980s and 1990s came great interest among businesspeople around the world in everything from Japanese management techniques to the Japanese language. Concurrently, justice officials became intrigued with Japan's apparent success in responding to the crime problem. In all of these areas, Japan's accomplishments were reflective of its cultural heritage and Eastern Asia legal tradition.

The analogy of the bonsai has been used to make a similar point. Americans admire the bonsai tree for its simple elegance, its sense of harmony, and the serenity imparted by its miniaturization. In some ways, the bonsai is considered a metaphor for Japanese society itself: orderly, efficient, peaceful, with citizens acting in unanimity. Yet, before foreigners covet the bonsai or, by analogy, Japanese society, it is important to see how it got this way. The bonsai's beauty is the result of wiring and molding the limbs of the tree so that it does not develop beyond certain limits. The aesthetics of Japanese society may result from similar wiring and molding. We should not ignore the wires when admiring the tree.

Because every society has been shaped by its own peculiar heritage, the analogy of the bonsai can be repeated for each merely by choosing an object linked to the particular country. The danger in undertaking a discussion of any country's "wiring and molding" is to make its cultural patterns stereotypes. Japan, especially, poses this danger because of its many paradoxes. For example, Japan is a conservative society with radical student groups; a contemplative self is admired by materialistic and consumerist citizens; and the Japanese strive for a closeness with nature while surrounded by a serious pollution problem. Obviously, it can be unwise and unfair to associate specific patterns with Japan or the Japanese. Nevertheless, anthropologists and others realize that broadly stated cultural values help make sense of the complexity and variation found in all societies. If we approach the issue with an understanding of the potential problem of developing stereotypes, the search for cultural values—and even cultural patterns—can be beneficial.

With that warning, we shall look at the wires before admiring the tree. That is, before appreciating the apparent efficiency and success of Japan's criminal justice system, we will inspect the cultural mold in which that system operates. We do that by considering the impact some Japanese cultural values may have on the criminal act and on society's response. A number of cultural patterns have been used to understand better the success of Japan's social control mechanisms, but here we concentrate on its homogeneous society, the emphasis on context and harmony of social relationships, and a respect for hierarchy and authority.

Homogeneity

Japan is ethnically homogeneous, with almost 99 percent of its population being Japanese. The largest single minority group is the Koreans, with Chinese, Brazilians, and Filipinos making up most of the rest of the foreigners. Also noteworthy are the *burakumin* (or village people). Although fully Japanese, these physically and culturally indistinguishable citizens are the recipients of serious prejudice and discrimination. Presumably, the burakumin formed a social class during feudal times that was perceived as an outcast group (Hendry, 1989; Parker, 2013; Reischauer, 1988; Upham, 1987). The burakumin of Tokugawa times were those people engaged in defiling or dirty occupations such as burying the dead or working with dead animals (e.g., butchers and leather workers).

The Emancipation Edict of 1871 granted the burakumin formal liberation from their feudal status of outcasts. Yet, as with minorities in other countries and in other times, legal emancipation did not have much impact on burakumin status. Official government policy helped perpetuate prejudice and discrimination by registering burakumin as "new commoners" in the family registries maintained at each citizen's place of origin (Upham, 1987). Because descent from a Tokugawa outcast is the only distinguishing feature of burakumin, these public registries provided easy identification of, and discrimination against, buraku individuals. The estimated 2 percent or 3 percent of today's population who fall into this group continue to have underprivileged status, which forces substantial numbers into associations with *bōryokudan* criminal gangs (Kaplan & Dubro, 1986). That process concerns Japanese justice officials because bōryokudan activity has increased in recent years.

In apparent contradiction to the idea that homogeneity declines with increased division of labor, the Japanese continue to express similar values and hold tightly to common norms. When virtually all the country's inhabitants know and agree upon what it means to be Japanese, the job of social control becomes remarkably easier. However, homogeneity in itself cannot explain low crime rates. Certainly, there are many worldwide examples of citizens who know and agree upon particular norms yet continue to violate them. Japanese culture must provide more than simple similarity among its people.

Contextualism and Harmony

An important correlate to homogeneity is contextualism, or relativism. As noted in Chapter 4's introduction to the Eastern Asia legal tradition, attention to the context and relations among objects encourages one to take a more holistic view of the environment. One result of this perspective is a belief that standards of morality and ethics are determined by reference to the group rather than to rigid legal codes or universal principles (Archambeault & Fenwick, 1988; Reischauer, 1988). Instead of there being absolute standards of morality, all behavioral standards are relative to the context in which people find themselves. That belief system helps explain atrocities (such as the 1937 Nanking massacre of Manchurians by Japanese forces) committed in the context of war by the same people who, in their own country, report more things being found than lost (Becker, 1988; Parker, 1984).

One way to view this apparent contradiction is through the concepts of *tatemae* (how things appear) and *honne* (the underlying reality). Early in the socialization process, Japanese children learn the importance of maintaining harmony (*wa*). Yet, because complete and continual harmony can be only an ideal, Japanese become rather adept at portraying harmony even where it does not exist. Often the ideal harmony that primary groups display on the surface disguises the reality of conflict underneath. The observer will usually see only the tatemae face because airing dirty laundry to outsiders brings shame on the primary group. That is, the group (whether it be the family, neighborhood, workplace, or even sports team) is faulty because it cannot maintain harmony.

Putting the concepts of contextualism and harmony together, we can appreciate some of the control techniques popular in Japan. It is possible that in certain situations (contextualism), a person's own internal motivations (honne) may lead to deviant behavior. However, conventions require an offender, victim, and control agent to handle the problem so that tatemae is achieved. Keeping this in mind will help us understand the Japanese preference for informal justice and a firm belief in social over individual rehabilitation. Control techniques that present harmony are more easily found outside the formal setting of justice agencies. Furthermore, because misbehavior is contextual, hence social, the treatment must also be social. Put deviants in a nurturing social environment, and they will get better—this is the philosophy.

Collectivism

From the earliest life stages, Japanese learn the importance of the group to their existence and well-being. There is probably no clearer way to express the point than by noting an aspect of Japanese child-rearing practices. Misbehaving children in America are often punished by being confined to the house and made to stay with the family. In Japan, parents are more likely to put the misbehaving child outside the house. The American child clamors to be let out; the Japanese child begs to be let in. As Bayley (1991, p. 143) puts it, American mothers chase their children around the block trying to get them to come home, but Japanese mothers are chased by their children so that they won't get left behind.

The family and group orientation of Japanese society continues a sense of collective responsibility present since pre-Confucian Japan. As explained in Chapter 4, individualism is present, but it takes a different form than in America. A sense of personal self-worth and identity in Japan stems from the groups to which one belongs. In this sense, individualism in Japan is achieved through one's ability to create, maintain, and guard relationships. For example, a Japanese woman is likely to introduce herself as a faculty member at Tokyo University and her husband as a worker at Toyota. Secondarily, specific occupations such as psychologist or janitor may be offered, but the group affiliation takes precedence.

The Work Group

The importance of the group in Japanese society results in a sense of obligation of one toward others and helps explain a preference for avoiding behavior that may bring embarrassment to the group.

Imtmphoto/123RF

The sense of collectivism attaches to family, employer, school, and other groups. The accompanying close ties to both formal and informal groups result in a sense of obligation of one toward the others. Such associations give the individual solid emotional support, but those same close ties also bring a strong sense of shame and embarrassment when a group member misbehaves. It is still not uncommon to find a boss resigning for the employee's misconduct, or parents apologizing for the behavior of even a fully grown child. Family members experience a sense of shame and embarrassment if a member's conduct brings dishonor on the family. Importantly, such group consciousness and family identity push most Japanese to avoid actions that may bring pain, shame, and punishment on the group (Archambeault & Fenwick, 1988; Becker, 1988).

Finally, we must note that collectivism links to contextualism because the way a reference group interprets a standard is more important than the abstract standard itself. The group is placed above the individual. For purposes of criminal justice, this means that the goal of keeping society moral and crime free must take precedence over a goal of protecting the letter of each individual's rights in Japan. As we see later, a criticism of the Japanese system is its apparent preference for the crime control model over the due process model. In addition, the importance of collectivism means that threatened exclusion from the group is more likely to produce conformity than is a formal punishment.

Hierarchies and Order

An appreciation for hierarchical arrangements among people is the final element of Japanese culture to consider here. Whereas citizens of some countries express considerable distrust of their social institutions, the Japanese are not among them—especially given their affinity for an ordered hierarchical society.

The link between preferring hierarchies and faith in social institutions proceeds as follows: Japanese hierarchies, which are not just grounded in power, are of great variety and based on differing social prescriptions and social obligations. Group consciousness combines with a sense of order to force cooperative relationships between most segments of the Japanese community and their justice agencies. The respect for one's position leads citizens to honor and trust justice system employees. Police, courts, and corrections officials are seen as guardians of society's morals as well as enforcers of the law. As a result, the people's faith in the agents of the system and the belief that decisions will be made according to what best serves society allow the Japanese people to give extensive discretion to the criminal justice agents.

YOU SHOULD KNOW!

The Importance of Confession

One reason for the effectiveness of Japan's criminal justice system is the tendency of Japanese citizens to confess their misbehavior. That tendency is also seen by some observers as one of the system's greatest problems. The predicament is outlined in Article 38 of Japan's Constitution (Japan National Diet, 1946):

> No person shall be compelled to testify against himself. Confession made under compulsion, torture or threat, or after prolonged arrest or detention shall not be admitted in evidence. No person shall be convicted or punished in cases where the only proof against him is his own confession.

Confession has played an important role in Japanese criminal cases since the early part of the Meiji period when defendants could not be found guilty without a confession—even being called "the king of evidence" by contemporary police and prosecutors (Buerk, 2009; Tamiya, 1983). Unfortunately, the requirement for a confession was accompanied by an acceptance of torture as a means to encourage the admission and Amnesty International (2012) reports continued use of such ill treatment as beatings, intimidation, sleep deprivation, and making the suspect stand in a fixed position for long periods. Some who admit guilt are plainly innocent—as exonerations show—but police and prosecutors are under great pressure to make suspects talk (Anonymous, 2015). Article 38, then, presents a dilemma wherein one horn recognizes the importance of confession and the other horn recognizes the protection against self-incrimination. To date, it appears that the tradition of confession takes precedence over the constitutional protection.

Saito (1990) suggests that any efficient state system is likely to cause human rights infringements, and the Japanese criminal justice system is no exception. His particular concern is with the process of pretrial detention, which Saito argues is used for interrogation and to obtain a confession. Saito's position is supported by Hataguchi (1990), who argues that confessions are routinely admitted into evidence despite the likelihood that they are the result of police coercion, and by human rights groups who believe forced "confessions" are rarely ruled inadmissible by courts.

Because the values of contextualism, harmony, collectivism, and order are firmly grounded in Japanese culture, they help explain the Japanese response to criminal offenders and how that response differs from the response in other countries. Importantly, however, the Japanese difference is more in the means to the end than in the end itself. For example, as with most Western systems, the Japanese corrections system is caught between the often conflicting punishment goals of rehabilitation and retribution. Western systems typically seek rehabilitation by encouraging the offender to become independent and responsible. The Japanese system encourages the offender to integrate voluntarily into the structured social order. In addition, the Japanese see the community, rather than an institution, as the more likely place for getting that voluntary integration. Because imprisonment is not considered a useful means for achieving the rehabilitative goal, a low incarceration rate is not really surprising.

Although retribution is seen as an appropriate and desirable goal rather than following an "eye for an eye" philosophy, Japan secures the goal through "disgrace" or "reintegrative shaming" (see Braithwaite, 1989). This approach would not likely work in many Western heterogeneous societies, but the value of collectivism makes retribution through disgrace very effective in Japan. The Japanese desire and need for group association and acceptance make alienation from the group a harsh and meaningful punishment. Because the impact of alienation and rejection does not increase over time, there is no need to have long prison sentences.

CRIMINAL LAW

Japanese law traces its foundation to 604 CE as reviewed in a variety of interesting books and articles (Ryavec, 1983; Wigmore, 1936), but we begin with the nineteenth-century developments. During the period 1868–1945, the Japanese legal system reflected the development of Japan as an institutionalized monarchy beginning with the Meiji Restoration.

The New Code of Laws was created in 1870 and then revised in 1873 to incorporate what was basically the current penal law in China (George, 1983). By the 1880s, increased contacts with America and Europe brought Japan additional ideas about legal systems. Those of France and Germany were particularly appealing. With the assistance of a French criminal law scholar, the 1873 code was replaced with an 1880 version heavily emphasizing French legal principles. Soon after the 1882 implementation of the 1880 code, the Japanese came to appreciate German law. The Germans seemed to share Japan's view of law as a system imposed by an absolute monarch (the German kaiser and the Japanese emperor), so the 1907 Japanese code was modeled on the German code of that time. Even so, the Japanese were ever mindful of their own traditions. For example, the first three books of the new Civil Code (General Principles, Property Rights, and Obligations) resembled the German Civil Code, but the fourth and fifth books on Family and Inheritance Law were clearly based on Japanese custom (Oppler, 1977).

In its modern form (1946–present), Japanese criminal law received instruction from the United States during the Allied occupation after World War II. The 1947 constitution reflects Western influence by stipulating a separation of legislative, administrative, and judicial powers; extensive protection of civil liberties; and introducing the American system of judicial review (Hendry, 1989; Ryavec, 1983). The occupation lawyers who supervised the legal reforms had to remember that the Japanese legal system was built on a foundation using both civil and common legal traditions in the context of local custom (Oppler, 1977).

Fortunately, the occupying forces understood that the legal system could not simply be replaced with one that worked in England, the United States, or France. Using considerable input from Japanese lawyers, a legal system was outlined that brought innovation yet maintained tradition (Oppler, 1977). Hendry (1989) describes the result as another example of a Western-like exterior hiding a clearly Japanese interior. The Ministry of Justice in Tokyo serves as an analogy for itself: The brick front reflects the Western influence, but the interior of the building—like the core of the legal system itself—reflects the Japanese spirit. As we saw while discussing cultural values, part of that spirit is informality. Upham (1987) draws on the concept of informality to position the Japanese legal system in a different light than other systems. A brief review of his comments will provide a context within which we can view the specifics of Japanese police, courts, and corrections.

Law by Bureaucratic Informalism

Chapter 4 identified legal informalism as a key characteristic of the Eastern Asia legal tradition. That legal informalism was seen, for example, in Chapter 9's discussion of the authority given to Chinese police to handle informally misbehaving youths. Such informal procedures are not always apparent when reviewing China's criminal justice process. The greater transparency of Japan's procedures makes it easier to identify instances of legal informalism. Upham (1987) calls this aspect of Japan's criminal justice system *bureaucratic informalism*, and that phrase seems to be a more accurate term for how Japan incorporates this feature of the Eastern Asia legal tradition.

As we saw earlier, Japanese society emphasizes, among other values, those of contextualism, harmony, collectivism, and order. Collectivism is of initial importance here because it helps explain bureaucratic informalism wherein informal responses to misbehaving individuals confirm the view that Japanese society is harmonious and conflict free. When sanctions are private, indirect, and ambiguous, they can be virtually invisible to society at large. In this manner, tatemae is securely harmonious and the group, including its disobedient members, maintains its respectable position. As we review the components of the Japanese criminal justice system, we will see several examples of justice personnel using informal sanctions. In fact, even when the formal process is imposed, we will see prosecutors and judges preferring responses that are private and unceremonious.

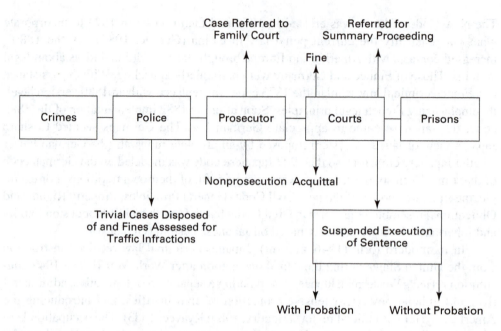

FIGURE 10.2   Flowchart of the Japanese Criminal Justice System for Adults

The formal process of Japanese criminal justice provides the basis and structure for the observations made in this chapter. As Figure 10.2 shows, the flow of adult cases is seemingly straightforward and rather reminiscent of flowcharts for the United States. That similarity allows us to approach the Japanese system from the traditional police, court, and corrections format. As we proceed through each of these stages, the informal system reinforcing the formal process is also discussed.

POLICING

The structure of Japanese policing was given close attention in Chapter 6, so discussion here can concentrate on its other aspects. Keeping with this chapter's theme of effectiveness and borrowing, we consider some reasons that law enforcement in Japan may be effective, and what, if anything, may transfer to America's police system.

Why Are the Japanese Police Effective?

The preceding heading "Why Are the Japanese Police Effective?" is somewhat misleading. It implies that the police are indeed effective, that we know why they are, and that the answer can be simply stated. It is hoped that you, the critical reader, will not be duped into such conclusions. The question is posed as a basis for discussion. If we accept Japan's comparatively low crime rate as a reflection of fact and if we believe that the police play a role in that low rate, we can at least dismiss problems regarding the term "effective." Similarly, if we accept the idea that aspects of police organization and citizen response affect how the police anywhere complete their work, we can identify possible reasons for any police agency's effectiveness or ineffectiveness. With these cautions in mind, let us draw on studies of Japanese policing in an attempt to understand what impact the police officer may have in Japan's comparatively low crime rate. Specifically, we direct our attention to (1) the deployment of police officers, (2) the working partnership with citizens, and (3) the police emphasis on a service role. These are not mutually exclusive categories, and all obviously work in concert to provide effective policing.

DEPLOYMENT OF POLICE OFFICERS A long-time problem for law enforcement officials has been determining the best way to distribute their forces over a geographic area. That deployment problem determines how the job is conducted and how supervision is carried out. Once police officers are dismissed from roll call, supervisors often lose any significant ability to monitor the officers' behavior. The supervision problem was a real concern to Henry Fielding when he initiated a patrol beat in mid-eighteenth-century England. A specified patrol area allowed more exact supervision of Fielding's men because absence from their particular area meant either a crime problem or a personnel problem.

Just as supervisors must know where their officers are, the officers need to be able to contact the supervisors. The classic scattering of officers throughout a geographic area made communication with supervisors rather difficult. The result could be officers who feel isolated and vulnerable. Boston responded to this problem in the 1870s by modifying its telegraph system in such a way that police call boxes could be positioned on city street corners so that officers could notify the supervisor that they were at their post (Rubinstein, 1973). The 1880 advent of two-way communication via the telephone call box meant that patrolmen could make hourly contact with the station house. Still, it remained difficult for the station to contact the officer. Rubinstein describes the horns, colored lights, and bells attached to the call boxes, which were activated from the station house when a supervisor wanted to contact the officer. The wireless radio and patrol cars provided the next technological advance. The cars allowed officers to patrol their territory more frequently, and the radio enabled the police station to quickly notify officers of a citizen's call for help.

Today, the use of patrol cars may seem not only the natural but maybe even the only way for a modern society to deploy its police. Japan has agreed in part, yet the country relies more heavily than many modern countries on a more static—or at least less mobile—type of deployment. In fact, its deployment system via the koban is offered by some as an explanation for police effectiveness (Bayley, 1991; Kim, 1987; Rake, 1987).

In addition to the use of radio patrol cars, Japan uses police boxes (recall descriptions in Chapter 6 of the koban and the chuzaisho) as a key means of police deployment. About 60 percent of Japan's police officers who are engaged in community policing (i.e., those assigned to patrol cars and police boxes) are posted at a koban or chuzaisho.

YOU SHOULD KNOW!
The Modern Koban

Police boxes continue to be widely found throughout Japan. The recognizable (and reassuring, to many Japanese citizens) red lamp above the entrance identifies these community policing structures for Japanese and foreigners alike. They are found in locations where people gather, such as parks, shopping areas, transportation hubs, and major intersections (Parker, 2013). Although varying widely in size, the police boxes (both koban and chuzaisho) generally have an office area and a simple kitchen and break room for officers. The residential police boxes (chuzaisho) also have living quarters for the officer and his or her family. Increasingly, both types of police boxes also incorporate a reception room (community room) where residents may meet.

All new police recruits begin their career at police boxes after receiving training at a prefectural police school.

At a typical koban, there is one supervisor and three police officers. One officer stays inside the koban doing administrative work while another is stationed outside the koban. The third officer patrols the area on foot. In addition to the officers, a police box may also have a counselor assigned. The counselors are not able to perform law-enforcement duties, but they can assist the officer in completing such tasks as giving directions, handling lost or found property, and responding to citizen questions. Similar duties are often performed by the wife of a police officer assigned to chuzaisho. Since the officer and family live at the residential police box, the wife must often receive residents who visit the chuzaisho when the officer is away. Wives at the chuzaisho receive a monthly residential police box allowance designed to reward their contribution to police activities (National Police Agency, 2005; Parker, 2013).

A Koban
Community policing in Japan relies in part on the widespread presence of neighborhood police stations or koban.

Takatoshi Kurikawa/Alamy Stock Photo

Tracing its origin to checkpoints the samurai established to protect the populace in feudal times, the koban now number about 6,300 and the chuzaisho around 6,600 (National Police Agency, 2005, 2015).

Japan's reliance on static deployment through fixed koban and chuzaisho posts, rather than dynamic deployment via constantly moving cars, occurs as much from necessity as from choice. Not only do the Japanese citizens strongly favor the koban, but the small proportion of Japanese land devoted to streets makes patrolling by car less feasible than in other countries. For example, only 20 percent of Tokyo's land area is composed of streets, compared with 28 percent in New York City, 43 percent in Washington, DC, and 44 percent in Boston (Gardner, 2011). Highly congested cities and streets mean that koban officers on bicycle or foot often beat patrol cars to scenes requiring police response.

The koban is a community fixture physically representing the link between police and citizens. It operates, and is perceived, as much like an assistance office as a police post. Koban officials spend much of their shift providing information about locations and addresses of homes and businesses tucked away in the confusing maze of often unnamed Japanese streets. They also act as the neighborhood lost and found, distribute crime prevention circulars, provide initial response to calls for assistance, and offer other services benefiting the community and citizens. The character of each koban is influenced by its surroundings; in some locations it may provide a community television set, whereas in others it serves as the primary time check and alarm clock (Bayley, 1991). Essentially, the needs of the neighborhood determine any unique traits found in individual koban.

The services provided at the koban and by the koban officers truly reflect the concept of community policing. The koban officers, who are not considered to know the area until after 2 years at the post, spend 56 hours on duty each week. This deployment system means that every part of Japan is continually under the supervision of a koban (or chuzaisho) officer who is familiar with, and known to, the residents of that area. Not surprisingly, koban officers and citizens develop a strong working relationship, which serves to make the police more effective.

THE CITIZEN AS PARTNER   During the informal stage of police development in England and the American colonies, policing relied on the efforts of individual citizens. Whether the citizen was issuing or answering the old "hue and cry" or was more actively serving as watchman or constable, policing depended on citizen participation. The growth of professional police work in the early twentieth century in the United States was accompanied by a philosophy that citizen involvement in policing was inappropriate. Instead, law

WEB PROJECT

Visiting a Koban

Search YouTube (http://www.youtube.com) for "Japan koban" and check out a few of the results. Also take a look at "Look at the 'top ten' koban shown" at http:// inventorspot.com/articles/top_ten_strange_unusual_japanese_6732. Write a paragraph that summarizes your impression of the koban's function in Japan.

enforcement was the duty of professional police officials who only incidentally had to interact with the law-abiding citizen. By the 1960s and 1970s, the pendulum was swinging back, and American police officials were recognizing the need for active citizen participation in crime prevention and reduction activities. In Japan, the tradition of police–citizen cooperation was never forsaken.

Building from a base that may stretch back some 600 years, Japan has established formal and informal associations that include crime prevention activities now linking the citizen and the police (Bayley, 1991; Kim, 1987; National Police Agency, 2015). Crime prevention associations exist from the central government level down to the neighborhoods, but the primary organization level is tied to police station jurisdictions. Association members cooperate with the police to maintain social order through activities such as distributing crime prevention literature and maintaining "contact points" where information and police assistance are available. Some crime prevention organizations may even organize civilian watches, which help monitor juvenile behavior, patrol streets, and assist police during emergencies.

Police response to these civilian efforts is one of support and encouragement. That cooperation requires Japanese police to place significant emphasis on nonenforcement activities and to interact with people other than those acting illegally. The result is a service orientation, which may also explain police effectiveness.

POLICING AS SERVICE Monkkonen (1981) reminds us that prior to the 1890s American policing had a strong service component. Police stations served many functions now handled by social welfare agencies, and police officers provided as much service as enforcement. Between the 1890s and 1920, the public service work of police departments disappeared or was substantially diminished. Couple that with the movement toward professionalism and the disinvolvement of a citizen-partner, and the United States was left with rather isolated police officers.

Mid-twentieth-century American police officers had few occasions to interact with the helpful law-abiding citizen or even the troubled resident who had fallen on hard times. Instead, daily association was (and essentially still is) primarily with society's riffraff. Even when they interact with a supposedly upstanding citizen, it is often because that citizen has crossed the boundary into deviance. No wonder police officers are accused of having a distorted image of John and Jane Citizen. When you constantly see people's misbehavior, it is easy to assume that people are basically bad.

The deployment system for Japanese police and the citizen–police partnership provides the Japanese officer a different view of people. Japanese police are informally called *Omawari-san* (the Honorable Mr. Walkabout), and their constant presence in the community gives them many opportunities to see people's good behavior. One result of this exposure to law-abiding citizens is the police officers' willingness to operate in a service capacity instead of constantly emphasizing their crime-fighter role.

The Japanese police officer's presence in the community is fittingly described by Bayley's (1991, p. 86) comparison of policing styles in America and Japan by suggesting that American police officers are like firefighters in the sense that they respond as required. Japanese police officers, on the other hand, are more like mail carriers because they have a daily round of low-key activities that relate them to the lives of the people with whom they work. The Japanese officer is consistently polite and businesslike during encounters with citizens and the officer's presence is considered rather routine and personal. Police involvement in activities seemingly unrelated to law enforcement is accepted and expected by Japanese citizens.

One of the best examples of nonenforcement activities and one that also emphasizes the citizen–police partnership is the "door-to-door visit" during which koban and chuzaisho officers periodically make routine visits to houses and businesses on their beat.

During these visits, the officers give advice on crime and accident prevention, listen to residents' concerns, and welcome suggestions for improvement of police services. The citizens in turn provide information about possible criminal activity in the area and may pass on rumors about neighborhood happenings (Bayley, 1991; Kim, 1987; National Police Agency, 2005, 2015). What may be considered an invasion of privacy in some countries is typically accepted in Japan as a way for police to gain knowledge of an area and its people.

The door-to-door visits are viewed as an important way to maintain a good relationship between police and citizen, but the National Police Agency (2005) is expressing concern about the increasing difficulty in carrying out these visits. As officers spend more time responding to occurrences of crimes and accidents, they have less time to conduct the visits. In addition, lifestyle changes have resulted in people being less likely to be at home and available (or willing, when they are home) to participate in the surveys. In an attempt to resolve this problem, some prefectural police have assigned older, more experienced officers to handle only the door-to-door visits.

The Japanese police officer's ability to play the potentially conflicting roles of authority figure and fellow citizen speaks well of both the officer and the citizen. Of course, it also reflects some of the cultural patterns discussed earlier in this chapter. Police officers represent one of the hardest-working groups among hardworking people. They view their fellow officers and supervisors as an extension of their family and take enormous pride in the successful performance of their roles. For their part, the citizens' respect for authority and orderliness, coupled with an acceptance of responsibility for each other's behavior, provides an atmosphere supporting police efforts. But, of course, the police are not the extent of the criminal justice system. We must also understand the role played by the courts.

JUDICIARY

Just as Japan's policing exhibits an intriguing combination of tradition, innovation, and imitation, so too does its contemporary court system. First, we examine the historical base for the adjudication system, and then we consider how the end result reflects aspects of Japanese cultural patterns. Especially meaningful in this section is the preference for compromise and conciliation and the importance of apology.

The Japanese judicial system certainly owes some of its features to the Chinese, but there always seems to have been a glimmer of features more typically associated with European legal traditions. For example, aspects of precedent and a role for adversaries have been present since the first developmental stage of Japanese legal process, but this does not appear to be the result of borrowing. Instead, the similarity to common law is an element that seems to have developed independent of outside influence. Since the 1600s, Japan's highly organized court system began developing a body of native law and practice based on judicial precedent. Though similar to the practice of stare decisis in English common law, Japan's development of judicial precedent cannot be attributed to borrowing from the common law tradition.

To see how judicial precedent has operated in Japan, it is necessary to describe the organization of courts. The regency domain was divided into three jurisdictions: metropolitan, rural, and ecclesiastical. The metropolitan judge received all suits in which the plaintiff was a townsperson, the exchequer judge got those with a country person plaintiff, and the Temple Judge accepted complaints from residents of church lands. When sitting as a single court, these three judges formed the supreme court, which had original jurisdiction in cases between parties from different jurisdictions. Actually, the men in these positions were not as busy as that description sounds. Each post was in fact held by two officials with each, in alternate months, sitting in the supreme court.

At other times, he officiated in his own jurisdiction. Even in his home province, lower magistrates heard most cases.

Within this structure, an independent system of case law developed without the need to cite Chinese or any other foreign authority. To make his point, Wigmore (1936) quotes at length a case that included formal and recorded consultation between judges, a search for precedent extending back nearly 100 years, the application of precedent, and the creation of new precedent. English case law had no advantage over this aspect of the Tokugawa legal system.

The Japanese desire to appease disputes is borrowed from the Chinese principle of conciliation as emphasized by Confucian philosophy. To achieve conciliation, each Japanese town and village was divided into *kumi*, or groupings of five neighboring families, with each responsible for the other's conduct. In times of disagreement, the five family heads met to settle the matter. In a dinner-party type of atmosphere, agreement was achieved in the midst of eating, drinking, and a friendly spirit. On those occasions when settlement was not reached, the complaint could be passed to a higher authority. Such appeal occurred more often in larger towns and cities. In the villages, the seeking of settlement outside the kumi or beyond the chief village officials was considered a dishonorable last resort.

Once a magistrate received a case from either a village or city, it could still be treated in a manner Western eyes may see as extralegal. Wigmore (1936) provides several examples of decisions that reflect an extremely flexible view toward the law. In an 1840 case, the magistrate of Komo County was asked to order a woman (Cho) and her four male family members to stop bothering farmer Uhei and his son Umakichi. Cho's family claimed Umakichi should marry Cho because prior relations (the exact nature of which are not specified) between the boy and girl made marriage the honorable thing to do. The magistrate investigated the case and apparently encouraged the two families to reach a settlement of their own accord. The records show that later in the same month as the first petition, Uhei asked the magistrate to dismiss the petition. Uhei explained in his second petition that the affair turned out to be unimportant and based on foolish statements. All parties were at peace, and Uhei credited the magistrate with bringing about the settlement. The petition asked the magistrate to shut his eyes to the case and not give it further consideration. Magistrate Shinomoto concurred, and no legal action was ever taken.

A more recent case suggests that 140 years did not significantly modify Japanese aversion to litigation and court activities (see Hendry, 1989, pp. 190–191). In 1983, a family's 3-year-old son drowned in an irrigation pond while he was in the care of a neighbor. The bereaved family filed a lawsuit claiming negligence by the neighbor, the contractor who had failed to fence in the pond, and against various levels of government. The district court ordered the neighbors to pay 5 million yen, but the other parties were exonerated. The case received considerable media coverage, and the bereaved family soon received hundreds of anonymous phone calls and some 50 letters and postcards condemning them for taking legal action against their neighbors. The father lost his job, and the other children in the family were subjected to ridicule at school. The neighbors, meanwhile, appealed the court's decision. This action elicited a similarly abusive response from the public. Apparently, appealing to the courts, even in self-defense, is regarded as being inappropriate, as are cases of disputes between neighbors.

These cases exemplify civil rather than criminal incidents, but the principle remains. Since the Tokugawa era, official conciliation procedures have provided alternatives to civil litigation and to criminal trials when the preferred informal conciliation efforts fail. The main difference between historical and modern procedures is the people playing the role of mediator. Where samurai and village officials served in the past,

IMPACT

WIRES AROUND THE BONSAI

This chapter emphasizes the general ideas of system effectiveness and borrowing. Japan has been cited for years as an example of a country with a low crime rate and an apparently effective criminal justice system. Its success is all the more intriguing when we realize that much of Japan's system is the result of borrowing from other countries and either modifying the ideas to fit in Japanese culture or modifying the culture to accept the new ideas. The result is a justice system looked upon by other countries, including some Japan has borrowed from, as a model for improving their own criminal justice procedures. This chapter concludes with a discussion of aspects of the Japanese system that could be transported to the United States. As a contrast to that optimism, this "Impact" section provides a necessary caution. Cultural differences make the transfer of some Japanese procedures unlikely and even undesirable for many Americans. It is just as important for a country to realize what it cannot adapt as it is to understand what is adaptable.

As this chapter notes, the beauty, simplicity, and harmony of the bonsai tree are not achieved without stifling freedom of growth by using wires and cutting to train the bonsai. Similarly, the unity, order, and safety of Japanese society are accomplished by, according to American values, some inhibition of personal freedoms. Consider, for example, the value of privacy.

Reasons given for the effectiveness of Japanese police included their working relationship with citizens and their service orientation. Those concepts sound innocent enough, but some Americans may be troubled by some of the techniques used in their practice. Consider, for example, the residential survey conducted by koban officers twice a year. Americans may not be so willing as Japanese to share personal and neighborhood information with police officers. It is possible that surveys by American police would result in such resentment as to offset any gains made by obtaining the information.

Parker (1984) writes about koban officers on patrol entering a home found unlocked and unoccupied. The officer leaves a calling card with his name on one side and a possible comment on the reverse warning the occupants about their poor crime prevention habits. Because police behavior in Japan reflects a moral norm as much as a legal one, Parker argues, such paternalism is acceptable in Japan. Many Americans may find such behavior to be overly intrusive.

Intrusive behavior does not only take place in the citizen's home. Japanese law allows police officers to stop and question people only if they have reasonable grounds for suspecting they have committed or are about to commit a crime, or have information about a crime. Despite that, Bayley (1991) found it to be standard patrol procedure to stop and question anyone whenever the officer found it useful. Because most arrests are made by koban and chuzaisho officers—and most of those are the result of field interrogations—the officers become very adept at on-street questioning and are usually able to elicit information and even consent to be searched.

To the extent that these features of the Japanese system are important to that system's effectiveness, Americans may wonder whether the trade-off of personal rights and due process would be worth the possibly lower crime rate.

police officers and lawyers act today. As we review the formal system of handling criminal disputes, we will necessarily refer to some of the informal procedures reflecting conciliation ideals.

Pretrial Activities

There is a saying about the American criminal process that "in the Halls of Justice, justice is in the halls." The implication is that much of the everyday work by justice officials takes place away from the formal courtroom environment. Police deals with informants, prosecution favors in return for testimony, plea negotiations, sentencing arrangements, and other activities constantly take place in informal settings.

At times those informal arrangements result in very formal activities (e.g., a formal contract stating a plea bargain agreement), but they may also simply remain an informal transaction. Japan's aversion to courtroom activities suggests that their "hallway justice" is even more pronounced than our own. This conclusion will be confirmed as we become familiar with the actors and actions involved at the pretrial stage.

POLICE ROLE Clearance rate for all penal code offenses in Japan is about 30 percent. Looking only at serious violent offenses, it appears that Japanese police clear 70 percent of the reported murder, robbery, rape, and assault cases (National Police Agency, 2015, Appendix 2). When compared with clearance rate for the same crime categories in the United States, Japan's police still seem to be doing an impressive job. The Uniform Crime Reports show a 48 percent clearance rate for violent crime in the United States (Federal Bureau of Investigation, 2014).

As with all comparative data, it is important to consider the impact of any reporting differences between countries. For example, cleared cases in Japan include cases disposed by police as trivial offenses in addition to those cases referred to public prosecutors (Ministry of Justice, 2014). The clearance rate for American police reflects a suspect being arrested, charged with committing an offense, and turned over to the court for prosecution (Federal Bureau of Investigation, 2014). In Japan, a crime is reported as cleared when the police tell the prosecutor the crime has been solved. No arrest is necessary. Even when an arrest is made, the police need not turn the suspect over in order to "clear" the crime (Araki, 1985; National Police Agency, 2012). By these definitions, Japanese police may well be expected to have a higher clearance rate than their American counterparts.

Japanese police have three choices in initiating cases. They can (1) send only the evidence to the prosecutor, leaving the suspect unarrested but still liable to prosecution, (2) arrest the suspect but decide not to detain him or her, or (3) arrest the suspect and recommend that the prosecutor detain him or her (Araki, 1985, p. 609). The first situation (evidence forwarded, suspect not), which is established by the local prosecutor's office, applies to most of the cases and allows police to clear a case and then discharge the suspect. In fact, the United Nations Asia and Far East Institute (UNAFEI) estimates that about 67 percent of suspects in non-traffic offenses are investigated and processed without arrest (UNAFEI, 2014). Each chief of the district public prosecutor's office

---

YOU SHOULD KNOW!
Suspect Rights

In 2006, Japan's House of Councilors passed a bill that improves the treatment of criminal suspects awaiting trial or sentencing. The law is aimed at the police detention centers (*daiyo kangoku*, or substitute prisons) where suspects may be detained when a regular detention center (e.g., jail) is not available. The substitute prison system has been harshly criticized both in Japan and internationally as a breeding ground for human rights violations. Suspects can be detained—solely under police authority—for up to 23 days for each charge. Since the 23-day period can be repeated over and over if there are multiple charges, suspects have been held in police detention for months.

The problem, critics argue, is that suspects are continually under the control of the police and there are no rules or regulations regarding length of interrogation. Further, lawyers' access to their clients during interrogations is restricted and there is no electronic recording of interviews by police.

The new law does not abolish the daiyo kangoku system, but it does require that investigating officers be separated from those who supervise the detainees. It also calls for prefectural police to establish panels of regular citizens and lawyers who can hear detainee complaints about their treatment. Despite these modifications, Amnesty International (2016) claims the daiyo kangoku system continues to facilitate torture and other ill-treatment as police seek to extract confessions during interrogation.

develops criteria permitting police to discharge persons committing less serious offenses when the crime and criminal are determined to be nondangerous.

The institutionalization of informal sanctioning is only one indication of the significant discretion given to Japanese police. Contextualism, as discussed earlier, plays an important role in understanding when and why police use their discretion to respond informally to offenses. Enforcement is influenced by where the offense occurred so that officers may respond according to the custom of each area (i.e., contextualism). In other instances, officers may believe that formal punishment would be inappropriately severe in a particular case and respond with anything from friendly warnings to ignoring evidence.

It is apparent that these examples of police discretion can just as accurately describe American, and almost any other, police officers as well. The difference lies more in the extent to which nonenforcement tactics are used than in their form or the situation provoking them. Generally, Japanese police officers make liberal use of policing tactics that avoid the formal justice process.

One reason that Japanese officers are likely to use informal tactics stems from their collectivist culture. Because the significance of the group is accepted by most Japanese, they are also aware of the obligations accompanying group membership. One of the most basic obligations is to refrain from embarrassing the group. If that obligation is not met, the dutiful group member will do his best to avoid public display of the misconduct. The police, being fully aware of this protocol, can use it to handle the situation informally. The primary method employed is to require an apology from the offender.

Americans may consider giving an apology to one's victim to be barely a slap on the offender's wrist. Yet this is where the cultural differences come into play. When a Japanese apologizes, he or she is admitting to having failed in his or her obligation to the group, an important concept to all concerned. Were that not bad enough, an apology also forces recognition of honne overcoming tatemae. It is no easy task to admit that one is responsible for disrupting the harmony, has failed in his or her duty to the group, and has jeopardized his or her group standing. The apology, in other words, can simultaneously be a punishment for the acutely embarrassed offender and an expression of remorse to compensate the victim.

Bayley (1991) relates several stories of observed police encounters that resulted in a formal apology as the police-imposed sanction. The tactic, which is always at the discretion of the officer, is used for minor violations ranging from traffic offenses and wandering drunks to inappropriate behavior toward fellow citizens. The apology as sanction is so commonly used that koban officers may keep a copy of an appropriate letter of apology to be used by remorseful offenders. At the same time, it is taken so seriously by Japanese citizens and police that some offenders are simply warned instead of being required to make a formal apology.

The police preference for nonenforcement strategies in responding to offenders is not unique to this stage of the Japanese criminal justice system. Of course, there are situations that require the police to respond formally and send the case to the next stage. However, as we will see, prosecutors and judges continue both the process and the propensity for informal sanctioning.

PROSECUTOR ROLE Prosecution in Japan falls under the authority of the Ministry of Justice and is under the direction of a prosecutor-general, who is appointed by the Cabinet. Neither the prefectural government nor any of the other subdivisions has any control of prosecution. So, unlike the police system, which has aspects of decentralization via prefectural involvement, prosecution is fully centralized (UNAFEI, 2014).

The prosecutor's primary activity is to gather information regarding the case and to provide information about the suspect to assist the judge in sentencing. Actually, these two activities define the role not only of prosecutors but also of police, defense, and even the trial itself (Castberg, 1990). This fact appeared to be true in our discussion of the pretrial activities of police, and we will soon appreciate its pertinence to the defense and in the trial, but we must begin with the prosecutor.

Given the vigorous investigation by police and the typical confession they are able to elicit, it may seem the prosecutor's job must require only minimum effort. Actually, there is still plenty to keep prosecutors busy because they must determine whether there is sufficient evidence to prosecute, initiate specific charges, and decide whether the prosecution should be suspended. Defendants in Japan cannot be found guilty solely on the basis of a confession, so prosecutors must have sufficient additional information to convince the judge of the defendant's guilt. Also, there is no plea bargaining in Japan, so determination of specific charges against the suspect is neither automatic nor always simple. Despite the time requirements for those activities, a spur-of-the-moment visit to a prosecutor's office is likely to find him pondering the appropriateness of suspending prosecution in a particular case.

The authority to suspend prosecution in a case is provided in Article 248 of the Code of Criminal Procedure, which requires prosecutors to consider these factors concerning the suspect and the crime (UNAFEI, 2014, p. 24):

- The offender's character, age, and situation (e.g., is the offender a young person or an elderly adult without a significant prior record?)
- The gravity of the offense
- The circumstances under which the offense was committed (e.g., whether the victim was partially at fault)
- Conditions subsequent to the commission of the offense (e.g., whether compensation has been made, the victim's feelings have been remedied)

Because prosecution is actually terminated in these cases, the term suspension is somewhat misleading. In any event, suspension of prosecution is an increasingly popular way for prosecutors to handle criminal cases. From a 1993 rate of 33 percent, suspension of prosecution increased to about 58 percent today.

Offenses ranging from homicide to gambling receive this prosecutorial response each year. However, as Table 10.1 shows, suspension of prosecution is especially used in embezzlement cases and in cases of negligent driving that causes death or injury. Not surprisingly, it is least often used in violent crime cases.

Article 248 is very general in setting criteria for prosecutors to use when deciding whether suspension of prosecution is appropriate. Reference to the "circumstances under which the offense was committed" concerns aggravating circumstances, such as excessive force or cruelty, which accompanied the crime. The "conditions subsequent to the commission of the offense" generally refers to apology and restitution by the suspect and forgiveness by the victim or victim's family. It is at this point that the defense attorney can begin an active role.

WEB PROJECT
Confessions and Exclusion of Evidence in Japan

The United Nations Asia and Far East Institute (UNAFEI) provides a very complete overview of the Japanese criminal justice system. Go to http://www.unafei.or.jp/english/pages/Publicationslist.htm and scroll down to find the most recent version of "Criminal Justice in Japan." Download the file and find Chapter 5: Trial Process, and then under "Rules of Evidence" look for the sections on "confession" and on "exclusionary rule." Write a paragraph explaining why you think a confession is not considered sufficient for a conviction. Write a second paragraph explaining why you believe the Japanese exclusionary rule is either more or less severe than the U.S. exclusionary rule.

TABLE 10.1	2013 Prosecution and Suspended Prosecution Percentages by Penal Code Offense		
		Prosecuted (%)	Suspended (%)
Total		33	65
Arson		48	22
Assault		34	64
Embezzlement		18	80
Homicide		31	11
Negligent driving causing death or injury		10	90
Rape		44	7
Robbery		54	9
Theft		41	52

Note: Based on White Paper on Crime 2013," Ministry of Justice (Appendix 2-3). Available at http://hakusyo1.moj.go.jp/en/nendo_nfm.html.

DEFENSE ATTORNEY ROLE In the United States, both suspects and the accused (defendants) enjoy the right to counsel (at government expense when necessary) from the earliest stages of the arrest process through the final stages of trial. Traditionally, Japan distinguished between the right to counsel for the suspect and the accused in a manner unfamiliar to Americans. Article 34 of Japan's constitution (Japan National Diet, 1946) states: "No person shall be arrested or detained without being at once informed of the charges against him or without the immediate privilege of counsel." Article 37 reads: "At all times the accused shall have the assistance of competent counsel who shall, if the accused is unable to secure the same by his own efforts, be assigned to his use by the State." In this manner, anyone "arrested" or "detained" had the "privilege of counsel," but because counsel in this case was a privilege rather than a right, the state was not obligated to pay for it. Therefore, indigents at the suspect stage were not provided counsel during the investigation/arrest process.

Once a Japanese suspect became an "accused" or defendant, Article 37 kicked in, and the state was obliged to provide competent counsel to assist the defendant during the trial phase. One result of the suspect/accused distinction was that few people held in pre-charge detention had access to an attorney. In fact, even suspects who could afford to hire a lawyer did not see their counsel very often because attorney access to the suspect was controlled by the investigating authorities.

The situation changed with the 2006 implementation of the 2004 Comprehensive Legal Support Law. That law established the Japan Legal Support Center (JLSC) under the Ministry of Justice and charged it with providing all citizens with information and services related to civil and criminal affairs. Regarding criminal affairs, this essentially meant the creation of a public defense system for detained criminal suspects charged with serious offenses (i.e., those punishable by death, life imprisonment, or a maximum prison sentence exceeding 3 years). Criminal defendants, who already had the right to court-appointed counsel, were affected by the new law only in terms of how that counsel was appointed. Today, at the court's request, the JLSC nominates attorneys as candidates to become court-appointed defense counsel to indigent suspects and defendants. The attorney fees are paid by the JLSC. Interestingly, if the defendant is eventually found guilty, he or she is obliged to pay the fees unless the court determines that payment is financially impossible for the offender (Ikenaga, 2013; UNAFEI, 2014).

Defense counsel's actual role in the Japanese proceedings is rather informal. For example, the attorney may accompany the defendant to contact the victim, or victim's family, so that appropriate apologies can be made and reparations offered. The defense attorney can advise the defendant regarding the proper way to show remorse and the appropriate restitution to offer. If counsel can obtain written statements of forgiveness and maybe even a victim's request for leniency toward the defendant, the prosecutor may be inclined to suspend prosecution. Should the victim's statements and requests for leniency not impress the prosecutor, defense counsel can always use them during the trial. In fact, because so many defendants have confessed, much of the defense role during trial is to present mitigating circumstances that may convince the judge to be sympathetic toward the defendant. However, even when there is no confession and the defendant is contesting the charge, a prime defense counsel role is to provide the judge with reasons to be compassionate (Castberg, 1990).

The pretrial activities of police, prosecutor, and defense attorney seem intent on avoiding formal sanctioning of suspects and defendants. This seeking of informal responses does not stop in those cases that actually do make it to a courtroom.

Court Structure and Trial Options

The public prosecutor's office typically handles around 1.4 million cases each year. About 65 percent of those are not prosecuted at all—because prosecution is suspended or due to insufficient evidence. Of the 35 percent going to court, the majority undergo summary proceeding (80 percent) and the remainder go to a trial court. More than 98 percent of the cases going to trial or summary proceedings result in a guilty plea or finding. Nearly all of those will receive a prison sentence, but 60 percent of those will have execution of that prison sentence suspended (Ministry of Justice, 2014, Table 2-3-1-1 and Figure 2-2-2-1; UNAFEI, 2014).

To emphasize the reluctance to impose formal sanctions, consider the numbers we would obtain by using these percentages on a hypothetical cluster of 1,000 offenders arriving at the prosecutor's office and not being transferred to family court (see Figure 10.3). Because about 650 of those would have either prosecution suspended or

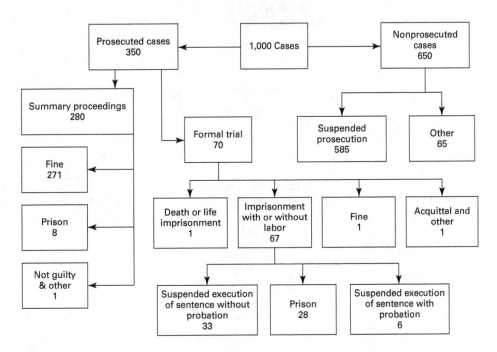

FIGURE 10.3 Dispositions by Prosecutor's Office of 1,000 Hypothetical Cases

no action toward prosecution even attempted, only 350 would even continue in the process. Of those 350 people being prosecuted, about 280 would plead guilty and have their case quickly handled through summary procedures for which they are not even present. Of the remaining 70 people going to formal trial, almost all would be convicted and sentenced to prison—an acquittal may occur but not often, or someone may be fined instead of imprisoned but, again, not often. About 39 of those convicted and sentenced to prison will have the execution of their sentence suspended. Only a few of those receiving a suspended execution of sentence will be placed on probation; the others will live in the community without any court supervision. Of the original 1,000 people, then, about 28 may actually be sent to prison.

It appears that the formal trial process is an infrequent occurrence in the Japanese criminal justice system. Even when adjudication is required, most of the cases are handled summarily instead of in a formal court setting. Following a brief review of Japan's court structure, we will look more closely at the summary procedures and regular trials.

COURT STRUCTURE   The Japanese court system has four levels composed of two trial courts and two appellate courts (see Figure 10.4). At the apex is Japan's Supreme Court, which was the primary judicial modification in the postwar constitution. The American influence is seen in the authority given to the Supreme Court, which has administrative control over all other courts and has the right to determine the constitutionality of all laws. This latter point, the concept of judicial review, presents an awkward situation because Japan's government is essentially parliamentary in nature. In most other such systems, nothing can override the parliament, but the right of judicial review gives Japan's judicial branch the authority to do just that. However, the Japanese Supreme Court has been reluctant to go against the Japanese Diet's political decisions and will typically defer to what the Diet majority voted (Reischauer, 1988). This is in contrast to the U.S. Supreme Court's vigorous use of judicial review to shape social and political developments.

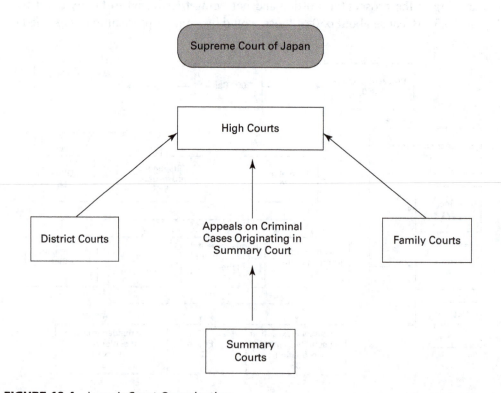

FIGURE 10.4   Japan's Court Organization

The Supreme Court consists of 1 chief justice and 14 justices. Cases, which are received on appeal, are initially assigned to one of three petty benches composed of five justices each. If the case concerns a constitutional issue, it is transferred to the Grand Bench, where all 15 justices sit (UNAFEI, 2014).

High courts are located in eight major cities in Japan. These courts serve as intermediate appellate courts with cases typically heard by a panel of three judges. Most of the high court cases come on appeal from the district or family courts, but criminal cases originating in summary court can also go directly to the high court.

The trial level courts for both criminal and civil offenses are the 50 district courts. Each of the 47 prefectures has one district court, but Hokkaido's size requires it to have an additional three. The district courts are the courts of first instance for all civil and criminal cases that are not exclusively reserved for summary courts (e.g., offenses punishable by fine or light sentence), family courts (e.g., offenses harmful to the welfare of juveniles), or high courts (e.g., offenses of insurrection). District court cases are heard by a single judge except in those cases involving possible death sentences, sentences to life imprisonment, or for crimes punishable by imprisonment for more than 1 year, which are heard by a panel of three judges (UNAFEI, 2014). Since 2009, for cases such as murder, robbery resulting in death or injury, rape resulting in death or injury, arson of an inhabited residence, and certain serious drug offenses, the panel of three professional judges is joined by six *Saiban-in* or lay judges.

Equal in number and location with the district courts, yet administratively independent, are the family courts. These courts, under a single judge or a three-judge panel, handle most domestic and juvenile (persons under age 20) matters. The only criminal matters heard in family court are those involving adults who have violated a child's well-being (typically less than 1 percent of family court cases).

Summary courts, in 438 locations nationwide, have original jurisdiction in minor criminal and civil cases. Cases heard in summary proceedings range from larceny to bodily injury, but the penalties imposed are limited to fines or imprisonment for no more than 3 years. The popularity of summary procedures with prosecutors and offenders makes the summary courts a good starting place in discussing Japan's adjudication process.

ADJUDICATION IN SUMMARY COURTS Japan has no grand jury system, so when the prosecutor decides to initiate formal proceedings the defendant is indicted through the filing of an information. Because there is no preliminary hearing, the next step is for the prosecutor to choose between a summary procedure and a regular trial. If the summary procedure is used, the case is handled in one of the country's summary courts. These courts also conduct a few formal trials, but the vast majority of their activities are summary proceedings.

If the defendant agrees (and that agreement is required for this procedure), the prosecutor can dispose of the case by sending the summary court judge the defendant's consent form, the evidence related to the case, and the prosecution's sentence recommendation (Araki, 1985; Castberg, 1990; UNAFEI, 2014). Neither party has the opportunity to appear before the summary court because the judge reviews the case outside the presence of either the prosecutor or defendant. However, there is a level of protection for both sides, because defense or prosecution can apply for a formal trial if either is dissatisfied with the ruling under summary procedures. The sanctions resulting from summary procedures are fines (both regular and minor), and they are used in both violent (e.g., bodily injury and assault) and nonviolent (e.g., embezzlement, gambling, and traffic violations) offenses.

ADJUDICATION WITH MODIFIED PUBLIC TRIALS If the charge is not a serious one (e.g., larceny) and the defendant is not contesting the facts, it is possible to have a formal, yet streamlined, trial (Araki, 1985; Castberg, 1990). These modified public trials can be held in either summary court or district court, but it is much more likely to be the former. Trial procedures are simplified, and great reliance is placed on information provided by the prosecutor as being an accurate reflection of the facts in the case. The judge's written work is simplified because this type of trial does not require written reasons for the decision, which can include fines or short-term (i.e., less than 3 years) detention.

ADJUDICATION WITH REGULAR TRIALS   District and family courts serve as the court of first instance for most contested criminal cases and for cases with which the defendant or prosecutor is not pleased with the result of a summary procedure. As noted earlier, criminal jurisdiction of family courts is limited to cases of domestic relations, juvenile delinquency, and cases in which adults violated laws protecting a child's welfare. The 50 district courts have jurisdiction over all criminal cases except insurrection (which must start in the high court), family court adult criminal cases, and crimes handled in summary court.

Although elements of both inquisitorial and adversarial procedures are found in Japan's courts, there is a greater emphasis on the adversarial model (UNAFEI, 2014). The judge controls the proceedings but the parties—especially the prosecutor—take an active role in developing the facts of the case. Inquisitorial elements are found in the single-stage procedure wherein evidence relevant to the defendant's guilt as well as evidence relevant to sentencing is heard during the trial.

Defendants have the right to remain silent and are not required to make any statement to the court. However, more than 90 percent of the defendants do in fact make a statement and admit their guilt. These noncontested cases are usually disposed of rather quickly. Because the defendant has confessed, the judge's role is to protect the accused's rights by examining all submitted evidence, occasionally requiring submission of more evidence, and determining an appropriate sentence.

When the defendant contests the charges, the Japanese court system follows its most formal procedures. In this type of trial, either there is a genuine dispute regarding the facts of the case or there is no confession. Depending on the charges, a single judge, a panel of judges, or a mixed panel of professional and lay judges serves as impartial adjudicator and fact finder.

Lay Judges

Between 1928 and 1943, Japan used a jury system for criminal cases. In its eventual format, the jury consisted of 12 literate male jurors over 30 years of age. Their verdict did not have to be unanimous—a simple majority was sufficient. During its 15-year existence, only 484 cases were tried by jury; defendants in more than 25,000 serious cases waived their right to a jury trial. Obviously, the idea did not catch on.

However, a recent reform to the justice system has once again given Japanese citizens a role in the adjudication process. Enacted in 2004 and implemented in 2009, the *Saiban-in* system adds lay judges (chosen by lot from among registered voters) to Japan's courts. Sitting with professional judges, the Saiban-in (citizen judge) hear from witnesses, examine evidence, and determine sentences in the most serious criminal cases. Panels are typically composed of three professional judges and six citizens, although in noncontested cases where the defendant has confessed and only sentencing remains, the court may use a panel with one professional and four lay judges. Each member of the panel has one vote, and decisions are by a majority vote that includes, in guilty decisions, at least one professional judge's ballot (Reichel & Suzuki, 2015).

Since the first Saiban-in trial in 2009, more than 42,000 people have served as lay judges. Nearly 7,500 defendants have been tried under the lay judge system and 7,300 were found guilty, including 22 who received the death sentence (Supreme Court of

Japan, 2015). This 97 percent conviction rate is about the same as was typical prior to implementation of the lay judge system. The high conviction rate is explained in part by noting that a trial is required even in cases where defendants have admitted guilt—with the admission simply being another piece of evidence to consider.

The lay judge system receives positive reviews from many sources. Japan's Supreme Court found it to be constitutional ("Lay judge system OK: Top court," 2011), practitioners and newspaper editorials make suggestions for improvement—but do not call for its elimination, and the formal review under the leadership of the Ministry of Justice had some general recommendations but gave an overall positive assessment.

Finally, it is important to note that Japan's experiment with citizen adjudicators is being closely watched in other Asian countries. The Japanese model may reflect Asian cultural values more closely than does the American jury system and, as a result, other Asian countries may find the Saiban-in system to be a more accommodating way to improve the quality of justice while enhancing public trust in the judiciary. For example, in 2013 South Korea's National Assembly gave official status to an advisory jury system that had been in an experimental stage since 2008. When the defendant agrees to this procedural addition, randomly selected civilian participants hear testimony and then deliberate on their own before consulting with professional judges regarding guilt and, as necessary, punishment (Kim, Park, Park, & Eom, 2013; Lee, 2009, 2010). Similarly, Taiwan is considering a proposal wherein a group of five randomly chosen citizens would sit with and advise three professional judges in serious criminal trials (Huang & Lin, 2013, 2014). To the extent Japan is able to set an Asian model for ordinary citizens to participate in deciding criminal cases, the Saiban-in system could be a major event of the early twenty-first century.

Judgments

Judges in district and family courts have several judgment types available. The defendant can, of course, be acquitted, but this occurs in less than 3 percent of the district court cases and less than 4 percent of cases in summary court (UNAFEI, 2014, p. 33). The high conviction rate in Japanese courts must be considered in light of the system's screening process and the defendant's tendency to confess. About 70 percent of the suspects are not arrested at all or are arrested and then released by the police. Then, as explained earlier and as shown in Figure 10.3, about 65 percent of the cases reaching the prosecutor are suspended and only about 20 percent of the cases that are prosecuted are heard in a formal trial. Even among that 20 percent, the majority of defendants do not contest the charges. Given these circumstances, a 96–97 percent conviction rate is not quite so surprising.

Allowable sentences for convicted offenders include the death penalty, life imprisonment, imprisonment with or without forced labor, or a fine. The execution of any sentence of imprisonment not exceeding 3 years or a fine not exceeding ¥500,000 (about $5000) can be suspended for 1–5 years if the defendant had not previously received (or received more than 5 years earlier) a sentence of imprisonment without work or a more severe penalty. Good behavior by the convicted offender for the period of suspension means the sentence will not be served. Since 2013, a partial suspension of execution has been possible. Prior to this new alternative, the only options were to serve the full sentence in prison, or to suspend execution of the entire sentence. Now, the offender can serve part of the sentence in prison and the remainder in the community—with reimprisonment possible for violations committed during the suspension (UNAFEI, 2014).

The majority of sentences (about 65 percent) are for 1–3 years (therefore may be eligible for suspension of execution) whereas fewer than 13 percent are for imprisonment longer than 3 years (UNAFEI, 2014). Neither the death sentence (given to about 10 offenders each year) nor life imprisonment (fewer than 50 each year) is handed down very often.

CORRECTIONS

Throughout the various shogunate periods, corrections (in its broadest sense) varied from the right of samurai to execute on the spot any misbehaving commoner to the use of prisons (*royas*) built in the fourteenth century as both pretrial holding facilities and places of punishments. Despite that historical base, the modern era of Japanese corrections did not begin until the late nineteenth and early twentieth centuries. The push toward modernization resulted from efforts during the Meiji Restoration to increase Japan's contact with the Western world. Actually, one of the stipulations made when revising treaties with the West required Japan to improve prison administration. Japan's response, as it was in so many other areas in the late nineteenth century, was to begin a search for a model to bring home.

By 1890 Japan had joined the International Penal and Penitentiary Congress and, with the assistance of Prussian penologist Kurt von Seebach, started the country's first national training institute for prison officers (Correction Bureau, 1990). Concern about the prison employees was not matched with concern for the inmates until the 1920s and the efforts of Japanese jurist Akira Masaki. His reminiscences provide a review of imitation and innovation as he describes the development of modern corrections in Japan (Masaki, 1964).

Masaki was sent abroad in 1928 to gather information on prison systems in other countries. Among his stops was the Hungarian farm prison, Kiss Halta, where he was impressed with the absence of iron bars and walls. The feature he would dwell upon, though, was the administrator's use of a prisoners' self-government policy controlled by a progressive stage system to modify prisoner behavior. A trip to the United States gave him an opportunity to see the classification system at Sing Sing prison (a system he found similar to a Belgian one he had earlier observed) and to visit the Elmira (New York) Reformatory, which he called the Mecca for criminologists (Masaki, 1964, p. 54).

American prisons at Sing Sing and Auburn (New York) and the naval prison at Portsmouth (New Hampshire) also provided Masaki an opportunity to gather more information on inmate self-government. He found that the process, as used in these prisons, had several defects, yet he believed that when properly implemented, inmate self-government could be the core of a treatment system.

In 1933, Masaki was finally able to try out some of his ideas gathered while abroad. Under orders from the director of the Prison Bureau, Masaki began to set up a progressive stage system. He used the classification procedure from Belgium and the United States to set up four specific stages of inmate categorization. Following the mark system observed at Elmira Reformatory (which had come to America from Australia via Ireland), Masaki awarded prisoners marks based on their work habits, good behavior, and showing responsibility and firm will. The marks allowed inmates to progress through the stages; with each promotion, they received more freedom and privileges.

At the second and first stages, self-government became an important aspect of the treatment plan. Inmates at these levels worked without the supervision of guards but instead under the leadership of a fellow prisoner they had selected. Unfortunately for Masaki, his program was criticized for being too lenient. Masaki admitted that some wardens forgot the need to instill a sense of responsibility in the prisoners, but he accepted the criticism and reported feelings of frustration with implementing a philosophy he believed to be correct. Today, the classification and progressive stage systems brought to Japan by Masaki remain important aspects of Japanese corrections, but the use of inmate self-government is not.

Community Corrections

Japan has both a low incarceration rate and a low percentage of persons under community supervision. This is surprising because one explanation for a low use of imprisonment may be the diversion of offenders into community-based programs rather than into prisons.

That is, in fact, what Japan does, but the release to the community is typically without any required supervision. Because the majority of offenders are returned to the community without correctional supervision, it is not fair to say that they are in a community-based program, yet clearly they have been given a community-based alternative!

PROBATION AND PAROLE Given the Japanese shared sense of shame and embarrassment when a group member misbehaves, it is not surprising that family and neighbors may resent offenders. An 1880s' case in which a discharged prisoner committed suicide after being rejected by family and community members led philanthropist Meizen Kinbara to establish a private aftercare halfway house (Parker, 1986). That facility provided shelter, employment, and guidance to released offenders with no place to return to in the community. Other private individuals and organizations, following Kinbara's lead, established a number of hostels throughout Japan. Halfway houses (officially, Offender Rehabilitation Facilities) remain an important part of Japan's corrections system, but we focus more on the probation and parole aspects.

Probation is available only as a complement to a suspended execution of sentence—rather than being available as a distinct sentencing option. Fewer than 10 percent of persons receiving a suspended sentence have probation conditions attached, so it actually is not used that often (UNAFEI, 2014). The probation period corresponds to the period of suspension of the execution of sentence that was given by the court.

There is no right to parole (early release from imprisonment), or even to apply for it, in Japan. Instead, the prison warden may request parole on the prisoner's behalf. The Regional Parole Board (RPB), which may also initiate its own parole examination, makes the actual decision regarding release on parole. A three-member RPB panel makes its decision on consideration of five factors: (1) the prisoner has served no less than one-third of the determinate sentence or 10 years of a life sentence, (2) the prisoner has shown remorse and a willingness to reform and rehabilitate, (3) there is no likelihood of recidivism during the proposed parole period, (4) parole supervision is a reasonable way to achieve reformation and rehabilitation, and (5) society will accept the parole (UNAFEI, 2014, p. 46). Parole from a prison sentence is a conditional release for the remaining term of the prisoner's sentence. Should a life-termer be paroled, that parole is for life unless he or she is granted a pardon.

Probation and parole supervision is carried out by probation officers, working under the Rehabilitation Bureau of the Ministry of Justice. That bureau administers rehabilitation services for the entire country out of its 50 probation offices that are located throughout the country in the jurisdictional areas of the district courts. The probation officers, who have a background in psychology, sociology, or education, provide aid and guidance to juvenile and adult offenders.

The probation officers are assisted in their endeavors by rehabilitation coordinators who must be qualified psychiatric social workers, public health nurses, or similarly qualified persons. These rehabilitation coordinators not only provide outpatient treatment but also coordinate the community-based treatment for outpatients among other agencies.

Assisting both the probation officers and the rehabilitation coordinators are some 50,000 volunteer probation officers (VPOs) across the country. The VPOs, under the direction of a probation officer, supervise and assist probationers and parolees by working with both the offender and the offender's family to encourage a successful adjustment. In addition, the VPOs help educate the public regarding the rehabilitative philosophy. This use of volunteers (unpaid except for expenses related to their activities) is considered desirable in Japan because the VPO is familiar with their community and able to give more effective guidance and aid than can a professional probation officer who may not be as familiar with the community (UNAFEI, 2014).

As in the United States, persons on probation or parole in Japan must abide by certain general conditions (e.g., live at a specified residence, refrain from criminal behavior, obtain permission before changing residence or taking trips, and maintain a sound attitude toward life). In addition to the general conditions, some probationers and parolees may be given special conditions relevant to their individual situation and needs. Special conditions may include avoiding contact with certain persons, going to certain places, or attending treatment programs. Failure to follow these restrictions on behavior can result in termination of probation or revocation of parole.

Prison Sentences

The supervision and treatment of inmates in all Japanese correctional institutions are the responsibility of the Correction Bureau of the Ministry of Justice. A result of this highly centralized structure is a unified and coordinated corrections system. The Correction Bureau operates nearly 190 penal institutions (including adult and juvenile prisons, their branches, and detention houses). Eight of the adult prisons and branches are designated for women prisoners—reflecting a more than 2.5 times increase in sentenced females since the mid-1990s. The number of sentenced inmates over age 60 has also increased (nearly tripling since the mid-1990s) and is now about 12 percent of the prison population. Unlike the United States, where an aging prison population results mostly from long mandatory sentences and restricted parole, the rise in Japan is driven chiefly by increased criminal behavior (mostly nonviolent) among older criminals (Ministry of Justice, n.d.; Onishi, 2007; UNAFEI, 2014).

In prison, the inmates have opportunities for work, education, and rehabilitation. Work assignments are in areas ranging from farming to metal- and woodwork. Vocational training is also available in such areas as auto mechanics. The inmates receive an incentive pay to encourage work and to provide funds for post-release. Education classes from elementary through high school and even university classes are matched to inmate needs and abilities. Rehabilitation programs include general guidance in appreciating the negative impact their actions had on crime victims and developing a law-abiding spirit and behavior. Depending on specific needs, treatment programs for drug abuse, sex offenses, job assistance, and other areas are also available.

COMING FULL CIRCLE

Japan is unique among countries of the world because of its comparatively low incarceration rate. That characteristic is all the more unusual because Japan emphasizes the same correctional objectives as most other countries: rehabilitation and retribution. Japan seeks to accomplish these objectives by a somewhat different route than other countries take. Whereas many Western countries seek rehabilitation by encouraging individualism, Japan secures it through an appeal to collectivism and social responsibility. Because association provides self-identity to the Japanese, rejection and alienation from the group (i.e., retribution) provide for society's revenge while making the offender lament.

Westerners often see the goal of retribution as conflicting with that of rehabilitation. The Japanese see it as a more harmonious relationship because both can be accomplished in the community with the aid of other citizens. The group in Japan serves as the dispenser of guilt feelings (retribution) and the provider of social support (rehabilitation). The cultural values of contextualism, harmony, collectivism, and order make achieving correctional goals difficult and inappropriate in an institution. On the other hand, those goals are more easily and properly realized in the community. Consequently, the use of imprisonment is somewhat infrequent.

When imprisonment is required, its explicit goal is to develop in the prisoner a willingness and ability to return to society as a law-abiding and productive member. Given the general societal importance of the work group and the pride in one's work-related accomplishments, it is logical that labor would have a special role in Japanese prisons. Through work, prison officials believe, inmates can learn values such as harmony, respect for authority, and the importance of the group.

There is a sense of having come full circle with this philosophy because these are the cultural patterns identified at the start of this chapter. The homogeneity of agreed-upon values means first that citizens are not so likely to misbehave and second that when norms are broken, the various agencies of social control will operate both informally and formally to emphasize and uphold those values. Even at the last stage in the process of corrections, prison officials respond to the offender in a manner designed to instill those cultural patterns that seem to make a law-abiding citizen. Therein lies the essence and simplicity of Japan's seemingly low crime rate—which brings us back to the bonsai tree.

Seductively simple and harmonious, the Japanese criminal justice system seems to call for imitation. Like the gardener and her bonsai, though, criminal justice policy makers must consider the necessary role restraining wires play in making both the tree and the justice system attractive.

WHAT MIGHT WORK

As this chapter's "Impact" section explains, the attractiveness of Japan's comparatively safe and orderly society seems partially achieved through tactics that citizens of other countries may find unacceptable. Some of the problems critics see in the Japanese justice system are intrusive police behavior toward law-abiding citizens, providing prosecutors with quasi-judicial duties, allowing judgments to be made without a public confrontation between defendant and judge, an apparent encouragement of self-incrimination, and severely restricted access to counsel for defense. Effective though they may be, proponents of due process (including those in Japan) are likely to express concern. However, this is certainly not a dilemma found only in Japan. Recall Chapter 3's discussion of the crime control model and the due process model. Japan may well exemplify the type of due process concessions that are necessary to control crime.

It is inappropriate to finish a book that hopes to encourage cross-cultural research, understanding, and appreciation with a suggestion that countries cannot effectively borrow from each other. In fact, although the "Impact" section emphasized problems that such borrowing may have, this entire chapter is built on the idea that borrowing is both possible and desirable. The question is not whether countries can learn from each other but how unfamiliar ideas can be made effective in a different setting.

A number of authors have made a variety of suggestions about adapting aspects of the Japanese criminal justice system in the United States (Bayley, 1992; Castberg, 1990; Parker, 1986). Some of the suggestions would require as much cultural as structural change whereas others require primarily structural change. Of course, the latter type is easier to implement and has the greatest chance for success because it would not pose significant challenges to cultural tradition.

For example, the centralization of policing would likely make law enforcement more efficient and effective. Yet that seemingly simple structural change directly opposes the long-held American values of decentralization and apprehension concerning a national police force. Some American communities are contracting with county or state officials to provide policing in their area, but even regional police forces in a particular state are not likely to be a popular tactic. If the United States moves away from its current decentralized multiple uncoordinated system, it seems more likely that we will model our system after that of a country such as Canada and its tendency to contract with a provincial or national agency to provide police services. Alternatively, we may inventively change American police structure through increased standardization brought about by national police accreditation standards and regional training facilities.

There are, however, some aspects of Japanese policing that should be easily adapted to the American setting. Interestingly, one of the most importable tactics is the one some observers see as Japan's most effective police strategy—deployment via the koban. Bayley (1991) argues that Japanese-style deployment is possible in the United States because there is no compelling cultural factor inhibiting its use. The Japan International Cooperation Agency (2014) explains that the koban system was adapted in Brazil's Sao Paulo state in 1997 and has since spread to other states. Following Brazil's lead, the Central American countries of Costa Rica, El Salvador, Guatemala, and Honduras have also expressed interest in learning community policing techniques—including the koban—from Japan.

A few U.S. cities have also tried this approach and found it to be quite effective. Neighborhood-based foot patrols, mini- or substations (some doubling as the officer's home), and home loan programs that encourage officers to move into troubled neighborhoods are some of the koban-inspired techniques being used in American jurisdictions.

Koban-like deployment is probably most likely to assist America's urban areas. Bayley recommends its use in places such as public housing projects, major shopping malls, and around transportation and community centers. Some of the storefront police posts found in such cities as Dallas and Houston, Texas, or Syracuse, New York, are similar in design and purpose to the koban.

Another example of adapting koban principles is found in the Portland (Oregon) Police Bureau (PPB). The PPB has implemented a variety of strategies that use police deployment and community interaction in a manner reminiscent of Japanese procedures. In the mid-1990s, the bureau aligned patrol district boundaries to closely correspond to neighborhood association boundaries and, using a five-precinct configuration, more closely aligned precinct boundaries with neighborhood coalition boundaries. Specific programs include the Neighborhood Response Team, which is a small team of officers who work on chronic call locations or other crime and livability problems referred to them by the police officer for that district. The Neighborhood Liaison Officer program connects officers to individual neighborhoods, and the Crisis Intervention Team officers receive specific training on defusing situations with people in a mental health crisis (City of Portland, 2007; Portland Police Bureau, 2016). The Neighborhood Response Team and Neighborhood Liaison Officer programs are popular with both the police bureau and the community, and the PPB continues to enhance each.

This discussion emphasizes ideas related to Japanese policing that may be transferable to the United States. Obviously, some aspects of Japan's court system and corrections process can also be helpful. Increased use of mediation, conciliation, and compromise in pretrial and even pre-charge stages could benefit from the Japanese experience. If greater use of volunteers in adult and juvenile probation, parole, and aftercare seems desirable, program directors may want to consider Japanese examples. Those in charge of providing productive work for prison inmates could benefit from examining prison labor procedures in Japan. There is no lack of possible alternatives to America's existing programs; the challenge lies in determining which, if any, foreign approaches are possible and appropriate here.

The Japanese example is particularly relevant for Americans because the United States played such an important role in structuring the contemporary Japanese system. In fact, as Castberg (1990) points out, the criminal justice provisions in both countries are essentially the same. Differences arise because the respective courts have not interpreted the provisions similarly. For example, each country's constitution protects against double jeopardy, but Japanese courts do not interpret that provision as preventing the prosecution from appealing not guilty verdicts. Likewise, search and seizure provisions are comparably stated, but Japanese courts do not require that arrest always precede search and seizure, nor are warrantless searches and seizures necessarily invalid as long as arrest takes place closely in time.

The point is that imitation and innovation go hand in hand. Japan borrowed from European, Asian, and North American countries but made sure that the new ideas were compatible with Japanese culture. Ensuring compatibility may require selective borrowing, may necessitate modifying the borrowed practice to fit a new cultural context, or could even mean using culture to gain acceptance for the new scheme. Whatever the technique, an understanding and appreciation for one's own cultural traditions are necessary for successful borrowing.

Summary

This book followed a descriptive approach focusing on primary components of a large number of countries rather than providing a detailed description of a few countries. In this manner, we showed the variability of systems but were not able to take a very close look at how any particular justice system operates—except for this chapter, which examines the Japanese criminal justice system in detail. Japan warrants specific attention for two reasons. First, by all indications, Japan has an effective criminal justice system if we measure effectiveness by low crime rate. Second, Japan's criminal justice system includes a blend of foreign ideas adapted to its particular cultural history. This borrowing is one of the goals that comparative criminal justice hopes to achieve. The key to successful borrowing is to make something with a foreign origin work in the context of the adapting country. Some practices that are very effective in one setting may not work at all in another. Concentrating on Japan provides an opportunity to see how cross-cultural borrowing can work and to consider which, if any, Japanese strategies may be effective in the United States.

Because peoples' cultural patterns may affect the transferability of policy and procedures, we briefly considered some of the obvious features of Japanese culture. Elements such as homogeneity, an emphasis on harmony, respect for hierarchy and authority, and reliance on collectivism help explain why and how the police, courts, and correctional agencies are effective in Japan. Upon looking at the three primary components of a criminal justice system, we saw how police deployment via the koban is a key feature in Japanese policing. Also important is the informal justice process that police officers and court personnel use. In fact, the reluctance to impose formal sanctions is apparent throughout the criminal justice operation and is a feature that sets the Japanese system apart from many others in the world.

This chapter's "Impact" section considers some of the problems that could be encountered if parts of Japan's system were implemented in the United States. Even after such cautions, the chapter concludes by noting some things the Japanese do that may be worthy of continued and even increased study by American policy makers. This, after all, is what comparative criminal justice is all about: What can we learn from each other and how can we work together?

Discussion Questions

- The chapter identifies four Japanese cultural patterns that may be helpful in understanding Japan's criminal justice system. Propose four American cultural patterns that could be used to understand the criminal justice system in the United States. Explain how each cultural pattern influences an aspect of the American criminal justice process.
- The Japanese koban is mentioned in several places in this chapter and it is quite likely that you have heard about it in other criminal justice classes. Discuss what you believe are key features of the koban as it operates in

Japan and which of its features (physical or conceptual) you believe could be adapted to your community.
- General supervision of probationers and parolees in Japan falls to the volunteer probation officer. Reasons given for this include the increased knowledge volunteers are likely to have regarding their community and the increased time available to professional probation officers to deal with more difficult cases. In your opinion, is this heavy reliance on volunteers a sound approach? Why or why not?

References

Amnesty International. (2012, November 7). Japan: End abusive detention system after murder conviction quashed. Justice systems. Retrieved from https://www.amnesty.org/en/latest/news/2012/11/japan-end-abusive-detention-system-after-murder-conviction-quashed/

Amnesty International. (2016). Japan. Report 2015/2016. Retrieved from https://www.amnesty.org/en/countries/asia-and-the-pacific/japan/report-japan/

Anonymous. (2015, December 5). Forced to confess: Criminal justice in Japan. *The Economist*, 16–18.

Araki, N. (1985). The flow of criminal cases in the Japanese criminal justice system. *Crime and Delinquency, 31*, 601–629.

Archambeault, W. G., & Fenwick, C. R. (1988). A comparative analysis of culture, safety, and organizational management factors in Japanese and U.S. prisons. *The Prison Journal, 68*, 3–23.

Bayley, D. H. (1991). *Forces of order: Policing modern Japan*. Berkeley, CA: University of California Press.

Bayley, D. H. (1992). Comparative organization of the police in English-speaking countries. In M. Tonry & N. Morris (Eds.), *Crime and justice: A review of research* (Vol. 21, pp. 509–545). Chicago, IL: University of Chicago Press.

Becker, C. B. (1988). Report from Japan: Causes and controls of crime in Japan. *Journal of Criminal Justice, 16*, 425–435.

Braithwaite, J. (1989). *Crime, shame, and reintegration*. Cambridge, England: Cambridge University Press.

Buerk, R. (2009, October 5). Japan urged to end 'false confessions'. *BBC News*. Retrieved from http://news.bbc.co.uk/2/hi/8290767.stm

Castberg, A. D. (1990). *Japanese criminal justice*. New York, NY: Praeger.

City of Portland. (2007). Neighborhood response team, Portland police. *Neighborhood Involvement*. Retrieved from http://www.portlandoregon.gov/oni/article/457873

Correction Bureau. (1990). *Correctional institutions in Japan 1990*. Tokyo: Ministry of Justice.

Dewan, S. (2009, August 1). The real murder mystery? It's the low crime rate. *The New York Times*. Retrieved from http://www.nytimes.com/

Federal Bureau of Investigation. (2014). Clearances. Crime in the United States 2013. Retrieved from https://ucr.fbi.gov/crime-in-the-u.s/2013/crime-in-the-u.s.-2013/offenses-known-to-law-enforcement/clearances/clearancetopic_final

Gardner, C. (2011, June 28). Density on the ground: Cities and building coverage. *Old Urbanist*. Retrieved from http://oldurbanist.blogspot.com/2011/06/density-on-ground-cities-and-building.html

George, B. J., Jr. (1983). Criminal law. *Encyclopedia of Japan* (Vol. 2, pp. 47–51). Tokyo: Kodansha.

Hataguchi, H. (1990). A few problems of criminal trial—A defense counsel's point of view. In V. Kusuda-Smick (Ed.), *Crime prevention and control in the United States and Japan* (pp. 41–44). Dobbs Ferry, NY: Transnational Juris.

Hendry, J. (1989). *Understanding Japanese society*. New York, NY: Routledge.

Huang, K.-C., & Lin, C.-C. (2013). Rescuing confidence in the judicial system: Introducing lay participation in Taiwan. *Journal of Empirical Legal Studies, 10*(3), 542–569. doi:10.1111/jels.12019

Huang, K.-C., & Lin, C.-C. (2014). Mock jury trials in Taiwan—Paving the ground for introducing lay participation. *Law and Human Behavior, 38*(4), 367–377. doi:10.1037/lhb0000080

Ikenaga, T. (2013). National report—Japan. International Legal Aid Group. Retrieved from http://international-legalaidgroup.org/index.php/papers-publications/conference-papers-reports/category/8-national-reports

Japan International Cooperation Agency. (2014, May 12). The 'koban' from Japan spreads from Brazil to Central America. *News*. Retrieved from http://www.jica.go.jp/english/news/field/2014/140512_01.html

Japan National Diet. (1946). *Constitution of Japan* (Vol. 2011). Retrieved from http://www.solon.org/Constitutions/Japan/English/english-Constitution.html

Johnson, D. T. (2002). *The Japanese way of justice: Prosecuting crime in Japan*. Oxford, UK: Oxford University Press.

Johnson, E. (2000). *Linking community and corrections in Japan*. Carbondale, IL: Southern Illinois University Press.

Kaplan, D. E., & Dubro, A. (1986). *Yakuza: The explosive account of Japan's criminal underworld*. Reading, MA: Addison-Wesley.

Kim, S., Park, J., Park, K., & Eom, J.-S. (2013). Judge–jury agreement in criminal cases: The first three years of the Korean jury system. *Journal of Empirical Legal Studies, 10*(1), 35–53. doi:10.1111/jels.12001

Kim, Y. (1987). Work—The key to the success of Japanese law enforcement. *Police Studies, 10*, 109–117.

Lay judge system OK: Top court. (2011, November 18). *The Japan Times*. Retrieved from http://www.japantimes.co.jp/text/nn20111118a6.html

Lee, J.-H. (2009). Getting citizens involved: Civil participation in judicial decision-making in Korea. *East Asia Law Review, 4*(Fall), 177–207.

Lee, J.-H. (2010). Korean jury trial: Has the new system brought about changes? *Asian-Pacific Law and Policy Journal, 12*(1), 58–71.

Masaki, A. (1964). *Reminiscences of a Japanese penologist*. Tokyo: Japan Criminal Policy Association.

Ministry of Justice. (2014). White paper on crime 2014. Retrieved from http://hakusyo1.moj.go.jp/en/nendo_nfm.html

Ministry of Justice. (n.d.). Facilities. Correction Bureau. Retrieved from http://www.moj.go.jp/ENGLISH/CB/cb-01.html

Monkkonen, E. H. (1981). *Police in urban America 1860–1920*. Cambridge, England: Cambridge University Press.

National Police Agency. (2005, August 31). Japanese community police and police box system. Police Policy Research Center. Retrieved from http://www.npa.go.jp/english/index.htm

National Police Agency. (2012, May 14). Crime in Japan in 2010. Police Policy Research Center. Retrieved from https://www.npa.go.jp/english/index.htm

National Police Agency. (2015, April 6). Police of Japan 2015. Overview of Japanese police. Retrieved from http://www.npa.go.jp/english/index.htm

Onishi, N. (2007, November 3). As Japan ages, prisons adapt to going gray. *The New York Times*. Retrieved from http://www.nytimes.com/2007/11/03/world/asia/03japan.html

Oppler, A. C. (1977). The reform of Japan's legal and judicial system under Allied occupation. *Washington Law Review* (special edition), 1–35.

Parker, L. C. (2013). *Crime and justice in Japan and China: A comparative view*. Durham, NC: Carolina Academic Press.

Parker, L. C., Jr. (1984). *A Japanese police system today: An American perspective*. Tokyo: Kodansha.

Parker, L. C., Jr. (1986). *Parole and the community based treatment of offenders in Japan and the United States*. New Haven, CT: University of New Haven Press.

Portland Police Bureau. (2016). Community policing strategic plans. Retrieved from http://www.portlandoregon.gov/police/29866

Rake, D. E. (1987). Crime control and police-community relations: A cross-cultural comparison of Tokyo, Japan, and Santa Ana, California. *Annals of the American Academy of Political and Social Science, 494*, 148–154.

Reichel, P. L., & Suzuki, Y. E. (2015). Japan's lay judge system: A summary of its development, evaluation, and current status. *International Criminal Justice Review, 25*(3), 247–262. doi:10.1177/1057567715588948

Reischauer, E. O. (1988). *The Japanese today: Change and continuity* (rev. ed.). Cambridge, MA: Belknap.

Rubinstein, J. (1973). *City police*. New York, NY: Farrar Straus & Giroux.

Ryavec, C. A. (1983). Legal system. *Encyclopedia of Japan* (Vol. 4, pp. 375–379). Tokyo: Kodansha.

Saito, T. (1990). 'Substitute prison': A hotbed of false criminal charges in Japan. *Northern Kentucky Law Review, 18*(3), 399–415.

Supreme Court of Japan. (2015). Saiban-in Seido no Jisshi Joukyou ni tsuite (Seido Shikkou-Heisei 27 1gatsu-matsu–Sokuhou). *Bulletin on State of the Lay Judge System—From Inception to January 2015*. Retrieved from www.saibanin.courts.go.jp/vcms_lf/h27_1_saibaninsokuhou.pdf

Tamiya, H. (1983). Confession. *Encyclopedia of Japan* (Vol. 1, p. 350). Tokyo: Kodansha.

UNAFEI. (2014). Criminal justice in Japan. Retrieved from http://www.unafei.or.jp/english/pages/Publicationslist.htm

Upham, F. K. (1987). *Law and social change in postwar Japan*. Cambridge, MA: Harvard University Press.

Westney, D. E. (1987). *Imitation and innovation: The transfer of western organizational patterns to Meiji Japan*. Cambridge, MA: Harvard University Press.

Wigmore, J. H. (1936). *A panorama of the world's legal systems* (Vol. library edition). Washington, DC: Washington Law Book Company.

Wilson, J. Q. (2011, May 28). Hard times, fewer crimes. *Wall Street Journal*. Retrieved from http://online.wsj.com/article/SB10001424052702304066504576345553135009870.html

APPENDIX A

World Maps

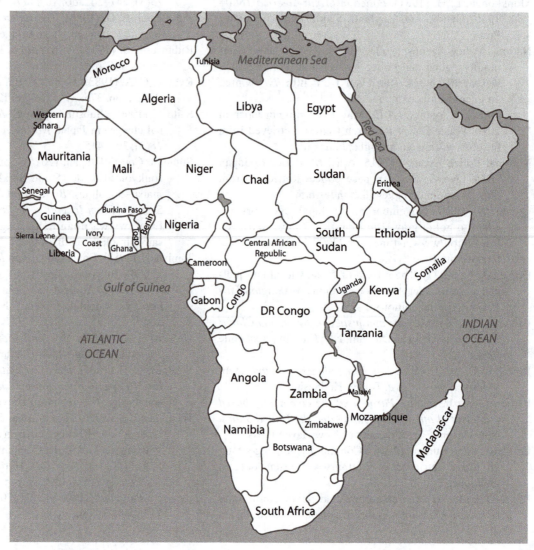

MAP A.1   AFRICA

Pavalena/Shutterstock

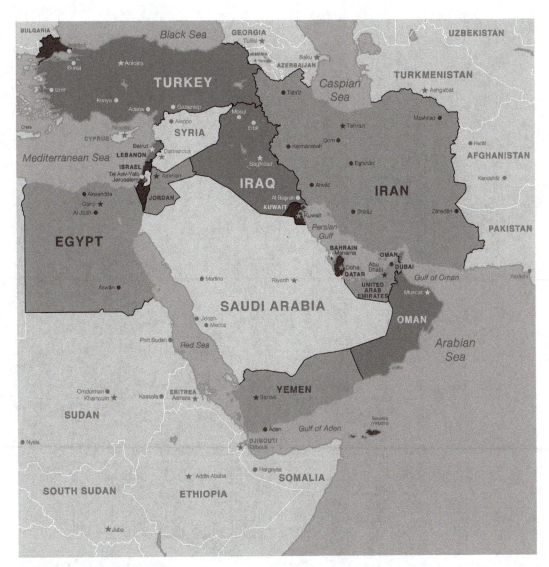

MAP A.2   MIDDLE EAST

Pingebat/Shutterstock

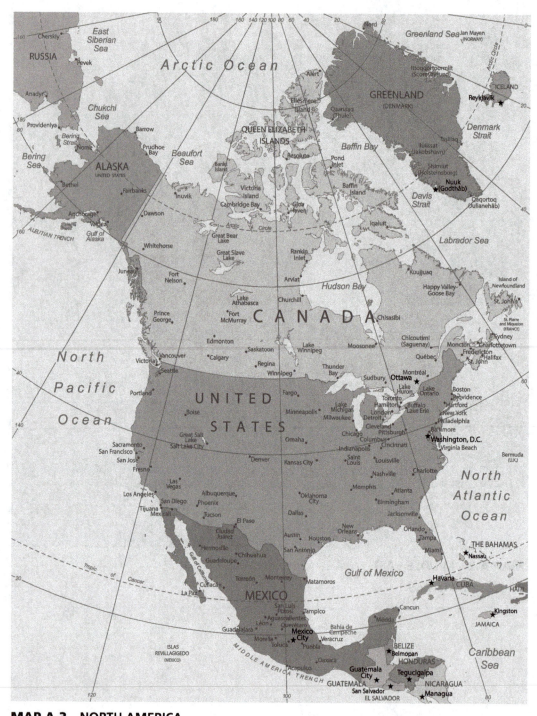

MAP A.3   NORTH AMERICA

Ekler/Shutterstock

MAP A.4   SOUTH AMERICA

Creative Jen Designs/Shutterstock

MAP A.5   CENTRAL AMERICA AND THE CARIBBEAN
Serban Bogdan/Shutterstock

MAP A.6   OCEANIA
Bogdanserban/Fotolia

MAP A.7   SOUTHEAST ASIA

Dikobrazik/Fotolia

MAP A.8   JAPAN AND KOREA

Pavalena/Shutterstock

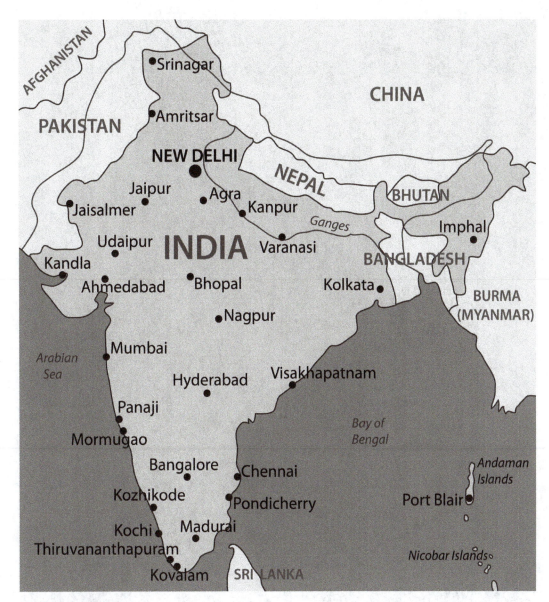

MAP A.9   INDIA

Pavalena/Shutterstock

MAP A.10 EUROPE
Ekler/Fotolia

APPENDIX B

Helpful Websites

The websites listed below provide good starting points for identifying helpful information about comparative crime and justice around the world. Many of the websites offer links to detailed information about law, police, courts, and corrections in various countries.

Crime and Society: A Comparative Criminology Tour of the World (http://www-rohan.sdsu.edu/faculty/rwinslow/index.html) provides user-friendly access to crime and justice information via a world map upon which you click your continent or country of interest.

Global Legal Monitor (http://www.loc.gov/law/foreign-news/) is an online publication from the Law Library of Congress covering legal news and developments worldwide.

Hauser Global Law School Program (www.nyulawglobal.org/globalex/index.html) offers a GlobalLex page where visitors find information of conducting research in the areas of international law, comparative law, and foreign law.

International Centre for Prison Studies (http://www.prisonstudies.org/) provides statistical information (e.g., prison population rate, official capacity, and percentage of women prisoners) for nearly every country in the world. Data for a specific country can be reached by clicking on a map or by searching on country name.

JuriGlobe: World Legal Systems (www.juriglobe.ca/eng/index.php) offers a visual portrayal of the world's legal traditions and encourages visitors to consider each of five systems (civil law, common law, customary law, Muslim law, and mixed law systems) according to such variables as geography, demographics, and economy.

Michigan State University Libraries http://staff.lib.msu.edu/harris23/crimjust/intsites.htm) lists foreign and international sites (some of which are annotated).

The International Monthly Accessions List (https://www.ncjrs.gov/imal.html) is a listing of documents on international and transnational topics added to the NCJRS Abstracts Database during the previous month. You can subscribe to the list and be notified as new material is added, or simply check it periodically for information on your country or topic.

The World Criminal Justice Library Network (http://andromeda.rutgers.edu/~wcjlen/WCJ/) provides a quick and easy way to find relevant links to justice agencies, statistics, and other topics related to countries around the world.

United Nations Office on Drugs and Crime (http://www.unodc.org/) provides links to many transnational crime topics.

INDEX